Praise for *SharePoint 2010 Development with Visual Studio 2010*

"The fact is, developers are either limited or liberated by the tools they use. This book brings a strong tools focus with Visual Studio 2010, and the authors are *the* experts when it comes to the tooling enhancements that vastly improve developing with SharePoint 2010. This book is the must-have SharePoint 2010 developer instruction resource for all ranges of experience, novice to expert."

—*John R. Durant, Senior Product Manager, Microsoft*

"I thoroughly enjoyed reading this SharePoint 2010 development book. Every chapter had useful information that was to the point and developer focused—a great addition to any SharePoint developer's library."

—*Greg Galipeau, Director, SharePoint Practice, Optimos Consulting*

"As a developer, you're always looking for new opportunities, and SharePoint offers plenty. Visual Studio 2010 adds a great set of tools for working with SharePoint 2010 and Eric Carter, Boris Scholl, and Peter Jausovec do an excellent job of explaining how to use them. After reading this book, you'll know what to do to begin building professional SharePoint solutions."

—*Robert Green, Senior Consultant, MCW Technologies*

"A really useful guide that every SharePoint developer should have in their bookcase."

—*Tomáš Herceg, Microsoft Visual Basic MVP*

"Carter, Scholl, and Jausovec have created an invaluable resource for professionals who need to learn the new Visual Studio Tools for SharePoint. With great walkthroughs and thorough explanations, this book is required reading for every SharePoint developer."

—*Scot Hillier, Microsoft SharePoint MVP, Scot Hillier Technical Solutions, LLC*

"If you're a .NET developer looking for a book to help you quickly get up to speed then *SharePoint 2010 Development with Visual Studio 2010* is *the* book. You won't get stumped or overwhelmed. It is laid out in an easy to consume way that will get you developing SharePoint apps in no time!"

—*Joel Oleson, Senior Architect & Evangelist, Quest Software*

D1307536

SharePoint 2010
Development with
Visual Studio 2010

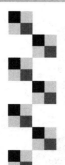

SharePoint 2010 Development with Visual Studio 2010

- Eric Carter
- Boris Scholl
- Peter Jausovec

✦✦ Addison-Wesley

Upper Saddle River, NJ • Boston • Indianapolis • San Francisco
New York • Toronto • Montreal • London • Munich • Paris • Madrid
Capetown • Sydney • Tokyo • Singapore • Mexico City

Many of the designations used by manufacturers and sellers to distinguish their products are claimed as trademarks. Where those designations appear in this book, and the publisher was aware of a trademark claim, the designations have been printed with initial capital letters or in all capitals.

The .NET logo is either a registered trademark or trademark of Microsoft Corporation in the United States and/or other countries and is used under license from Microsoft.

Microsoft, Windows, Visual Basic, Visual C#, and Visual C++ are either registered trademarks or trademarks of Microsoft Corporation in the U.S.A. and/or other countries/regions.

The authors and publisher have taken care in the preparation of this book, but make no expressed or implied warranty of any kind and assume no responsibility for errors or omissions. No liability is assumed for incidental or consequential damages in connection with or arising out of the use of the information or programs contained herein.

The publisher offers excellent discounts on this book when ordered in quantity for bulk purchases or special sales, which may include electronic versions and/or custom covers and content particular to your business, training goals, marketing focus, and branding interests. For more information, please contact:

U.S. Corporate and Government Sales
(800) 382-3419
corpsales@pearsontechgroup.com

For sales outside the United States please contact:

International Sales
international@pearson.com

Visit us on the Web: informit.com/aw

Library of Congress Cataloging-in-Publication Data
Carter, Eric.
  SharePoint 2010 development with Visual Studio 2010 / Eric Carter, Boris Scholl, Peter Jausovec.
    p.   cm.
  Includes index.
  ISBN 978-0-321-71831-0 (pbk. : alk. paper)
  1. Microsoft SharePoint (Electronic resource) 2. Intranets (Computer networks) 3. Web servers. 4. Microsoft Visual studio. I. Scholl, Boris. II. Jausovec, Peter. III. Title.
  TK5105.875.I6C367 2010
  006.7—dc22   2010022236

ISBN-13: 978-0-321-71831-0
ISBN-10:   0-321-71831-3
Text printed in the United States on recycled paper at Edwards Brothers in Ann Arbor, Michigan.
Second printing, February 2011

*To my wife, Tamsyn, and our children, Jason, Hayley,
Camilla, Rand, Elizabeth, and Miles*
—*Eric Carter*

*To my wife, Christina, and our son, Anton,
who was born while I was working on the book*
—*Boris Scholl*

To Nives and my family
—*Peter Jausovec*

Contents at a Glance

Contents

Figures

Tables

Foreword

Over the last decade, we've seen SharePoint evolve from a collaboration application to a business collaboration platform. With SharePoint's growing popularity, organizations have looked to extend SharePoint beyond traditional collaboration to scenarios such as human workflow, document processing, line-of-business portals, Internet sites, and more. Before the arrival of SharePoint 2010, developers spent a great deal of effort developing SharePoint applications and going through a number of manual steps and processes.

With the SharePoint 2010 release, we really focused on the developer audience by investing in out-of-the-box tools and features to make the SharePoint development experience familiar. We received very clear feedback from developers that they wanted an experience similar to developing using ASP.NET applications, including out-of-the-box Visual Studio templates and an F5 experience for rapid development, debugging, and deployment. We listened and delivered with the SharePoint 2010 and Visual Studio 2010 releases.

I fundamentally believe that with the release of SharePoint 2010 the number of SharePoint developers will double. That's a significant jump given that we estimate hundreds of thousands of developers have worked on a SharePoint project in the last six to twelve months. This growth will be driven by the expected increase in SharePoint customers along with the business opportunity this will bring to developers everywhere; it's a great time to be a SharePoint developer.

Whether you're a .NET developer with no SharePoint experience or an experienced SharePoint 2003 or 2007 developer, this book will help you take advantage of the rich SharePoint 2010 platform and Visual Studio 2010 tools! Beyond just describing the basics, this book dives into some of the best practices that all SharePoint developers should know. This book is special because it's written by experts Boris, Eric, and Peter—people with deep real world experience *and* product insight: a SharePoint developer book by SharePoint developers!

—Arpan Shah
Director, SharePoint
June 2010

Preface

In late 2007, we had just put the final touches on Visual Studio 2008. For the Visual Studio Tools for Office (VSTO) team, the 2008 release was an important one. Visual Studio 2008 was the team's first major investment in SharePoint projects. Visual Studio 2008 included two projects to build SharePoint Workflow: the Sequential and State Machine Workflow Projects.

In some ways, however, our Visual Studio 2008 investment in SharePoint development was too little and too late. All around us, SharePoint development was taking off. When we attended Microsoft developer conferences and talked about VSTO, the level of interest in SharePoint was unbelievable. Although we had a great set of developer tools for the Office client in VSTO, SharePoint support in Visual Studio was still very limited.

During this time, a group of us began to seriously survey the SharePoint development space to determine how we could catch up. This space is vast and a large part of our effort was to figure out what would be possible to do in the next two years to best support SharePoint developers. In addition, a vibrant ecosystem for SharePoint development was springing up all around us, so we knew that it was also important to have a great extensibility model to allow third parties to plug into Visual Studio. Our focus was on delivering a solid set of basic support for SharePoint development, particularly in making it easy to build and deploy SharePoint solutions.

This book tries to put in one place all the information you need to succeed using Visual Studio to program against SharePoint Foundation. The first three chapters form an introduction to SharePoint development, including extensive coverage of the SharePoint UI and how to extend SharePoint, an introduction to Visual Studio, and an introduction to the SharePoint object models. The remaining chapters take you through Visual Studio's support for creating the various elements of a SharePoint solution, including lists, workflow, and connections to business data.

This book is unique in that it focuses on Visual Studio throughout the book where most books only mention Visual Studio in a few chapters. Our focus is on showing you what Visual Studio provides to make SharePoint development easy. We also introduce SharePoint Designer as a tool to fill in some of the gaps left by Visual Studio, showing you ways to easily create some SharePoint elements.

The goal of this book is to allow you to be productive in SharePoint development by relying on Visual Studio—it won't require you to have a deep understanding of everything going on behind the scenes in Share-Point because Visual Studio takes care of a lot of this for you. Visual Studio really makes SharePoint development much more accessible to a new developer, similar to how MFC and Visual Basic made Windows development accessible to a broader range of developers.

This book provides an insider view of all the rich features of Visual Studio that were created to enable you to develop SharePoint solutions. We participated in the design and implementation of many of these features. Therefore, we can speak from the unique perspective of living and breathing Visual Studio support for SharePoint for the past two years. Programming SharePoint with Visual Studio is powerful and fun. We hope you enjoy using Visual Studio to develop SharePoint solutions as much as we enjoyed writing about it and creating it.

—Eric Carter, Boris Scholl, and Peter Jausovec

Acknowledgments

Although there are only three names on the cover, no book of this magnitude gets written without the efforts of many dedicated individuals.

Eric Carter would like to thank his entire family for the patience they showed while "Dad" was working on his book: Jason, Hayley, Camilla, Rand, Elizabeth, and Miles; and his wife Tamsyn. He would also like to thank all his colleagues in Visual Studio who made the last 10 years so enjoyable—thanks everyone and I miss working with you every day.

Boris Scholl would like to thank his wife, Christina, for the amazing support and patience she showed while he was working on the book, even though she was pregnant with their firstborn, Anton Scholl. In addition he would like to thank all his colleagues in Visual Studio and his friends and colleagues in the SharePoint Community, in particular Arpan Shah, who has been a mentor for Boris ever since he started working in the SharePoint area.

Peter Jausovec would like to thank his wife, Nives, for her constant support and encouragement during countless weekends spent working on the book.

Many thanks to everyone at Addison-Wesley who made this book possible. Joan Murray and Olivia Basegio provided expertise, guidance, encouragement, and feedback through every step of the process. Thanks are also due to the production and marketing teams at Addison-Wesley, especially John Fuller and Anna Popick, along with compositor and project manager Kim Arney, copyeditor Julie DeSilva, proofreader Linda Begley, and indexer Richard Evans.

A huge thank-you to everyone at Microsoft who over the last three years contributed to Visual Studio 2010 features for SharePoint development. Many people from different disciplines—design, development, education, evangelism, management, marketing, and testing—dedicated their passion and energy toward bringing SharePoint development support to Visual Studio. We could not have written this book without the efforts of all of them. One could not ask for a better group of people to have as colleagues.

We also acknowledge leaders like KD Hallman, S. Somasegar, Julia Liuson, and Jason Zander for their support and encouragement of our delivering a great developer experience for SharePoint development in Visual Studio. It is impossible to mention everyone who worked on this project, but in particular we acknowledge the impact of the leaders of the project, including Donald Drake, Jay Schmelzer, Jing Lou, Svetlana Loksh, Reza Chitsaz, Lubo Birov, and Mike Morton. We also acknowledge leaders in the SharePoint space, including Mike Ammerlaan, Rob Howard, Maxim Lukiyanov, Rolando Jimenez Salgado, Thomas Mechelke, Arpan Shah, and Richard Riley.

A considerable number of industry experts in SharePoint gave the Visual Studio team valuable feedback over the past two years. Many thanks to everyone who came so far to give so much of their time and expertise by participating in Software Design Reviews and using early versions of the product. Their suggestions made Visual Studio 2010 a better product than the one we originally envisioned. In particular, we want to make mention of Ted Pattison, Andrew Connell, Todd Bleeker, Waldek Mastykarz, Scot Hillier, Wouter Van Vugt, and Robert Green.

Many thanks to our technical reviewers, whose always-constructive criticism was a huge help. They helped us remove a huge number of errors in the text; those that remain are our own. We thank Mike Morton, Andrew Whitechapel, Tomáš Herceg, Greg Galipeau, Maarten van Stam, and Matt Ranlett for their reviews and contributions to this project.

About the Authors

Eric Carter is a development manager in the Bing team at Microsoft. Previously, he worked as a development manager in the Visual Studio team at Microsoft. He helped invent, design, and implement many of the features that are in Visual Studio today. Also while at Microsoft he worked on Visual Studio Tools for Office, Visual Studio Tools for Applications, the Visual Studio Macros IDE, and Visual Basic for Applications for Office 2000 and Office 2003.

Eric has written three books for Addison-Wesley: *Visual Studio Tools for Office: Using C# with Excel, Word, Outlook, and InfoPath*; *Visual Studio Tools for Office: Using VB with Excel, Word, Outlook, and InfoPath*; and *Visual Studio Tools for Office 2007: VSTO for Excel, Word, and Outlook*.

Boris Scholl is a program manager on the Visual Studio team in Redmond working on Microsoft Visual Studio 2010 SharePoint developer tools. Before joining the Visual Studio product team he worked as senior technical product manager in the Office Server group in Redmond focusing on developer readiness and SharePoint integration with Project Server. He also spent five years as a senior consultant in the Microsoft European Information Worker of Excellence and Microsoft Project Server World Wide Center of Excellence, working on large Project Server and SharePoint server projects across the globe that focused on development, Line-of-Business integration, and performance. Boris started his IT career in 1995, working as a developer at a startup company. He began his Microsoft career in 1999 and has been working on portal technologies ever since.

Boris is a frequent speaker at large events in Europe and the United States.

Peter Jausovec joined the Visual Studio team in Redmond after graduating from the University of Maribor in Slovenia. During his college years he worked on various projects involving Visual Studio Tools for Office. In 2007 he started working as a Software Development Engineer in Test on Microsoft Visual Studio 2010 SharePoint developer tools. He helped with testing and designing the Microsoft Visual Studio 2010 SharePoint developer tools; his main focus was on SharePoint workflow.

■ 1 ■

Introduction to SharePoint

What Is SharePoint Development?

In this chapter, we will introduce you to basic SharePoint concepts and give you an overview of the building blocks of SharePoint solutions. Development in SharePoint is an interesting hybrid of several Microsoft technologies and styles of development. For example, when you build a custom web part or custom application page in SharePoint, it will feel very similar to creating a web part or web page with ASP.NET. This may make you think that SharePoint development is just like ASP.NET development. But just when you are feeling confident, you hit the barrier of packaging and deployment. To deploy that web part or web page, you will have to use SharePoint's packaging and deployment system, which is a system that uses custom XML files to define what SharePoint calls "features." Those features are packaged with their associated files into a .WSP file (basically a CAB file renamed to .WSP). Finally, you must run a command line tool on the SharePoint server to process the WSP file and install the web part or web page.

If you want to customize the behavior of a SharePoint list, development in SharePoint begins to feel more like the customization of a rich client application such as Office. You create a .NET assembly that handles a set of events raised by a particular SharePoint list. You interact with SharePoint's object model much like Office customizations interact with the Office object model. Then you use SharePoint's packaging and deployment system to install your .NET assembly.

If you want to create a custom SharePoint list, a custom content type, or a site definition, development in SharePoint begins to feel like declarative programming. SharePoint has a custom XML language called CAML, which is used to define key objects such as lists, columns, and content types. This XML language can be difficult to learn and manipulate to get the results you want. In this book, we will typically recommend using Share-Point Designer as the "WYSIWYG" editor for editing the XML that defines these custom SharePoint types. As before, you then use SharePoint's pack-aging and deployment system to install your custom SharePoint types.

If you want to develop custom workflows in SharePoint, another Microsoft technology must be learned—the Windows Workflow Founda-tion. SharePoint's workflow features are often used to automate workflow that people participate in for items in a list or even workflow that occurs at a site level. If you have worked with workflow, this will feel familiar to you—it is yet another style of development used within SharePoint. Typi-cally your workflow also interacts with the SharePoint object model to get interesting things to happen.

SharePoint can feel like ASP.NET at times, like event-driven customiza-tions at other times, like declarative programming, like workflow pro-gramming, and like code focused on automating an object model at other times. This can make SharePoint programming difficult—you have to get comfortable with many styles of programming to get interesting things done.

Where Is the List Command?

Another challenge of SharePoint solutions is that they tend to be a loosely coupled collection of various types of customizations that all work together in a solution to produce the desired application experience. Because they are loosely coupled, it is sometimes difficult to figure out where to start and how to get your various SharePoint customizations to work together to produce the result you want. Bill Gates, in a review of

SharePoint, put it this way: "Where is the SharePoint *list* command for a SharePoint page?"—meaning how do you go to a SharePoint page and do the equivalent of the *list* command that was available in the Basic language. Ideally this hypothetical *list* command would give you a nice listing of all the code that is running in that web page that is creating the page experience; then you could easily modify the code, rerun it, and change the experience of the SharePoint page.

Unfortunately, SharePoint has no *list* command. For a particular SharePoint page, you could have multiple things going on, none of which are obvious from looking at just one piece of code. Consider for example a SharePoint page that is tracking work items for a development team with a nice web part showing the work items that are currently "in flight" for the development team like the one shown in Figure 1-1.

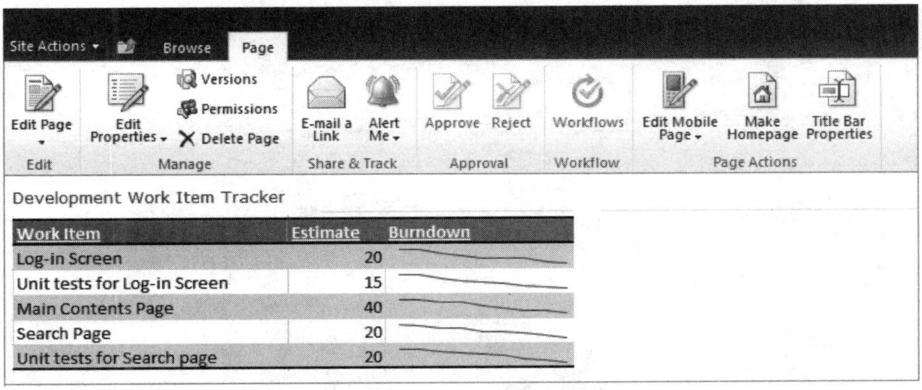

Figure 1-1: A SharePoint page with a web part tracking "in flight" development work items

If you view the source for this page in the web browser, you won't be getting the full "listing" for what is going on in the web page. You will only see the HTML and script code that is currently being rendered by the browser. To understand how the page works, you really need to look at the ASP.NET code that is compiled to create the web part. Chances are that the ASP.NET web part is talking to the SharePoint object model to get data to display—so you have to understand the SharePoint object model. Also, the work item list that the web page is showing is probably a custom list, one that was defined using the custom XML language we referred to earlier. And that custom list might have custom behavior associated with it when the list is manipulated—either in list event handler code or in custom workflow associated with the list. Also, there is behavior in the web page that is provided by SharePoint itself that can be modified by changing the site definition, style sheets, or master pages used by the site. Very quickly you realize that a simple SharePoint solution can be defined by multiple elements as shown in Figure 1-2. These elements may be unfamiliar to you now, but we will explain these elements throughout this book.

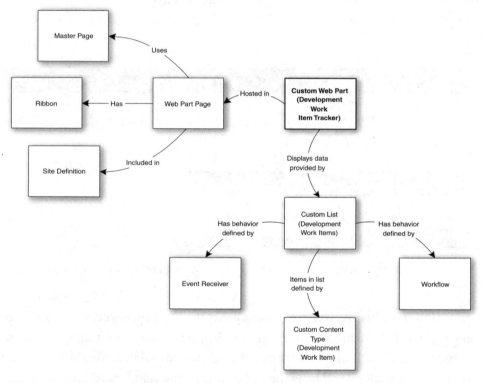

Figure 1-2: Potential elements in the code behind Figure 1-1

How Do I Play My Changes Back?

You may be familiar with using either the SharePoint web user interface or SharePoint Designer to modify and configure a SharePoint site. The problem with this approach is that the changes made to the site are not version controlled in a way that you can revert a particular change or play back the same set of modifications to an existing site. You can create and configure a list and save it as a list template or create and configure a site and save it as a site template, which can then be used when creating a new list or a new site. But what if you want to add some functionality to an existing site without starting from scratch?

Once I witnessed a development team who had written down everything they had done to create a particular SharePoint application using SharePoint Designer. They were deploying the application from test to production by pointing SharePoint Designer at the production site and manually executing every step they had written down to configure the test site. Obviously this is not optimal and points to the major problem you face when trying to develop a SharePoint application using SharePoint Designer—all changes you make are made to the live site and no record is created of the changes you make so you can apply them to a different site. This severely limits your ability to use SharePoint Designer in a complete Software Development lifecycle. We will discuss an approach later in this section that allows you to use SharePoint Designer and/or the SharePoint web interface to create certain definitions that you can then export and import into Visual Studio so they can be easily deployed.

Visual Studio to the Rescue

It is perhaps exaggeration to say that Visual Studio is going to rescue you from the variety of styles and complexity of interrelated components that make up SharePoint development. But Visual Studio is uniquely suited to helping you in your SharePoint development. Visual Studio excels at supporting multiple styles of development. It has visual design experiences for ASP.NET development, for workflow development, and has a good environment for building up the classes that are used to handle events in

SharePoint. Visual Studio also has a good environment for editing XML that can be used when designing the SharePoint objects that are defined by XML.

Visual Studio allows you to create a project or multiple projects to contain the various types of SharePoint elements that make up a SharePoint solution. So you might not be able to use the *list* command on a particular SharePoint web page, but at least you can see in one Visual Studio project or solution the multiple types of elements that make up a SharePoint solution as shown by Figure 1-3 for our simple "work items" system. In Figure 1-3 you can see that the code behind our work item tracking system has a web part project item, a sequential workflow project item, an event receiver, and a list definition. All of these elements work together to provide the Share-Point experience in Figure 1-1.

Figure 1-3: A Visual Studio view of the elements behind the SharePoint web page in Figure 1-1

When you use Visual Studio to develop a SharePoint solution, everything you do is captured in code and XML in your Visual Studio project. You can use version control to track the changes you make to your application over time and revert them if necessary. When you deploy your solution, it can be deployed to an existing site and retracted from that same site if necessary. In short, Visual Studio gives you a consistent way to put everything your application does in source code files and play it back.

Visual Studio helps you as a SharePoint developer by taking care of a lot of the complexity around packaging and deploying your SharePoint solution. In SharePoint development prior to Visual Studio 2010, this aspect of SharePoint development was particularly tedious and time consuming. In Visual Studio 2010, visual designers for packaging and deployment make it very easy to deploy your SharePoint solution.

SharePoint Designer—Your SharePoint Development Sidekick

In addition to your copy of Visual Studio 2010, you should have a copy of SharePoint Designer 2010. Although Visual Studio 2010 provides a great environment for visually designing web pages and web parts, workflow, and writing code intensive components like event receivers—Visual Studio 2010 provides no visual designers for key SharePoint items like custom lists, custom content types, and custom site columns. Visual Studio 2010 will let you hand-edit the XML definitions of these elements and it can provide you with some IntelliSense support based on the element you are editing, but it isn't a lot of fun and it is error prone. In the future, it is our hope that Visual Studio will add visual designers for these items, but for now the safest way to develop the items is to design them using the visual designers in SharePoint Designer. This approach gets around the "How Do I Play My Changes Back" problem by exporting changes you've made to a SharePoint element to something called a WSP file and then importing the modified SharePoint definitions into Visual Studio so they can be deployed with your Visual Studio solution. This book will use this approach where applicable.

Introduction to SharePoint Site Collections and Sites

Before we get too far ahead of ourselves, let's look at what a SharePoint server is, what makes it run, how it is structured, and how you start developing for it. As we work through this chapter, we are going to create a new

SharePoint site collection with a top-level SharePoint site in it. This will require you to have SharePoint 2010 set up on a machine to follow along. With SharePoint 2010, you can now install SharePoint onto a 64-bit Windows 7 or Windows Vista operating system in addition to Windows Server 2008. Appendix A, "Preparing for SharePoint Development," describes how to set up a machine to run SharePoint 2010.

Also, as we introduce SharePoint features and capabilities in this chapter, we will call out "Extension Points" as we go along—places where you can extend SharePoint and add your own content and functionality. This should give you an idea of the kinds of solutions you will later build in this book.

We will look at SharePoint from three different perspectives to give you a broad introduction to SharePoint capabilities and concepts. First, we will use the SharePoint web UI that an end user or the owner of a SharePoint site would use to modify the content and settings associated with a SharePoint site. Second, we will use the Central Administration web UI that a server administrator uses to configure a SharePoint server to further explore how SharePoint servers work and are configured. Finally, we will look at Visual Studio's Server Explorer view, which provides a developer-centric perspective on a SharePoint site.

Creating a New Child Site in an Existing Site Collection

When SharePoint is first installed, a default site collection is automatically created for you, rooted at http://yourmachinename. What is a site collection you might ask? A site collection is a container that always has a top-level SharePoint site in it and can contain any number of additional child SharePoint sites as well. These child sites can be parented off of the top-level SharePoint site in the site collection or off of any children sites or their children. This means you can create hierarchies of sites rooted at the top-level SharePoint site in the site collection.

You may want to create separate site collections to put related groups of sites together—for example, the sales department of your company may want to have one SharePoint site collection and the marketing department may want to have a separate site collection. This allows each department to have its own users and security settings and share them within the subsites contained in a site collection.

Let's create a new child site off of the default SharePoint site collection. Go to your top-level SharePoint site URL. My machine name is ecarter1, so my top-level SharePoint site URL is http://ecarter1. There you will see a page like the one shown in Figure 1-4. This is the top-level SharePoint site that is created for you when you install SharePoint.

Figure 1-4: The top-level SharePoint site page

In the top left corner of this page is a Site Actions menu. This provides actions associated with the top-level SharePoint site in your default site collection. The Site Actions menu is only shown if you have the right permissions. In this case, I am a member of the "Team Site Owners" group, which gives me full control and results in all available site actions being shown. Click on the Site Actions menu and then click on New Site as shown in Figure 1-5.

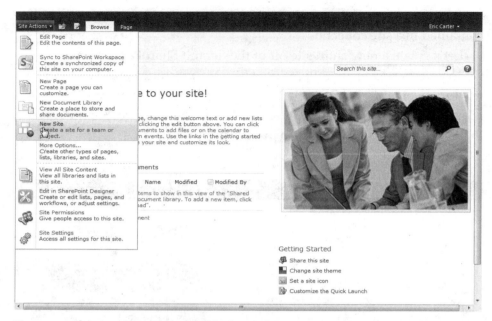

Figure 1-5: Creating a new site using the SharePoint Site Actions menu

The Create dialog comes up as shown in Figure 1-6. In this dialog, you can choose a site template to be used for the new site. A site template defines the initial set of pages and features that are available for the Share-Point site you create using the template. In Figure 1-6 we have chosen the Blank Site template. You can then give the new site a name and a URL. For our site we chose to name it "My Child Site" and picked "mychildsite" for the URL. Note that the URL is rooted off of the top-level site URL, so for our example, the final URL for the newly created child site will be http://ecarter1/mychildsite. Finally, click the Create button to create the new child site.

The newly created child site is then opened in the browser as shown in Figure 1-7. Note the URL of the newly created child site in the browser URL box.

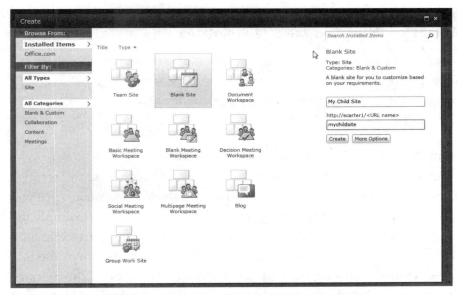

Figure 1-6: Creating a new child site using the Create dialog

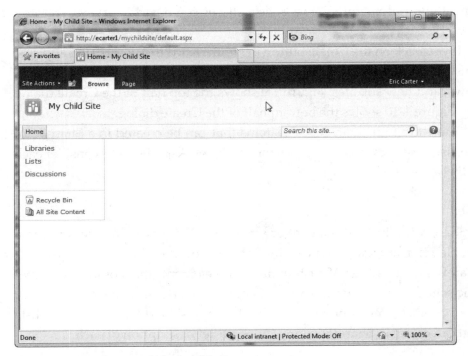

Figure 1-7: A newly created blank child site

Extension Point: Custom Site Templates

You can create your own site template that can be displayed in the Create dialog. This site template can specify the initial set of pages, libraries, and lists and other content that is available to the site.

Content That Can Be Created in a SharePoint Site

Now that we have created an empty child site, let's examine the settings and content available in the new child site. You should first make sure you are on the home page for the newly created child site—in our example the home page for the child site is located at http://ecarter1/mychildsite/default.aspx. From the home page for the child site, drop down the Site Actions menu and choose View All Site Content. The All Site Content page is shown as displayed in Figure 1-8. Because the site template we picked was a blank site, there is no content created—specifically, there are no document libraries, picture libraries, lists, discussion boards, surveys, subsites, or workspaces.

If you click on the Create button in Figure 1-8, the Create dialog appears. This dialog gives you the option to create libraries, lists, pages, site workflows, and new subsites. Figure 1-9 shows the top half of the Create dialog and Figure 1-10 shows the bottom half of the Create dialog.

There are four main types of items that can be created in a SharePoint site: lists, libraries, pages, and new subsites/workspaces. Let's consider each of these item types in turn.

Lists

A SharePoint list is at the core of what SharePoint is about—in fact some people refer to SharePoint as simply being composed of "lists of lists." A SharePoint list is a list of custom data with elements that conform to a specific schema—for example, a list of contacts in which each item in the list has a contact name, phone, etc. Table 1-1 shows the different kinds of lists you can create in SharePoint and gives a brief description of each.

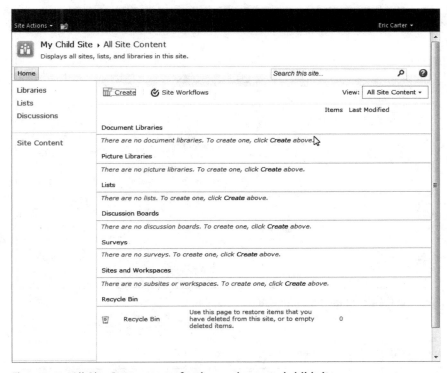

Figure 1-8: All Site Content page for the newly created child site

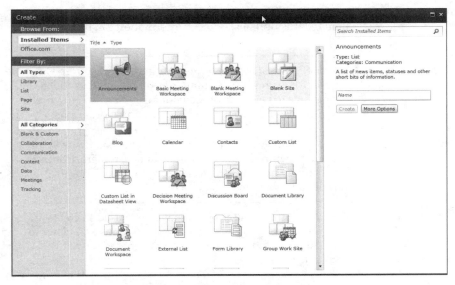

Figure 1-9: The Create dialog—top half of the dialog

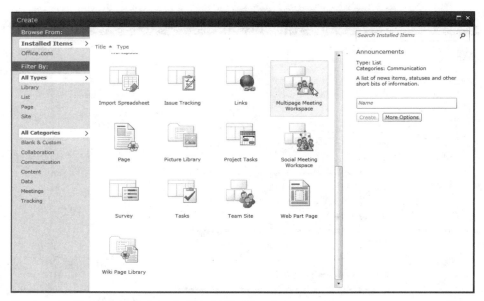

Figure 1-10: The Create dialog—bottom half of the dialog

TABLE 1-1: Lists That Can Be Created in a Blank SharePoint Site

List Type	Description
Announcements	A SharePoint list in which announcements such as news items, status updates, or other information can be stored and shared.
Calendar	A SharePoint list in which calendar items can be stored and shared, for example, upcoming meetings or events that a team needs to be aware of. Calendar lists can also be synced with Microsoft Outlook or other compatible programs.
Contacts	A SharePoint list in which contacts can be stored, for example, team member names or important customers. Contact lists can also be synced with Microsoft Outlook or other compatible programs.
Custom List	A SharePoint list that is blank that can be used to create a list to store custom data. You can add columns and views to the list to match the data and display what you want for your list.

TABLE 1-1: Lists That Can Be Created in a Blank SharePoint Site *(Continued)*

List Type	Description
Custom List in Datasheet View	A SharePoint list that is blank that can be used to create a list to store custom data. This list starts out with a datasheet view as the default view rather than a standard list view. A datasheet view is a grid view similar to what you would find in Access or Excel. You can add columns and views to the list to match the data and display what you want for your list.
Discussion Board	A SharePoint list that manages a discussion. This type of list supports discussion threads and has settings to allow moderation of a discussion board—for example, approval for posts before they appear publicly.
External List	An external list is a special SharePoint list that shows data coming from a third-party database or line of business system. External lists are discussed in detail in Chapter 6, "Working with Business Data."
Import Spreadsheet	A SharePoint list created by importing the columns and rows from an existing spreadsheet.
Issue Tracking	A SharePoint list that tracks issues or problems associated with a project or product; allows you to assign, track, and prioritize issues in the list.
Links	A SharePoint list that stores links to other web pages.
Project Tasks	A SharePoint list that stores tasks that can be displayed in a Gantt Chart view or synchronized with Microsoft Project or other compatible programs.
Survey	A SharePoint list that contains questions that you want to ask in a survey. Has functionality to allow you to create questions and view responses for the questions.
Tasks	A SharePoint list that allows you to store tasks assigned to a person or team. A tasks list is also used in workflow as we will see in Chapter 8, "SharePoint Workflow."

Extension Point: Custom List Type

In Chapter 4, "SharePoint Lists," we'll see that you can create your own list type that can be displayed in the Create dialog shown in Figure 1-9—for example, you could create a "Candidates List" that is preconfigured to track people interviewing for a job.

Let's create a list from the Create dialog and explore the capabilities and options associated with a list in SharePoint. To create a list, use the Create dialog shown in Figure 1-9. Select Custom List from the list of items that are available to be created. Name the list Interview Candidates in the text box at the right side of the Create dialog. Finally click the Create button to create the new custom list.

After you create the new list, SharePoint opens the main web page for the list as shown in Figure 1-11. Notice the List tab is selected. This tab contains a number of commands for working with the list. As we work through these commands you will see the capabilities of a SharePoint list.

Looking at the ribbon in Figure 1-11 we can see first that a list by default has what is called a Standard View and a Datasheet View. The Standard View is the web-based view that is currently showing. The Datasheet View provides a spreadsheet-like view of the list as shown in Figure 1-12. Here we have also clicked on the Show Task Pane button in the Datasheet section of the ribbon, which displays additional commands in a task pane to the right of the Datasheet View that let you use the data in the list with Access and Excel.

You can create additional views and change which view is the default view. To create a new view, click the Create View button in the Manage Views section of the ribbon. When you click the Create View button, a page appears allowing you to choose from a variety of view formats as shown in Figure 1-13. In addition to the Standard View and Datasheet View formats, you can also choose to display the list as a calendar, a Gantt chart, custom forms and reports created in Access, or custom views created in SharePoint designer.

Figure 1-11: A SharePoint list's Standard View

Figure 1-12: A SharePoint list's Datasheet View

Figure 1-13: SharePoint list view formats

For this example, let's choose a Standard View by clicking on the Standard View icon in Figure 1-13. The next page that appears is the Create View page shown in Figure 1-14. This page lets you set the name of your custom view and whether it should be the default view for the list. In addition, this page has expandable sections that let you apply a range of settings, including which columns should be displayed, sorting order, whether a filter should be applied to limit the items displayed, whether editing can occur inline, whether to group the list by particular columns, whether to show totals for a particular column, and whether folders should be allowed in the list.

Figure 1-15 shows the Columns section of the Create View page where you can set which columns are displayed and in which order. Notice that even though we created a blank custom list, it is preconfigured with a number of columns that are common to most SharePoint lists. In the Columns section, let's check the Created and Created By columns to show them in our custom list view. Then click the OK button at the bottom of the page to create the custom view.

The resulting custom view is shown in Figure 1-16. Note that the Created and Created By columns are visible in this view.

Figure 1-14: SharePoint Create View page

Extension Point: Custom List Views

You can define one or more custom views and install them to a Share-Point site along with a custom list type. We will see how to do that in Chapter 4, "SharePoint Lists."

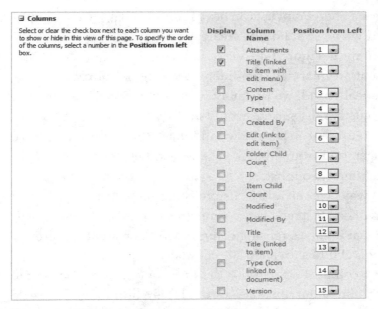

Figure 1-15: SharePoint list view columns settings

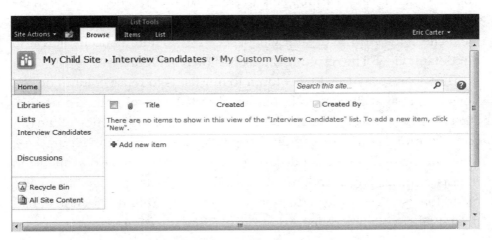

Figure 1-16: A Custom View called "My Custom View"

We've seen that a SharePoint list can have multiple views in a variety of view formats and we've seen how to create a custom view. But when we looked at the columns in Figure 1-15, we didn't have the necessary column names to represent an interview candidate (the original purpose of this list). Now, in the real world, we probably would have created a Contacts list rather than a custom list since it would already have many of the columns required to represent an interview candidate. But for the purposes of this example, we started from a blank custom list. Let's examine how to add additional columns to our list.

There are two ways we can add a custom column to our list. First we'll show the process of create a new list column and second we'll show a different technique that involves reusing column definitions that are already available in the SharePoint site called site columns.

To create a list column, we can use the List tab of the ribbon. In the Manage Views section of the ribbon (Figure 1-11) is a button called Create Column. When you click that button, the dialog shown in Figure 1-17 appears. This allows you to pick the name for the column and the type of the column along with additional settings that are appropriate to the type you pick. In this case, we are going to create a column called "Phone Interview Completed" and set the Yes/No. The default value will be No and we'll check the Add to default view check box to automatically add it to our default view. The resulting dialog is shown in Figure 1-18.

The second way to add a column to our list is to reuse column definitions available at the site collection level called site columns. To do this, click the List Settings button in the List tab in the Settings section of the ribbon (Figure 1-11). The List Settings page appears as shown in Figure 1-19. Many of the things you can do using the List ribbon are also available in the List Settings page. And, in this case, the List Settings page has a command that isn't available in the ribbon. Note in the Columns section in Figure 1-19 there is a link called Add from existing site columns.

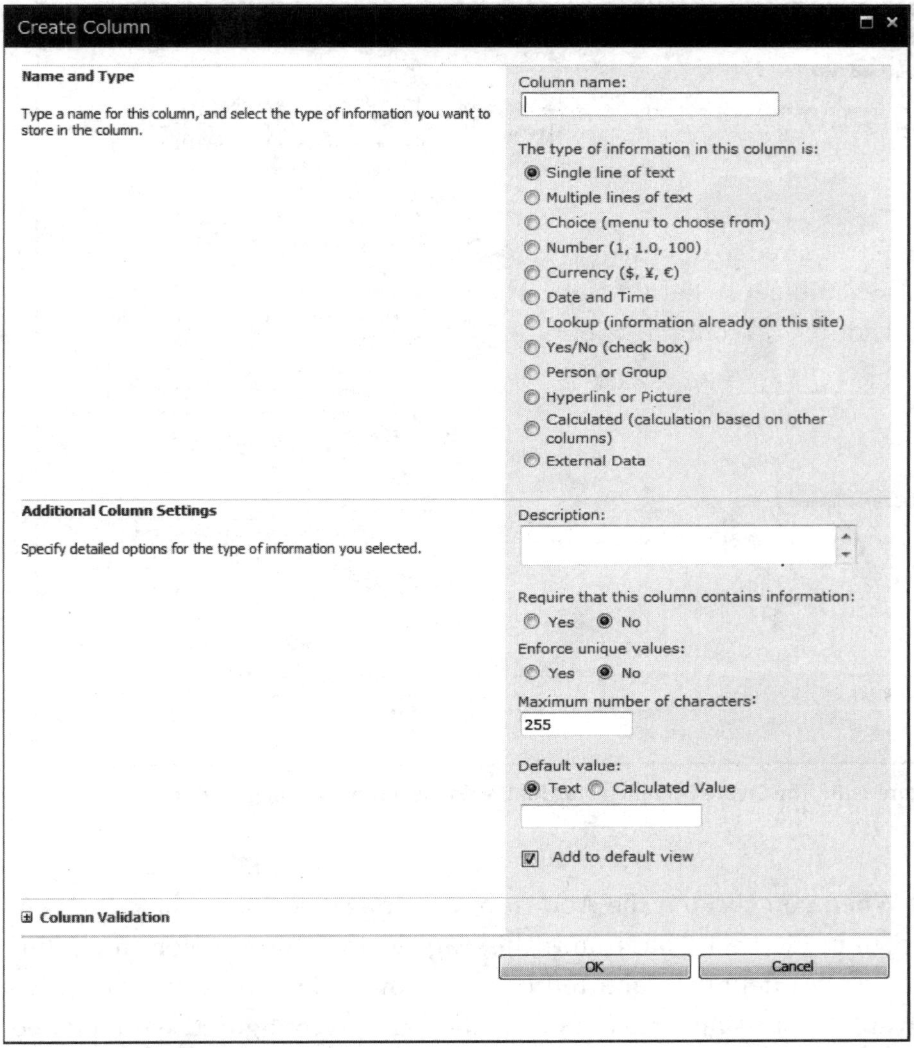

Create Column   □ ×

Name and Type

Type a name for this column, and select the type of information you want to store in the column.

Column name:

[   ]

The type of information in this column is:

- ◉ Single line of text
- ○ Multiple lines of text
- ○ Choice (menu to choose from)
- ○ Number (1, 1.0, 100)
- ○ Currency ($, ¥, €)
- ○ Date and Time
- ○ Lookup (information already on this site)
- ○ Yes/No (check box)
- ○ Person or Group
- ○ Hyperlink or Picture
- ○ Calculated (calculation based on other columns)
- ○ External Data

Additional Column Settings

Specify detailed options for the type of information you selected.

Description:

[   ]

Require that this column contains information:
○ Yes ◉ No

Enforce unique values:
○ Yes ◉ No

Maximum number of characters:
[255]

Default value:
◉ Text ○ Calculated Value
[   ]

☑ Add to default view

⊞ **Column Validation**

[OK   ]   [Cancel   ]

Figure 1-17: The Create Column dialog

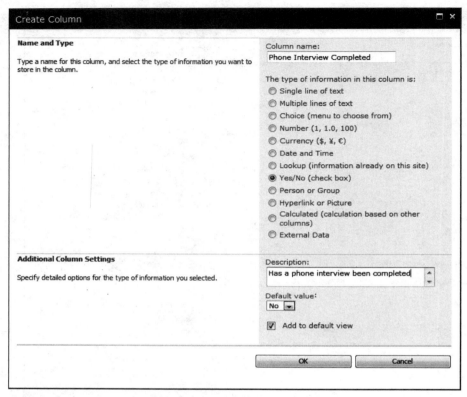

Figure 1-18: The Create Column dialog for the Phone Interview Completed column

When you click on the Add from existing site columns link, the page shown in Figure 1-20 appears. This page lets you browse for an existing site column definition and reuse the column definition in your list. One advantage of using site columns is they are preconfigured with a name, data type, and default behavior so you don't have to spend a lot of time setting the column up. Here we have filtered to show site columns used in Core Contact and Calendar lists. We then selected three columns from site column definitions to use in our list: E-Mail, Full Name, and Referred By. Finally, clicking OK adds the columns to the list and to the default view for the list.

Several other settings should be mentioned from the General Settings section of the List Settings page in Figure 1-19. First, the List Settings page

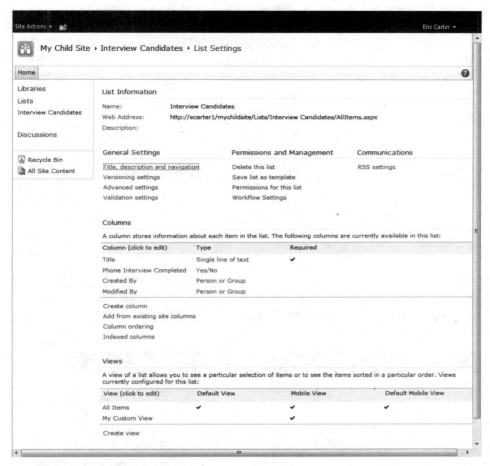

Figure 1-19: The List Settings page

provides a Versioning settings link that when clicked on displays the Versioning Settings page shown in Figure 1-21. Versioning settings allows you to set whether items added to a list remain in draft state until they have been approved. Visibility of items in this draft state can be controlled so they are not visible in public views. For example, you could have a list to which anyone can post news items, but the news items are not visible to everyone until a site owner approves them. You can also specify whether a versioning history is saved for each item in a list, thereby allowing you to track changes made to an item and revert to a previous version of an item.

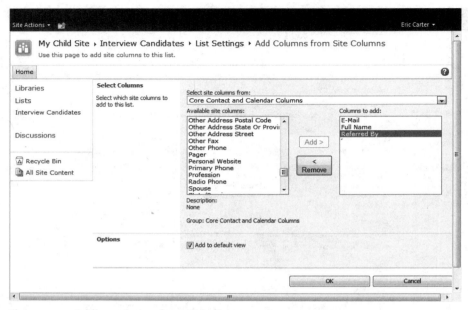

Figure 1-20: Adding columns from site columns

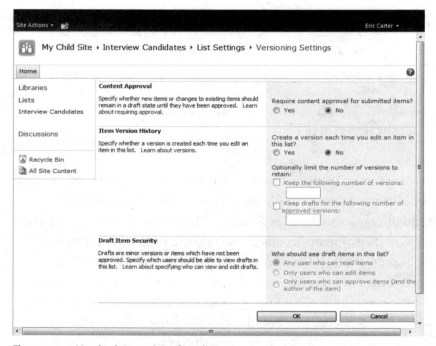

Figure 1-21: Versioning settings for a list

Extension Point: Custom Site Columns

You can define one or more custom site column types and install them to a SharePoint site. You typically do this when the built-in column types are not sufficient for your needs—for example, maybe you would want to create a custom site column that could contain and display barcode information for a product. To do that you might want to create a custom validator to validate that the bar code entered is correct and maybe a custom view form to display the bar code. We will see how to create a custom site column in Chapter 4, "SharePoint Lists."

The General Settings section of the List Settings page in Figure 1-19 also has a link to an Advanced Settings page that controls the list settings described in Table 1-2. There is also a Validation Settings link that allows you to specify a formula that validates the data in a particular column when new items are added to a list. For example, you could require that the "Retail Price" column of an item is greater than the "Sales Price" column for the same item and display a user message if the formula evaluates to False.

TABLE 1-2: Advanced Settings for a List

Advanced Settings	Description
Content Types	Controls whether users can create multiple types of items within one list. This is discussed more in the next section on Document libraries.
Item-level Permissions	You can configure a list so that users can only see items that they have created or see items created by all users. You can also configure a list so users can create and edit all items in the list, edit only items created by them, or have read-only permissions and no permissions to create or edit.
Attachments	A list can be configured so items in it can have attached files.

Continues

TABLE 1-2: Advanced Settings for a List *(Continued)*

Advanced Settings	Description
Folders	Lists can have a folder structure in which a new folder command is available, and items can be organized into folders or you can disable the creation of folders in a list.
Search	You can opt to exclude items in a list from appearing in search results.
Offline Client Availability	SharePoint allows users to download a list for use in an offline client like SharePoint Workspace. You can turn this on or off to either allow or disallow this scenario for a list.
Datasheet	As we saw earlier, a list can be displayed in a datasheet view. This setting allows you to allow or disallow the bulk editing of data in the datasheet.
Dialogs	SharePoint can use dialogs to display a "new item", "edit item", and "display item" form for items in a list—if you disallow dialogs, these forms will be displayed in new web pages.

In the Permissions and Management section of the List Settings page in Figure 1-19, there are several links that allow you to control permissions for the list and manage other aspects of the list. The first link in this section called "Delete this list" allows you to delete the list from SharePoint. The second link called "Save list as template" allows you to save the list as a template that can then be used to create new lists. We will describe this feature more in Chapter 4, "SharePoint Lists," but this allows you to reuse a list you have created in another solution.

Clicking the link "Permissions for this list" brings up the Permissions page for the list shown in Figure 1-22. In SharePoint there are three SharePoint permission groups created by default for a list: Team Site Members, Team Site Owners, and Team Site Visitors. There are also three permission levels used by default in a list: Contribute, Full Control, and Read. As you might expect, Team Site Members have Contribute permission, meaning they can add, edit, and delete items in existing lists and document librar-

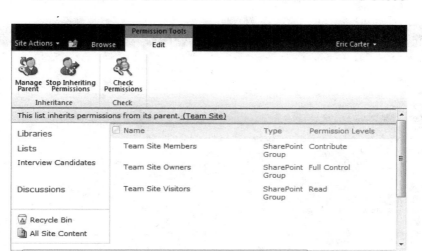

Figure 1-22: Permission settings for a list

ies. Team Site Owners have Full Control permission meaning they have all permissions available, including the permissions to create, modify, and delete lists and libraries. Team Site Visitors have read-only access to the web site.

If you click on the link for a particular permission group, you can add and remove users from it as shown on the Site Actions page in Figure 1-23. A key part of SharePoint is the permission system that allows you to create custom permission groups and even custom permission sets. SharePoint allows you even more fine-grained control over permission granted to a particular group. There are more granular permissions available for working with lists, sites, and personal views and web pages. For example, you could create a new permission group with a custom permission level that is almost the set of permissions in Contribute but does not include deletion of item privileges. You might do this because you want to enforce a policy that allows items in a particular list to be deleted only by members of a particular group and not by general users of the SharePoint list. A complete discussion of all the permissions that can be used in creating permission levels and groups is beyond the scope of this book, but can be found discussed here: http://office.microsoft.com/en-us/sharepointtechnology/HA101001491033.aspx.

Figure 1-23: Permission group membership page

The final setting in the Permissions and Management section of the List Settings page in Figure 1-19 is a setting to control the workflow associated with a list. We will consider workflow more in Chapter 8, "SharePoint Workflow," but for now it is sufficient to know that you can associate custom workflow with a list—essentially executable code that runs when items in the list are created or changed.

Extension Point: Custom Workflow

You can define one or more custom workflows and install them to a Share-Point site. Workflow can also include forms that are displayed when the workflow is started and configured for a list. The workflow can be associated with a particular list as well. For example, you might create a custom interview workflow that codifies the steps and the people that must be involved when scheduling an interview with a candidate for a job position.

We've considered in some detail the options available in the List tab of the List Tools section of the ribbon and the List Settings page for a list. All of these tools help configure the list and operate at the list level. Users typically will use the Items tab of the List Tools section of the list to add, edit, and delete items from the list. Let's consider some of the experiences around the item-editing experience in a list. The Items tab of the ribbon is shown in Figure 1-24. In this example, no items have yet been added to the list so most of the ribbon buttons are disabled. Clicking the New Item button allows the user to create a new item in the list.

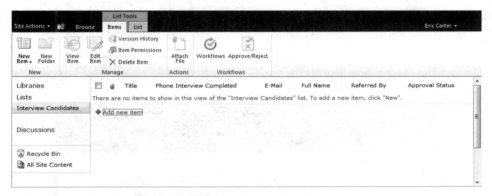

Figure 1-24: Interview Candidates list page

When you click on the Add new item button, the New Item dialog appears as shown in Figure 1-24. This dialog lets you enter the column values for the item, attach a file (if Attachments is enabled for the list), and save the new item to the list.

Once you've added a new item to the list, you can then start to use other buttons in the ribbon. The View Item button, shown in Figure 1-25, allows you to view whatever list item is checked in a View dialog as shown in Figure 1-26.

Items in a list can also be edited by clicking the Edit Item button in the Items tab of the List Tools section of the ribbon. When you click this button, the Edit Item dialog appears as shown in Figure 1-27.

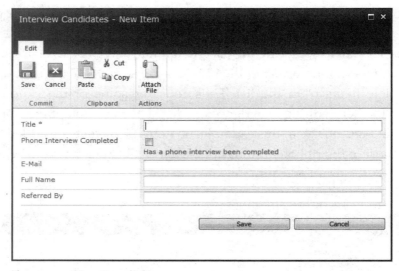

Figure 1-25: New Item dialog

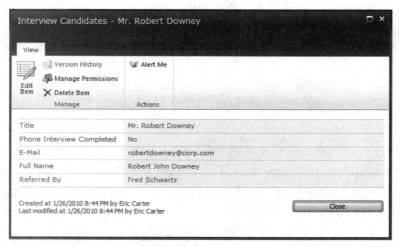

Figure 1-26: View dialog

Extension Point: Custom New, View, and Edit Item Dialogs

You can define custom new, view, and edit item dialogs for a list that can also run code to validate the creation and editing of items.

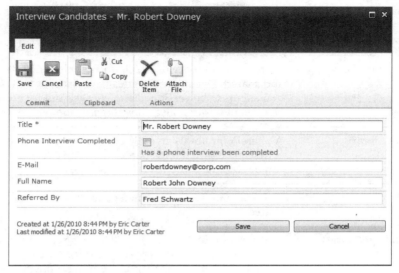

Figure 1-27: Edit item dialog

The Items tab of the List Tools section of the ribbon also has buttons to work with workflows associated with items in the list.

Extension Point: Custom Actions in the Ribbon

You can customize the ribbon that is shown for a particular SharePoint page. For example, we could add a button (also called a custom action) to the Items tab for this list that performs a custom action on a selected candidate in the list such as sending the candidate an e-mail message.

Libraries

A library is a specialized SharePoint list focused on managing documents and files. A library is where you can store and manage files and share them with other members of the SharePoint site. Table 1-3 shows the different kinds of libraries you can create in SharePoint Foundation and gives a brief description of each.

TABLE 1-3: Libraries That Can Be Created in a Blank SharePoint Site

Library Type	Description
Document Library	A SharePoint library in which documents can be stored and shared. Document libraries have features that allow documents to be versioned and checked out for editing. Document libraries also allow organization by folders.
Form Library	A SharePoint library in which business forms stored as XML can be stored and shared. Forms in a forms library can be edited by Microsoft InfoPath 2010.
Picture Library	A SharePoint library in which pictures can be stored and shared.
Wiki Page Library	A SharePoint library in which wiki pages can be stored and shared. Wiki pages are easily edited by end users and allow for easy collaborative editing. Wiki pages can also be easily linked to each other.

SharePoint Foundation versus SharePoint Server

Note that this chapter and this book are primarily focused on SharePoint Foundation, the most basic version of SharePoint. In SharePoint Server, there are additional features available. For example, in SharePoint Server you can also create an Asset Library and a Data Connection Library.

As you might expect, the differences between a document library and a list are small and most of the extension points available for a list are also available for a SharePoint library. We will note the extension points in this section as well, even though many are duplicates from the previous list section.

Let's create a document library from the Create dialog and explore the capabilities and options associated with a document library in SharePoint. To create a document library, start in the page shown in Figure 1-8 by going to the home page for your site, dropping down the Site Actions menu, and choosing View All Site Content. The Create dialog shown in Figure 1-9 appears. Select Document Library from the list of items that are available to be created. Click on the More Options button in the right side of the dialog. This lets you fill in more details about the document library that you want to create as shown in Figure 1-28. For this example, we'll give this document library the name "Expense Reports" and set the description to "A place to put expense reports." SharePoint lets you choose whether you want the document library displayed as a link in the Quick Launch area—the side bar at the left side of the SharePoint page. It also lets you choose whether to use document versioning, which will let you track all the revisions made to documents in the document library. Choose Yes for this option. Finally SharePoint lets you choose the document template to be used for new files created in the document library. Here we'll choose Microsoft Excel spreadsheet from the Document Template drop-down list. Finally click the Create button to create the new document library.

Extension Point: Custom Library Type

In Chapter 4, "SharePoint Lists," we'll see that you can create your own library type that can be displayed in the Create dialog—for example, you could create an "Expenses Library" that is preconfigured to track expense reports.

Extension Point: Custom Word and Excel Document Templates with Visual Studio

In Chapter 7, "SharePoint Content Types," we'll see that you can create your own customized document template and associate it with a document library. This document template can also have .NET code associated with it by using Visual Studio's Excel and Word Template Projects. The .NET code you associate with the Excel and Word templates runs whenever the document is opened by the user.

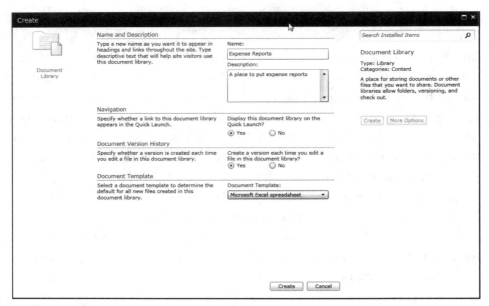

Figure 1-28: Create options for creating a document library

After you create the new document library, SharePoint opens the main web page for the document library. We've clicked on the Documents tab of the ribbon and pressed the New Document button to create a new Excel spreadsheet in the library, which we saved with the name "My Expense Report." The resulting document library with the Documents tab activated is shown in Figure 1-29. The Documents tab lets users create new documents—in this case Microsoft Excel spreadsheets because we chose that as the default Document Template for the library. Users can also upload existing documents and create folders in the document library to further organize content.

Extension Point: Custom Actions in the Ribbon

You can customize the ribbon that is shown for a particular SharePoint page. For example, we could add a button (also called a custom action) to the ribbon of this documents library that would submit an expense report from this list to the finance department for further processing.

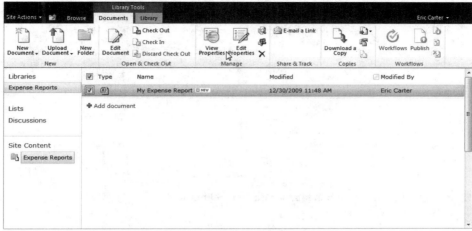

Figure 1-29: The Documents ribbon tab for a document library

Users can edit documents in the document library and they can also check the document in and out so revision history is maintained. They can view and edit the properties associated with a document such as the name of the document and the title to be used for the document. They can also e-mail a link to the document to a colleague, download a copy of the document to their local machines, and send a copy of the document to another document library where it can be synchronized with the master copy in this document library. From the Documents tab of the ribbon, you can also manage workflow associated with a particular document. We'll introduce workflow later in this chapter.

If you click on the Library tab of the ribbon, you will see a number of settings and commands that impact the entire document library as shown in Figure 1-30. The Library tab provides commands to switch between a standard view and a datasheet view. It also provides commands to modify and create new views on the document library—a document library always has at least one view and can have multiple additional views. A view for a document library specifies the columns that are shown for the document (e.g., name, modified by, etc.) and the order in which those columns are shown. It also specifies which columns to sort and in what order.

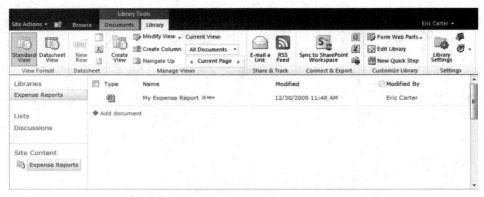

Figure 1-30: The Library ribbon tab for a document library

Extension Point: Custom Document Properties

In this document library, the properties associated with the document are fairly boring—just the name of the document file and a title. Later in Chapter 7, "SharePoint Content Types," we'll see that you can create custom document properties that are associated with a document and editable and viewable in the document library—for example, you could expose the total expense amount for the expense report as a property that could be edited without opening the document and could be displayed as a column in the SharePoint document library view.

Figure 1-31 shows the page that appears when you click on the Modify View button in the Library tab to modify the currently active view. Table 1-4 summarizes the types of view settings that are configurable in the Edit View page. Note that a similar page appears when modifying the view for a SharePoint list.

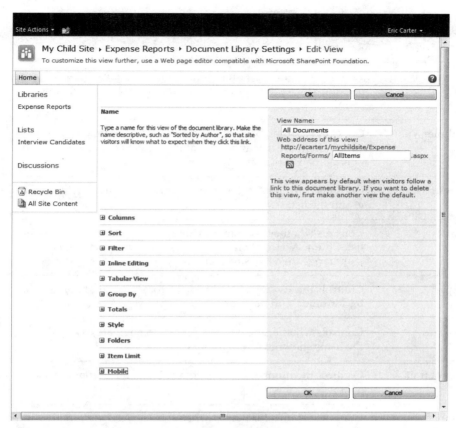

Figure 1-31: The Edit View page for a document library view

TABLE 1-4:   View Settings Associated with a List or Document Library View

View Setting	Description
Columns	Controls which columns are displayed for the view and the order in which the columns are displayed
Sort	Controls the primary and optional secondary column to sort the list by and the sort order
Filter	Sets a filter to be used for a list to control which items are shown

Continues

TABLE 1-4: View Settings Associated with a List or Document Library View *(Continued)*

View Setting	Description
Inline Editing	Controls whether an edit button is enabled for each row of the list, allowing editing of the row without showing a separate form.
Tabular View	Controls whether individual item check boxes are provided for each item in the list, allowing multiple items to be selected and operated on at the same time.
Group By	Controls a primary and optional secondary column by which to group the list.
Totals	Controls whether a summary value is shown for columns in the list. Count, Average, Maximum, and Minimum can be used to summarize the values in a column.
Style	Controls the styles used by the list—for example, shading, background, and borders.
Folders	Controls whether the list uses folders to navigate or whether the list is shown without folders.
Item Limit	Controls the number of items to display at once from the list in a view.
Mobile	Controls settings for the list when it is viewed by a mobile device.

Figure 1-32 shows the Columns section of the page that lets you choose the columns for items in the document library that are displayed in the view. You can check the check boxes next to each column name to control whether that column displays in the current view. You can also choose the order in which the columns display using the drop-down list next to each column name.

When defining a view, you can also specify filters that can hide or show items in the document library based on the values of columns—for example, you could create a view with a filter that only shows documents in the document library that have been modified by you. There are a number of

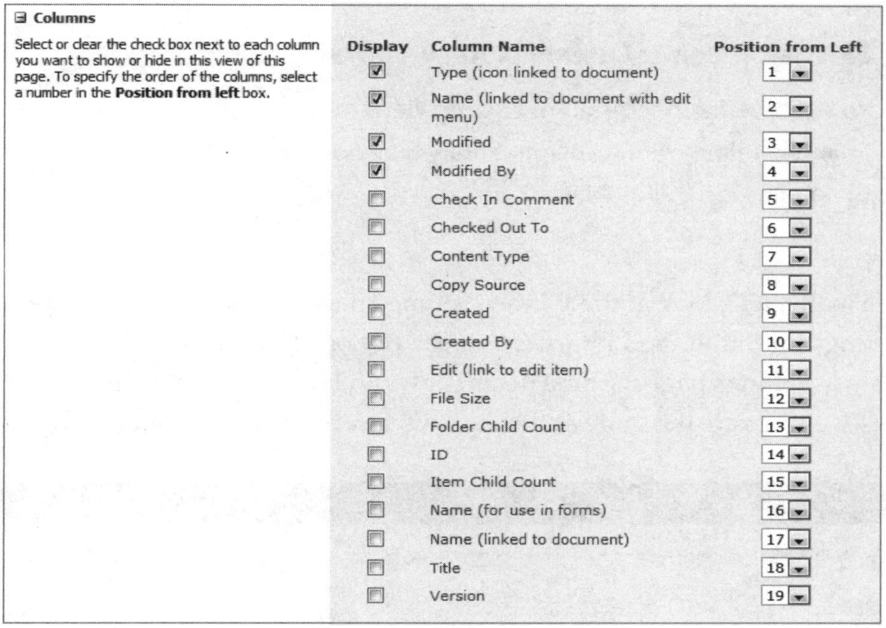

Figure 1-32: The Columns section of the Edit View page

other settings as shown in Figure 1-31—to explore the settings available for views, click on the Create View button in the Library tab of the ribbon to create a new view for the document library or click on the Modify View button in the Library tab to modify the currently active view.

Extension Point: Custom Site Columns

You can define one or more custom site column types and install them to a SharePoint site. You typically do this when the built-in column types are not sufficient for your needs—for example, maybe you would want to create a custom site column that could contain and display barcode information for a product. To do that you might want to create a custom validator to validate that the bar code entered is correct and maybe a custom view form to display the bar code.

Extension Point: Custom Library Views

You can define one or more custom views and install them to a SharePoint site along with a custom library type. We will see how to do that in Chapter 4, "SharePoint Lists."

Finally, let's look at the Library Settings page by clicking on the Library Settings button in the Library tab of the ribbon. This causes the Document Library Settings page to come up as shown in Figure 1-33. Note that most of these settings are the same as the ones we saw for lists earlier in the chapter.

Figure 1-33: The Document Library Settings page

The Document Library Settings page has a lot of the same kinds of commands as those shown on the Library tab of the ribbon. One command of interest is accessed by clicking the Advanced settings link on this page. The top setting in advanced settings lets you turn on the management of content types as shown in Figure 1-34. Click Yes to allow management of content types then click the OK button at the bottom of the page.

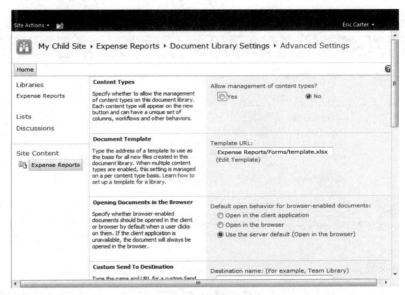

Figure 1-34: Advanced Settings: Allow management of content types

Content types define the columns and document associated with a class of list items—for example, one list could contain both an Excel template-based Expense Report that has a custom column called "Total Expenses" and a Word template-based Invoice with a custom column called "Invoice Amount." The Expense Report and the Invoice are both examples of content types. Content types are used in all SharePoint lists—for example, the Calendar list in SharePoint uses a content type called Event, which defines the columns associated with each event listed in the Calendar.

Content types are a concept that were there all along in the document library as well, but when you say Yes to allow management of content types you can actually see the content type associated with the document library.

If you navigate back to the Document Library Settings page (this will happen automatically after you click the OK button on the Advanced Settings page) you will now see a new section in the Document Library Settings page called Content Types as shown in Figure 1-35. As you can see, the document library already has a content type associated with it called Document. If you click on the Document link in the Content Types section, the settings page for the Document content type will appear as shown in Figure 1-36.

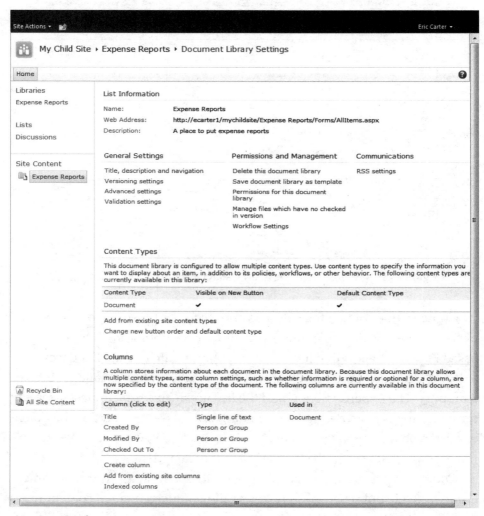

Figure 1-35: The Document Library Settings page with content type management turned on

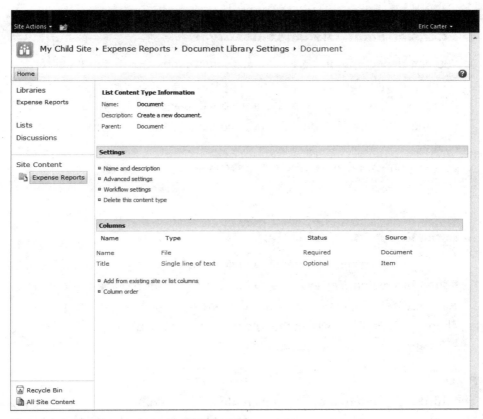

Figure 1-36: The Document content type settings

As you can see in Figure 1-36, a content type goes beyond just specifying a document template file to also specifying custom columns associated with the document and the workflow associated with the document. Furthermore, looking at Figure 1-35 you can see that you can optionally have multiple content types available in one document library. For example, one document library could have a content type for an expense report that is an Excel workbook and a second content type for an invoice that is a Word document. This same concept applies to SharePoint lists. You could have a list that contains both Appointments and Contacts.

Note that the other options and behaviors we saw in the SharePoint Lists section earlier in this chapter also apply to document libraries, including the ability to use workflow, and the ability to have new, view, and edit forms.

Extension Point: Custom Content Types

You can define one or more custom content types and install them to a SharePoint site. These content types can then be used by end users in the lists they create. Content types can have a document template associated with them that can include .NET code. Content types can also have custom columns and workflow associated with them. We will see how to create a custom Content Type in Chapter 7, "SharePoint Content Types."

Extension Point: Custom Forms

You can create a custom form to be displayed when an item in a library is edited or created. For example, a custom form can replace the default form you get when you click on a document in a document library and choose Edit Properties from the Document tab of the ribbon.

Pages

The third type of item that you can create in SharePoint is a page. There are two main types of pages you can create in SharePoint as shown in Table 1-5: a wiki page that can be edited in the browser that can contain text, images, tables, and other content and a web part page that can contain web parts. A web part is a reusable control that can be displayed in a web page and customized by the user of the page containing the web part.

TABLE 1-5: Pages That Can Be Created in a SharePoint Site

Page Type	Description
Page	This is a wiki page that can be edited in the web browser and can contain text, images, tables, links to other wiki pages, list data, and other content.
Web Part Page	This is a page that has a standard layout in which web parts can be displayed and the display of each web part can be customized.

In this section we will consider the creation of a web part page. Creation of a wiki page is a cool feature of SharePoint, but we won't be using wiki pages in this book. Let's create a web part page from the Create dialog and explore the capabilities and options associated with a web part page in SharePoint. To create a web part page, open the page shown in Figure 1-8 by going to the home page for your site, dropping down the Site Actions menu, and choosing View All Site Content. In the All Site Content page, click the Create button. The Create dialog shown in Figure 1-9 appears. Click on Page in the Filter By section to show only the Pages you can create. The Page and Web Part Page are shown as seen in Figure 1-37. Click the Web Part Page then click the Create button.

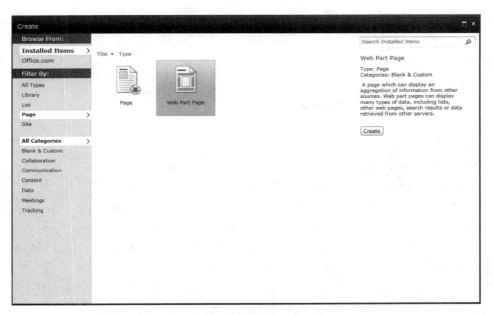

Figure 1-37: Pages that can be created in a SharePoint site

When you click the Create button, the New Web Part Page appears as shown in Figure 1-38. This page allows you to name your web part page, select a layout for your page, and select a location to save your web part page. Here we've named our page My Web Part Page. The layout we chose has one region in which web parts can be placed. Finally, we save the page

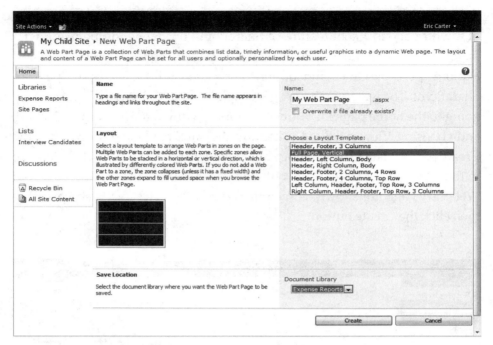

Figure 1-38: The New Web Part Page

to the Expense Reports document library. You can also save it to other document libraries associated with the web site.

After you click the Create button to create your web part page, the page will appear in an edit mode as shown in Figure 1-39. In this mode, you can add web parts to your page. To add a web part, just click on the Add a Web Part link and the UI shown in Figure 1-40 will appear.

The UI in Figure 1-40 shows several categories of web parts that are available by default. The Lists and Libraries category contains web parts that are preconfigured to display libraries and lists that are already added to the SharePoint site. The other web parts that are available are described in Table 1-6.

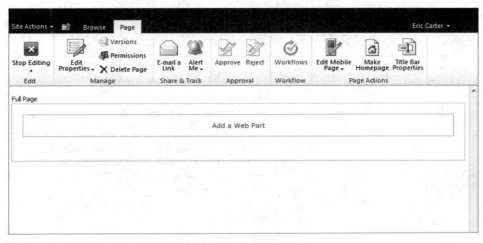

Figure 1-39: Edit view for the newly created web part page

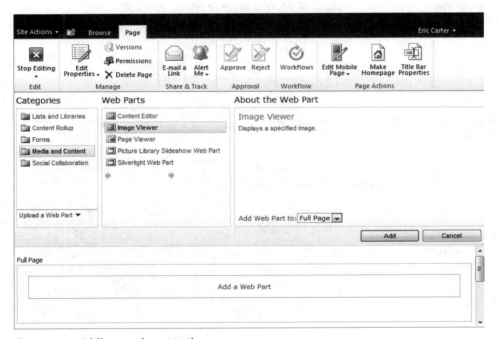

Figure 1-40: Adding a web part to the page

TABLE 1-6:   Some Web Parts That Can Be Added to a Web Part Page

Web Part	Description
Relevant Documents	Displays documents that are relevant to the user viewing the page.
XML Viewer	Displays XML transformed via an XSLT file.
HTML Form	Allows you to use simple HTML and HTML controls in your page and connect them to other web parts in the page.
Content Editor	Displays rich text.
Image Viewer	Displays an image file.
Page Viewer	Displays another web page in an IFrame.
Picture Library Slideshow	Displays a slideshow of pictures from a picture library (a special kind of document library).
Silverlight Web Part	Displays a Silverlight application.
Site Users	Displays users of the SharePoint site.
User Tasks	Displays tasks associated with the current user.

Extension Point: Custom Web Parts

You can create a custom web part that can be displayed in a SharePoint web part page. For example, you could create a custom web part that displays data from a list in a custom way or that displays other data. For more information on creating a custom web part, see Chapter 9, "SharePoint Web Parts."

We will add an Image Viewer web part to our web part page. After selecting the Image Viewer web part as shown in Figure 1-40, click the Add button to add the web part to the page. The web part is displayed as shown in Figure 1-41. Note that the page is still in an editing mode.

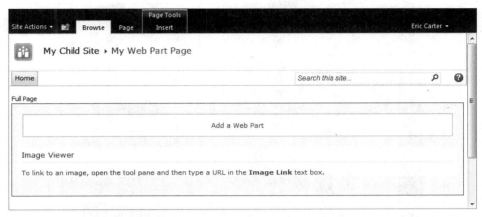

Figure 1-41: A web part page with an Image Viewer web part

Extension Point: Custom Silverlight Application

One of the web parts that is available in Table 1-6 is a Silverlight web part. The Silverlight web part lets you run a Silverlight application within a SharePoint web part page. For more information on using the Silverlight web part, see Chapter 9, "SharePoint Web Parts."

To configure the web part, hover over the web part; a check box will appear. Click the check box to select the web part. A new ribbon section appears called Web Part Tools with a tab called Options. If you click on the Options tab, a button called Web Part Properties is displayed as shown in Figure 1-42. Clicking the Web Part Properties button displays a sidebar to the right of the web part where various properties of the web part can be configured. In this case you can specify a URL for the image displayed by the web part.

When you are done configuring the page and any web parts in the page, click the Page tab and the Stop Editing button to show the page in its final form as shown in Figure 1-43.

Figure 1-42: Configuring the Web Part Properties for the Image Viewer web part

Figure 1-43: The Final Web Part Page with one Image Viewer web part

Subsites and Workspaces

The fourth type of item that you can create in SharePoint is a subsite or workspace. A workspace and subsite are the same thing: a SharePoint site populated with some initial lists, libraries, and pages. When you create a subsite or workspace, SharePoint creates a SharePoint site that is a child of the SharePoint site you create the subsite or workspace from. There are a number of different subsites and workspaces that are defined by Share-Point that you can create, as shown in Table 1-7.

TABLE 1-7: Subsites That Can Be Created in a Blank SharePoint Site

Subsite Type	Description
Basic Meeting Workspace	A site used to plan, organize, and capture the results of a meeting. This workspace is preconfigured with lists to manage the agenda, attendees, and documents generated by the meeting.
Blank Meeting Workspace	A site used to plan, organize, and capture the results of a meeting. This site doesn't have any pre-created lists in it.
Blank Site	A blank SharePoint site like the one we created at the start of this chapter.
Blog	A site to post blog pages in.
Decision Meeting Workspace	A site used to track and record tasks and decisions made in meetings.
Document Workspace	A site used to collaborate on a document.
Group Work Site	A site used to help a team work together. It includes a group calendar, shared document library, and other preconfigured lists.
Multipage Meeting Workspace	Similar to the Basic Meeting Workspace; it includes additional web pages that can be customized.
Social Meeting Workspace	A site to organize a social meeting.
Team Site	A site to organize, author, and share information in document libraries, calendar lists, and other preconfigured lists.

Extension Point: Custom Sites or Workspaces

You can create a custom site template that can be listed as a site or workspace that users can create. For example, you could create a custom site template that defines a SharePoint site created for tracking a particular interview candidate—maybe the site includes a wiki for notes on the candidate, a picture library for pictures taken the day the candidate interviewed, and so on.

To create a subsite or workspace, open the page shown in Figure 1-8 by going to the home page for your site, dropping down the Site Actions menu, and choosing View All Site Content. In the All Site Content page, click the Create button. The Create dialog shown in Figure 1-9 appears. Click on Site in the Filter By section to show only the sites you can create. The sites you can create are shown in Figure 1-44.

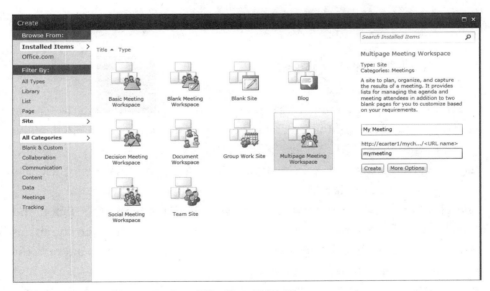

Figure 1-44: Sites That Can Be Created in SharePoint Site

In Figure 1-44 we have selected the Multipage Meeting Workspace and set the name of the site to My Meeting and the URL to http://ecarter1/mychildsite/mymeeting. The URL emphasizes that this is going to be a child site of the original site we created called mychildsite. When you click the Create button, a new subsite is created as shown in Figure 1-45.

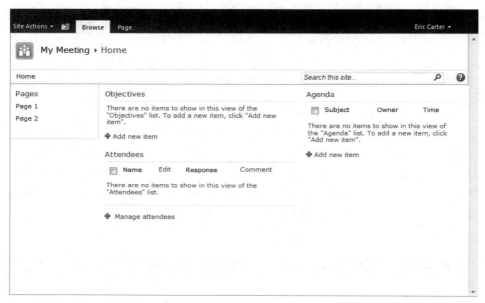

Figure 1-45: The My Meeting workspace

The Multipage Meeting Workspace site is an interesting site to look at because it has many of the precreated SharePoint elements we have talked about in this chapter. The home page for the site is a web part page, which has three web parts in it, one displaying the Objectives SharePoint list, one displaying the Attendees SharePoint list, and one displaying the Agenda SharePoint list. To verify this, you can click the Page tab in the ribbon and then the Edit Page button, which will then show you that the page layout has left, center, and right columns to which web parts can be added, but only the left and center columns contain web parts as shown in Figure 1-46. You also may notice that two additional web part pages were created with the workspace, one called Page 1 and the other called Page 2. Links to these pages are accessible from the quick launch area on the left side of the main site page.

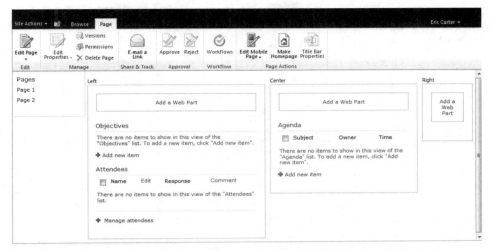

Figure 1-46: The web part page and web parts used to create the home page for the My Meeting Workspace

Next, drop down the Site Actions menu for the My Meeting Workspace and choose View All Site Content. This shows the SharePoint lists that are created with this workspace as shown in Figure 1-47: Agenda, Attendees, and Objectives.

Finally, if you navigate back to the parent site of the workspace (in our example http://ecarter1/mychildsite), drop down the Site Actions menu for My Child Site, and choose View All Site Content. You will see that under Sites and Workspaces the workspace My Meeting is now listed as a child site.

Examining the Settings of a Site and Site Collection

Now that we have explored the type of content that can be created in a SharePoint site, let's look at the settings available for a site and for a site collection. Let's go again to the child site we created at http://ecarter1/mychildsite/default.aspx. From the Site Actions menu pick Site Settings. The Site Settings page shown in Figure 1-48 will appear.

Let's compare the site settings for our child site with the site settings for our top-level site. This, as you may remember, is also where we find site collection settings. We go again to the top-level site at http://ecarter1 and from the Site Actions menu pick Site Settings. The Site Settings page

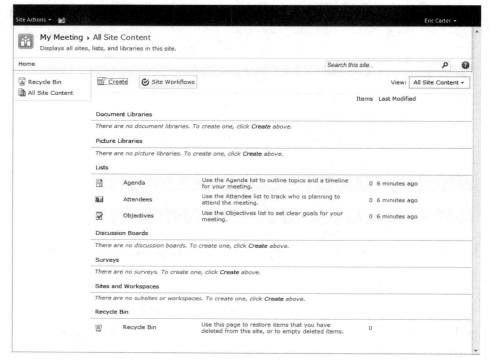

Figure 1-47: Lists that are Created in the My Meeting Workspace

shown in Figure 1-49 appears. We have drawn a box around each part of the Site Settings page that is added for a Site Collection so you can see the settings that are available at the site collection level that are not available at the site level.

We will now examine each category of Site and Site Collections settings and briefly consider what these settings control. In the tables in this section, settings that are only available at the Site Collection level are shown with gray shading.

Users and Permissions

Let's consider the permissions, users, and groups for a SharePoint site and site collection. First we'll look at people and groups. From the Site Settings page shown in Figure 1-48, click the People and groups link. This brings up the Team Site Members page shown in Figure 1-50. The Team Site Members page shows one of several groups that are created in a standard Share-

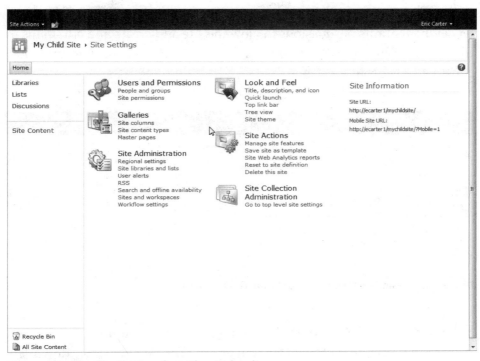

Figure 1-48: The Site Settings for a SharePoint site

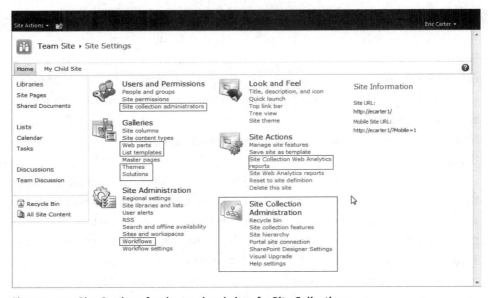

Figure 1-49: Site Settings for the top-level site of a Site Collection

Point site. The Team Site Members group has the Contribute permission level which grants permissions to view the site and create and edit items in the site. We will consider permission levels in a moment. For now, let's consider how groups are managed.

Figure 1-50: Team Site Members People and Groups page

Using the New drop-down in the page shown in Figure 1-50, you can add users to the Team Site Members group. The Actions drop-down lets you e-mail or call/message users in the group as well as remove users from the group. The Settings drop-down lets you manage settings for the group such as the name and permission level associated with the group.

The Group Settings page (which is displayed when you choose Group Settings from the Settings drop-down) is shown in Figure 1-51. In the Group Settings page you can modify the name of the group, set a description for the group, and select users or groups who can modify the group and the group membership. You can also control who can see the members of the group and whether e-mail requests can be made to join or leave the group.

Consider again the page shown in Figure 1-50. Although this page shows the Team Site Members group when you invoke it from the Site Settings page, you can also access other groups from the side bar at the left. The other groups that are shown by default are the Team Site Visitors group and the Team Site Owners group. The Team Site Visitors group has the Read permission level, which grants users permission to view the site but not to create or modify any items. The Team Site Owners group has the Full Control

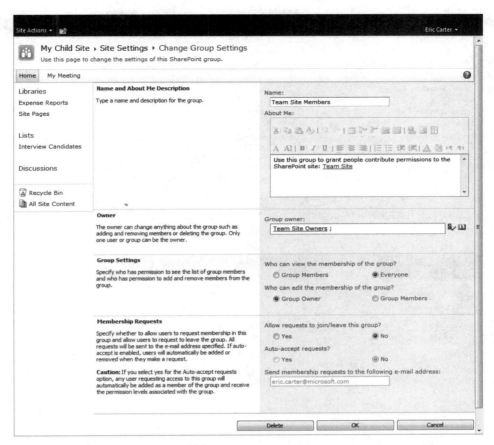

Figure 1-51: Group Settings for a SharePoint group

permission level, which grants full control of all content and settings of the site. To see all the groups defined for the site, click the Groups link at the left side of the page shown in Figure 1-50. This will show the All Groups page in Figure 1-52. The All Groups page has a New drop-down that lets you create additional SharePoint groups.

Now that we've seen how groups are created and managed and how users are added to a group, let's consider permission levels in SharePoint. From the Site Settings page shown in Figure 1-48, click the Site permissions link. This brings up the Permissions page shown in Figure 1-53. The permissions page shows the SharePoint groups and the permission levels associated with each group.

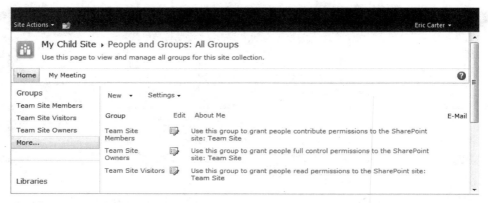

Figure 1-52: The All Groups page

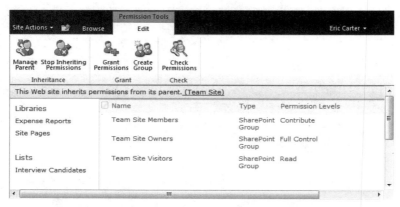

Figure 1-53: The permissions page for the child site

The Permission Tools ribbon shown in Figure 1-53 has a number of commands for working with permissions. First, because we are currently working with a child site and not the site associated with the site collection, permissions are inherited from the parent site. The buttons in the Inheritance ribbon group has commands for managing that inheritance. Clicking the Manage Parent button will take you to the Permissions settings for the parent group. You can also click the Stop Inheriting Permissions button if you want the child site to stop inheriting permissions from the parent site.

In the Grant section of the ribbon in Figure 1-53 is a Grant Permissions button and a Create Group button. The Grant Permissions button lets you specifically grant a permission level to a user. This is not the preferred way of doing this—you should instead add a user to a SharePoint group that is associated with a particular permission level. The Create Group button lets you create a new SharePoint group from this page. Finally, the Check Permissions button lets you enter the name of a user or group and see what permission levels they have.

Because the permission levels are inherited from the parent site, you must click on the Manage Parent button to get to the permissions page for the parent site if you want to edit the permission levels. Clicking the Manage Parent button takes you to the top-level site for the site collection's Permissions page shown in Figure 1-54.

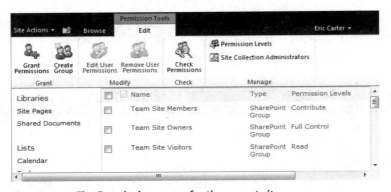

Figure 1-54: The Permissions page for the parent site

The Permissions page for the parent site has several additional buttons used for editing permission levels associated with SharePoint groups. If you click on the check box next to the Team Site Members group and then click the Edit User Permissions button, the dialog shown in Figure 1-55 appears. Here you can see that the Team Site Members group has the Contribute permission level. This dialog also describes what the other default permission levels allow.

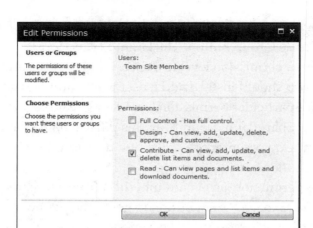

Figure 1-55: The permissions levels for the Team Site Members group

Returning to the permissions page in Figure 1-54, you can also edit built-in permissions levels or create your own custom permissions level by clicking the Permission Levels button. Clicking the Permissions Levels button displays the Permissions Levels page shown in Figure 1-56.

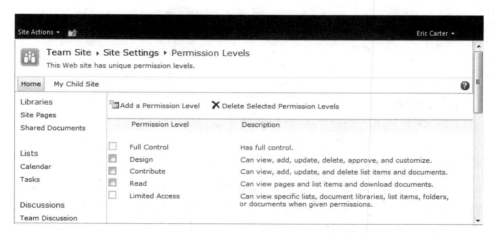

Figure 1-56: Permissions Levels page

From this page you can click the Add a Permission Level button to create a new custom permission level. Permission levels can contain a number of more granular permissions shown in Table 1-8. Table 1-8 also shows which built-in permission levels have which permissions.

TABLE 1-8: SharePoint Permissions and Default Permission Levels

Permission	Description	Design	Contribute	Read
List Permissions				
Manage Lists	Create and delete lists, add or remove columns in a list, and add or remove public views of a list.	X		
Override Check Out	Discard or check in a document that is checked out to another user.	X		
Add Items	Add items to lists and add documents to document libraries.	X	X	
Edit Items	Edit items in lists, edit documents in document libraries, and customize web part pages in document libraries.	X	X	
Delete Items	Delete items from a list and documents from a document library.	X	X	
View Items	View items in lists and documents in document libraries.	X	X	X
Approve Items	Approve a minor version of a list item or document.	X		
Open Items	Add items to lists and add documents to document libraries.	X	X	X
View Versions	View past versions of a list item or document.	X	X	X
Delete Versions	Delete past versions of a list item or document.	X	X	
Create Alerts	Create alerts.	X	X	X
View Application Pages	View forms, views, and application pages; enumerate lists.	X	X	X

Continues

TABLE 1-8: SharePoint Permissions and Default Permission Levels *(Continued)*

Permission	Description	Design	Contribute	Read
Site Permissions				
Manage Permissions	Create and change permission levels on the web site and assign permissions to users and groups.			
View Web Analytics Data	View reports on web site usage.			
Create Subsites	Create subsites such as team sites, Meeting Workspace sites, and Document Workspace sites.			
Manage Web Site	Grants the ability to perform all administration tasks for the web site as well as manage content.			
Add and Customize Pages	Add, change, or delete HTML pages or web part pages, and edit the web site using a Microsoft SharePoint Foundation-compatible editor.	X		
Apply Themes and Borders	Apply a theme or borders to the entire web site.	X		
Apply Style Sheets	Apply a style sheet (.CSS file) to the web site.	X		
Create Groups	Create a group of users that can be used anywhere within the site collection.			
Browse Directories	Enumerate files and folders in a web site using SharePoint Designer and Web DAV interfaces.	X	X	
Use Self-Service Site Creation	Allows users to create a web site using Self-Service Site Creation.	X	X	X
View Pages	View pages in a web site.	X	X	X
Enumerate Permissions	Enumerate permissions on the web site, list, folder, document, or list item.			
Browse User Information	View information about users of the web site.	X	X	X

TABLE 1-8:   SharePoint Permissions and Default Permission Levels *(Continued)*

Permission	Description	Design	Contribute	Read
Manage Alerts	Manage alerts for all users of the web site.			
User Remote Interfaces	Use SOAP, Web DAV, the Client Object Model, or SharePoint Designer interfaces to access the web site.	X	X	X
Use Client Integration Features	Use features that launch client applications; without this permission, users will have to work on documents locally and upload their changes.	X	X	X
Open	Allows users to open a web site, list, or folder in order to access items inside that container.	X	X	X
Edit Personal User Information	Allows a user to change his or her own user information, such as adding a picture.	X	X	
Personal Permissions				
Manage Personal Views	Create, change, and delete personal views of lists.	X	X	
Add/Remove Personal Web Parts	Add or remove personal web parts on a Web Part Page.	X	X	
Update Personal Web Parts	Update web parts to display personalized information.	X	X	

Galleries

Continuing our tour of Site Settings, we next consider galleries. Galleries are lists built into SharePoint that contain elements that are used in the SharePoint site—for example, site column definitions, web parts, and site content types. Table 1-9 lists the different galleries available at the site or site collection level.

TABLE 1-9: Galleries

Gallery	Description
Site Columns	A gallery containing site column definitions that can be used to define columns in a list.
Site Content Types	A gallery containing content types that can be used to define the items in a list or document libraries. Creating a custom content type is described in Chapter 7, "SharePoint Content Types."
Web Parts	A gallery containing web parts available to be used in web part pages. We show how to create custom web parts in Chapter 9, "SharePoint Web Parts."
List Templates	A gallery containing list templates that can be used to create new lists. We consider how to create list templates in Chapter 4, "SharePoint Lists."
Master Pages	A gallery containing master pages for the web site—a master page sets the look for the overall layout of a SharePoint page and is considered in more detail in Chapter 10, "SharePoint Pages."
Themes	A gallery containing themes that are used to configure fonts and colors for the web site.
Solutions	A gallery containing user solutions that include custom code and can be run in a sandbox. We show how to create user solutions throughout this book, starting in Chapter 2, "Introduction to SharePoint Development in Visual Studio 2010."

Rows with a gray background are only available at the site collection level and not at the site level.

Extension Point: Galleries

Almost all Galleries can have custom-developed items added to them, as we will see throughout this book. These custom gallery items can then be used by the SharePoint user to provide a customized SharePoint experience. For example, you can define your own site columns that would appear in the site columns gallery, your own site content types that would appear in the site content types gallery, your own web parts that would appear in the web parts gallery, and so on.

Site Administration

The Site Administration settings provide commands for administering various features of the SharePoint site. These Site Administration settings and their descriptions are listed in Table 1-10.

TABLE 1-10:   Site Administration Settings

Site Setting	Description
Regional Settings	Configures site settings such as time zone, time format, calendar format, and locale.
Site Libraries and Lists	Provides a quick way to access the list and library settings page for all site document libraries and lists.
User Alerts	Configures alerts that users have configured for when content changes on the site.
RSS	Configures RSS feed settings for the site; SharePoint lists and libraries can be subscribed to via RSS.
Search and Offline Availability	Configures whether the contents of the site are included in search results, whether content displayed in web parts is indexed, and whether items in the site can be downloaded to offline clients like SharePoint Workspace.
Sites and Workspaces	Provides a quick way to access and delete any child sites, document workspaces, or meeting workspaces associated with this site.
Workflows	Lists all workflows that are currently available in the site collection.
Workflow Settings	Allows you to manage workflows for the site. Workflow is described in more detail in Chapter 8, "SharePoint Workflow."

Rows with a gray background are only available at the site collection level and not at the site level.

Look and Feel

The Look and Feel settings provide commands for configuring the appearance of the SharePoint site. These settings are described in Table 1-11.

TABLE 1-11: Look and Feel Settings

Site Setting	Description
Title, Description, and Icon	Changes the title, description, icon, and URL for the SharePoint site.
Quick Launch	Edit the contents of the quick launch area typically displayed on the left side of the SharePoint site. The quick launch area provides shortcuts to libraries, lists, and other important content on your site. It consists of headings that are links to URLs internal or external to the site. You can also create navigation links as children of the headings. By default, the quick launch area has three headings linked to corresponding internal content: Libraries, Lists, and Discussions.
Top Link Bar	Edit the links that appear in the top link bar of the SharePoint site.
Tree View	Configure whether a tree view is displayed in the quick launch area of the SharePoint site. The tree view shows all the content and subsites of the SharePoint site in the quick launch area as shown in Figure 1-57. Configures whether the quick launch area is displayed or not.
Site Theme	Sets the theme used for the web site, which impacts fonts and colors used by the site. This does not impact the layout of the site nor any pages that have been individually themed. Themes can be found in the Theme Gallery, which is stored in the top-level SharePoint site associated with the site collection. New themes can be added to the Theme Gallery and used in the SharePoint sites associated with the site collection.

Extension Point: Creating Custom SharePoint Features

Creating custom SharePoint features and installing them to a SharePoint server is the fundamental way you add functionality to SharePoint. Visual Studio has many features that allow you to configure and package SharePoint features. This is described in more detail in Chapter 11, "Packaging and Deployment."

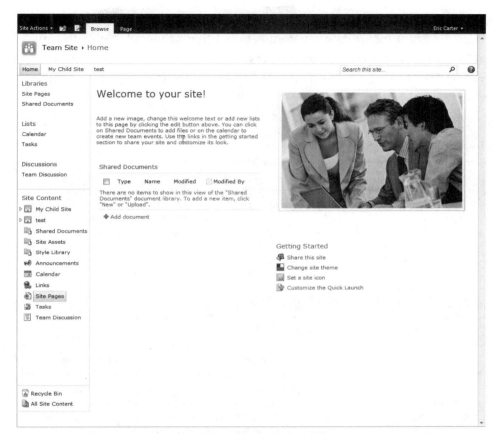

Figure 1-57: The Quick Launch Area for the top-level SharePoint Site with the Tree View turned on

Site Actions

The Site Actions settings provide several commands used for managing the SharePoint site. These commands are described in Table 1-12.

Two of the Site Actions described in Table 1-12 deserve additional mention. The Manage site features command lets you manage the features that are activated for the SharePoint site. A SharePoint feature has a confusing name that means more than you might think. A SharePoint *feature* is a special term used in SharePoint to refer to the mechanism whereby a developer packages and makes available SharePoint customizations. When you click on the Manage Site Features link in the Site Settings, you are presented with the page shown in Figure 1-58. This page lets you activate and deactivate features (think SharePoint customizations) that are available in the site— activating a site turns the feature on and enables the functionality it provides, deactivating a feature turns the feature off and removes the functionality it provides.

TABLE 1-12: Site Actions

Site Actions	Description
Manage Site Features	Manages the features that are activated for the SharePoint site. Features are a key concept in SharePoint development described in Chapter 11, "Packaging and Deployment."
Save Site As Template	Saves the site as a site template file (.WSP file).
Site Collection Web Analytics Reports	Gives a report of how the site collection is being used, including storage use, number of users, and how often the site collection is visited.
Site Web Analytics Reports	Gives a report of the number of page views per day, number of unique visitors per day, number of referrers, top pages, top visitors, top referring links, and top browsers for the site.
Reset to Site Definition	Removes all the customizations made to a particular web part page or all web part pages on the site.
Delete This Site	Deletes the SharePoint site.

Rows with a gray background are only available at the site collection level and not at the site level.

Site features can be installed for a particular site or site collection using a command line tool called stsadm.exe that is run on the SharePoint server machine. We will see later how new SharePoint features can be created in Visual Studio and how Visual Studio installs and uninstalls features as part of the process of running a SharePoint solution.

The second Site Action that deserves additional mention is the Save site as template functionality. This command lets you take the current Share-

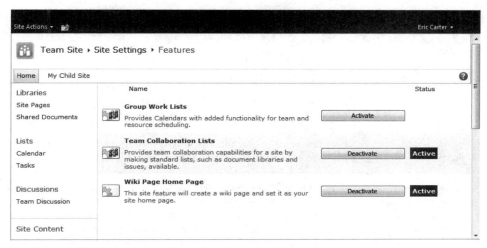

Figure 1-58: The Features Page for a SharePoint Site

Point site and save it as a .WSP file. This is significant because Visual Studio can then import the .WSP file and let you bring items you have defined in a live SharePoint site into Visual Studio for reuse and further modification. In Chapter 4, "SharePoint Lists," we will see this approach—we first create a custom SharePoint list using the SharePoint web UI, then we export the SharePoint site as a .WSP file. Finally, we import the .WSP file into Visual Studio and select the components defined as part of the SharePoint list to import. This same approach can be used when creating SharePoint components in SharePoint designer—to reuse these components in a Visual Studio solution you can use the Save site as template command to create a .WSP file then import the desired component into Visual Studio.

Site Collection Administration

The Site Collection Administration settings provide several commands used for managing the Site Collection. These settings are only available when you view the Site Settings for the top-level SharePoint site associated with the site collection as is shown in our example http://ecarter1. The Site Collection Administration commands are described in Table 1-13.

TABLE 1-13: Site Collection Administration Commands

Site Collection Administration Command	Description
Recycle Bin	The recycle bin allows a site collection administrator to restore items that were accidentally deleted.
Site Collection Features	Displays a page like the one shown in Figure 1-58 that displays features that are installed at the site collection level.
Site Hierarchy	Displays all the sites created within the site collection.
Portal Site Connection	Sets an optional parent site for the site collection, which is then used in breadcrumbs and other navigation for the site.
SharePoint Designer Settings	Controls settings specific to SharePoint Designer, such as whether SharePoint designer can be used in the site collection.
Visual Upgrade	Controls whether the site collection and sites use the latest SharePoint user interface.
Help Settings	Manages the help files used for the web site.

The Central Administrative View of a SharePoint Server

We have now considered the content that can be created in a SharePoint site and most of the major settings that can be configured for a SharePoint site. Hopefully the discussion thus far has given you a good overview of what is possible in a SharePoint site. We now consider the Central Administration page for a SharePoint server, which will provide you with additional insight into how a SharePoint server works.

To invoke the Central Administration page for a SharePoint server, navigate to the root of your server using a different port—in our example http://ecarter1:23283/. The port number could be set differently on your machine; search the Start menu for the "SharePoint 2010 Central Administration" link by typing "sharepoint central" in the search box of the Start menu as shown in Figure 1-59. You can also find this link by navigating to the All Programs > Microsoft SharePoint 2010 Products folder and click on the SharePoint 2010 Central Administration shortcut.

Figure 1-59: Searching for the SharePoint 2010
Central Administration command in the Start menu

When you click on SharePoint 2010 Central Administration in the Start menu, a browser window will open to the Central Administration page shown in Figure 1-60. The Central Administration page has commands in eight categories: Application Management, Monitoring, Security, General Application Settings, System Settings, Backup and Restore, Upgrade and Migration, and Configuration Wizards. We will consider all of these categories in this section.

Web Applications

First, however, the Central Administration page introduces two new concepts we haven't considered yet and must now introduce. Previously we introduced the concept of a Site Collection and a SharePoint Site. We have seen that a Site Collection has at least one top-level SharePoint site associated with it. We've also seen that a SharePoint site can have additional

Figure 1-60: SharePoint Central Administration page

child SharePoint sites, which in turn can have children sites and so on. Clearly a Site Collection or a Site is the parent of other SharePoint sites, but what is the parent of a Site Collection?

The Central Administration page introduces the concept of a web application. A web application is functionally the container or parent for one or more Site Collections. A web application is also a place where the underlying technology powering SharePoint shows through because a web application maps to the web application concept in ASP.NET. If you're not familiar with ASP.NET, that's OK—you can still start developing some SharePoint extensions without being an ASP.NET expert. ASP .NET knowledge becomes necessary when you want to develop web parts and stand-alone customized web pages that are integrated into Share-Point—these are called Application pages and are described in Chapter 10, "SharePoint Pages." ASP.NET knowledge is also required when we talk about workflow association and initiation forms and master pages. If you don't know ASP.NET, for now it is sufficient to know that it is a .NET tech-nology that allows you to use C# and VB.NET code to write web applications that are then hosted by IIS—Internet Information Server. So under the covers, SharePoint is built on web applications that are ASP.NET based and are hosted by IIS.

If you click on the Manage web applications link in the Application Management section shown in Figure 1-60, the page shown in Figure 1-61 appears. This page shows the web applications that are created by default when you install SharePoint. Note that there is a web application at port 80 called "SharePoint -80," which is the web application that maps to the URL http:// ecarter1 and the web application that is hosting the SharePoint site collection we have explored in this chapter. There is also a second web application at port 23283 called "SharePoint Central Administration v4," which is the web application that hosts the SharePoint Central Administration pages.

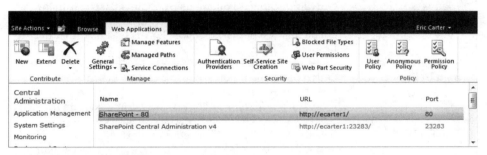

Figure 1-61: Web Applications management page

There are a number of settings and policies that are configurable at the web application level that impact any site collections and sites hosted in that web application. We will consider these by exploring the Web Applications ribbon tab and the commands available there.

The New button in the Web Application ribbon tab creates a new Web application—note that this ribbon is only available when you launch Internet Explorer as an administrator. In the dialog that appears when you create a new web application, there are a number of options you can set; these are described in Table 1-14. This table should start to give you an idea of some of the things that are set at the web application level.

TABLE 1-14: Create New Web Application Setting

Web Application Setting	Description
Authentication	Configures whether the web application uses Claims Based Authentication or Classic Mode Authentication.
IIS Web Site	Configures whether to use an existing IIS web site or create a new IIS web site to host the web application.
Security Configuration	If Authentication is set to Classic Mode Authentication, you can select either Kerberos or NTLM to be the Authentication provider and you can decide whether to allow anonymous access and whether to use SSL. If Authentication is set to Claims Based Authentication, you can choose whether to allow anonymous access and whether to use SSL.
Claims Authentication Type	Only applicable if you are using Claims Based Authentication; this lets you set whether Windows authentication is enabled and whether to enable Forms Based Authentication via ASP.NET.
Sign In Page URL	Only applicable if you are using Claims Based Authentication; this lets you use either a default Sign In page provided by SharePoint or your own customized Sign In page.
Public URL	Sets the root URL that is used for pages within the web application; by default it is set to the current server name and port, e.g., http://ecarter1:29302.
Application Pool	Chooses whether to use an existing application pool or whether to create a new application pool to be used by this web application. An application pool is a unit of isolation in IIS that can isolate one web application from another (if you run them in separate application pools). An application pool maps to one or more worker processes created by IIS in which to run your actual code. Using a separate application pool can ensure that a SharePoint site running in one application pool cannot impact or access data in a SharePoint site running in another application pool.
Database Name and Authentication	Sets the database server and database name for the SharePoint "content" database in which SharePoint data and user configuration are stored for SharePoint sites running within this web application.

TABLE 1-14: Create New Web Application Setting *(Continued)*

Web Application Setting	Description
Fallover Server	Fallover database server if you are using SQL Server database mirroring for the SharePoint content database.
Search Server	Specifies the search server that you want to use for the web application; when you install SharePoint on your machine, you also install Microsoft SharePoint Foundation search server. You typically will use only this server. In more complex topologies, you might be running SharePoint and associated services and servers on multiple machines so you might pick a SharePoint search server running on a different machine.
Service Application Connections	Configures the Service Applications used by the web application. In a standard SharePoint Server install, you will have a Service Application for Business Data Connectivity Services and a second Service Application for Usage and Health data collection. For more information on Business Data Connectivity Services see Chapter 6, "Working with Business Data."
Customer Experience Improvement Program	Specifies whether the web application will collect web site analytics to improve the customer experience.

Extension Point: Custom Forms-Based Authentication and Sign in Pages

SharePoint allows you to provide a custom forms-based authentication implementation in ASP.NET as well as provide your own sign in page. For example, you could write your own forms-based authentication implementation that looks up user names and passwords in an existing company database.

Other commands available in the Web Applications ribbon tab include the Extend command. This button lets you make your web application with all of its content available in multiple IIS web sites. This command is typically used when you want to make the same content available to both intranet and extranet users.

Table 1-15 lists additional web application settings that are available via the General Settings drop-down in the Web Applications tab of the ribbon. The goal here is not to give an exhaustive guide of how to administer a SharePoint site, but to give you an idea of the capabilities and options that you have at the web application level in SharePoint.

TABLE 1-15:   General Web Application Setting

Web Application Setting	Description
Default Time Zone	Sets the time zone used for sites that are created in the web application.
Default Quota Template	Sets quotas that are used by default for site collections, including limits on the maximum storage available in a site collection and how sandboxed solutions are limited in their use of resources.
Presence Settings	Enables or disables online presence information being shown for people in sites hosted by the web application.
Alerts	Configures the defaults for alerts for the web application— whether they are on or off and how many alerts a user can create.
RSS Settings	Controls whether RSS feeds are enabled or not within the web application.
Blog API Settings	Controls whether the MetaWeblog API is enabled for the web application and authentication method for the Blog API.
Browser File Handling	Configures whether additional security headers are added to documents served by the web application requiring the browser to show a download prompt for certain types of files.

TABLE 1-15: General Web Application Setting *(Continued)*

Web Application Setting	Description
Web Page Security Validation	Sets whether security validations expire or not and the expiration period for a security validation.
Send User Name and Password in E-Mail	Sets whether to send users their user names and passwords by e-mail.
Master Page Setting for Application _Layouts Pages	Chooses whether pages in the _Layouts folder of SharePoint will use the site master page or a default SharePoint master page. For more information, see Chapter 10, "SharePoint Pages."
Recycle Bin	Sets whether or not to use the Recycle Bin feature in the web application.
Maximum Upload Size	Sets the maximum size to allow for a single upload to a site.
List View Threshold	Allows you to set the maximum number of items that a database operation can involve at one time.
Object Model Override	Allows code with sufficient permission to request more items than the list view threshold would grant in a programmatic query.
List View Lookup Threshold	Allows you to set the maximum number of Lookup, Person/Group, or workflow status fields that a database query can involve at one time (since these are costly to lookup).
Daily Time Window for Large Queries	Sets a time window when large queries can be executed.
List Unique Permissions Threshold	Sets the maximum number of unique permissions that a list can have at once.
HTTP Request Monitoring and Throttling	Throttles low-priority requests in the event of HTTP request overload.

Continues

TABLE 1-15:   General Web Application Setting *(Continued)*

Web Application Setting	Description
Change Log	Specifies how long entries are kept in the change log.
User-Defined Workflows	Sets whether users can create their own workflows built out of predeployed workflow building blocks (without custom code).
Workflow Task Notifications	Sets whether users without access to the site are notified of assigned workflow tasks.
Mail Settings	Configures an SMTP mail server that SharePoint uses to send e-mail alerts, invitations, and administrator notifications.
Text Message Service Settings	Configures a URL for an SMS sending service to be used to send SMS-based alerts.
SharePoint Designer Settings	Sets whether SharePoint Designer can be used to edit sites in this web application, whether master pages and layout pages can be customized, and other settings related to SharePoint Designer.

Table 1-16 summarizes the remaining commands in the Web Application Ribbon Tab.

TABLE 1-16:   Additional Commands in the Web Application Tab of the Ribbon

Web Application Tab Command	Description
Manage Features	Allows you to manage SharePoint features that are installed at the web application level.
Managed Paths	Configures which paths within the URL namespace of the web application are managed by SharePoint.
Service Connections	Specifies which Service Applications are used by the web application (by default this includes the Business Data Connectivity Service and the Usage and Health data collection service).

TABLE 1-16: Additional Commands in the Web Application Tab of the Ribbon *(Continued)*

Web Application Tab Command	Description
Authentication Providers	Configures the Authentication providers used for the web application.
Self-Service Site Creation	Configures whether users can create their own sites from within SharePoint.
Blocked File Types	Configures the file types that cannot be added to the web application. For example, .exe files are one file type that is blocked by default.
User Permissions	Configures which permissions (shown in Table 1-8) cannot be used in the web application. For example, you could disallow the "Create Alerts" permission at the web application level so no one could use it in sites hosted by the web application.
Web Part Security	Configures whether web parts can be connected to each other to pass data and values between each other, whether users can access the online web part gallery to add additional web parts not installed on the SharePoint site, and whether users with contributor permission can edit scriptable web parts.
User Policy	Sets the user account and permissions used for the web application.
Anonymous Policy	Chooses whether anonymous access is allowed to sites hosted by the web application and what permissions anonymous users have.
Permission Policy	Sets permission policies (in terms of the permissions granted as shown in Table 1-8) that are then used for User Policy and Anonymous Policy settings.

Farms

The second concept that the Central Administration page introduces is the concept of a Farm. Until this point, we have assumed that SharePoint runs on one machine. But in reality, one of the greatest strengths of SharePoint is its ability to run on several machines collectively called a farm. SharePoint allows you to build a solution that can start out on a single machine but scale to many machines if necessary. SharePoint can manage the deployment of your solution to a farm of machines, which makes it much easier to deploy a scalable web solution. The Farm concept comes up occasionally in Share-Point development, for example when you are trying to decide at what scope to deploy a SharePoint feature—at the farm level, the web application level, the site collection, or site level. Also, the term "Farm Solution" is used for a full trust solution that must be deployed as a SharePoint feature or set of SharePoint features. The alternate to a "Farm Solution" is a "Sandboxed Solution," which requires less trust but is limited to customizing a smaller subset of SharePoint functionality.

Application Management

From the Central Administration page shown in Figure 1-60, we now consider each of the subcategories of Central Administration: Application Management, System Settings, Monitoring, Backup and Restore, Security, Upgrade and Migration, and General Application Settings. If you click on the Application Management link in Figure 1-60, the page shown in Figure 1-62 appears.

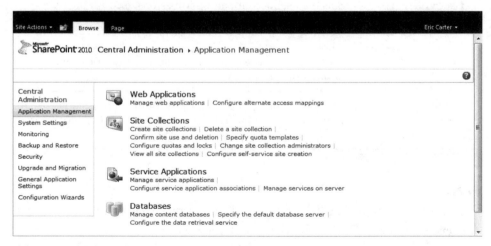

Figure 1-62: Web Application Management page

We've already considered the Manage web applications link in some detail. The Configure alternate access mappings link lets you configure alternate URLs that map to a web application.

The Site Collections group of commands let you configure existing site collections and add new site collections to a web application. As we mentioned earlier, a web application can have one or more site collections that it is hosting. If you click the Create Site Collections link, a page appears where you have to pick an existing web application that will host your new site collection, a title and description for your new site (which will be the top-level site for the newly created site collection), a URL typically created by appending /sites/ to the top-level URL of your web application and then appending the name of the new site collection, a site template to be used for the top-level site for the new site collection, the primary and secondary site collection administrator, and a quota template that sets limits on storage and other resources used by the site collection. So as a specific example, if we were to create a second site collection in our http://ecarter1 web application, the original site collection's URL is http://ecarter1. The second site collection's URL if the site collection was called mysecondsitecollection would be http://ecarter1/sites/mysecondsitecollection.

The Site Collections group of commands has many functions. You can delete an existing site collection, modify quota templates that describe limits on disk space and resources used by sandboxed solutions that are then used in site collections settings, lock a site collection so it cannot be modified, configure the administrators for the site collection, view all site collections on the server, and configure whether self-service site creation is enabled for a site collection.

The Service Applications group of commands lets you manage and configure service applications such as the Business Data Connectivity Service and the Usage and Health data collection service. Clicking Manage service applications shows a list of service applications that are available and provides links to configure additional settings specific to each service application. The Manage services on server link lets you see which services are running on the server that SharePoint uses and stop and start those services if needed. It also provides links to configure additional settings specific to some of those services. The Manage Services page is shown in Figure 1-63. This page is also interesting because it shows that SharePoint is actually a collection of several services, including search, a timer service that runs jobs on a timer, a sandboxed code service that runs sandboxed solutions, and other components.

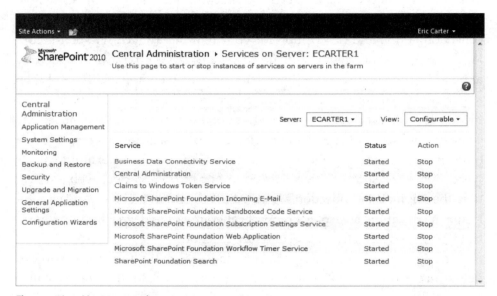

Figure 1-63: Manage services page

The Databases group of commands allows you to manage the content database associated with your web application and SharePoint sites within that web application. SharePoint stores some of the content of the Share-Point Site in the content database and other content of the SharePoint site resides on disk. You can also configure whether data access technologies like OLEDB, SOAP Passthrough, and XML-URL are allowed to process direct queries against the content database.

System Settings

If you click on the System Settings link in Figure 1-60, the page shown in Figure 1-64 appears. This page lets you manage settings related to the multiple servers that make up a SharePoint farm, e-mail and SMS settings, and settings related to both farm solutions and sandboxed solutions.

Figure 1-64: System Settings page

If you click on Manage servers in this farm, the Servers in Farm page is displayed as shown in Figure 1-65. This page displays each of the servers that make up the SharePoint farm as well as the services running on each machine in the server. In our example, only one server is running: ECARTER1. This page also introduces another SharePoint concept—the configuration database. The configuration database is another database in addition to the content database that stores information necessary to configure a SharePoint solution across one machine or across multiple machines in a farm.

The E-Mail and Text Messages group of commands lets you configure an outbound SMTP server that is used by the SharePoint server to send e-mail, an inbound SMTP service that is used to receive e-mail, and a text message service that can be used to send SMS messages. The inbound SMTP service allows a SharePoint site to receive e-mail messages and store them in SharePoint lists. SharePoint lists can be given their own e-mail addresses so they can receive and store incoming messages.

The Farm Management group of commands lets you manage features that are installed at the farm level using the Manage farm features link.

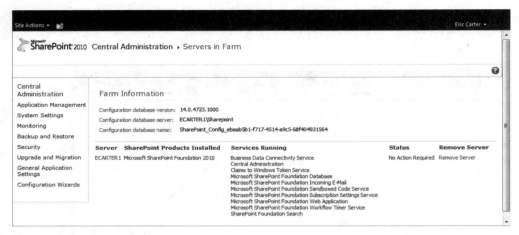

Figure 1-65: Servers in Farm page

When you develop features for SharePoint in Visual Studio, you can set their scope so they will install at the farm level. There is also a link to Manage farm solutions. Finally, the Manage user solutions link shows a page that gives you control over how sandboxed solutions are run, as shown in Figure 1-66. You can choose to block specific solution packages with this page. You can also configure where sandboxed solutions run in a farm—either on the same machine where the request came in or on a machine using solution affinity.

The most important thing to know about sandboxed solutions is that they give SharePoint a safer, more isolated way to run custom code at the expense of applying some limitations to what the code can do. But in general, you will want to try to first write your solution as a sandboxed solution and then if you run into limitations, consider writing it as a full trust farm solution. It is also to your advantage to write a sandboxed solution because in many environments, SharePoint administrators may choose to only enable sandboxed solutions to ensure the stability of their SharePoint installations.

Monitoring

If you click on the Monitoring link in Figure 1-60, the page shown in Figure 1-67 appears. This page lets you monitor and report on the health of your SharePoint server. This page also serves to introduce another SharePoint extension point—the timer job.

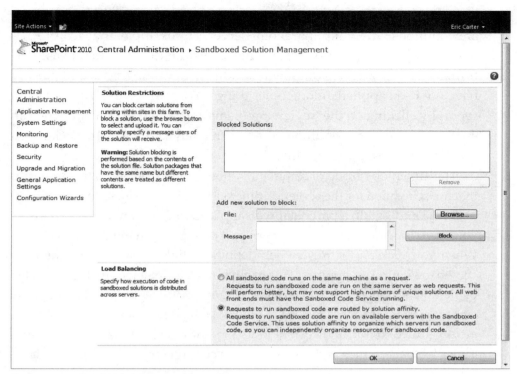

Figure 1-66: Sandboxed Solution Management page

Figure 1-67: Monitoring page

In the Health Analyzer group of commands, you can review problems and solutions with your SharePoint server. For example, the Health Analyzer will detect if you are running low on disk space, if your database performance is poor due to fragmented indices, and if upgrades and patches have not been applied among other things. You can see the current health report by clicking on the Review problems and solutions link and you can explore the types of conditions the health analyzer detects by clicking on the Review rule definitions link.

The Timer Jobs group of commands allows you to review all the timer jobs that are scheduled for the server. A timer job can be scheduled to run at a regular time and within a particular web application. You can define and install your own timer jobs and run them as part of a larger SharePoint application. When you click on the Review job definitions link in Figure 1-67, the page shown in Figure 1-68 appears. This page shows the timer jobs that are installed by default as part of a SharePoint installation and also provides links to view currently running jobs, a history of timer jobs that have already run, jobs that are scheduled to run, and current timer job status. Figure 1-69 shows the Edit Timer Job page, which is shown when you click on one of the links associated

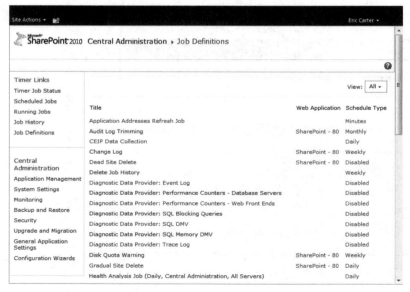

Figure 1-68: Job Definition page

with a timer job definition in Figure 1-68. This page lets you see information about the job, when it was last run, when it is scheduled to run, and provides buttons to run the job now or disable the job.

Figure 1-69: Edit Timer Job page

Extension Point: Timer Jobs

You can write your own custom timer jobs that can run within a particular web application and run on a recurring schedule.

The Reporting group of commands lets you configure diagnostics and logging occurring in the SharePoint server. It also lets you create health reports such as showing the slowest pages in the SharePoint server.

Backup and Restore

The Backup and Restore group of commands lets you backup your farm, restore from a backup, and configure backup settings. You can also backup a single site collection and export a site or a SharePoint list to a file.

Upgrade and Patch Management

The Upgrade and Patch Management group of commands lets you check to make sure your servers and databases are up-to-date and patched.

Security

The Security group of commands is described in Table 1-17.

TABLE 1-17:   Security Commands

Security Command	Description
Manage the Farm Administrators Group	Allows you to manage the users that are farm administrators—these users have full access to all settings in the farm and can take ownership of any SharePoint site on the farm.
Approve or Reject Distribution Groups	Allows you to approve or reject distribution groups that are created when a SharePoint group is created and an e-mail distribution group for the group is requested.
Configure Managed Accounts	Allows you to configure "managed accounts" that are used by the SharePoint services on the server so that the password for these accounts is automatically changed on a recurring basis.
Configure Service Accounts	Configures which SharePoint services are associated with which accounts—you can also configure the services to use one of your managed accounts.
Configure Password Change Settings	Configures settings around when to send e-mail when passwords expire and need to be changed.
Specify Authentication Providers	Configures the authentication settings for the web site: whether to use windows or forms-based authentication, whether to use anonymous access, etc.
Manage Antivirus Settings	Settings related to antivirus scanning, which controls whether documents are scanned when uploaded and downloaded.
Define Blocked File Types	Sets which file extensions are blocked from being saved or retrieved from SharePoint sites, such as .exe files.

TABLE 1-17: Security Commands *(Continued)*

Security Command	Description
Manage Web Part Security	Configures whether web parts can be connected to each other to pass data and values between each other, whether users can access the online web part gallery to add additional web parts not installed on the SharePoint site, and whether users with contributor permission can edit scriptable web parts.
Configure Self-Service Site Creation	Configures whether users can create their own sites from within SharePoint.
Configure Information Rights Management	Configures whether Information Rights Management is used on the SharePoint server.

A Visual Studio View of SharePoint: The Server Explorer

We've now seen a view of SharePoint content and settings through the lens of what you can do in SharePoint in the web user interface. We've also seen a view of SharePoint through the lens of the Site Administration tools. Our final view of SharePoint for this chapter will be through the lens of Visual Studio. We will use Visual Studio to take a closer look at the top-level site that was created when SharePoint was installed as well as the new child site and content we have created in this chapter.

The SharePoint features in Visual Studio require administrator privileges so Visual Studio must be run as an administrator. To launch Visual Studio as an administrator, locate the "Microsoft Visual Studio 2010" shortcut in the Start menu under All Programs > Microsoft Visual Studio 2010. Right click on the Microsoft Visual Studio 2010 shortcut. You can choose "Run as administrator" from the context menu that appears to run Visual Studio as an administrator.

Alternatively, if you just want to make Visual Studio start up with administrator privileges every time you launch it, you can change the Microsoft Visual Studio 2010 shortcut properties to always run as administrator. To do this, right click on the Microsoft Visual Studio 2010 shortcut and choose Properties. Click the Compatibility tab as shown in Figure 1-70.

Then check the "Run this program as an administrator" check box and press OK.

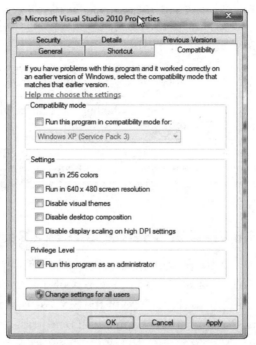

Figure 1-70: Setting the Microsoft Visual
Studio 2010 shortcut to start as administrator

Now use the modified Microsoft Visual Studio 2010 shortcut or the "Run as administrator" command in the context menu to launch Visual Studio with administrator privileges. Once Visual Studio starts, use the View menu and choose Server Explorer to show the Server Explorer window. Visual Studio 2010 lets you browse the structure of a SharePoint site using the Server Explorer window. Expand the SharePoint Connections node and expand the subnode under that to see the contents of the SharePoint server on your developer machine as shown in Figure 1-71. In Figure 1-71 we have also expanded the Sites subnode to show the child site we created called "My Child Site." The Sites subnode shows any child sites for the SharePoint sites.

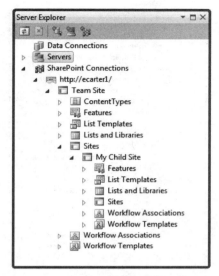

Figure 1-71: Visual Studio's Server Explorer
view of the SharePoint Site and child site

Visual Studio's Server Explorer view surfaces a lot of the content and structure of a SharePoint site that is of interest to a developer. Consider the nodes under the Team Site node (our top-level site in our site collection). There are seven subnodes displayed by Visual Studio: ContentTypes, Features, List Templates, Lists and Libraries, Sites, Workflow Associations, and Workflow Templates. We've already seen the Sites subnode in Figure 1-71. Let's consider the rest of these subnodes in turn.

ContentTypes

Visual Studio displays all the 52 content types that are installed by default on a SharePoint site as shown in Figure 1-72. Figure 1-73 shows the properties window that is displayed when you select one of the content types in Server Explorer. If the Properties window isn't visible, use the View menu to display the Properties window. The Properties window shows key properties of the content type. Note that the properties in the Properties window are all read-only, you can't directly modify the server with the server explorer. Also, when you expand the content type in Server Explorer, you will be able to see the fields associated with the content type as shown in Figure 1-74.

Figure 1-72: Server Explorer view of
ContentTypes

Figure 1-73: Properties associated with a content type

Figure 1-74: Fields associated with a content type

Features

The next subnode displayed in the Server Explorer under the SharePoint site is the Features node. If you expand this node, you can see all 33 features that are installed in the SharePoint site by default as shown in Figure 1-75. You can see by this list that SharePoint features aren't just created by third-party developers—the implementation of SharePoint itself uses features built into the system. This is extremely useful as you learn SharePoint development because you can look at the features that are part of a standard SharePoint installation and learn how to build your own features. As before, when you click on a feature node in the Server Explorer, the Properties window shows additional information about the node as shown in Figure 1-76. In this case, one interesting property to point out is the FeatureDefinitionScope property that shows that the Announcement Lists feature is defined at the Farm level, which means it is available to sites running in the farm.

List Templates

The next subnode displayed in Server Explorer is the List Templates node as shown in Figure 1-77. Below the node are the various list templates that are installed in the SharePoint site. These templates can be used to create new lists. Figure 1-78 shows the Properties window that is displayed for the Announcements list template. In this case, an interesting property to point out is the FeatureId property. This indicates that the list template was installed as part of a feature. If you compare the DefinitionId property for the Announcements Lists feature in Figure 1-76 with the FeatureId property in Figure 1-78 you can see that it matches. This lets you know that the Announcements list template was installed by the Announcements Lists feature as you might expect.

Lists and Libraries

The Server Explorer also shows the lists and libraries that have been created in a SharePoint site. If you expand the Lists and Libraries subnode under the SharePoint site, you will see the Document Libraries subnode with document libraries below it and the Lists subnode with lists below it. This view shows not only the Shared Documents library but also all the

Figure 1-75: Server Explorer view of features

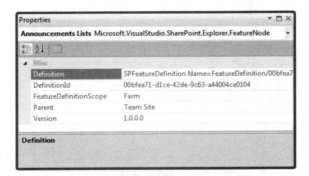

Figure 1-76: Properties associated with a feature

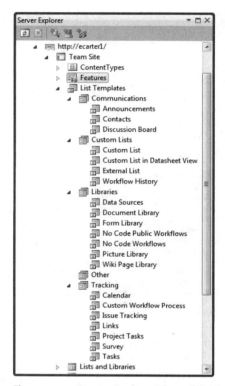

Figure 1-77: Server Explorer View of list templates

Figure 1-78: Properties associated with a list template

galleries as document libraries (Figure 1-79)—the Galleries we have seen in this chapter are really just special document libraries. It also shows the lists that are created by default in a SharePoint site. When you expand a document library or list, you can see additional nodes associated with the list or library. In Figure 1-80, you can see the fields associated with the Announcements list. You can also see that there are two Views associated with the list and no Workflow Associations have been made with the list.

Figure 1-79: Server Explorer View of lists
and libraries

Workflow Associations and Templates

Figure 1-81 shows the final two subnodes in the Server Explorer. The Workflow Associations node shows any workflow associations that have been made in the site. The Workflow Templates node shows any workflow templates that are installed in the site. We will consider workflow in more detail in Chapter 8, "SharePoint Workflow."

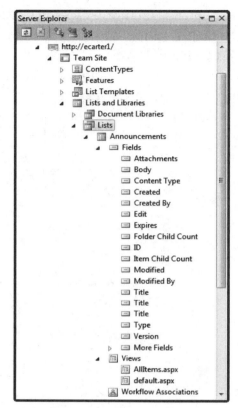

Figure 1-80: Server Explorer view of children of a list: fields, views, and workflow associations

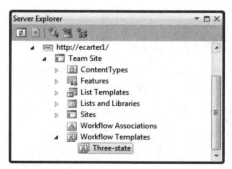

Figure 1-81: Server Explorer view of Workflow Templates

Conclusion

In this chapter we've introduced SharePoint from several perspectives: the perspective of a user of SharePoint's web UI, the perspective of a Share-Point administrator, and the perspective given by Visual Studio's Server Explorer. In the process of looking at SharePoint through these three perspectives, we've introduced a lot of the vocabulary and concepts you need that we will build upon in this book as we consider SharePoint development with Visual Studio. We've also identified many of the extension points—places where you can extend SharePoint with your own code.

In the next chapter we'll do a tour around the Visual Studio development tools for SharePoint to get you familiar with what is available. We'll also build our first SharePoint solution.

2

Introduction to SharePoint Development in Visual Studio 2010

Visual Studio 2010 provides the templates and tools you need to develop complete SharePoint solutions. In this chapter you will create your first SharePoint solution and we will introduce you to some of the projects, project item templates, and tools that are in Visual Studio 2010 for SharePoint development.

Creating a SharePoint Solution

First, make sure you have followed the setup instructions in Appendix A, "Preparing for SharePoint Development." Once your machine is set up, you will need to launch Visual Studio as an administrator. The SharePoint projects in Visual Studio require administrator privileges to interact with SharePoint. To launch Visual Studio as an administrator, locate the Microsoft Visual Studio 2010 shortcut in the Start Menu under All Programs > Microsoft Visual Studio 2010. Right click on the Microsoft Visual Studio 2010 shortcut. You can choose Run as administrator from the context menu to run Visual Studio as an administrator.

Alternatively, if you just want to make Visual Studio start up with administrator privileges every time you launch it, you can change the Microsoft Visual Studio 2010 shortcut properties to always run as administrator. To do this, right click on the Microsoft Visual Studio 2010 shortcut and choose Properties. Click the Compatibility tab as shown in Figure 2-1. Then check the Run this program as an administrator check box and press OK.

Figure 2-1: Setting the Microsoft Visual Studio
2010 shortcut to start as administrator

Now use the modified Microsoft Visual Studio 2010 shortcut or the Run as administrator command in the context menu to launch Visual Studio with administrator privileges. Once Visual Studio has started up, choose New > Project... from the File menu. This brings up the New Project dialog. Select Visual C# as the language from the tree view control on the left. Then expand the Visual C# node and select SharePoint under the Visual C# node. Expand the SharePoint node and click the 2010 node. This will display all the available SharePoint project types as shown in shown in Figure 2-2.

Figure 2-2: SharePoint projects in the New Project dialog in Visual Studio

Visual Studio has 12 basic SharePoint project types; they are listed in Table 2-1. The most basic SharePoint project type is the empty SharePoint Project. This project begins empty but lets you create and add any Share-Point project items you want to it as you go along. So in an empty SharePoint project you could add a web part, a list definition, and so on.

TABLE 2-1: SharePoint Project Types

Project Type	Description
Empty SharePoint Project	An empty SharePoint project; as with all projects in this table, you can add and remove arbitrary SharePoint item types once they are created.
Visual Web Part	A SharePoint project prepopulated with a visual web part project item; web parts are controls written using ASP.NET that users can place in a SharePoint web part page.

Continues

TABLE 2-1:   SharePoint Project Types *(Continued)*

Project Type	Description
Sequential Workflow	A SharePoint project prepopulated with a Sequential Workflow project item; when you create a workflow, you are writing a program that is structured as a multistep process that may be long running, waiting for humans or external systems to complete tasks or other processes before continuing. A sequential workflow proceeds in a linear top-to-bottom fashion.
State Machine Workflow	A SharePoint project prepopulated with a State Machine Workflow project item; a state machine workflow uses concepts such as states, events, and transitions to model more complex business processes with multiple possible paths through the workflow.
Business Data Connectivity Model	A SharePoint project prepopulated with a Business Data Connectivity Model project item; a business data connectivity model allows you to define a data model and code that lets you integrate external data into SharePoint.
Event Receiver	A SharePoint project prepopulated with an Event Receiver project item; an event receiver handles events that are raised by lists and other key objects in SharePoint. For example, an event receiver could execute custom code when a new item is added to a SharePoint list.
List Definition	A SharePoint project prepopulated with a List Definition project item; a list definition defines the schema of a list along with other things that define the list, such as views and forms used by the list.
Content Type	A SharePoint project prepopulated with a Content Type project item; a content type defines the schema for an item in a list— examples of content types in SharePoint include the Contact content type and the Announcement content type. Content types can also be associated with document libraries, allowing you to create a specialized document type, such as an expense report content type complete with a document template, such as an Excel workbook or Word document, to be used when a new expense report is created.
Module	A SharePoint project prepopulated with a Module project item; a module is used when creating deployments to provision the SharePoint site with one or more files that are needed by a solution—for example, you might use this to deploy a custom document to a document library or some other custom resource like an image file or an application page.

TABLE 2-1: SharePoint Project Types *(Continued)*

Project Type	Description
Site Definition	A SharePoint project prepopulated with a Site Definition project item; a site definition is a template that is used when creating a new SharePoint site and defines all the initial content in that site—for example, the subsites that we saw in Chapter 1, Table 1-7 are all backed by custom site definitions.
Import Reusable Workflow	A SharePoint project created by importing a workflow that was initially created in SharePoint Designer.
Import SharePoint Solution Package	A SharePoint project created by importing a .WSP SharePoint Solution Package exported from SharePoint or SharePoint Designer.

A second class of SharePoint project is prepopulated with one particular SharePoint project item type. This class includes the Visual Web Part, Sequential Workflow, State Machine Workflow, Business Data Connectivity Model, Event Receiver, List Definition, Content Type, Module, and Site Definition projects. These projects are empty SharePoint projects that have one SharePoint project item preadded to them—the item type specified by the project type designation. So, for example, the Content Type SharePoint project is an Empty SharePoint project with a Content Type project item preadded to it. As with the Empty SharePoint project type, you can continue to add SharePoint project item types to this class of projects or even remove from them the initially preadded SharePoint project item type.

A third class of SharePoint projects is populated by a wizard that runs when the project is first created. This class of SharePoint projects includes the Import Reusable Workflow and Import SharePoint Solution Package. The Import Reusable Workflow project creates a SharePoint project by importing a workflow from a workflow created in SharePoint or SharePoint Designer. The Import SharePoint Solution Package project creates a SharePoint project by importing a .WSP file exported from SharePoint Designer.

It is worth noting at this point that you have two general options for how you structure your SharePoint solutions. You can use a single project and add as many SharePoint project items as you need to that project. Or you can divide your solution into multiple projects. A key limitation of a project is that a single project can only produce a single .NET assembly (a .DLL file). So in cases where you need to factor your solution to produce multiple .NET assemblies you need to create multiple projects. You might also choose to divide your solution into multiple projects if you are developing a solution with other developers. This can make it easier for a solution to be simultaneously worked on by multiple developers.

Later in this chapter we will discuss in more detail what each of these project items and projects do. For now, let's start by creating an Empty SharePoint Project. As shown in Figure 2-2, you can specify a name and location for your project. You can also optionally add the project to source control by checking the Add to Source Control check box. Once you've set the name and location for your project, click the OK button to create the project.

A second dialog will appear to configure the site URL and security level for the newly created project as shown in Figure 2-3. The site URL should designate the SharePoint site where you want to deploy and test your SharePoint solution. As discussed in Chapter 1, a particular machine can host multiple SharePoint sites. If you click the Validate button, Visual Studio will verify that the URL you have typed corresponds to an already created SharePoint site.

In order for you to successfully deploy and debug your SharePoint solution, you must also have the proper permissions on the SharePoint site you designated with the site URL. Your user account must be added as the Site Owner or Site Collection Administrator for the site URL. In some cases, a customization you build may be deployed at the site level and at other times a customization may only be deployable at the site collection level. For more information on setting up the SharePoint site properly so you can deploy and debug, see Appendix A, "Preparing for SharePoint Development."

In the same dialog shown in Figure 2-3, you must choose the trust level for the SharePoint solution. After the project is created, you can change the trust level later by using the Properties window for the project as shown in Figure 2-5 (see page 114). The property to change is the Sandboxed Solution property—if this is set to False the solution will have a Farm solution trust level.

Sandboxed solutions run in a secure, monitored process. Sandboxed solutions can be deployed without requiring SharePoint administrative privileges. If you choose a sandboxed solution, you can only use project item types that are valid in sandboxed solutions.

If you choose the option "Deploy as a farm solution," Visual Studio will deploy the solution as a fully trusted farm solution. If you choose a farm solution, you can use all available SharePoint project item types in your project, but deployment will require administrative privileges and the solution will run in full trust.

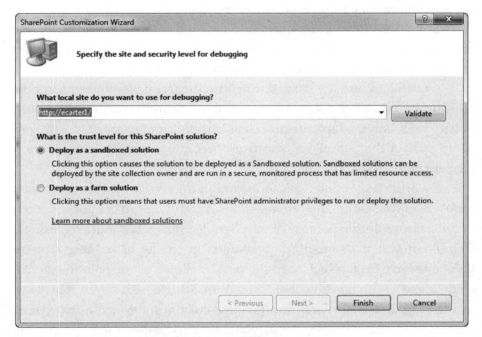

Figure 2-3: Debugging options for empty projects

For this example, choose Deploy as a sandboxed solution. Click the Finish button as shown in Figure 2-3 to complete the creation of the project.

Sandboxed Solutions versus Farm Solutions

Early in the project creation process, Visual Studio asks you to decide between using a sandboxed solution or a farm solution. It is worth considering in more detail the difference between a sandboxed solution and a farm solution and when to choose one over the other.

Prior to SharePoint 2010, all solutions you could create were farm solutions. In Chapter 1 we saw that SharePoint solutions are deployed to a farm that could consist of one to many servers. Each server in the farm can have multiple web applications running on it. A web application can in turn have one or more site collections, and a site collection has one or more sites. Farm solutions can impact the entire SharePoint system and are available to all site collections and sites in the farm. This is sometimes desirable, but sometimes can have undesired effects because a farm solution that is misbehaving can impact all sites and site collections in the system.

In SharePoint 2010, you can create a new type of solution called a sandboxed solution. Sandboxed solutions are deployed at the site collection level rather than the farm level, so this lets you isolate a solution so it is only available to one site collection within the farm. Sandboxed solutions also run in a separate process from the main SharePoint IIS web application process, and the separate process is throttled and monitored with quotas to protect the SharePoint site from becoming unresponsive due to a misbehaving sandboxed solution.

It is worth mentioning that sandboxed solutions solve an organizational problem as well—in many organizations it is difficult to get permission to install a farm solution because of the possible impact that could have on the SharePoint system. System administrators in charge of running a SharePoint site have been reluctant in the past to allow custom solutions to run on their sites. With the advent of SharePoint 2010, there is now a robust system in place to monitor and throttle these custom solutions so that system administrators don't have to worry about a custom solution bringing the entire SharePoint site down. In addition, with sandboxed solutions, users can upload solutions without requiring administrator approval.

So if sandboxed solutions are so great, why are farm solutions still around at all in SharePoint 2010? Well, because of the need to restrict and throttle a sandboxed solution so that it cannot negatively impact the entire site, there are restrictions on the kinds of solutions you can build with a sandboxed solution. The most significant restrictions disallow creation of application pages, visual web parts, or code-based workflows with a sandboxed solution. You can, however, create a web part without using the visual designer and deploy it in a sandboxed solution—we will see how to work around this particular limitation in Chapter 9, "SharePoint Web Parts."

So in the end, the choice between sandboxed and farm solutions should come down to whether or not you need to create an application page or a workflow with code in it. For these kinds of solutions, you should pick a farm solution. For all other solutions, pick a sandboxed solution. The only other reason to use a farm solution over a sandboxed solution is if you really have some code that needs to run at the web application or farm level, perhaps because it needs to interact with or move data between multiple site collections. In this case, you would create a farm solution as well.

Exploring an Empty SharePoint Project

Returning now to the project we just created, let's inspect the structure of an empty SharePoint project as shown in Figure 2-4. First, click on the root node, Solution 'SharePointProject1' in our example. In the Properties win-

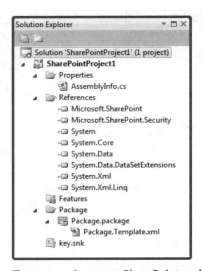

Figure 2-4: An empty SharePoint project

dow, you will see the properties associated with the solution. The two most interesting properties are the Active config and the Startup project properties. Active config sets whether to build debug or release assemblies. By default this starts out as Debug | Any CPU. Typically, during development you will use debug, but when you are ready to deploy the solution you will use Release | Any CPU setting. The Startup project will set which project's startup settings will be used when you press F5 when there are multiple projects in the solution. Since in typical solutions all projects will be deploying to the same SharePoint site URL, this won't matter much in practice unless you are building one solution that creates multiple deployments.

Now, click on the Project node, SharePointProject1, in our example. In the Properties window are a number of SharePoint specific properties as shown in Figure 2-5. Table 2-2 describes the functions of each of these properties. Two of the properties you configured during project creation can be changed here: Site URL—which designates the SharePoint site where you deploy and test your SharePoint solution, and Sandboxed Solution—which when set to True indicates that the solution will be a sandboxed solution and when set to False indicates that the solution will be a farm solution.

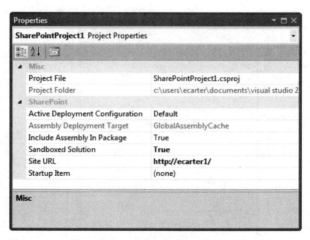

Figure 2-5: SharePoint project Properties window

TABLE 2-2: SharePoint Project Properties

Project Properties	Description
Project File	The name of the Visual Studio project file.
Project Folder	The name of the folder where the project file is saved.
Active Deployment Configuration	If set to Default, this does the standard deployment when deploying a SharePoint solution. If set to No Activation then when a solution is deployed to the SharePoint site, Visual Studio won't try to activate the solution. For more information, see Chapter 11, "Packaging and Deployment."
Assembly Deployment Target	Sets where the assembly created by this project will be deployed; for sandboxed solutions, this property is disabled because in a sandboxed solution the management of where the assembly is loaded and runs is controlled by SharePoint. For a farm solution, this can be GlobalAssemblyCache or WebApplication. For some SharePoint solutions, the assembly must go in the global assembly cache, for others it can be put at the web application level in a directory specific to the web application. For more information see Chapter 9, "SharePoint Web Parts."
Include Assembly in Package	Sets whether the assembly created by this project is packaged into the .WSP file created when the project is built; you will typically set this to True unless you have a project that is only used for deploying CAML-based SharePoint artifacts like a list definition.
Sandboxed Solution	If set to True, the project will deploy as a partially trusted sandboxed solution, if set to False, the project will deploy as a fully trusted farm solution.
Site URL	The URL for the SharePoint site where you want to deploy and test your SharePoint solution.
Startup Item	The item in the project that will be started when you press F5. For example, if you have an application page in your project, it will open the application page in the browser when you press F5.

Next, consider the Properties folder in the Solution Explorer. In this folder, you will find an AssemblyInfo.cs file that contains the attributes that will be added to the assembly that is created when the project is built. Almost all of these attributes are identical to the ones you would find when creating a simple class library project. The only one that is new is the Allow-PartiallyTrustedCallers attribute. This attribute is used for partially trusted solutions (sandboxed solutions or farm solutions that have Assembly Deployment Target set to WebApplication as we saw in Table 2-2). For projects that have Assembly Deployment Target set to GlobalAssembly-Cache, the AllowPartiallyTrustedCallers attribute can be removed.

The References folder in the Solution Explorer contains all the referenced assemblies for the project. The set of referenced assemblies are identical to the ones you would find when creating a simple class library project with two additions: Microsoft.SharePoint and Microsoft.SharePoint.Security. The Microsoft.SharePoint assembly contains the server object model for Share-Point that you will use when writing code against SharePoint. The Microsoft .SharePoint.Security assembly contains code access security objects that are used for partially trusted solutions.

The Features folder is a special folder that is found only in a Visual Studio SharePoint project. This folder contains SharePoint features that have been created for the project. A SharePoint project can contain zero or more features. By default, when you add a new SharePoint item to a SharePoint project that requires a feature, Visual Studio will create a new feature automatically or reuse an existing feature if there is already a feature in the project with the same scope (Farm, Site, Web, or Web Application). For more information on working with features, see Chapter 11, "Packaging and Deployment."

The Packages folder is another special folder that is found in SharePoint projects. This folder contains information that allows the project to create a package file or .WSP file. Package files are used to deploy SharePoint features to a SharePoint site. By default, when you add a new SharePoint item to a SharePoint project that results in the creation of a new feature, that new feature will automatically be added to the package file associated with the project. For more information on working with packages, see Chapter 11, "Packaging and Deployment."

The next file you will find in a SharePoint project is the key.snk file. This is a strong name key that is used to sign the output assembly of the project.

Mapped Folders, Deployment, and the Hive

One item you will often find in a SharePoint project that isn't found in our example is a mapped folder. Mapped folders give you a way to take resources and other files in your project and add them to folders in the Visual Studio project that are mapped to file system locations where those files need to be deployed on the SharePoint server. For example, imagine you have an application page you have developed that needs to deploy a file to the SharePoint server's images folder. To do this you would right click on the Project node and choose Add, then SharePoint Images Folder. This creates a mapped folder in the project called Images. Any folders you add to the images folder will be created on disk (if they aren't already there) and the contents of those folders will be copied to the SharePoint server's images folder when the project is deployed.

It is time for another aside regarding SharePoint terminology. We've just implied that SharePoint has an images folder—what is this and what other special folders does SharePoint have? When you build a deployment for SharePoint you build a SharePoint package, which is basically a CAB file (like a ZIP file if you aren't familiar with the CAB format) that has in it a set of files and instructions that are used to install your SharePoint solution. The instructions are encapsulated in one or more SharePoint Feature files, which consist of XML markup that is read at install time. A special program called stsadm.exe takes the SharePoint package file (which is a CAB file with a .WSP extension) and reads the SharePoint feature files in the package to determine how to install the SharePoint solution. These SharePoint feature files in turn can refer to additional files that are packaged within the SharePoint package. Stsadm.exe then does two major things—it adds information to the SharePoint content database and it copies files to the file system. So a SharePoint solution typically modifies the SharePoint content and configuration databases and adds files to the file system of the SharePoint server machine.

There are three general locations where SharePoint copies files to the file system of the server during deployment. The first location is the global assembly cache of the server machine. Solutions that have assemblies that need full trust will copy to this directory when Assembly Deployment Target is set to GlobalAssemblyCache as we saw in Table 2-2.

The second location is directories specific to a web application (which is an IIS concept we described in Chapter 1). One of those web application-specific directories is the bin directory. This is where assemblies are deployed if you set the Assembly Deployment Target property to WebApplication. To determine where the web application directory is, launch the Internet Information Services (IIS) manager on the SharePoint server (use the search box in the Start menu to search for it). Once you've launched the IIS manager, expand the Sites folder and find the web application you are interested in—in a default install it will be called SharePoint -80 as shown in Figure 2-6. Right click on the SharePoint -80 node, and pick Explore from the context menu. This will open the base directory for your web application as shown in Figure 2-7. Of interest here are several directories and files you may use. The web.config file is used to configure ASP.NET specific settings—you have to modify this file for some SharePoint development scenarios we will see later in this book. The bin folder is the bin directory associated with the web application where assemblies are sometimes deployed. There are other directories here that are used for web part development, such as the wpresources folder.

The third location of interest for deployment is known in the SharePoint developer world as *the hive*, which is the location on disk where SharePoint installs feature definitions, site definitions, and other content used to provision the web site. SharePoint builds on its own extensibility model—many of the features in the SharePoint web site correspond to actual files you can inspect and learn from in these directories. The hive can be found at Program Files\Common Files\Microsoft Shared\Web Server Extensions\14. Some of the folders found in the hive are shown in Figure 2-8.

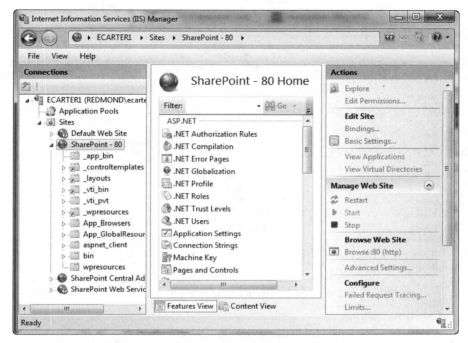

Figure 2-6: The Internet Information Services (IIS) Manager showing the web application
SharePoint -80

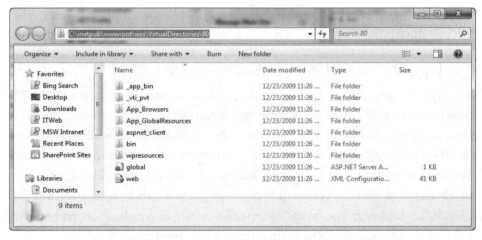

Figure 2-7: Directories and files associated with the SharePoint -80 web application

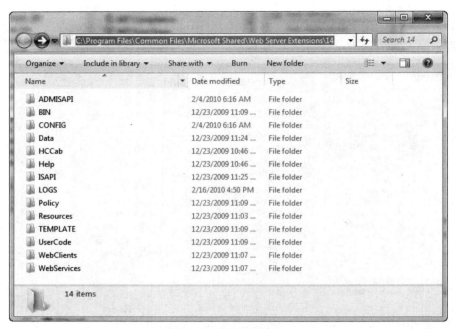

Figure 2-8: Directories and files in the SharePoint hive

When you add a mapped folder in Visual Studio by right clicking on the Project node and choosing Add, then SharePoint Mapped Folder, you will see the dialog shown in Figure 2-9, which lets you view all the folders in the hive to which you might want to deploy items. In Figure 2-9, we have expanded the TEMPLATE folder, which is the main place to which you will deploy items. In this folder, you can see there is an IMAGES folder, where you can deploy arbitrary images you want to use from web parts or application pages. There are other directories as well—for example, the SiteTemplates folder, where you install Site Definitions files and the LAYOUTS folder, where you can find the master page being used for the SharePoint server. You will typically create a subdirectory within the LAYOUTS folder if you want to install your own application pages. We will learn more about the hive throughout this book.

Figure 2-9: Adding a Mapped Folder in Visual
Studio to the Layouts folder

SharePoint Project Items

So now that we've seen the basic structure of an empty SharePoint project
and learned a little bit more about deployment, let's consider what happens when we add a SharePoint project item to the SharePoint project. To
add a SharePoint project item, right click on the Project node in Server
Explorer (titled SharePointProject1 in our example) and choose Add, then
New Item… from the context menu. The Add New Item dialog shown in
Figure 2-10 appears. There are a number of SharePoint project items that
can be added to a SharePoint project. Table 2-3 lists the project item types
and briefly describes each one. It also lists the chapter in this book where
each project item type is described in detail.

Figure 2-10: Add New Item dialog

TABLE 2-3:   SharePoint Project Item Types

Project Item Type	Description	Described in Chapter
Application Page	An ASP.NET web page that is displayed within a SharePoint site	Chapter 10, "SharePoint Pages"
Business Data Connectivity Model	A business data connectivity model allows you to define a data model and code that lets you integrate external data into SharePoint.	Chapter 6, "Working with Business Data"
Content Type	A content type defines the schema for an item in a list—examples of content types in SharePoint include the Contact content type and the Announcement content type. Content types can also be associated with document libraries, allowing you to create a specialized document type such as an "Expense	Chapter 7, "SharePoint Content Types"

TABLE 2-3: SharePoint Project Item Types *(Continued)*

Project Item Type	Description	Described in Chapter
Content Type *(continued)*	Report" content type complete with a document template (e.g., an Excel workbook or Word document) to be used when a new expense report is created.	Chapter 7, "SharePoint Content Types"
Empty Element	An empty element is used to create a SharePoint project item that has a single XML file called Elements.xml associated with it. In this file you can define SharePoint elements that aren't natively supported yet by Visual Studio, such as a site column for a list. This element can then be referenced by other project items and installed with the rest of the solution.	Chapter 11, "Packaging and Deployment"
Event Receiver	An event receiver handles events that are raised by lists and other key objects in SharePoint. For example, an event receiver could execute custom code when a new item is added to a SharePoint list.	Chapter 5, "SharePoint Event Receivers"
List Definition	A list definition defines the schema of a list along with other things that define the list, such as views and forms used by the list.	Chapter 4, "SharePoint Lists"
List Definition from Content Type	Allows you to create a list definition based on a content type already in the project or on the local SharePoint server	Chapter 4, "SharePoint Lists"
List Instance	A list instance allows you to create an instance of a list as part of your solution; for example, you could have a project with a custom list definition called Expense Reports and two instances of that list, one called "International Expense Reports" and one called "Domestic Expense Reports."	Chapter 4, "SharePoint Lists"
Module	A module is used when creating deployments to provision the SharePoint site with one or more files that are needed	Chapter 11, "Packaging and Deployment"

Continues

TABLE 2-3:   SharePoint Project Item Types *(Continued)*

Project Item Type	Description	Described in Chapter
Module *(continued)*	by a solution—for example, you might use this to deploy a custom document to a document library or some other custom resource (e.g., an image file or an application page). A module has an Elements.xml file that you can edit to specify the file or files associated with the module.	Chapter 11, "Packaging and Deployment"
Sequential Workflow	A multistep process that can be long running, waiting for humans or external systems to complete tasks or other processes before continuing. A sequential workflow proceeds in a linear top-to-bottom fashion.	Chapter 8, "SharePoint Workflow"
State Machine Workflow	A state machine workflow uses concepts such as states, events, and transitions to model more complex business processes with multiple possible paths through the workflow.	Chapter 8, "SharePoint Workflow"
User Control	User controls are ASP.NET controls that can be deployed and reused by application pages or web parts. For example, you might create a custom user control that provides a drop-down control with custom behavior you want to reuse in several application pages and web parts.	Chapter 9, "SharePoint Web Parts"
Visual Web Part	Web parts are controls written using ASP.NET that users can place in a SharePoint web part page. The Visual Web Part project gives you a user control that you can visually edit combined with a class deriving from ASP.NET's web part class that hosts the user control.	Chapter 9, "SharePoint Web Parts"
Web Part	Web parts are controls written using ASP.NET that users can place in a SharePoint web part page. The Web Part project does not use ASP.NET user controls or the visual designer for an ASP.NET user control; instead it has you edit a class deriving from ASP.NET's web part class.	Chapter 9, "SharePoint Web Parts"

Table 2-3 shows the SharePoint project items available when you right click on the Project node item and choose Add New Item. In addition, there are four more SharePoint project items that are only available when you right click on an existing item in a SharePoint project and then choose Add > New Item… . It can be confusing that these items don't appear if you have the Project node selected but only when you have an existing project item selected. But this reinforces the idea that these project items only make sense when used in conjunction with other SharePoint project items. These four additional project items are listed in Table 2-4.

TABLE 2-4: SharePoint Project Item Types Dependent on Other Project Item Types

Project Item Type	Description	Described in Chapter
Business Data Connectivity Resource Item	Dependent on Business Data Connectivity (BDC) Model; allows you to add a resource file to your BDC solution to provide localized names for a BDC model.	Chapter 7, "SharePoint Content Types"
Global Resources File	Dependent on having other SharePoint project items in the project; allows you to add a resource file to provide localized names that can be used by any feature or element file in the solution.	Chapter 11, "Packaging and Deployment"
Workflow Association Form	Dependent on having a Sequential or State Machine workflow in the project; an ASP.NET form that can be displayed when a workflow is associated with a SharePoint list, document library, or site. This can be used to configure initial settings for the workflow.	Chapter 9, "SharePoint Web Parts"
Workflow Initiation Form	Dependent on having a Sequential or State Machine workflow in the project; an ASP.NET form that is displayed when an instance of a workflow is begun for an item in a list or document library or for a site workflow.	Chapter 8, "SharePoint Workflow"

For the purposes of this chapter, let's create an event receiver. An event receiver handles events that are raised by lists, items in a list, webs (Share-Point sites), and workflow. To create an event receiver, select Event Receiver from the list of project item types that can be added, as shown in the Add New Item dialog in Figure 2-10. Accept the default name (EventReceiver1) and press the Add button. The SharePoint Customization Wizard dialog appears. Here you can choose the type of event receiver you want to create, as shown in Figure 2-11.

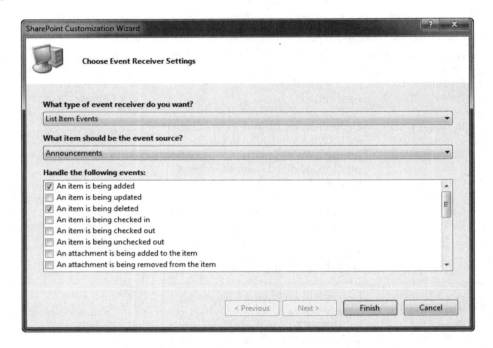

Figure 2-11: The SharePoint Customization Wizard dialog configured to handle list item events for the Announcements list

There are five types of event receivers you can create: a list event receiver, a list item event receiver, a list e-mail event receiver, a web (SharePoint site) event receiver, and a list workflow event receiver. List item, list workflow, and list e-mail event receivers act on a specific list instance that you must also elect in the dialog in Figure 2-11. List and web event receivers pertain to a web scope and act on the current SharePoint site to which you are deploying.

For this example, let's create an event receiver that handles list item events for the Calendar list associated with the SharePoint site. To do this, pick List Item Events from the first drop-down in the dialog and select Announcements as the specific list for which we will handle events. After making these selections, the list box at the bottom of the dialog shows the different list item events that can be handled by your code. Check the check boxes next to An item is being added, An item is being deleted, An item was added, and An item was deleted. The dialog should look like Figure 2-11. Then press the Finish button.

Visual Studio adds the SharePoint project item representing an event receiver. The resulting project structure now looks like Figure 2-12.

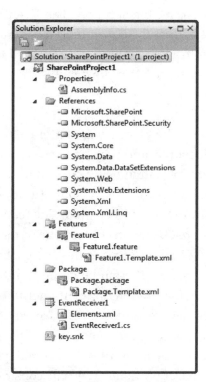

Figure 2-12: A SharePoint project with a single SharePoint project item for an Event Receiver

Exploring a SharePoint Project Item

Now that we have added our first SharePoint project item to this project, we will explore some of the new things we can see in the project with the addition of a SharePoint project item. First note that there is a project item icon in Solution Explorer titled EventReceiver1, and parented under that icon are two additional items: an XML file called Elements.xml and a code file called EventReceiver1.cs. As we will see throughout this book, this is a common pattern for many SharePoint project items.

The root SharePoint project item node "EventReceiver1" has properties that configure the event receiver. This root node is actually a folder that contains two files. The Elements.xml file contains the XML that is used to describe the customization to SharePoint and is read by stsadm.exe as part of installing and configuring the solution. The EventReceiver1.cs file contains custom code that defines the behavior of the SharePoint customization and will be compiled into an assembly to be deployed to the SharePoint site. Let's consider each of these files in more detail.

The Elements.xml File

The first file to consider is the Elements.xml file. This is sometimes referred to as an Element Manifest file, and is an XML file that contains information that describes the SharePoint item being created to SharePoint, in this case an event receiver. Behind the scenes, Visual Studio will refer to this Elements.xml file in a feature file it has created. The feature file in turn is contained by a package—a package can contain one or more features as shown in Figure 2-13. When Visual Studio deploys the package, each feature file and associated Elements.xml file will be copied to the SharePoint server. SharePoint will read the feature file that will refer to the Elements.xml file. The Elements.xml file, as we will see, in turn refers to event handlers defined in an assembly. Once SharePoint has read the feature file and associated Elements.xml and assembly files, it can make the feature available for activation in the SharePoint site. We will consider the Visual Studio project support for features and packages in more detail later in this chapter and in Chapter 11, "Packaging and Deployment." Note that in this diagram, one feature has custom code associated with it represented by a

.NET assembly. It is possible for multiple features to use code written within the same assembly.

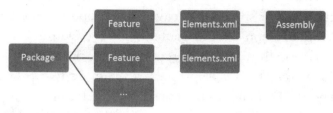

Figure 2-13: The relationship among a package, a feature, element manifests, and an assembly

When you click on the Elements.xml file node in the Solution Explorer, you will see several properties in the Properties window that can be configured as shown in Figure 2-14. Note that the properties in the Properties window change if you click in the contents of the Elements.xml file, so be sure you've clicked on the node in the Solution Explorer tree view. These properties are organized into three categories: Advanced, Misc, and Share-Point. Let's consider the properties in each of these three categories.

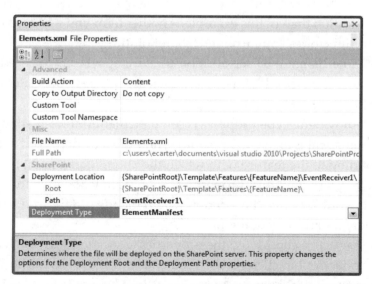

Figure 2-14: The properties associated with the Elements.xml file node

Under the Advanced category of properties there are four properties: Build Action, Copy to Output Directory, Custom Tool, and Custom Tool Namespace. These properties tell Visual Studio how to process the Elements.xml file and you should just leave these properties set to their original values—Build Action is set to Content, Copy to Output Directory is set to Do not Copy, and the other two properties have no setting.

Under the Misc category of properties there are two properties—the File Name and the Full Path to the file so you can locate where it is stored on disk. As with the Advanced properties, there is no good reason to change these properties; they should be left set to their original values.

Finally, the SharePoint category of properties includes the property Deployment Location with child properties Root and Path and the property Deployment Type. The Deployment Location property tells you where on the SharePoint server the Elements.xml file will be deployed when you build and deploy the solution. In our example, it is set to {SharePointRoot}\Template\ Features\{FeatureName}\EventReceiver1\. In our example, {SharePointRoot} is a substitution token that will be replaced by the actual root file location where SharePoint features are deployed on a server, typically a path such as "C:\Program files\Common Files\Microsoft Shared\web server extensions\14\, although SharePoint could be installed to a different drive or program file location than in this example. Another term you will hear used for this set of directories found under {SharePointRoot} is *the SharePoint hive*. {FeatureName} is another substitution token that will be replaced by the name of the feature that this SharePoint project item file is associated with, in our example: Feature1.

The Deployment Type property is set to ElementManifest—this reflects that Elements.xml is an element manifest and must be deployed to a folder corresponding to the feature with which the SharePoint project item file is associated. Changing this property would be a bad idea for this file because it would change the location where the file is deployed to one not appropriate for an element manifest.

Now that we've considered the properties associated with the Elements. xml file node, double click on the Elements.xml file node in the Solution Explorer window to open the contents of the Elements.xml file. The contents of the file are shown in Listing 2-1. Note that this is representative of the contents of an Elements.xml file for an event receiver. But for other SharePoint project item types—for example a list definition—the contents of the Elements.xml file will look quite different. This can be confusing to new SharePoint developers because they think that all Elements.xml files have similar contents when in truth, the contents of Elements.xml are specific to the SharePoint project item type.

Listing 2-1: The Elements.xml file defining event receivers for four list item events

```xml
<?xml version="1.0" encoding="utf-8"?>
<Elements xmlns="http://schemas.microsoft.com/sharepoint/">
<Receivers ListTemplateId="104">
  <Receiver>
    <Name>EventReceiver1ItemAdding</Name>
    <Type>ItemAdding</Type>
    <Assembly>$SharePoint.Project.AssemblyFullName$</Assembly>
    <Class>SharePointProject1.EventReceiver1.EventReceiver1</Class>
    <SequenceNumber>10000</SequenceNumber>
  </Receiver>
  <Receiver>
    <Name>EventReceiver1ItemDeleting</Name>
    <Type>ItemDeleting</Type>
    <Assembly>$SharePoint.Project.AssemblyFullName$</Assembly>
    <Class>SharePointProject1.EventReceiver1.EventReceiver1</Class>
    <SequenceNumber>10000</SequenceNumber>
  </Receiver>
  <Receiver>
    <Name>EventReceiver1ItemAdded</Name>
    <Type>ItemAdded</Type>
    <Assembly>$SharePoint.Project.AssemblyFullName$</Assembly>
    <Class>SharePointProject1.EventReceiver1.EventReceiver1</Class>
    <SequenceNumber>10000</SequenceNumber>
  </Receiver>
  <Receiver>
    <Name>EventReceiver1ItemDeleted</Name>
    <Type>ItemDeleted</Type>
    <Assembly>$SharePoint.Project.AssemblyFullName$</Assembly>
    <Class>SharePointProject1.EventReceiver1.EventReceiver1</Class>
    <SequenceNumber>10000</SequenceNumber>
  </Receiver>
</Receivers>
</Elements>
```

The contents of the Elements.xml file have a root element called Elements. Elements has a child element called Receivers. Receivers contains a

Receiver element for each of the four event receivers we defined for our Event Receiver project item. Each Receiver element contains 5 subelements listed in Table 2-5. You might also notice the ListTemplateId attribute, which is set to 104. To find out where this magic number comes from, use the Server Explorer that we saw in Chapter 1 to browse the site. Under Team Site, List Templates, Communications select the Announcements list template. In the Properties window, you will see that its Type_Client property is 104. The number 104 tells SharePoint to associate the event receiver with the Announcements list definition.

TABLE 2-5: Subelements Contained within the Receiver Element in Elements.xml

Element	Description
Name	The name of the receiver
Type	The type of the event handler; this name is defined by SharePoint and must also match the name of the method defined in the class handling the event.
Assembly	The full name of the assembly where the event handler for this event is defined; Visual Studio allows a token to be used here, $SharePoint.Project.AssemblyFullName$, which will be replaced with the full name of the assembly when the project is built.
Class	The fully qualified name of the class where the event handler for this event is defined, e.g., SharePointProject1.EventReceiver1.EventReceiver1
SequenceNumber	The number inside the SequenceNumber element defines the order in which events are executed. If there are two or more event receivers and they are handling the same events, the one that has the smallest number in the SequenceNumber element is executed first.

As you might imagine, the Elements.xml or element manifest for other SharePoint project item types contains different content that defines that particular SharePoint project item type. Every Elements.xml file, regardless of type, has a root element called Elements, however.

The Code File (EventReceiver1.cs)

Below the SharePoint project item node "EventReceiver1" you will see a code file called EventReceiver1.cs, shown in Listing 2-2. This contains a class that derives from Microsoft.SharePoint.SPItemEventReceiver. Event handlers are added with calls to the base class implementation of the event handler. Note that the names of these event handlers map to the names used in the Elements.xml file.

Listing 2-2: EventReceiver1.cs

```
using System;
using System.Security.Permissions;
using Microsoft.SharePoint;
using Microsoft.SharePoint.Security;
using Microsoft.SharePoint.Utilities;
using Microsoft.SharePoint.Workflow;

namespace SharePointProject1.EventReceiver1
{
  /// <summary>
  /// List Item Events
  /// </summary>
  public class EventReceiver1 : SPItemEventReceiver
  {
    /// <summary>
    /// An item is being added.
    /// </summary>
    public override void ItemAdding(SPItemEventProperties properties)
    {
      base.ItemAdding(properties);
    }

    /// <summary>
    /// An item is being deleted.
    /// </summary>
    public override void ItemDeleting(SPItemEventProperties properties)
    {
      base.ItemDeleting(properties);
    }

    /// <summary>
    /// An item was added.
    /// </summary>
    public override void ItemAdded(SPItemEventProperties properties)
    {
```

```
      base.ItemAdded(properties);
    }

    /// <summary>
    /// An item was deleted.
    /// </summary>
    public override void ItemDeleted(SPItemEventProperties properties)
    {
      base.ItemDeleted(properties);
    }
  }
}
```

We will add some code to the ItemDeleting and ItemAdded event as shown in Listing 2-3. In ItemDeleting, we first call the base ItemDeleting method. Then we use the properties parameter that is passed to the function and use the ListItem property. The ListItem property is a parameterized property to which we can pass a field name to read and write a field from the item being deleted from the list. We use the ListItem property to access the Title field and append the Title field with an asterisk. Next, we call the Update method on the ListItem to update the item being deleted with the new Title. Finally, we use the Cancel property on the properties parameter to cancel the deletion of the item. We can stop an item from being deleted in the ItemDeleting event because this event is fired before the item is deleted—the ItemDeleted event happens after the item is deleted, so putting this code into that event would not work.

We also add code to the ItemAdded event. Here, we again use the List-Item property on the properties parameter passed to the event. We modify the Title to add the string " added" to it after it is added to the list. We then call the Update method on the ListItem to update the item that was added so our change will be shown in the list.

Listing 2-3: EventReceiver1.cs with custom event handlers for ItemDeleting and ItemAdded

```
using System;
using System.Security.Permissions;
using Microsoft.SharePoint;
using Microsoft.SharePoint.Security;
using Microsoft.SharePoint.Utilities;
using Microsoft.SharePoint.Workflow;
```

```csharp
namespace SharePointProject1.EventReceiver1
{
  /// <summary>
  /// List Item Events
  /// </summary>
  public class EventReceiver1 : SPItemEventReceiver
  {
    /// <summary>
    /// An item is being added.
    /// </summary>
    public override void ItemAdding(SPItemEventProperties properties)
    {
      base.ItemAdding(properties);
    }

    /// <summary>
    /// An item is being deleted.
    /// </summary>
    public override void ItemDeleting(SPItemEventProperties properties)
    {
      base.ItemDeleting(properties);
      SPWeb web = properties.OpenWeb();
      properties.ListItem["Title"] =
        properties.ListItem["Title"] + "*";
      properties.ListItem.Update();
      properties.Cancel = true;
    }

    /// <summary>
    /// An item was added.
    /// </summary>
    public override void ItemAdded(SPItemEventProperties properties)
    {
      base.ItemAdded(properties);
      SPWeb web = properties.OpenWeb();
      properties.ListItem["Title"] =
        properties.ListItem["Title"] + " added";
      properties.ListItem.Update();
    }

    /// <summary>
    /// An item was deleted.
    /// </summary>
    public override void ItemDeleted(SPItemEventProperties properties)
    {
      base.ItemDeleted(properties);
    }
  }
}
```

The Root Project Item Node or Folder (EventReceiver1)

When you click on the root level SharePoint project item node Event-
Receiver1, you will see several properties in the Properties window that
can be configured as shown in Figure 2-15. First note that the Properties
window indicates that EventReceiver1 is a folder—the Properties window
says Folder Properties. The properties for EventReceiver1 are organized
into three categories: Misc, SharePoint, and SharePoint Events. Let's consider the properties in each of these three categories.

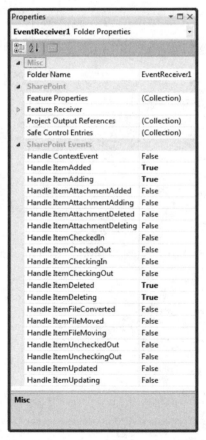

Figure 2-15: The properties associated
with the EventReceiver1 node

Misc Properties   The sole property under the Misc category in Figure 2-15 is Folder Name. If you change the name of the project item node—either by changing the Folder Name property or by renaming the project item node in the Solution Explorer, it will automatically change some but not all areas in the project that refer to the project item node. For example, if you were to rename EventReceiver1 to EventReceiver2, Visual Studio automatically fixes up the feature "Feature1" associated with the SharePoint project item to refer to the new project item name. But it doesn't change the names of the files contained in the (now EventReceiver2) folder or any of the classes that were created. So after changing the node to EventReceiver2, the code file is still titled EventReceiver1.cs and the class inside the code file is still titled EventReceiver1. More critically, the Elements.xml file still refers to EventReceiver1.

You could manually rename EventReceiver1.cs to EventReceiver2.cs and even refactor the class contained in the newly renamed EventReceiver2.cs file to be EventReceiver2. In this case, the Elements.xml file will be updated correctly. But in some cases the Elements.xml file will not be updated correctly after a refactor. For example, if you change the namespace that your class is defined in from SharePointProject1.EventReceiver1 to SharePointProject1.MyEventReceiver, the Elements.xml file will not be updated to have the right fully qualified class names in the Class elements. You would have to manually update the Elements.xml file to ensure it contains the new SharePointProject1.MyEventReceiver namespace or the project won't run successfully.

SharePoint Properties   Continuing with our exploration of the properties associated with the root level SharePoint project item node EventReceiver1, you will see a number of properties under the category SharePoint in Figure 2-15. Feature Properties is a collection of key value pairs that are used when deploying the feature associated with the event receiver to SharePoint. These properties are deployed with the feature and can be accessed later in SharePoint using the SPFeaturePropertyCollection object. So for example, you might use feature properties to associate some configuration information or other static data with your feature.

The Feature Receiver set of properties includes the subproperties Assembly and Class Name. You can use these properties to specify an assembly and class name that you want to handle events that are raised when the Feature associated with your EventReceiver1 item is raised. You can create a class in your current solution and refer to it or include another assembly in your SharePoint package—for more information on how to include additional assemblies in your SharePoint package, see Chapter 11, "Packaging and Deployment."

Events that your feature receiver can handle include FeatureInstalled, FeatureUninstalling, FeatureActivated, and FeatureDeactivating. So you could write code that runs when your EventReceiver1 is installed and uninstalled from the SharePoint site, maybe to add additional resources or lists required on install and remove those additional resources or lists on uninstall. We will discuss feature event receivers more in Chapter 5, "SharePoint Event Receivers."

Project Output References are used to tell Visual Studio about any dependent assemblies your project item requires to run. For example, maybe your event receiver uses a helper class library called HelperLibrary .dll. You can use the Project Output References project to tell Visual Studio about the helper class library and then Visual Studio will package the dependent assembly in the final solution. For more on Project Output References, see Chapter 11, "Packaging and Deployment."

Finally Safe Control Entries is used to designate whether an ASPX control or web part is trusted and can be used by users on the site. In the context of an Event Receiver, this property is not applicable and doesn't do anything. We will see this property used in Chapter 9, "SharePoint Web Parts."

SharePoint Events Properties   In Figure 2-15, under the category SharePoint Events are a number of properties that correspond to the list of events we saw earlier in the wizard shown in Figure 2-11. For the events that we checked earlier, the properties Handle ItemAdded, Handle ItemAdding, Handle ItemDeleted, and Handle ItemDeleting are set to True. To add and remove events that this event receiver handles you can change which SharePoint event "Handle" properties are set to True or False. To see the impact of setting a property that was previously set to False to True, open the Elements.xml file and the EventReceiver1.cs files under the Event-Receiver1 node and arrange your windows so these files are visible while you change "Handle" properties under the SharePoint Events category to True or False. You will notice that setting a property like Handle Item-CheckedIn, which was previously False to True, adds a block of XML to the Elements.xml file and adds a new event handler to the EventReceiver1 .cs file. If you then set that property back to False, you will see that Visual Studio removes the block of XML that it previously added from the Elements.xml file, but leaves the event handler it added to the Event-Receiver1.cs file intact. It leaves the code in EventReceiver1.cs intact because you might have written some code in the handler and Visual Studio wants to preserve any code you wrote. Also, having an inactive event handler in EventReceiver1.cs (inactive because it isn't registered in the Elements.xml file) will have no ill-effect on your remaining active event handlers (active because they *are* registered in the Elements.xml file).

Features and Packages in a Visual Studio Project

We've now explored the properties and files that are associated with a new SharePoint project item. We've seen the Elements.xml file, the code file associated with an event receiver, and the properties associated with each of these files and the root EventReceiver1 folder for the SharePoint project item.

You may have noticed that when we added the event receiver project item to our blank solution, some new items appeared under the Features folder. Let's examine the Features and Package folders in the SharePoint project to start to get an idea of what Visual Studio does to package and deploy our SharePoint solution.

Features

Just to make things a little more interesting, let's create a second event receiver. Follow the steps we did earlier in the chapter to create a second event receiver called EventReceiver2. For the second event receiver, choose List Item Events as the type of event receiver to create, use Calendar as the event source, and handle the event when an item is being added.

Now double click on the project item called Feature1 under the Features folder. The Visual Studio Feature designer appears as shown in Figure 2-16. Note that we now have two event receivers in our solution, EventReceiver1 and EventReceiver2, and Feature1 is configured to install both event receivers.

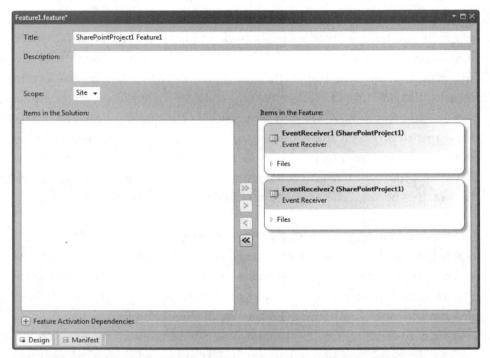

Figure 2-16: Visual Studio's Feature designer with two SharePoint project items to deploy

It is possible to add features to the Features folder. For example, maybe you want EventReceiver1 and EventReceiver2 to be deployed as separate features. You could create a separate feature called "Feature2" and install EventReceiver1 in Feature1 and EventReceiver2 in Feature2. Doing this would enable the event receivers to be installed and uninstalled separately. Another reason you might need to have separate features is when you have SharePoint project items you want to deploy that need to be installed at a different scope. If you drop down the Scope drop-down in Figure 2-16, you can see that a feature can be installed to one of four scopes: Farm, Site (the Site Collection Level), Web (the Site level), and Web-

Application (all sites hosted by an IIS web application). Due to historical reasons, SharePoint sometimes uses the word Site to refer to a Site Collection and Web to refer to a SharePoint Site.

Let's create a second feature by right clicking on the Features folder and choosing Add Feature. A new Feature called Feature2 is created. In the Feature designer that will appear for Feature2, click on the EventReceiver2 SharePoint item and click the > button to move the feature from the left-hand list to the right-hand list. Then back in the Feature1 designer, ensure that EventReceiver2 is not installed by Feature1 by clicking on Event-Receiver2 and pressing the < button to move it from the right-hand list to the left-hand list. The resulting Feature1 designer is shown in Figure 2-17. This shows that Feature1 will now install only EventReceiver1 not Event-Receiver2. The right-hand list contains the features that will be installed; the left-hand list contains other items in the solution that have not been added to this feature. Also in Figure 2-17, we have expanded the Files outline and the

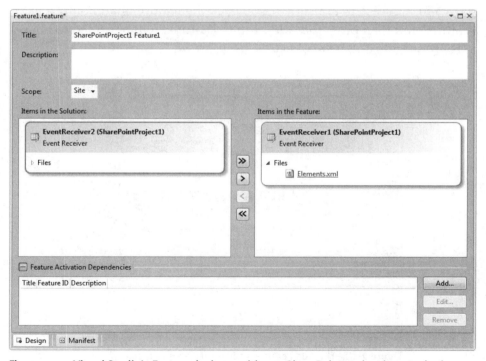

Figure 2-17: Visual Studio's Feature designer with one SharePoint project item to deploy

Feature Activation Dependencies area of the Feature designer. We will discuss these two areas of the designer next.

The Files outline shows the actual files that will be included in the feature to install the associated SharePoint project item. In this case, you can see that the Elements.xml file will be included. The assembly built with the current project is also implicitly included in the feature, even though it doesn't show in this designer.

Also, at the bottom of the dialog you can now see the Feature Activation Dependencies area of the Feature designer. Here you can add dependencies that your feature has on other features in the solution or on other features that must be installed in advance to the SharePoint site where this feature will be installed. For example, you might have a situation in which you've created two features in your solution but Feature1 needs Feature2 to be installed first. Let's enforce this constraint. Click the Add… button in the Feature Activation Dependencies area for Feature1 to specify that Feature2 is a dependency. When you click the Add… button, the dialog shown in Figure 2-18 appears. If you click the feature SharePointProject1. Feature2 and then press the Add button, Feature2 will be added to the list of Feature Activation Dependencies for Feature1.

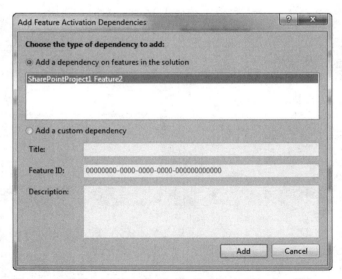

Figure 2-18: The Add Feature Activation Dependencies dialog

You also might want to add a dependency on another custom or built-in SharePoint feature. For example, you might need to ensure that the Announcement Lists feature is installed on the SharePoint site because your event receiver modifies or creates announcement lists. If announcement lists are not there, your event receiver will fail. The dialog shown in Figure 2-18 also lets you add dependencies to SharePoint features not in your solution by specifying the Feature ID of the feature on which you are dependent. As you might remember from Chapter 1, you can use the Server Explorer and the Properties window to determine the Feature ID for a particular feature as shown in Figure 1-76's DefinitionID. This ID could be added as a custom dependency for our Feature1 using the dialog in Figure 2-18.

Package Designer

Features in a project are useless unless they are deployed into what is called a Package or a .WSP file. Visual Studio helps you configure the Package created by your solution with the Package Designer. To see the Package Designer, double click on the Package.package project item under the Package folder in your solution. The designer shown in Figure 2-19 appears.

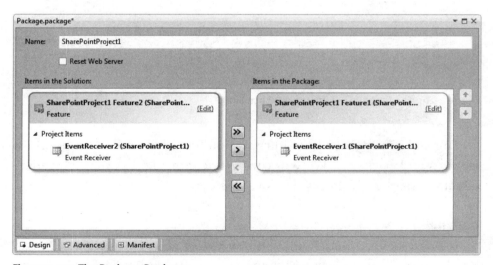

Figure 2-19: The Package Designer

When you first open the designer it won't exactly match Figure 2-19 because Visual Studio will automatically place both features we created into the items to install in the package that is created by the project. We used the < button to remove Feature2 from the package because we don't really want to install EventReceiver2 since we have no code added to it yet. Each project can build only one package, but you can have a package created by other projects in your solution. Visual Studio also lets you mix and match where features come from—that is, a feature can come from Project1 in a solution but be installed by the Package built by Project2.

If you click on the Advanced button at the bottom of the Package Designer, options are provided to add additional assemblies to the package—either assemblies created by other projects in the solution or additional external assemblies. The Advanced page of the Package Designer is shown in Figure 2-20.

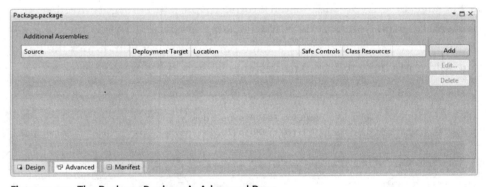

Figure 2-20: The Package Designer's Advanced Page

This has given you a brief introduction to Visual Studio's support for features and packages. We will consider features and packages in more detail in Chapter 11, "Packaging and Deployment."

Building

So we now have a SharePoint solution with two event receivers: Event-Receiver1 and EventReceiver2, two features: Feature1 and Feature2, and one package: Package.package. Feature1 includes EventReceiver1, Feature2 includes EventReceiver2, but Package.package only includes Feature1, so the EventReceiver2 will not be packaged or installed. If we build currently, we will get a missing dependency error because we made Feature2 a dependency for Feature1 and Feature2 is not currently being packaged. Use the Feature designer's Feature Activation Dependencies area for Feature1 to remove the dependency on Feature2 by clicking the Remover button.

We are now ready to build our project in preparation for running and debugging it. When you build the project by choosing Build Solution from the Build menu, the Output window indicates pretty much what you would expect—it says that a DLL has been built in the Debug folder of your project called SharePointProject1.dll. When we go to the bin\debug directory for the project in Windows Explorer, you will see the DLL and the PDB for the DLL, which contains debugging information. If you package the project by choosing Package from the Build menu, you will see something a little different, as shown in Figure 2-21. You will now find in addition to the DLL and PDB files, there is a .WSP file. This is the SharePoint package file that the Feature and Package Designer helped us to create.

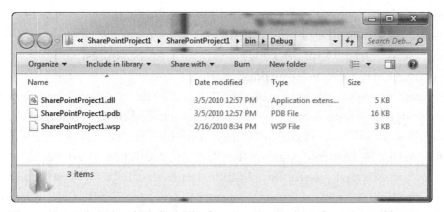

Figure 2-21: What Visual Studio built after choosing Package from the Build menu

Let's look at the .WSP file in a little more detail. Click the SharePointProject1.wsp file in the bin\debug folder of your project. Copy the SharePointProject1.wsp then Paste to make a copy of the .WSP file. Rename its extension from .WSP to .CAB. Remember we said that a .WSP file was actually a .CAB file? Now that we've renamed it to a .CAB file, you should be able to double click on it and see the contents of the .WSP file as shown in Figure 2-22.

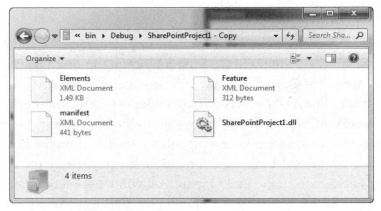

Figure 2-22: Inside the .WSP File

As you can see, there are 4 files inside the .WSP file: Elements.xml, Feature.xml, manifest.xml, and the assembly created by our project (a copy of the one we saw in the debug directory). Let's look at the contents of these files briefly. Drag Elements.xml, Feature.xml, and manifest.xml out of the renamed .CAB file to your desktop.

Manifest.xml is shown in Listing 2-4 and is the top-level manifest for the .WSP file. It tells about any assemblies included in the package (in this case SharePointProject1.dll). Additional assemblies could be included if you use the Advanced page of the Package Designer to add additional project or external assemblies. Manifest.xml also lists any features contained in the Package, in this case Feature1. You can see what manifest.xml will look like within Visual Studio by double clicking on the Package.package project item to show the Package Designer then clicking on the Manifest button at the bottom of the Package Designer. The same file shown in Listing 2-4 will be shown.

Listing 2-4: Manifest.xml inside the .WSP file

```xml
<?xml version="1.0" encoding="utf-8"?>
<Solution xmlns="http://schemas.microsoft.com/sharepoint/"
  SolutionId="00257823-9b84-48c4-814a-fd754b21073f"
  SharePointProductVersion="14.0">
  <Assemblies>
    <Assembly Location="SharePointProject1.dll"
      DeploymentTarget="GlobalAssemblyCache" />
  </Assemblies>
  <FeatureManifests>
    <FeatureManifest Location="SharePointProject1_Feature1\Feature.xml"
      />
  </FeatureManifests>
</Solution>
```

Feature.xml is shown in Listing 2-5 and corresponds to Feature1 of our two features. In fact, you can see this XML file by double clicking on Feature1.feature to show the Feature designer, then clicking the Manifest button at the bottom of the form. This XML file describes the Feature and tells about the manifests included in the feature. Because Feature1 includes EventReceiver1, there is one Elements.xml file associated with Event-Receiver1, which is the same Elements.xml file that we found under the EventReceiver1 folder.

Listing 2-5: Feature.XML inside the .WSP file

```xml
<?xml version="1.0" encoding="utf-8"?>
<Feature xmlns="http://schemas.microsoft.com/sharepoint/"
Title="SharePointProject1 Feature1" Id="d4050cd0-e7d5-48b0-88a2-fb4257b461b7"
Scope="Site">
  <ElementManifests>
    <ElementManifest Location="EventReceiver1\Elements.xml" />
  </ElementManifests>
</Feature>
```

Elements.xml is just the same file we saw under the EventReceiver1 folder as shown in Listing 2-6. As you can see, there is no magic here, the .WSP file packages up files we've already been able to see in the Package and Feature designers and the Elements.xml file we edited in Visual Studio associated with EventReceiver1.

Listing 2-6: Elements.xml inside the .WSP File

```xml
<?xml version="1.0" encoding="utf-8"?>
<Elements xmlns="http://schemas.microsoft.com/sharepoint/">
  <Receivers ListTemplateId="104">
    <Receiver>
      <Name>EventReceiver1ItemDeleting</Name>
      <Type>ItemDeleting</Type>
      <Assembly>$SharePoint.Project.AssemblyFullName$</Assembly>
      <Class>SharePointProject1.EventReceiver1.EventReceiver1</Class>
      <SequenceNumber>10000</SequenceNumber>
    </Receiver>
    <Receiver>
      <Name>EventReceiver1ItemAdded</Name>
      <Type>ItemAdded</Type>
      <Assembly>$SharePoint.Project.AssemblyFullName$</Assembly>
      <Class>SharePointProject1.EventReceiver1.EventReceiver1</Class>
      <SequenceNumber>10000</SequenceNumber>
    </Receiver>
    <Receiver>
      <Name>EventReceiver1ItemDeleted</Name>
      <Type>ItemDeleted</Type>
      <Assembly>$SharePoint.Project.AssemblyFullName$</Assembly>
      <Class>SharePointProject1.EventReceiver1.EventReceiver1</Class>
      <SequenceNumber>10000</SequenceNumber>
    </Receiver>
    <Receiver>
      <Name>EventReceiver1ItemAdding</Name>
      <Type>ItemAdding</Type>
      <Assembly>$SharePoint.Project.AssemblyFullName$</Assembly>
      <Class>SharePointProject1.EventReceiver1.EventReceiver1</Class>
      <SequenceNumber>1000</SequenceNumber>
    </Receiver>
  </Receivers>
</Elements>
```

Debugging

Now that we've built our project and created the .WSP file, let's debug our solution. To debug the solution, press F5 or choose Run from the Debug menu. Now we see much more activity in the Output window as shown in Listing 2-7. The Build phase does what we saw before—compiles a DLL from any code in the project and builds a package. Then in Deploy several things of interest happen. First, there are some steps to Retract the previous version of the solution. This is so the edit code, run, edit code and run again cycle will work. Visual Studio automatically removes the package and features you installed on your last debug session before deploying your updated package to ensure that you will always have the most recent version of your solution on the server and that the old one won't conflict with the new one. You can also manually Retract a solution from the Server using the Retract command from the Build menu—for example, if you want to ensure that the Server you were testing on doesn't have your solution on it when you are done.

The next thing that Visual Studio does is deploy your .WSP file to the server—the equivalent of using stsadm.exe on the .WSP file at the command line. This installs the package, but there is also a second step after installation called activation. An installed solution is still not active for the web site. Visual Studio also activates the features in the solution to ensure they are installed and active on the web site. Visual Studio will also do an IIS Application Pool recycle if necessary—this ensures that the most current version of the site is running with your new solution installed on it. Finally, Visual Studio launches the site URL in a browser window.

Listing 2-7: Output when you start the solution

```
------ Build started: Project: SharePointProject1,
  Configuration: Debug Any CPU ------
  SharePointProject1 -> C:\Users\ecarter\Documents\
  Visual Studio 2010\Projects\SharePointProject1\SharePointProject1\
  bin\Debug\SharePointProject1.dll
  Successfully created package at:
  C:\Users\ecarter\Documents\Visual Studio 2010\
  Projects\SharePointProject1\SharePointProject1\
  bin\Debug\SharePointProject1.wsp
------ Deploy started: Project: SharePointProject1,
  Configuration: Debug Any CPU ------
Active Deployment Configuration: Default
Run Pre-Deployment Command:
  Skipping deployment step because a pre-deployment command
  is not specified.
Recycle IIS Application Pool:
  Skipping application pool recycle because no matching package
  on the server was found.
Retract Solution:
  Skipping package retraction because no matching package
  on the server was found.
Add Solution:
  Adding solution 'SharePointProject1.wsp'...
  Deploying solution 'SharePointProject1.wsp'...
```

```
Activate Features:
  Activating feature 'Feature1' ...
Run Post-Deployment Command:
  Skipping deployment step because a post-deployment command
  is not specified.
========== Build: 1 succeeded or up-to-date,
  0 failed, 0 skipped ==========
========== Deploy: 1 succeeded, 0 failed, 0 skipped ==========
```

Let's see if our event receiver is working. As you may remember, we tied our event receiver to the Announcements list. First, let's set a break point in EventReceiver1.cs. Click on the ItemAdded event in that file and add a breakpoint by clicking in the left margin of the code editor. Now, go back to the web browser that Visual Studio opened up for you and navigate to the Announcements list. To get there, click on the Site Actions dropdown in the top left corner of the page and choose View All Site Content. On the page that appears, scroll down to the Lists section and click on the Announcements list. Click on the Add new announcement link at the bottom of the list as shown in Figure 2-23.

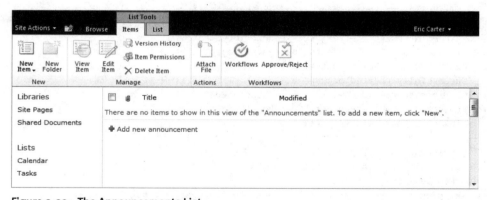

Figure 2-23: The Announcements List

In the dialog that pops up, type some text for your new announcement, something like "Test" as shown in Figure 2-24. Then click the Save button.

When you click the Save button your breakpoint should be hit in the debugger in the ItemAdded event. You can step through the code to watch it modify the newly added item by appending the text "added" to it using

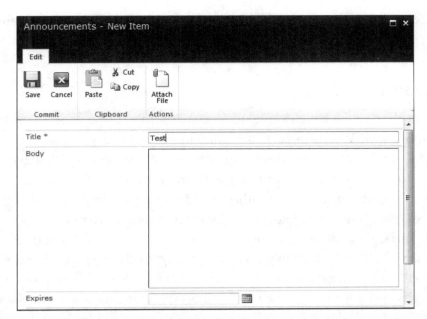

Figure 2-24: Creating a new announcement

the F10 key. Press F5 to continue. You will now see the announcement list in the browser with the newly added announcement with the text "added" appended to the text you entered "Test."

You can also click the check box next to the newly added announcement and press the Delete Item button to try to delete it. For this case, the event receiver we created called ItemDeleting runs and cancels the deletion of the announcement. SharePoint shows the dialog in Figure 2-25, notifying the user that the announcement cannot be deleted.

Figure 2-25: An Event Receiver canceled the Request dialog

To stop debugging, close the browser window or choose Stop Debugging from the Debug window.

Conclusion

In this chapter we have examined Visual Studio's support for SharePoint development. We have seen the SharePoint projects you can create in Visual Studio and all the project item types you can create. We have created a simple Visual Studio project with an event receiver and learned the basic structure of a Visual Studio SharePoint project in which there are SharePoint project item folders for each SharePoint project item you create that contain a code file (EventReceiver1.cs, in our example) and an Elements.xml file. We have explored the properties that are associated with SharePoint project items and their associated files. We have also seen how features and packages work in Visual Studio and examined the Feature and Package designers as well as the .WSP file created by Visual Studio. Finally, we have seen how deployment and debug work in the Visual Studio environment.

In the next chapter we will give an overview of the SharePoint object model because you will need to be familiar with the SharePoint object model to write useful SharePoint solutions.

◼ 3 ◼
Introduction to the SharePoint Object Model

Introduction

No matter how much you know about the SharePoint UI and Visual Studio's support for SharePoint development, you will eventually need to work with the SharePoint object model to get things done. It is impossible to completely describe the SharePoint object model in this book, but we will try to make you familiar with the most important objects in the SharePoint object model and show some of the most frequently used methods, properties, and events on these objects.

There's More Than One Object Model

We have said that there is *a* SharePoint object model, but really there are *four* SharePoint object models. The first object model has been around the longest and is known as the SharePoint Server object model. This is the object model you will use for any SharePoint code that runs on the SharePoint server. We will mainly focus on this server-side object model in this chapter and in this book. The remaining three object models are new in SharePoint 2010 and are used by client code running in the browser or in a client application that needs to talk to SharePoint. There is a client object model catered to .NET 3.5 and higher client applications, another one for

Silverlight applications, and the final one for Jscript code. The client object models have a subset of the objects found in the server-side object model. In general, the client object models mirror the server-side object model, so once you have learned about the server-side object model the client object models will look familiar. We will learn more about the client-side object models for SharePoint lists in Chapter 4, "SharePoint Lists."

Key Objects in the SharePoint Object Model

The first step in learning the SharePoint object model is getting an idea for the most commonly used objects in the object model. The object model has thousands of types in it, so initially it is hard to figure out which types are going to be most commonly used. One way of determining the most commonly used types in the object model is to do a web search against all the types in the object model and rank the types by how many web pages talk about these object model types. The result of such a study is shown in Table 3-1.

TABLE 3-1: Most Commonly Used SharePoint Object Model Objects Ordered by Number of References to the Object on the Web

SharePoint Object	Description
Microsoft.SharePoint.SPList	A SharePoint list that can be used to modify the contents of a list.
Microsoft.SharePoint.SPWeb	A SharePoint site.
Microsoft.SharePoint.SPUser	A SharePoint user.
Microsoft.SharePoint.SPContext	The context of an HTTP request that gives information, such as the current web application, site collection, list, etc.
Microsoft.SharePoint.SPListItem	An item in a SharePoint list.
Microsoft.SharePoint.SPSite	A SharePoint site collection.

TABLE 3-1: Most Commonly Used SharePoint Object Model Objects Ordered by Number of References to the Object on the Web *(Continued)*

SharePoint Object	Description
Microsoft.SharePoint.SPFile	A file in a SharePoint site, for example, a web part page, a file in a folder, or an item in a document library.
Microsoft.SharePoint.SPField	A column defined for a SharePoint list.
Microsoft.SharePoint.SPQuery	A query (in CAML) that can be used to return required list items (SPListItem)
Microsoft.SharePoint.SPSecurity*	Provides a method called RunWith-ElevatedPrivileges that lets you run code with more permissions than the one the current user has.
Microsoft.SharePoint.Administration.SPWebApplication*	An IIS web application that has methods and properties for modifying web application settings and administering at the web application level.
Microsoft.SharePoint.Administration.SPFarm*	A SharePoint Farm that has methods and properties for modifying farm settings and administering at the farm level.
Microsoft.SharePoint.SPException	An exception thrown by SharePoint.
Microsoft.SharePoint.SPListItem-Collection	The collection of SPItem objects from a SharePoint list (SPList) or query (SPQuery).
Microsoft.SharePoint.Library.SPRequest	This object represents SharePoint's connection to native unmanaged code. In many cases, if you do not dispose correctly of SharePoint objects, the SPRequest object associated with them will proliferate and will be referred to in error messages.
Microsoft.SharePoint.SPFolder	A SharePoint folder in a list or document library.

Continues

TABLE 3-1:   Most Commonly Used SharePoint Object Model Objects Ordered by Number of References to the Object on the Web *(Continued)*

SharePoint Object	Description
Microsoft.SharePoint.Utilities. SPUtility	A utility class that provides useful methods such as SendEmail used to send an e-mail from a SharePoint site
Microsoft.SharePoint.SPSite-DataQuery	A query that can act against multiple lists in multiple sites in the same site collection.

* Not available in sandboxed solutions.

Figure 3-1 shows a diagram that describes how all of these commonly used objects relate to each other in the SharePoint object model.

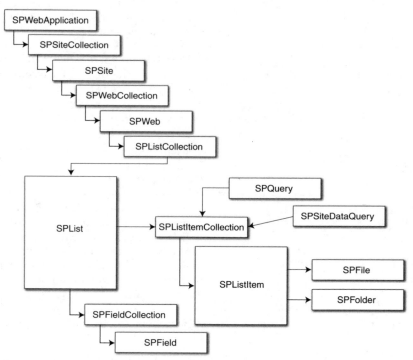

Figure 3-1: The relationships among commonly used objects in the SharePoint object model

The Disposable Pattern in SharePoint Development

In Table 3-1, you might have noticed the comment about SPRequest. The SPRequest object is something that you don't typically use directly as it represents SharePoint's connection from managed objects like SPSite to the unmanaged part of SharePoint. But it will appear in error dialogs when you don't dispose of a managed object correctly. This section will talk about the patterns you must use when using the SharePoint object model to ensure disposal of objects that implement IDisposable.

If you don't properly dispose of objects in the SharePoint object model that implement IDisposable, you will have memory usage problems in your application. Under heavy load, SharePoint may perform poorly or even exit when memory allocation fails. So it is critical to properly dispose of these IDisposable objects. The objects to be most careful of are SPSite and SPWeb, which must be disposed of because they consume large amounts of unmanaged memory.

But I Thought Garbage Collection Took Care of Memory Management?

You might wonder why you must dispose of these objects yourself and why garbage collection doesn't just take care of these things. The answer is that an object like SPSite uses a mix of managed and unmanaged code. The memory usage of the managed side of SPSite is monitored by the .NET garbage collector, and when enough memory is used by the managed code, the garbage collector will kick in. The problem is that the .NET garbage collector doesn't watch the unmanaged code's use of memory and the unmanaged memory use is much greater than the managed memory use. So you can quickly run out of memory on the unmanaged side without .NET ever feeling like it needs to do a garbage collection.

There are several coding patterns you should use in your code when working with SPWeb and SPSite and other objects that implement IDisposable. The first pattern to know about is the Dispose method. The basic idea behind using the Dispose method is you call it on an IDisposable object when you are done with it. At the point you call Dispose on the object the managed and unmanaged memory associated with the object is reclaimed. The object is also no longer usable after you call Dispose on it—any subsequent calls to the object will result in an error. A simple example using Dispose is shown in Listing 3-1.

Listing 3-1: Using Dispose with an SPSite object

```
SPSite mySite = new SPSite("http://mysite");

// do something with mySite

mySite.Dispose();  // disposes of memory used by mySite

// don't use mySite anymore after Dispose or an error will occur
```

C# actually provides a more elegant way of doing this than the Dispose method. C# has a keyword in the language called *using*. This keyword allows you to ensure that the object that you are using is disposed when the object goes out of scope. It also makes your code more clear and makes it impossible for you to accidentally call into the object after it has been disposed because it also goes out of scope when you are done with it, as shown in Listing 3-2.

Listing 3-2: The using clause with SPSite

```
using (SPSite mySite = new SPSite("http://mysite"))
{
  // do something with mySite

} // mySite gets disposed here and goes out of scope

// can no longer use mySite in code here because it is out of scope
```

You can also combine the using statements as shown in Listing 3-3 to have multiple items within a using clause and dispose of them together when the clause ends.

Listing 3-3: Combined using clauses

```
using (SPSite mySite = new SPSite("http://mysite"))
using (SPWeb myWeb = mySite.OpenWeb())
{
  // do something with mySite and myWeb

} // mySite and myWeb gets disposed here and go out of scope
```

A third pattern you may use in your code is try, catch, finally when working with code that you anticipate will raise exceptions you need to handle. For code like this, it is essential to make sure that you dispose of IDisposable objects in the finally block of your code. The finally block of a try, catch, finally construct is always called whether an exception is thrown or not.

Listing 3-4 shows an example of using the try, catch, finally pattern with an SPSite object.

Listing 3-4: Using Dispose in the finally block of try, catch, finally code

```
SPSite mySite = null;

try
{
  SPSite mySite = new SPSite("http://mysite");
  // do something with mySite that potentially raises an exception
}
catch (Exception e)
{
  // handle exception here
}
finally
{
  if (mySite != null)
    mySite.Dispose();
}
```

There are cases in your code where you may be creating objects that are IDisposable that may not be as obvious. For example, you may have a foreach loop that iterates over a collection that returns SPSite or SPWeb objects. For these cases you use a try, finally block in the iterator to ensure that each IDisposable object created in the foreach loop is disposed of properly, as shown in Listing 3-5.

Listing 3-5: Using Dispose with an object in a foreach loop

```
using (mySite = new SPSite("http://mysite"))
{
  SPSite = iteratedSite = null;
  foreach (iteratedSite in mySite.WebApplication.Sites)
  {
    try
    {
      // use iteratedSite
    }
    finally
    {
      if (iteratedSite != null)
        iteratedSite.Dispose();
    }
  }
}
```

A foreach clause is just one example of a construct that you might not realize is creating IDisposable objects. There are several other ways you can create IDisposable objects in your code that you may not dispose of properly. Fortunately, Microsoft provides a tool to help you detect and track down objects you aren't disposing of properly called the SharePoint Dispose Checker tool. That tool is found here: http://code.msdn.microsoft.com/SPDisposeCheck.

This section introduced this issue and provided you with some patterns you can use to properly dispose of IDisposable objects in the SharePoint object model. For a more detailed discussion of this issue, be sure to read the MSDN article "Best Practices: Using Disposable Windows SharePoint Services Objects" found here: http://msdn.microsoft.com/en-us/library/aa973248.aspx. Also valuable is the MSDN article "Best Practices: Common Coding Issues When Using the SharePoint Object Model" found here: http://msdn.microsoft.com/en-us/library/bb687949.aspx.

Sandboxed Solutions

Although sandboxed solutions use the Server object model, only a subset of the Server object model is available to sandboxed solutions. For example, Table 3-1 showed some objects that aren't available in sandboxed solutions as indicated by an asterisk. Visual Studio helps you out in this regard—when you are editing code in a sandboxed solution, Visual Studio IntelliSense only shows the objects, properties, and methods that are available in a sandboxed solution. An example of this is shown in Figures 3-2 and 3-3. Figure 3-2 shows an event receiver in a farm solution and Figure 3-3 shows an event receiver in a sandboxed solution. In both figures, IntelliSense for the SPFolder object is shown. Note that in Figure 3-3, the sandboxed solution, fewer properties and methods are shown because many properties and methods of SPFolder are not available in sandboxed solutions.

```
public override void ItemAdding(SPItemEventProperties properties)
{
  base.ItemAdding(properties);
  properties.ListItem.Folder.|
}
```
```
AddProperty
Audit
ContainingDocumentLibrary
ContentTypeOrder
CopyTo
Delete
DeleteProperty
DocumentLibrary
EffectiveAuditMask
```

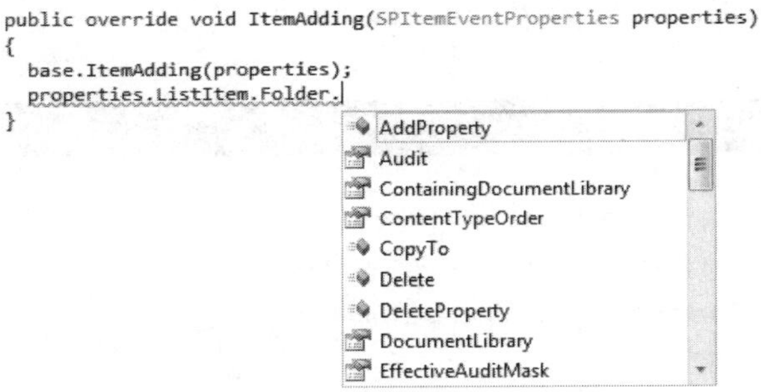

Figure 3-2: IntelliSense for SPFolder in a farm solution

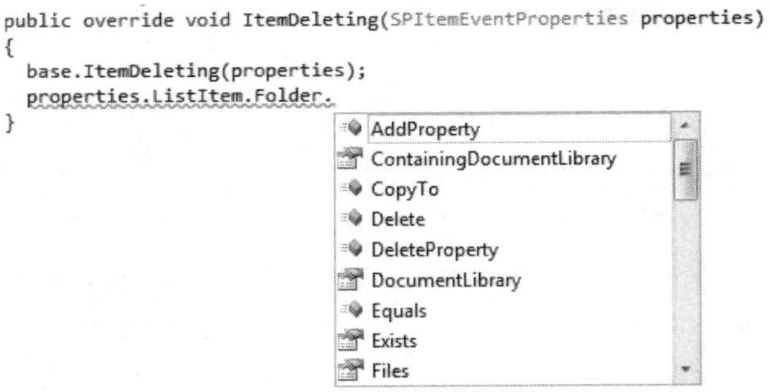

```
public override void ItemDeleting(SPItemEventProperties properties)
{
  base.ItemDeleting(properties);
  properties.ListItem.Folder.
}
```
```
AddProperty
ContainingDocumentLibrary
CopyTo
Delete
DeleteProperty
DocumentLibrary
Equals
Exists
Files
```

Figure 3-3: IntelliSense for SPFolder in a sandboxed solution

Although the IntelliSense helps you figure out what is and isn't available in sandboxed solutions, unfortunately the compiler does not. For example, consider this code for an ItemAdding event handler in a farm solution in Listing 3-6. This same code—namely the line starting with "int iCount" can be pasted into a sandboxed solution. Even though we see from Figure 3-3 that the ContentTypeOrder property is not available to a sandboxed solution, the code will still compile. The error is not detected until runtime—when the sandboxed event handler runs a runtime error is raised as shown in Figure 3-4.

Listing 3-6: ItemAdding handler in a Farm Solution

```
public override void ItemAdding(SPItemEventProperties properties)
{
  base.ItemAdding(properties);
  int iCount = properties.ListItem.Folder.ContentTypeOrder.Count;
}
```

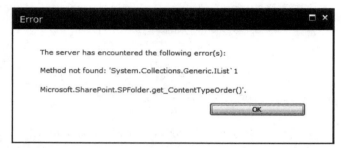

Figure 3-4: Runtime error thrown when code not valid in a sandboxed solution is used

Throughout the rest of the chapter, we'll continue to mark methods and properties that aren't available in sandboxed solutions with an asterisk in tables where they appear. We will also provide code samples for both farm and sandboxed solutions.

A Little Set Up

In the remaining pages of this chapter, we're going to write a bunch of code, and we want you to be able to follow along. So let's set up some simple Visual Studio SharePoint projects with a couple of SharePoint project items in which we will write code samples throughout this chapter. First, we want to create an empty SharePoint project with full trust (a farm solution) by following these steps:

1. Open Visual Studio 2010 with administrator privileges.
2. Click File > New > Project….
3. Expand the Visual C# > SharePoint > 2010 node and select the Empty SharePoint Project template.
4. Name the project "FarmProject" and click OK to start the SharePoint Customization Wizard.
5. Select Deploy as a farm solution, and click Finish to create the project.

Next, we want to create an empty SharePoint project that is a sandboxed solution by following these steps:

1. Right click on the Solution node in Solution Explorer and choose Add > New Project….
2. Expand the Visual C# > SharePoint > 2010 node and select the Empty SharePoint Project template.
3. Name the project "SandboxedProject" and click OK to start the SharePoint Customization Wizard.
4. Select "Deploy as a sandboxed solution" and click Finish to create the project.

In the FarmProject, we are going to add a Visual Web Part and a List Item Event handler. To add the Visual Web Part, follow these steps:

1. Right click on the FarmProject node in Solution Explorer and choose Add > New Item….
2. Select Visual Web Part and name the item VisualWebPart1.
3. Click the Add button to add the Visual Web Part to the project.
4. Double click on the VisualWebPart1 project item. This will open the designer for the web part in Source view.
5. Click the Design tab at the bottom of the web part designer to show the Visual design view.

6. Drag and drop a Label control from the Toolbox to the design view. If the Toolbox is not visible, show it by choosing View > Toolbox. This will add a Label called Label1.

7. With Label1 selected, click the events icon (a yellow lightning bolt icon) at the top of the Properties window to show the events for the label. If the Properties window is not visible, show it by choosing View > Properties window.

8. Double click on the Load event to add a Label1_Load event handler. We will write our Visual Web Part sample code in this event handler.

9. At the top of the code where the Label1_Load event handler is shown, add the using statements "using Microsoft.SharePoint"; and "using System.Text"; The VisualWebPart1UserControl.ascx.cs file should now look like Listing 3-7.

For brevity, we will only show the Label1_Load handler in this chapter without the additional code shown in Listing 3-7. So when you see a Label1_Load handler in this chapter, refer back to this listing to see the complete VisualWebPart1 definition.

Listing 3-7: VisualWebPart1UserControl.ascx.cs with Label1_Load event handler and using Microsoft.SharePoint.

```
using Microsoft.SharePoint;
using System;
using System.Web.UI;
using System.Web.UI.WebControls;
using System.Web.UI.WebControls.WebParts;
using System.Text;

namespace FarmProject.VisualWebPart1
{
  public partial class VisualWebPart1UserControl : UserControl
  {
    protected void Page_Load(object sender, EventArgs e)
    {
    }

    protected void Label1_Load(object sender, EventArgs e)
    {
    }
  }
}
```

Next, in the FarmProject, we are going to add a List Item Event Receiver:

1. Right click on the FarmProject node in Solution Explorer and choose Add > New Item….
2. Select Event Receiver and name the item EventReceiver1.
3. Click the Add button to add the Event Receiver to the project.
4. The SharePoint Customization Wizard dialog appears. Set the "What type of event receiver do you want?" dropdown to List Item Events. Set the "What item should be the event source?" dropdown to Announcements. Finally, check the check box "An item is being added" to handle the ItemAdding event for the Announcements list as shown in Figure 3-5.

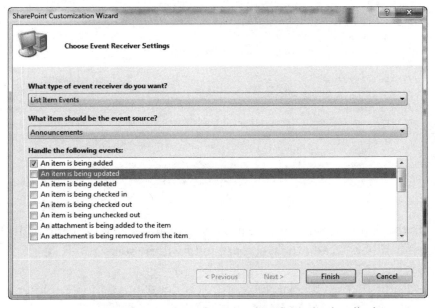

Figure 3-5: The SharePoint Customization Wizard configured to handle the ItemAdding event

5. Click the Finish button to add the Event Receiver to the project.
6. Double Click on EventReceiver1 to show the code for the ItemAdding event receiver. Add the using statement "using System.Text"; to the top of the code file. The file should look like Listing 3-8.

For brevity, we will only show the ItemAdding event handler in this chapter without the additional code shown in Listing 3-8. So when you see a ItemAdding event handler in this chapter, refer back to Listing 3-8 to see the complete event receiver definition.

Listing 3-8: Event Receiver handling the ItemAdding event

```
using System;
using System.Security.Permissions;
using Microsoft.SharePoint;
using Microsoft.SharePoint.Security;
using Microsoft.SharePoint.Utilities;
using Microsoft.SharePoint.Workflow;
using System.Text;

namespace FarmProject.EventReceiver1
{
  /// <summary>
  /// List Item Events
  /// </summary>
  public class EventReceiver1 : SPItemEventReceiver
  {
    /// <summary>
    /// An item is being added.
    /// </summary>
    public override void ItemAdding(SPItemEventProperties properties)
    {
      base.ItemAdding(properties);
    }
  }
}
```

In the SandboxedProject we are going to add a web part and a List Item event handler. To add the web part, follow these steps:

1. Right click on the SandboxedProject node in Solution Explorer and choose Add > New Item….

2. Select Web Part and name the item WebPart1.

3. Click the Add button to add the web part to the project.

4. Double click on WebPart1 to show the code. Add the using statement "using System.Text"; to the top of the code file. To the CreateChildControls method we add a line of code to create a label control and set its text as shown in Listing 3-9.

For brevity, we will only show the CreateChildControls method in this chapter without the additional code shown in Listing 3-9. So when you see a CreateChildControls event handler in this chapter, refer back to Listing 3-9 to see the complete event receiver definition.

Listing 3-9: Web part code with CreateChildControls creating a label

```
using System;
using System.ComponentModel;
using System.Web;
using System.Web.UI;
using System.Web.UI.WebControls;
using System.Web.UI.WebControls.WebParts;
using Microsoft.SharePoint;
using Microsoft.SharePoint.WebControls;
using System.Text;

namespace SandboxedProject.WebPart1
{
  [ToolboxItemAttribute(false)]
  public class WebPart1 : WebPart
  {
    protected override void CreateChildControls()
    {
      Label label1 = new Label();
      Controls.Add(label1);
      label1.Text = "Hello World!";
    }
  }
}
```

Now let's add a List Item event receiver to the SandboxedProject.

1. Right click on the SandboxedProject node in Solution Explorer and choose Add > New Item….

2. Select Event Receiver and name the item EventReceiver1.

3. Click the Add button to add the Event Receiver to the project.

4. The SharePoint Customization Wizard dialog appears. Set the "What type of event receiver do you want?" drop-down to List Item Events. Set the "What item should be the event source?" drop-down to Announcements. Finally, check the check box "An item is being deleted" to handle the ItemDeleted event for the Announcements list.

5. Click the Finish button to add the Event Receiver to the project.

6. Double Click on EventReceiver1 to show the code for the ItemAdding event receiver. Add the using statement "using System.Text"; to the top of the code file. The file should look like Listing 3-10.

For brevity, we will only show the ItemDeleting event handler in this chapter without the additional code shown in Listing 3-10. So when you see an ItemDeleting event handler in this chapter, refer back to Listing 3-10 to see the complete event receiver definition.

Listing 3-10: Event receiver handling the ItemDeleting event

```
using System;
using System.Security.Permissions;
using Microsoft.SharePoint;
using Microsoft.SharePoint.Security;
using Microsoft.SharePoint.Utilities;
using Microsoft.SharePoint.Workflow;
using System.Text;

namespace SandboxedProject.EventReceiver1
{
    /// <summary>
    /// List Item Events
    /// </summary>
    public class EventReceiver1 : SPItemEventReceiver
    {
        /// <summary>
        /// An item is being deleted
        /// </summary>
        public override void ItemDeleting(SPItemEventProperties
            properties)
        {
            base.ItemDeleting(properties);
        }
    }
}
```

To recap, we will see code samples for these four basic methods throughout this chapter:

1. **Label1_Load** (FarmProject Visual Web Part)
2. **ItemAdding** (FarmProject Announcements List Item Event Handler)
3. **CreateChildControls** (SandboxedProject Web Part)
4. **ItemDeleting** (SandboxedProject Announcements List Item Event Handler)

We also need to build our projects and set up SharePoint so we can see these four methods execute properly. Choose Deploy Solution from the Build menu to build and deploy the FarmProject and SandboxedProject to the SharePoint site.

Next, let's create a site page that hosts our two web parts. Go to the home page of your SharePoint site. Then follow these steps to create a site page that hosts the two web parts we have created:

1. From the SiteActions menu in the top left corner of the web page, choose New Page.
2. In the New Page dialog, name the new page Test Page and then click the Create button.
3. SharePoint will open the new page in editing mode. Click on the Insert tab in the ribbon in the Editing Tools ribbon tab group.
4. Click the Web Part button in the Insert ribbon. This will bring up the view shown in Figure 3-6. Click Custom in the Categories list to show the custom web parts we have created: VisualWebPart1 from the FarmProject and WebPart1 from the SandboxedProject.

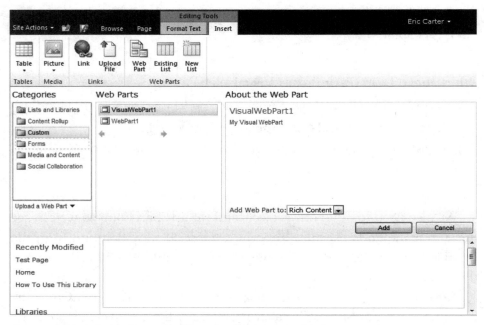

Figure 3-6: Creating a site page to host VisualWebPart1 and WebPart1

5. In the Web Parts list, click VisualWebPart1 then click the Add button.

6. Click the Web Part button in the Insert ribbon. This will bring up the view shown in Figure 3-6 again. Click Custom in the Categories list to show the custom web parts. Then click WebPart1 and click the Add button.

7. In the Web Parts list, click VisualWebPart1 then click the Add button.

8. The web page should now look like Figure 3-7. Click the Save button in the quick access toolbar area of the ribbon at the top left corner of the page.

If you return to the home page of the SharePoint site, you should be able to access the Test Page you created by clicking on the Site Pages link under the Libraries heading in the left sidebar. This brings up the Site Pages library as shown in Figure 3-8. Click on the Test Page item in the list to view the test page and the two web parts.

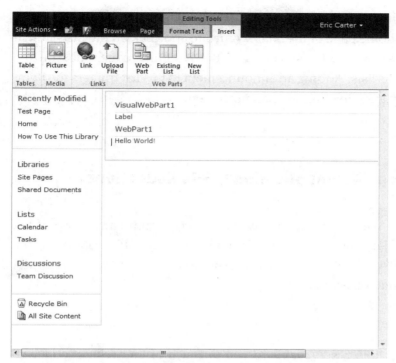

Figure 3-7: The completed test page with VisualWebPart1 and WebPart1

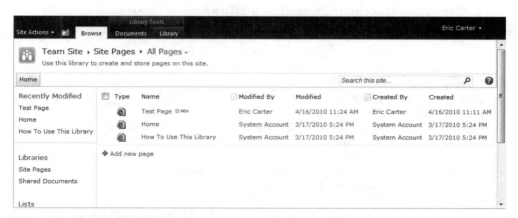

Figure 3-8: The Site Pages library

To get to the Announcements lists from which our two event handlers run, go to the home page of the SharePoint site and click on the Lists link in the left sidebar. In the Lists section of the resulting page, click on the Announcements lists. Adding an announcement to this list triggers the Item-Adding event and deleting an announcement from this list triggers the ItemDeleting event.

From the Top: Web Applications, Site Collections, and Sites

In this section, we will consider the five objects that are at the top of the SharePoint object model tree: SPContext, SPFarm, SPWebApplication, SPSite, and SPWeb. From these objects you can navigate to most of the rest of the SharePoint object model.

SPContext

The SPContext object is available to you in much of the web page or web part code you write and provides the context of the HTTP request, as well as giving you access to critical objects in the SharePoint object model. Table 3-2 shows the most commonly used properties and methods of SPContext.

TABLE 3-2: Commonly Used Properties and Methods of SPContext

Property or Method	Description
Web	Returns the SPWeb object that represents the site associated with the context
Site	Returns the SPSite object that represents the site collection associated with the context
Current	A static property that returns the SPContext object for the current HTTP request

TABLE 3-2:   Commonly Used Properties and Methods of SPContext *(Continued)*

Property or Method	Description
List*	Returns the SPList object associated with the context
File*	Returns the SPFile object that is associated with the SPListItem object returned by the Item property
Fields*	Returns the SPFieldCollection that contains the SPField objects associated with the SPListItem or SPContentType of the context
ListItem*	Returns the SPListItem object associated with the context object
ListId*	Returns the GUID of the list associated with the context object
ItemId*	Returns the integer ID of the item that is associated with the context object

* Not available in sandboxed solutions.

Listing 3-11 shows a CreateChildControls implementation in a sandboxed solution web part that uses the properties and methods in Table 3-2 that are available for sandboxed solutions. Note that the static property Current is used to get the current SPContext. The current site collection and web site are then retrieved and the URL of each is displayed. In the case of this web part being displayed on the root site of a site collection, the URLs for the site collection will be the same as the URL for the root site. Also, we remind you of the unfortunate naming of object model objects. In your mind, you have to remap "SPWeb" and "web" to "SharePoint site" and "SPSite" and "site" to "SharePoint site collection" when you read this code. Also, note that we are aggressively declaring temporary variables here for the purpose of showing the types of objects returned by the properties and methods being shown—in production code you wouldn't need to declare as many temporary variables as we do in the listings in this chapter.

Listing 3-11: Using SPContext in the CreateChildControls method for a web part in a sandboxed solution

```
protected override void CreateChildControls()
{
  StringBuilder output = new StringBuilder();

  SPContext context = SPContext.Current;

  SPSite site = context.Site;
  output.AppendFormat("Site collection URL: {0}<P>", site.Url);
  SPWeb web = context.Web;
  output.AppendFormat("Site URL: {0}<P>", web.Url);

  Label label1 = new Label();
  Controls.Add(label1);
  label1.Text = output.ToString();
}
```

Why Don't We Need to Dispose of the SPSite and SPWeb Objects in This Sample?

We just talked about disposing SPSite and SPWeb and here we aren't doing it. According to SharePoint best practices, SPSite and SPWeb objects returned by SPContext.Site, SPContext.Current.Site, SPContext.Web, and SPContext.Current.Web should not be explicitly disposed by user code.

Listing 3-12 shows a visual web part handler in a farm solution that uses the remaining properties in Table 3-2 that are available in farm solutions. The output of the code is shown in Listing 3-13. Note the multiple ways to get a list item ID and list ID.

Listing 3-12: Using SPContext in the Label1_Load visual web part handler in a farm solution

```
protected void Label1_Load(object sender, EventArgs e)
{
  StringBuilder output = new StringBuilder();

  SPContext context = SPContext.Current;
  SPSite site = context.Site;
  output.AppendFormat("Site collection URL: {0}<P>", site.Url);
```

```
SPWeb web = context.Web;
output.AppendFormat("Site URL: {0}<P>", web.Url);

SPList list = context.List;
output.AppendFormat("List title: {0}<P>", list.Title);
output.AppendFormat("List ID: {0}<P>", list.ID);

SPItem item = context.Item;
output.AppendFormat("Item ID: {0}<P>", item.ID);

SPFile file = context.File;
output.AppendFormat("File: {0}<P>", file.Name);

SPFieldCollection fields = context.Fields;
output.AppendFormat("Field count: {0}<P>", fields.Count);

SPListItem listItem = context.ListItem;
output.AppendFormat("List Item ID: {0}<P>", listItem.ID);

Guid listId = context.ListId;
output.AppendFormat("List ID: {0}<P>", listId);

int itemID = context.ItemId;
output.AppendFormat("Item ID: {0}<P>", itemID);

Label1.Text = output.ToString();
}
```

Listing 3-13: Output of Listing 3-12

```
Site collection URL: http://ecarter1
Site URL: http://ecarter1
List title: Site Pages
List ID: cbf2b026-2ab1-4185-bc2b-daee3cb800f3
Item ID: 4
File: Test Page.aspx
Field count: 8
List Item ID: 4
List ID: cbf2b026-2ab1-4185-bc2b-daee3cb800f3
Item ID: 4
```

The last example we will consider for SPContext is kind of an "anti-example." SPContext is a concept used in web pages and web controls that is not available to event receivers. So our code in Listing 3-14 shows how an event receiver can access all the same values shown in Listing 3-12 but without using an SPContext. Because our standard ItemAdding event handler doesn't yet have a SharePoint item created to look at, we have written an event handler for ItemUpdating for this example. Note that we check if the file returned is null because in a list, the list item doesn't necessarily have a file associated with it.

Listing 3-14: "SPContext-Less" ItemUpdating event handler in a farm solution

```
public override void ItemUpdating(SPItemEventProperties properties)
{
  StringBuilder output = new StringBuilder();

  using (SPSite site = properties.OpenSite())
  using (SPWeb web = properties.OpenWeb())
  {
    output.AppendFormat("Site collection URL: {0}<P>", site.Url);
    output.AppendFormat("Site URL: {0}<P>", web.Url);

    SPList list = properties.List;
    output.AppendFormat("List title: {0}<P>", list.Title);
    output.AppendFormat("List ID: {0}<P>", list.ID);

    SPItem item = properties.ListItem;
    output.AppendFormat("Item ID: {0}<P>", item.ID);

    SPFile file = properties.ListItem.File;
    if (file != null)
      output.AppendFormat("File: {0}<P>", file.Name);

    SPFieldCollection fields = properties.ListItem.Fields;
    output.AppendFormat("Field count: {0}<P>", fields.Count);

    SPListItem listItem = properties.ListItem;
    output.AppendFormat("List Item ID: {0}<P>", listItem.ID);

    Guid listId = properties.ListId;
    output.AppendFormat("List ID: {0}<P>", listId);

    int itemID = properties.ListItemId;
    output.AppendFormat("Item ID: {0}<P>", itemID);
  }

  properties.AfterProperties["Body"] = output.ToString();
  base.ItemUpdating(properties);
}
```

SPFarm

The SPFarm object represents a SharePoint farm and has a number of methods and properties that let you modify settings at the farm level. Some of the most commonly used properties and methods are shown in Table 3-3. The SPFarm object is not available to sandboxed code.

TABLE 3-3: Commonly Used Properties and Methods of SPFarm

Property or Method	Description
Services*	Returns the SPServiceCollection object that contains all the services that are available in the farm
Local*	Static property that returns the SPFarm object for the local server
Update()*	Tells the server farm to save its state and update the rest of the farm
Products*	Returns a collection of GUIDs for the products that are installed in the farm
Solutions*	Returns an SPSolutionCollection object that contains all the solutions that are available in the farm
Servers*	Returns an SPServerCollection object that contains all the physical computers that are in the farm
Create(…)*	Static Create method with several overloads that can programmatically create a new farm and return an SPFarm object for the newly created farm
Open(..)*	Static Open method with several overloads that can programmatically open a farm and return an SPFarm object for the newly created farm
Join()*	Adds the local computer to the farm

* Not available in sandboxed solutions.

Listing 3-15 shows the usage of the Local property to get an SPFarm instance representing the current farm. It then iterates through the services that are available in the farm and prints them. You can see in Listing 3-16 the services that are running in the farm. It also iterates over the solutions that are installed in the farm using the Solutions property to get an SPSolutionCollection. In Listing 3-16, you can see that on the server where we ran this code, five solutions were installed. Finally, Listing 3-15 uses the Servers property to iterate over all the servers in the farm. In this case, Listing 3-16 only shows one server being output because this code was run on a developer machine with only one machine in the farm.

Listing 3-15: Using SPFarm in the Label1_Load visual web part handler in a farm solution

```
protected void Label1_Load(object sender, EventArgs e)
{
  output = new StringBuilder();

  SPFarm farm = SPFarm.Local;
  output.AppendFormat ("Farm services:<P>");

  foreach (SPService svc in farm.Services)
  {
    output.AppendFormat ("{0} - {1} <P>", svc.Name, svc.Status);
  }

  output.AppendFormat ("Farm solutions:<P>");
  SPSolutionCollection solutions = farm.Solutions;
  foreach (SPSolution solution in solutions)
  {
    output.AppendFormat ("{0}<P>", solution.Name);
  }

  output.AppendFormat ("Farm servers:<P>");
  SPServerCollection servers = farm.Servers;
  foreach (SPServer server in servers)
  {
    output.AppendFormat ("Server name: {0}<P>", server.Name);
  }

  Label1.Text = output.ToString();
}
```

Listing 3-16: Output of Listing 3-15

```
Farm services:
WSS_Administration - Online
SPAdminV4 - Online
SPUserCodeV4 - Online
SPTraceV4 - Online
```

```
SPTimerV4 - Online
SecurityTokenService - Online
SPSearch4 - Online
c2wts - Online
spworkflowtimerv4 - Online

Farm solutions:
contenttypeproject1.wsp
eventreceiverproject1.wsp
farmproject.wsp
sharepointproject1.wsp
sharepointproject2.wsp

Farm servers:
Server name: MYSPMACHINE
```

SPWebApplication

The SPWebApplication object gives you access to settings and state for the IIS web application associated with the SharePoint site collection you are working with. Table 3-4 shows some of the commonly used properties and methods of the SPWebApplication object. None of the properties or methods of SPWebApplication are available to sandboxed solutions.

TABLE 3-4: Commonly Used Properties and Methods of SPWebApplication

Property or Method	Description
Sites*	Returns an SPSiteCollection containing SPSite objects representing each site collection associated with the web application
Update(...)*	Saves any changes you have made to the web application using the SPWebApplication object and makes them take effect in the server farm
Features*	Returns an SPFeatureCollection containing SPFeature objects representing all the features that are active in the web application
Delete()*	Deletes the web application
Lookup(...)*	Static method that takes a Uri as a parameter and returns an SPWebApplication for the given Uri

Continues

TABLE 3-4: Commonly Used Properties and Methods of SPWebApplication *(Continued)*

Property or Method	Description
Provision()*	Provisions the web application
Policies*	Returns the SPPolicyCollection containing SPolicy objects defined for the web application
DisplayName*	Returns the name of the web application
WebService*	Returns the SPWebService object associated with the web application
WebConfig-Modifications*	Returns a collection of SPWebConfigModification objects that represents modifications made to the web.config file associated with the web application
Content-Databases*	Returns the SPContentDatabaseCollection containing SPContentDatabase objects representing the content databases associated with the web application

* Not available in sandboxed solutions.

Listing 3-17 shows some of the most commonly used properties and methods of SPWebApplication. Note that to use SPWebApplication in our code we must add a using statement: "using Microsoft.SharePoint.Administration"; first. We get a web application by using the static Lookup method with the Uri of our web server. Next, we print the name of the web application using the DisplayName property. The Sites property is used to iterate over the site collections hosted by the web application. We likewise iterate over the features and policies that are active in the web application. Finally, we get the web service associated with the web application and print its ID. We also display the count of web config modifications, and the number of content databases associated with the web application. The output of running List 3-17 on a typical development server is shown in Listing 3-18.

Listing 3-17: Using SPWebApplication in the Label1_Load visual web part handler in a farm solution

```
protected void Label1_Load(object sender, EventArgs e)
{
  StringBuilder output = new StringBuilder();

  SPWebApplication webApplication = SPWebApplication.Lookup (new Uri
    ("http://localhost"));
  output.AppendFormat ("Web application name: {0}<P>",
    webApplication.DisplayName);

  SPSiteCollection sites = webApplication.Sites;
  output.AppendFormat ("Site Collection count: {0}<P>", sites.Count);

  SPFeatureCollection features = webApplication.Features;
  output.AppendFormat ("Feature count: {0}<P>", features.Count);

  SPPolicyCollection policies = webApplication.Policies;
  output.AppendFormat ("Policy count: {0}<P>", policies.Count);

  SPWebService webService = webApplication.WebService;
  output.AppendFormat ("Web service name: {0}<P>", webService.Id);

  Collection<SPWebConfigModification> modifications =
    webApplication.WebConfigModifications;
  output.AppendFormat ("Web config modification count: {0}<P>",
    modifications.Count);

  SPContentDatabaseCollection contentDatabases =
    webApplication.ContentDatabases;
  output.AppendFormat ("Content database count: {0}<P>",
    contentDatabases.Count);

  Label1.Text = output.ToString();
}
```

Listing 3-18: Output of Listing 3-17

```
Web application name: SharePoint - 80
Site Collection count: 1
Feature count: 1
Policy count: 1
Web service name: 9d4c062b-d1f7-43c3-b2b0-450c2fe69415
Web config modification count: 0
Content database count: 1
```

SPSite

The SPSite object seems misnamed due to changes over the years in Share-Point terminology. This object represents a site collection in SharePoint. Some of the most commonly used properties and methods of the SPSite object are shown in Table 3-5. Several commonly used properties and methods are not available in sandboxed solutions.

TABLE 3-5: Commonly Used Properties and Methods of SPSite

Property or Method	Description
Url	Returns the URL to the root web site associated with the site collection
ID	Returns a GUID that uniquely identifies the site collection
OpenWeb(...)	A method with several overloads that returns the SPWeb object (a site) specified by the indentifier (GUID or URL) passed as a parameter to the method
Features	Returns an SPFeatureCollection object containing a collection of SPFeature objects representing the features that are installed and activated in the site collection
Solutions*	Returns an SPUserSolutionCollection object containing a collection of SPUserSolution objects representing the user solutions (sandboxed solutions) that have been installed and activated in the site collection
Usage*	Returns a UsageInfo object that gives information about the site, such as storage, number of visits, and site usage
Delete(...)*	A method with several overloads that deletes the site collection
Close()	Closes the SPSite object and releases all resources associated with the object; this is the equivalent of calling Dispose on the object
Exists(uri as Uri)	Static method that returns True if a site collection exists at the given Uri
RootWeb	Returns an SPWeb object representing the root web site in the site collection

TABLE 3-5: Commonly Used Properties and Methods of SPSite *(Continued)*

Property or Method	Description
AllWebs	Returns an SPWebCollection object containing a collection of SPWeb objects representing all the web sites in the site collection
Cache	Returns an SPSiteCollectionPropertyCache that is a thread safe cache in which small amounts of data associated with the site collection can be stored
Owner	Gets and sets the SPUser representing the owner of the site collection
WebApplication*	Returns the SPWebApplication object associated with the site collection
AllowUnsafeUpdates	Gets and sets a bool value representing whether updates can be made to the content database as a result of a GET request or without requiring a security validation
Port	Returns the port number used by the site collection
ReadOnly	ReadOnly gets or sets whether the site collection is read-only—you might make the site collection read-only during a long operation that requires that the site collection not change while you are updating it
Zone	Returns an SPUrlZone object representing which zone the site collection is in (intranet, Internet, etc.)
ServerRelativeUrl	Returns the server-relative URL of the root SPWeb in the site collection
ContentDatabase*	Returns the SPContentDatabase object used by the site collection
EventReceivers	Returns an SPEventReceiverDefinitionCollection object, which is a collection of SPEventReceiverDefinition objects representing each registered event receiver registered at the site collection level
HostName	Returns the name of the server on which the site collection is hosted

* Not available in sandboxed solutions.

Listing 3-19 shows some of the most commonly used properties and methods of SPSite in a code listing. First, the exists method is used to make sure there is a site collection at http://localhost. Next, a new SPSite object is created for http://localhost. SPSite is one of those objects we must be careful to dispose of, so we put it into a try, finally block and call Close in the finally block.

Next we print the URL and Id of the site collection. Then we use the OpenWeb method with no parameter—this gets the lowest-level site (SPWeb object) for the URL we used when creating the SPSite object (http://localhost). We then print the title of that site and call the Close method on the SPWeb object to ensure it is disposed.

Next, we use the Features and Solutions properties and print the number of features and solutions that are active in the site collection. The Usage property is used to print the number of visits to the web site. We then use the RootWeb property to display the URL of the root web associated with the site collection.

The AllWebs property is used to display the count of all the web sites in the site collection. The site collection owner and name of the web application hosting the site collection is displayed. We also display whether unsafe updates are allowed for the site collection. Then the port associated with the site collection is displayed, whether the site is read-only, and the URL zone for the site collection.

The server relative URL is displayed along with the name of the content database used for the site collection. The number of event receivers and the name of the host server for the site collection is displayed. The output of Listing 3-19 is shown in Listing 3-20.

Listing 3-19: Using SPSite in the Label1_Load visual web part handler in a farm solution

```
protected void Label1_Load(object sender, EventArgs e)
{
  StringBuilder output = new StringBuilder();

  output.AppendFormat("Site exists: {0}<P>",
    SPSite.Exists(new Uri("http://localhost")));

  SPSite site = null;
  try
  {
```

```csharp
site = new SPSite("http://localhost");
output.AppendFormat("Site URL: {0}<P>", site.Url);
output.AppendFormat("Site ID: {0}<P>", site.ID);

SPWeb web = null;
try
{
  web = site.OpenWeb();
  output.AppendFormat("Opened web: {0}<P>", web.Title);
}
finally
{
  if (web != null)
    web.Close();
}

SPFeatureCollection features = site.Features;
output.AppendFormat("Feature count: {0}<P>", features.Count);

SPUserSolutionCollection solutions = site.Solutions;
output.AppendFormat("Solution count: {0}<P>", solutions.Count);

SPSite.UsageInfo usage = site.Usage;
output.AppendFormat("Total # of hits: {0}<P>", usage.Visits);

using (SPWeb rootWeb = site.RootWeb)
{
  output.AppendFormat("Root web URL: {0}<P>", rootWeb.Url);
}

SPWebCollection allWebs = site.AllWebs;
output.AppendFormat("All webs count: {0}<P>", allWebs.Count);

SPUser user = site.Owner;
output.AppendFormat("User: {0}<P>", user.Name);

SPWebApplication webApplication = site.WebApplication;
output.AppendFormat("Web application: {0}<P>",
  webApplication.Name);

bool allowUnsafeUpdates = site.AllowUnsafeUpdates;
output.AppendFormat("Allow unsafe updated: {0}<P>",
  allowUnsafeUpdates);

int port = site.Port;
output.AppendFormat("Port: {0}<P>", port);

bool readOnly = site.ReadOnly;
output.AppendFormat("Read Only: {0}<P>", readOnly);
```

```
    SPUrlZone zone = site.Zone;
    output.AppendFormat("URL Zone: {0}<P>", zone);

    string serverRelativeUrl = site.ServerRelativeUrl;
    output.AppendFormat("Server relative URL: {0}<P>",
      serverRelativeUrl);

    SPContentDatabase contentDatabase = site.ContentDatabase;
    output.AppendFormat("Content database: {0}<P>",
      contentDatabase.Name);

    SPEventReceiverDefinitionCollection eventReceivers =
      site.EventReceivers;
    output.AppendFormat("Event receiver count: {0}<P>",
      eventReceivers.Count);

    string hostName = site.HostName;
    output.AppendFormat("Host name: {0}<P>", hostName);
  }
  finally
  {
    if (site != null)
      site.Close();
  }
}
```

Listing 3-20: Output of Listing 3-19

```
Site exists: True
Site URL: http://ecarter1
Site ID: c3f408ca-e02d-4d39-bf96-cfaf7c2aa13c
Opened web: Team Site
Feature count: 7
Solution count: 0
Total # of hits: 0
Root web URL: http://ecarter1
All webs count: 15
User: Eric Carter
Web application: SharePoint - 80
Allow unsafe updated: False
Port: 80
Read Only: False
URL Zone: Default
Server relative URL: /
Content database: WSS_Content
Event receiver count: 2
Host name: ecarter1
```

SPWeb

The SPWeb object represents a site in the site collection (and can easily be confused with SPSite, which represents a site collection and not a site). Commonly used properties and methods of SPWeb are shown in Table 3-6.

TABLE 3-6: Commonly Used Properties and Methods of SPWeb

Property or Method	Description
ID	Returns a GUID that uniquely identifies the site
Url	Returns the top-level URL for the site
Lists	Returns an SPListCollection object that contains SPList objects representing all the lists in the site
Name	Gets and sets the name of the site
Update()	Method that updates the database with any changes you have made to the SPWeb object
Title	Gets and sets the title for the site
Site	Returns the SPSite object representing the parent site collection for this site
Files	Returns an SPFileCollection object that contains SPFile objects located in the root directory of the site
Created	Returns the DateTime for when the site was created
Features	Returns an SPFeatureCollection object that contains SPFeature objects representing all the features activated for the site
Description	Gets and sets the description used for the site
Configuration	Returns the ID of the site definition used for the site
Properties*	Returns an SPPropertyBag object containing key value pairs for settings associated with the site
Delete()	Method that deletes the site

Continues

TABLE 3-6: Commonly Used Properties and Methods of SPWeb *(Continued)*

Property or Method	Description
Navigation	Returns an SPNavigation object that allows access to the quick launch area and the top navigation bar of the site
Language	Returns the LCID identifying the locale used for the site
Close()	Closes the SPWeb object and releases all resources associated with the object; this is the equivalent of calling Dispose on the object
Webs	Returns an SPWebCollection object that contains SPWeb objects representing all the immediate child sites of this site
Workflows	Returns an SPWorkflowCollection object that contains SPWorkflow objects representing all workflow instances that have run or are running in the site
Folders	Returns an SPFolderCollection object that contains SPFolder objects representing all the subfolders in the site's root folder
Exists	Returns True if the site represented by the SPSite object exists
Author	Returns the SPUser object for the user who created the site
Theme	Returns the name of the theme that is used in the site
Alerts	Returns an SPAlertCollection object that contains SPAlert objects representing alerts that have been created for the site
AllowUnsafe-Updates	Gets and sets a bool value representing whether updates can be made to the content database as a result of a GET request or without requiring a security validation
Audit*	Returns an SPAudit object representing the audit log for the site
ParentWeb	Returns an SPWeb object representing the parent site for the current site
RootFolder	Returns an SPFolder object representing the root folder for the site

TABLE 3-6: Commonly Used Properties and Methods of SPWeb *(Continued)*

Property or Method	Description
Provisioned	Returns True if the site has been provisioned
Locale	Returns a CultureInfo object that can be used to specify the settings used for time, currency, and numeric fields on the site
Modules	Returns an SPModuleCollection object that contains SPModule objects representing the modules used on the site
CurrentUser	Returns an SPUser object representing the current user of the site
ServerRelativeUrl	Gets and sets the server-relative URL of the site
WebTemplate	Returns the name of the site definition or site template used to create the site
MasterUrl	Gets and sets the URL for the master page used by the site
EnsureUser(string)	Method that takes as a string the login name of a user and ensures that the user is added as a user for the site; returns an SPUser object representing the user
GetSiteData(SP-SiteDataQuery)	Method that queries across all lists in the site using the settings specified in the parameter of type SPSiteDataQuery; returns a DataTable as a result. SPSiteDataQuery is discussed in more detail later in this chapter.
ListTemplates	Returns an SPListTemplateCollection object that contains SPListTemplate objects for each list definition and list template available on the site
RegionalSettings	Returns an SPRegionalSettings object that allows you to configure the regional settings (e.g., time zone) for a site

* Not available in sandboxed solutions.

Listing 3-21 shows some code in a sandboxed solution that uses some of the most frequently used properties and methods of SPWeb. The lines of code that access the two properties that don't work with a sandboxed solution

(Properties and Audit) are commented out. Listing 3-22 shows the output of Listing 3-21.

Listing 3-21: Using SPWeb in the CreateChildControls Web Part method in a sandboxed solution

```
protected override void CreateChildControls()
{
  StringBuilder output = new StringBuilder();

  using (SPWeb web = SPContext.Current.Web)
  {
    Guid webId = web.ID;
    output.AppendFormat("Web ID: {0}<P>", webId);

    string url = web.Url;
    output.AppendFormat("Web URL: {0}<P>", url);

    SPListCollection lists = web.Lists;
    output.AppendFormat("List count: {0}<P>", lists.Count);

    string name = web.Name;
    output.AppendFormat("Web name: {0}<P>", name);

    string title = web.Title;
    output.AppendFormat("Web title: {0}<P>", title);

    using (SPSite parentSite = web.Site)
    {
      output.AppendFormat("Site URL: {0}<P>", parentSite.Url);
    }

    SPFileCollection files = web.Files;
    output.AppendFormat("File count: {0}<P>", files.Count);

    DateTime created = web.Created;
    output.AppendFormat("Date Created: {0}<P>", created);

    SPFeatureCollection features = web.Features;
    output.AppendFormat("Feature count: {0}<P>", features.Count);

    string description = web.Description;
    output.AppendFormat("Description: {0}<P>", description);

    short configuration = web.Configuration;
    output.AppendFormat("Configuration: {0}<P>", configuration);
```

```
//Microsoft.SharePoint.Utilities.SPPropertyBag propertyBag =
//  web.Properties;
//output.AppendFormat("Property count: {0}<P>", propertyBag.Count);

Microsoft.SharePoint.Navigation.SPNavigation navigation =
  web.Navigation;
output.AppendFormat("Navigation (Home title): {0}<P>",
  navigation.Home.Title);

uint language = web.Language;
output.AppendFormat("Language: {0}<P>", language);

SPWebCollection webs = web.Webs;
output.AppendFormat("Web count: {0}<P>", webs.Count);

Microsoft.SharePoint.Workflow.SPWorkflowCollection workflows =
  web.Workflows;
output.AppendFormat("Workflow count: {0}<P>", workflows.Count);

SPFolderCollection folders = web.Folders;
output.AppendFormat("Folder count: {0}<P>", folders.Count);

bool exists = web.Exists;
output.AppendFormat("Site exists: {0}<P>", exists);

SPUser author = web.Author;
output.AppendFormat("Author: {0}<P>", author.Name);

string theme = web.Theme;
output.AppendFormat("Theme: {0}<P>", theme);

SPAlertCollection alerts = web.Alerts;
output.AppendFormat("Alert count: {0}<P>", alerts.Count);

bool allowUnsafeUpdates = web.AllowUnsafeUpdates;
output.AppendFormat("Allow unsafe updates: {0}<P>",
  allowUnsafeUpdates);

//SPAudit audit = web.Audit;
//output.AppendFormat("Audit entry count: {0}<P>",
//  audit.GetEntries().Count);

SPWeb parentWeb = null;
try
{
   parentWeb = web.ParentWeb;
  if (parentWeb != null)
```

```
    {
      output.AppendFormat("Parent web URL: {0}<P>", parentWeb.Url);
    }
    else
    {
      output.AppendFormat("Parent web is not set.");
    }
  }
  finally
  {
    if (parentWeb != null)
      parentWeb.Close();
  }

  SPFolder rootFolder = web.RootFolder;
  output.AppendFormat("Root folder: {0}<P>", rootFolder.Name);

  bool provisioned = web.Provisioned;
  output.AppendFormat("Provisioned: {0}<P>", provisioned);

  System.Globalization.CultureInfo culture = web.Locale;
  output.AppendFormat("Locale: {0}<P>", culture.Name);

  SPModuleCollection modules = web.Modules;
  output.AppendFormat("Modules: {0}<P>", modules.Count);

  SPUser currentUser = web.CurrentUser;
  output.AppendFormat("Current user: {0}<P>", currentUser.Name);

  string serverRelativeUrl = web.ServerRelativeUrl;
  output.AppendFormat("Server relative URL: {0}<P>",
    serverRelativeUrl);

  string webTemplate = web.WebTemplate;
  output.AppendFormat("Web template: {0}<P>", webTemplate);

  string masterUrl = web.MasterUrl;
  output.AppendFormat("Master URL: {0}<P>", masterUrl);

  System.Data.DataTable siteData = web.GetSiteData(new
    SPSiteDataQuery());
  output.AppendFormat("Site data row count: {0}<P>",
    siteData.Rows.Count);

  SPListTemplateCollection listTemplates = web.ListTemplates;
  output.AppendFormat("List template count: {0}<P>",
    listTemplates.Count);
```

```
    SPRegionalSettings regionalSettings = web.RegionalSettings;
    SPTimeZone timeZone = regionalSettings.TimeZone;

    output.AppendFormat("Time zone: {0}<P>", timeZone.Description);
  }

  Label label1 = new Label();
  Controls.Add(label1);
  label1.Text = output.ToString();
}
```

Listing 3-22: Output of Listing 3-21

```
Web ID: 8c9a5dc5-fbfb-41de-9251-422c9b91d1a1
Web URL: http://ecarter1
List count: 15
Web name:
Web title: Team Site
Site URL: http://ecarter1
File count: 1
Date Created: 3/18/2010 12:23:57 AM
Feature count: 23
Description:
Configuration: 0
Navigation (Home title): Home
Language: 1033
Web count: 0
Workflow count: 0
Folder count: 11
Site exists: True
Author: Eric Carter
Theme:
Alert count: 0
Allow unsafe updates: False
Parent web is not set.Root folder:
Provisioned: True
Locale: en-US
Modules: 1
Current user: Eric Carter
Server relative URL: /
Web template: STS
Master URL: /_catalogs/masterpage/v4.master
Site data row count: 10
List template count: 21
Time zone: (UTC-08:00) Pacific Time (US and Canada)
```

Working with Lists

In this section we will cover the major objects that are used when working with lists: SPList, SPListItem, SPListItemCollection, SPFolder, SPFile, and SPField.

SPList

The SPList object represents a list on a SharePoint site. Some of the most commonly used properties and methods are shown in Table 3-7. All the properties and methods in Table 3-7 except for the Audit property and the GetDataTable method are available to sandboxed solutions.

TABLE 3-7:　Commonly Used Properties and Methods of SPList

Property or Method	Description
Update(…)	Method that updates the content database with any changes you have made to the list using SPList methods and properties
Version	Returns an integer value representing the version number for the list
Items	Returns an SPListItemCollection that contains SPListItem objects representing each item in the list
Title	Gets and sets the title for the list
ID	Returns the GUID that uniquely identifies the list
Created	Returns a DateTime object representing the date and time the list was created
Lists	Returns the SPListCollection object representing the parent list collection that the list is in—for example, the other lists in the site
Fields	Returns the SPFieldCollection object that contains SPField objects for each field used by the list
Description	Gets and sets the description for the list

TABLE 3-7: Commonly Used Properties and Methods of SPList *(Continued)*

Property or Method	Description
RoleAssignments	Returns the SPRoleAssignmentCollection object that contains SPRoleAssignment objects that assign a user or group a role assignment with regards to the list
Forms	Returns an SPFormCollection object that contains SPForm objects representing the create, edit, and display forms for the list
Delete()	Method that deletes the list
Views	Returns an SPViewCollection object that contains SPView objects for each view associated with the list.
Folders	Returns an SPListItemCollection object that contains SPListItem objects for each folder in the list
Author	Returns an SPUser object representing the user who created the list
Hidden	Gets and sets whether the list is hidden from the SharePoint UI
GetItems(...)	Overloaded method that returns an SPItemCollection containing list items specified by a SPQuery or SPView object
AddItem(...)	Overloaded method that adds a new list item to the list
Audit*	Returns an SPAudit object representing the audit log for the list
GetItemById(int)	Method that returns the SPListItem with the integer ID specified by the parameter passed to the method
ParentWeb	Returns the parent SPWeb object associated with the list
RootFolder	Returns the SPFolder object that contains all the files associated with the list
Recycle()	Method that puts the list in SharePoint's "Recycle bin" and returns the GUID associated with the list

Continues

TABLE 3-7: Commonly Used Properties and Methods of SPList *(Continued)*

Property or Method	Description
DefaultItemOpen	Gets and sets a member of the DefaultItemOpen enumeration that sets whether the list item should be opened in the browser (DefaultItemOpen.Browser) or a rich client application (DefaultItemOpen.PreferClient)
ContentTypes	Returns an SPContentTypeCollection object that contains SPContentType objects representing the content types being used by the list
DefaultView	Returns an SPView object representing the default view for the list
DataSource	For lists that have an external data source (see Chapter 6, "Working with Business Data") this property returns an SPListDataSource object representing the external data source for the list
BreakRole-Inheritance(…)	Overloaded method that controls whether the list uses role assignments set by the parent web site or whether it maintains its own unique role assignments
ItemCount	Returns the total number of items and folders in the list
BaseType	Returns an SPBaseType enumeration representing the base type of the list, e.g., SPBaseType.GenericList, SPBaseType.DocumentLibrary, etc.
EventReceivers	Returns an SPEventReceiverDefinitionCollection object, which is a collection of SPEventReceiverDefinition objects representing each registered event receiver registered for the list
BaseTemplate	Returns an SPListTemplateType enumeration that represents the type of list template used for the list, e.g., SPListTemplateType.Survey, SPListTemplateType.Links, etc.
OnQuickLaunch	Gets and sets whether the list is shown in the Quick Launch area of the home page for the site
Ordered	Gets and sets whether users can reorder the items in the list

TABLE 3-7: Commonly Used Properties and Methods of SPList *(Continued)*

Property or Method	Description
GetDataTable(...)*	Method that takes an SPQuery object and other parameters and returns a System.Data.DataTable object representing the result of the query
WorkflowAssociation	Returns an SPWorkflowAssociationCollection that contains SPWorkflowAssociation objects representing all the workflow templates that are associated with the list
DefaultViewUrl	Returns the URL for the default view for the list

* Not available in sandboxed solutions.

Listing 3-23 shows some code for the Label1_Load event in a farm solution that uses many of the properties and methods in Table 3-7. For this code to work, be sure you have an announcements list with at least one item in it.

Listing 3-23 starts by getting the lists associated with the web site where the code is running. It then gets the Announcements list. It displays the title, version, number of items in the announcements list, the ID for the list, the date it was created, the count of other lists in the site, the number of fields used in the list, and the description of the list. It then displays the number of forms, views, and folders associated with the list. Finally it displays the author of the list, whether the list is hidden, and the count of items in the list. It also calls the Audit property to get the number of audit entries; in a sandboxed solution this code will fail.

Next, Listing 3-23 gets the first item in the list and displays its title. It displays the URL of the parent web site. It also displays the root folder name (Announcements in this case). It displays the default way items are opened; in this case they are opened in the browser. Next, the number of content types associated with the list is displayed and the name of the default view. If the list has an external data source, the data source is displayed.

Finally, the count of items in the list is displayed again, this time using the ItemCount property. The base type (Generic List) is displayed, whether the list is in the quick launch sidebar or not, whether the list is ordered, and the number of workflow associations for the list, and the default view URL for the list. Listing 3-24 shows the output for Listing 3-23.

Listing 3-23: Using SPList in the Label1_Load visual web part handler in a farm solution

```csharp
protected void Label1_Load(object sender, EventArgs e)
{
  StringBuilder output = new StringBuilder();
  SPListCollection lists;

  using (SPWeb web = SPContext.Current.Web)
  {
    lists = web.Lists;
  }

  // Get Announcement list
  SPList list = lists["Announcements"];

  string title = list.Title;
  output.AppendFormat("Title: {0}<P>", title);

  int version = list.Version;
  output.AppendFormat("Version: {0}<P>", version);

  SPListItemCollection items = list.Items;
  output.AppendFormat("Item count: {0}<P>", items.Count);

  Guid id = list.ID;
  output.AppendFormat("ID: {0}<P>", id);

  DateTime created = list.Created;
  output.AppendFormat("Created: {0}<P>", created);

  SPListCollection parentLists = list.Lists;
  output.AppendFormat("Parent list count: {0}<P>", parentLists.Count);

  SPFieldCollection fields = list.Fields;
  output.AppendFormat("Field count: {0}<P>", fields.Count);

  string description = list.Description;
  output.AppendFormat("Description: {0}<P>", list.Description);

  SPRoleAssignmentCollection roleAssignments = list.RoleAssignments;
  output.AppendFormat("Role assignment count: {0}<P>",
    roleAssignments.Count);
```

```
SPFormCollection forms = list.Forms;
output.AppendFormat("Form count: {0}<P>", forms.Count);

SPViewCollection views = list.Views;
output.AppendFormat("View count: {0}<P>", views.Count);

SPListItemCollection folders = list.Folders;
output.AppendFormat("Folder count: {0}<P>", folders.Count);

SPUser author = list.Author;
output.AppendFormat("Author: {0}<P>", author.Name);

bool hidden = list.Hidden;
output.AppendFormat("Hidden: {0}<P>", hidden);

SPListItemCollection listItems = list.GetItems();
output.AppendFormat("Item count: {0}<P>", listItems.Count);

SPAudit audit = list.Audit;
output.AppendFormat("Audit entry count: {0}<P>",
  audit.GetEntries().Count);

SPListItem firstItem = list.GetItemById(1);
output.AppendFormat("First item title: {0}<P>", firstItem.Title);

using (SPWeb parentWeb = list.ParentWeb)
{
  output.AppendFormat("Parent web URL: {0}<P>", parentWeb.Url);
}

SPFolder rootFolder = list.RootFolder;
output.AppendFormat("Root folder name: {0}<P>", rootFolder.Name);

DefaultItemOpen defaultItemOpen = list.DefaultItemOpen;
output.AppendFormat("Default item open: {0}<P>", defaultItemOpen);

SPContentTypeCollection contentTypes = list.ContentTypes;
output.AppendFormat("Content type count: {0}<P>",
  contentTypes.Count);

SPView defaultView = list.DefaultView;
output.AppendFormat("Default view title: {0}<P>", defaultView.Title);

bool hasExternalDataSource = list.HasExternalDataSource;
if (hasExternalDataSource)
{
  SPListDataSource dataSource = list.DataSource;
  output.AppendFormat("Data source: {0}<P>", dataSource.ToString());
```

```
    }
    else
    {
      output.AppendFormat("List doesn't have an external data source.");
    }

    int itemCount = list.ItemCount;
    output.AppendFormat("Item count: {0}<P>", itemCount);

    SPBaseType baseType = list.BaseType;
    output.AppendFormat("Base type: {0}<P>", baseType);

    bool onQuickLaunch = list.OnQuickLaunch;
    output.AppendFormat("On Quick Launch: {0}<P>", onQuickLaunch);

    bool ordered = list.Ordered;
    output.AppendFormat("Ordered: {0}<P>", ordered);

    Microsoft.SharePoint.Workflow.SPWorkflowAssociationCollection
      workflowAssociations = list.WorkflowAssociations;
    output.AppendFormat("Workflow association count: {0}<P>",
      workflowAssociations.Count);

    string defaultViewUrl = list.DefaultViewUrl;
    output.AppendFormat("Default view URL: {0}<P>", defaultViewUrl);

    Label1.Text = output.ToString();
}
```

Listing 3-24: Output of Listing 3-23

```
Title: Announcements
Version: 0
Item count: 6
ID: 135fca58-6841-4295-954f-42c38bbe1471
Created: 3/10/2010 12:54:35 AM
Parent list count: 17
Field count: 57
Description: Use this list to track upcoming events, status updates or other
team news.
Role assignment count: 3
Form count: 3
View count: 2
Folder count: 0
Author: System Account
Hidden: False
Item count: 6
Audit entry count: 0
```

```
First item title: Get Started with Microsoft SharePoint Foundation!
Parent web URL: http://ecarter1
Root folder name: Announcements
Default item open: Browser
Content type count: 2
Default view title: All items
List doesn't have an external data source.
Item count: 6
Base type: GenericList
On Quick Launch: False
Ordered: False
Workflow association count: 0
Default view URL: /Lists/Announcements/AllItems.aspx
```

SPListItem

The SPListItem object represents an item in a SharePoint list. The most commonly used properties and methods of the SPListItem object are shown in Table 3-8. Only the Audit property is not available for sandboxed solutions.

TABLE 3-8: Commonly Used Properties and Methods of SPListItem

Property or Method	Description
Web	Returns an SPWeb object representing the site the list item is associated with
Item	Overloaded property that can get and set field values associated with the list item by passing in the GUID for the field, the index of the field in the field collection, or the field's display name
Name	Gets and sets the name of the list item—for a document library this is the file name including the file extension
Url	Returns the site-relative URL for the list item
Xml	Returns the data in the list item as a string in the XMLDATA format
ID	Returns an integer that identifies the item

Continues

TABLE 3-8: Commonly Used Properties and Methods of SPListItem *(Continued)*

Property or Method	Description
Update()	Method that saves the changes made to the list item by using the SPListItem object's methods and properties
File	For a list item in a document library, this property returns an SPFile object for the document, otherwise it returns null
Properties	Returns a Hashtable object with metadata associated with the item in key value pairs
Title	Returns the title of the list item
Fields	Returns an SPFieldCollection object that contains SPField objects for each column associated with the list item.
Folder	If the list item is a folder, this property returns the SPFolder object for the list item, otherwise it returns null
Delete()	Method that deletes the list item
Level	Returns a member of the SPFileLevel enumeration to indicate whether the list item is published, is a draft, or is checked out
Copy(...)	Static method that takes a source URL and destination URL and can copy a list item from the source to destination location
Tasks	Returns an SPWorkflowTaskCollection object that contains SPWorkflowTask objects representing workflow tasks associated with the list item
Workflows	Returns an SPWorkflowCollection object that contains SPWorkflow objects for any workflow instances that are currently running against the list item
Versions	Returns an SPListItemVersionCollection object that contains SPListItemVersion objects representing previous versions of the list item
Attachments	Returns an SPAttachmentsCollection object that contains SPAttachment objects representing any attachments that are associated with the list item

TABLE 3-8: Commonly Used Properties and Methods of SPListItem *(Continued)*

Property or Method	Description
ContentType	Returns an SPContentType object that represents the content type associated with the list item
Audit*	Returns an SPAudit object representing the audit log for the list item
DisplayName	Returns the display name for the list item
Recycle()	Method that puts the list item in SharePoint's recycle bin and returns the GUID associated with the list item
UniqueId	Returns a GUID that uniquely identifies the list item
ListItems	Returns the parent SPListItemCollection to which this list item belongs
SystemUpdate()	An alternate to the Update method that updates the list item without changing the modified or modified by values for the list item
ParentList	Returns the SPList object that is the parent of the list item
BreakRole-Inheritance(...)	Overloaded method that controls whether the list item uses the role assignments set by the parent list or whether it maintains its own unique role assignments
CopyTo(string)	Copies the list item to the URL specified in the string parameter

* Not available in sandboxed solutions.

Listing 3-25 shows the use of many of the commonly used properties and methods of SPListItem. This code works with your Shared Documents library and requires that there be at least one document in that library.

Listing 3-24 first gets the current SharePoint site and gets the SPList object for the Shared Documents library. Next, it gets an SPListItem for the first item in the Shared Documents library. It displays the SharePoint site associated with that item. It then displays the name, URL, XML, ID, and file name for the item. The properties associated with the item are then retrieved and the count displayed. The title of the item and number of fields associated with the item are displayed. If the first item in the list is a folder, the name of the folder is displayed. The level at which the file is located is displayed; in this case the level is Published. The number of workflow tasks associated with the item and the number of workflows associated with the item are displayed.

Next, the number of versions stored for this item is displayed. If the item has attachments, the count of attachments is also displayed. The name of the content type for the item is displayed as well as the unique ID for the item, the number of other list items in the list, and the name of the list that the item is in. The output for Listing 3-25 is shown in Listing 3-26. In this case, the first item in our list is a Word document.

Listing 3-25: Using SPListItem in the Label1_Load visual web part handler in a farm solution

```
protected void Label1_Load(object sender, EventArgs e)
{
  StringBuilder output = new StringBuilder();
  SPList list = null;
  using (SPWeb web = SPContext.Current.Web)
  {
    list = web.Lists["Shared Documents"];
  }

  SPListItem item = list.Items[0];

  using (SPWeb associatedWeb = item.Web)
  {
    output.AppendFormat("Web URL: {0}<P>", associatedWeb.Url);
  }

  string name = item.Name;
  output.AppendFormat("Name: {0}<P>", name);

  string url = item.Url;
  output.AppendFormat("URL: {0}<P>", url);

  string xml = item.Xml;
  output.AppendFormat("XML: {0}<P>", xml);

  int id = item.ID;
  output.AppendFormat("ID: {0}<P>", id);
```

```csharp
SPFile file = item.File;
output.AppendFormat("File name: {0}<P>", file.Name);

System.Collections.Hashtable properties = item.Properties;
output.AppendFormat("Property count: {0}<P>", properties.Count);

string title = item.Title;
output.AppendFormat("Title: {0}<P>", title);

SPFieldCollection fields = item.Fields;
output.AppendFormat("Field count: {0}<P>", fields.Count);

SPFolder folder = item.Folder;
if (folder != null)
{
  output.AppendFormat("Folder name: {0}<P>", folder.Name);
}
else
{
  output.AppendFormat("Folder is null.");
}

SPFileLevel fileLevel = item.Level;
output.AppendFormat("File level: {0}<P>", fileLevel);

Microsoft.SharePoint.Workflow.SPWorkflowTaskCollection workflowTasks
  = item.Tasks;
output.AppendFormat("Workflow task count: {0}<P>",
  workflowTasks.Count);

Microsoft.SharePoint.Workflow.SPWorkflowCollection workflows =
  item.Workflows;
output.AppendFormat("Workflow count: {0}<P>", workflows.Count);

SPListItemVersionCollection versions = item.Versions;
output.AppendFormat("Version count: {0}<P>", versions.Count);

try
{
  SPAttachmentCollection attachments = item.Attachments;
  output.AppendFormat("Attachment count: {0}<P>", attachments.Count);
}
catch (System.ArgumentException)
{
  output.AppendFormat("Attachment column does not exist.");
}

SPContentType contentType = item.ContentType;
output.AppendFormat("Content type name: {0}<P>", contentType.Name);
```

```
    SPAudit audit = item.Audit;
    output.AppendFormat("Audit entry count: {0}<P>",
      audit.GetEntries().Count);

    string displayName = item.DisplayName;
    output.AppendFormat("Display name: {0}<P>", displayName);

    Guid uniqueId = item.UniqueId;
    output.AppendFormat("Unique ID: {0}<P>", uniqueId);

    SPListItemCollection listItems = item.ListItems;
    output.AppendFormat("Parent list item collection count: {0}<P>",
     listItems.Count);

    SPList parentList = item.ParentList;
    output.AppendFormat("Parent list title: {0}<P>", parentList.Title);

    Label1.Text = output.ToString();
}
```

Listing 3-26: Output of Listing 3-25

```
Web URL: http://ecarter1
Name: My Document.docx
URL: Shared Documents/My Document.docx
XML:
ID: 1
File name: My Document.docx
Property count: 15
Title:
Field count: 73
Folder is null.
File level: Published
Workflow task count: 0
Workflow count: 0
Version count: 1
Attachment column does not exist.
Content type name: Document
Audit entry count: 0
Display name: My Document
Unique ID: 539dc70c-fcf1-486f-b00d-988939440a86
Parent list item collection count: 1
Parent list title: Shared Documents
```

SPListItemCollection

The SPListItemCollection object represents a collection of SPListItem objects and can be obtained in a variety of ways including from the Items method of SPList and via a query using SPQuery or SPSiteDataQuery. The most commonly used properties of SPListItemCollection are shown in Table 3-9. Of these properties and methods, only the method EnsureList-ItemsData is not available to sandboxed solutions.

TABLE 3-9: Commonly Used Properties and Methods of SPListItemCollection

Property or Method	Description
List	Returns the parent SPList object associated with the collection
Item(...)	Overloaded parameterized property that takes either the GUID associated with the list item or the index in the collection to return a single SPListItem object
Add(...)	Overloaded method that can create a new SPListItem; note that the newly created SPListItem object must have its Update method called for the item to be successfully added
Xml	Returns all the data in the collection as a string in the XMLDATA format
Fields	Returns an SPFieldCollection object that contains an SPField object representing all the fields that are available in the collection
Count	Returns the number of list items in the collection excluding folders
Delete(int)	Method that deletes the list item in the collection at the index specified by the int parameter
GetItemById(int)	Method that returns the list item in the collection with the integer ID specified by the int parameter
GetDataTable()	Method that returns the list items as a System.Data .DataTable object
ListItemCollection-Position	Returns an SPListItemCollectionPosition that can return collections of list items for a given page of a list

Continues

TABLE 3-9: Commonly Used Properties and Methods of SPListItemCollection *(Continued)*

Property or Method	Description
EnsureListItemsData()*	Method that ensures that the items in the collection are current
DeleteItemById(int)	Method that deletes the list item in the collection with the integer ID specified by the int parameter
ReorderItems(…)	Method that can reorder list items in a list

* Not available in sandboxed solutions.

Listing 3-27 shows some code in Label1_Load that uses common properties and methods of SPListItemCollection. The code gets the SPWeb object from the current context and then gets the Announcements list. Then the code does something that is questionable—it sets the AllowUnsafeUpdates property of SPWeb to True. We will return to this shortly to explain why this code is required to make this listing work and then why this is generally a bad idea.

Next we add an SPListItemCollection object to our code for the Announcements list. After displaying the list name and item count, it then uses the Add method to add a new list item. It sets the title for the new list item, then calls Update on the new SPListItem object. Here is where the code will fail if AllowUnsafeUpdates is not set to True. SharePoint does not allow you to add new items when code is running as a result of an HTTP GET—in this case, the code is running to render the web part as part of an HTTP GET. This is to prevent cross-site scripting attacks and to prevent a web page from modifying lists as a result of a page view triggered by a URL. A safe way to add a new list item to a list is to do so when you are processing an HTTP POST—for example when you are processing a button push in your web part or page. For the purpose of this discussion, and to get our code in Load to add a new item, we have set AllowUnsafeUpdates to True, but this is not a practice you should follow.

After adding the new list item, we display the count. We then use the Delete method to delete the item we just added. Finally, we display the number of fields used in the list and we get a DataTable object and display the number of rows in the table. The output for Listing 3-27 is shown in Listing 3-28.

Listing 3-27: Using SPListItemCollection in the Label1_Load visual web part handler in a farm solution—uses the bad practice of setting AllowUnsafeUpdates to True

```
protected void Label1_Load(object sender, EventArgs e)
{
  StringBuilder output = new StringBuilder();
  SPList list = null;
  using (SPWeb web = SPContext.Current.Web)
  {
    list = web.Lists["Announcements"];
    web.AllowUnsafeUpdates = true; // don't do this in real code!

    SPListItemCollection items = list.Items;

    output.AppendFormat("list name: {0} = list name: {1}<P>",
      list.Title, items.List.Title);

    output.AppendFormat("list count: {0}<P>", items.Count);
    SPListItem newItem = items.Add();
    newItem["Title"] = "Test item" +
      System.DateTime.Now.ToShortTimeString();
    newItem.Update();
    output.AppendFormat("list count: {0}<P>", items.Count);
    output.AppendFormat("new item: {0}<P>",
      items[items.Count - 1].Title);
    items.Delete(items.Count-1);

    output.AppendFormat("fields in list: {0}<P>", items.Fields.Count);

    System.Data.DataTable table = items.GetDataTable();
    output.AppendFormat("data rows count: {0}<P>", table.Rows.Count);
  }

  Label1.Text = output.ToString();
}
```

Listing 3-28: Output of Listing 3-27

```
list name: Announcements = list name: Announcements
list count: 11
list count: 12
new item: Test item6:06 PM
fields in list: 56
data rows count: 11
```

SPFolder

The SPFolder object represents a folder in a SharePoint list. Commonly used properties and methods of SPFolder are shown in Table 3-10. To get an SPFolder object, you typically start with an SPListItem object and use the Folder property that will return an SPFolder if the list item is a folder, otherwise it returns null. Of the properties in Table 3-10, only the Audit property is not available to sandboxed solutions.

TABLE 3-10: Commonly Used Properties and Methods of the SPFolder

Property or Method	Description
Name	Returns the name of the folder
Url	Returns the site-relative URL of the folder
Files	Returns an SPFileCollection object that contains SPFile objects representing all the files found in the folder
Item	Returns the SPListItem object that corresponds to the folder
Update()	Method that saves the changes made to the folder by using the SPFolder object's methods and properties
Properties	Returns a Hashtable object with metadata associated with the folder in key value pairs
SubFolders	Returns an SPFolderCollection object that contains SPFolder objects for all the subfolders contained within the folder
Exists	Returns a bool value that indicates whether the folder exists
Delete()	Method that deletes the folder
Recycle()	Method that puts the folder in SharePoint's recycle bin and returns the GUID associated with the folder
Audit*	Returns an SPAudit object representing the audit log for the folder

TABLE 3-10: Commonly Used Properties and Methods of the SPFolder *(Continued)*

Property or Method	Description
CopyTo(string)	Copies the folder and its contents to the URL specified by the string parameter
ServerRelativeUrl	Returns the server-relative URL for the folder
ParentFolder	Returns the SPFolder object representing the parent folder of this folder
MoveTo(string)	Moves the folder and its contents to the URL specified by the string parameter
ParentWeb	Returns an SPWeb object representing the parent site for the folder
ParentListID	Returns the GUID that uniquely identifies the parent list for the folder
ItemCount	Returns the count of children of this folder including subfolders

* Not available in sandboxed solutions.

Listing 3-29 shows an ItemDeleting event receiver for the Announcements list that prevents the deletion of an item if it is a folder. To make this sample work, you may need to go to the list settings for the Announcement list, click on the Advanced Settings link, and set the "Make 'New Folder' command available" setting to Yes. Once you have created a folder in the list, try to delete it. The code in Listing 3-29 will detect that the deleting item is a folder (since properties.ListItem.Folder returns a non-null result). It then displays the URL, number of files in the folder, and number of subfolders in the folder. Finally, it uses properties.ErrorMessage to set the error displayed to the output and sets properties.Cancel = true to prevent the deletion of the folder. The output for Listing 3-29 is shown in Listing 3-30.

Listing 3-29: Using SPFolder in the ItemDeleting event receiver handler in a sandboxed solution

```
public override void ItemDeleting(SPItemEventProperties properties)
{
  base.ItemAdding(properties);
  StringBuilder output = new StringBuilder();
  SPFolder folder = properties.ListItem.Folder;

  if (folder != null)
  {
    // trying to delete a folder
    output.AppendFormat("Prevented deletion of the folder {0}\n",
      folder.Name);
    output.AppendFormat("Folder url: {0}\n", folder.Url);
    output.AppendFormat("Folder contains {0} files\n",
      folder.Files.Count);
    output.AppendFormat("Folder contains {0} subfolders",
      folder.SubFolders.Count);

    // Prevent deletion
    properties.ErrorMessage = output.ToString();
    properties.Cancel = true;
  }
}
```

Listing 3-30: Output of Listing 3-29

```
Prevented deletion of the folder Test
Folder url: Lists/Announcements/Test
Folder contains 0 files
Folder contains 0 subfolders
```

SPFile

The SPFile object represents a file in SharePoint—for example, web part pages, or a file in a document library or folder. Table 3-11 shows some of the most commonly used properties and methods of SPFile. To get an SPFile object, you typically start with an SPListItem object and use the File property that will return an SPFile object if the list item is a file, otherwise it returns null.

TABLE 3-11: Commonly Used Properties and Methods of SPFile

Property or Method	Description
Web	Returns the SPWeb object representing the site where the file is found
Name	Returns the name of the file including the file extension
Url	Returns the site-relative URL of the file
Properties	Returns a Hashtable object with metadata associated with the file in key value pairs
Update()	Method that saves the changes made to the file after using the SPFile object's methods and properties
Versions	Returns an SPFileVersionCollections object that contains SPFileVersion objects representing prior versions of the file
Length	Returns the size of the file in bytes
Item	Returns the SPListItem object associated with the file
Convert()*	Method that can be used to convert the file from one format to another
Level	Returns a member of the SPFileLevelEnumeration to indicate whether the file is published, is a draft, or is checked out
Title	Returns the display name for the file
Exists	Returns a bool value that indicates whether the file exists
Delete()	Method that deletes the file
Author	Returns an SPUser object representing the user who created the file or uploaded it originally
Publish(string)	Method that publishes the file with the comment specified by the string parameter
OpenBinary(..)	Overloaded method that returns a byte array for the file contents

Continues

TABLE 3-11:   Commonly Used Properties and Methods of SPFile *(Continued)*

Property or Method	Description
Recycle()	Method that puts the file in SharePoint's recycle bin and returns the GUID associated with the file
GetLimitedWeb-PartManager(…)*	If the file is a web part page, this method returns the SPLimitedWebPartManager object associated with the web part page
ServerRelativeUrl	Returns the server-relative URL for the file
CheckOut(…)	Overloaded method that checks out the file if it is in a document library
CheckOutType	Returns a member of the SPCheckOutType enumeration that indicates whether the file is checked out for editing on the server (Online), checked out for editing on the client (Offline) or not checked out (None)
Approve(string)	Method that approves the file for content approval with the comment specified by the string parameter
MoveTo(…)	Overloaded method that moves the file to a destination URL specified by input parameters to the method
InDocumentLibrary	Returns True if the file is in a document library
CheckIn(…)	Overloaded method that checks a file into a document library with a comment specified by a string input parameter
EventReceivers	Returns an SPEventReceiverDefinitionCollection object that is a collection of SPEventReceiverDefinition objects representing each registered event receiver registered for the file

* Not available in sandboxed solutions.

Listing 3-31 shows an ItemDeleting event receiver for the Document Library (Shared Documents) that prevents the deletion of an item if it is a file. Listing 3-31 first detects whether the item being deleted is a file by using properties.ListItem.File to get the SPFile object associated with the list item. If this returns a non-null result, the code prints the URL and name of the file. It next iterates through the document properties associated with the file and prints them. This is an interesting part of this listing because it shows that document properties associated with a document—properties you can see if you right click on the document in Windows Explorer and choose Properties—can be seen by the SharePoint object model. This gives you another way to exchange data between a Windows Client or Office application and SharePoint—you can move data back and forth within document properties. Experiment with this code; try setting properties in Windows Explorer, such as Comments, Tags, etc., within the Details tab of the properties window for the file that appears when you right click on the file in Windows Explorer and choose Properties. You will then see your edited properties displayed by the code shown in Listing 3-31.

Listing 3-31 then displays the file length, title, and author and sets the ErrorMessage that will be displayed to the output string and cancels the deletion of the file. The output for Listing 3-31 is shown in Listing 3-32. The output doesn't quite fit in the allocated space for the ErrorMessage property, so a debugger was used to get the full string.

Listing 3-31: Using SPFile in the ItemDeleting event receiver handler in a sandboxed solution

```
public override void ItemDeleting(SPItemEventProperties properties)
{
  base.ItemAdding(properties);
  StringBuilder output = new StringBuilder();
  SPFile file = properties.ListItem.File;

  if (file != null)
  {
    // trying to delete a file
    output.AppendFormat("Prevented deletion of the file {0}\n",
      file.Name);
    output.AppendFormat("Url: {0}\n", file.Url);

    System.Collections.Hashtable fileProperties = file.Properties;
    foreach (System.Collections.DictionaryEntry e in fileProperties)
    {
      output.AppendFormat("Key {0}, value {1}\n", e.Key, e.Value);
    }

    output.AppendFormat("File length : {0}", file.Length);
    output.AppendFormat("Title: {0}", file.Title);
    output.AppendFormat("Author: {0}", file.Author);
```

```
    // Prevent deletion
    properties.ErrorMessage = output.ToString();
    properties.Cancel = true;
  }
}
```

Listing 3-32: Output of Listing 3-31

```
Prevented deletion of the file FY2011 budget.xlsx
Url: Shared Documents/FY2011 budget.xlsx
Key vti_candeleteversion, value true
Key vti_modifiedby, value DOMAIN\ecarter
Key vti_rtag, value rt:05E78C89-D009-4D12-B280-FA611E6BD9C6@00000000001
Key _Comments, value
Key vti_title, value
Key vti_parserversion, value 14.0.0.4756
Key vti_contentversionisdirty, value false
Key vti_sourcecontrolversion, value V1.0
Key Subject, value
Key vti_setuppathversion, value 4
Key vti_previewexists, value false
Key vti_level, value 1
Key ContentType, value
Key vti_etag, value "{05E78C89-D009-4D12-B280-FA611E6BD9C6},1"
Key vti_canmaybeedit, value true,Key vti_foldersubfolderitemcount, value 0
Key vti_timelastmodified, value 4/27/2010 5:32:16 PM
Key _Status, value
Key vti_timecreated, value 4/27/2010 5:32:16 PM
Key vti_folderitemcount, value 0
Key vti_contenttag, value {05E78C89-D009-4D12-B280-FA611E6BD9C6},1,2
Key ContentTypeId, value 0x010100EE2B1B0BE92B594A8B14915C58656008
Key vti_filesize, value 2424680
Key vti_sourcecontrolcookie, value fp_internal
Key vti_thumbnailexists, value false
Key vti_author, value ecarter
Key _Author, value John Danielson
Key _Category, value
Key Keywords, value
Key vti_replid, value rid:{05E78C89-D009-4D12-B280-FA611E6BD9C6}
Key vti_docstoreversion, value 1
Key vti_stickycachedpluggableparserprops, value Subject Keywords _Status
vti_title _Author _Category ContentType _Comments
Key vti_metainfoversion, value 1
Key vti_docstoretype, value 0,
File length : 2424680
Title:
Author: DOMAIN\ecarter
```

SPField

An SPField object represents a column in a list—for example, a document library has a column called Modified By and a column called Modify Date. The most commonly used properties and methods of SPField are shown in Table 3-12.

TABLE 3-12:   Commonly Used Properties and Methods of SPField

Property or Method	Description
Type	Gets and sets the SPFieldType enumeration for the column that sets the type of the column (e.g., SPFieldType.Text, SPFieldType.Note, SPFieldType.DateTime, SPFieldType.Boolean, etc.)
Id	Returns a GUID that uniquely identifies the column
Update()	Method that saves the changes made to the column after using the SPField object's methods and properties
Title	Gets and sets the display name of the column
Version	Gets the version number of the column as an int
Description	Gets and sets the description of the column
Required	Gets and sets a bool value that controls whether the column must contain a value when the associated item is created or edited
Group	Gets and sets a string value that determines which group of site columns the column belongs to, e.g., Base Columns, Core Contact, and Calendar Columns, etc.
Hidden	Gets and sets a bool value that controls whether the column is displayed or not
Delete()	Method that deletes the column
InternalName	Returns the internal name that is used for the column

Continues

TABLE 3-12:   Commonly Used Properties and Methods of SPField *(Continued)*

Property or Method	Description
FieldRendering-Control*	Returns the SPMobileBaseFieldControl class that renders the column in web pages
DisplaySize	Gets and sets the display size for the column
Scope	Returns the site-relative path to the SharePoint list where the column is used
SchemaXml	Gets and sets the schema XML that defines the column in CAML format
Sealed	Returns True if other columns can be derived from this column
StaticName	Gets and sets the internal name of the column
DefaultValue	Gets and sets the default value of the column as a string
ParentList	Returns an SPList object for the parent list that uses the column
ShowInEditForm	Gets and sets a bool value that controls whether the column is displayed in the form used to edit a list item. Similar properties exist for the display form (ShowInDisplay-Form), the new item form (ShowInNewForm), the list settings page (ShowInListSettings), the list view (ShowInViewForms), and the version history (ShowInVerrsionHistory)
TypeDisplayName	Returns the display name of the column as a string

* Not available in sandboxed solutions.

Listing 3-33 shows a helper method called AddRow, which helps to build a table that we construct in CreateChildControls. Our web part will generate a table showing all the columns associated with the Announcements list and uses properties such as Type, Id, Title, Description, Required, Group, Hidden, and DefaultValue.

The output for Listing 3-33 is the table displayed by the web part as shown in Figure 3-9.

Listing 3-33: Using SPField in a web part in a sandboxed solution

```
protected void AddRow(Table tbl, params object[] paramlist)
{
  TableRow tr = new TableRow();

  foreach (object o in paramlist)
  {
    TableCell tc = new TableCell();
    Label label = new Label();
    if (o != null)
      label.Text = o.ToString();
    tc.Controls.Add(label);
    tr.Cells.Add(tc);
  }
  tbl.Rows.Add(tr);
}

protected override void CreateChildControls()
{
  Table tbl = new Table();

  SPList list = null;
  using (SPWeb web = SPContext.Current.Web)
  {
    list = web.Lists["Announcements"];
    AddRow(tbl, "Type", "Id", "Title", "Description", "Required", "Group",
      "Hidden", "DefaultValue");

    foreach (SPField field in list.Fields)
    {
      AddRow(tbl, field.Type, field.Id, field.Title, field.Description,
        field.Required, field.Group, field.Hidden, field.DefaultValue);
    }
  }
  Controls.Add(tbl);
}
```

WebPart1

Type	Id	Title	Description	Required	Group	Hidden	DefaultValue
Counter	1d22ea11-1e32-424e-89ab-9fedbadb6ce1	ID		False	Custom Columns	False	
ContentTypeId	03e45e84-1992-4d42-9116-26f756012634	Content Type ID		False	Custom Columns	True	
Computed	c042a256-787d-4a6f-8a8a-cf6ab767f12d	Content Type		False	_Hidden	False	
Text	fa564e0f-0c70-4ab9-b863-0177e6ddd247	Title		True	Custom Columns	False	
DateTime	28cf69c5-fa48-462a-b5cd-27b6f9d2bd5f	Modified		False	Custom Columns	False	
DateTime	8c06beca-0777-48f7-91c7-6da68bc07b69	Created		False	Custom Columns	False	
User	1df5e554-ec7e-46a6-901d-d85a3881cb18	Created By		False	Custom Columns	False	
User	d31655d1-1d5b-4511-95a1-7a09e9b75bf2	Modified By		False	Custom Columns	False	
Boolean	26d0756c-986a-48a7-af35-bf18ab85ff4a	Has Copy Destinations		False	Custom Columns	True	
Text	6b4e226d-3d88-4a36-808d-a129bf52bccf	Copy Source		False	Custom Columns	True	
Integer	d4e44a66-ee3a-4d02-88c9-4ec5ff3f4cd5	owshiddenversion		False	Custom Columns	True	
Integer	f1e020bc-ba26-443f-bf2f-b68715017bbc	Workflow Version		False	Custom Columns	True	
Integer	7841bf41-43d0-4434-9f50-a673baef7631	UI Version		False	Custom Columns	True	
Text	dce8262a-3ae9-45aa-aab4-83bd75fb738a	Version		False	Custom Columns	True	
Attachments	67df98f4-9dec-48ff-a553-29bece9c5bf4	Attachments		False	Custom Columns	True	
ModStat	fdc3b2ed-5bf2-4835-a4bc-b885f3396a61	Approval Status		False	Custom Columns	True	0
Note	34ad21eb-75bd-4544-8c73-0e08330291fe	Approver Comments		False	Custom Columns	True	
Computed	503f1caa-358e-4918-9094-4a2cdc4bc034	Edit		False	Custom Columns	False	
Computed	bc91a437-52e7-49e1-8c4e-4698904b2b6d	Title		False	Custom Columns	False	
Computed	82642ec8-ef9b-478f-acf9-31f7d45fbc31	Title		False	Custom Columns	False	
Computed	5f190d91-3dbc-4489-9878-3c092caf35b6	Title		False	Custom Columns	True	
Computed	b1f7969b-ea65-42e1-8b54-b588292635f2	Select		False	Custom Columns	True	
Integer	50a54da4-1528-4e67-954a-e2d24f1e9efb	Instance ID		False	Custom Columns	True	
Number	ca4addac-796f-4b23-b093-d2a3f65c0774	Order		False	Custom Columns	True	
Guid	ae069f25-3ac2-4256-b9c3-15dbc15da0e0	GUID		False	Custom Columns	True	
Guid	de8beacf-5505-47cd-80a6-aa44e7ffe2f4	Workflow Instance ID		False	Custom Columns	True	
Lookup	94f89715-e097-4e8b-ba79-ea02aa8b7adb	URL Path		False	Custom Columns	True	
Lookup	56605df6-8fa1-47e4-a04c-5b384d59609f	Path		False	Custom Columns	True	
Lookup	173f76c8-aebd-446a-9bc9-769a2bd2c18f	Modified		False	Custom Columns	True	
Lookup	998b5cff-4a35-47a7-92f3-3914aa6aa4a2	Created		False	Custom Columns	True	
Lookup	30bb605f-5bae-48fe-b4e3-1f81d9772af9	Item Type		False	Custom Columns	True	
Lookup	423874f8-c300-4bfb-b7a1-42e2159e3b19	Sort Type		False	Custom Columns	True	
Computed	ba3c27ee-4791-4867-8821-ff99000bac98	Effective Permissions Mask		False	Custom Columns	True	
File	8553196d-ec8d-4564-9861-3dbe931050c8	Name		False	Custom Columns	False	
Lookup	4b7403de-8d94-43e8-9f0f-137a3e298126	Unique Id		False	Custom Columns	True	
Lookup	6d2c4fde-3605-428e-a236-ce5f3dc2b4d4	Client Id		False	Custom Columns	True	
Lookup	c5c4b81c-f1d9-4b43-a6a2-090df32ebb68	ProgId		False	Custom Columns	True	
Lookup	dddd2420-b270-4735-93b5-92b713d0944d	ScopeId		False	Custom Columns	True	
Text	39360f11-34cf-4356-9945-25c44e68dade	File Type		False	Custom Columns	False	
Computed	4ef1b78f-fdba-48dc-b8ab-3fa06a0c9804	HTML File Type		False	Custom Columns	True	
Computed	3c6303be-e21f-4366-80d7-d6d0a3b22c7a	Edit Menu Table Start		False	Custom Columns	True	
Computed	1344423c-c7f9-4134-88e4-ad842e2d723c	Edit Menu Table Start		False	Custom Columns	True	
Computed	2ea78cef-1bf9-4019-960a-02c41636cb47	Edit Menu Table End		False	Custom Columns	True	
Computed	9d30f126-ba48-446b-b8f9-83745f322ebe	Name		False	Custom Columns	True	
Computed	5cc6dc79-3710-4374-b433-61cb4a686c12	Name		False	Custom Columns	True	
Computed	224ba411-da77-4050-b0eb-62d422f13d3e	Name		False	Custom Columns	True	
Computed	081c6e4c-5c14-4f20-b23e-1a71ceb6a67c	Type		False	Custom Columns	False	
Computed	105f76ce-724a-4bba-aece-f81f2fce58f5	Server Relative URL		False	Custom Columns	True	
Computed	7177cfc7-f399-4d4d-905d-37dd51bc90bf	Encoded Absolute URL		False	Custom Columns	True	
Computed	7615464b-559e-4302-b8e2-8f440b913101	File Name		False	Custom Columns	True	
Lookup	687c7f94-686a-42d3-9b67-2782eac4b4f8	Property Bag		False	Custom Columns	True	
Integer	43bdd51b-3c5b-4e78-90a8-fb2087f71e70	Level		False	Custom Columns	True	
Boolean	c101c3e7-122d-4d4d-bc34-58e94a38c816	Is Current Version		False	Custom Columns	True	
Lookup	b824e17e-a1b3-426e-aecf-f0184d900485	Item Child Count		False	Custom Columns	False	
Lookup	960ff01f-2b6d-4f1b-9c3f-e19ad8927341	Folder Child Count		False	Custom Columns	False	
Note	7662cd2c-f069-4dba-9e35-082cf976e170	Body		False	Custom Columns	False	
DateTime	6a09e75b-8d17-4698-94a8-371eda1af1ac	Expires		False	Custom Columns	False	

Figure 3-9: Table output by the web part in Listing 3-33

We've now covered the major object model objects that you will use when working with lists in SharePoint. Chapter 4, "SharePoint Lists," has additional practical code examples of working with SharePoint lists.

Working with Queries

SPQuery

The SPQuery object allows you to construct queries to return specific items in a list. Commonly used properties and methods of SPQuery are shown in Table 3-13. We have already seen several methods that take an SPQuery and return an SPListItemCollection, including SPList.GetItems and SPList.GetDataTable.

TABLE 3-13: Commonly Used Properties and Methods of SPQuery

Property or Method	Description
Query	Gets and sets the query in CAML. This means you must know how to construct a query in CAML to use this object. We will show some examples later in this section.
Folder	For a query on a document library, this property can set or get the folder used to restrict the quer.y
ViewFields	Gets and sets the columns that are returned by the query using a CAML expression.
RowLimit	Gets and sets a limit for the number of items that should be returned by a query.
ViewAttributes	Gets and sets additional parameters to the query in CAM, for example whether the scope of the query should include just files in a particular folder or should recursively include files in subfolders.

The tricky thing with SPQuery is you have to come up with a Query string and the language the query is defined in is a SharePoint specific language called CAML—collaborative application markup language. It is beyond the scope of this book to completely describe CAML, but we will show you an example query and how it is used with SPQuery. Another reason we don't describe CAML in depth is that with SharePoint 2010 you can now use LINQ to create queries that we describe in Chapter 4, "Working with SharePoint Lists."

CAML is constructed as a block of XML. For example, to search our announcements lists for items with a title that contains the word "Test," you would use a block of CAML. This block orders the results by Title and finds items whose titles contain the word *Test*.

```
<OrderBy>
  <FieldRef Name='Title' />
</OrderBy>
<Where>
  <Contains>
    <FieldRef Name="Title" />
    <Value Type="Text">Test</Value>
  </Contains>
</Where>
```

Note the use of the XML element <Contains>. This is an operator that tells SharePoint to find Titles that contain the word *Test*. Other operators include <EQ> for equals, <NEQ> for not equal, <GT> for greater than, <GEQ> for greater than or equal, <LT> for lower than, <IsNull> for is null, and <BeginsWith> for begins with.

Listing 3-34 shows code in a web part that uses this CAML query string and places results in a table in a web part.

Listing 3-34: Using SPQuery in a web part in a sandboxed solution

```
protected void AddRow(Table tbl, params object[] paramlist)
{
  TableRow tr = new TableRow();

  foreach (object o in paramlist)
  {
    TableCell tc = new TableCell();
    Label label = new Label();
    if (o != null)
      label.Text = o.ToString();
    tc.Controls.Add(label);
    tr.Cells.Add(tc);
  }
  tbl.Rows.Add(tr);
}
```

```
protected override void CreateChildControls()
{
  Table tbl = new Table();

  SPList list = null;
  using (SPWeb web = SPContext.Current.Web)
  {
    list = web.Lists["Announcements"];
    AddRow(tbl, "Title");

    SPQuery query = new SPQuery();
    query.Query = "<OrderBy>" +
      "<FieldRef Name='Title' />" +
      "</OrderBy>" +
      "<Where>" +
      "<Contains>" +
      "<FieldRef Name='Title' />" +
      "<Value Type='Text'>Test</Value>" +
      "</Contains>" +
      "</Where>";

    SPListItemCollection items = list.GetItems(query);

    foreach (SPListItem item in items)
    {
      AddRow(tbl, item.Title);
    }
  }
  Controls.Add(tbl);
}
```

SPSiteDataQuery

The SPSiteDataQuery is like a powered up version of SPQuery—it can execute a query across multiple lists in a site where SPQuery can only find items in one particular list. The SPSiteDataQuery object is commonly used with the SPWeb object's GetSiteData method as a parameter that specifies the query to perform. Commonly used properties and methods of the SPSiteDataQuery object are shown in Table 3-14.

TABLE 3-14:   Commonly Used Properties and Methods of SPSiteDataQuery

Property or Method	Description
Lists	Gets and sets an XML string in CAML that configures which lists to include in the query
Query	Gets and sets an XML string in CAML that defines the query to perform
Webs	Gets and sets an XML string in CAML that specifies which sub webs to include in the query
ViewFields	Gets and sets an XML string in CAML that specifies the columns the query should return
RowLimit	Gets and sets a limit for the number of rows the query should return

Listing 3-35 shows an example site collection wide query using SPDataQuery. We create an SPDataQuery, then set the Lists property to select lists with a basetype of 0—this will select all basic lists, but not document libraries. Next we use a CAML query similar to the one we used in Listing 3-34 but this time without an <OrderBy> clause. We set the Webs property with CAML that says to search all webs within the site collection. We set the Fields property to return just one field, the Title column. We also set a row limit—a good practice when using an SPDataQuery to ensure you don't accidentally run a query that brings back everything on the site. We then get an SPWeb object and call the GetSiteData method passing in the SPDataQuery. This returns a DataTable that we enumerate that generates a table from the results in our web part.

In each returned DataRow we output the values of four columns. The ListId GUID identifies the list the item was found in; the WebId GUID identifies the web site the item was found in; the ID identifies each item and the Title identifies the actual value of our Title column, which we requested by setting the ViewFields property.

Listing 3-35: Using SPDataQuery in a web part in a sandboxed Solution

```
protected void AddRow(Table tbl, params object[] paramlist)
{
  TableRow tr = new TableRow();

  foreach (object o in paramlist)
  {
    TableCell tc = new TableCell();
    Label label = new Label();
    if (o != null)
      label.Text = o.ToString();
    tc.Controls.Add(label);
    tr.Cells.Add(tc);
  }
  tbl.Rows.Add(tr);
}

protected override void CreateChildControls()
{
  Table tbl = new Table();

  SPSiteDataQuery query = new SPSiteDataQuery();
  query.Lists = "<Lists BaseType='0'/>";
  query.Query =
      "<Where>" +
      "<Contains>" +
      "<FieldRef Name='Title' />" +
      "<Value Type='Text'>Test</Value>" +
      "</Contains>" +
      "</Where>";

  query.Webs = "<Webs Scope='SiteCollection'/>";
  query.ViewFields = "<FieldRef Name='Title'/>";
  query.RowLimit = 10;

  using (SPWeb web= SPContext.Current.Web)
  {
    System.Data.DataTable table = web.GetSiteData(query);

    if (table.Rows.Count > 0)
      AddRow(tbl, table.Columns[0].ColumnName,
        table.Columns[1].ColumnName,
        table.Columns[2].ColumnName,
        table.Columns[3].ColumnName);

    foreach (System.Data.DataRow row in table.Rows)
    {
```

```
        AddRow(tbl, row[0].ToString(), row[1].ToString(),
          row[2].ToString(), row[3].ToString());
    }
  }
  Controls.Add(tbl);
}
```

Working with Users

SPUser

The SPUser object represents a user of the SharePoint site. Commonly used properties and methods of SPUser are shown in Table 3-15.

TABLE 3-15: Commonly Used Properties and Methods of SPUser

Property or Method	Description
Update()	Method that saves the changes made to the user after using the SPUser object's methods and properties
Name	Gets and sets the name of the user
Email	Gets and sets the e-mail address of the user
ID	Returns an int ID for the user
Xml	Returns a string representing the user's data in XML
Groups	Returns an SPGroupCollection object that contains SPGroup objects for each group of which the user is a member
Notes	Gets or sets a string value storing notes for the user
LoginName	Returns the user name of the user
Alerts	Returns an SPAlertCollection object that contains SPAlert objects for each alert created by the user
UserToken*	Returns an SPUserToken object that identifies how the user was authenticated
Sid*	Returns a unique security ID as a string for the network account used by the user

* Not available in sandboxed solutions.

Listing 3-36 shows some code in an ItemUpdating event handler that grabs the user with user name DOMAIN\ecarter and takes the new title of the item being updated in the Announcements list and sets the user's e-mail to that title. It then constructs some output that displays the ID of the user, the number of groups of which the user is a member, and the number of alerts the user has, and puts those into the Notes for the user. Finally, the SPUser's Update method is called to save the changes.

Listing 3-36: Using SPUser in ItemUpdating event receiver in a farm solution

```
public override void ItemUpdating(SPItemEventProperties properties)
{
  if (properties.List.Title.CompareTo("Announcements")==0)
  {
    SPWeb web = properties.Web;
    SPUser user = web.AllUsers[@"DOMAIN\ecarter"];
    user.Email = properties.AfterProperties["Title"].ToString();

    StringBuilder output = new StringBuilder();
    output.AppendFormat("User's ID is {0}\n", user.ID);
    output.AppendFormat("User is a member of {0} groups\n",
     user.Groups.Count);
    output.AppendFormat("User has {0} alerts\n", user.Alerts.Count);

    user.Notes = output.ToString();
    user.Update();
    base.ItemUpdating(properties);
  }
```

Other Important SharePoint Objects

SPException

The SPException object represents an exception thrown by SharePoint. So often your code will have to interact with this object to detect errors that occur at runtime. The commonly used properties and methods of the SPException object are shown in Table 3-16. Also, SPException inherits from .NET's Exception class, so all the methods and properties associated with a standard .NET exception are also available.

TABLE 3-16: Commonly Used Properties and Methods of SPException That Are Specific to SPException and Not the Exception Base Class

Property or Method	Description
ErrorCode	Returns an int value that uniquely identifies the exception
NativeErrorMessage	Returns the error message as a string that was returned from SharePoint's unmanaged code
NativeStackTrace	Returns the stack trace for SharePoint's unmanaged code as a string

SPUtility

The SPUtility object has a ton of useful static methods that you can use in your SharePoint solution. Table 3-17 lists some of the most commonly used static methods.

TABLE 3-17: Commonly Used Static Methods of SPUtility

Method	Description
Redirect(…)*	Overloaded static method that can redirect an HTTP request
SendEmail(…)*	Overloaded static method that sends e-mail from a SharePoint web site
GetGenericSetup-Path(string)*	Static method that takes a site-relative URL and returns the local path where that subdirectory is stored. For example, passing "Lists/Announcements" would return C:\Program Files\Common Files\Microsoft Shared\Web Server Extensions\14\Lists\Announcements.
CreateISO8601DateTime-FromSystemDate-Time(DateTime)	Static method that takes a DateTime object and returns a string with that DateTime object represented in ISO8601 format
ResolvePrincipals(…)	Overloaded static method that retrieves an SPPrincipalInfo object representing a SharePoint user or group used in security policies

TABLE 3-17: Commonly Used Static Methods of SPUtility *(Continued)*

Method	Description
HandleAccess-Denied(Exception)*	Static method that handles access-denied exceptions in the same way Windows SharePoint does
GetLocalizedString(…)	Static method that gets a localized string given a source, resource file, and language id
FormatDate(…)	Static method that returns a formatted date/time string for the date and the date format specified
ParseDate(…)	Companion static method to FormatDate—converts a formatted date time string to a DateTime object
AlternateServerUrlFrom-HttpRequestUrl(Uri)	Static method that takes a request URL and returns the outgoing URL as a Uri

* Not available in sandboxed solutions.

Conclusion

In this chapter, we have looked at some of the most commonly used objects, properties, and methods in the SharePoint server object model. In the next chapter, we will look at creating lists in SharePoint in depth and consider more code samples to create and manipulate lists. We will also introduce and work with the client object models for SharePoint.

4

SharePoint Lists

Introduction to SharePoint Lists

SharePoint 2010 has a variety of functionalities, including enterprise content management and search, but at its core, SharePoint is about collaboration and document management. These types of solutions require a flexible model that allows users to store, manage, and share all kinds of data. In SharePoint you can have tasks or issues assigned to members in a team, documents, or any other kind of structured data shared across groups of users. SharePoint uses lists and content types that define the data in the lists to implement these collaboration scenarios. Out of the box, SharePoint provides a huge variety of list templates but there are scenarios that require extending existing lists or creating lists that are better suited for your particular business scenario. In this chapter we will discuss how to create and customize lists as well as how to work with custom list data.

Creating Lists

Before we create our first SharePoint list we need to look into the terminology. If this is your first encounter with SharePoint there might be some confusion around what a list definition, a list template, and a list instance is. It's important for us to understand the difference between these objects as these terms are used by Visual Studio and the official SharePoint documentation.

A *list definition* defines a schema for a SharePoint list. It contains information on what views are being used, which columns and content types are being used, and other metadata information. A list definition is an XML file written in the Collaborative Application Markup Language (CAML), a markup language specific to SharePoint. A list is made up of several columns. Columns define the name, the type of the column (for example a Yes/No type), whether the value is required to be entered for the list item to be valid, etc. Columns are created from existing site column definitions that are defined at the SharePoint site level but you can also create a list column that is used only for a particular list and not available to other lists. A list column can be one of several types: single line of text, multiple lines of text, choice, number, currency, date & time, yes/no check box, hyperlink or picture, lookup (for information already on the site), calculated (based on values in other columns), and person or group. Site column definitions are more powerful than custom list columns because you can also define additional behavior, such as the editing UI that is shown when an item in the list is edited in the details view.

A *list template* can either be created by end users through the SharePoint user interface using an existing list as a pattern or using an existing list instance. If based on a user-created list it is called a *custom list template*.

A custom list template includes everything that defines the list, including list columns and site columns used by the list, content types used by the list, views defined for the list, and so on.

List Templates versus List Definitions

A list template may sound a lot like a list definition—but they are effectively the same thing, a pattern for a SharePoint list. They differ mainly in how they are created: list templates are created in SharePoint or SharePoint designer, list definitions in Visual Studio.

A *list instance* is an instance of a specific SharePoint list definition or list template. All of its data is stored in the relevant content database. This is typically a list in SharePoint used by end users to enter and view data and it is based on either a list template or list definition. A list instance can be created in many ways, but commonly by:

- Creating an empty list manually and then defining it column by column with the SharePoint UI.
- Creating a new list manually by selecting a list template to base it on.
- Using the SharePoint object model.
- Using a list definition referenced from a site definition when a site is created.

So, for example, you might create multiple list instances from a calendar list template for a given SharePoint site—maybe one list instance for a vacation calendar, another list instance for an events calendar, and another list instance for important milestones for your team's project. Each of these list instances could use the same list template or list definition defining a SharePoint list containing calendar items.

SharePoint 2010 comes with a number of list templates that are designed to meet common business requirements. If these templates don't meet your specific requirements you can use them as a template for the list you want to create so that you don't need to build a new list definition from scratch. Table 4-1 shows the list templates available in SharePoint Foundation 2010.

TABLE 4-1:   SharePoint Foundation List templates

List Template	Description
Announcements	Used for sharing news; an expiration date can be set for each announcement in the list.
Calendar	List that tracks team events, social events, milestones, etc.; the calendar list can be optionally synchronized with Microsoft Outlook.
Contacts	List for storing contact information with optional Microsoft Outlook integration.

Continues

TABLE 4-1:   SharePoint Foundation List templates *(Continued)*

List Template	Description
Custom List	An empty list definition; it is supposed to be extended with custom columns. This list type is also used when Microsoft Excel spreadsheets are exported to lists.
Custom List in DataSheet View	List displaying Access datasheets; in order to use this type of list you need to enable SharePoint support in Office Professional.
Discussion Board	List for storing a threaded discussion.
Tasks	List for task items that can optionally be integrated with SharePoint workflow and Microsoft Outlook.
Links	List for managing hyperlinks
Project Tasks	List of tasks with support for Gant Chart rendering. Data from the list can be integrated into Microsoft Project Server through Project Web Access.
Survey	List used for creating surveys to collect feedback on certain topics.
Issue Tracking	List for tracking issues.
Document Library	Standard document library used to store Word, Excel, and other documents.

A *site column* is a column definition that is defined at a site level and is available for reuse amongst child sites. SharePoint comes with a set of pre-installed site column definitions. As a developer, you can define new site column definitions that can be installed at a site level and used across multiple lists. You might create a custom site column definition if you have a data type that cannot be easily represented and edited using the built-in site columns. For example, you might want to create a site column definition that stores a credit card number complete with a custom editing and verification experience to ensure that the value entered is a valid credit card number.

A *list view* defines how the list is displayed to the user. A list view includes information that tells SharePoint which list columns to display, the order in which to display them, and the sorting and filtering to use when displaying the list. A SharePoint list can have several different list views defined for it—for example, a list showing sports teams could have a view that displays the sports teams sorted by season records, a second view that displays the sports teams sorted by geography, and each list view can have a different set and ordering of columns. A list view can also be set to display in a grid view similar to how Microsoft Access displays a data table or the more traditional web view used as the default for most SharePoint lists.

A *content type* is a reusable definition of the schema used by a list item (see Chapter 7, "SharePoint Content Types" for more information on content types). Content types are stored at a site level so they can be reused in the site and across all the child sites and lists in and under the site in which they are defined. Built-in content types available by default in SharePoint include those representing a contact, task, document, and so forth. A list may contain one or more content types—for example, you could have a document library that contains only documents or you could have the document library contain additional more specialized content types, such as "Expense Report" or "Invoice" that have custom data and templates used for them. This makes a list even more flexible because it can contain multiple data types.

Fields versus List and Site columns

Sometimes you hear "field" used interchangeably with list and site column. This is because a field refers to the XML element (‹Field›) that describes a list or site column in the SharePoint schema (CAML). A field element contains a complete description of a list or site column, such as display name, and whether the field is required. The term "field" also appears in the object model where the object SPField represents a site or list column.

Building List Instances Using SharePoint Designer

We will first explore how to create a list instance then we will show how to take a list instance and save it as a list template so it can be reused by other lists. Later in this chapter we will also show how to create a list definition. The easiest way to create a SharePoint list instance is to use SharePoint Designer because Visual Studio doesn't come with a visual list designer. We will consider how to create a SharePoint list instance using only Visual Studio, but we will mainly focus on using SharePoint Designer to create list instances.

Let's create our first list using SharePoint Designer. We'll create a list that allows users to add authors, their book titles, and their ISBN numbers. On the Sites start screen of SharePoint Designer, use the Open Site button in the Open SharePoint Site group. Figure 4-1 shows the SharePoint Designer Sites start screen.

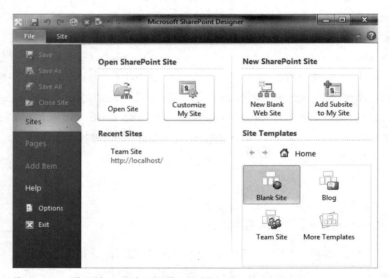

Figure 4-1: The SharePoint Designer Sites start screen

In the Open Site dialog enter the URL for the site in which you want to create a new list instance as shown in Figure 4-2. We will use http://localhost because this is the default SharePoint site on a development machine.

After SharePoint Designer has connected to the SharePoint site the home screen for the site appears providing us with information about the opened

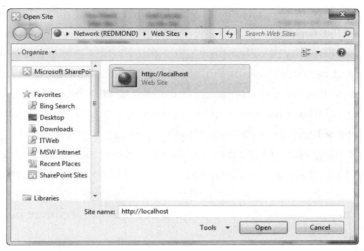

Figure 4-2: The Open Site dialog

site. In the left navigation pane as shown in Figure 4-3, click on Lists and Libraries to bring up the Lists and Libraries screen. The Lists and Libraries screen is displayed with the active lists and document libraries for the site.

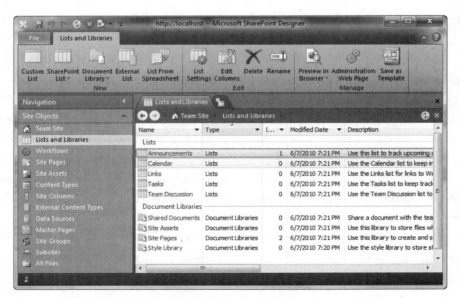

Figure 4-3: The Lists and Libraries screen

A document library is a special type of a list. SharePoint differentiates a specialized list type like a document library from standard lists through the use of a different base list type identifier in the CAML markup for the list. Standard lists such as announcements, calendar, links, and tasks have the base type 0, whereas document libraries have a base type of 1. There are other specialized list types in SharePoint including the survey and discussion lists, which use a different base type than 0 or 1. The list base type for a survey list is 4 and for a discussion list 3. The base list type identifier is important to be aware of because base list type identifiers limit the site columns that can be used in a particular list. For example, there are site columns that are only available to a document library that cannot be used in a standard list type.

Creating a List Instance

Let's create a list instance using an already available list template. We see in Figure 4-3 that this site already has a list template for a Links list available. Already defined in this Links list template are default columns, including a URL column used to store the URL information for a particular link. Now if we create a new list instance based on the Links list template we will automatically get the URL column in our list instance. Note too in Figure 4-3 that there are 0 items next to the links template. This indicates that although there is a links list template available in the site, no list instances using that template have been created yet.

Let's create a links list instance by clicking on the SharePoint List drop-down button in the ribbon and selecting Links from the drop-down. Figure 4-4 shows the drop-down that appears when you click the SharePoint List button.

In the Create list or document library dialog, name the list "Addison-Wesley Links," leave the description blank as shown in Figure 4-5, and press the OK button.

Our new list now appears in the Lists section of the Lists and Libraries screen. Figure 4-6 shows the new list in the Lists and Libraries screen.

Click on the link "Addison-Wesley Links" to get to the page that allows us to view and manage settings for the list. Let's have a look at the list instance

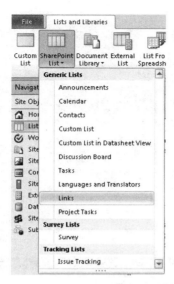

Figure 4-4: Creating a new SharePoint list instance based on the Links list template

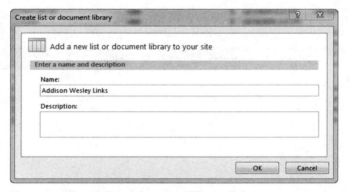

Figure 4-5: Create list or document library dialog

we have just created. In the ribbon of this screen click the "Preview in Browser" button. Figure 4-7 shows our list instance Addison-Wesley Links.

If we compare our list instance with the list template Links you'll notice that their definitions are identical. This is because we have just created an instance of the list template Links. Our goal is to customize the list, so that it meets our specific requirements, which are to add a new column to store

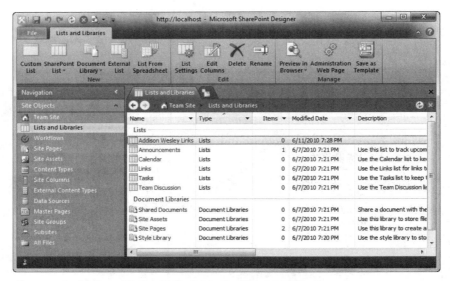

Figure 4-6: Addison-Wesley Links list in the Lists and Libraries screen

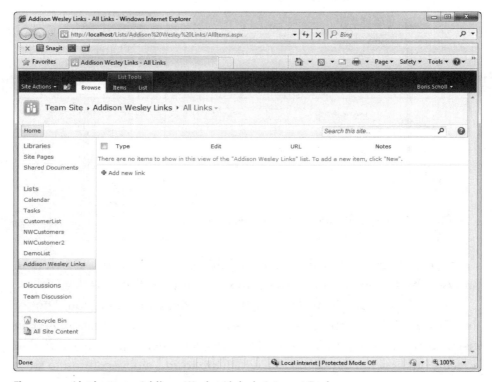

Figure 4-7: List instance Addison-Wesley Links in Internet Explorer

an ISBN number and author information. To customize the list we start in the Lists and Libraries screen shown in Figure 4-6. Hover your mouse over the Addison-Wesley Links entry and click on the hyperlink. This will take you to the view and manage settings for this page list shown in Figure 4-8.

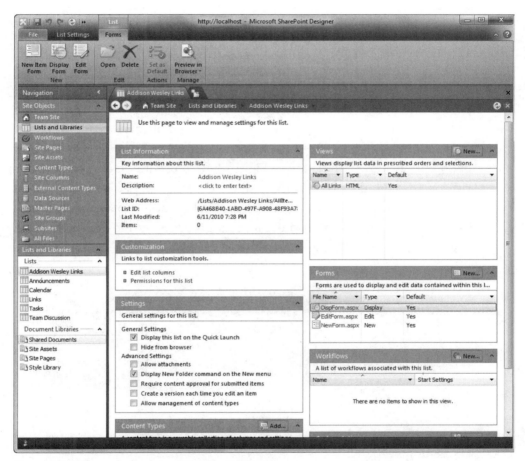

Figure 4-8: View and manage settings for this list page

In the Customization section click the Edit list columns link. Figure 4-9 shows the customization section.

When you click the Edit list columns link, the Columns Editor page comes up and shows the two columns that are already defined in our list: URL and Notes.

Figure 4-9: Customization section

Adding Existing Site Columns and Creating New Custom List Columns for a List

Now we want to add two columns to our Addison-Wesley Links list: Author and ISBN number. SharePoint Designer allows us to create new custom list columns or add existing site columns to a list. As you recall, a site column is a column definition that is stored at the site collection level available to all child sites. Author is a site column definition that already exists for use in document libraries. So in this case we can use the Add Existing Site Column ribbon button shown at the top of Figure 4-10 to use this site column in our Addison-Wesley Links list. Click on the Add Existing Site Column ribbon button to bring up the site columns picker dialog shown in Figure 4-11. The picker lists all the available site columns grouped by the type of lists in which they are typically used.

Figure 4-10: Columns Editor Page

Figure 4-11: Site Columns Picker dialog

Before you create a new custom list column you should always check if there is an existing site column that you can reuse because SharePoint comes with a huge variety of site columns that meet most requirements. To find the Author column, type *Author* into the search field of the Site Columns Picker. The Author site column will be displayed in the dialog. Double click on the Author site column to add it to your Addison-Wesley Links list.

Custom List Columns versus Site Column Definitions

You might wonder what benefit you get if you reuse a site column definition instead of creating a custom list column. The benefits are these: Site
columns are reusable in lists across multiple SharePoint sites and help to
ensure consistency of metadata across sites and lists.

Next we need to create the ISBN column because there is no existing site column definition for an ISBN number. You can verify this by using the Add Existing Site Column ribbon button to bring up the Site Columns Picker dialog and search for ISBN. Back in the Column Editor page shown in Figure 4-10, click on the Add New Column ribbon drop-down button. In the drop-down menu that appears select Single Line of Text. Change the column name from the default of NewColumn1 to ISBN. The Column Editor page should now look like Figure 4-12. Click the Save button (the floppy disk icon) in the quick access toolbar at the top left of the SharePoint Designer window to save the changes.

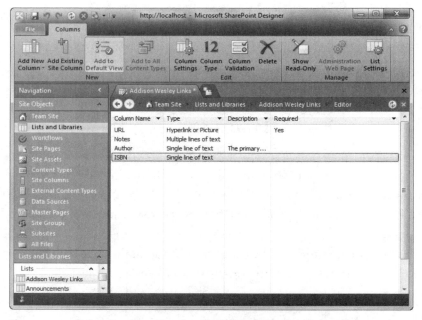

Figure 4-12: Columns editor showing the Addison-Wesley Links columns

Now let's see how our new Addison-Wesley Links list instance looks in the browser. Go back to the page used to view and manage settings for this list by either using the breadcrumb navigation or using the back button placed to the left of the breadcrumb navigation. Once you are back on the view and manage settings for this list page, click on the Preview in Browser button in the ribbon. Figure 4-13 shows the list in the browser with Author and ISBN added to the list.

Congratulations! You just created your first list instance using SharePoint Designer. Of course we are not done with our exploration of creating list instances even though users could now start using this list to enter data. We

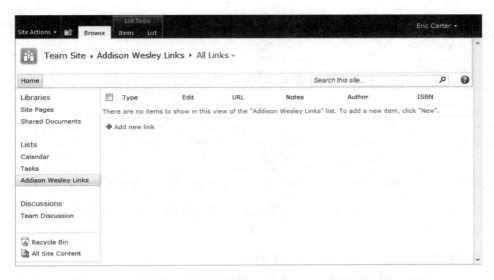

Figure 4-13: Addison-Wesley Links list with two custom columns: Author and ISBN

still need to look at all the other sections in the view and manage settings for this list page. Close the browser to return to this screen shown in Figure 4-8. The section beneath Customization is called Settings. It contains general settings as well as advanced settings that influence the behavior of the list and its items for the list. Table 4-2 lists the settings and their purposes.

TABLE 4-2: List Settings

Name	Description
Display this list on the Quick Launch	Indicates whether the list should show up in the Quick Launch menu of the home page or not: the default is Yes.
Hide from browser	The list is not accessible in the browser meaning site visitors cannot see the list.
Allow attachments	Indicates if you can use attachments with a list item.
Display New Folder command on the New menu	Allows users to create folders in the list if checked.

Continues

TABLE 4-2: List Settings *(Continued)*

Name	Description
Require content approval for submitted items	Indicates whether items or files that are added to the list need to be approved by users that are members of the approvers group in the approval workflow.
Create a version each time you edit an item	If checked, SharePoint creates a new version of an item each time it is edited and adds it to the version history.
Allow management of content types	Allows end users to add multiple content types to the list.

Enabling the Use of Content Types in a List

We want to enable the management of content types in this list by setting the last setting described in Table 4-2, Allow management of content types. Content types are explained in detail in Chapter 7, "SharePoint Content Types." For now, all you need to know is that a content type is a reusable collection of columns and settings that you can use for data in your list. In order to add a new content type to a list or have users add new content types while they are working on the list in the browser, the setting Allow management of content types needs to be checked—otherwise, the concept of content types will be hidden from the user of the list. We've already done that, and now we can have a look at how to add a new content type. Click the Add button in the section Content Types in the view and manage settings for this list page. Figure 4-14 shows the Content Types section of the view and manage settings for this list page.

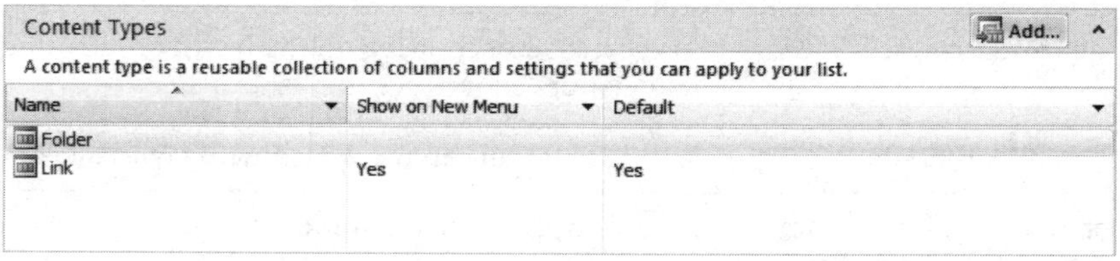

Figure 4-14: Content Types section

If you click the Add... button in the Content Types section, the Content Types Picker dialog appears as shown in Figure 4-15. The Content Types Picker lists all of the content types available for the site.

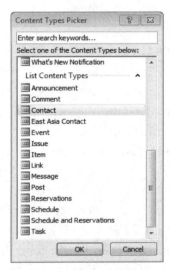

Figure 4-15: Content Types Picker Dialog

To select a content type just click on the one you want to add to your list, e.g., Task, and click the OK button. This will add the content type to the content type table in the Content Types section and it will then be available in your list. We will learn how to create and use content types in Chapter 7, "SharePoint Content Types."

You may wonder what the impact is of adding "Task" to the available content types in our Addison-Wesley Links list. Basically, this now allows us to add three types of items to the list. As you may have noticed in Figure 4-14, the user can add a folder that is a special content type that can contain other items. The user can also add a Link that is the default content type for the list and is shown on the New menu. By adding Task to the available content types, a user can now use the ribbon for the list, and by clicking on the New Item drop-down button in the list, they will see Task as an available item that can be added to the list. As you may notice, there is a mismatch between our default view for our list that shows columns like "ISBN" that don't exist for the Task content type. This is OK—SharePoint will only show column values for the Task item that match columns defined for the default view and leave the rest blank.

Creating a Custom View for a List

The next section shown in the view and manage settings for this list page is the views section. Views are enabled by a special web part that SharePoint uses to display SharePoint list data. Views allow you to display the list data in a certain order, define filters for your data, and configure other settings for viewing the data in a list. The actual view columns, controls, and data are displayed by a web part called the XsltListViewWebPart. The default view for a list is a page named AllItems.aspx. SharePoint Designer provides a full web page designer experience to customize a SharePoint list's views.

Let's see how we can create a new view for our list. Clicking the New button in the Views section shown in the top right corner of Figure 4-8 causes the Create New List View dialog to appear as shown in Figure 4-16. In the Create New List View dialog, name the new view "MyLinks." Leave the check box for Make this the default view unchecked because we don't

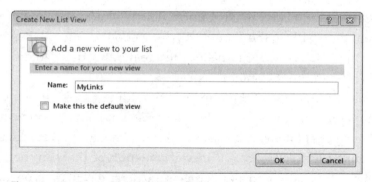

Figure 4-16: Create New List View dialog

want this view to be used by default. Click the OK button. The new list is added to the views section.

Click on the MyLinks link in the view and manage settings for this list page to bring up the List View designer. This will take a while as SharePoint Designer creates the web part page for the view, creates a web page for the view (in our case MyLinks.aspx), and renders the master page. Once the page is rendered you can start editing the page by using the List View Tools section of the ribbon. You can only edit the content region part of the page shown in the blue highlighted box in Figure 4-17. The List View Tools ribbon group is highlighted and the Options tab is selected in the ribbon.

There are four tabs in the List View Tools section allowing us to design the view page. The Options tab allows you to add, change, or edit options for the list itself or for its content. Let's add another column to our view. Note that this is different than when we added the Author and ISBN columns before—in that example we were changing the definition of our list. In this case we are changing which existing columns in the list are displayed by a particular view.

Click on the Add/Remove Columns button in the ribbon in the Options page. A dialog with all the fields defined in the list appears. Available fields are defined by the type of list template you used and any additional fields you added (either from site columns or as custom list columns). Also remember that available fields will be a merge of all fields coming from all content types that are valid in the list. In Figure 4-18 we have selected Title field and clicked the Add >> button to ensure the Title field is added to the bottom of the list on the right and shown in our view.

Click the OK button. SharePoint Designer updates the view immediately to show the Title field. Table 4-3 lists other functionalities available in the Options tab.

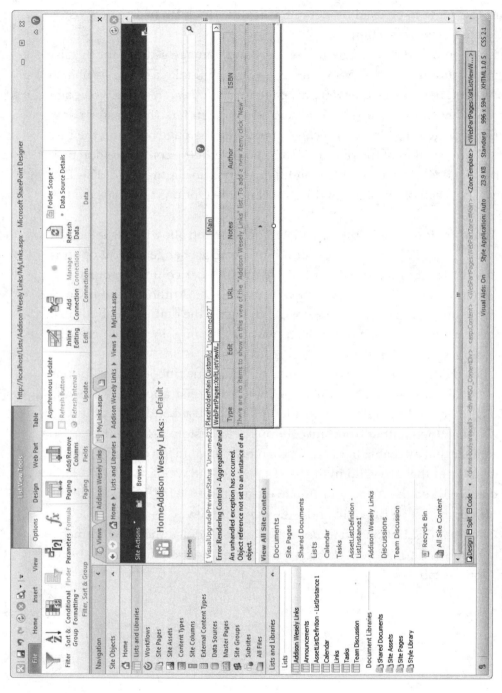

Figure 4-17: List View designer

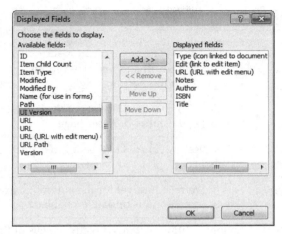

Figure 4-18: Displayed Fields dialog

TABLE 4-3: Options Tab Functions

Name	Functionality
Filter	Allows you to specify filter criteria to limit the items that should be displayed.
Sort & Group	Allows you to sort and group items in a column.
Conditional Formatting	Displays items in a certain way based on their values. For example, you can set up conditional formatting to display all negative values in a number column in red.
Finder (Only available in External Lists)	Selects the default finder method in an external list; see Chapter 6, "Working with Business Data," for more information on finder methods.
Parameters	You can define query string parameters for the view. This allows you to filter the view based on the value passed in by query parameters.
Formula	You can insert a formula to be displayed for a particular field in the view.
Paging	Sets the paging criteria for the view; the default setting is to display 30 items per page.

Continues

TABLE 4-3:   Options Tab Functions *(Continued)*

Name	Functionality
Add/Remove Columns	Allows you to add and remove columns from the list as we saw earlier in this section.
Asynchronous Update	Enables asynchronous update of the list data without refreshing the entire browser page.
Refresh Button	Adds a Refresh button to the view if asynchronous update is enabled.
Refresh Interval	Sets the refresh interval for the automatic update of the content if asynchronous update is enabled.
Inline Editing	Enables editing of items directly in cells of the web page
Add Connection	Add a connection to another web part; for more information see Chapter 9, "SharePoint Web Parts."
Manage Connections	If a connection is defined the properties of the connection can be changed here.
Refresh Data	Refreshes the data displayed.
Folder Scope	Specifies the scope of the view; for example you can set if the view shows content from all folders or only from the currently active subfolder.
Data Source Details	Opens or closes the data view details task pane, which allows you to get a detailed view of the data source used for this view.

Now that we have added another column in our view we can go ahead and add some data to our list instance. Click the Save button in the Share-Point Designer's quick access toolbar. After the view has been saved, click the Home tab in the ribbon tabs. On the Home tab, click the Preview in Browser drop-down button. In the drop-down that appears click on a resolution to bring up the browser. Figure 4-19 shows the Preview in Browser button in the List Settings tab of the ribbon.

Once the new view is displayed in the browser you can add some sample data to see the new view in action. There are three more List View Tools tabs available when editing a SharePoint list view. The Table tab allows you to

Figure 4-19: Preview in Browser button in the List Settings tab of the ribbon

define and edit a table-based view for the list. You will be able to understand the functionalities to create a table view right away if you are familiar with the table tools in other Office applications.

The Design tab and the Web Part tab provide additional functionality to customize views. The Design tab allows you to customize the design and behavior of your view. There is also a great functionality available to help you create sample data for a new view. Table 4-4 describes the functionality in the Design tab.

TABLE 4-4: Design Tab Functions

Name	Functionality
Sample Data	Generates sample data for your view.
Totals Row	Displays a totals row at the bottom of the view for each column
View Style	You can select from different styles for the list within your view. The following styles are available: Basic Table Boxed, no labels Boxed Newsletter Newsletter, no lines Shaded Preview Pane
Options	Toolbar options for your list within the view; the default is none.

Continues

TABLE 4-4: Design Tab Functions *(Continued)*

Name	Functionality
Insert Control	Allows you to insert data view controls such as check boxes and textboxes to the view .
Form Action	Available when a form action button or a hyperlink is selected in the view; a form action button is a button control that can be added to the form, which has actions such as Commit, Refresh, Cancel, Navigate to Source, and Navigate to Page. Those actions can be added by clicking the Form Action button in the ribbon.
Customize XSLT	Allows you to customize the XSLT used to generate the view. You can customize the entire view or only one item in the view.
Revert XSLT	Reverts the XSLT back to the default XSLT.
Data View Preview	Sets the preview of the data list based on the value selected in the drop-down.

The Web Part tab allows you to save and customize the XsltListView-WebPart and make it available to others. Remember that the XsltListView-WebPart is a web part provided by SharePoint that actually displays your custom view. Table 4-5 describes the functionality in the Web Part tab.

TABLE 4-5: Web Part Tab Functions

Name	Functionality
Web part Title	The title of the web part; by default it is set to the name of the view.
Properties	Launches the properties dialog for the web part; the most common properties are exposed in the ribbon as well. These are explained in this table.
Chrome Type	Sets the chrome type for the web part. Available chrome types are: Default None Title and Border Title only Border only

TABLE 4-5:   Web Part Tab Functions *(Continued)*

Name	Functionality
Chrome State	State of chrome type.
Width	Width of the web part in pixels; you can set this property in the properties dialog as well.
Height	Height of the web part in pixels; you can set this property in the properties dialog as well.
Add Connection	Add a connection to another web part (see Chapter 9, "SharePoint Web Parts").
Manage Connection	If a connection is defined the properties can be changed here.
Minimize	Allows the user to minimize the web part.
Close	Allows the user to close the web part.
Hide	Allows the user to hide the web part.
Zone Change	Allows the user to change the web part zone for this web part.
Connections	Allows connections for this web part to other web parts.
Edit in Personal View	Allows the user to edit the web part in the personal view; SharePoint has a personal and a shared view. In a shared view all users see the same view and all changes made by all users to the page. In personal view you have your own personalized page showing just your changes.
To Site Gallery	Saves the web part to the site gallery.
To File	Saves the web part as a web part file.

Deploying Your List Instance

To allow your list to be used in other SharePoint sites you can save it as a list template. From the view and manage settings for this list page shown in Figure 4-8, click on Save as Template in the ribbon. Figure 4-20 shows the ribbon with the Save as Template button.

Figure 4-20: Save as Template button in the ribbon of the view and manage settings for this list page

Clicking on the Save as Template button will open a SharePoint application page asking for information for the template you want to create shown in Figure 4-21. In the File name box enter AddisonWesleyLinks. For the name, enter the template name—this is the name that the end user will see. We've typed "AddisonWesleyLinks" again but an end user might prefer "Addison-Wesley Links." Leave the Include Content check box unchecked. Checking this would save the currently added items in the list as part of the list template—useful if you want the list prepopulated with some data.

Click the OK button to save the list as a list template. The confirmation page comes up as shown in Figure 4-22. Note that it has saved the list template to something called the "list template gallery." The list template gallery is a site-collection–level document library that stores list templates that can be used to create lists in the site collection. The list template gallery can be seen in Figure 4-23.

In the list template gallery, right click on the list template AddisonWesleyLinks and select Save Target As…. Save the list as an .STP file to disk. Now you can import this file to other SharePoint servers where you want to use this list. To do this, copy the .STP file to a location on disk on the destination server. Next, go to the top-level site for the site collection where you want to use the list template and drop down the Site Actions menu on the top left corner of the page. Select Site Settings, which will take you to the Site Settings page shown in Figure 4-24.

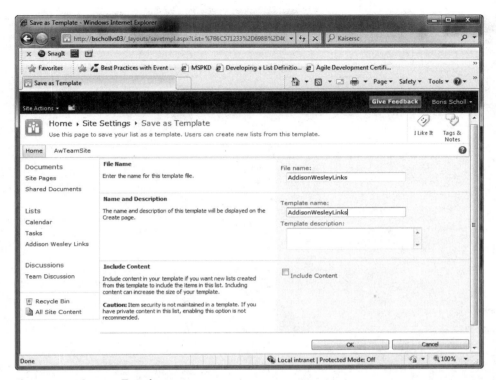

Figure 4-21: Save as Template page

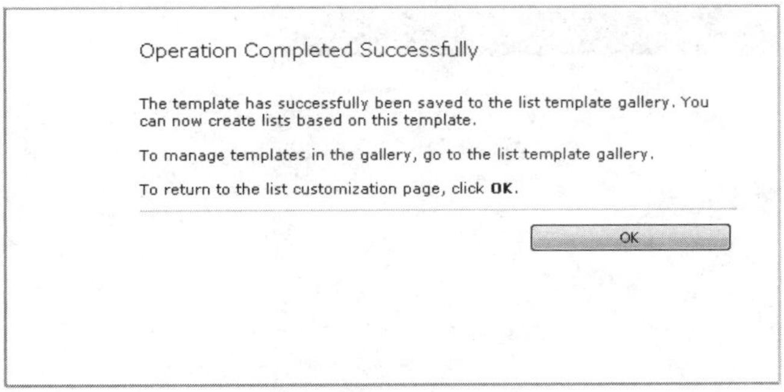

Operation Completed Successfully

The template has successfully been saved to the list template gallery. You can now create lists based on this template.

To manage templates in the gallery, go to the list template gallery.

To return to the list customization page, click **OK**.

OK

Figure 4-22: Save as Template confirmation page

Figure 4-23: List Template Gallery

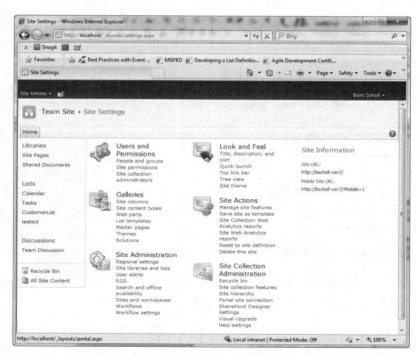

Figure 4-24: Site Settings page for top-level site in a site collection

Inheritance by Copy

You might wonder what happens if users create list instances based on your Addison-Wesley Links list template but then later you change the list template—maybe to add a new column such as "Publish Date." Is there a way to republish the list template so that existing lists that used the old list template will be updated to have the new column? Unfortunately there is no automatic inheritance of new columns for lists created through a list template when the list template changes. The good news is that you can use Visual Studio 2010 and the feature upgrade actions to propagate the changes to lists created from that definition. In other words you would create a new list definition in Visual Studio 2010 in the first place and deploy it to the server. Now you want to change the list and add a new column. First update the list definition in Visual Studio 2010 to contain the new column definition. Next add an ‹UpgradeActions› and ‹CustomUpgradeAction› element to the feature XML (for more information on features see Chapter 11, "Packaging and Deployment"). The ‹CustomUpgradeAction› would define the step to add the new column. Once deployed all the lists created from the list definition would inherit the new column. For more information on ‹UpgradeActions› see http://msdn.microsoft.com/en-us/library/aa544511(v=office.14).aspx.

In the Site Settings page under Galleries, click the List templates link. This will take you to the List Template Gallery. In the List Template Gallery select the Documents tab in the ribbon to make document-related operations appear (remember that the List Template Gallery is a document library). In the Documents tab, click on the Upload Document button and drop-down and select Upload Document as shown in Figure 4-25.

Browse to the destination folder that contains your .STP file, leave the Overwrite existing files check box checked, and click the OK button. Figure 4-26 shows the Upload Template dialog.

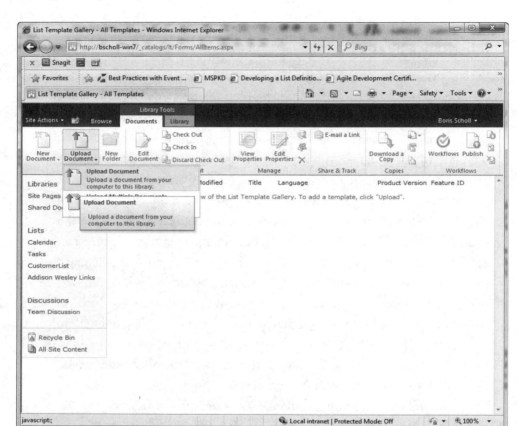

Figure 4-25: Using the Upload Document button to upload a List Template to the List Templates Library of a site collection

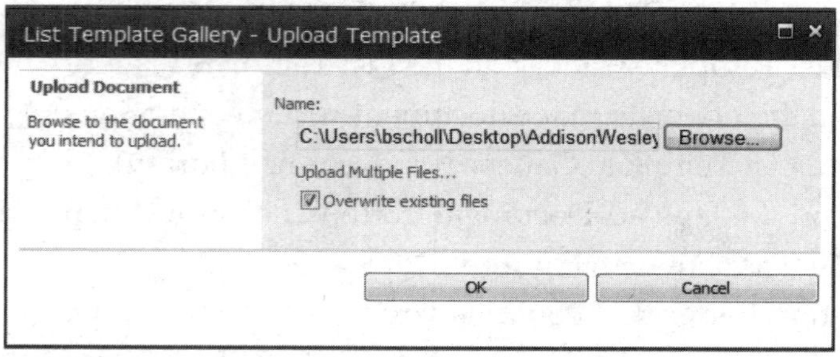

Figure 4-26: The Upload Template dialog

The template is now imported into the destination system and is ready to be used.

Missing Dependencies

Another question that might come up as you consider moving list templates from one SharePoint server to another—what happens if a list template references something that was available on the source server but isn't available on the destination server? For example, what if our Addison-Wesley Links list template referred to a custom Site Column definition that was installed on our original server but wasn't available on the destination server? The list template will contain the schema XML file of the list itself, which basically means all the fields and columns are included and will be available on the destination server with one exception. If the list contains custom field types or site columns referencing objects that cannot be expressed in the schema XML, i.e., an assembly that is referenced by a field, only the field markup will be included in the template.

Importing Your List into Visual Studio

The main goal of this chapter so far has been to introduce you to SharePoint Designer and its visual editors for creating list instances and how to create list templates based on those list instances. But you might be saying to yourself at this point, "I thought this was a Visual Studio book—what's with all this SharePoint Designer stuff?" Well, as we mentioned at the start of this chapter, Visual Studio has no visual design experience for lists or list templates (unless you consider editing a super hairy XML file as a visual experience). So the strategy we are recommending when you need to create a list for a Visual Studio solution is to create the list or list instance in SharePoint Designer then import it into Visual Studio. In this section, we will show you how to import artifacts you have created in SharePoint Designer into Visual Studio.

You may want to import a list instance into Visual Studio for many reasons, for example you may have created a list instance and you now want to attach an event receiver to it to implement business logic for items added to that list. In order to deploy the event receiver you need to have both your list instance definition and your event receiver in Visual Studio. The easiest way to do this is to use the Import SharePoint Solution Package project in Visual Studio 2010.

Before we can create an Import SharePoint Solution Package project in Visual Studio we need to create a SharePoint solution package. SharePoint solution packages are stored in .WSP files (see Chapter 11, "Packaging and Deployment" for more information on SharePoint solution packages). As SharePoint only creates solution packages for entire sites we unfortunately cannot just save our list as .WSP file. We will have to save the entire site as a .WSP file then import that into Visual Studio using the Import SharePoint Solution Package project. A dialog will be displayed in Visual Studio when the .WSP file is imported that will allow us to pick out of the .WSP file the elements corresponding to the list we want to bring into our Visual Studio project.

What If I Have an Existing Project into Which I Want to Import the List?

You may have noticed that we said a new project called an "Import Share-Point Solution Package" project must be created to import our list. What if we already have a SharePoint project created—can the list be imported into an existing project? The answer unfortunately is no. However, this isn't as big of a limitation as you would think because SharePoint solutions are typically made up of multiple projects and you can still create a single deployment even though your solution is made up of multiple projects.

Let's create a .WSP solution package for the site that we created the Addison-Wesley Links list in. In your browser go to the top-level site that contains the Addison-Wesley Links list. Click on Site Actions to show the Site Actions menu of the site as shown in Figure 4-27.

Figure 4-27: Site Actions Menu

In the Site Actions menu click the Site Settings item. This will open up the Site Settings page for the site. Figure 4-28 shows the Site Settings page.

In the Site Settings page, click the Save site as template link in the Site Actions section. This will take you to the Save as Template page. This is a similar page to the Save as Template page we saw when saving our Addison-Wesley list as a list template in Figure 4-21. Remember though that a list template is an .STP file and we are about to create a .WSP file.

Enter "MyHomePage" in the File name and Template name boxes. In the Template description box enter "Includes the Addison-Wesley links list"

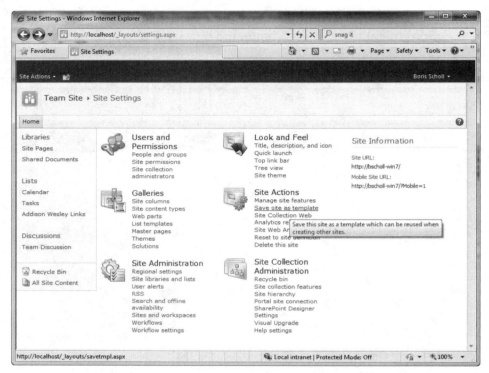

Figure 4-28: Site Settings page

and leave the Include Content check box unchecked and click the OK button. Figure 4-29 shows the Save as Template page with information entered.

Workaround for Client Operating Systems

If you are developing on Windows Vista or Windows 7 you need to make sure that SharePoint can access the folder "C:\Windows\ServiceProfiles\ NetworkService\AppData\Local\Temp\" as it needs to create a temporary folder for the solution. In Windows 7 or Vista browse to the folder. The OS will ask you if you are sure that you want to access this folder. Say yes. This will make the folder accessible to your account, which has to be in the administrator group.

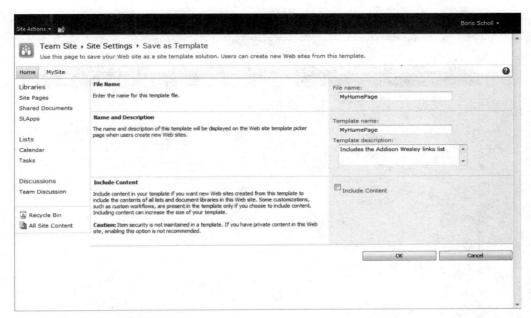

Figure 4-29: Save as Template page

Once the .WSP file has been created successfully you will get the confirmation page shown in Figure 4-30, which indicates that the site template (.WSP file) has been saved in the solution gallery. The solution gallery is a special document library stored in the top-level site for a Site Collection.

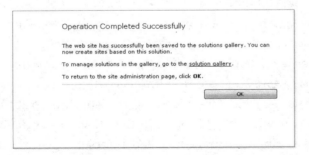

Figure 4-30: Save as Template confirmation page

Click on the solution gallery link in the dialog shown in Figure 4-30 to see the template in the solution gallery. Figure 4-31 shows the solution template gallery with our template MyHomePage.

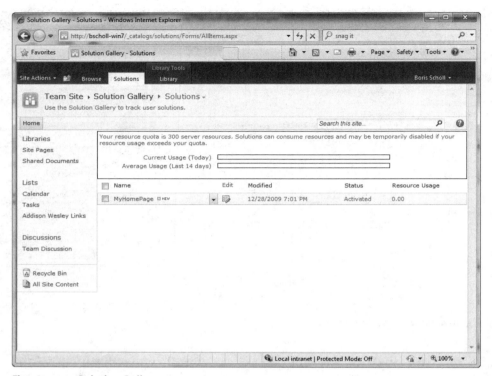

Figure 4-31: Solution Gallery

As the last step we need to save the .WSP template file to disk. Right click on the link MyHomePage and select Save Target As… in the context menu and save the template to a directory on your disk. Figure 4-32 shows the context menu with the Save Target As… command.

We have now created a .WSP file that contains our entire site with our Addison-Wesley Links list along with everything else in the site (content types, other lists, etc.). Next we need to start Visual Studio 2010. With Visual Studio 2010 open select New Project. In the New Project dialog select 2010 under the SharePoint node in the Installed Templates tree and choose Import SharePoint Solution Package and name the project AddisonWesleyLinksList. Figure 4-33 shows the New Project dialog.

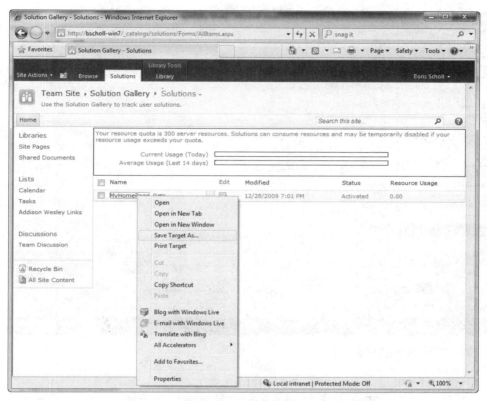

Figure 4-32: Context menu for a Solutions template in the Solution Gallery

Can I Import a List Template Into a Sandboxed Solution?

The short answer is Yes.

The SharePoint Customization Wizard comes up. Here you can select the site you want to use for debugging and the trust level for the solution. Chose Deploy as farm solution and click the Next button. Figure 4-34 shows the SharePoint Customization Wizard.

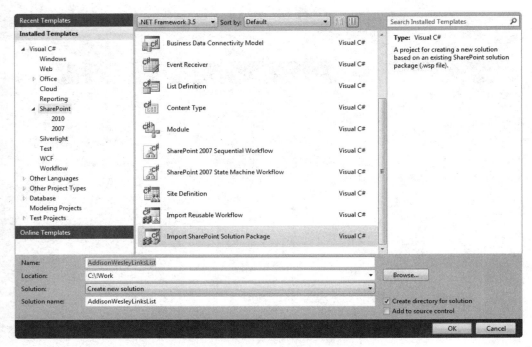

Figure 4-33: New Project dialog

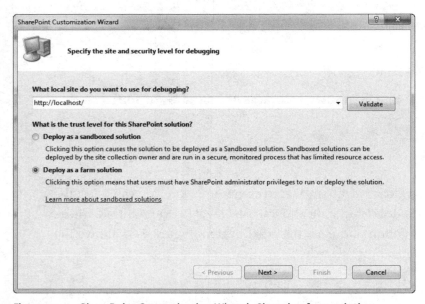

Figure 4-34: SharePoint Customization Wizard: Choosing farm solution

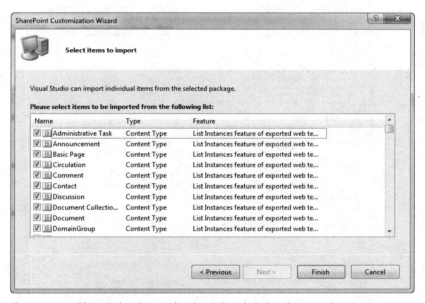

The next step allows us to select the solution package we want to import. Click the Browse button. In the Open dialog click the Browse… button to browse to the directory that contains the MyHomePage solution package and select the .WSP file, in our example titled "MyHomePage.WSP." Next, click the Open button. Once the solution package is selected, click the Next button to get to the next wizard step.

Figure 4-35 shows the SharePoint Customization wizard step that allows you to select specific items out of the contents of the .WSP file. As you can see, there are a ton of items in the .WSP file. As the solution package contains the entire SharePoint site you will find all the content types, fields, modules, list instances etc. in the item list.

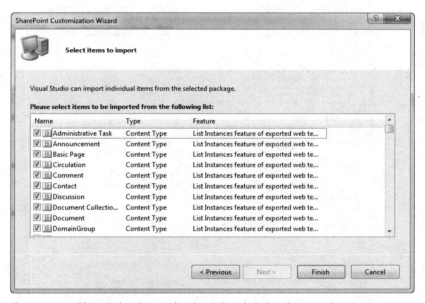

Figure 4-35: SharePoint Customization Wizard: Select items to import

As we only want to import the Addison-Wesley Links list we need to uncheck all the other items. Here we employ a little user interface trick. Click anywhere in the data list and press CTRL + A to select all the items. With all the items in the list selected, uncheck the first item. This will uncheck all other items in the list as well.

Now that everything is unchecked, scroll down to the item Addison-Wesley Links list and check the item. Then click the Finish button. We don't need to worry about the dependencies the list might have. Visual Studio 2010 will automatically detect the dependencies and provide us with the opportunity to include those once we press the Finish button.

As we predicted, we next get a warning that our list has some dependencies that weren't unchecked and a message that this could lead to a broken solution. Visual Studio has detected all the dependencies that our Addison-Wesley Links list has and now offers to include these as well. Click the Yes button and let Visual Studio include all the dependent objects. Figure 4-36 below shows the Selection Dependency Warning dialog.

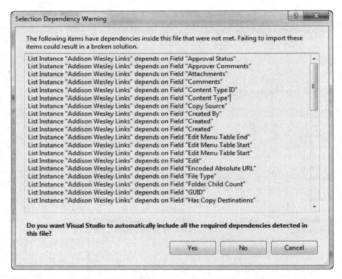

Figure 4-36: Selection Dependency Warning dialog

What Are All These Dependencies?

Our Addison-Wesley Links list seemed simple enough, but there are a ton of dependencies here. What does it all mean? As we examine the list of dependencies Visual Studio displays in Figure 4-36, you will see they fall into these categories: Fields and Content Types. Our list uses those fields and

content types. Visual Studio detects all the dependencies and provides us
with the opportunity to include all of them. That is useful if we don't know
the target system and want to ensure that all the fields or content types our
list uses exist on the target system.

After the import completes, Visual Studio creates a project that contains
our list and all the items it depends on as shown in Figure 4-37. Now we
can add other SharePoint project items to this project and create a new
solution that uses the imported list.

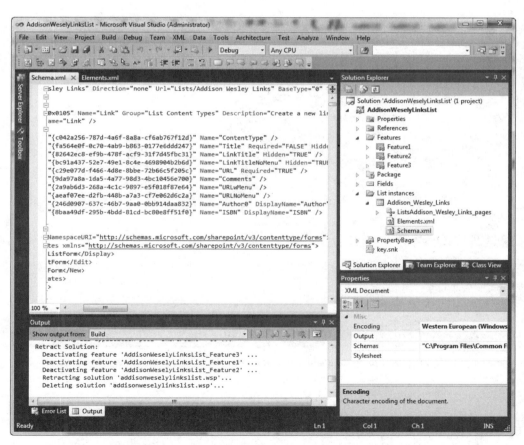

Figure 4-37: A Visual Studio Project that contains the Addison-Wesley Links list instance
definition and detected dependencies

Creating List Definitions and Instances Using Visual Studio 2010

As we have seen SharePoint Designer is a really great RAD (rapid application development) tool that allows you to create list instances based on templates, but what do you do if there is no template that meets your requirements or your company or customers have so many custom requirements for columns and views that it would require a lot of effort to implement? The answer: build a List Definition.

Let's create a new List Definition in Visual Studio by starting Visual Studio 2010. Select New Project. In the New Project dialog select List Definition. Name it "MyListDefinitionProject" and click the OK button. Figure 4-38 shows the New Project dialog with the List Definition template selected.

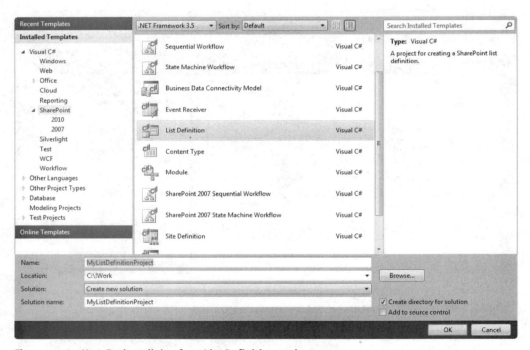

Figure 4-38: New Project dialog for a List Definition project

After you click the OK button to create the List Definition project, the SharePoint Customization Wizard appears. In the text box What local site do you want to use for debugging? enter "http://localhost." Set the trust level to Deploy as farm solution and click the Next button.

So Can I Create a List Definition in a Sandboxed Solution?

The answer is Yes. Sandboxed solutions allow list templates or list defini-tions to be created and deployed as part of the solution.

The next wizard step lets you set the name and type of the list definition as shown in Figure 4-39. Visual Studio suggests a name based on your project name. Change the name to MyListDefinition. In the drop-down What is the type of the list definition? select Custom List. Leave the check box Add a list instance for this list definition checked. You should usually leave this checked as it makes it easier to test your list definition. If you don't check this check box, Visual Studio won't create an instance of your list when you go to debug it, and this will force you to create an instance of the list manually using SharePoint's UI. Click the Finish button to com-plete the creation of the project.

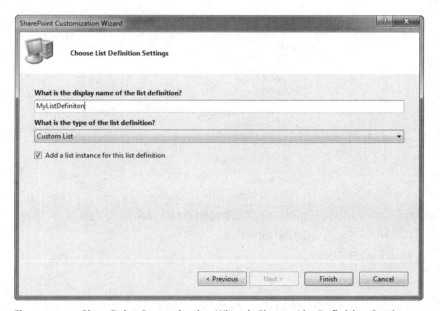

Figure 4-39: SharePoint Customization Wizard: Choose List Definition Settings

Where Did Addison-Wesley Links Go?

When you drop down the drop-down for What is the type of the list definition? our custom list template Addison-Wesley Links is not displayed. Custom list templates deployed to your machine won't be listed in the drop-down because Visual Studio only allows you to create list definitions based on the base list templates deployed to every SharePoint server.

When you click the Finish button, Visual Studio creates all the files needed for a list definition and a list instance and opens the Elements.xml file. Figure 4-40 shows the structure of the project that is created in the Solution Explorer window. The Elements.xml file is a manifest that is used by SharePoint to make the list definition available to SharePoint UI. Important attributes of the Elements.xml file are shown in Table 4-6.

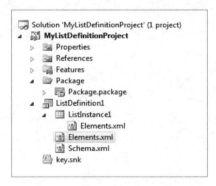

Figure 4-40: The project created for a list definition

TABLE 4-6: Elements.xml Attributes for List Definitions

Attribute	Description
Name	The name of the list template: by default the name is always ListDefinition1. If you want to change the name of a list definition, rename the list definition folder in the Solutions Explorer. Visual Studio will update the Elements.xml file. (Note: If you change the name directly in the XML you need to manually update the name of the folder associated with the list definition).
Type	Provides a unique identifier for the list definition. Visual Studio sets this value to 10000. You should always keep the value between 10000 and 10099 as those values are not taken by other templates. If there is already a list definition of the type you provided for your list you will get an error indicating that there is already a list definition of that type in SharePoint.
BaseType	Defines the default schema for lists created from this schema; Visual Studio defaults to use base types whose value will always be 0, which are generic lists. Below is a list of all the list base types: 0 (Generic List) 1 (Document Library) 3 (Discussion Forum) 4 (Survey) 5 (Issues List)
OnQuickLaunch	If set to True list instances created from this list definition will show up in the QuickLaunch bar in SharePoint.
SecurityBits	A two-digit string that defines the item level permissions in the list; Visual Studio sets it to 11, which means that users with sufficient permissions can read and edit list items.
Sequence	Sequence specifies the ordering priority to use for the list template on the Create page. If you want to order your template differently on the Create page, you can increase or decrease this number to move it relative to other list definitions you have developed.
DisplayName	This is the name you entered in wizard step "Choose List Definition Settings" to represent the display name of the list definition.
Description	Description of the list definition.
Image	URL to an icon to represent the list; ITGEN.png is the default icon for lists.

Let's see how we can edit the Elements.xml file. First, rename the list definition by right clicking the project item folder ListDefinition1 in the Solution Explorer and selecting Rename in the context menu. Rename the folder to MyListDefinition. Visual Studio will automatically update the Name attribute in Elements.xml.

If we deployed the list definition right now, instances of this list definition would look like a standard custom list. To change that, we will need to modify the Schema.xml file. The Schema.xml file contains the actual definition of our list in CAML. Open the Schema.xml file by double clicking the file in the Solution Explorer window. It doesn't make much sense to create a list definition without also creating a new content type, so we will add XML to Schema.xml that will define a new content type to be used by our list. The content type we will add defines asset items that can be used for an inventory list.

In the Schema.xml file locate the <ContentTypes> element and replace the <ContentTypeRef> element and its contents with the XML shown in Listing 4-1. The content type defines a Title field, an AssetCost field, an AssetCategory field, an AssetCount field, and an AssetTag field.

Listing 4-1: CAML for the Content Type Asset Items

```
<ContentType
  ID="0x0100247971ABF81E4ac9B96C7C6287D18774"
  Name="Asset Items"
  Group="Sample Content Types"
  Description="Asset item content type."
  Version="0">
  <FieldRefs>
    <FieldRef
      ID="{fa564e0f-0c70-4ab9-b863-0177e6ddd247}"
      Name="Title"
      Required="TRUE"
      DisplayName ="Description"/>
    <FieldRef
      ID="{76B3E608-4ED1-4F8F-ADFE-95AE9CCF438E}"
      Name="AssetCost"
      Required="TRUE"
      ShowInNewForm="TRUE"
      ShowInEditForm="TRUE"/>
    <FieldRef
      ID="{8E6C31CE-0BE3-4BB9-A763-A33554D6DCA4}"
      Name="AssetCategory"
```

```
         Required="TRUE"
         ShowInNewForm="TRUE"
         ShowInEditForm="TRUE"/>
      <FieldRef
        ID="{B1428D3B-7F1D-479C-9029-731D9BC96935}"
        Name="AssetCount"
        Required="TRUE"
        ShowInNewForm="TRUE"
        ShowInEditForm="TRUE"/>
      <FieldRef
        ID="{995C00C3-EABF-49CB-9967-D7A30A9E3D45}"
        Name="AssetTag"
        Required="TRUE"
        ShowInNewForm="TRUE"
        ShowInEditForm="TRUE"/>
    </FieldRefs>
</ContentType>
```

Now locate the <Fields> element in your Schema.xml file and add within the Fields element the XML shown in Listing 4-2. Note that there are foreign key relationships between these Field IDs and the FieldRef IDs from the content type.

Listing 4-2: CAML to Define the Fields in the List Definition

```
<Field ID="{76B3E608-4ED1-4F8F-ADFE-95AE9CCF438E}"
   DisplayName="Cost"
   Type="Number"
   Required="TRUE"
   StaticName="AssetCost"
   Name="AssetCost"
   SourceID="http://schemas.microsoft.com/sharepoint/v3">
<Field ID="{8E6C31CE-0BE3-4BB9-A763-A33554D6DCA4}"
   DisplayName="Category"
   Type="Choice"
   Required="TRUE"
   StaticName="AssetCategory"
   Name="AssetCategory"
   SourceID="http://schemas.microsoft.com/sharepoint/v3">
   <CHOICES>
     <CHOICE>Books</CHOICE>
     <CHOICE>Computers</CHOICE>
     <CHOICE>Other</CHOICE>
   </CHOICES>
</Field>
<Field ID="{B1428D3B-7F1D-479C-9029-731D9BC96935}"
   DisplayName="Items in Stock"
   Type="Number"
```

```
   Required="TRUE"
   StaticName="AssetCount"
   Name="AssetCount"
   SourceID="http://schemas.microsoft.com/sharepoint/v3" />
<Field ID ="{995C00C3-EABF-49CB-9967-D7A30A9E3D45}"
   DisplayName ="Asset Tag"
   Type = "Text"
   Required ="TRUE"
   StaticName ="AssetTag"
   Name ="AssetTag"
   SourceID ="http://schemas.microsoft.com/sharepoint/v3"/>
```

The last thing we need to do is to add the fields to be displayed to the two <ViewFields> elements in the Schema.xml. The ViewFields element defines which fields are displayed in a view, for example the view that is shown when you want to create a new list item. Locate both ViewFields elements and add the XML shown in Listing 4-3.

Listing 4-3: CAML for the Fields to be Added to the ‹ViewFields› Elements

```
<FieldRef Name="AssetCost" />
<FieldRef Name="AssetCategory" />
<FieldRef Name="AssetCount" />
<FieldRef Name="AssetTag" />
```

You Lost Me at CAML

In this section we have started to introduce CAML. It may seem like a bunch of magic XML that Listings 4-1 through 4-3 ask you to paste into your Schema.xml file. "OK, I can cut and paste," you say, "but how am I supposed to build my own custom CAML?" This is one of the greatest weaknesses right now of the Visual Studio support for SharePoint—there are no visual designers for lists and other key CAML-based SharePoint items. So how do you figure out how to edit these CAML-based files? There are several answers, none of which are entirely satisfying. First, you can read the SharePoint documentation for how you define a list in CAML. Second, you can steal CAML code—for example, in the first section of this chapter, we created a list in SharePoint Designer, exported the site as a .WSP file, then imported it into Visual Studio. If you look at the Schema.xml file created in that project, you can track down the XML that you would need to put in other custom list definitions to create a field such as the Author field. In the future, we hope third parties and Microsoft create a good visual design experience for list definitions so the CAML in this chapter can go away.

Our list definition, MyListDefinition, is now ready to be used, but before we deploy the list definition let's look at the list instance that was created for us by Visual Studio. In the Solution Explorer window, expand the node ListInstance1. Double click on the Elements.xml file below List-Instance1. This Elements.xml file is the manifest that tells SharePoint how to create an instance of our list. Table 4-7 shows the attributes used in the list instance Elements.xml file.

TABLE 4-7: Elements.xml Attributes for List Instances

Attribute	Description
Title	The title of the list instance; by default the title is always "ProjectName – ListDefinition1." If you want to change the title of the list instance, rename the project item folder that parents Elements.xml in the Solution Explorer. Visual Studio will update Elements.xml automatically. (Note: If you change the name in Elements.xml directly you will need to manually update the list instance project item folder manually.)
OnQuickLaunch	Sets whether the list instance will show up in the Quick-Launch bar in SharePoint.
TemplateType	TemplateType corresponds to the type attribute of the list definition's Schema.xml file. If you change the type in the list definition's Schema.xml file you need to update the TemplateType property in this file to match.
Url	The URL by which the list instance can be accessed.
Description	Description of the list instance.

To finish up our first list definition and list instance created with Visual Studio, rename the list instance folder in Solution Explorer by right clicking on the ListInstance1 project item folder and selecting Rename in the context menu. Rename the list instance to AssetList. Hit F5 to deploy the list definition and instance to SharePoint. The list instance MyListDefinitionProject-AssetList is added to the SharePoint site as shown in Figure 4-41.

Figure 4-41: MyListDefinition - AssetList in the browser

Now we can add items to the list by clicking the Items tab under List Tools in the SharePoint ribbon. Select New Item. Enter SharePoint 2010 Development with Visual Studio 2010 as a description and $50 for the cost. Select Books in the Category drop-down; enter 1 for Items in Stock and ISBN-13: 9780321718310 as the Asset Tag. Figure 4-42 shows the New Item dialog.

Adding a List Instance to an Existing Project

We've seen how to add a list instance by checking the Add a list instance for this list definition in the SharePoint Customization Wizard that is dis-

Figure 4-42: AssetList create New Item dialog

played when you create a new List Instance project. Let's also look at how to add a new list definition to an existing project.

We will add a new list instance to our existing MyListDefinition project. In Solution Explorer right click on the MyListDefinition project node, and in the context menu select Add and then New Item. In the Add New Item dialog select List Instance and name it MyAssetItems and click the Add button. Visual Studio contacts SharePoint to receive information on which lists are available. As shown in Figure 4-43 the SharePoint Customization Wizard comes up to allow you to enter information for the list instance you want to create.

To define our new list instance, we first need to enter the display name to be used for the list instance. Visual Studio prepopulates the name and other fields in the wizard—these values are similar to what we got when we allowed Visual Studio to create a list instance along with our list definition. The main difference is that we can now select a list definition for the instance. The drop-down Which list do you want to instantiate? lists all the list definitions available on your development machine. Because we have a list definition in our project already, Visual Studio sets the list definition to be used to the list definition in the project, in our case MyListDefinition\MyListDefinition. In the Description field enter "List Instance added to a project" and click the Finish button. The Elements.xml of the new list

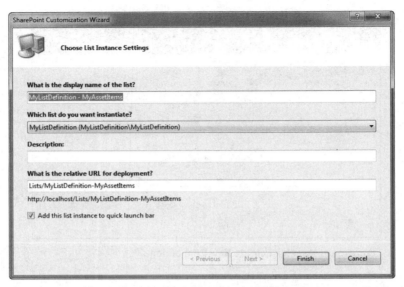

Figure 4-43: SharePoint Customization Wizard—Choose List Instance Settings

instance is opened in Visual Studio's XML editor. Figure 4-44 shows Visual Studio after the new list instance is added to the project.

List Definitions in the Current Project versus List Definitions in the Local Debugging Site

When the list instance wizard shown in Figure 4-43 is shown, it displays: Which list do you want to instantiate? It is asking you to choose the list definition to instantiate from the list definitions installed in the local SharePoint debugging site and the list definitions in the current project. Be careful that you don't add a dependency to a list definition that won't be available on your final production site. Make sure you pick a stock list definition that is available to all SharePoint sites, or even better, pick a list definition that is defined by the current project rather than in the current debugging site. In this case, we pick MyListDefinition (MyListDefinition\ MyListDefinition). The information in parentheses tells us that the list definition is part of the current project and not the local debugging site.

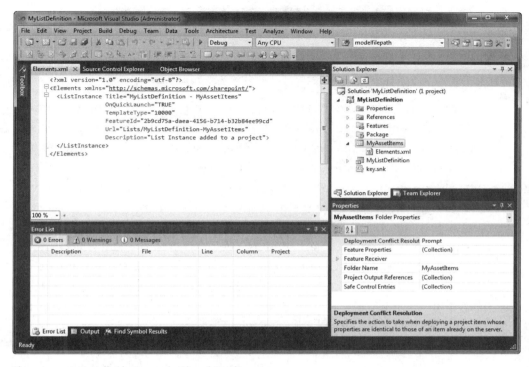

Figure 4-44: New list instance in Visual Studio

You can deploy the new list instance by hitting F5 or by right clicking on the solution and selecting Deploy in the context menu.

New List Definitions from Existing Content Types

Visual Studio also allows us to create a list definition from an existing content type, which we will discuss in Chapter 7, "SharePoint Content Types."

So far in this chapter we have seen how to create list instances using SharePoint Designer as well as how to create list definitions and list instances using Visual Studio. Although Visual Studio doesn't offer a visual designer it is the only tool that allows us to create list definitions. Next let's look into how lists can be created programmatically using SharePoint's object model.

Creating Lists Programmatically

In some situations you might want to create list instances programmatically, for example, you may develop a .NET application that adds lists to SharePoint, or you may have some business logic running on the SharePoint server that creates a new list instance based on certain conditions. SharePoint Foundation offers two types of object models to interact with SharePoint sites, the server-side object model (Microsoft.SharePoint.dll) and the client-side object model. The client-side object model actually consists of three separate object models: the .NET-based client object model (Microsoft.SharePoint.Client.dll), which is used by applications written in .NET 3.5 or later; the Silverlight client object model (Microsoft.SharePoint. Silverlight.Client.dll), which is used in Silverlight applications; and the ECMAScript object model, which is used in browser applications.

As we shall see, all of the object models allow you to create lists and list items, but let's look into when to use which object model. Each client object model provides a subset of the server object model, which means that not all objects accessible through the server object model are available in the client object model. For example, objects that are higher than site-collection level, such as web application and farm objects in the SharePoint object model hierarchy, cannot be accessed through the client object models. This makes sense if we think about security and performance. Also the client object models are intentionally kept small for Silverlight and ECMAScript to allow fast loading of the object models at runtime.

So when should we use the server side object model? The recommendation is that you use it whenever you build an application or an application page that is hosted within SharePoint and running on the SharePoint server. You also need to use it if you want to access list information across site collections because the client object models only work in the site collection in which the calling application is hosted.

Beware the .NET 3.5 Framework Client Profile

You cannot use the .NET 3.5 Framework Client profile (a subset of the full .NET Framework 3.5 SP1 that targets client applications, such as WPF, WCF, Windows Forms and Console applications) with the client-side SharePoint object models because the SharePoint client libraries have a reference to System.Web, which is not part of the Client Profile subset.

The Server-Side Object Model

Let's build an application page (see Chapter 10, "SharePoint Pages," for more information on application pages) that allows a user to select a site collection and create a list for a selected site within the site collection based on the user input. An application page is a page developed using ASP.NET that sits within the SharePoint URL hierarchy and interacts with the SharePoint server-side object models. You typically create an application page when you want to create some very custom UI that displays within SharePoint but doesn't need to be customized by each individual user because application pages don't support per-user customization. If you need per-user customizations, you should create a web part instead as described in Chapter 9, "SharePoint Web Parts."

Open Visual Studio 2010 and select New Project. In the New Project dialog navigate to SharePoint under Installed Templates and select 2010. Create an Empty SharePoint project and name it "ListwithServerOm." Click the OK button. In the SharePoint Wizard select Deploy as Farm Solution and click the Finish button. Once the project is created go to the Solution Explorer and right click on the project node to bring up the context menu. In the context menu select Add and then New Item. The Add New Item dialog comes up. Select Application Page. Figure 4-45 shows the Add New Item Dialog.

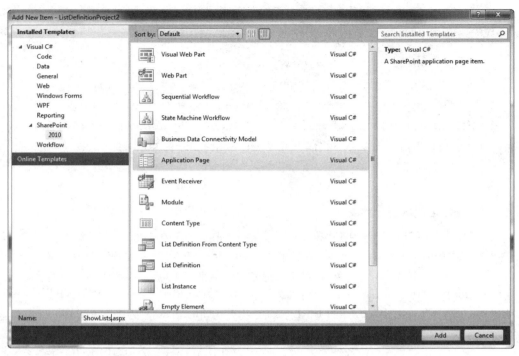

Figure 4-45: Add New Item dialog

What about Application Pages with Sandboxed Solutions?

Forget about it. Application pages are not available to sandboxed solutions.

Name the application page ShowLists.aspx. Visual Studio creates the application page and opens the Source View of the application page. Unfortunately, Visual Studio does not support a WYSIWYG Design View for application pages, so we need to edit the .ASPX file directly. Locate the placeholder with the ContentPlaceHolderID property "PlaceHolderMain." Open the Visual Studio Toolbox by either using the shortcut CTRL+ALT+ X or by using the View menu and selecting Toolbox. Drag a DropDown-List control into the placeholder area and rename it from DropDownList1 to cboSiteCollections. The drop-down will list the site collections in your environment. Drag another DropDownList control to the placeholder and name it cboWebs. It will show the available webs that can be used for creating a new list. Then we need a TextBox control to enter the list name for the list we want to create; name it txtListName.

Finally we need to add a Button control to use its event handler to implement the code for the list creation. Change the button's ID property to btnClick and its Text property to "Create List." Now we need to add a new property that points to the event handler in the code. To do that, place your cursor after the "Create List" in the button element and type "onClick." While typing "onClick" Visual Studio's IntelliSense prompts you to complete the attribute. Enter "btnClick_Click" as the value of the onClick property.

In content tags for the placeholder PageTitle change the string "Application page" to "Create List." This will change the title of the page. The last thing we need to do is to change the page title in the title area. Locate the content tags for the placeholder PageTitleInTitleArea and replace the string "My Application Page" with "List Creation Page." Listing 4-4 shows the content placeholders after editing.

Listing 4-4: Main Placeholder with DropDownList

```
<asp:Content ID="PageHead" ContentPlaceHolderID="PlaceHolderAdditionalPageHead"
  runat="server">
</asp:Content>

<asp:Content ID="Main" ContentPlaceHolderID="PlaceHolderMain" runat="server">
  <asp:DropDownList ID="cboSiteCollections" runat="server">
  </asp:DropDownList>
  <asp:DropDownList ID="cboWebs" runat="server">
  </asp:DropDownList>
  <asp:TextBox ID="txtListName" runat="server"></asp:TextBox><asp:Button
    ID="btnClick" runat="server" Text="Create List" onClick="btnClick_Click" />
</asp:Content>

<asp:Content ID="PageTitle" ContentPlaceHolderID="PlaceHolderPageTitle"
  runat="server">
Create List
</asp:Content>

<asp:Content ID="PageTitleInTitleArea"
  ContentPlaceHolderID="PlaceHolderPageTitleInTitleArea" runat="server" >
List Creation Page
</asp:Content>
```

You Lost Me at ASPX

Yes, it is quite disappointing that Visual Studio doesn't support a WYSI-WYG design view for application pages. If you don't know ASP.NET, Listing 4-4 can be quite disconcerting. To start to learn ASP.NET, check out the ASP.NET web site for some great tutorials and http://asp.net.

Now that we have finished the design of our application page we can go ahead and start implementing the logic. Right click anywhere in the Source View window where we've been editing the ASPX file and select View Code as shown in Figure 4-46.

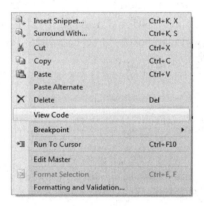

Figure 4-46: Context menu with
View Code item

The code editor shows the code behind our application page that runs when the page is opened. The first thing we need to do is to add a using directive. Add the following using statement to the top of the code behind file:

```
using Microsoft.SharePoint.Administration;
```

The Administration namespace is part of the assembly Microsoft.SharePoint, which contains the implementation of the server-side object model.

Each Visual Studio SharePoint project has this assembly referenced by default.

Next, we need to implement an event handler for the button control. Add the empty event handler shown in Listing 4-5 to the class ShowLists.

Listing 4-5: Empty Event Handler for button btnClick

```
public void btnClick_Click(object sender, EventArgs e)
{
}
```

Now we can start writing the code to enumerate site collections and sites and eventually add them to the drop-down boxes. Listing 4-6 shows the code that enumerates the site collections and adds all sites available in the site collection selected to the drop-down. First we create a Farm object that represents our local SharePoint installations. Then we implement code in the Page_Load event to iterate through all the web applications in our farm as the site collections might be defined under different web applications. Objects of the class SPWebApplication class represent web applications in a SharePoint Farm. Finally we iterate through all the site collections in a web application and add their URLs to our drop-down box cboSiteCollections by obtaining an object of type SPSite, which represents a site collection in a SharePoint environment. What we have implemented so far can only be done through the server-side object model; site collection objects are not available in the client-side object models.

Now that we have our site collection objects, we need to implement the code that iterates through the sites available using objects of the SPWeb class. At the end of the Page_Load event we call the method GetWebs, which takes the site collection URL as a parameter. The method first creates a new site collection object for the site URL specified. Note that the SPSite and SPWeb objects implement the IDisposable interface. To dispose of the object correctly we employ the using statement. We iterate through all the webs available by creating objects of the SPWeb class and adding their URL properties as items to the drop-down control cboWebs.

Yes, the Object Model Naming is Confusing

SPSite should be an object that represents a SharePoint site. Actually it is an object that represents a SharePoint Site Collection. SPWeb is the object that represents a SharePoint site. This is because of naming changes that occurred in later versions of SharePoint. Renaming these objects in the object model to reflect the new nomenclature would break all existing SharePoint code.

Therefore, you must train your brain to see "site collection" when it sees "Site" in the object model and "site" when it sees "Web." Also, rather than fight this, we name methods "GetWebs" to reflect the object model naming and declare local variables holding an SPWeb object web. Keep doing the mental search-and-replace of Site for SiteCollection and Site for Web.

Listing 4-6: Code for Adding All Site Collections and Web Sites in a Farm to Drop-Down Lists

```
public partial class ShowLists : LayoutsPageBase
{
  SPFarm farm = SPFarm.Local;

  protected void Page_Load(object sender, EventArgs e)
  {
    if (!Page.IsPostBack)
    {
      SPWebService service = farm.Services.GetValue<SPWebService>("");
      foreach (SPWebApplication webapp in service.WebApplications)
      {
        foreach (SPSite site in webapp.Sites)
        {
          string url = site.Url;
          cboSiteCollections.Items.Add(url);
        }
        cboSiteCollections.Items[0].Selected = true;
        GetWebs(cboSiteCollections.SelectedItem.ToString());
      }
    }
  }
  private void GetWebs(string siteCollectionUrl)
  {
```

```
    using (SPSite siteselected = new SPSite(siteCollectionUrl))
    {
      foreach (SPWeb web in siteselected.AllWebs)
      {
        try
        {
          string url = web.Url;
          string name = web.Name;
          System.Web.UI.WebControls.ListItem item = new
            System.Web.UI.WebControls.ListItem(url,name);
          cboWebs.Items.Add(item);
        }
        finally
        {
          if(web != null)
            web.Dispose();
        }
      }
      cboWebs.Items[0].Selected = true;
    }
  }
  public void btnClick_Click(object sender, EventArgs e)
  {
  }
}
```

Listing 4-7 shows the code to fill in our previously empty handler btnClick_Click that creates a new list. Before creating the list we need to get the right site collection to create the list under by instantiating a new object of the SPSite class and pass the site collection selected in constructor of the SPSite class. As we want to be able to create the list under all sites listed in the drop-down control cboWebs we need to create an SPWebCollection object that has all sites in the site collection. Now we can create an SPWeb object that represents the site under which we want to create the list.

We also need to check if a list with the same name already exists. We do that by enumerating the lists in the site and comparing the list title with the name the user input for the new list. If there is no such list, the list object will be null and we can add the new list by using the Add method of the Lists collection in the web object. The first parameter is the list title, the second one the description, and the third one the list type. The SPListTemplate-Type enum contains all the list templates available.

Once the list is added to the site we use the GUID returned by the Add method to assign our new list to the list object and set the OnQuickLaunch property to True. Finally we call the Update method to save the changes to the content database.

Listing 4-7: Create New List Using Server Object Model

```
public void btnClick_Click(object sender, EventArgs e)
{
  using(SPSite site = new SPSite(cboSiteCollections.
                      SelectedItem.ToString()))
  {
    SPWebCollection webs = site.AllWebs;
    using (SPWeb web = webs[cboWebs.SelectedValue])
    {
      SPList list = null;
      foreach (SPList currentList in web.Lists)
      {
        if (currentList.Title == txtListName.Text)
        {
          list = currentList;
          break;
        }
      }
      if (list == null)
      {
        Guid listID = web.Lists.Add(txtListName.Text,
                    "List created by server om",
                    SPListTemplateType.Links);
        list = web.Lists[listID];
        list.OnQuickLaunch = true;
        list.Update();
      }
    }
  }
}
```

Let's see if the code works. In the Solution Explorer right click on ShowLists.aspx and select Set as Startup Item. Figure 4-47 shows the context menu.

Now hit F5 to bring up the application page in debug mode. Figure 4-48 shows the application page with the site collection drop-down and the sites drop-down. The sites drop-down has two entries because there are two sites in this site collection.

Figure 4-47: Set as Startup Item context menu

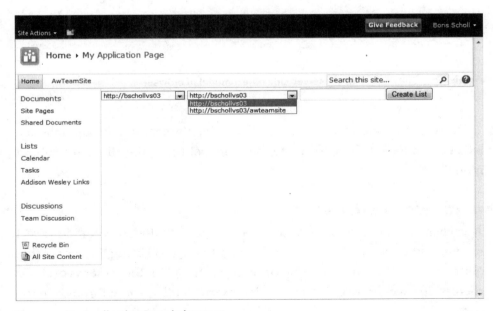

Figure 4-48: Application Page in browser

In the text box enter "Server OM List" as the name for the list, and click the Create List button. Refresh the page by using the CTRL+F5 keys on your keyboard (which will also clear the browser cache). In the left navigation bar click on Server OM List to bring up the list we just created as shown in Figure 4-49.

Figure 4-49: List created using server-side object model in browser

Now that we know how to create lists using the server-side object model, let's have a look at how to create the same list using the client-side object model.

The Client-Side Object Model

The client-side object models are consistent with the server-side object model, so the code looks somewhat similar to the code using the server-side object model. There are some big differences though in the patterns used for client-side execution versus server-side execution that show through in the code.

Let's start our exploration of creating lists using the client-object model by creating the same list that we've built before using the server-side model. Open Visual Studio 2010 and create a new Windows application by clicking File, New, Project. Select Windows and chose a Windows Forms Application. Name the application "ListWithClientOm" and click the Create button. In the Toolbox expand the section All Windows Forms, and drag a new TextBox control onto the form and name it txtSite. Keep in mind that we don't have access to the SPWebApplication object in the client-side object model, so we can't enumerate all the available site collections on the server. Instead, we'll require that the user enters the URL manually for the site collection.

Now drag another TextBox onto the form and change its Name property to txtListName. Finally we need to add a Button control. Change its Name property to btnClick and its Text property to Create List. Figure 4-50 shows the resulting Windows Form.

Figure 4-50: Windows User input form

Before we can implement the code that creates the list we need to reference the two assemblies that are required to develop against the client-side object model. As shown in Figure 4-51 right click on the References folder in the Solution Explorer and select Add Reference.

In the Add Reference dialog select the Browse tab and browse to c:\Program Files\Common Files\Microsoft Shared\Web Server Extensions\14\ISAPI. Select Microsoft.SharePoint.Client.dll and Microsoft.SharePoint.Client.Runtime.dll as shown in Figure 4-52, and click the OK button.

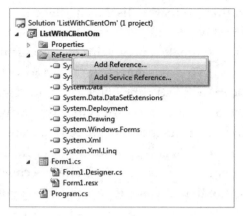

Figure 4-51: Add Reference

Figure 4-52: Add Reference Dialog—Selecting Client
Object Model Assemblies

Double click on the button Create List in the Windows Forms designer
to create the event handler in the code editor. We need to add two using
directives to access the client object model. To avoid ambiguous references
add the following statement to the other using directives:

```
using ClientOM = Microsoft.SharePoint.Client;
using Microsoft.SharePoint.Client;
```

We need to use the fully qualified names for the Form class from which our class Form1 derives because there is a conflicting Form type in the Microsoft.SharePoint.Client namespace. Rewrite the class definition from

```
public partial class Form1: Form
```

to

```
public partial class Form1: System.Windows.Forms.Form
```

Now we can add the code to the event handler for the Create List button to create a new list. Listing 4-8 shows the code for creating a new list using the client-side object model. As we've done in our server-side sample, we first check if the list already exists. To do this, we need to create a new ClientContext object. The ClientContext object serves as the main entry point for accessing the client object model. In addition it is used to access site collections or sites and their dependent client objects. By default the client-side object model uses Windows authentication, which means that the user who executes the client application needs to have sufficient permissions on the target SharePoint site. If your SharePoint server is using forms authentication you need to set the AuthenticationMode property of the ClientContext object to ClientAuthenticationMode.Forms-Authentication. The ClientContext constructor initializes a context either for a site collection or a site. In our case we pass in the value of the textbox txtSite, which can either be the URL to a site collection or a site.

Next we create an object representing the SharePoint site under which we want to create the list. Creating the Web object is pretty much identical to what we had to do when using the server-side object model—and yes, it is still called a Web object, although the SP has been mercifully dropped.

The next part of the code is very different to the code we wrote on the server to check if there is already a list with the same name. First we create a ListCollection object to store all the lists defined in the web site. Next, we create a new variable to store the new list name entered by the user. To store the result of the method `LoadQuery` of the `clientContext` object we define a new collection `resultCollection` of type IEnumerable<List>. Then we use the LINQ query expression syntax `collList.Include` and the

LINQ lambda expressions `list => list.Title,list => list.Id` to only return the list properties Title and ID. Because we only want to check if there is a list with the same title we don't need to return all the data for a list and slow down the performance of the query. The last part of the query applies the condition for the list title.

After we have loaded the collection into the context object we need to execute the query against the site by using `clientContext.ExecuteQuery()`. Calling either the Load(…) or LoadQuery(...) method and calling the Execute-Query() method on the ClientContext object always has to be done before you can access value properties. That's the biggest difference to the server-side object model.

Why Isn't the Client Object Model Just Like the Server Object Model?

If you think about this for a second, you'll probably figure it out. The main difference is that the server object model is designed for code that is running on the server in the same process as the SharePoint server. The client object model is designed for code that is running out of process from the SharePoint server typically on a different machine. So the client object model is designed to batch up requests and actions so that it can minimize the traffic over the wire from the machine using the client object model to the SharePoint server servicing the requests.

Next we check if there is a list object in the collection and if not we use the ListCreationInformation object to assign the values for the new list (Listing 4-8). Finally we need to call the ExecuteQuery method again to persist the newly created list in the database.

Listing 4-8: Creating a New List Using Client Object Model

```
public void btnClick_Click(object sender, EventArgs e)
{
  ClientContext clientContext = new ClientContext(txtSite.Text);
  Web webSite = clientContext.Web;
```

```
ListCollection collList = webSite.Lists;
string listName = txtListName.Text;

IEnumerable<ClientOM.List> resultCollection =
                clientContext.LoadQuery(
                collList.Include(
                list => list.Title,
                list => list.Id).Where(list =>
                list.Title == listName));
clientContext.ExecuteQuery();

int i = resultCollection.Count();
if (i == 0)
{
  ListCreationInformation listCreationInfo = new
    ListCreationInformation();
  listCreationInfo.Title = txtListName.Text;
  listCreationInfo.TemplateType = (int)ListTemplateType.Links;
  listCreationInfo.QuickLaunchOption = QuickLaunchOptions.On;
  List newList = webSite.Lists.Add(listCreationInfo);
  clientContext.ExecuteQuery();
}
}
```

Now we can test our Windows Application. Hit F5 to run the application. In the form that comes up enter "http://localhost" as the site name in the top textbox to create the new list under the default site. In the bottom textbox, enter "Client OM List" as the name for the list we want to create, and click the Create List button. Figure 4-53 shows the form with the data added.

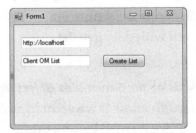

Figure 4-53: Form for creating a new list

Now the new list should be available. Open the browser and go to your SharePoint homepage. The new list is available in the quick launch section on the left hand side of the page. Figure 4-54 shows the new list.

Figure 4-54: List created with Client OM

Programmatically Modifying Data in Lists

Now that we know how to programmatically create lists and how to use the client and server object models, we can start looking at how to create, read, update, and delete items in a list. Again we will first look at how to do this with the server-side object model and then how to use the client-side object model to work with list items. Finally, we will look at using LINQ to SharePoint to work with data in a list.

Working with Items in a List Using the Server-side Object Model

The very first thing we need to know if we want to add items to a list is, of course, the list name. But as we learned before, lists are children of a SharePoint site (the SPWeb object), so we also need to know in advance which site the list is a child of before we can add items to it. That means our first task is to create an SPWeb object. Once we have an SPWeb object we can use either the GetList() method or the Lists[] collection of the SPWeb object to access the list.

There are two approaches we can choose when creating SPWeb objects depending on the context the code runs in. In an ASP.NET application, information about the current application, each user session, the current HTTP request, the requested page, etc., is stored in the HTTP context object. The first approach takes advantage of the HTTP context object. Within a SharePoint HTTP context we can use the Microsoft.SharePoint. SPContext class to obtain information for the current application, such as the current site collection, the current SharePoint site or list object if the application that needs to access the object is in the same context. That means your application has to be in the same HTTP context when you want to create an SPWeb based on the SPContext class. Note that SPSite and SPWeb objects returned by SPContext.Site, SPContext.Current.Site, SPContext.Web, and SPContext .Current.Web do not need to be disposed as SPContext objects are managed by the SharePoint framework. (See more about dispose patterns in Chapter 3, "Introduction to the SharePoint Object Model.")

For example, code we wrote in the application page we created earlier in this chapter can access the root site as an SPWeb object using the code such as `SPWeb web = SPContext.Current.Web` because it is in the same HTTP context as the root SharePoint site.

That works fine if we want to access a list in the same site in which our code is running. But if we want to access a list under a different SharePoint site in the same site collection we need to go up to the site collection object first and call either the OpenWeb() method or use the AllWebs[] collection to return the desired SPWeb object for the SharePoint site we are interested in. Listing 4-9 shows how to obtain an SPWeb object from an SPContext class using the OpenWeb() method and the AllWebs[] collection. As you can see, using the AllWebs collection has the advantage that you need only know the name of the site, not the entire URL. This code could be used in the Page_Load event of the application page we created earlier in this chapter.

Listing 4-9: Obtaining an SPWeb object from an SPContext

```
SPSite siteCollection = SPContext.Current.Site
using (SPWeb webSite =
  siteCollection.OpenWeb("http://localhost/mysubweb"))
{
  // Use webSite variable here to access lists in mysubweb
}

SPSite siteCollection = SPContext.Current.Site
using (SPWeb webSite = siteCollection.AllWebs["MyWebSite"])
{
  // Use webSite variable here to access lists in MyWebSite
}
```

The second option is to use the SPSite constructor to instantiate an object representing the site collection with which you want to work. This option can be used if you are calling objects in a different site collection from the one in which the running code is or you are writing code somewhere that has no access to an HTTP context, e.g., a Windows application. You can refer to Listing 4-7 to see how to use the SPSite object's constructor.

Once we have obtained the desired SPWeb object, we can access the list to which we want to add the items. Let's assume there is a list named Budget-List and the list has three columns: Title, Budget, and Usage. (You can easily create such a list by either using SharePoint Designer or the SharePoint UI itself). First we obtain an SPListItemsCollection object by accessing the Items property of the SPWeb's List collection object. The BudgetList list can be easily accessed by using the name indexer for the list collection. Once we have the items collection we can add a new list item. The last thing to do is to assign values to the new list item. This is done by using an indexer on the list item. For example item["Budget"] accesses the budget column in the budget list. Finally we call SPListItem's Update method to persist the new item. Listing 4-10 shows how to add a new item to the BudgetList list.

Listing 4-10: Adding a New List Item Using the Server Object Model

```
SPSite siteCollection = SPContext.Current.Site
using (SPWeb webSite = siteCollection.RootWeb)
{
  SPListItemCollection listItems = webSite.Lists["BudgetList"].Items;
  SPListItem item = listItems.Add();
```

```
  item["Title"] = "New Budget Request";
  item["Budget"] = Convert.ToDouble("5000");
  item["Usage"] = "Morale Fund";
  item.Update();
}
```

What do we need to do if we want to update this newly created item? Of course first we need to find it again in the collection. There are two ways to accomplish this. The first one is iterating through an item collection and comparing the value of each item to some condition to find the item we are interested in. Then we can access the values of each column for the item by using the indexer on the list item. Listing 4-11 shows how to update the Morale Fund item in the BudgetList.

Listing 4-11: Inefficient Code That Updates a List Item Using the Items Collection

```
SPSite siteCollection = SPContext.Current.Site
using (SPWeb webSite = siteCollection.RootWeb)
{
  SPListItemCollection listItems = webSite.Lists["BudgetList"].Items;
  foreach (SPItem item in listItems)
  {
    if ("Morale Fund" == item["Usage"].ToString())
    {
      item["Title"] = "Updated Budget Request";
      item["Budget"] = Convert.ToDouble("5000");
      item.Update();
    }
  }
}
```

Code You Don't Want to Copy

Listing 4-11 has some pretty inefficient code—it illustrates some concepts for iterating a collection, but it would be a very bad idea to copy this code and use it in a live web site as it iterates over every item in a list, which is expensive. We will now see a better way to do this using GetItems() and LINQ to SharePoint later in the chapter.

The second option is to use the GetItems() method on an SPList object. This method uses an SPQuery object to query the list for items that meet a certain condition. You have to build a string containing a CAML query to retrieve the items meeting the condition. The advantage over the first approach is that only items meeting a certain condition are returned, which brings performance improvements by limiting the data returned. Building query strings using CAML is an advanced topic and we won't go too deep into the syntax. The SharePoint SDK is a great place to learn more about this topic.

Listing 4-12 shows code that accomplishes the same item update in Listing 4-11 but much more efficiently. First we create an SPList object representing the BudgetList. Then we create a new SPQuery object and assign a query string to its query property. The query string contains the condition to return all items for which Usage value is equal to "Morale Fund." The items returned by the query are assigned to the listItems collection of type SPListItemCollection. For simplicity we assume there is only one item meeting this criteria, so we can directly access it by accessing the first item in the items collection. After that we can update the Title value again and finally call the Update() method on it to commit the change.

Listing 4-12: Updating a List Item Accessed through SPQuery

```
SPSite siteCollection = SPContext.Current.Site;
using (SPWeb webSite = siteCollection.RootWeb)
{
  SPList list = webSite.Lists["BudgetList"];
  SPQuery query = new SPQuery();
  query.Query = "<Where><Eq><FieldRef Name='Usage'/>
                <Value Type='Text'>
                Morale Fund</Value></Eq></Where>";
  SPListItemCollection listItems = list.GetItems(query);
  SPItem item = listItems[0];
  item["Title"] = "Newly Updated Budget";
  item.Update();
}
```

The last item operation using the server object model is deleting an item. Once you have returned the item you want to delete by one of the methods above you simply can call SPListItem's Delete method.

Working with Items in a List Using the Client-side Object Model

Let's look at how to create, read, update, and delete list items by using the client object model. Again we will focus on the managed .NET Client object model. You can find further information on the ECMA client object model at http://msdn.microsoft.com/sharepoint. We will discuss the Silverlight client object model in Chapter 9, "SharePoint Web Parts," when we discuss Silverlight web parts.

We will reuse our sample BudgetList from the server-side object model samples. The first task we will look at is how to create list items. Keep in mind that the client application needs to reference the assemblies Microsoft. SharePoint.Client and Microsoft.SharePoint.Client.Runtime. Listing 4-13 shows the code that creates a new budget item. First we create a new ClientContext object for the site collection our list is in. Next we get the List object for the BudgetList by using the GetByTitle method on the Lists collection object. Before we can add the new item we need to create a new ListCreationInformation object and set its properties. This object will be passed in as a parameter for the AddItem method on the List object. Finally we call the Update method on the ListItem object and ExecuteQuery on the ClientContext object. Without calling ExecuteQuery nothing would be posted to the server and we couldn't create the item.

Listing 4-13: Creating a New List Item Using Managed Client Object Model

```
string siteUrl = "http://localhost";
ClientContext clientContext = new ClientContext(siteUrl);

List list = clientContext.Web.Lists.GetByTitle("BudgetList");

ListItemCreationInformation itemCreateInfo =
  new ListItemCreationInformation();
ListItem item = list.AddItem(itemCreateInfo);

item["Title"] = "New Budget item!";
item["Budget"] = Convert.ToDouble("10000");
item["Usage"] = "Marketing budget";
item.Update();

clientContext.ExecuteQuery();
```

Updating a list item using the client object model works similarly to the server-side object model. We can either iterate through a list item collection or use a CAML query. Listing 4-14 shows how to update an item that was retrieved by using a CAML query. First we need to create a Client-Context object that passes our top-level site URL into the constructor. Once we have obtained the client context we can get a List object representing the BudgetList by using the GetByTitle method on the Lists collection. Next we need to create a new CamlQuery object that we can pass as a parameter to the GetItems method on the List object.

If we don't define a query and only pass in the object we would get all the items in the list. Because we are looking for one particular item we define the query that returns all the items that have the value "Marketing budget" in the Usage column. A request to SharePoint is made to return the list items defined by the query. We call the Load and ExecuteQuery method on the ClientContext object.

In our case there is only one item meeting these criteria. We can access this item using ListItemCollection's index accessor (collListItem[0]). We can now access the Title column and update the title of the item. Then we need to call item.Update() and eventually the ExecuteQuery method on the ClientContext again to persist the changes to the database.

Listing 4-14: Retrieving and Updating a List Item Using the Client Object Model

```
string siteUrl = "http://localhost";
ClientContext clientContext = new ClientContext(siteUrl);

List list = clientContext.Web.Lists.GetByTitle("BudgetList");

CamlQuery camlQuery = new CamlQuery();
camlQuery.ViewXml = "<View><Query><Where><Eq><FieldRef Name='Usage'/>"+
                    "<Value Type='Text'>Marketing budget</Value>
                    </Eq></Where></Query></View>";
ListItemCollection collListItem = list.GetItems(camlQuery);
clientContext.Load(collListItem);
clientContext.ExecuteQuery();

ListItem item = collListItem[0];
item["Title"] = "Updated budget request";
item.Update();

clientContext.ExecuteQuery();
```

The last operation we need to look at is the deletion of an item. Before we can delete an item we need to retrieve the ListItem for the item we want to delete. We use the same approach we used for updating an item to retrieve the item. Once we have the item we call the ListItem's Delete method on the item. This will delete the item from the database. Listing 4-15 shows the code for deleting an item with the value "Marketing budget" in the Usage column. There is one thing to point out when deleting items. SharePoint maintains the integer IDs of items within collections, even if they have been deleted, which basically means that the ID of items in the list don't necessarily reflect their positions, so it's always a good practice to query items based on other criteria before deleting them.

Listing 4-15: Deleting a List Item Using the Client Object Model

```
string siteUrl = "http://localhost";
ClientContext clientContext = new ClientContext(siteUrl);

List list = clientContext.Web.Lists.GetByTitle("BudgetList");

CamlQuery camlQuery = new CamlQuery();
camlQuery.ViewXml = "<View><Query><Where><Eq><FieldRef Name='Usage'/>"+
                    "<Value Type='Text'>Marketing budget</Value>
                    </Eq></Where></Query></View>";
ListItemCollection collListItem = list.GetItems(camlQuery);
clientContext.Load(collListItem);
clientContext.ExecuteQuery();

ListItem item = collListItem[0];
item.DeleteObject();

clientContext.ExecuteQuery();
```

LINQ to SharePoint–SPLINQ

SharePoint 2010 introduces LINQ to SharePoint also called SPLINQ to query list data. So what exactly is SPLINQ? SPLINQ allows you to write strongly typed queries against lists. If you haven't worked with LINQ you should read *Essential LINQ* published by Addison-Wesley.

Using SPLINQ has a couple of advantages over CAML-based queries. First of all CAML is hard to use because it is an XML-based query language that is unique to SharePoint. This basically means that if you are not familiar with the CAML syntax you need to invest some time to learn it. Secondly CAML offers no compile time validation for the queries as queries are just strings that are used with objects like SPQuery, which means that during compile your query will never be checked for syntax errors. Furthermore, if your syntax is not correct you won't get an error during runtime, the query just won't return any items. That makes it extremely hard to analyze issues caused by faulty CAML-based queries.

To use SPLINQ, we first need to know where to find the list data we want to work with. SharePoint 2010 exposes list data through a REST (Representational State Transfer) service that you can consume in your projects. The underlying technology used by SharePoint to expose list data through REST is called WCF data services. You can find more info on WCF data services here: http://msdn.microsoft.com/en-us/data/bb931106.aspx.

The actual WCF data service that SharePoint provides is called List-Data.svc, and it sits in the _vti_bin directory of the site collection associated with the list in which you want to work with. In a default SharePoint site collection you can access the listdata.svc by entering the URL http://localhost/_vti_bin/listdata.svc. In order to use the service you need to have the ADO.NET client runtime installed on your machine. See Appendix A for more information on how to install the ADO.NET client runtime. Figure 4-55 shows the data returned by the listdata.svc in the browser. If you can't see any data in your own browser, be sure to turn off the feed reading view in your browser. In Internet Explorer go to Internet Options in the Tools menu. In the Internet Options dialog select the content tab and click Settings in the Feeds and Web Slices section. In the Advanced section uncheck Turn on feed reading view.

In order to use the objects returned by the listdata.svc service we need to generate the entity classes for the list objects returned by the service and add those entity classes to the application that is supposed to work with the list data. There are two ways to do that.

The first way is to use SPMetal.exe, which is a command line tool that generates the entity classes that is located in %ProgramFiles%\Common Files\Microsoft Shared\web server extensions\14\BIN. For more information on SPMetal see the SharePoint SDK http://msdn.microsoft.com/en-us/library/ee538255(office.14).aspx.

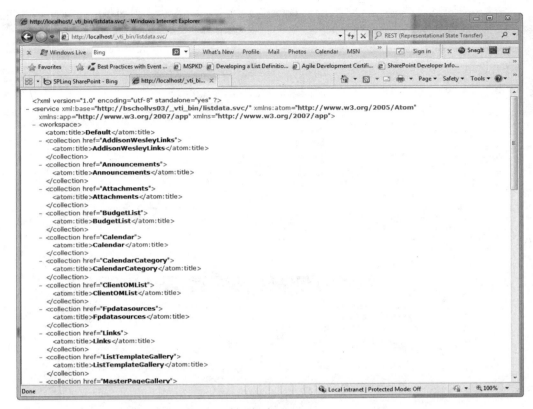

Figure 4-55: Listdata.svc results displayed in the browser

The second way is to use the Add Service Reference feature in Visual Studio 2010. We will use this option throughout this book. Let's build a console application that uses SPLINQ to work with list data. Open Visual Studio 2010 and select New Project. Under Installed Templates select Windows and then Console Application and name the console application "ListDataClient." Once the project is created we need to add a new Service Reference to the listdata.svc service. Right click on the References folder in the Solution Explorer and select Add Service Reference in the context menu. Figure 4-56 shows the context menu of the References folder.

In the dialog enter the URL of the listdata service that we described earlier and click the Go button. Visual Studio now downloads the data returned by the service. Once successfully downloaded, use the Namespace textbox to set a namespace for the entity classes. For this example, we will pick

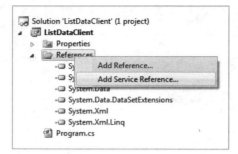

Figure 4-56: Add Service Reference context menu

MyLists. Figure 4-57 shows the dialog after successfully downloading the service data.

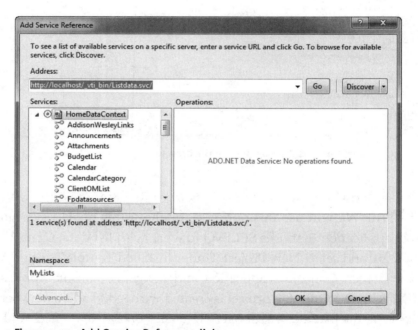

Figure 4-57: Add Service Reference dialog

Click the OK button. In the background Visual Studio adds all the references needed by the ADO.NET data services to the project, creates the entity classes for the lists and adds them as a data source. If you are interested in examining all the entity classes created you can see all the list entity classes created by right clicking MyLists under the Service References folder and selecting View in the Object Browser.

Next we need to manually add a reference to the Microsoft.SharePoint.Linq assembly. Right click on the References folder and select Add Reference. In the Add Reference dialog that appears click the Browse tab and browse to %ProgramFiles%\Common Files\Microsoft Shared\web server extensions\14\\ISAPI; select the Microsoft.SharePoint.Linq assembly. Figure 4-58 shows the dialog with the assembly selected.

Figure 4-58: Add Reference dialog with
Microsoft.SharePoint.Linq selected

Next we need to add two using directives to the project. The first one is System.Net, which we need to access the default credentials in the credential cache. Visual Studio runs under an account that has no rights to do anything but read the list data from the service so we need to pass our credentials to be able to update, create, and delete list data. The second one is the using statement for the Microsoft.SharePoint.Linq assembly. Double click the Application.cs file and add these two statements to the top of the code file:

```
using System.Net;
using Microsoft.SharePoint.Linq;
```

Now we are all set and can start implementing the code. Let's start our SPLINQ exploration by creating a new item in the BudgetList that we have referred to before in this chapter. Listing 4-16 shows the code that creates a new budget item. The first line creates a new DataContext object. The DataContext class allows you to connect to SharePoint, access data, and send changes back to the server. Unlike the context objects we have seen before, the DataContext class is strongly typed (it was generated when we added the service reference) and therefore it knows about the specific lists on the server—for example it has an AddToBudgetList method that is strongly typed to the BudgetList that is available in our site collection. The DataContext class takes the server URL as a parameter of the constructor.

Once we have a new DataContext object we create a new BudgetListItem object—another strongly typed object that was created in the MyLists namespace when we added the service reference. After that, some properties of the BudgetListItem object are set and we can add the budget object to the context by using the AddToBudgetList method, so that it is tracked by the DataContext. Before we can save the chances we need to add the default credentials to the context, so that our program has the permission to create a new item. Finally we call the SaveChanges method to save the new item back to SharePoint.

Listing 4-16: Creating a New Item Using SPLINQ

```
MyLists.HomeDataContext context = new MyLists.HomeDataContext(
  new Uri("http://localhost/_vti_bin/listdata.svc"));

MyLists.BudgetListItem budget = new MyLists.BudgetListItem();

budget.Budget = 20;
budget.Title = "Budget request from LINQ";
budget.Usage = "Buy a LINQ Book";

context.AddToBudgetList(budget);
context.Credentials = CredentialCache.DefaultCredentials;
context.SaveChanges();
```

If you don't have items in the list already run the code a couple of times and update the budget properties for each run. Now that you have a couple of budget items in the list, you can replace the code in your console app that creates a new item with the code shown in Listing 4-17. The first two lines of code are identical to the ones we implemented for creating a new item.

The first line of the code gets the data context object. Then we need to use the default credentials from the credential cache again in order to be able to access the data. In the next line the local variable budgetListItems is initialized with a LINQ query expression returning an IEnumerable of BudgetListItem. The query expression operates on the BudgetList source by applying the select operator. This expression also uses the orderby operator to order the result by Budget.

Lastly we iterate through the collection and print out the values for the Budget, Usage, and Title properties of that item.

Listing 4-17: Retrieving All Items in a List Using SPLINQ

```
MyLists.HomeDataContext context = new MyLists.HomeDataContext(
  new Uri("http://localhost/_vti_bin/listdata.svc"));
context.Credentials = CredentialCache.DefaultCredentials;

IEnumerable<MyLists.BudgetListItem> budgetListItems =
  from b in context.BudgetList
  orderby b.Budget
  select b;

foreach (MyLists.BudgetListItem item in budgetListItems)
{
  Console.WriteLine("{0} {1} {2}", item.Budget, item.Usage,
    item.Title);
}
```

This small sample should give you an idea about how great and easy it is to work with list data using SPLINQ. You want to retrieve items meeting a certain criteria, for example items with a budget greater than $200. You just add a where clause with that condition to the LINQ query. The query will return only the items meeting that criteria. Listing 4-18 shows code that only returns the budget items whose Budget value is $20, updates the value of the first found item to 21, and writes it back to the server. Because we only care that one item meets the criteria we can use the Single() operator to only return one element. Before we can write it back to the store we need to call the UpdateObject method so the data context knows that the object has been modified. This step is needed, otherwise no change would occur on the server.

Listing 4-18: Updating an Item in a List Using SPLINQ

```
MyLists.HomeDataContext context = new MyLists.HomeDataContext(
  new Uri("http://localhost/_vti_bin/listdata.svc"));
context.Credentials = CredentialCache.DefaultCredentials;

MyLists.BudgetListItem item =
  (from b in context.BudgetList
   where b.Budget == 20
   orderby b.Budget
   select b).Single();

item.Budget = 21;
context.UpdateObject(item);
context.SaveChanges();
```

To delete the same item we only need to replace the UpdateObject method with the DeleteObject method as shown in Listing 4-19.

Listing 4-19: Deleting an Item in a List Using SPLINQ

```
MyLists.HomeDataContext context = new MyLists.HomeDataContext(
  new Uri("http://localhost/_vti_bin/listdata.svc"));
context.Credentials = CredentialCache.DefaultCredentials;

MyLists.BudgetListItem item =
  (from b in context.BudgetList
   where b.Budget == 21
   orderby b.Budget
   select b).Single();

context.DeleteObject(item);
context.SaveChanges();
```

In the last four examples we learned how to use SPLINQ to implement basic Create/Read/Update/Delete (CRUD) operations. Of course SPLINQ is much more powerful. You can implement queries across multiple lists with relationships and more. You can find further information on SPLINQ in the SharePoint Software Development Kit (SDK).

List Relationships—What Are Those?

OK, we can't cover everything about SharePoint, the book would be 1500 pages long. But here's a quick idea about list relationships. Think about a list with customers that is the parent list and a list with orders that is the child list. SharePoint allows you to set referential integrity constraints on the child items by specifying a delete behavior. For example, we could enforce that customers who have an order cannot be deleted. List relationships can be defined through the user interface or through the object model using the SPRelatedField class.

Conclusion

In this chapter we looked at creating lists and list templates in SharePoint Designer and creating list instances and list definitions in Visual Studio. Further we discussed how to programmatically create lists using the server object model and the client object model. We also looked into which scenarios should use which object model. We spent the end of the chapter looking into various ways to work with list data itself. We created CRUD samples for list items using the server-side object model, the client-side object model, and LINQ to SharePoint.

■ 5 ■

SharePoint Event Receivers

E vent receivers are used for responding to events raised by SharePoint on lists, features, items, or workflows. This chapter provides an overview of what type of event receivers are supported in Visual Studio 2010, how they work, and how to use them.

Introduction to Event Receivers

Events are part of almost every development project you have ever worked on and SharePoint is no different. Because SharePoint is composed of site collections, sites, lists, and items you can imagine that each of these Share-Point objects can raise different types of events. Events provide a powerful way to signal various state changes and are useful if you have to implement business rules tied to SharePoint objects such as lists.

For example, consider a document library that contains draft documents. Imagine that the business rules for the document library require that every time a document gets uploaded that has been reviewed and marked as ready, the document needs to be moved to a second document library that has the final documents. It would be quite painful if you needed to do this manually—instead, you could use list event receivers that subscribe to the events that are raised when an item in the list is added or updated. The event receiver can then read the document properties and, based on the document property values, move the document to the document library containing the final documents.

In order to respond to SharePoint events we use something called an event receiver. An event receiver is just a .NET class that contains methods that are called when a specific event is raised. The assembly that is compiled from the .NET class is installed to SharePoint and registered in a way that SharePoint knows to call into the assembly when certain events occur.

Events in SharePoint are triggered in response to changes, creation, and deletion of SharePoint features, items, lists, sites, or workflows. You can probably already imagine all the benefits event receivers can have. You can make your existing SharePoint solutions even more powerful by using event receivers to handle various events raised by SharePoint.

Events in SharePoint 2010

The simplest classification of events would be to separate them into two groups: synchronous and asynchronous events. Synchronous events, also called "before" events, are events that are raised right before the actual event happens. An example of a synchronous event would be ItemAdding or ItemDeleting. At the time we respond to ItemAdding event for example, the actual item is not added to the list yet, instead it is in the process of being added to the list or library. Before the item is added, code in the event handler needs to execute. This means that synchronous events stop the execution flow until the code in the event handler is run. That is why synchronous events are typically used to validate data prior to completing an action in SharePoint. For example, we could handle the ItemAdding event for a list item and use custom logic, validation, and rules to decide if an item should be added to the list or not. Synchronous events typically have a Cancel parameter passed to them that allows the code to cancel the event and prevent the SharePoint action being monitored from happening. A perfect example of a synchronous event that could be canceled is trying to upload a document with .exe or any other extension that is not allowed in document libraries or lists. Behind the scenes, SharePoint is using a synchronous event that verifies the file extension and displays an error message like the one in Figure 5-1 if the file extension is not allowed.

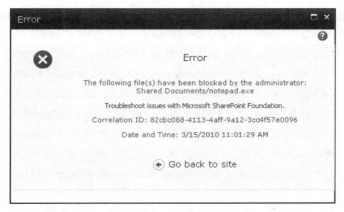

Figure 5-1: Error message when file can't be uploaded

Compared to synchronous events, asynchronous events are mostly used for starting a business process that can occur in parallel with a SharePoint action, because they don't stop or block execution of the flow. A common use for asynchronous events, or "post" events as they are also called, would be a document library with associated workflow. If you configured your workflow to be started each time a document is uploaded something similar to an event receiver is used to start that workflow once a document is uploaded (an ItemAdded event triggers the workflow).

Several objects in the SharePoint hierarchy (site collections, sites, lists, items, etc.) emit both synchronous and asynchronous events. These different levels in the SharePoint hierarchy can trigger events:

- List events
- List Item events
- List email events
- Site events
- List workflow events
- SharePoint Feature events

Event receiver projects in Visual Studio 2010 are implemented as .NET classes that derive from a particular SharePoint event receiver class corresponding to the object to which you want to listen to events. If you want to respond to events that occur on a SharePoint list, your event receiver class must derive from the SPListEventReceiver class. Other classes used for event receiver base classes include SPItemEventReceiver, SPWebEventReceiver, SPEmailEventReceiver, SPWorkflowEventReceiver, and SPFeatureReceiver. All these classes, except for SPFeatureReceiver, derive from a common base class named SPEventReceiverBase. These classes have some necessary plumbing for listening and responding to events that are being raised.

Each event receiver method with the exception of some events in e-mail event receiver and feature event receiver has a single argument that is derived from the SPEventPropertiesBase. This parameter allows us to obtain information about the event and to respond to that event accordingly. Properties common to all event receivers are listed in Table 5-1.

TABLE 5-1: Common Event Receiver Properties

Property Name	Description
Cancel	Boolean value that determines if event is canceled or not; if set to true the event will be canceled. The default value is false.
ErrorMessage	Sets the error message that is displayed if an event is canceled.
EventType	An enum that corresponds to the event type (e.g., ItemAdding, ItemDeleting, etc.).
ReceiverData	String that contains the data of the receiver.
RedirectUrl	Used together with Status property; it contains the redirect URL in case event is canceled.
SiteId	Contains the GUID of the SharePoint site.
Status	Set to Continue if event is not canceled. In case Cancel is set to true, the value of this property changes to CancelWithError. You can also use this property together with RedirectUrl. If you set the RedirectUrl and change this property to CancelWithRedirectUrl, SharePoint will redirect the user to the RedirectUrl in case the event is canceled when Cancel is set to true.
Web	Returns an instance of the SPWeb object for the SharePoint site.

Every event receiver has other properties that are specific to the type of the event receiver. Properties specific to each event receiver will be described later in this chapter.

List Events and SPListEventReceiver

List events are raised when the metadata of the list has changed or the list itself is modified. With list event receivers we can respond to the following events:

- FieldAdded
- FieldAdding
- FieldDeleted
- FieldDeleting
- FieldUpdated
- FieldUpdating
- ListAdded
- ListAdding
- ListDeleted
- ListDeleting

The argument passed to list event receiver methods is of type SPListEventProperties. Table 5-2 lists the properties that are specific to the SPListEventProperties object.

TABLE 5-2: Properties of the SPListEventProperties Object

Property Name	Description
FeatureId	Feature GUID.
Field	SPField instance that is affected by the event; this property is set to null if you access it in non-field events.
FieldName	Name of the column (field) that is being affected by the event.

Continues

TABLE 5-2:   Properties of the SPListEventProperties Object *(Continued)*

Property Name	Description
FieldXml	XML definition of the column that is being affected by the event.
List	SPList instance that is being affected by the event.
ListId	GUID of the list that is being affected by the event.
ListTitle	Title of the list that is being affected by the event.
TemplateId	Property contains the list template Id.
UserDisplayName	Display name of the user whose action triggered the event.
UserLoginName	Login name of the user whose action triggered the event.
WebId	Contains the GUID identifying the SharePoint site.
WebUrl	URL of the SharePoint site.

Apart from the properties in Table 5-2, the SPListEventProperties object has two SharePoint specific methods: InvalidateList and InvalidateWeb. In case you modify the list or site you should call either InvalidateList or InvalidateWeb, which invalidates the out-of-date list or site and prepares it to be refreshed. For example, if you perform an operation in the event receiver that modifies the state of the SPWeb object you would call the InvalidateWeb method to invalidate the object and make SharePoint update the SharePoint site to match the SPWeb object.

List Item Events and SPItemEventReceiver

List item events are raised when specific actions are performed on list items. Since there is no universal list item event receiver that would catch events for all items regardless of the list they are in you need to provide an event source. In this case the event source is a SharePoint list template. So, for example, if you create a list item event receiver for the Announcements list you will also receive events for any other list that is using Announcement list as a list template. Compared to the list events, this event receiver has many more events we can respond to:

- ItemAdded
- ItemAdding
- ItemDeleted
- ItemDeleting
- ItemCheckedIn
- ItemCheckingIn
- ItemCheckedOut
- ItemCheckingOut
- ItemUncheckedOut
- ItemUncheckingOut
- ItemUpdated
- ItemUpdating
- ItemAttachmentAdded
- ItemAttachmentAdding
- ItemAttachmentDeleted
- ItemAttachmentDeleting
- ItemFileMoved
- ItemFileMoving
- ItemFileConverted
- ContextEvent

Most of the events in the previous list are self-evident—when an item is added the ItemAdded event fires, when you check-in or checkout a Share-Point list item ItemCheckedIn and ItemCheckedOut are fired. If you want to respond to an event that fires when a user adds an attachment to an item or moves a file you would use ItemAttachmentAdded and ItemFileMoved events.

How about ItemFileConverted and ContextEvent? SharePoint 2010 includes document converters that can convert an XML document into a web page for example. If you are using document converters and an item is converted, an ItemFileConverted event fires. You could use this event for example to log the document conversion.

Even though ContextEvent shows up in the list of events you could subscribe to, there's no developer scenario in which this event could be used. This event is a dummy event for triggering real list item events that are hosted outside of the list event receivers.

Table 5-3 contains the properties that are specific to the SPItemEvent-Properties object.

TABLE 5-3: Properties of the SPItemEventProperties Object

Property Name	Description
AfterProperties	Hashtable of string/value pairs that correspond to the fields in a SharePoint item after the event has occurred. For example, you could use AfterProperties["vti_title"] to get the document title in the ItemUpdating or Item-Updated event.
AfterUrl	URL of the item after the event has occurred.
BeforeProperties	Hashtable of string/value pairs that correspond to the fields in a SharePoint item before the event has occurred. For example, if you have a document with the title "My Document" and you change it to "Your Document" the value of BeforeProperties["vti_title"] (in ItemUpdating or ItemUpdated event) would be "My Document," whereas the value of AfterProperties["vti_title"] would be "Your Document." Also note that BeforeProperties are only available for document libraries.
BeforeUrl	URL of the item before the event has occurred.
Context	Context (SPEventContext) of the item event.
CurrentUserId	User ID whose action caused the event.
FileSystemObject-TypePropertyName	Contains the name of the file system object type.
List	SPList instance that contains the item.
ListId	List instance ID.

TABLE 5-3: Properties of the SPItemEventProperties Object *(Continued)*

Property Name	Description
ListItem	SPListItem instance that is affected by the event.
ListItemId	List item ID.
ListTitle	Title of the list.
RelativeWebUrl	Server-relative URL of the web site where the event occurs.
UserDisplayName	Display name of the user whose action triggered the event.
UserLoginName	Login name of the user whose action triggered the event
Versionless	Boolean value indicating whether the item tracks versioning.
WebUrl	Absolute URL of the site in which the event occurs.
Zone	SPUrlZone enumeration.

Just as with the list event receiver, the SPItemEventProperties object also contains methods for invalidating a list item or site: InvalidateListItem and InvalidateWeb can be used when the list item or site has been changed as a result of the event handler. As you might remember from Chapter 3, "Introduction to the SharePoint Object Model," the OpenWeb method can be used to get an SPWeb object.

Two of the interesting properties from Table 5-3 are AfterProperties and BeforeProperties. These two properties can be used to get the item properties before the item was changed (added, deleted, updated, checked-in, etc.) and after the change has happened. However, getting the before and after properties doesn't always work as expected. For example what would you expect BeforeProperties to contain in an ItemAdded or ItemAdding event? Since the item was just added (or it's being added) to the SharePoint list there are no BeforeProperties—the item didn't exist in the list before. But if you handle an ItemUpdated or ItemUpdating event you could use Before-Properties to get the properties on an item before it was changed. And here's the second gotcha—the previous sentence only applies if you are using SharePoint document library. Trying to use BeforeProperties in an event receiver on a SharePoint list (e.g., the Announcements list) doesn't work; use the ListItem property instead. To illustrate the different property values in most common events, refer to Tables 5-4 and 5-5. Note that N/A in both tables means that the property value is either not set or it's set to null.

TABLE 5-4: BeforeProperties, AfterProperties, and ListItem Values When Using a SharePoint List

Event	BeforeProperties	AfterProperties	ListItem
ItemAdding	N/A	New value	N/A
ItemAdded	N/A	New value	New value
ItemDeleting	N/A	N/A	Original value
ItemDeleted	N/A	N/A	N/A
ItemUpdating	N/A	Changed value	Original value
ItemUpdated	N/A	Changed value	Changed value

TABLE 5-5: BeforeProperties, AfterProperties, and ListItem Values When Using a SharePoint Document Library

Event	BeforeProperties	AfterProperties	ListItem
ItemAdding	N/A	N/A	N/A
ItemAdded	N/A	N/A	New value
ItemDeleting	N/A	N/A	Original value
ItemDeleted	N/A	N/A	N/A
ItemUpdating	Original value	Changed value	Original value
ItemUpdated	Original value	Changed value	Changed value

List E-mail Events and SPEmailEventReceiver

List e-mail event receivers can be used to respond to events when the selected list receives an e-mail message. In contrast to other event receivers that can be used to respond to multiple different events, this event receiver exposes only one event: EmailReceived.

Instead of the event receiver specific properties parameter being passed to the method, EmailReceived has three parameters as shown in Listing 5-1.

Listing 5-1: The EmailReceived Method of List E-Mail Event Receiver

```
public override void EmailReceived(SPList list, SPEmailMessage emailMessage,
  string receiverData)
{
  base.EmailReceived(list, emailMessage, receiverData);
}
```

The SPList parameter represents the list that received the e-mail message. SPEmailMessage is the actual e-mail that was send to the list. You can use this parameter to get to the parts of the e-mail message and read the sender information, body of the e-mail, and any attachments. The last parameter (receiverData) is a string and it contains the event receiver definition data.

Web Events and SPWebEventReceiver

Web events are raised when an event happens on a SharePoint site (confusingly called a "Web" in the object model) or when a SharePoint site collection is being deleted (confusingly called "Site" in the object model). A web event receiver can be used to respond to the following events:

- SiteDeleted
- SiteDeleting
- WebAdding
- WebDeleted
- WebDeleting
- WebMoved
- WebMoving
- WebProvisioned

Table 5-6 shows the properties that are specific to the SPWebEvent-Properties object that is passed as a parameter to your event handler methods.

TABLE 5-6:   Properties of SPWebEventProperties Object

Property Name	Description
FullUrl	Absolute URL of the SharePoint site where the event occurs.
NewServerRelativeUrl	Server-relative URL that represents the address of the site after it has been moved.
ParentWebId	GUID of the parent site.
ServerRelativeUrl	Server-relative URL that represents the SharePoint site before it was moved or the current server-relative URL if the SharePoint site was renamed.
UserDisplayName	Display name of the user whose action triggered the event.
UserLoginName	Login name of the user whose action triggered the event.
Web	SPWeb object representing the SharePoint site where the event occurred.
WebId	SharePoint site ID where the event occurred.

As with the list and list item event receiver, the SPWebEventProperties object has an InvalidateWeb method that must be called if your event receiver changes the SharePoint site in any way during the event.

List Workflow Events and SPWorkflowEventReceiver

A list workflow event receiver can be used to respond to events that are specific to workflow behavior. To use this event receiver a SharePoint list instance needs to be specified. The SharePoint list instance serves as the event source for the event receiver. The following events can be responded to with the list workflow event receiver:

- WorkflowCompleted
- WorkflowStarted

- WorkflowStarting
- WorkflowPostponed

In previous versions of SharePoint, workflows were not able to raise events and there was no point to having a list workflow event receiver. In SharePoint 2010 one can respond to all the events in the above list and use them to send out a notification when workflow is postponed or completed. Based on the value of the CompletionType property of the SPWorkflow-EventProperties object that is passed as a parameter to your event handler, an action can be performed if errors occur during workflow execution, if workflow is terminated, or if there was an error starting the workflow.

Table 5-7 lists the properties of the SPWorkflowEventProperties object that is passed as a parameter to each list workflow event method.

TABLE 5-7: Properties of the SPWorkflowEventProperties Object

Property Name	Description
ActivationProperties	SPWorkflowActivationProperties instance in which you can access the properties of workflow activation, such as HistoryList, TaskList, List, etc.
AssociationData	String that contains workflow association data.
CompletionType	Enumeration that describes how workflow was completed; this property can be set to the following values: Completed, Errored, ExternallyTerminated, FailedOn-Start, InternallyTerminated, or NotApplicable.
ErrorException	Property that contains exception information.
InitiationData	String that contains workflow initiation data.
InstanceId	Workflow instance GUID.
PostponedEvent	Enumeration used to specify what type of workflow action was postponed in case of resource constraints; this property can be set to the following values: Load, None, or Start.
RelativeWebUrl	Server-relative URL of the SharePoint site where the event occurs.

Continues

TABLE 5-7:   Properties of the SPWorkflowEventProperties Object *(Continued)*

Property Name	Description
TerminatedByUserId	ID of the user who terminated the workflow.
WebUrl	Absolute URL of the site where the event occurs.

SharePoint Feature Event Receiver

Feature event receivers are similar to other event receivers that can be created with Visual Studio 2010. Since there is no separate project template to create feature event receivers a SharePoint project needs to be created first and then a feature event receiver can be added to the desired feature. From the implementation standpoint, feature event receivers inherit from a different base class (SPFeatureReceiver) than other event receivers mentioned in this chapter.

With feature event receiver we can respond to the following events that are triggered on SharePoint feature:

- FeatureActivated
- FeatureDeactivating
- FeatureInstalled
- FeatureUninstalling
- FeatureUpgrading

Feature events can be used to set up the environment when a feature is installed (FeatureInstalled event) and do clean-up work when a feature is deactivating (FeatureDeactivating) or uninstalled (FeaturedUninstalled).

Just as the base class of the feature event receiver is different from the base class of other event receivers, so is the SPFeatureReceiverProperties type that is passed as a parameter to the event handler methods. The biggest difference is that the common properties described at the beginning of this chapter don't apply to SPFeatureEventReceiverProperties. Table 5-8 lists the properties of the SPFeatureReceiverProperties object.

TABLE 5-8: Properties of SPFeatureReceiverProperties Object

Property Name	Description
Definition	SPFeatureDefinition object that contains the information about the feature definition.
Feature	SPFeature object that contains the information about the feature.
UserCodeSite	SPSite object for the site collection where a solution that includes this feature is deployed.

One additional exception to note—the FeatureUpgrading event is passed two additional parameters: a string called upgradeActionName and a string dictionary containing additional named parameters.

Creating Event Receivers in Visual Studio

In order to understand how event receivers are created in Visual Studio, we should start with a simple event receiver project. Follow the steps below to create a C# Event Receiver project.

1. Open Visual Studio.
2. Select File > New > Project or press Ctrl + Shift + N.
   The New Project dialog is displayed.
3. Select "Event Receiver" under Visual C# > SharePoint > 2010 node.
4. Type "MyEventReceiver" in the Name textbox and click OK.
   The SharePoint Customization Wizard is displayed as shown in Figure 5-2.
5. Select the Deploy as a farm solution option and click the Next button to move to the second wizard page.

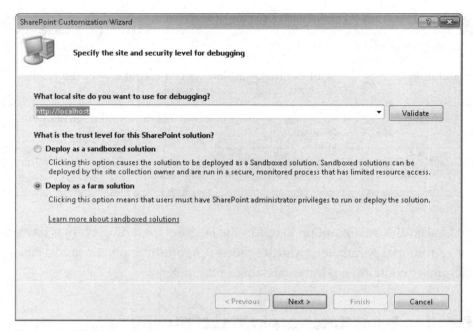

Figure 5-2: The first wizard page of the SharePoint Customization Wizard

Can I Create Sandboxed Event Receivers?

Yes, you can create both sandboxed as well as farm solution event receivers. The reason we are creating a farm solution is because later in the chapter we are going to add an application page to the project. Application pages can't be deployed with sandboxed solutions.

The Choose Event Receiver Settings wizard page is displayed as shown in Figure 5-3. The first drop-down contains the list of event receivers that you can create with the Event Receiver project template. As mentioned before, Feature event receivers cannot be created with this template. Later in this chapter we will show how to create a feature event receiver.

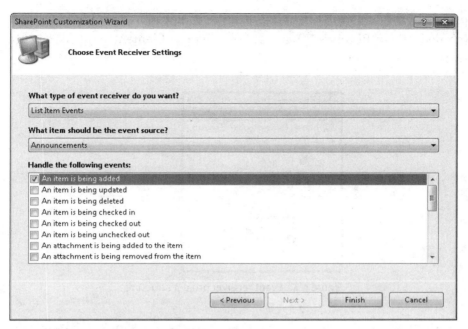

Figure 5-3: Event Receiver Settings wizard page

6. Select "List Item Events" from the first drop-down.

7. Select "Announcements" from the second drop-down.

   This drop-down enables us to select the event source for the event receiver. Some types of event receivers, such as list and web, don't have an event source and in that case this drop-down is disabled.

8. Click the "An item is being added" event to select it.

   Code that is generated after the project is created contains the event handlers for any events that were selected in this list. After the project is created you can still add additional event handlers through the Properties window.

9. Click Finish to create the project.

   The resulting event receiver project structure shown in Figure 5-4 is not any different from other SharePoint projects. Just as with other SharePoint project items, a SharePoint event receiver is placed in a project item folder (named "EventReceiver1") and it contains the Elements.xml file and the code file.

Figure 5-4: Event receiver project structure

The Elements.xml file describes the event receiver to SharePoint when the event receiver is deployed. The contents of this file are shown in Listing 5-2.

Listing 5-2: Event Receiver Definition in Elements.xml File

```xml
<?xml version="1.0" encoding="utf-8"?>
<Elements xmlns="http://schemas.microsoft.com/sharepoint/">
  <Receivers ListTemplateId="104"
    <Receiver>
      <Name>EventReceiver1ItemAdding</Name>
      <Type>ItemAdding</Type>
      <Assembly>$SharePoint.Project.AssemblyFullName$</Assembly>
      <Class>MyEventReceiver.EventReceiver1.EventReceiver1</Class>
      <SequenceNumber>10000</SequenceNumber>
    </Receiver>
  </Receivers>
</Elements>
```

Events we selected in the wizard are defined in this XML file. Type and Name elements represent the event receiver method name and event type. The number inside the SequenceNumber element defines the order in which events are executed. If there are two or more event receivers and they are handling the same events, the one that has the smallest number in the SequenceNumber element is executed first.

The Type element contains the name of the event we are responding to and the Assembly and Class elements tell SharePoint the assembly and class where the event method is located. You may see strange $ signs around the value in the Assembly element. This indicates that Visual Studio is using a replaceable parameter or a token to define the assembly. This token will be resolved to the actual name of the assembly when the project is packaged.

Tokens Sound Cool. Tell Me More!

Tokens or replaceable parameters can be used for Visual Studio for SharePoint items whose actual values are not known at design time. SharePoint tokens function like Visual Studio template tokens (e.g., $safeprojectname$, $guid1$, etc.). All tokens begin and end with a dollar sign ($) character and they are replaced with actual values when the Share-Point project is packaged. For more information about the tokens specific to SharePoint projects, see Chapter 11, "Packaging and Deployment."

If you double-click the EventReceiver1.cs code file to open it you will notice that the file contains an EventReceiver1 class that inherits from the correct base event receiver class (SPItemEventReceiver) and contains the event handler for the method we selected in the wizard. Your code should look like Listing 5-3.

Listing 5-3: Generated C# Class for the Item Event Receiver

```
/// <summary>
/// List Item Events
/// </summary>
public class EventReceiver1 : SPItemEventReceiver
{
  /// <summary>
  /// An item is being added.
  /// </summary>
  public override void ItemAdding(SPItemEventProperties properties)
  {
    base.ItemAdding(properties);
  }
}
```

What happens if you want to respond to additional events after you've created the project? It's very common that you would want to add new events or remove events you already selected in the wizard. One way to add or remove events would be to manually update the EventReceiver1 class and override additional methods. You could then update the Elements.xml file as well. Fortunately, Visual Studio provides an easier way to do this.

We will add an event handler to handle the asynchronous ItemAdded event. Follow these steps to add an additional event handler:

1. Click the EventReceiver1 project item folder in the Solution Explorer window.
2. Open the Properties window.

   With the EventReceiver1 folder selected you can press F4 to open the Properties window.
3. In the Properties window find the Handle ItemAdded property under SharePoint Events.
4. Click the drop-down next to Handle ItemAdded property and change it to True.

   Figure 5-5 shows the Properties window that is shown when the EventReceiver1 folder is selected.

As soon as the Handle ItemAdded property value is changed from False to True, an event handler for the selected property is added to the code file and a new Receiver element is added to Elements.xml that describes the event.

Removing events is just as simple as adding them. Instead of changing the property value to True we would set it to False.

Removing Event Handlers

You should note that when you remove the event handler (change the property from True to False), the corresponding Receiver element is removed from the Elements.xml file, but the event handler code in the event receiver code file is not removed. You will have to remove it manually to complete the removal of the event handler.

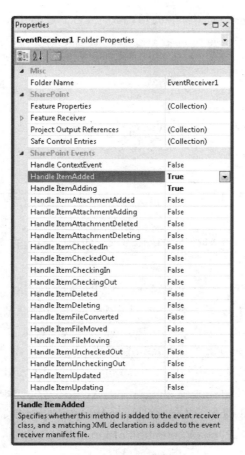

Figure 5-5: Event receiver project item
properties

We have an event handler for the ItemAdding event and we should write some code to validate the item before it is added to the list. This is our scenario: we want to make sure that each announcement being added to the list has an expiration date set. To enforce this rule we are going to use the ItemAdding event and check the value of the column "Expires." If the date is not set (it is either null or empty) we are going to cancel the event and display an error message. The code to implement this scenario is shown in Listing 5-4.

Listing 5-4: Code in ItemAdding Method to Check the Expiration Date

```
public override void ItemAdding(SPItemEventProperties properties)
{
  base.ItemAdding(properties);
  string expirationDate = properties.AfterProperties
    ["Expires"].ToString();

  if (string.IsNullOrEmpty(expirationDate))
  {
    properties.Cancel = true;
  }
}
```

What's Up with base.ItemAdding—Why, When, and Where Do I Call It?

Base class method ItemAdding (or any other base class method) should be called at the end of your event. Unfortunately that's not the case if you want to cancel the event. If we call the base method after we cancel the event we get an unexpected behavior: The event would not be canceled. Therefore always call the base class method at the end of your handler, except if you are trying to cancel the event, in that case call the base method at the start of the handler as we do in Listing 5-4.

Press F5 to deploy the project and test the code. The Internet browser opens to the homepage of the SharePoint site. Click the Lists link to open the site content page. Next, click the Announcements list link on the page to navigate to the Announcements list. Click the Add new announcement link to add a new announcement; make sure you don't set the expiration date. Click Save. An error page is displayed just like the one in Figure 5-6.

If you managed to decipher the error page you will notice it actually does contain an error message: An event receiver has canceled the request. Let's be honest, this error message is useless for the end user. Only developers would care about an event receiver being canceled. Because we are writing solutions for users we need to make the error message more helpful. We should make sure that we tell the users what went wrong. On top of everything else, the error page that is displayed doesn't look very appealing

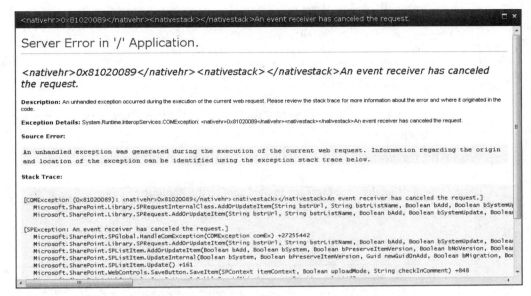

Figure 5-6: SharePoint error when event is canceled

either. The good news is that with the help of the Status and RedirectUrl properties we can redirect the users to a custom-made error page.

We should expand the scenario and specify that we want to display a specific end user-friendly error message: Please enter the expiration date. This error message should be displayed on a custom error page. For our custom error page we are going to create an ASP.NET application page.

1. Right click the project name and select Add > New Item. The Add New Item dialog opens.

2. Select the Application page template and name it "Custom-ErrorPage.aspx."

3. Click Add to add the application page to the project.

4. Drag and drop a Label control on the application page. Since there's no visual designer for application pages you have to drag the controls to the markup view. Locate the <asp:Content ID="Main" …> element and make sure you put the Label inside that element. We should rename the control to lblErrorMessage and make the font bold and larger. The updated Main content element is shown in Listing 5-5.

Listing 5-5: Label Control on the Application Page

```
<asp:Content ID="Main" ContentPlaceHolderID="PlaceHolderMain" runat="server">
   <asp:Label ID="lblErrorMessage" runat="server" Text="Label"
     Font-Bold="true" Font-Size="Large"></asp:Label>
</asp:Content>
```

5. Right click the CustomErrorPage.aspx and select View Code to open the code view.

6. Add the code from Listing 5-6 to the Page_Load handler.

Listing 5-6: Setting the Error Message to the Label on the Application Page

```
protected void Page_Load(object sender, EventArgs e)
{
  lblErrorMessage.Text = Request.Params["Error"];
}
```

We are using the Request property to read the parameter called "Error," which contains the error message and then set it to the Text property of the label on the application page. This means we also have to set the parameter called Error somewhere else. Our event receiver code should be the place where we set the "Error" parameter. Open the EventReceiver1.cs file and update the code in the ItemAdding method to match the code in Listing 5-7. We want to redirect the users to the custom error page and pass the Error parameter to the error handling page containing a user-friendly error message. We do this by encoding the Error parameter into the RedirectUrl used for the error page.

Listing 5-7: Canceling the Event and Redirecting Users to Custom Error Page

```
public override void ItemAdding(SPItemEventProperties properties)
{
  base.ItemAdding(properties);
  string expirationDate = properties.AfterProperties
    ["Expires"].ToString();

  if (string.IsNullOrEmpty(expirationDate))
  {
    string errorMessage = "Please enter the expiration date.";
    properties.Cancel = true;
    properties.Status = SPEventReceiverStatus.CancelWithRedirectUrl;
```

```
    properties.RedirectUrl =
      "/_layouts/MyEventReceiver/CustomErrorPage.aspx?Error=" +
      errorMessage;
  }
}
```

In the above code we are setting the Status property to CancelWithRedirectUrl, which means that in the case of the event being canceled, users are going to be redirected to the URL specified in the RedirectUrl property. We set the RedirectUrl to point to the application page we created, and we also pass the error message by encoding the "Error" parameter into the URL.

We should try our solution to see if it works. Press F5 to start debugging. Navigate to the Announcements list and add a new announcement without entering the expiration date. This time we should see a more user-friendly error message on a custom error page as shown in Figure 5-7.

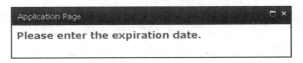

Figure 5-7: A custom error page

Instead of creating a custom error page we could re-use the built-in error page to display a custom error message. To do that we need to set the ErrorMessage property to contain the custom error message and instead of canceling the event with redirect URL we set the Status property to SPEventReceiverStatus.CancelWithError.

Creating Feature Event Receiver Projects

Feature event receivers are very similar to the other event receivers we described earlier. The main difference with feature event receiver is the scope at which they operate and where you go to create them in Visual Studio.

As the name suggests feature event receivers can be used to respond to events that are being raised at the SharePoint feature level. Visual Studio

2010 doesn't include a separate project template for feature event receivers, which means we can't create feature event receiver projects in the same way we created other event receivers. Instead of using the template a feature event receiver can be added to a SharePoint feature in a SharePoint project with a few mouse clicks.

In this example we are going to programmatically create five SharePoint lists: an announcement list, a contacts list, a document library, a links list, and a task list. We will create them when a feature is activated and, because we want to be good citizens of SharePoint land, we are going to clean up after ourselves and delete those lists when the same feature is deactivated. You should always make sure you clean up the solutions you deploy to the SharePoint server by handling feature events. Otherwise, the server can become cluttered with various SharePoint objects that are not used.

Open Visual Studio 2010 and create an empty SharePoint project.

1. Select New > Project... from the File menu in Visual Studio.
2. In the New Project dialog under Visual C#, select SharePoint and 2010.
3. Select Empty SharePoint project template.
4. Name the project "MySharePointLists" and click OK. Accept the defaults in the wizard, and click Finish to create the project. Because we are using an empty project, there is nothing in the project yet. In order to use feature event receivers we need a feature first.
5. Right click the Features folder and select Add Feature. Figure 5-8 shows the context menu for the Features folder, which has only one command. After you click the menu item Feature1 is added to the project and the feature designer opens. Now that the project has a feature we can add a feature event receiver to it.

Figure 5-8: Add Feature Context menu item

6. Right click Feature1 and select Add Event Receiver from the context menu.

The code file for Feature1.EventReceiver.cs shown in Listing 5-8 is added to the project.

Listing 5-8: Feature1.EventReceiver.cs

```csharp
using System;
using System.Runtime.InteropServices;
using System.Security.Permissions;
using Microsoft.SharePoint;
using Microsoft.SharePoint.Security;

namespace MySharePointLists.Features.Feature1
{
    /// <summary>
    /// This class handles events raised during feature activation,
    /// deactivation, installation, uninstallation, and upgrade.
    /// </summary>
    /// <remarks>
    /// The GUID attached to this class may be used during packaging
    /// and should not be modified.
    /// </remarks>

    [Guido("a89c77b4-dc95-4b41-8c0a-31367c22ba3c")]
    public class Feature1EventReceiver : SPFeatureReceiver
    {
        // Uncomment the method below to handle the event raised
        // after a feature has been activated.

        //public override void Feature Activated(
        //  SPFeatureReceiverProperties properties)
        //{
        //}

        // Uncomment the method below to handle the event raised
        // before a feature is deactivated.

        //public override void FeatureDeactivating(
        //  SPFeatureReceiverProperties properties)
        //{
        //}

        // Uncomment the method below to handle the event raised
        // after a feature has been installed.

        //public override void FeatureInstalled(
        //  SPFeatureReceiverProperties properties)
        //{
        //}
```

```
        // Uncomment the method below to handle the event raised
        // before a feature is uninstalled.

        //public override void FeatureUninstalling(
        //   SPFeatureReceiverProperties properties)
        //{
        //}

        // Uncomment the method below to handle the event raised
        // when a feature is upgrading.

        //public override void FeatureUpgrading(
        //   SPFeatureReceiverProperties properties,
        //   string upgradeActionName,
        //   System.Collections.Generic.IDictionary<
        //      string, string> parameters)
        //{
        //}
    }
}
```

The feature event receiver class is structured similarly to the other event receivers discussed earlier. But you will notice that all methods are already in the class and they are commented out. Instead of choosing events in the wizard or toggling the setting in the Properties window, for feature events we only need to uncomment the code for the events we want to handle.

What about the Elements.xml file? Where is the information about the event receiver stored? For feature event receivers this information is stored in the Feature.xml file instead. This file contains all necessary information needed for the feature event receiver to be deployed and correctly registered, including the event receiver assembly and class.

If we wanted to change these values in the Feature.xml file we can do so using the feature designer by double-clicking the Feature1.feature file. The event receiver assembly and event receiver class values are displayed in the Properties window. As before, a token is used to specify the assembly in class. Table 5-9 shows the replaceable parameters and sample values to which these parameters resolve when a project is deployed.

TABLE 5-9: A Feature's Receiver Assembly and Receiver Class Properties

Property Name	Property Value	Resolved Value
Receiver Assembly	$SharePoint.Project. AssemblyFullName$	MyLists, Version=1.0.0.0, Culture=neutral, PublicKeyToken= 6b8440479dc58448
Receiver Class	$SharePoint.Type.453d7f23-a25a-4bea-a02f-9b094482c727. FullName$	MyLists.Features.Feature1. Feature1EventReceiver

The receiver assembly property resolves to the fully qualified name of the assembly that contains the assembly name, version, culture, and a public key. The receiver class resolves to the full class name. One interesting part of the receiver class property value is the GUID, which is used in the token to distinguish between different event receiver classes—this GUID is used to disambiguate between multiple features in a project.

The same GUID in the receiver class property value is an attribute of the event receiver class in the code file as shown in Listing 5-9.

Listing 5-9: GUID Attribute on the Event Receiver Class

```
[Guid("453d7f23-a25a-4bea-a02f-9b094482c727")]
public class Feature1EventReceiver : SPFeatureReceiver
```

About Changing the GUID

Generally you shouldn't have to change the GUID in either the class file or Feature.xml file, but if you do, make sure the GUID in the code file matches the one in the Feature.xml file.

Now we are ready to write code that is triggered when our feature is activated that will create lists. We will also write code to delete the same lists when the feature is deactivated. Open the code file (Feature1.Event-Receiver.cs) and uncomment the FeatureActivated and FeatureDeactivating methods. Before we add code to the event handler we need to define our list names. Add the code in Listing 5-10 to the event receiver class.

What's the Difference Between Installing and Activating?

A SharePoint feature can be activated for its scope only after it is successfully installed on the SharePoint server. And, if a feature is installed it can't be used on the SharePoint until it's activated. Think about it this way: You must turn the key to activate the engine in your car before you can drive the car. Having a car "installed" in your garage doesn't mean you can drive it—you have to "activate" it first.

Listing 5-10: Defining the List Names in Event Receiver Class

```
private string news = "My News";
private string contacts = "My Contacts";
private string docs = "My Documents";
private string links = "My Links";
private string tasks = "My Tasks";
```

Now that we defined the list names we can write the code that adds the lists to SharePoint when the feature is activated. Uncomment the FeatureActivated method then add the code in Listing 5-11 to the method.

Listing 5-11: Code for Adding the Lists to the SharePoint

```
public override void FeatureActivated(SPFeatureReceiverProperties properties)
{
  SPWeb web = properties.Feature.Parent as SPWeb;
  web.Lists.Add(news, news, SPListTemplateType.Announcements);
  web.Lists.Add(contacts, contacts, SPListTemplateType.Contacts);
  web.Lists.Add(docs, docs, SPListTemplateType.DocumentLibrary);
  web.Lists.Add(links, links, SPListTemplateType.Links);
  web.Lists.Add(tasks, tasks, SPListTemplateType.Tasks);
}
```

To add the lists to SharePoint we need to set a reference to the Share-Point site where the lists should be created. For more information on using the SharePoint object model see Chapter 3, "Introduction to the SharePoint Object Model" and for more information on working with lists see Chapter 4, "SharePoint Lists." We are using the Parent property of the feature to get to the SPWeb object for the SharePoint site. Once we have an SPWeb object we call the Add method on Lists to add the lists. Creating a list is simple: we just need to pass the list title, the description, and the list template type to the Add method. Note that the Add method has multiple overrides and we could pass different parameters, such as custom XML schema, list instance feature definition, and quick launch options.

Deleting lists is just as easy as adding them. Uncomment the Feature-Deactivating method and add the code from Listing 5-12 to the method.

Listing 5-12: Code to Remove Lists from the SharePoint

```
public override void FeatureDeactivating(SPFeatureReceiverProperties
  properties)
{
  SPWeb web = properties.Feature.Parent as SPWeb;
  web.Lists[news].Delete();
  web.Lists[contacts].Delete();
  web.Lists[docs].Delete();
  web.Lists[links].Delete();
  web.Lists[tasks].Delete();
}
```

Again, we need the SPWeb object to access the Lists property. We are using the indexer and we pass in the list name to get to the specific list. Finally we call the Delete method to delete each list.

Deploying and Debugging Event Receiver Projects

Event receiver projects can be deployed in the same manner as every other SharePoint project. You can either use the Build menu in Visual Studio 2010 to deploy the project or select Deploy Solution to deploy the whole solution. If you have multiple projects in the solution and you only want to deploy a specific project, you can right click the project name that you want to deploy

and click the Deploy menu item in the context menu. There's not much difference in debugging either. In general all event receiver projects, except for
feature event receivers, can be debugged in the same way as any other
SharePoint project.

Due to the special nature of feature event receivers, the debugging experience for those event receivers is a bit different. Depending on the feature
event that we want to debug we have to change the deployment configuration from Default to No Activation or use stsadm.exe to manually deploy the
feature. In this section we are going to show you how to use No Activation
deployment to debug FeatureActivated and FeatureDeactivating methods,
as well as how to set up Visual Studio 2010 and manually deploy the Share-
Point feature using stsadm.exe to debug FeatureInstalled and Feature-
Uninstalling events.

What Is stsadm.exe?

stsadm.exe is a command-line tool used for the administration of the
SharePoint servers and sites. The stsadm.exe tool needs to run on the
server itself and in order to use it you must be a member of the Administrators group on the server.

We are going to start with the FeatureActivated and FeatureDeactivating
events. As mentioned before, if we use the default deployment configuration to deploy the feature event receiver project we created earlier, the
breakpoint in the FeatureActivated event will not get hit, because Visual
Studio activates the feature before the debugger is ever attached. Since the
No Activation deployment configuration doesn't contain the activate features step, which activates the feature in Default deployment configuration, it will allow us to debug the FeatureActivated event.

Let's show how this works on the feature event receiver sample we
built earlier. Follow the steps below to insert breakpoints and use No Activation deployment to debug the project.

1. Double-click on Feature1.EventReceiver.cs to open the code view.

2. Go to the FeatureActivated method and press F9 to insert the breakpoint.

3. Go to the FeatureDeactivating method and press F9 to insert the breakpoint.

4. Click the project name in Solution Explorer and open the Properties window. With project selected you can press F4 to open the Properties window.

5. In the Properties window change the Active Deployment Configuration property from Default to No Activation. You can refer to Figure 5-9.

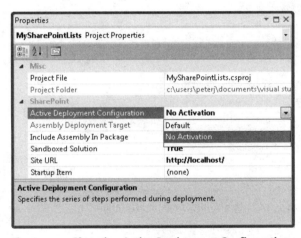

Figure 5-9: Changing Active Deployment Configuration

Deployment Configurations

You can create new deployment configurations in the SharePoint tab in project properties. A more detailed explanation of configurable deployment is found in Chapter 11, "Packaging and Deployment."

6. Press F5 to start debugging.

   Because the feature will not be activated before debugging starts due to our use of the No Activation deployment configuration, we will have to activate the feature manually.

7. When the Internet browser opens, drop down the Site Actions menu and select Site Settings. A site settings page like the one in Figure 5-10 is displayed.

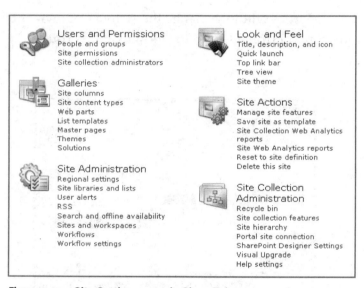

Figure 5-10: Site Settings page in SharePoint

8. Click the Manage site features link under the Site Actions header.

   A web page with a list of features similar to the one shown in Figure 5-11 appears.

9. Find the "MySharePointLists Feature1" feature that we created and click the Activate button next to the feature name to activate it. As soon as you click the Activate button, the breakpoint on the Feature-Activated method is hit.

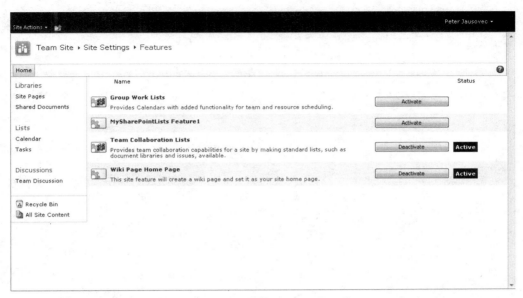

Figure 5-11: List of features available in the SharePoint site

10. Press F5 to continue debugging. The Internet browser will get the focus and the status column next to the "MySharePointLists Feature1" is now set to active.

11. Click the Deactivate button to deactivate the feature. A warning page like the one in Figure 5-12 is displayed.

12. Click the Deactivate this feature link. Once again, a breakpoint is hit, this time on the FeatureDeactivating method.

13. Press SHIFT + F5 to stop debugging or simply close the Internet browser.

With the help of No Activation deployment we can debug the feature activation and deactivation events. Debugging the FeatureInstalled and FeatureUninstalling events is trickier than debugging the feature activated or deactivating events. The commands for installing and uninstalling the feature are part of the deployment and retraction process. The feature gets

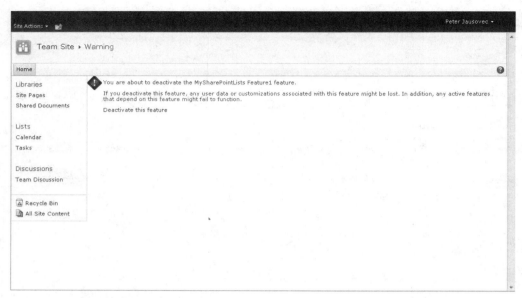

Figure 5-12: Deactivating the feature

installed in the Add Solution deployment step and uninstalled during the Retract Solution step. When we start debugging (press F5) the deployment steps are executed and as the last step the Add Solution step is called. Once this step is completed the debugger is attached. It doesn't help us much to have the debugger attached after the code we wanted to debug (e.g., FeatureInstalled event) is already executed.

One way we could debug the code inside the FeatureInstalled and FeatureUninstalling events is to run the stsadm.exe to manually add and deploy the solution. We can do that through Visual Studio 2010 in order to hit a breakpoint. Follow these steps to prepare the project, and then run the stsadm.exe to manually add and deploy the feature.

1. Open Feature1.EventReceiver.cs.

2. Uncomment the FeatureInstalled method and insert a breakpoint to that method.

3. Uncomment the FeatureUninstalling method and insert a breakpoint to that method.

4. Right click the project name and select Retract. We want to retract the project first to make sure we don't get any errors when we are manually deploying it.

5. Right click the project name and select Rebuild. This command rebuilds the project and updates the project assembly.

6. Right click the project name and select Package. Since we are manually deploying the project we need the updated .WSP file.

7. Click Start > All Programs > Accessories and open the Command Prompt as administrator. To run the program as administrator you can right click the Command Prompt and select Run as Administrator.

8. Navigate to the folder where stsadm.exe is located by executing the command below in the command prompt:

```
cd X:\Program Files\Common Files\Microsoft Shared\Web server
   Extensions\14\BIN\
```

Replace X: with your system drive letter (usually C:).

9. From the Command window, run the stsadm.exe command below to add the SharePoint solution to the solution store.

```
stsadm.exe -o addsolution -filename
   C:\MySharePointLists\bin\Debug\MySharePointLists.wsp
```

File Paths That Contain Spaces

Make sure you change the above path to the .WSP file to the path where you created your project. If the path to your project contains spaces, put the whole path in quotes (e.g., "C:\My Projects\MySharePointLists\bin\Debug\MySharePointLists.wsp").

Any Tricks to Quickly Get to the Project Path?

It happens quite often that you want to navigate to the project path. Within Visual Studio 2010 you can right click the project name and select Open Folder in Windows Explorer.

10. The next step is to deploy the solution. Run the command below from the command window to deploy the solution to SharePoint.

```
stsadm.exe –o deploysolution –name MySharePointLists.wsp –local –allowgac
```

Because the .WSP file is already in the solution store we don't need to specify the full path to the above command. The local parameter is used for synchronously deploying the feature on the local computer. With the allowgac parameter we are telling the stsadm.exe to put the assemblies in a global assembly cache. If we don't specify the allowgac parameter, an error message will be displayed.

11. Switch back to Visual Studio 2010.

12. Right click on the project name and select Properties. The property pages for the project are opened.

13. Click the Debug tab.

14. Under the Start Action select Start external program and click the button next to the textbox. A browse dialog is opened.

15. From the Select File dialog navigate to the file X:\Program Files\Common Files\Microsoft Shared\Web server Extensions\14\ BIN\stsadm.exe where X: is your system drive letter (usually C:).

16. Click Open to close the dialog.

17. Type the text below for the Command line arguments textbox under Start Options.

```
-o installfeature -name MySharePointLists_Feature1 -force
```

We have specified that we want to run stsadm.exe with the above arguments. Because we specified an external program Visual Studio 2010 will automatically attach to the stsadm.exe process and the breakpoint in FeatureInstalled method will be hit. At this point MySharePointLists project properties should look like Figure 5-13.

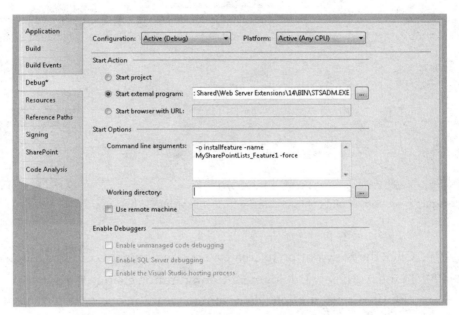

Figure 5-13: Debug tab with command line arguments to start stsadm.exe

18. Click the SharePoint tab to open the configurable deployment settings. SharePoint configurable deployment settings are displayed in Figure 5-14.

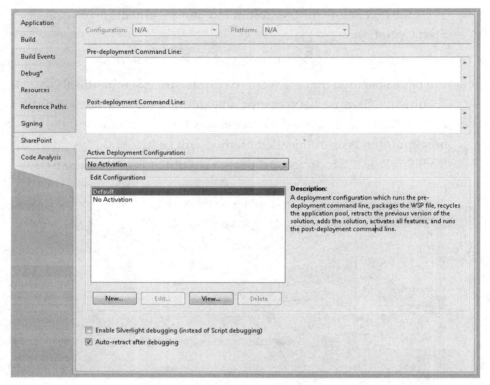

Figure 5-14: SharePoint configurable deployment settings

19. Click the New button to create a new deployment configuration.

20. In the Add New Deployment Configuration change the name to "Empty Configuration." We want to create an empty deployment configuration because we already manually deployed the feature. Refer to Figure 5-15.

21. Click OK to close the dialog.

22. Change the Active Deployment Configuration to "Empty Configuration."

23. Press F5 and verify the breakpoint is hit.

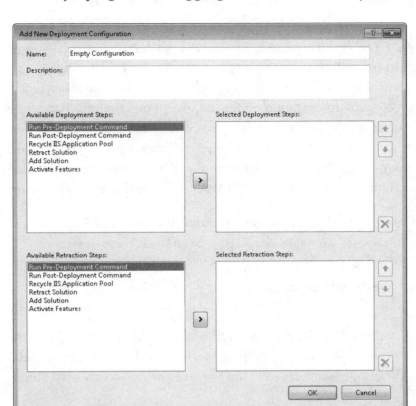

Figure 5-15: New 'Empty Deployment' configuration in the dialog

At this point the stsadm.exe should run and the breakpoint on the FeatureInstalled method will be hit. How about FeatureUninstalling? Since the feature is already added to the solution store, it is deployed and installed already—we only need to uninstall it. We can change the command line arguments we set in step 17 to uninstall the feature and hit a breakpoint in FeatureUninstalling. Click the Debug tab in the Project Properties window and change the command line arguments to these:

```
-o uninstallfeature –name MySharePointLists_Feature1 –force
```

Make sure a breakpoint is set on the FeatureUninstalling method and press F5 to run the project. Stsadm.exe with the specified command line arguments will run and the breakpoint on the method is hit.

Even if you decide that debugging these events is too much work you can still get some information about the exceptions that are happening in the FeatureInstalled method. If any exceptions are thrown during the deployment process, the deployment process will fail. To demonstrate this create a new empty project and add a feature and feature event receiver to it. Next, uncomment the FeatureInstalled method and add the code in Listing 5-13.

Listing 5-13: Throwing an Exception from FeatureInstalled Method

```
public override void FeatureInstalled(SPFeatureReceiverProperties
  properties)
{
  throw new Exception("Exception in FeatureInstalled");
}
```

Try deploying the project. At the Add Solution step the FeatureInstalled method is called and an exception is thrown. The deployment fails and an error message is displayed in the Error List window of Visual Studio:

```
Error occurred in deployment step 'Add Solution': Exception in
  FeatureInstalled
```

Even though you didn't go through all the steps to set up the debugging you can still get some valuable information. Sometimes the exception information could be enough but for some cases you might have to go through the above steps to debug the code.

Conclusion

The purpose of this chapter was to give you an overview of event receiver project templates in Visual Studio 2010. Event receivers are a powerful way to implement business rules in a SharePoint environment. We learned about the SharePoint events that developers can leverage and respond to. In the list event receiver sample we showed how to cancel an event and use an application page to display custom errors to the users. Using feature event receivers we can respond to events that occur when a feature is installed, uninstalled, activated, deactivated, or upgraded. These events can be used to prepare the environment before a feature is installed and activated and to do clean-up work once a feature is uninstalled or deactivated. We also learned how to debug feature event receiver events use No Activation deployment and how to debug FeatureInstalled and Feature-Uninstalling events.

■ 6 ■
Working with Business Data

Introduction to Business Connectivity Services

There are a lot of scenarios in which you might want to integrate data from external systems into SharePoint. External systems are any systems that store data outside of SharePoint. For example your company might store its customer information in a CRM system or its HR data in an HR system, but use SharePoint for its corporate intranet. Now wouldn't it be nice if all employees could create, read, update, and delete data from the CRM and HR systems from a familiar SharePoint site?

SharePoint 2010 offers this capability through the Business Data Connectivity Services or BCS, which is an improved version of what was formerly known as the Business Data Catalog in SharePoint 2007. In all SKUs of SharePoint 2010 developers can use the BCS to declaratively surface external data, commonly called business data, to Office client applications and SharePoint. BCS is the recommended way of integrating external data provided by web services, WCF services, databases, and .NET assemblies into SharePoint and Office client applications.

Another advantage of working with business data using BCS is that the end user can work with a familiar UI with lists and web parts, the data can be made searchable through SharePoint Search and the user's security context and credentials can be passed through to the external system. What developers need to implement for BCS is an entity data model that describes the external data and interfaces. The external data objects are defined through External Content Types or ECTs, which contain identifiers and methods that define the fields of external data and indicate to the business data connectivity runtime how to pull external data out of the external system.

A SharePoint list can be associated with an external content type and such a list is called an external list. An external list associated with a customer external content type allows the user to see the customers in the external system displayed in a SharePoint List. The user can interact with the customer data just like the user interacts with a regular SharePoint list.

There are two major tools that allow you to integrate business data using BCS: Visual Studio 2010 and SharePoint Designer 2010. We will first consider how to integrate business data using SharePoint Designer.

Creating External Content Types Using SharePoint Designer

To begin our exploration of Business Connectivity Services, let's create a simple external content type representing customer data coming from an external database using SharePoint Designer 2010. We will be using the Microsoft Northwind sample database for the samples in this chapter. The Northwind database can be downloaded from http://go.microsoft.com/fwlink?linkid=64296.

To get started, open SharePoint Designer and click on the Open Site Button to show the Open Site dialog in Figure 6-1. For the Site Name we need to enter the SharePoint root site where we want to create an external list containing data defined by an external content type. We will use the default site at http://localhost.

Once SharePoint Designer has successfully connected to our site, SharePoint Designer's home screen appears. This screen provides us with an overview of site objects in the left navigation pane and additional information such as general site information, permissions, settings, and a list of available subsites for this site. Because we want to create an external content type, click the item External Content Types in the left navigation pane as shown in Figure 6-2.

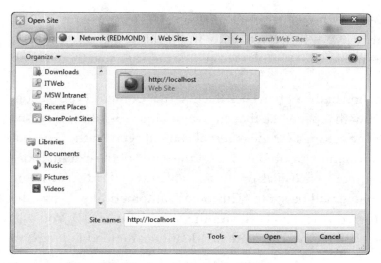

Figure 6-1: SharePoint Designer's Open Site dialog

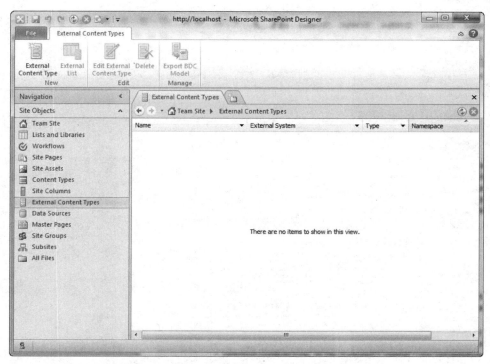

Figure 6-2: SharePoint Designer's home screen

SharePoint Designer now queries the Business Data Store to retrieve all the external content types that are already in the store. Since we haven't deployed an external content type yet we get the message that there are no items to show.

In the New section of the ribbon click the External Content Type button. We are presented with a page like that shown in Figure 6-3 that allows us to view and manage settings for the external content type. In the External Content Type Information group box, we set the name of the external content type to "Customer." Next click on the textbox next to the display name and the display name will be set to "Customer" automatically. Leave the Namespace set to your root site URL and the Version to 1.0.0.0. You will notice that if you click on the There are no identifiers defined link next to

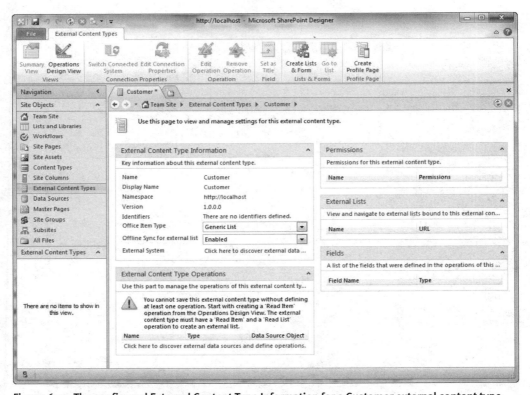

Figure 6-3: The configured External Content Type Information for a Customer external content type

the Identifiers label that nothing happens. That's because we don't have any business data associated with our external content type yet. Leave the Office Item Type set to Generic List. The Office Item Type setting allows you to configure data in a list to sync with built-in Outlook types such as appointments, contacts, and tasks. The possible Office Item Types that you can choose are shown in Table 6-1.

TABLE 6-1: Office Item Types

Item Type	Description
Generic List	The external content type will be represented as an external list only and cannot be synced to Outlook 2010.
Appointment	Will be available as an external list and can be synced to Outlook 2010 as an appointment in a calendar folder.
Contact	Will be available as an external list and can be synced to Outlook 2010 as a contact in a contacts folder.
Task	Will be available as an external list and can be synced to Outlook 2010 as a task in a task folder.
Post	Will be available as an external list and can be synced to Outlook 2010 as a post in a mail folder.

The External Content Type Information group box should now have the settings shown in Figure 6-3.

The next step is to connect the external content type to the external data source. Let's click on the "Click here to discover external data..." link. A page called Operation Designer opens that allows you to define the connection to external data and define the operations for the external data source. Figure 6-4 shows the Operation Designer page.

Clicking on the Add Connection button will pop up a dialog that lets you select the external system you want to connect to as shown in Figure 6-5. Table 6-2 lists the available external data source types. Because we want to connect to a database, select SQL Server and click the OK button.

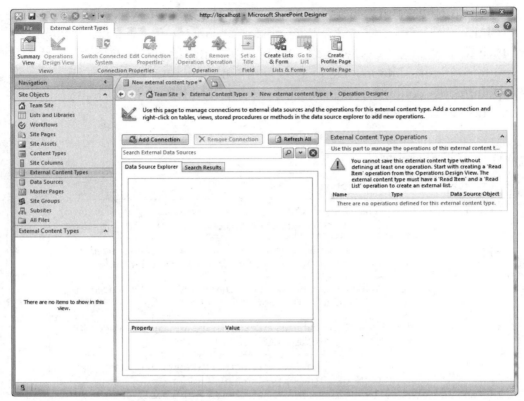

Figure 6-4: The Operation Designer page

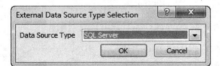

Figure 6-5: The External Data Source Type Selection dialog

TABLE 6-2: External Data Source Types

Data Source Type	Description
.NET Type	A custom .NET assembly provides the external data.
SQL Server	A SQL Server database provides the external data.
WCF Service	A WCF Service provides the external data.

Next you will need to enter the SQL Server connection data. Figure 6-6 shows the SQL Server Connection dialog. It allows you to either connect with the current user account, an impersonated Windows Identity, or an impersonated Custom Identity. The latter two require a Secure Store ID. (See more information on how to connect using a Secure Store ID at http://msdn.microsoft.com/en-us/library/ee556780(office.14).aspx).

Figure 6-6: SQL Server connection dialog

What Is the Secure Store?

The Secure Store Service in SharePoint 2010 is a single sign-on service that allows you to store and map credentials such as account names and passwords used for connecting to external systems. Those credentials can be associated with identities known on the system running the BCS service and thus the BCS service is able to connect to the external systems without needing to enter the credentials for the external system.

If we had selected .NET Assembly or WCF Service we would have seen a different dialog that would have allowed us to enter the information for those objects. Enter the information for your SQL Server and Northwind database and click the OK button.

Once successfully connected to the Northwind database the tables, views, and other elements defined in the database will show up in the Data

Source Explorer. Expand the Tables node and right click on the Customers table. As shown in Figure 6-7 the context menu that appears provides a list of operations you can implement for the external content type.

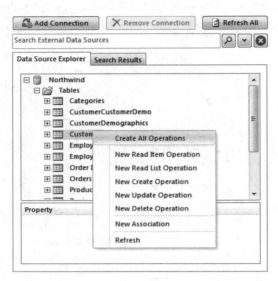

Figure 6-7: Data Source Explorer in the Operation Designer

Because we want our users to be able to create, read, update, and delete Customer data select "Create All Operations." The Operations Wizard pops up.

The first page of the Operations Wizard dialog gives you a summary of the created methods. Figure 6-8 shows the first page of the Operations Wizard.

Click the Next button to configure the parameters for all of the CRUD (Create, Read, Update, Delete) methods in the Parameters Configuration page of the Operations Wizard as shown in Figure 6-9.

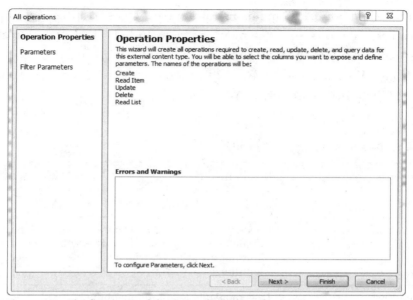

Figure 6-8: The first page of the Operations Wizard

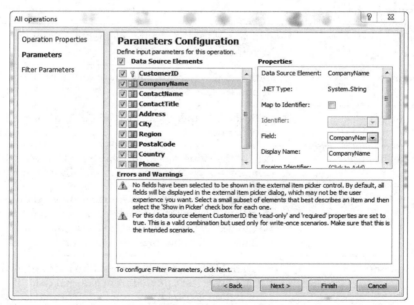

Figure 6-9: The Parameters Configuration page of the Operations Wizard

In the Data Source Elements list of the Parameters Configuration page you can select and unselect elements to be included. The Data Source Elements correspond to the fields defined in your Customer table in the database. In the Properties section you can set the properties for each element. Table 6-3 lists all the properties available.

TABLE 6-3: Data Source Elements Properties

Property	Description
.NET Type	.NET type of the data source element.
Map to Identifier	Check the box if the data source element will be a unique identifier for the data. This will enable the Identifier drop-down, which allows you to select an Identifier.
Identifier	Lists of available identifiers in the ECT.
Field	The actual field.
Display Name	The display name of the data source element .
Foreign Identifier	Indicates if the data source element is a foreign key identifier.
Required	Indicates whether the data source element is required or not.
Read-Only	Indicates whether the data source element is read-only or not.
Office Property	One of the values listed in Table 6.1 if the data source element will be associated with an Office Item type.
Show In Picker	Specifies whether the data source element should be shown in the picker; the picker is a form in the SharePoint UI that allows the user to read, enter, and update information for an external content type.
Timestamp Field	Sets a field to contain the time stamp indicating when the field was last updated from external data. This information is used by search to determine when to update the search index with the updated external data.

The Error and Warnings section of the Parameters Configuration page shows two warnings as shown in Figure 6-10.

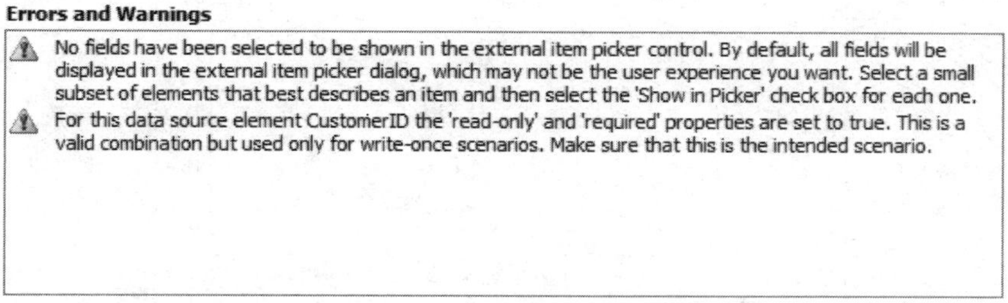

Errors and Warnings

⚠ No fields have been selected to be shown in the external item picker control. By default, all fields will be displayed in the external item picker dialog, which may not be the user experience you want. Select a small subset of elements that best describes an item and then select the 'Show in Picker' check box for each one.

⚠ For this data source element CustomerID the 'read-only' and 'required' properties are set to true. This is a valid combination but used only for write-once scenarios. Make sure that this is the intended scenario.

Figure 6-10: The Errors and Warnings section of the Parameters Configuration page

The first warning tells us that if we don't set any of the elements in the "Show in Picker" property to True then all the fields will show up in the picker. If you only want some of the elements to show up in the picker you need to select the ones you want displayed.

The second warning indicates that the identifier CustomerID is required and read-only. Although this is a valid setting you should consider if this is what you want. Think about a table that has an identifier and that identifier is an autoincrement field. Every time you create a new entry in that table the identifier is automatically created. In this case the identifier would not be required for an Insert operation and would be read-only for all other operations—this is called a "Write Once" scenario. On the other hand you can have a table that expects you to create an identifier for an entry that is created, but the identifier is not an autoincrement field. In that case the identifier would be required and could not be read-only. Based on your requirements you might want to adjust those settings as described above. For now, accept the default settings, ignore the warnings, and click the Next button.

The Filter Parameters Configuration page shown in Figure 6-11 allows you to configure filter parameters and default values. This is highly recommended to restrict returning large result sets. Importing models without filters, for example through Windows Power Shell comandlets or through the admin UI will succeed but with a warning that there is no limit filter applied.

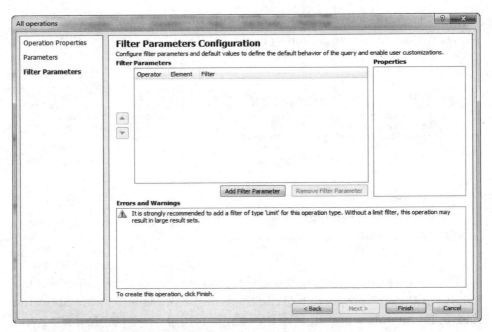

Figure 6-11: The Filter Parameters Configuration page

We will create a filter for Country. This will make it so users will be prompted to filter customers by country, thereby ensuring that less data will typically be returned. Click the Add Filter Parameter button and a new row is added to the Filter Parameters data grid. Figure 6-12 shows the Filter Parameters data grid with the new row.

In the Element drop-down select Country, and in the Filter row click the "(Click to Add)" link to add a filter based on this element. The Filter Configuration dialog appears as shown in Figure 6-13.

In the Filter Configuration dialog name your filter "CountryFilter." Select Comparison for the Filter Type, Equals for the operator, and leave the Filter Field value set to Country. Table 6-4 lists all the filter types available.

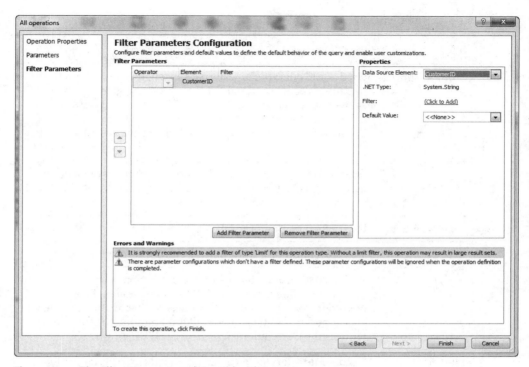

Figure 6-12: The Filter Parameters data grid with new row

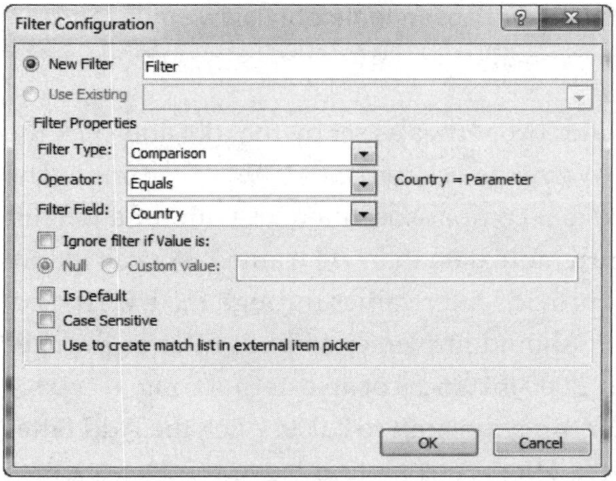

Figure 6-13: The Filter Configuration dialog

TABLE 6-4: Filter Types

Filter	Description
Comparison	Used while querying an external system, this value represents a pattern of regular and wildcard characters that is matched against the value of a particular field of the set of Entity-Instances. The external system returns only those Entity-Instances whose field values match the specified pattern.
Limit	Used while querying an external system and the value of this filter can be interpreted as a limit on the number of external items (EntityInstances) that are returned when the method that it belongs to is called.
Page Number	Used when paging of result sets is required.
Timestamp	The timestamp of the latest search crawl.
ActivityID	ActivityID is used when calling an operation on the external system. Its value is set to a GUID that represents the current operation context. If no such value is available, this filter generates a random GUID. On SharePoint Foundation 2010, this filter uses the CorrelationID.
Wildcard	Used while querying an external system; an external system can compare a ComparisonFilter value with the value of a particular field of a set of external content type instances and only those external content type instances in which the field values pass the comparison test are returned.

We leave the remaining Filter properties as set by the tool and click the OK button. The Errors and Warnings section shows two warnings. The first one indicates that we have a comparison filter set without a default value and the query may return more data than we wanted. We can ignore this warning because we will provide filter values through the UI. The second warning suggests that we should implement a limit filter as the runtime cannot return more than 2,000 instances of an external content type.

So let's create another filter to set the limit to 2,000. Click the Add Filter Parameter button again. In the Properties section leave the Data Source Element set to CustomerID. Next click the "(Click to Add)" link in the Filter row. In the Filter Configuration dialog leave New Filter selected, and name your filter "CustomerLimit." In the Filter properties section select

Limit as the Filter Type. Leave the other settings as created by SharePoint Designer and click the OK button. Finally, set the Default Value to 2,000 by typing "2000" in the Default Value drop-down box. The Filter Parameters Configuration wizard page should now look like Figure 6-14.

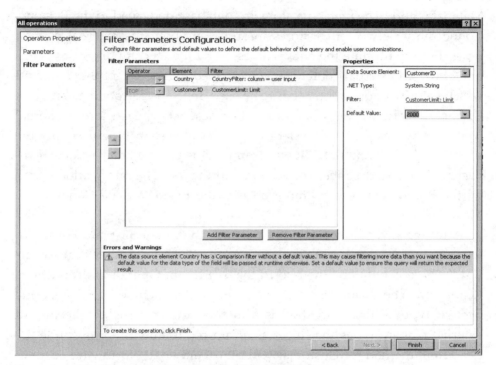

Figure 6-14: The Filter Parameters Configuration page for Customer

Click the Finish button. The external content type Customer is now defined. It is CRUD capable and is searchable within SharePoint through SharePoint Search. SharePoint Designer automatically adds properties to external content types that allow the SharePoint Search engine to crawl external content types.

We could also add an association to associate it with another external content type such as the Orders table. We will take a deeper look into associations later in this chapter. The next step is to create a UI so that users can work with the data defined by the Customer external content type.

In the SharePoint Designer ribbon section entitled List & Forms shown in Figure 6-3, click the button Create Lists & Form. A message box comes up telling you that you need to save the external content type before a list and form can be created. Click the Yes button to save. A progress bar appears saying that the data is now being saved to the Business Data Connectivity Metadata Store. The metadata store is a database dedicated to the Business Connectivity Services that stores information about the external content types. During runtime the data is accessed by the UI components to determine how an external content type is defined, where to get the data, and which security information needs to be used. In the background, SharePoint Designer creates the metadata model that describes the Customer external content type using an LobSystem type. An LobSystem type describes the source of the external data. In our example it is of type database. The Lob-System type also describes connection information. The information stored by the LobSystem type is imported into the Business Data Connectivity Metadata Store.

After the save has successfully finished, the Create List and Form dialog pops up as shown in Figure 6-15. In the List Name enter "Customer-List." There is only one method in the Read Item Operation drop-down, Read Item. The Read Item method is the finder method of this external content type. A finder method is a method that returns a collection of external content types that meet a certain requirement. For example the Read Item method for Customer will return either all Northwind customers if we don't set the country filter or only the customers for a certain country if we apply the country filter. An external content type can have more than one finder method, but because our external content has only one finder method defined we cannot select another one. Also there is only Northwind in the System Instance drop-down because we only have one LobSystemInstance defined. An LobSystemInstance describes the connection to an external data source, in our case it describes the connection information to the SQL Server hosting the Northwind database. An external content type can have more than one LobSystemInstance, for example one for a test database and one for a production database. At this point we leave the Create InfoPath Form check box unchecked. The Create List and Form dialog should now look like Figure 6-15.

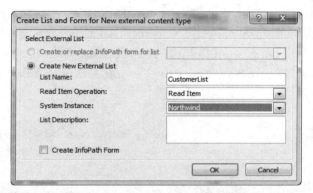

Figure 6-15: The Create List and Form dialog for Customer

Click the OK button. A progress bar tells us that SharePoint Designer started creating the external list for Customer. Once it is done the dialog closes, which tells us that SharePoint Designer has finished the creation of the external list CustomerList. Click Lists and Libraries in the Navigation pane on the left-hand side. The tab Lists and Libraries comes up and you can locate the external list CustomerList at the bottom in the External Lists section. Click the CustomerList link to get to the page that allows you to view and manage settings for the external list CustomerList.

What Is an External List?

An external list is a list that is backed by an external content type. An external list has the look and feel of a normal list, as well as the same functionality. The columns of the external list are defined by the data source elements or type descriptors of the external content types. External lists can be accessed through the SharePoint object model but they don't expose the data through the WCF data service listdata.svc (see Chapter 4, "SharePoint Lists," for more information on working with lists).

Before we can test our list we need to set the permission for the external content type in the Business Data Connectivity Metadata Store. This requires farm admin rights, which you should have already for the account that installed SharePoint on your development machine. Go to the SharePoint Central Administration page by selecting All Programs in the Windows start menu > Microsoft SharePoint 2010 Products > SharePoint 2010 Central Administration. Figure 6-16 shows the Central Administration page.

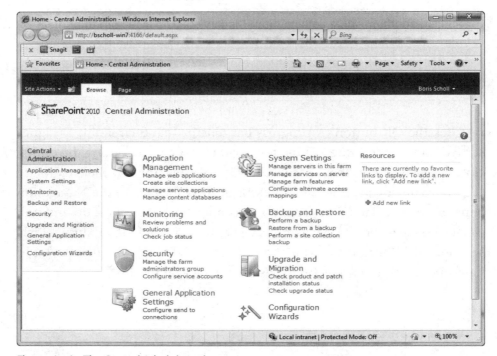

Figure 6-16:　The Central Administration page

Under Application Management click the link Manage service applications. This will take you to the Manage service applications page, which lists all the service applications in your SharePoint environment. Figure 6-17 shows the Service Applications page.

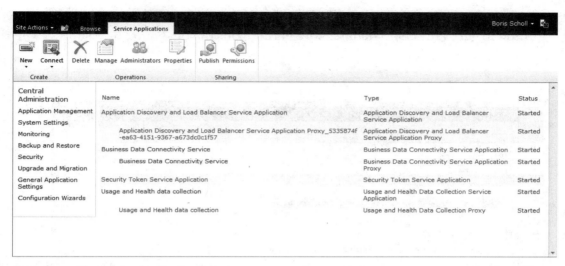

Figure 6-17: The Service Applications page

In the Service Applications page click the Business Data Connectivity Service link of type Business Data Connectivity Service Application Proxy. This is usually the second Business Data Connectivity Service entry. This will take you to the View External Content Types page as shown in Figure 6-18.

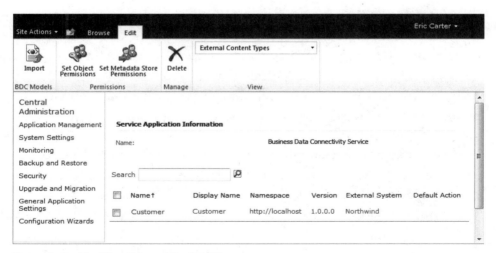

Figure 6-18: The View External Content Types page

In the ribbon of that page click the Set Metadata Store Permissions button to get to the Set Metadata Store Permissions dialog. Figure 6-19 shows the dialog.

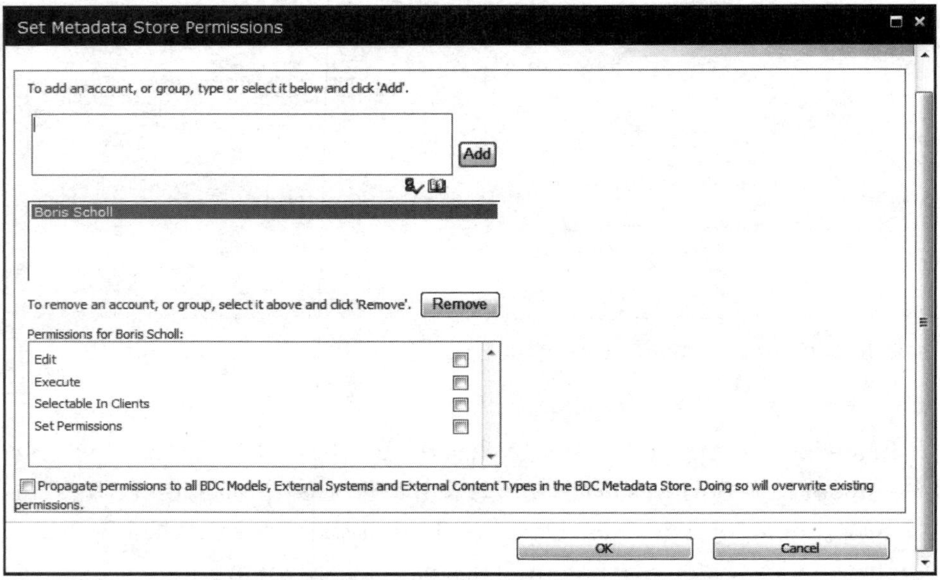

Figure 6-19: The Set Metadata Store Permissions dialog

Enter your user account in the first list box and click the Add button. Once SharePoint has verified your account it will appear in the second list box and you will be able to set permissions for your account.

If you are in a production environment you will always provide the minimal rights necessary. The security settings are as follows:

- **Edit** enables you to edit the security settings for the metadata store. The Set Metadata Store Permissions button will be enabled. You should only select Edit in your development environment

- **Execute** enables you to create, read, update, and delete external content type data.

- **Selectable in Clients** is needed to create external lists and web parts that use external content types.
- **Set Permissions** allows the user to set permissions on any object in the metadata store.

For now you can check all the check boxes for your account because we will need them when we create external content types in Visual Studio. Your Metadata Store Permissions dialog should now look like Figure 6-20.

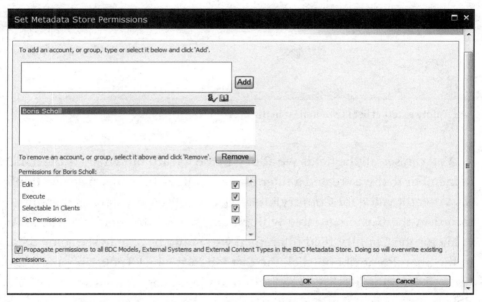

Figure 6-20: The Metadata Store Permissions dialog with permission settings entered

Now we can verify that CustomerList works. Go to the top-level Share-Point site in which you created the external list under http://localhost. In the Quick Menu on the left side of the page click on CustomerList. The browser opens the list as shown in Figure 6-21.

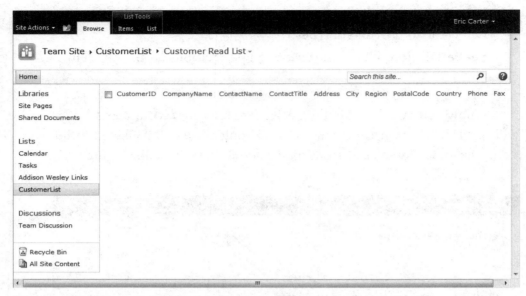

Figure 6-21: Empty external list CustomerList in the browser

You can see all the fields we added in the wizard but where is the data? Remember that we created a filter on the Country field. Because we didn't set a default value for CountryFilter, we cannot see any data as there is no record in the Customer table with an empty Country field. So let's set a value for the Country field filter, then we should be able to see some data. In the SharePoint ribbon click the List tab in the List Tools ribbon group. Next click on the Modify View button in the Manage Views section of the ribbon as shown in Figure 6-22.

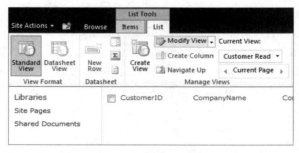

Figure 6-22: The Modify View button in the List tab for the CustomerList ribbon

The Edit View page shown in Figure 6-23 appears. In the Edit View page scroll down to Data Source Filters. Figure 6-23 shows the two filters we created before.

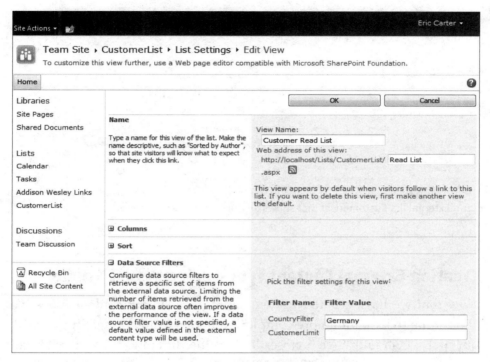

Figure 6-23: The Data Source Filters section in the Edit View page

Enter "Germany" as the value for the CountryFilter, we don't need to enter a value for the CustomerLimit filter as we set the default value to 2000. Click the OK button. Figure 6-24 shows the result after setting Germany as the filter value for the filter CountryFilter.

Click on the Items tab in the List Tools section of the ribbon. The external list dynamically enables appropriate CRUD operations based on the metadata that was provided when you designed the external content type. Because we created all of the CRUD operations for the external content type Customer, you can now create items, update items, delete items, and of course modify the filters to see customers from other countries as well.

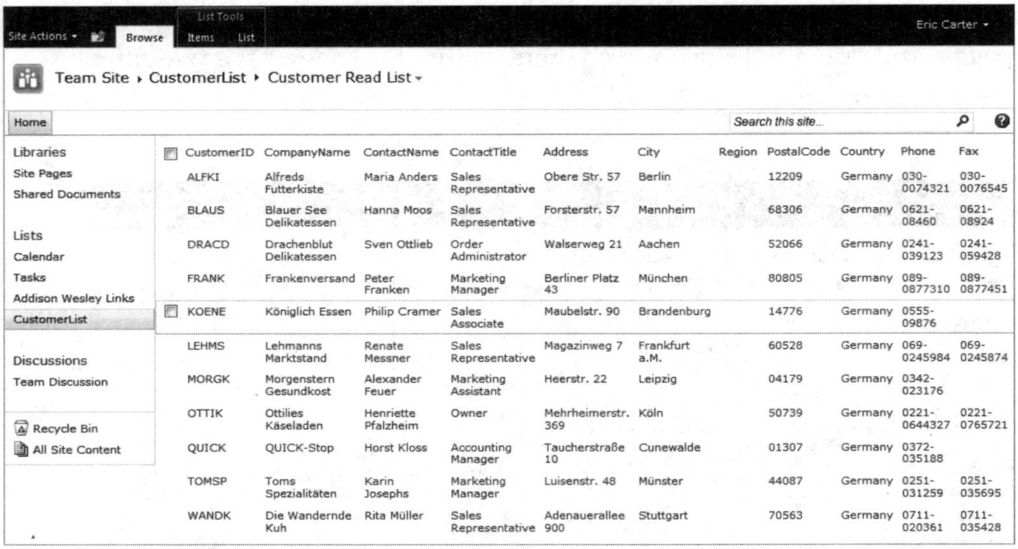

Figure 6-24: External list CustomerList that shows all the customers from Germany

Creating External Content Types Using Visual Studio

Now that we have a better understanding of external content types it's about time to look into more complex scenarios using Visual Studio 2010, but first we should have a closer look at the differences between Share-Point Designer and Visual Studio 2010.

Besides targeting different user groups there are three other major differences between Visual Studio and SharePoint Designer when it comes to creating external content types. First, Visual Studio will only allow you to build external content types whose data is provided by .NET assemblies, which basically means that the code written in the assembly serves as a proxy for working with external data. This allows the developer to implement custom security, implement business rules, and aggregate data from different sources.

Second, Visual Studio uses a different concept for creating an external content type than SharePoint Designer 2010. SharePoint Designer connects directly to a live SharePoint site and writes the external content type directly in the Business Data Store. Visual Studio creates a model file (*.bdcm file) defining all the external content types. This file gets packaged together with the project output assembly and is eventually deployed as a .WSP file to SharePoint. This is useful if you work within a source control system as you can check in the model file along with your source code.

Third, Visual Studio provides a little bit more freedom and functionality with regards to method types, search implementation, and associations. We will discuss this in more detail over the next pages of this chapter.

Can I Import BDC Models Created in SharePoint Designer?

Yes but there are some limitations. To import a BDC model created in SharePoint Designer you need to export it from the BDC metadata store. This can be done in the SharePoint Administration web site under Application Management › Manage Service Applications › Business Data Connectivity Service › Select BDC Models in the View section of the ribbon › Click the Export button. This will allow you to save the .bdcm file to disk. Now you can add it as an existing item to a Visual Studio SharePoint project. As we have learned, the Visual Studio BDC designer only supports BDC models backed by .NET assemblies, so when you import a BDC model Visual Studio asks whether you want to add a LobSystem .NET assembly or not. If you decide not to add one, Visual Studio disables the designer but imports the model. You can modify the model in XML view and deploy it using Visual Studio; you just don't have designer support.

Before we can start building our first external content type with Visual Studio we need to look at the deployment options available with Visual Studio. All SharePoint SKUs except SharePoint Foundation allow a .WSP file to install a BDC model. SharePoint Foundation does not support importing .WSP files containing BDC models. If you are using SharePoint Foundation there are two decent workarounds to solve this problem. One workaround is to use a Windows PowerShell Script that uploads the BDC model and the project output assembly to the BDC Metadata Store. The downside of that option is that you need to also deploy the output assembly to the GAC manually and attach the debugger manually if you want to debug your code. A second option is to create a custom feature event receiver that implements the deployment logic needed to import and install a BDC model and deploy the custom feature event receiver to your SharePoint Foundation machine along with the BDC model. You can either create a single feature event receiver in an empty SharePoint project or add the feature event receiver to your Business Data Connectivity model project. The advantage of the latter solution is that once the feature event receiver has been deployed you can take advantage of Visual Studio's deployment and F5 capabilities. The feature event receiver only needs to be deployed once as SharePoint will call it every time a BDC model is deployed.

You can find the steps to deploy a custom feature event receiver to deploy BDC models to SharePoint Foundation in the deployment section of this chapter. The code is found in the MSDN code gallery located at http://code.msdn.microsoft.com/BDCSPFoundation. A third alternative is to install Microsoft SharePoint Search Express on your SharePoint Foundation server, which is freely available, is a superset of SharePoint Foundation, and supports installing BDC models.

Remember that you must grant the Farm administrator permissions to the metadata store otherwise you won't be able to select the external content type in the picker. We've done that already, so we don't need to do that again.

Build a Simple External Content Type in Visual Studio

To understand how to build an external content type in Visual Studio, let's start with a "Hello World" project. To create a Business Connectivity Model in Visual Studio 2010, select New > Project... from the File menu. Then select the SharePoint 2010 project node and pick the Business Data Connectivity Model project as shown in Figure 6-25. Name the new project "HelloWorld" and click the OK button.

The SharePoint Customization Wizard dialog appears; here you can enter your debugging site. Because you are creating this project from scratch and you don't have an external content type yet, pick the default site URL. As Figure 6-26 shows, you don't have the option to choose between sandboxed solutions and farm solutions because BCS models must be deployed as farm solutions. This is because the assembly used by a BCD model must be

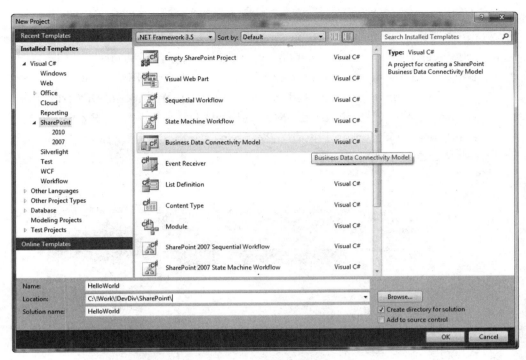

Figure 6-25: Creating a new Business Data Connectivity Model project

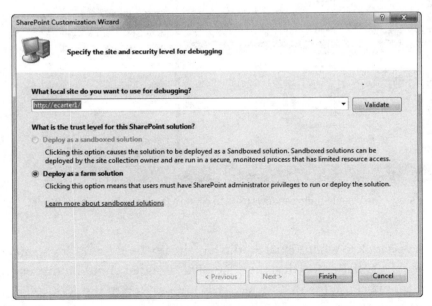

Figure 6-26: SharePoint Customization Wizard for a Business Data Connectivity Model project

deployed to the BCS database, and this requires full trust. During development you will find the BCS assembly in the GAC, but this only happens in the development environment so you can debug your code—in a production environment the assembly will be deployed to the BCS database.

After the project is created, Visual Studio opens up the BDC designer surface, the BDC Explorer, the Method Details window, and the Properties window—all shown in Figure 6-27. These are the main windows you will use to create a BDC model.

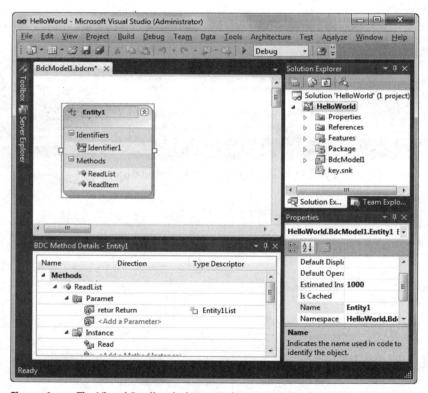

Figure 6-27: The Visual Studio windows used to create a Business Connectivity Model

Let's have a look at what Visual Studio has already built for us. If you are used to the ADO.NET entity designer, the BDC designer should look very familiar to you because the BDC designer is built on top of the ADO.NET entity designer. The designer surface shows the external content types defined in the Business Connectivity Model and allows the user to add new entities and associations by dragging them from the Toolbox. The designer surface is prepopulated with an external content type called Entity1. Visual Studio refers to external content types as entities because the underlying BDC schema only knows about entities and not external content types. Entity1 has an Identifier property called Identifier1 and two methods defined, a Finder method called ReadList and a Specific Finder method called ReadItem. A Finder method is a method that returns a collection of entities and a Specific Finder method is a method that returns a single entity. An external content type needs to have at least one Finder method defined because this is the method called by SharePoint to get data when an external content type is selected to be rendered in an external list or a business data web part.

Click on the Entity1 shape to display the method definitions in the Method Details window (at the bottom of Figure 6-27). The Method Details window shows the method structure and allows you to create and delete methods, parameters, method instances, and filter descriptors for an entity (content type). You should always create your methods using the Method Details window as opposed to right clicking on the entity shape and selecting New method if you want to create one of the CRUD (create, read, update, and delete) methods. Using the <Add a Method> option in the Method Details window will automatically create the right method signature for you. Figure 6-28 shows a closer view of the Method Details window for Entity1.

The method ReadList (the Finder method that Visual Studio created for the entity) has one parameter called returnParameter and one method instance called ReadList.

There are two additional pieces of information stored in the model for the parameter returnParameter. First, a Direction is defined that is set to Return. A method parameter can have different directions. In addition to Return, the direction can be In—which means that the parameter is an input parameter; Out—which means the parameter is an output parameter; and In/Out—which means the parameter is an input and output

Figure 6-28: Method Details window for Entity1

parameter. This direction type is equivalent to a "ref" parameter in the C# programming language.

The second piece of information stored in the model for returnParameter is a Type Descriptor with the name Entity1List. A type descriptor is metadata used by the BCS runtime to describe type information about a parameter. In this case the type descriptor Entity1List describes a collection of objects of type Entity1.

Let's dig a little bit deeper into the world of type descriptors. Click on the Type Descriptor cell for returnParameter in which the type descriptor Entity1List is displayed, and select <Edit> from the drop-down menu that displays as shown in Figure 6-29.

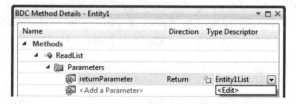

Figure 6-29: <Edit> drop-down for the type descriptor
Entity1List associated with returnParameter

Clicking on <Edit> will take you to the BDC Explorer, which is only visible when the BDC designer window is open. The BDC Explorer gives you a hierarchical view of the model and allows you to copy, paste, and delete type descriptors. This functionality will be very helpful, as we will see later.

In the BDC Explorer, you will see a node for our parameter returnParameter. Click to expand the Entity1List node under returnParameter and then click again to expand the Entity1 node. Now you can see the details of the type descriptor that describes returnParameter. At the highest level is Entity1List, one level down Entity1, and one level below that there is Identifier1 and Message. Figure 6-30 shows the expanded type descriptor Entity1List in the BDC Explorer.

Figure 6-30: Expanded type descriptor Entity1List in the BDC Explorer window

In order to understand how a type descriptor relates to code, we need to click on Entity1List in the BDC Explorer and look at the Properties window where the Type Name property is displayed. The Type Name property of Entity1List is:

```
System.Collections.Generic.IEnumerable[
  [HelloWorld.BDCModel1.Entity1, BDCModel1]]
```

As you recall, the way we started down this rabbit hole was by using the Method Details window to determine that the ReadList method had a parameter called returnParameter with a TypeDescriptor called Entity1List. We know that the method ReadList returns returnParameter (because returnParameter's direction was Return). We then navigated to the BDC Explorer window to look at the Entity1List type descriptor, which defines returnParameter's type. We found that the Entity1List's type name is an IEnumerable of Entity1 objects.

Let's have a look at the code to verify this is correct. Right click on the method ReadList in the Entity1 shape and select View Code. As you can see in the code, there is a method called ReadList(), which returns IEnumerable <Entity1>. If you go back to the BDC Explorer and look at the type name property of the type descriptor Entity1, it says HelloWorld.BDCModel1 .Entity1. From the solution explorer window open the file Entity1.cs. You can see that the class Entity1 is defined in the namespace HelloWorld .BDCModel1 and has two properties: Identifier1 and Message of type string. If you look at the Type Name property of Identifier1 and Message using the BDC designer and the Properties window, you will see System.String which matches the properties defined in the class. So as you can see our type descriptor accurately describes the types used by our ReadList method. Figure 6-31 shows the relationship between the type descriptors and the actual code.

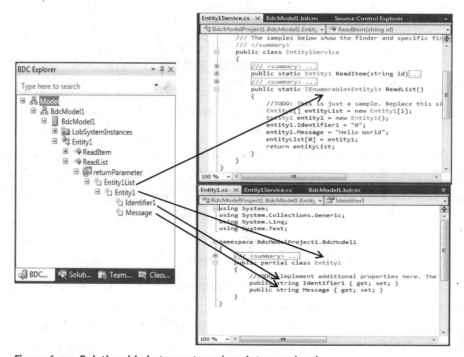

Figure 6-31: Relationship between type descriptors and code

There are additional properties defined for a type descriptor that help the BDC runtime to know how to move data between SharePoint and our custom assembly. Table 6-5 shows a list of properties for type descriptors (type name is TypeDescriptor).

TABLE 6-5: Type Descriptor Properties

Property	Description
Associated Filter	Sets the filter used for this type descriptor.
Creator Field	Set to True if the type descriptor is used in the create forms to create a new ECT; these forms are used as user input forms to create a new object of an ECT.
Custom Properties	Custom properties for the type descriptor; we will look into custom properties in more detail later in the chapter.
Default Display Name	Default display name of the type descriptor in the SharePoint UI.
Foreign Identifier Association Name	Specifies the name of the Association referenced by the type descriptor; if the type descriptor does not reference an Association, this attribute must not be present. When this attribute is present, the IdentifierName attribute must also be present. The ForeignIdentifierAssociationName attribute must be specified when the Identifier referenced by this type descriptor is related to an Association and the Identifier is contained by a source Entity of the Association.
Foreign Identifier Association Entity	Specifies the namespace of the Entity that contains the Association referenced by the type descriptor. If the type descriptor does not reference an Association, this attribute must not be present. When this attribute is present, the ForeignIdentifierAssociationEntityName and ForeignIdentifierAssociationName attributes must also be present. The default value of this attribute is the namespace of the Entity that contains the Method containing the Parameter that contains the type descriptor.
Identifier	Specifies the Identifier if the type descriptor represents an Identifier.
Identifier Entity	The entity in which the Identifier is defined.

Continues

TABLE 6-5:   Type Descriptor Properties *(Continued)*

Property	Description
Is Cached	Specifies whether the type descriptor is used frequently.
Is Collection	This property is checked if the type descriptor represents a collection, such as an Array, IEnumerable, etc.; checked by default in the return type descriptors of Finder methods.
LOB Name	Specifies the name of the data structure that is represented by the type descriptor; the default value of this attribute is the name of the type descriptor. For example, a line-of-business (LOB) system data structure named "CN1A" can be represented by a type descriptor with a Name attribute equal to "Customer Name," if the LobName attribute of this type descriptor is equal to "CN1A."
Name	Name of the type descriptor.
Pre-Updater Field	Specifies whether data structure represented by the type descriptor stores the latest data value received from the external system of a field for MethodInstances of type Updater. When this attribute is specified UpdaterField attribute must not be specified.
Read-Only	Indicates whether the type descriptor is read only.
Significant	Specifies whether values stored by the data structure represented by this type descriptor are included in calculating a hash code or comparing values stored in the data structures; for example, a type descriptor representing a customer's last name is taken into account when determining whether a record has been modified, thus it is significant, whereas the type descriptor representing the date on which the customer record was last modified typically is not taken into account to determine whether a record has been modified, thus it is not significant.
Type Name	The .NET type that implements the type descriptor.
Updater Field	Set to True if the type descriptor is used in the update forms to update an ECT.

Hopping back now to Figure 6-28, you can see that the method ReadList has one method instance that is also called ReadList. You might wonder why we need a method instance. In the BCS runtime a method points to an abstract piece of business logic in the backend system, which is the project output assembly in the Visual Studio case. Methods are not directly executable. They become executable only when associated with a method instance.

A method instance has a type that tells the runtime how to handle external content types. Click on the ReadList instance in the Method Details window to show its properties in the Properties window. The Type is set to Finder, which tells us that this method will return a collection of Entity1 objects. Table 6-6 shows all the method types available. Remember Visual Studio will create the correct signatures for the create, read, update, and delete methods if you create the methods by clicking on the <Add a Method> line in the Method Details window. If you need to create a method other than a CRUD method choose blank method and choose the desired type in the type property of the method instance. A full list of methods supported by BCS can be found on MSDN http://msdn .microsoft.com/en-us/library/ee557363(office.14).aspx.

TABLE 6-6: Method Instance Types and Method Signatures Created by Visual Studio

Type	Description	Signature
Finder	Returns a collection of all entity objects.	EntityDataType GetEntityById(IdType1 id1, etc...)
Specific Finder	Returns an entity object based on the id.	IEnumerable<EntityDataType> GetEntities ()
Creator	Creates a new entity object.	void CreateEntity(EntityDataType fields)
Updater	Updates an existing entity object.	void UpdateEntity(EntityDataType fields)
Deleter	Deletes an entity object.	void DeleteEntity(id1Type id1, etc...)

Table 6-7 shows the properties that can be set on a method instance (type name is MethodInstance).

TABLE 6-7:   All Method Instance Properties

Property	Description
Custom Properties	Custom properties for the method instance.
Default	Specifies whether the method instance is the default among all method instances sharing its type within the containing external content type.
Default Display Name	The default display name in the SharePoint UI.
Is Cached	Indicates if the Business Connectivity runtime should cache the object in memory; this can be used if a method is frequently executed.
Name	Name of the method instance.
Return Parameter Name	Specifies the name of the Parameter that contains the return type descriptor of the method instance; the Direction attribute of the Parameter must be a ParameterDirection attribute with a value of either Out, InOut, or Return.
Return Type Descriptor	The path of the type descriptor that represents the result of executing the method instance. Visual Studio offers a picker for it, so that you can select the type descriptor in a dropdown rather than entering a path.
Type	Specifies the type of the method instance.

If you now look at the method ReadItem in the Method Details window in Figure 6-28, you should be able to tell what it does. The only difference to ReadList is that it has an In parameter named id with a type descriptor named Identifier1 and a return parameter named returnParameter with a type descriptor named Entity1. The MethodInstance type is Specific Finder, which tells us that the method only returns one object of Entity1, the one whose id matches the input parameter.

The last piece of the puzzle is how the BCS runtime knows where to find the methods we just looked at. Basically everything you see in the designer ends up in the metadata model as XML. For example, Entity 1 is an entity element with a couple of attributes. You can set the values of the attributes in the Properties window when the entity is selected. Click on Entity1 in the BDC designer to see its properties in the Properties window. Click on the ... next to Collection for the Custom Properties property and look at the name value pair of this property. As Figure 6-32 shows the property name is Class and its value shows the fully qualified name of the service class Entity1Service. The value also shows the LobSystem instance name BDCModel1. Later in this chapter we will see what LobSystem instances are used for, but for now it's only important to know that the Class property of an entity points to the class that is used for this entity and that's how the BCS runtime knows what .NET class to create to call the methods we have defined. Normally you don't need to worry about this property because Visual Studio generates it for you.

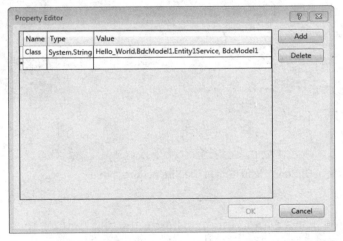

Figure 6-32: Custom Property Class element in Property Editor dialog

Now you have enough knowledge to understand how everything fits together so it's time to build, deploy, and debug the project. Highlight the method ReadList in the entity shape and click View Code. Set a breakpoint at the first line in the method. Also set a breakpoint at the first line in the method

ReadItem. When you press F5 to run the project, Visual Studio validates the model, and if the validation succeeds it deploys the model to the metadata store. (Remember that this will not work if you are using SharePoint Foundation, see the workarounds at the beginning of this section to make this work on SharePoint Foundation.) Once the deployment is successful it opens http://localhost in the browser and hooks up the debugger.

Visual Studio does not create an external list that uses the external content type for you—you must create the external list manually. To do this, use the SharePoint UI and click the Site Actions menu then, More Options… as shown in Figure 6-33.

Figure 6-33: More Options menu item in the Site Actions menu

When you select More Options… from the Site Actions menu, a Create dialog appears. In the Create dialog select Data in the left menu. Figure 6-34 shows the Create items dialog.

Select External List in the page and click the Create button. A New External List page appears shown in Figure 6-35. Name the external list "Hello World," leave the description blank, and set the Quick Launch radio button to Yes.

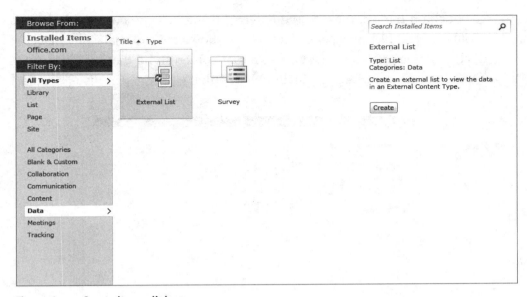

Figure 6-34: Create items dialog

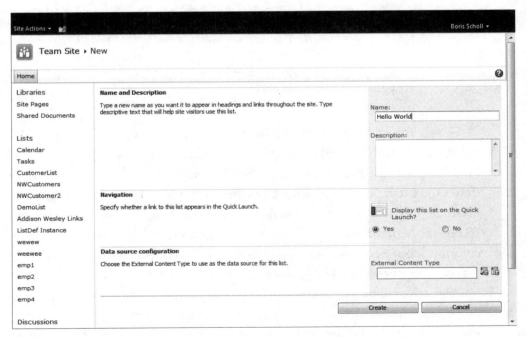

Figure 6-35: New external list page

Click on the icon next to the External Content Type box. The External Content Type Picker appears. Figure 6-36 shows the External Content Type Picker dialog and the Customer external content type that we created in SharePoint Designer along with BdcModel1 that we created in Visual Studio.

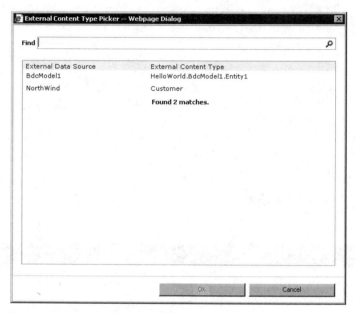

Figure 6-36: External Content Type Picker

Select the line with BdcModel1 as data source and HelloWorld .BdcModel1.Entity1 as external content type and click the OK button. In the new External List page click the button Create. Even before the list is rendered the breakpoint in ReadList, our finder method, is hit. Hit F5 again to leave the method. Before the list shows up it breaks again, so we need to hit F5 one more time. Now the list shows up, as shown in Figure 6-37, with two columns Identifier1 and Message with values 0 and Hello World. Hover your mouse over the Identifier row with the value 0. Click on the drop-down button and select view item. Now we hit the second breakpoint in the GetItem, our specific finder method. Hit F5 again to leave the method. A dialog comes up and shows us the details for the item. Hit the close button. Congratulations, you've just created your first external content type with Visual Studio.

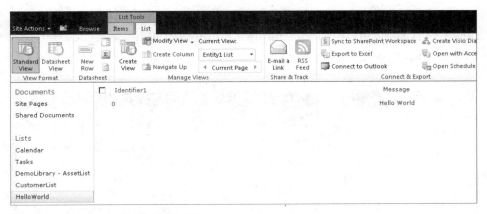

Figure 6-37: External list Hello World

Let's summarize: We can say that the method ReadList of type Finder shows all the entities in the External List—in our case there was only one entity. The columns in the External List are defined by the child type descriptors of the external content type returned by the Finder method. The Specific Finder method is called when a user wants to see the details of a specific item and the fields in the details form are defined by the child type descriptors of the external content type returned by the Specific Finder method.

Build a CRUD-enabled External Content Type

Let's apply what we know to build a second external content type with Visual Studio. Create a new Visual Studio project. This time select an empty SharePoint project and name it Employees.

The advantage of creating an Empty SharePoint project first is that we don't need to rename the SharePoint project item folder and model file (which are set by default to Entity1 in a Business Data Connectivity project). Instead, the name of our external content type can be set at creation when we add a new BDC project item to the empty SharePoint project. In the Share-Point Wizard select Deploy as Farm Solution and click the Finish button. Once Visual Studio has opened up go to the Solution Explorer and right click on the Employees project node.

In the context menu click Add > New Item. In the dialog select Business Data Connectivity Model, name it EmployeeModel, and click the Add button. Figure 6-38 shows the New Item dialog.

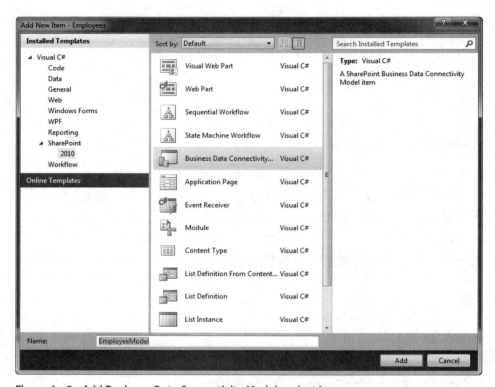

Figure 6-38: Add Business Data Connectivity Model project item

Once the BDC Model has been added, go to the Solution Explorer window and delete the Entity1.cs file. As we already know Entity1.cs contains the definition of Entity1 that was created for us in the Business Data Connectivity model EmployeeModel. This class is called a data class. In this sample we will add a LINQ to SQL class to back our EmployeeModel rather than the default Entity1 class.

Right click on the folder EmployeeModel and select Add > New Item. In the dialog under Installed Templates navigate to Visual C# > Data. Select LINQ to SQL Classes. Name the class Employee.dbml and click the Add button. Figure 6-39 shows the dialog for adding a data class.

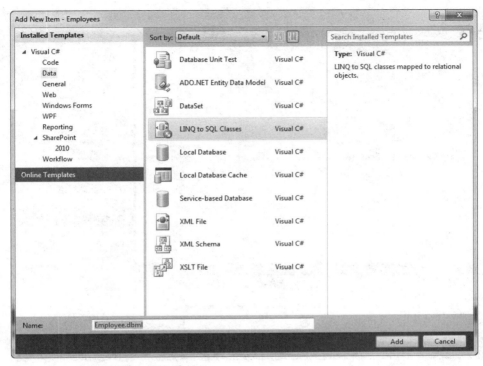

Figure 6-39: Add a LINQ to SQL Class

What Is LINQ to SQL?

LINQ to SQL is a feature of .NET Framework version 3.5 that provides a run-time infrastructure for managing relational data as objects. We're using it for our samples because we are accessing the NorthWind database and LINQ to SQL allows us to access the data in the database with less code. For more information on LINQ to SQL check http://msdn .microsoft.com/en-us/library/bb425822.aspx.

The LINQ to SQL designer opens. Click on the Server Explorer link in the left part of the designer as shown in Figure 6-40.

The Server Explorer window will appear. In the Server Explorer window add a new data connection by right clicking on the Data Connections

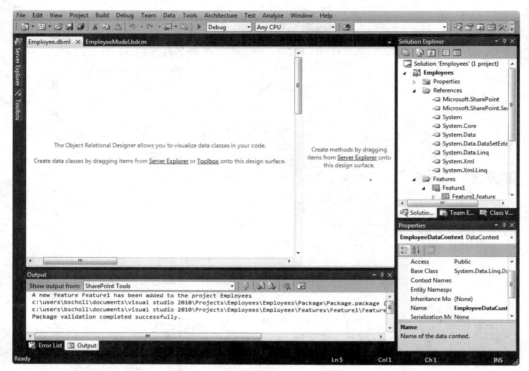

Figure 6-40: Server Explorer link in LINQ to SQL Designer

node. Figure 6-41 shows the Add Connection... item in the Data Connections context menu.

Select Add Connection... item. In the Choose Data Source dialog select Microsoft SQL Server and click the Continue button as shown in Figure 6-42.

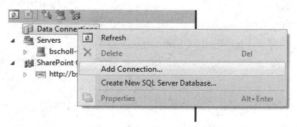

Figure 6-41: Add Connection... item in the Data
Connections context menu

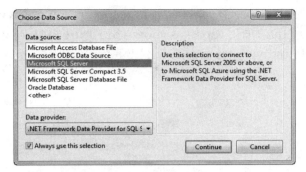

Figure 6-42: Choose Data Source dialog

In the Add Connection dialog enter a server name (if you installed the Northwind database to your default SQL Express instance you need to enter .\sqlexpress). Leave Use Windows Authentication checked. In the Connect to a database section select Northwind in the drop-down and click the OK button. Figure 6-43 shows the Add Connection dialog.

Figure 6-43: Add Connection dialog

In the Server Explorer expand the …\sqlexpress.Northwind.dbo node and navigate to the Tables node as shown in Figure 6-44. Now we need to and drag the Employees table onto the LINQ to SQL designer.

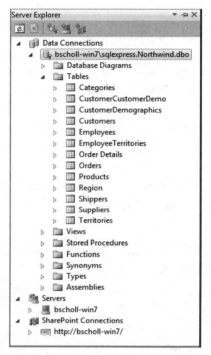

Figure 6-44: Expanded tree in the
Server Explorer

After dragging the Employees table from the Server Explorer window to the LINQ to SQL Designer surface, Visual Studio should now look like Figure 6-45. Don't get confused; the entity presented is not the external content type, it is the entity describing the database table for LINQ to SQL. LINQ to SQL generates a class that we will use as our data class. You can close the Employee.dbml file because we don't need it anymore.

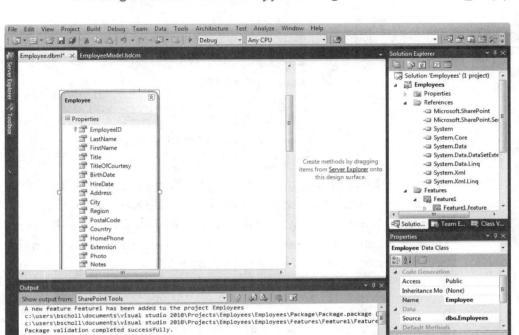

Figure 6-45: LINQ to SQL designer with entity Employee in Visual Studio 2010

Our data class was created by LINQ to SQL and is located in the Employee.designer.cs file. The BDC designer is now our focus again where we can start designing our model.

Once you have a data class there are a couple of steps that you can apply to make the designing of the external content types in models easier. Following we will list all those steps based on our sample.

1. **Rename the entity shape.** In the BDC designer rename Entity1 to Employee by clicking on the name Entity1. Visual Studio will rename the service file and the service class name for you. It will also update the class property of the entity. Figure 6-46 shows the renaming of the entity.

Figure 6-46: Rename Entity1

2. **Rename the Identifier and set the Type Name property.** Click on
   Identifier1. In the Properties window select the Name property of
   Identifier1 and change it to EmployeeID. Because the type of EmployeeID is an integer we need to set the Type Name property of EmployeeID to System.Int32 as shown in Figure 6-47.

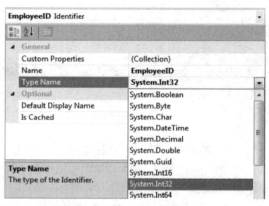

Figure 6-47: Rename Identifier and set Type
Name property

3. **Rename the default methods.** Highlight the method ReadlList in the
   entity shape and change the Name property to ReadEmployeeList in
   the Properties window. Highlight the method ReadlItem in the entity
   shape, and change the Name property to ReadEmployee in the Properties window. The Method Details window should now look like
   Figure 6-48.

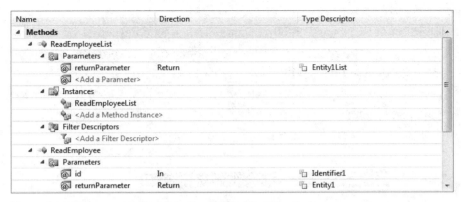

Figure 6-48: Renamed methods in the Method Details window

4. **Define the type descriptor representing the external content type Employee for the return parameter of the Finder method.** In the Method Details window click on the drop-down for the type descriptor Entity1List cell and select <Edit>. This will set the focus to the BDC Explorer window. In the Properties window rename the type descriptor from Entity1List to EmployeeList. In the drop-down of the Type Name property, select the Current Project tab and select Employee. It's important that you leave the Is Enumerable check box checked because this type descriptor defines a collection of Employees. Now you have defined the type descriptor that represents an IEnumerable of Employees. Figure 6-49 shows the Type Picker Control.

Let's move on and define the Employee external content type itself.

Why Do We Need to Define Employee Again, Isn't EmployeeList Sufficient?

The first time we defined the type descriptor that describes a collection of Employees. When the BDC runtime executes the method ReadEmployeeList it knows that it is of type Finder. That makes the runtime expect a collection of external content type objects to be returned, in our case a collection of Employees. In other words the first type descriptor (Employee-List) only tells the runtime that the method is about to return a collection of Employees. At this moment it doesn't know what the employee external content type looks like. And that's why we need to create the Employee type descriptor.

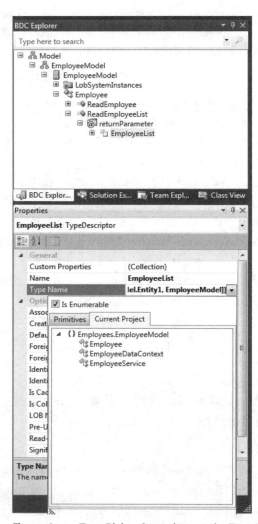

Figure 6-49: Type Picker Control to set the Type Name for EmployeeList

In the BDC Explorer we highlight Entity1 underneath Employee-List. Now we need to change its name to Employee in the Properties window. Also we need to set the Type Name property to Employee. In the drop-down for the Type Name property, select the Current Project tab and select Employee. Note this time we leave the IsEnumerable check box unchecked (Figure 6-50).

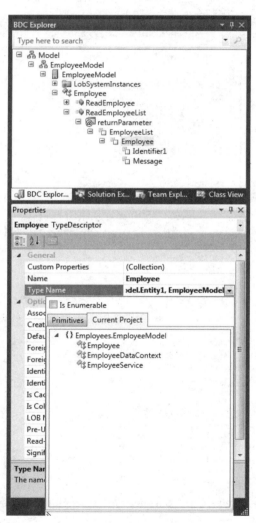

Figure 6-50: Type Picker Control to set the type for Employee

Now we need to define what data we want the end users to work with. Let's say the only information we really need for employees is the first name and the last name. That means we only need to create child type descriptors that represent the employee's id and the first and last names. We start with renaming Identifier1 to EmployeeID. Highlight Identifier1 in the BDC Explorer and change its name to EmployeeID in the Properties window. Also change the Type Name property to System.Int32. Figure 6-51 shows the renamed type descriptor.

Figure 6-51: Renamed type descriptor EmployeeID

Wait a Minute; Didn't We Already Create an EmployeeID?

Yes we did. This time we created a type descriptor that describes the identifier of the external content type. The first time we renamed the actual identifier. Have a look at the Identifier property of the type descriptor EmployeeID in Figure 6-51. Its value is set to EmployeeID, which is the actual employee identifier. You need to set this property if a type descriptor describes an identifier of an entity.

In the next step we need to create a type descriptor for the first name. Change the name of the type descriptor Message (which is a left over from the default entity) to FirstName. We don't need to change the Type Name property because FirstName is defined as a String already.

To finish our external content type Employee we need to add a new type descriptor to describe the last name. Right click on the type descriptor Employee and select Add Type Descriptor. Figure 6-52 shows the context menu to add a new type descriptor.

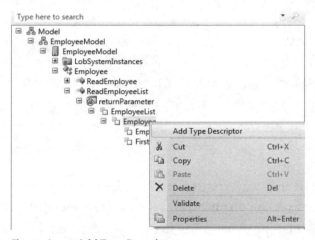

Figure 6-52: Add Type Descriptor

Visual Studio will always create a child of the selected type descriptor and set its Type Name property to System.String by default. Because LastName is also type String in our LINQ to SQL class, we only need to change the name of the newly added type to LastName. Figure 6-53 shows the entire EmployeeList type descriptor.

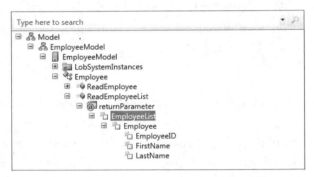

Figure 6-53: EmployeeList type descriptor in the BDC Explorer

Why Don't We Need to Define All Properties of an Employee?

What we've just done gives us a great example of an external content type. Even though we use data that is defined by an Employee object that retrieves data from an Employee table in the database, we can describe the external content type the way we want. In our case we don't need all properties of an Employee so we just defined our external content type to have first name and last name. On the other hand we could now add type descriptors to our external content type to describe aditional data from our LINQ to SQL class or some other data source.

Now that we have the ReadEmployeeList method completely defined we can go ahead and define the remaining methods.

5. **Copy the type descriptors to the Specific Finder method.** Designing the first type descriptor was a little bit painful, but from now on Visual Studio will do the work for us.

The feature of the BDC Explorer that we can take advantage when working with type descriptors is the copy type descriptor functionality. Because the method ReadEmployee returns one employee based on the EmployeeID we will copy the EmployeeID type descriptor first. In the BDC Explorer expand the parameter id of the ReadEmployee method and expand the nodes below the ReadEmployeeList method. Figure 6-54 shows the expanded parameter node of parameter Employee with EmployeeID selected.

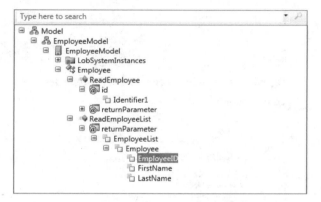

Figure 6-54: The selected type descriptor EmployeeID

Right click on the type descriptor EmployeeID under the ReadEmployeeList method. In the context menu select Copy as shown in Figure 6-55.

Now go back to the method ReadEmployee and select the parameter id. Right click on it and select Paste. A message tells you that there is already a TypeDescriptor and asks if you want to replace it. Select yes. Figure 6-56 shows the Paste command in the type descriptor context menu. We've now reused our EmployeeID type descriptor for the id parameter of ReadEmployee.

Next we need to repeat this step for the returnParameter of the ReadEmployee type descriptor as the method ReadEmployee returns an Employee. Copy the Employee type descriptor from the method ReadEmployeeList by right clicking on the type descriptor Employee in the BDC Explorer and choosing Copy.

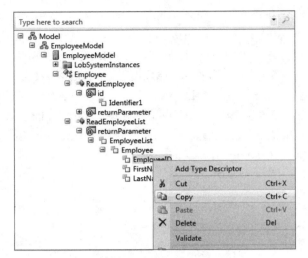

Figure 6-55: The Copy command in the type descriptor context menu

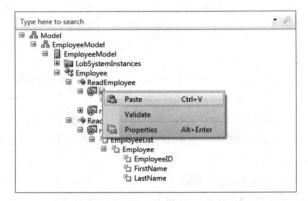

Figure 6-56: The Paste command in the type descriptor context menu

Next, select the parameter returnParameter in the method Read-Employee. Right click on it and select Paste in the context menu. You will be asked again if you want to replace the existing type descriptor, select Yes. As you can see in Figure 6-57 Visual Studio copies the entire type descriptors with all their properties. That saves a lot of time and limits the errors if the first one is defined correctly.

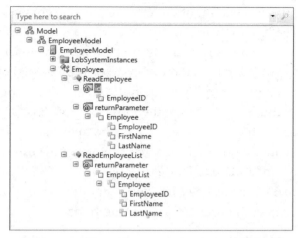

Figure 6-57: The type descriptor Employee copied to the
ReadEmployee method's returnParameter

6. **Create other methods.** As we want to create a CRUD enabled external content type we also need to add methods to Create, Update, and
Delete Employees.

Select the entity Employee in the BDC designer, so that the Method
Details window for our external content type appears. In the Method
Details window scroll all the way down to the row <Add a Method>.
As shown in Figure 6-58 click the drop-down button so that all the
available methods that can be added show up and select Create Creator
Method.

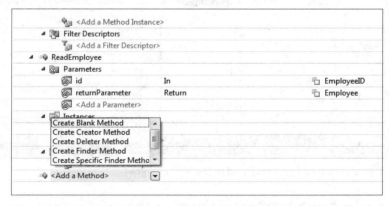

Figure 6-58: Drop-down box for <Add a Method> in the Method Details window

As you can see in Figure 6-59 Visual Studio creates a new method called Create with the right signature.

Rename the method in the Properties window to CreateEmployee.

Now we need to repeat the steps to create a deleter and an updater method. Remember that Visual Studio creates the right signatures for CRUD methods if you create them from the Method Details window as opposed to the entity shape. Once the methods are created rename the Delete method from Delete to DeleteEmployee and the updater method from Update to UpdateEmployee.

Figure 6-60 shows the BDC designer with external content type Employee and all necessary CRUD methods.

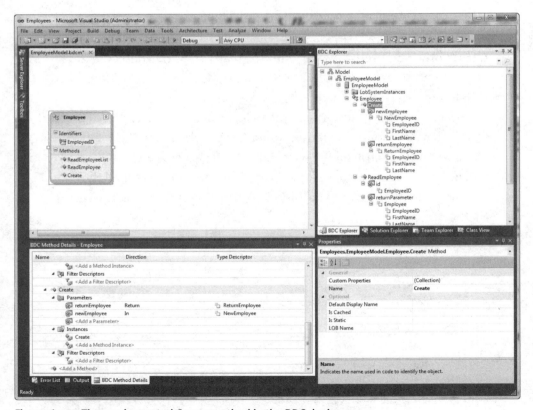

Figure 6-59: The newly created Create method in the BDC designer

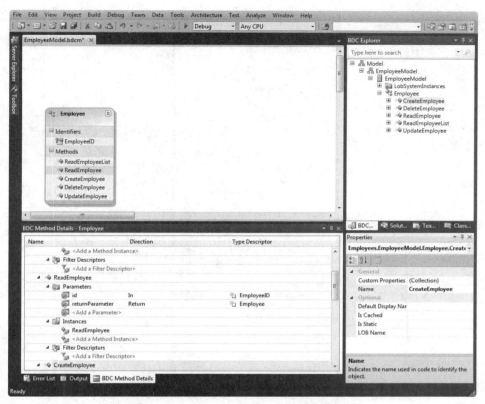

Figure 6-60: The external content type Employee with CRUD operations

We are almost done. The last thing we need to do is to set the property Read-only to True for the type descriptor EmployeeID in the specific finder method ReadEmployee's return parameter "returnParameter."

Go to the BDC Explorer and navigate to the method ReadEmployee. Expand its node and further expand the node of the return parameter "returnParameter." Expand the tree of the type descriptor Employee and navigate to the type descriptor EmployeeID. In the Properties window for EmployeeID locate the property ReadOnly and set it to True as shown in Figure 6-61.

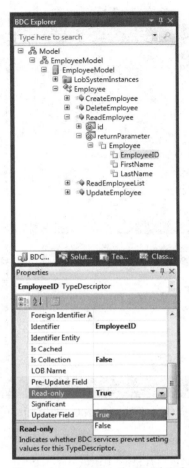

Figure 6-61: Setting the Read-Only
property of the type descriptor EmployeeID

There is one last thing we should point out with regards to creating methods. As you have seen in the drop-down you can also create a blank method. This requires you to add the parameters manually, set the type descriptors manually and set the type of the method instance correctly. Table 6-6 shows the method types for which Visual Studio automatically creates the correct signatures. To cover all of the other types would go way beyond the scope of this book. If you want further information on all the other method types see http://msdn.microsoft .com/en-us/library/ee557363(office.14).aspx.

You Lost Me. Why Do We Need to Manually Adjust the Type Descriptor for EmployeeID in ReadEmployee?

Unfortunately you always need to make manual adjustments when you create an updater method. The first one is the one we have just implemented: setting the type descriptor of the external content type's id to read-only in the specific finder method. The reason for that is that the EmployeeID is an identity field in the database. The database auto increments the field when a new record is added to a table (the "write once" scenario) and after that the field is read-only. When a user wants to update or create an Employee object, the SharePoint UI calls the specific finder method to determine how the update or create form should look. Because the user is not allowed to update the identifier or enter a new one after a record is created, we need to set the property to Read-only.

If you are not using the "write once" model, you need to provide a value for the external content type's identifier. In that case you need to add another parameter to the updater method, which has the direction in and the type descriptor of the external content type's identifier. The Pre-Updater Field property of that identifier needs to be set to True. That tells the runtime which identifier needs to be updated as the value of the old identifier is also passed in. In that scenario you don't need to set the Read-only property of the type descriptor of the external content type's id to True.

Store the Connection Information and Make It Accessible During Runtime

Before we can start implementing the code we should think about a way to handle connection strings. BCS uses LobSystemInstance objects to provide authentication and connection string information to the BCS runtime. The information is provided through properties added to the LobSystem-Instance object in the BDC Explorer. There are standard connection properties you can use for database and WCF service LobSystems. The information provided in those properties would enable the BCS runtime to connect to the

LobSystems. Because Visual Studio only builds models based on .NET Assembly LobSystems, we cannot take advantage of those properties because the project output assembly itself acts as a proxy to the external system, which means that we need to provide the connection information in the code.

We can achieve the storing of connection information by adding custom properties to the LobSystemInstance object.

Can't I Just Hard Code the Connection Information in the Code or Use a Settings File?

Yes you can hard code the connection information in the code. The only caveat is that you won't be able to change the information in SharePoint Designer when opening the external content type. No, you cannot store the information in a settings file because the project output assembly will be uploaded to the database and the settings file won't be accessible.

We should also keep in mind that each LobSystemInstance object needs to have a unique name. Visual Studio has already created an LobSystemInstance object called EmployeeModel in the project. We will add custom properties to EmployeeModel to store to store connection information. Let's rename the LobSystemInstance. In the BDC Explorer locate the Lob-SystemInstances folder and expand it. Figure 6-62 shows the expanded LobSystemInstances folder in the BDC Explorer.

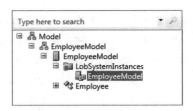

Figure 6-62: The LobSystemInstances folder in the BDC Explorer

In the Properties window change the name from EmployeeModel to EmployeeModelConnect. Before we can create a custom property for the connection string we need to copy the connection information from our existing connection in Server Explorer.

Open the Server Explorer and click on the connection to the Northwind database. In the Properties window copy the value of the connection string property to the clipboard. Figure 6-63 shows the Server Explorer and its Properties window.

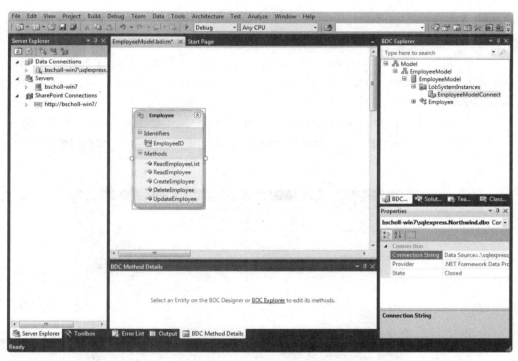

Figure 6-63: Connection string property of the connection to the Northwind database

Now double click on the EmployeeModel.bdcm file to bring up the BDC Designer again. In the BDC Explorer navigate to the LobSystemInstance EmployeeModelConnect.

In the Properties window click on (Collection) in the Custom Properties value as shown in Figure 6-64.

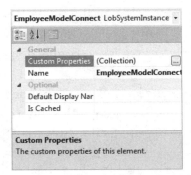

Figure 6-64: Custom Properties for the

LobSystemInstance EmployeeModelConnect

Click on the … button in that cell to bring up the Property Editor. In the Name column enter "NWConnection," which will be the name of our property, in the Type drop-down select System.String and in the Value column you need to paste the connection string from the clipboard and hit OK. Figure 6-65 shows the Property Editor with the newly added property.

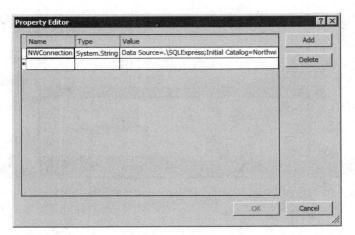

Figure 6-65: Property Editor

But how can our code access the property during runtime? The answer is we need to implement an interface in our service class to access the property.

First we need to add a reference to the Microsoft.BusinessData assembly which is located in the GAC. It is not a good practice to reference assemblies in the GAC so we will copy the Microsoft.BusinessData.dll assembly out of GAC. Go to the Start menu and choose Run... and type in C:\Windows\ assembly\gac_msil. Find Microsoft.BusinessData folder, and then copy Microsoft.BusinessData.dll to the folder C:\Program Files\Common Files\ Microsoft Shared\Web Server Extensions\14\ISAPI.

In the Solution Explorer right click on references and select Add Reference. Switch to the Browse tab and browse to C:\Program Files\Common Files\Microsoft Shared\Web Server Extensions\14\ ISAPI, locate the Microsoft.BusinessData.dll, select it and click the OK button.

Add the following using statement to the EmployeeService class:

```
using Microsoft.BusinessData.SystemSpecific;
```

Finally we need to have EmployeeService implement the IContextProperty interface. Visual Studio helps you with this. As soon as you have added the interface name to the `EmployeeService` class a smart tag appears as shown in Figure 6-66 that gives you two options to implement the interface. Select implement interface 'IContextProperty' and Visual Studio will generate the code for you. You need to remove the `throw new NotImplementedException` in the getter and setter of the properties because the BCS runtime will call these methods when context variables are read and written.

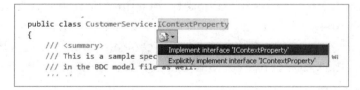

Figure 6-66: Implement Interface smart tag

Now that we are done with implementing the connection information and the last step is to implement the actual code.

7. **Implement the methods.** As you can see there are a lot of methods with squiggles in our class. Basically you can delete all of the methods with squiggles, because Visual Studio has also created the correct ones. The reason for these redundant methods lies in how Visual Studio does code management.

How Does Visual Studio Code Management Work?

When you create a method in the designer, the tool will generate a static method in the service class. Visual Studio creates static methods because the BDC runtime performs slightly better when accessing static methods. The problem is that when we work with the IContextProperty interface we need to remove the static modifier from the methods because the interface itself is not static and thus we wouldn't be able to access its properties. Also if you plan to open the external content types that are defined in the model in SharePoint Designer you need to change the finder methods to return type IList<> instead of IEnumerable<> manually. Before it creates a new method it looks at the method name, method return type, if the method is static or not, the method parameter count, the parameter type, and the parameter order. If it cannot find a method with a similar signature and name it will create a new one. If you rename the method the method name in the code is updated. Also when you update the Type Name property of a parameter's type descriptor the parameter's type in the code is updated.

Listing 6-1 shows the code after deleting the redundant method signatures and adding the logic to create, read, update, and delete the employee external content type. The code also contains a method that reads the value of our custom property NWConnection and returns the connection string.

Listing 6-1: Code for Creating, Reading, Updating, and Deleting an Employee External Content Type

```
public class EmployeeService:IContextProperty
{
  public IEnumerable<Employee> ReadEmployeeList()
  {
```

```csharp
  EmployeeDataContext ctx =
    new EmployeeDataContext(GetConnectionString());
  return ctx.Employees;
}

public Employee ReadEmployee(Int32 id)
{
  EmployeeDataContext ctx =
  new EmployeeDataContext(GetConnectionString());
  return ctx.Employees.Single(e=>e.EmployeeID == id);
}

public Employee CreateEmployee(Employee newEmployee)
{
  EmployeeDataContext ctx =
    new EmployeeDataContext(GetConnectionString());
  ctx.Employees.InsertOnSubmit(newEmployee);
  ctx.SubmitChanges();

  Employee emp = ctx.Employees.
    Single(e => e.EmployeeID == newEmployee.EmployeeID);
  return emp;
}

public void DeleteEmployee(int employeeID)
{
  EmployeeDataContext ctx =
    new EmployeeDataContext(GetConnectionString());
  Employee emp = ctx.Employees.
    Single(e => e.EmployeeID == employeeID);
  ctx.Employees.DeleteOnSubmit(emp);
  ctx.SubmitChanges();
}

public void UpdateEmployee(Employee employee)
{
  EmployeeDataContext ctx =
    new EmployeeDataContext(GetConnectionString());
  Employee emp = ctx.Employees.
    Single(e => e.EmployeeID == employee.EmployeeID);
  emp.FirstName = employee.FirstName;
  emp.LastName = employee.LastName;
  ctx.SubmitChanges();
}

internal string GetConnectionString()
{
  Microsoft.BusinessData.MetadataModel.Collections.
    INamedPropertyDictionary dic =
    this.LobSystemInstance.GetProperties();
```

```
    if (dic.ContainsKey("NWConnection"))
    {
      return dic["NWConnection"].ToString();
    }
    return null;
  }

  public Microsoft.BusinessData.Runtime.
    IExecutionContext ExecutionContext
  {
    get;
    set;
  }

  public Microsoft.BusinessData.MetadataModel.
    ILobSystemInstance LobSystemInstance
  {
    get;
    set;
  }

  public Microsoft.BusinessData.MetadataModel.
    IMethodInstance MethodInstance
  {
    get;
    set;
  }
}
```

8. The only thing left to do is to deploy the solution, create an external
    list, and test to see if it works. We already learned how to debug and
    deploy models, so let's set a breakpoint in the first line of the method
    ReadEmployeeList and hit F5. Once the browser comes up create an
    external list and name it "Employees." Before the list is rendered you
    hit the breakpoint as expected. Now you can go ahead and try all
    operations. Note: Delete won't work because the Employees table in
    the database ensures referential integrity.

      Since the external content type Employee has CRUD methods
    defined that allow you to create, delete, and update employees; the
    external list has enabled those commands in the UI as well as shown
    in Figure 6-67.

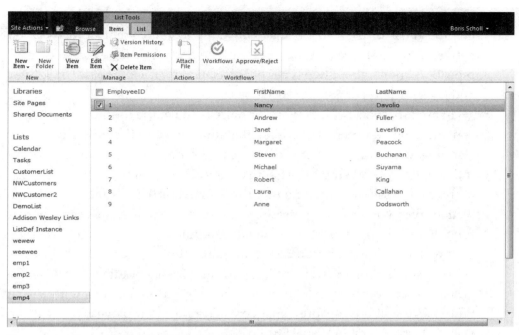

Figure 6-67: External list with CRUD operations enabled

In eight steps we went through the recommended way to create a CRUD-enabled external content type with Visual Studio. The biggest difference between doing this in SharePoint Designer versus Visual Studio is that by using Visual Studio it's in the developer's power to write the data access logic. In our sample above, if you wanted to add some custom business logic, i.e., checking for valid area codes etc. or custom security rules before saving data, there is no way to do that in SharePoint Designer, whereas in Visual Studio you can.

Build Associations Between External Content Types

At this point you should be familiar with creating single CRUD-capable external content types using Visual Studio. We will now look into how to create external content types that are in relation to each other. For example, in the Northwind database employees have a relationship with orders. Assume you wanted to display the relationship in the UI, meaning you want to see all the orders entered by an employee to figure out which employee has the most orders. To do that you need to implement an association between an employee external content type and an order external content type. BCS knows about two types of associations; *foreign key-based* or *fk-based* and *foreign key-less* or *fk-less* associations.

In an fk-based association one or more fields of the destination external content type represent the ids of the source external content type. For example, order (destination external content type) has a field for storing the id of the related employee (source external content type).

In an fk-less association neither the source nor the destination external content type has a field representing the id of the related external content type. For example, a business contact external content type can be associated with one or more account external content type instances.

You can use both SharePoint Designer and Visual Studio to create an fk-based association but you can only create fk-less associations with Visual Studio. We will use our previously created project Employees to create an fk-based association in Visual Studio.

Open the previously created project Employees in Visual Studio. We will use LINQ to SQL again to access the orders table in the database. First we will add the Order table to our already existing LINQ to SQL model Employee .dbml. In the Solution Explorer double click the Employee.dbml file. Open the Server Explorer and navigate to the Northwind database. Expand the Tables node and select Orders. Drag the Orders table to the designer and place it next to the Employee entity. That's all we need to do to update our LINQ to SQL model. Figure 6-68 shows the LINQ to SQL designer after adding the Orders table.

Now we need to define the Order external content type. In the Solution Explorer double click on EmployeeModel.bdcm to bring up the BDC designer. Open the toolbox and drag a new entity to the design surface and rename it Order. Figure 6-69 shows the newly added external content type Order.

Add a new identifier by right clicking on the Order entity shape; select Add new Identifier as shown in Figure 6-70. Name it OrderID and change the Type Name property to System.Int32 by using the type picker in the Properties window shown for the identifier.

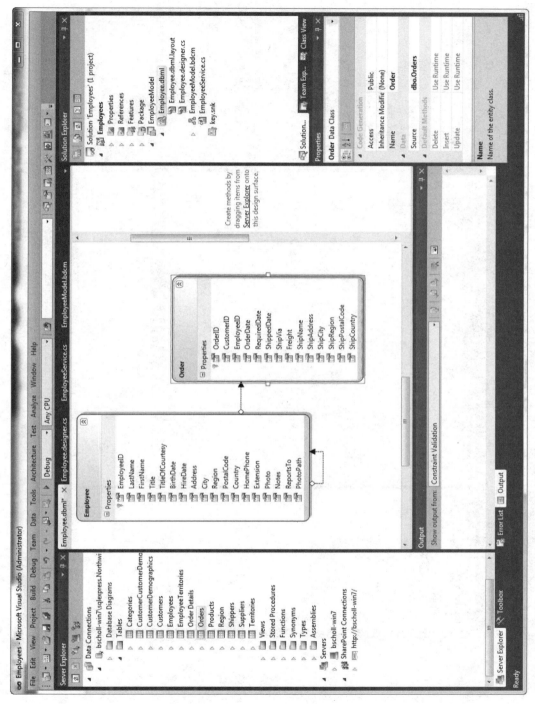

Figure 6-68: Order added to the LINQ to SQL designer

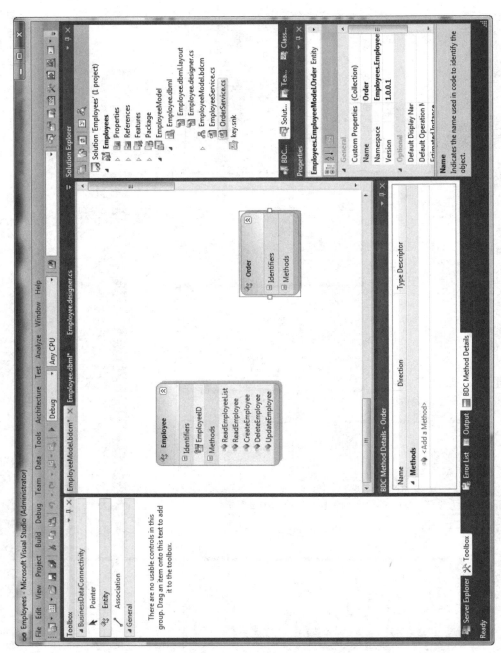

Figure 6-69: Create a new external content type from the toolbox

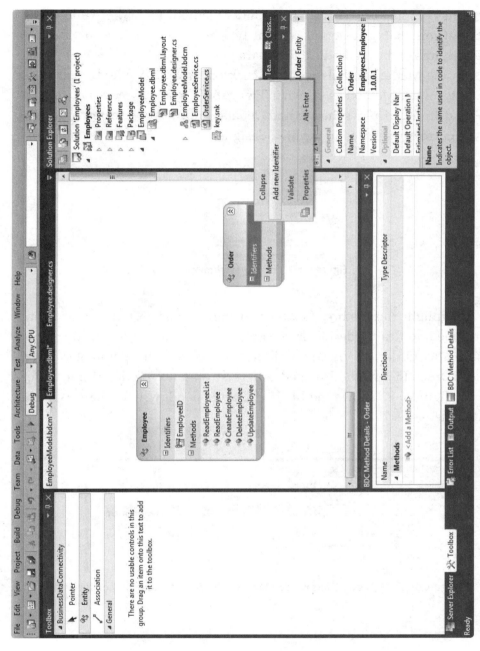

Figure 6-70: Adding an identifier to the Order external content type

433

The next step is to create a new Finder method. This is very interesting; it confirms that an external content type in BCS is defined by the type descriptors of the method's return parameter.

In the Method Details window click on <Add a Method> and select Create Finder Method as shown in Figure 6-71. You may have noticed that Visual Studio displays the Method Details window for the external content type currently selected in the BDC designer.

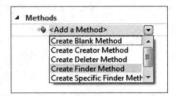

Figure 6-71: Create new finder method

Highlight the method ReadList in the Method Details window and rename it to ReadOrderList in the Properties window. We already named our entity Order, so Visual Studio has created a return parameter for the ReadOrdersList method named orderList with a type descriptor Order-List. Figure 6-72 shows the Method Details window with the newly created method.

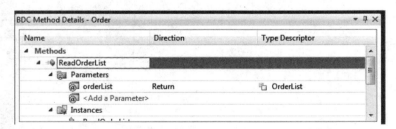

Figure 6-72: Method Details window with ReadOrderList finder method for orders

Now we need to define the type descriptor for our orders external content type. Click on the OrderList type descriptor and select <Edit> to get to the BDC Explorer. It is still up to us to define the type descriptor because Visual Studio does not know how an order external content type is defined, but it already set some properties based on the selection to create a Finder method. Because a Finder method always returns a collection the Type Name property of OrderList is already set to an IEnumerable of System.String, which is the default type for type descriptors created by Visual Studio. Visual Studio also created a child type descriptor Order. Figure 6-73 shows the type descriptor OrderList in the BDC Explorer.

Figure 6-73: OrderList type descriptor
in BDC Explorer

Now we need to set the right Type Name property for the type descriptor OrderList and design the Order type descriptor itself. Click on Order-List in the BDC Explorer then the Type Name property in the Properties window to bring up the type picker. Switch to the Current Project tab and select the Order class as shown in Figure 6-74.

Visual Studio knows that this is the top-level type descriptor of the return parameter of a Finder method, so we don't need to select the IsEnumerable check box because Visual Studio has already done that. Let's define the Order

Figure 6-74: Set Type Name property for
OrderList type descriptor

type descriptor next. Since we've already learned how to do that, we will skip explaining it in detail. You should add all the Order properties defined in the data class as child type descriptors to the Order type descriptor. Table 6-8 shows the list of child type descriptors and their type names for the Order type descriptor.

TABLE 6-8: Child Type Descriptors of the Order Type Descriptor

Name	Type Name
CustomerID	System.String
EmployeeID	System.Int32
OrderID	System.Int32
Freight	System.Decimal
OrderDate	System.DateTime
RequiredDate	System.DateTime
ShipAddress	System.String
ShipCity	System.String
ShipCountry	System.String
ShipName	System.String
ShippedDate	System.DateTime
ShipPostalCode	System.String
ShipRegion	System.String
ShipVia	System.Int32

The Order type descriptor should now look like Figure 6-75.

Now we can take advantage of Visual Studio's create method functionality again. In the Method Details window click on <Add a Method> and in the drop-down select Create Specific Finder Method. Visual Studio creates the correct signature for us, so that you only need to rename the method. In the Properties window for the method rename the method to ReadOrder as shown in Figure 6-76. The last method we create is an Updater method using the <Add a Method> drop-down again. Select the "Create Updater Method" item. We also need to mark the type descriptor OrderID as read-only because the schema doesn't allow the OrderID field to be updated.

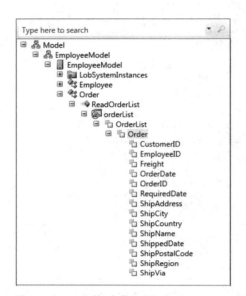

Figure 6-75: Fully defined Order type descriptor in the BDC Explorer

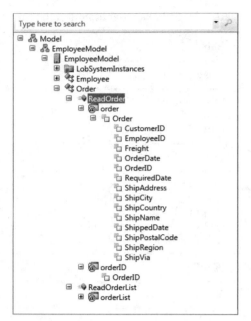

Figure 6-76: Specific Finder for the Orders external content type in the BDC Explorer

For this example we will only create a Finder, Specific Finder, and an Updater method for the Order external content type. Of course we could also implement Create and Delete for Order, but the Finder, the Specific Finder, and the Updater are the only methods we really need to build and demonstrate an association. Click on ReadOrder and in the drop-down select <View Code>. You will notice that Visual Studio takes you to the file OrderService.cs, which has the OrderService class defined. The is perfect to remind us that Visual Studio code management will only create service classes for external content types. First we have to add `using Microsoft`
`.BusinessData.SystemSpecific;` to the code file, so that we are able to access the connection string. Next, we need to add code to all three methods to retrieve the Order data from the database and enable the update of the data. Because Visual Studio has all methods as static methods we need to remove the static modifier again so that we can access the LobSystemInstance property NWConnection and implement the IContextProperty interface.

Listing 6-2 shows the code that reads the order data from the database.

Listing 6-2: Implementation of the Order's Finder, Updater, and Specific Finder

```
public partial class OrderService:IContextProperty
{
  public IEnumerable<Order> ReadOrderList()
  {
    EmployeeDataContext ctx =
      new EmployeeDataContext(GetConnectionString());
    return ctx.Orders;
  }

  public Order ReadOrder(int orderID)
  {
    EmployeeDataContext ctx =
      new EmployeeDataContext(GetConnectionString());
    return ctx.Orders.Single(o=>o.OrderID == orderID);
  }

  internal string GetConnectionString()
  {
    Microsoft.BusinessData.MetadataModel.Collections.
      INamedPropertyDictionary dic =
      this.LobSystemInstance.GetProperties();

    if (dic.ContainsKey("NWConnection"))
    {
      return dic["NWConnection"].ToString();
    }
    return null;
  }

  public void UpdateOrder(Order order)
  {
    EmployeeDataContext ctx
      = new EmployeeDataContext(GetConnectionString());
    Order neworder =
      ctx.Orders.Single(o => o.OrderID == order.OrderID);

    neworder.CustomerID = order.CustomerID;
    neworder.EmployeeID = order.EmployeeID;
    neworder.OrderDate = order.OrderDate;
    neworder.RequiredDate = order.RequiredDate;
    neworder.ShippedDate = order.ShippedDate;
    neworder.ShipVia = order.ShipVia;
    neworder.Freight = order.Freight;
    neworder.ShipName = order.ShipName;
    neworder.ShipAddress = order.ShipAddress;
    neworder.ShipCountry = order.ShipCountry;
    neworder.ShipCity = order.ShipCity;
```

```
    neworder.ShipRegion = order.ShipRegion;
    neworder.ShipPostalCode = order.ShipPostalCode;
    ctx.SubmitChanges();
}

public Microsoft.BusinessData.Runtime.
    IExecutionContext ExecutionContext
{
    get;
    set;
}

public Microsoft.BusinessData.MetadataModel.
    ILobSystemInstance LobSystemInstance
{
    get;
    set;
}

public Microsoft.BusinessData.MetadataModel.
    IMethodInstance MethodInstance
{
    get;
    set;
}
}
```

With our Order entity implemented we can go ahead and build an Association between Employee and Order. In the Toolbox window click on the Association icon and move your cursor to the Employee external content type. Your cursor should now display an Association icon. Click somewhere on the Employee entity shape to start drawing the line. Draw the line to the Order external content type and click somewhere on the entity shape. Visual Studio always considers the source entity to be where you started drawing the line, in our case Order. Figure 6-77 shows the Association editor.

We can leave the association name as proposed by Visual Studio (EmployeeToOrderAssociation). The drop-down boxes for Source Entity and Destination Entity are disabled. This is because we've drawn the line from Employee to Order, thus Visual Studio knows what the destination entity is and what the source entity is. The association type is always set to fk-based by default. Because we want to create an fk-based association we leave it checked.

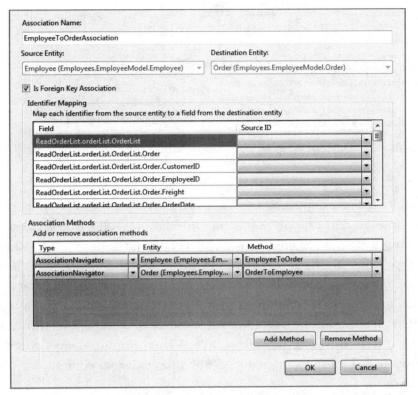

Figure 6-77: Association editor dialog after drawing an association from Employee to Order

In the Identifier Mapping section you need to map the identifier of Employee's EmployeeID to the type descriptor in the Orders entity that represents the EmployeeID. This is necessary for the BCS runtime to know how those external content types are related.

Select EmployeeID in the Source ID column and map it to the type descriptor representing the EmployeeID in the Field column (ReadOrderList .orderlist.OrderList.Order.EmployeeID). Figure 6-78 shows the drop-down.

You need to do this for all type descriptors representing the EmployeeID in the destination external content type. Also if the source external content type has more than one identifier you need to do this for all the identifiers.

In database scenarios the id and foreign key id don't need to have the same name, but the id and foreign key id names *do* need to exactly match in

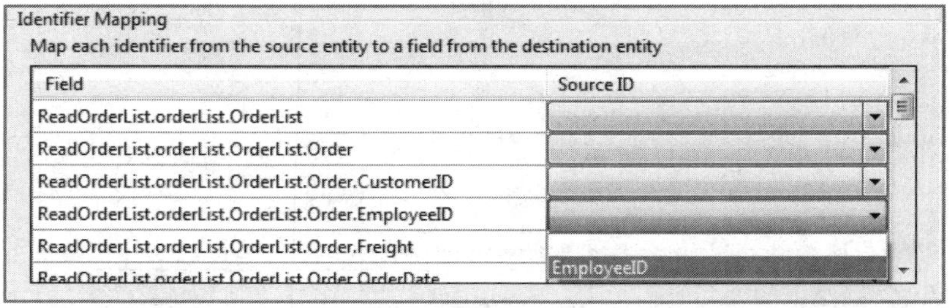

Figure 6-78: Identifier mapping

BCS scenarios. For example, if your id is EmployeeID, the type descriptor representing the fkid cannot be named OrderEmployeeID, it must also be named EmployeeID; keep this in mind when you build fk-based associations.

In the Methods section we can define the Association Methods. Visual Studio creates two methods by default, in our case EmployeeToOrder and OrderToEmployee. The methods created are of type AssociationNavigator, which means that one navigates from source to destination entity and the other one from destination to source. Visual Studio always chooses the names based on the source and destination external content types in an association.

The first method created for our sample allows you to navigate from Employee to Order—the method will return all orders for an employee. The second method allows us to get all employees for an order—sometimes referred to as a reverse navigator method. Such functionality doesn't make much sense based on the Northwind database schema, because the method will only return one employee. We will leave the method as is but this will give us an understanding of a navigator from destination to source external content type.

You can add and remove additional association methods by using the Add Method and Remove Method buttons. Table 6-9 shows all the properties in the Association Editor.

Click the OK button. The dialog disappears and you can see a line between Employee and Order, indicating the external content types are now associated. Figure 6-79 shows the association in the designer.

TABLE 6-9: Association Editor Properties

Property	Description
Association Name	Name of the association
Source Entity	The source entity of the association
Destination Entity	The destination entity of the association
Is Foreign Key Association	Indicates whether it is a foreign-key association
Source ID	The identifiers of the Source ID
Field	The type descriptors defining the return parameters of the methods in the destination entity
Type	Association method type
Entity	Entity on which the method is to be created
Method	Name of the method

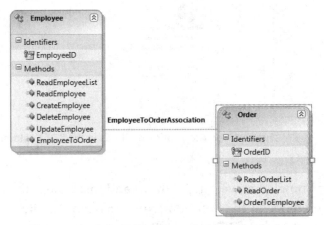

Figure 6-79: EmployeeToOrderAssociation in the designer

Let's have a closer look at what was created when you hit the OK button. A new method was added to both external content types: Employee-ToOrder on the employee external content type and OrderToEmployee on the order external content type.

For our exploration we focus on the EmployeeToOrder method because both method signatures are identical. Select the Employee shape in the BDC designer to show the Method Details window for this method. The method has two parameters: employeeID is an *in* parameter with a type descriptor for EmployeeID and orderList is a *return* parameter with a type descriptor describing an IEnumerable of Orders.

We can summarize that an association is basically a method that allows users to navigate from one external content type to another, in our case from Employee to Order. Figure 6-80 shows the newly created association methods in the BDC Explorer.

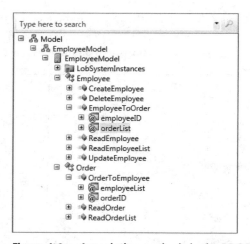

Figure 6-80: Association methods in the BDC Explorer

With this knowledge we can go ahead and implement the code for our association method. In the Solution Explorer open the file EmployeeService.cs. Locate the method EmployeeToOrder and add the code shown in Listing 6-3.

Listing 6-3: Code for Association Method EmployeeToOrder

```
public IEnumerable<Order> EmployeeToOrder(int employeeID)
{
  EmployeeDataContext ctx = new
    EmployeeDataContext(GetConnectionString());
  return ctx.Orders.Where(o => o.EmployeeID == employeeID);
}
```

The EmployeeToOrder method takes an employeeID as an in parameter and returns an IEnumerable of Orders for the given employee. The nice thing about using LINQ is that it really reduces the lines of code you need to implement. The line `context.Orders.Where(o => o.EmployeeID == employeeID);` applies a filter to return only the orders for an employee with that particular id.

Now open OrderService.cs and locate the method OrderToEmployee to implement the code. Listing 6-4 shows that the OrderToEmployee method takes an orderID as an in parameter and returns an IEnumerable of Employee.

Listing 6-4: Code for Association Method OrderToEmployee

```
public  IEnumerable<Employee> OrderToEmployee(int orderID)
{
  EmployeeDataContext ctx = new
    EmployeeDataContext(GetConnectionString());

  return ctx.Employees.Where(e => e.EmployeeID ==
    ctx.Orders.Where(o => o.OrderID == orderID).
    Select(o => o.EmployeeID).Single());
}
```

In the Northwind database an order has only one employee assigned to it. Since our employee external content type doesn't have an orderID property we need to get the employeeID for this particular order first. The employeeID is returned by this part of the LINQ statement:

```
ctx.Orders.Where(o => o.OrderId == orderID).Select(o => o.employeeID).Single());
```

Once we have the employeeID for the order we can apply the filter to the employee object.

```
e => e.EmployeeId ==ctx.Orders.Where(o =>…….
```

With the OrderToEmployee method implemented we can deploy the model and see if it works, but before we do that we should look at our UI options for displaying associations.

The best UI components for working with associations are profile pages or business data web parts because they provide the richest functionality and user experience. Unfortunately those components are only available in SharePoint Server. SharePoint Foundation only offers UI support for associations in external lists.

Let's see what our model looks like now. Deploy the model by hitting F5. Visual Studio will show several warnings as shown in Figure 6-81. These warnings are caused by the Visual Studio model validator indicating that the BDC runtime doesn't know how DateTime data types are defined and therefore uses UTC. You will always get a warning when using DateTime types in your models but you can ignore them.

	Description	File	Line	Column	Project
⚠ 1	The TypeDescriptor 'OrderDate' is of a DateTime type, but there is no Interpretation describing how the back-end interprets the DateTime value. The DateTime value is therefore assumed to be UTC.	EmployeeModel.bdcn	151	27	Employees
⚠ 2	The TypeDescriptor 'RequiredDate' is of a DateTime type, but there is no Interpretation describing how the back-end interprets the DateTime value. The DateTime value is therefore assumed to be UTC.	EmployeeModel.bdcn	152	27	Employees
⚠ 3	The TypeDescriptor 'ShippedDate' is of a DateTime type, but there is no Interpretation describing how the back-end interprets the DateTime value. The DateTime value is therefore assumed to be UTC.	EmployeeModel.bdcn	157	27	Employees
⚠ 4	The TypeDescriptor 'OrderDate' is of a DateTime type, but there is no Interpretation describing how the back-end interprets the DateTime value. The DateTime value is therefore assumed to be UTC.	EmployeeModel.bdcn	175	23	Employees
⚠ 5	The TypeDescriptor 'RequiredDate' is of a DateTime type, but there is no Interpretation describing how the back-end interprets the DateTime value. The DateTime value is therefore assumed to be UTC.	EmployeeModel.bdcn	176	23	Employees

Figure 6-81: Warnings when model contains type descriptors of type DatetTme

Once the browser comes up, go to Site Actions, More Options, and in the Create dialog select Data. In the main area of the page choose type External List and click the Create button, then the New External List page appears.

Name the external list Orders and click the second icon next to the External Content Type textbox to bring up the External Content Type Picker dialog. Figure 6-82 shows the dialog.

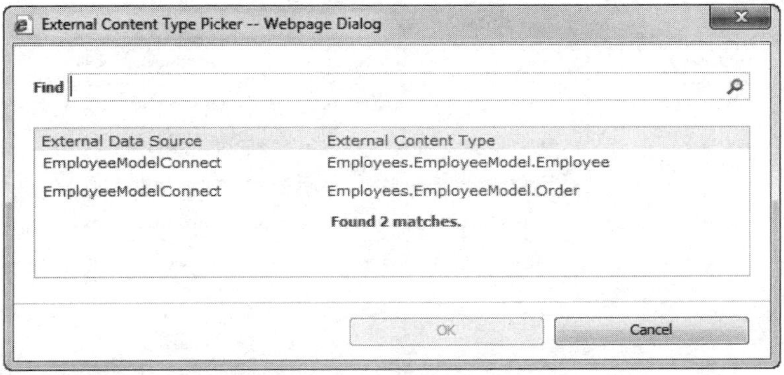

Figure 6-82: External Content Type Picker dialog

Select Order and click OK then Create. Once the list is created select one item and click Edit Item in the context menu as shown in Figure 6-83.

The edit item dialog comes up. As you can see in Figure 6-84, it enables us to update all the properties we have defined through type descriptors in the updater method's in parameter. You will also notice that OrderID is not displayed, because we set the type descriptor of the OrderID in the return parameter of the order's specific finder to read-only. That also tells us that the UI for the edit, read item, and create forms are driven by the type descriptors of the external content type's specific finder.

Now look at the Employees.EmployeeModel.Employee field. This is actually the foreign key identifier for employees in the orders table. When we created the association we mapped the employeeID identifier to the type descriptors of the orders methods return parameters employeeID. That makes the form render this field as a picker rather than a normal text-box. Now click on the picker icon to bring up the picker. We have a foreign key-based association so we can pick any of the employees and assign the employee to the order. Figure 6-85 shows the picker for employees.

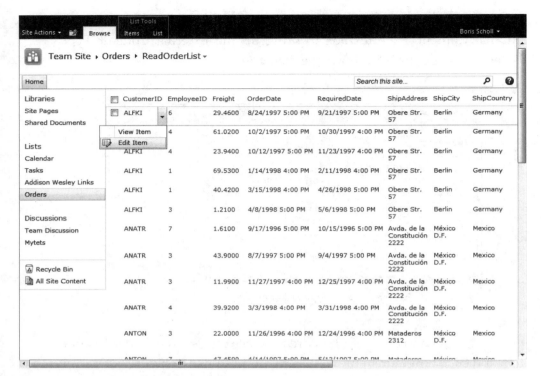

Figure 6-83: Edit Item context menu item

Select any of the employees in the list and click the OK button to assign the new value. Back in the Edit Item dialog click the Save button to save the changes to the database.

That Is All? But I Wanted to See All Orders for One Particular Employee!

Unfortunately one of the limitations of associations in external lists is that there is no way to show us all orders for an employee. If we wanted this functionality in SharePoint Foundation we need to write custom web parts that use the BCS API to call our association methods. SharePoint Server comes with Business Data Web Parts that allow you to graphically display associations. Those are not covered here because this book targets SharePoint Foundation.

Figure 6-84: Edit Item dialog

As mentioned above Visual Studio also supports creating fk-less associations but we won't cover them in this book. The only out-of-the-box UI to render those associations is Business Data Web Parts that provide read-only functionality. As we know these are not available in SharePoint Foundation. Fk-less associations are fully supported at the API level so if you want to do more than the simple read-only scenarios supported by the Business Data Web Parts you need to implement the entire UI and work with associations at the API level.

As we have seen, BCS uses associations to enable the user to browse related external content types. You should keep in mind that most of the associations you will implement are fk-based, which gives you the choice between using SharePoint Designer and Visual Studio to create them.

The same recommendation for which tool to use for creating external content types applies for associations as well. If you just need to create simple

Figure 6-85: Entity Picker

fk-based associations without custom logic, custom security, data aggrega-
tion, and have no need for source control then SharePoint Designer is certainly a good choice, but as soon as you want to have more control over the
implementation of any of the previously mentioned items, there is no other
choice but Visual Studio.

Custom Properties

Now that we've looked into how to create and work with external content
types we should look into how we can influence their behaviors. For example you may want to have SharePoint Search crawl an external content
type so that it shows up in your intranet search or you may want to map an
external content type to Office Item Types (see Table 5-1) so that a user can
take a list offline. To accomplish these behaviors you need to implement
Custom Properties. You actually already know how to do this because you
did it when you created a custom property for the connection string earlier
in this chapter.

There are two types of custom properties: the custom ones you create
and the predefined ones that the runtime and other tools, such as the Office

client, understand. There is only one scenario in which you want to create your own custom property and that's creating properties that store connection strings, authorization, and authentication information on a LobSystemInstance as we've done before.

Custom properties can be added to every object in the BDC Explorer. Just Click the ... button next to the Custom Properties property in the Properties window to bring up the Custom Properties Editor, then enter the name, the type, and the value for the custom property you want to add. If you want to get an overview of all the properties available simply click on the question mark in the Custom Property Editor. As mentioned before external content types created by SharePoint Designer are searchable out of the box. To make the Employee external content type created in Visual Studio searchable in the same way as the one created in SharePoint Designer you need to add the custom properties shown in Table 6-10. All properties are of type System.String.

TABLE 6-10:   Custom Properties Needed to Enable Search

Name/Level	Value	Purpose
ShowInSearchUI LobSystemInstance (i.e., the EmployeeModelConnect object in this chapter)	Blank	This is a property that specifies that an LobSystemInstance in the application model file should be displayed in the search UI as indexable.
RootFinder Finder<MethodInstance>level (i.e., ReadEmployee method in this chapter)	Blank	This designates that the Finder method specified will be used to enumerate the roots.
UseClientCachingForSearch on the "RootFinder" at <MethodInstanceLevel> and on the AssociationNavigators at <MethodInstanceLevel> (i.e., ReadEmployee and EmployeeToOrder methods in this chapter)	Blank	This specifies whether the backend can return the content during enumeration. If the backend being crawled can return all indexable data (less than 8k in size when zipped) during the enumeration, the search system will index this data without subsequent round-trips.

The properties above will only enable basic search functionality on an external content type. In SharePoint Designer you cannot change this behavior. Visual Studio again gives you more possibilities because you can implement more Search properties.

Deployment Considerations for External Content Types Using Visual Studio

Visual Studio provides two deployment modes. The default mode is "Incremental," which means that only changes will be deployed after the initial deploy; this mode increases the deployment performance drastically. Now you might wonder why this is needed because you probably won't have more than between 8 and 10 external content types in a model anyways. Well it is not so much the number of external content types in a model as it is the number of type descriptors. Just think about how many type descriptors are defined in the Employee external content type we have used throughout the chapter. Now multiply this number by 10 and add the number of parameters, methods, and method instances to it and you will end up with quite a large number of objects that need to be deployed and imported into the metadata store. That's why it is a good practice to leave the default setting Incremental Update set to True while you are developing.

Sometimes you will want to switch to full deployment mode (e.g., Incremental Update set to False). Doing a full deployment will always clean up the entire store. Why is that necessary? For example, you might find that the runtime is still using an old version of an external content type after you changed the identifier. How is that possible? Visual Studio increases the version number of the external content type with every change you make. Once the external content type gets deployed the runtime sets the already deployed external content type with an older version to inactive and the newly imported one to active. So over time you have a lot of inactive external content types in the metadata store. But the runtime also selects the external content type based on its identifier, so if we change the identifier and the identifier doesn't match a new external content type the runtime will use an older external content type. If you deploy a model in full deployment mode the runtime will entirely retract the old model and delete all the inactive versions of the external content types defined in the model, which will prevent older external content types from being used.

You should also switch to full deployment mode if you want to package the model to be deployed to a test environment. Deployment modes can be switched by clicking on the model name in the BDC Explorer and changing the value of Incremental Update in the Properties window to True to enable incremental deployment and to False to enable full deployment. Figure 6-86 shows the Incremental Update property in the Properties window for the model node.

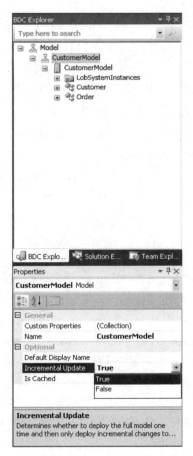

Figure 6-86: Incremental Update Property

The last consideration for deploying BDC models with Visual Studio is the target SKU of SharePoint. As we mentioned before if you cannot upgrade to SharePoint Server or install the freely available Microsoft Share-Point Search Express edition, you either need to write a feature event receiver that imports a .WSP containing a BDC model or you need to use a Windows PowerShell commandlet for the deployment if you are working on SharePoint Foundation. We need to do the following steps in our project to implement the feature event receiver (see Chapter 5, "SharePoint Event Receivers," for more information on creating feature event receivers).

1. Add a new feature event receiver by right clicking on the feature in the Feature folder and selecting Add event receiver.

2. Replace the code with the code found in the code gallery http:// code.msdn.microsoft.com/BDCSPFoundation.

3. Add the .NET reference: System.Web, version=2.0.0.0.

4. Ensure a reference to the Microsoft.BusinessData assembly is added.

5. Select the EmployeeModel project item folder and update the Feature Receiver properties as follows:

   Assembly = $SharePoint.Project.AssemblyFullName$
   ClassName = Employees.Features.Feature1. ImportModelReceiver

6. Double click Feature1.Feature, update Receiver Class = Employees.Features.Feature1. ImportModelReceiver

The code for importing a BDC model in a feature event receiver can be found at http://code.msdn.microsoft.com/BDCSPFoundation. In a nut-shell this code parses the BDCM file for all relevant model information such as finding the LobSystem, LobSystemInstances, external content types, type descriptors, etc., and uses the BCS APIs to persist this information in the BCS metadata store. There are also comments inline that further explain the code. Once the feature event receiver is deployed we don't need to implement this again for another project because SharePoint persists this feature event receiver in the content database.

Conclusion

Using the new Business Connectivity Services in SharePoint 2010, developers now have a powerful way to integrate business data into SharePoint. They can create external content types describing business data with SharePoint Designer and Visual Studio. We saw how to create external content types with each of the tools. We also learned the differences between creating external content types with SharePoint Designer and Visual Studio. While SharePoint Designer provides a power user approach that lets us implement all the basic operations on an external content type, Visual Studio is the recommended approach if you need to aggregate data from different external systems or add custom business logic and custom security. In addition we looked at creating associations with Visual Studio, which allows end users to see external content types that are related.

■7■
SharePoint Content Types

In this chapter we are going to discover the world of SharePoint content types. We are going to learn about the content types that ship with SharePoint 2010 and how to create new content types from the SharePoint UI and from Visual Studio 2010. Since this book is focused on SharePoint development with Visual Studio 2010 we are going to show you how to deploy the content type together with site columns and a list definition in a single Visual Studio solution. At the end of the chapter we will touch on Visual Studio Tools for Office (VSTO) customized documents. We will also show how to use content type information in Word 2010 documents and how to update that information.

Introduction to Content Types

As the name suggests, content types are about SharePoint content. In the SharePoint world content is everything. Content on the SharePoint server includes everything from documents to contacts, from tasks to calendar items. All of this content can easily turn into a mess if it's not managed correctly. To make everyone's life easier there has to be a way to manage all that content.

One way of managing the content on SharePoint is to group it by its type—for example, you could group all Word documents together. That doesn't sound too bad, but it would be better if we could group those documents based on the type of information and data they contain. You probably wouldn't want to group employee resumes, trip reports, and legal documents all together. Even though those are all Word documents, the contents are very different.

What content types can provide is a way to define the type of the content stored in SharePoint and proper fields to associate with that content. For example, I wouldn't want to associate a lawyer's name field with resumes or trip reports, but I would really like to have that field associated with every legal document across all of my SharePoint sites.

Considered another way, if you think of a SharePoint document library—there's nothing special about it, it's just a place to store arbitrary documents. But as soon as you apply a content type to that library it offers you a way to store more information about the document outside of the actual document by associating additional fields with the document. For example, why should I have to open every document to get some piece of information if I could store that information in a field in my document library.

Content Type Definition

To come up with a more formal definition of a content type we can say that a content type is a collection of settings that can be applied to different types of content. Throughout this chapter when we refer to content we usually mean a document, picture, task, or something similar that can be stored on a SharePoint site or in a SharePoint list. Content in SharePoint is usually stored in SharePoint lists and that means content types can be applied to different SharePoint lists. SharePoint supports storing multiple content types in one document library. You can store your trip reports with resumes together in the same document library even though they use different content types. Only one content type can be applied to a particular item in a document library or list. Document can't be both a resume and a trip report.

Each content type has a distinctive set of properties and metadata that describe the content. This can include fields that are associated with the content type that can be displayed as columns in the list or document library. It can also include a specific document template used when creating instances of the content type. For example, if we create a content type called Trip-Report we could also create a Word document template and associate it with the content type TripReport. This Word template could define the layout for each trip report. Then, when we associate the TripReport content type with a particular SharePoint list or library, the content type shows up in the New menu when creating new items. Figure 7-1 shows an example of the New menu in a document library that supports multiple content types—in this case a Document content type, a Link to a Document content type, and a Form content type.

Figure 7-1: New Menu in a Share-
Point Library That Is Associated with
Multiple Content Types

SharePoint Site Columns

We mentioned that content types can be associated with additional meta-data—specifically this means that content types can be associated with site columns or list columns. These are then displayed for each item in a Share-Point list or document library. List columns are "one off" columns that are only used for one content type. Usually we won't want to use list columns because of their "one off" nature. Instead we want to use an existing site column or create a new site column when existing site columns don't do the job. So before we continue our content type discussions, let's look more closely at site columns since they are an important component of a content type definition.

Each site column in SharePoint consists of four components:

- Column name
- Column type

- Column group name
- Additional column settings

The Column name is the name that represents the site column. One shouldn't underestimate the importance of carefully naming a site column. When naming the columns it's good to keep in mind that the column name is going to be used throughout the SharePoint UI. It will also be the name that is displayed in the header row of a column when viewing a SharePoint list or document library. The same name is used in the Document Panel and content controls in Office Word 2010 documents. We will talk about the Document Panel and content controls later in this chapter.

If you have worked with SharePoint before, you know that there are different types of columns that can be displayed in SharePoint lists and document libraries. Each column has an associated data type. The column type in SharePoint defines the type of data you want the column to store. For example, the column type of the start date column in a task item is Date and time, the column type of a title column for a document library is Single line of text, and the column type of a description column is Multiple lines of text.

SharePoint supports the following column data types:

- Single line of text
- Multiple lines of text
- Choice (menu to choose from)
- Number (1, 1.0, 100)
- Currency ($, ¥, €)
- Date and Time
- Lookup (looks up values from a list already on the site)
- Yes/No (check box)
- Person or Group
- Hyperlink or Picture
- Calculated (calculation based on other columns)

Column group name is not a required setting for a site column, but it's a good practice to group all site columns into a meaningful column group so you can find them easier and faster when creating new content types. When possible, you should put your site column into a predefined column group rather than creating your own column group. Predefined column groups that are already defined in SharePoint are listed below:

- Base Columns
- Core Contact and Calendar Columns
- Core Document Columns
- Core Task and Issue Columns
- Custom Columns
- Extended Columns

Every predefined column group already contains site columns that can be used when creating new content types. When developing new content types you should first look to see if there is an existing site column you can use rather than creating a new site column. For example, if you need a Description column or a Title column, use the site columns already defined in SharePoint rather than creating your own. You should only create your own site column if none of the existing site columns meet your needs.

The fourth component of the site column includes more detailed options one can set for a site column. For example, you can set the column as "required," which means that users must enter the data for that column otherwise an error is displayed. You can also enforce that the value set in a site column be unique, you can configure a default value, and set the maximum number of characters allowed for the column value. Depending on the type of the column there are additional settings that can be specified.

Later in this chapter we are going to show how to create new site columns from Visual Studio 2010, but for now let's show how to create a new site column from within the SharePoint UI:

1. Open the SharePoint site home page in the Internet browser.
2. Click the Site Actions menu.
3. Select the Site Settings item in the menu as shown in Figure 7-2.
   The Site Settings page is opened.

Figure 7-2: The Site Actions menu

4. In the Site Settings page, click the Site Columns link under the Galleries header.

   A page showing the list of column groups and columns is displayed as shown in Figure 7-3.

5. To create a new site column, click the Create link at the top of the Site Columns page.

   The New Site Column page is displayed as shown in Figure 7-4.

6. Type "MyColumn" in the Column name textbox.

7. Leave the column type set to Single line of text.

8. Click the New group radio button and type "My Columns" into the textbox.

   Note that here you can choose to reuse an existing site column group by clicking the Existing group radio button. There are additional settings we could specify, but let's just leave the column as it is.

9. Click OK to create the column.

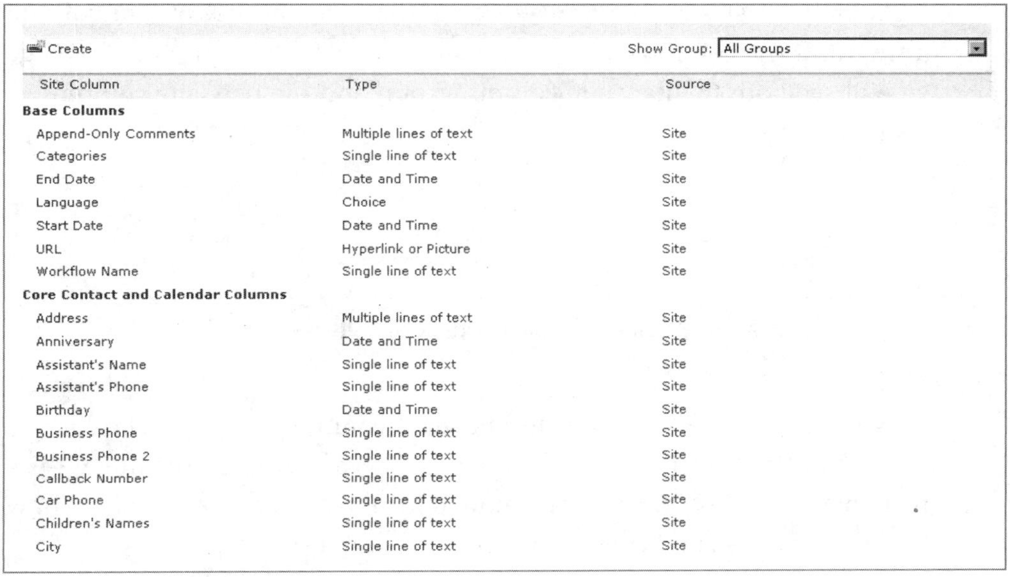

Create		Show Group:	All Groups
Site Column	Type	Source	
Base Columns			
Append-Only Comments	Multiple lines of text	Site	
Categories	Single line of text	Site	
End Date	Date and Time	Site	
Language	Choice	Site	
Start Date	Date and Time	Site	
URL	Hyperlink or Picture	Site	
Workflow Name	Single line of text	Site	
Core Contact and Calendar Columns			
Address	Multiple lines of text	Site	
Anniversary	Date and Time	Site	
Assistant's Name	Single line of text	Site	
Assistant's Phone	Single line of text	Site	
Birthday	Date and Time	Site	
Business Phone	Single line of text	Site	
Business Phone 2	Single line of text	Site	
Callback Number	Single line of text	Site	
Car Phone	Single line of text	Site	
Children's Names	Single line of text	Site	
City	Single line of text	Site	

Figure 7-3: The Site Columns page

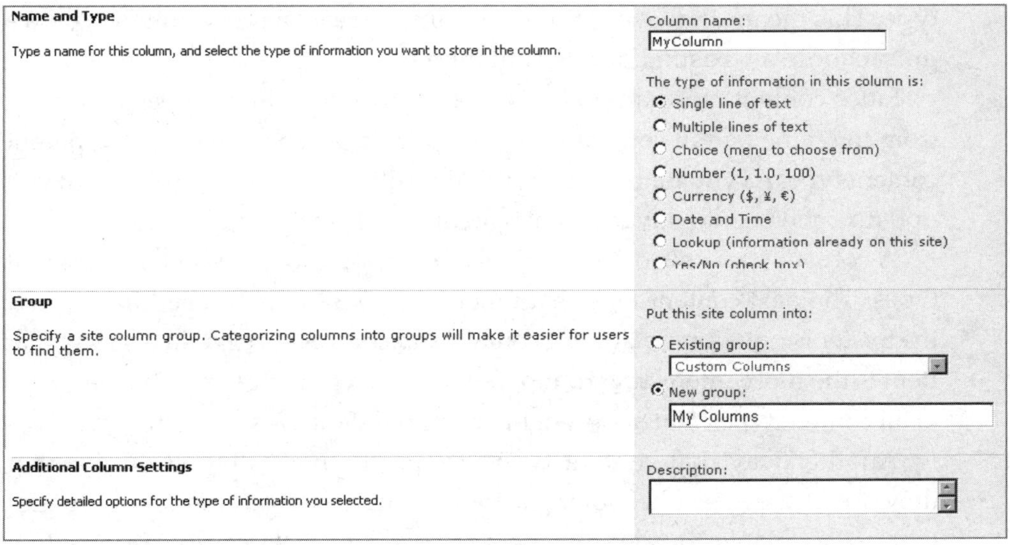

Name and Type

Type a name for this column, and select the type of information you want to store in the column.

Column name:

MyColumn

The type of information in this column is:
- Single line of text
- Multiple lines of text
- Choice (menu to choose from)
- Number (1, 1.0, 100)
- Currency ($, ¥, €)
- Date and Time
- Lookup (information already on this site)
- Yes/No (check box)

Group

Specify a site column group. Categorizing columns into groups will make it easier for users to find them.

Put this site column into:
- Existing group:
  Custom Columns
- New group:
  My Columns

Additional Column Settings

Specify detailed options for the type of information you selected.

Description:

Figure 7-4: New Site Column page

After the last step we are redirected back to the list of site column groups and site columns. If we scroll all the way to the bottom of the page we will see both the new site column group and the new site column we created as shown in Figure 7-5.

My Columns

MyColumn   Single line of text   Site

Figure 7-5: A newly created site column group and site column

We've now seen how to create a new site column group and site column in the SharePoint UI. But site columns are just a means to an end until we use them in a content type. So we will now return to content types and see how they are organized and created and how they can use site columns.

Content Type Hierarchy

All content types in SharePoint are organized in a hierarchy. Each content type in SharePoint inherits its attributes and settings from a parent content type. This means that every time we want to create a new content type we must choose an existing parent content type.

Since content types are in a hierarchy, all child content types inheriting from the same parent content type are updated when we update the parent content type. As you might expect, this doesn't work in reverse order—if you update a child content type no changes are made to the parent content type.

A content type called "System" is at the root of the hierarchy of content types. The next content type that inherits from System is called Item. Since the System content type doesn't contain any columns we could also say that Item is the more interesting root parent of every content type. The hierarchy of all content types that are predefined in SharePoint is shown in Figure 7-6.

Another way that content types are partitioned is based on whether they are at the site collection or list level. Site content types are templates that are available throughout the site collection. We could also create a content type directly at the list level, but this would mean that the content type is only available to that list and to none of the other sites or lists.

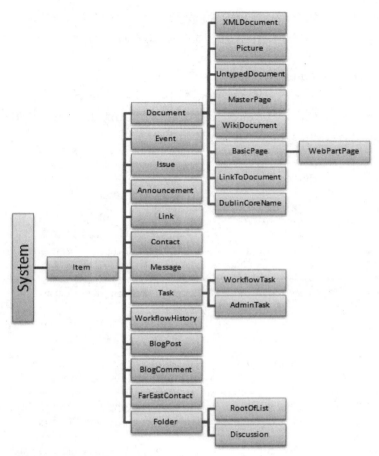

Figure 7-6: Content types hierarchy

Just as site columns are organized into site column groups, content types are organized into content type groups. SharePoint ships with the following groups of content types:

- Document Content Types
- Folder Content Types
- Group Work Content Types
- List Content Types
- Special Content Types

In the following sections we are going to explore these different content type groups and the content types that are in each group.

Document Content Types

Document content types are meant to be used with document libraries. Content types in the document content type group, their descriptions, and their parent content types are shown in Table 7-1.

TABLE 7-1: Document Content Types

Content Type	Parent Content Type	Description
Basic Page	Document	Used for creating new basic SharePoint pages
Document	Item	Used for creating new documents
Dublin Core Columns	Document	The Dublin Core metadata element set
Form	Document	This content type is used when users need to enter some data in a form
Link to a Document	Document	Used for creating a link to a document that is stored in a different document library
List View Style	Document	Used for creating new list view styles
Master Page	Document	User for creating a SharePoint master page
Picture	Document	A picture that is stored in a picture library
Web Part Page	Basic Page	A page that can host SharePoint web parts
Wiki Page	Document	Used for creating new wiki pages

The content type Dublin Core Columns deserves more explanation. Dublin Core Columns are a set of metadata elements that are used to describe resources online, such as text, video, sound, images, and web pages. This content type contains columns such as Contributor, Creator, Format, Language, Publisher, Rights Management, etc. These are used for describing the items and make them easier to find online. If you wonder about the name, this content type was named after the first workshop where the metadata was defined that was held in Dublin, Ohio.

Folder Content Types

Content types in the folder group are used for SharePoint folders as the name suggests. This group contains content types that are used for grouping SharePoint artifacts in folders. The three content types in this group are shown in Table 7-2.

TABLE 7-2: Folder Content Types

Content Type	Parent Content Type	Description
Discussion	Folder	Used for creating new discussion topics
Folder	Item	Used for creating new folders
Summary Task	Folder	Used for grouping and describing related tasks

Group Work Content Types

Group Work content types are used for organizing content that tracks work being done by a group on the SharePoint site. This group consists of the content types shown in Table 7-3.

TABLE 7-3: Group Work Content Types

Content Type	Parent Content Type	Description
Circulation	Item	Used for creating new circulation
Holiday	Item	Used for adding new holidays
New Word	Item	Used for adding new words to a list

Continues

TABLE 7-3: Group Work Content Types *(Continued)*

Content Type	Parent Content Type	Description
Official Notice	Item	Used for adding new official notice
Phone Call Memo	Item	Used for adding new phone call memos
Resource	Item	Used for new resources
Resource Group	Item	Used for new resource groups
Timecard	Item	Used for adding new timecard data
Users	Item	Used for adding new users to the list
What's New Notification	Item	Used for adding new notifications

List Content Types

Content types in this group are probably the most used content types in SharePoint. This group contains content types for creating basic Share-Point list items. Content types in this group are shown in Table 7-4.

TABLE 7-4: List Content Types

Content Type	Parent Content Type	Description
Announce-ment	Item	Used for creating new announcements
Comment	Item	Used for creating new comments
Contact	Item	Used for storing information about business or personal contacts
East Asia Contact	Item	Used for storing information about business or personal contacts

TABLE 7-4: List Content Types *(Continued)*

Content Type	Parent Content Type	Description
Event	Item	Used for creating new meetings, deadlines, or other events
Issue	Item	Used for tracking issues or problems
Item	System	Used for creating new list items
Link	Item	Used for creating new links
Message	Item	Used for creating new messages
Post	Item	Used for creating new blog posts
Reservations	Event	Used for reserving a resource like a conference room
Schedule	Event	Used for creating new appointments
Schedule and Reservations	Event	Used for creating new appointments and reserving resources, this content type is a combination of Reservations and Schedule content type
Task	Item	Used for creating tasks or work items

The list content types group contains a content type that is the parent of all other content types—Item. The Item content type inherits from the System content type, which is a hidden content type that doesn't contain any columns.

Special Content Types

This group contains only one content type that is used for unknown document types. It allows users to upload arbitrary documents to a document library. For example, you could use an Unknown Document Type content type to upload a PDF document or any other custom document to a document library.

Content Types in Visual Studio 2010

Now that we explained SharePoint content types, it is time to show how to develop one in Visual Studio. Developing new content types with Visual Studio 2010 can be achieved in three steps:

- Create site columns if existing ones can't be reused
- Create a content type
- Assign the content type to one or more lists

Before we dive into these specific steps, we will explain how to create a content type project and explore the content type project structure. Start by opening Visual Studio 2010 and follow the steps below to create a new content type project.

1. Click File > New > Project in Visual Studio 2010.

   The New Project dialog opens.

2. Select the Content Type project template under Visual C# > Share-Point > 2010.

3. Name the project "MyFirstContentType" and click OK.

   The first page of the SharePoint Customization Wizard is displayed as shown in Figure 7-7. Select the Deploy as a farm solution radio button.

4. Click Next.

   On the second page of the SharePoint Customization Wizard we can choose the base content type as shown in Figure 7-8. Our new content type will inherit from the selected base content type.

5. Select Picture from the drop-down and click the Finish button to create the content type project.

   The content type project is created and the structure of the project is shown in Figure 7-9.

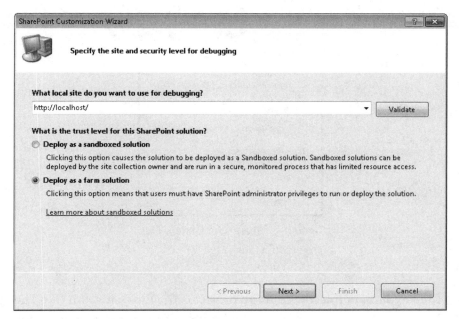

Figure 7-7: SharePoint Customization Wizard

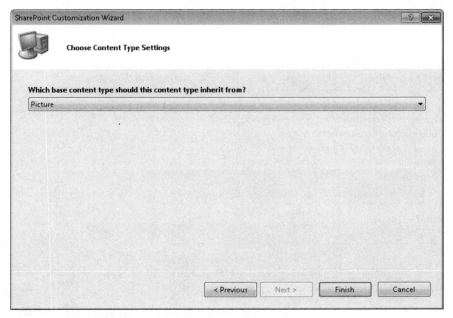

Figure 7-8: Choosing the base content type in the Wizard

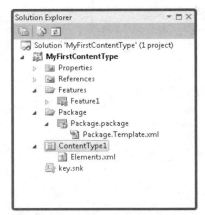

Figure 7-9: SharePoint Content Type project structure

The key item in the content type project is the Elements.xml file. This is the file where we are going to define the site columns and all other content type settings. The initial contents of the Elements.xml file are shown in Listing 7-1.

Listing 7-1: Elements.xml for a Content Type Project Item

```xml
<?xml version="1.0" encoding="utf-8"?>
<Elements xmlns="http://schemas.microsoft.com/sharepoint/">
  <!-- Parent ContentType: Picture (0x010102) -->
  <ContentType ID="0x01010200452a819252d447e09d9ab11d39b6fca1"
    Name="MyFirstContentType - ContentType1"
    Group="Custom Content Types"
    Description="My Content Type"
    Inherits="TRUE"
    Version="0">
    <FieldRefs>
    </FieldRefs>
  </ContentType>
</Elements>
```

The ContentType element within the Elements.xml file defines a single content type and is prepopulated with values for required and optional attributes. Table 7-5 describes the most common attributes used in the ContentType element in the Elements.xml file.

TABLE 7-5: ContentType Element Attributes

Attribute Name	Description
ID	This attribute specifies the content type ID. The ID consists of a parent content type ID, two zeros, and a GUID to uniquely identify the content type.
Name	The content type name.
Group	The name of the content type group.
Description	The content type description.
Inherits	Used for field/site column inheritance.
Version	Content type version number.

At this point, we can actually deploy the content type but this content type wouldn't be very interesting. At this point it is identical to its parent—in our example, the Picture content type. The Picture content type uses site columns specific to pictures, including Date Picture Taken, Picture Size, and Keywords.

We are going to remove the Date Picture Taken and Picture Size site columns from our new content type so they won't be inherited. To remove or add site columns to the content type we can use the FieldRefs element, which was an empty element in Listing 7-1. Add the XML shown in Listing 7-2 to the FieldRefs element in the Elements.xml file.

Listing 7-2: FieldRefs Element in Elements.xml

```
<FieldRefs>
  <!-- Date Picture Taken -->
  <RemoveFieldRef ID="{a5d2f824-bc53-422e-87fd-765939d863a5}" />
  <!-- Picture Size -->
  <RemoveFieldRef ID="{922551b8-c7e0-46a6-b7e3-3cf02917f68a}" />
</FieldRefs>
```

You are probably wondering where we got the IDs for the two site columns we removed in Listing 7-2. You can use the SharePoint Server Explorer to get the IDs. To open the SharePoint Server Explorer, click the Tools menu and select Add SharePoint Connection. Next, type the SharePoint site URL and click OK to add the connection to Server Explorer. In order to get to the site column name, expand the connection node you just added and under the ContentTypes node, find the desired content type. Under each content type you will find the site columns (called fields in this UI). From here, getting to the site column ID is very simple. With the site column name selected, open the Properties window and locate the ID property value. That's the ID of the site column you want to use when referring to site column in the Field-Refs element. Figure 7-10 shows the Server Explorer with the Picture Size site column selected.

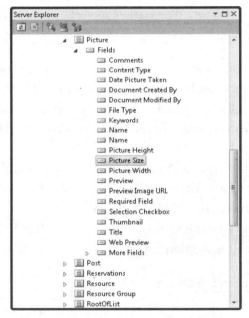

Figure 7-10: Server Explorer

Before we deploy the solution there is one more thing we need to do—we must remove the Inherits attribute because if we don't we won't be able to delete the field references. If Inherits is set to TRUE, it will force our content type to have all the same site columns the parent does regardless of our use of RemoveFieldRef elements in Listing 7-2. The final contents of Elements.xml file are shown in Listing 7-3.

Listing 7-3: Final Elements.Xml for a Content Type That Removes Date Picture Taken and Picture Size from the Base Picture Content Type

```xml
<?xml version="1.0" encoding="utf-8"?>
<Elements xmlns="http://schemas.microsoft.com/sharepoint/">
  <!-- Parent ContentType: Picture (0x010102) -->
  <ContentType ID="0x01010200452a819252d447e09d9ab11d39b6fca1"
    Name="MyFirstContentType - ContentType1"
    Group="Custom Content Types"
    Description="My Content Type"
    Version="0">
    <FieldRefs>
      <!-- Date Picture Taken -->
      <RemoveFieldRef ID="{a5d2f824-bc53-422e-87fd-765939d863a5}" />
      <!-- Picture Size -->
      <RemoveFieldRef ID="{922551b8-c7e0-46a6-b7e3-3cf02917f68a}" />
    </FieldRefs>
  </ContentType>
</Elements>
```

We should deploy the project at this point and verify that the two site columns are not included in the new content type.

1. In Visual Studio press F5 to start debugging and deploy the project.

   The Site Content Types page will open in the Internet browser and the deployed content type will be displayed on that page as shown in Figure 7-11.

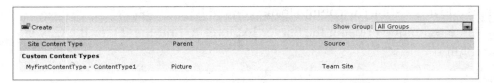

Figure 7-11: SharePoint Site Content Type Page

2. Click the MyFirstContentType – ContentType1 link to open the content type.

   A page with content type information opens as shown in Figure 7-12. Notice the site columns we removed are no longer part of the content type.

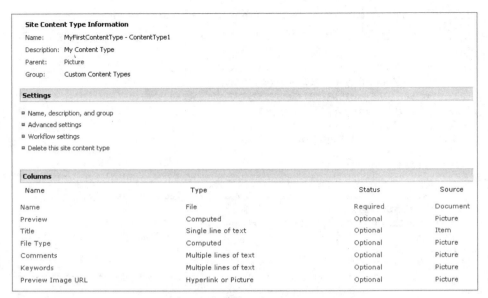

Site Content Type Information

Name: MyFirstContentType - ContentType1
Description: My Content Type
Parent: Picture
Group: Custom Content Types

Settings

▫ Name, description, and group
▫ Advanced settings
▫ Workflow settings
▫ Delete this site content type

Columns

Name	Type	Status	Source
Name	File	Required	Document
Preview	Computed	Optional	Picture
Title	Single line of text	Optional	Item
File Type	Computed	Optional	Picture
Comments	Multiple lines of text	Optional	Picture
Keywords	Multiple lines of text	Optional	Picture
Preview Image URL	Hyperlink or Picture	Optional	Picture

Figure 7-12: Content type with Date Picture Taken and Picture Size removed

Removing columns from the content type was easy. How about adding new columns using existing site columns? Just for fun, let's say we want the postal code to be included with every picture. Since a site column for postal codes already exists in SharePoint we can just reference it in our content type. In Listing 7-4 we show how this is done—this time we use the FieldRef element rather than the RemoveFieldRef element. The FieldRef element lets us add an existing site column to our content type. To get the ID, we used the same technique of using the Server Explorer to find the ID for the City site column.

Listing 7-4: Using the FieldRef element to add a column from an existing site column to a content type

```
<FieldRefs>
  <!-- Date Picture Taken -->
  <RemoveFieldRef ID="{a5d2f824-bc53-422e-87fd-765939d863a5}" />
  <!-- Picture Size -->
  <RemoveFieldRef ID="{922551b8-c7e0-46a6-b7e3-3cf02917f68a}" />
  <!-- Postal code -->
  <FieldRef ID="{9a631556-3dac-49db-8d2f-fb033b0fdc24}" DisplayName="Where was
    this picture taken?"/>
</FieldRefs>
```

Notice we also provided a display name for this column. Let's try deploying the project again and see if the content type is updated. Follow the same steps as above. The column list of the deployed content type is shown in Figure 7-13.

Columns			
Name	Type	Status	Source
Name	File	Required	Document
Preview	Computed	Optional	Picture
Title	Single line of text	Optional	Item
File Type	Computed	Optional	Picture
Comments	Multiple lines of text	Optional	Picture
Keywords	Multiple lines of text	Optional	Picture
Preview Image URL	Hyperlink or Picture	Optional	Picture
Where was this picture taken?	Single line of text	Optional	

Figure 7-13: Columns in the content type

In order to use the content type we have just created, we should create a new picture library and assign this content type as the default content type for the picture library. To do this, follow these steps:

1. Open the SharePoint site home page in the Internet browser.
2. Click the Libraries link.
3. Click the Create link.

    The Create dialog opens.

4. Select the Picture Library as the type of item you want to create.
5. Type "My Photos" in the textbox to the right of the Create dialog and click the Create button to create the library as shown in Figure 7-14.

    A new Picture library is created and the page for the new library is opened.

6. Click the Settings menu and select Picture Library settings as shown in Figure 7-15.
7. Click on the Advanced settings link under the General Settings.

    In order to use the new content type we need to allow the management of content types for this library.

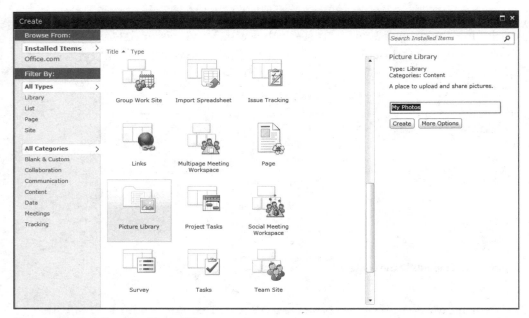

Figure 7-14: Creating New Picture Library

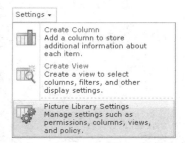

Figure 7-15: Picture Library settings

8. Select Yes for the Allow management of content types question.

9. Click OK to accept changes and return to the library settings page.

Now, the Content Types section is available and we can add an exist-ing content type to the library.

10. Click the Add from existing site content types link.

Figure 7-16 shows the Select Content Types page that opens.

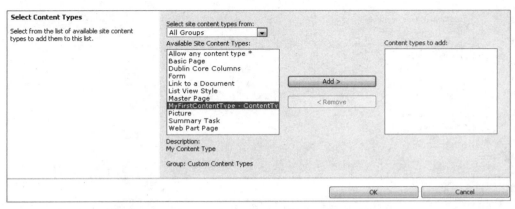

Figure 7-16: Select Content type MyFirstContentType – ContentType1

11. Select MyFirstContentType – ContentType1 from the list of available site content types.

12. Click the Add button to add the content type to the library.

13. Click OK to add the content type.

   We are now redirected to the library settings page and, as you can see in Figure 7-17, the MyFirstContentType content type is added to the library.

Content Types

This document library is configured to allow multiple content types. Use content types to specify the information you want to display about an item, in addition to its policies, workflows, or other behavior. The following content types are currently available in this library:

Content Type	Visible on New Button	Default Content Type
Picture	✔	✔
MyFirstContentType - ContentType1	✔	

Add from existing site content types
Change new button order and default content type

Figure 7-17: Content Type in the library

14. Because we want to use only this new content type in the library we should remove the Picture content type. Click the Picture link in the Content Types section shown in Figure 7-17.

   The information page for the Picture content type shown in Figure 7-18 is opened.

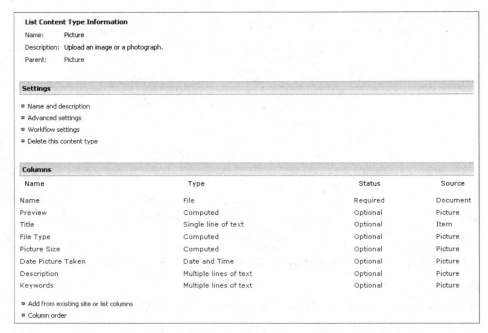

Figure 7-18: Content Type Information page

15. Under Settings, click the Delete this content type link to remove the Picture content type from the picture library.

16. Click OK in the confirmation dialog to delete the content type.

   The picture library now contains only the content type we created. We should try uploading a picture now.

17. Click the My Photos link to open the library.

18. Click the Upload button and browse to an existing picture.

19. Click OK to upload the picture.

   An Edit form like the one in Figure 7-19 is displayed. Notice the form doesn't contain the column we removed and it contains the "Where was this picture taken?" column.

20. Click OK to add the picture to the library.

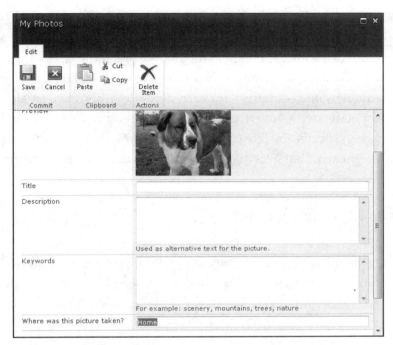

Figure 7-19: Edit Item form

We now know how to add columns to our content type using existing site column definitions but what if we want to use a column like "Camera model" that doesn't exist yet? We could create a site column from the SharePoint UI as we demonstrated earlier in this chapter, or we could do it from within Visual Studio 2010.

In order to create a new site column from within Visual Studio 2010 we are going to use the Empty Element project item template. Follow the steps below to create a new site column with empty element project item, reference it in the content type, and then deploy both the site column and the content type to SharePoint.

1. Right click the MyFirstContentType project node in the Solution Explorer and select Add > New Item.
2. Select the Empty Element template from the Add New Item dialog.

3. Name the element "SiteColumns" and click Add to add it to the project. An empty element project item is just what the name suggests it is. It contains an empty Elements.xml file. We are going to use this Elements.xml file to create site columns. We can use the Field element to create new site columns—for each new site column we create we must specify an ID, Name, and Type of the column. It's also a good practice to specify the Site column group name as well as the display name—the text that gets displayed in forms and column headers.

How Do I Specify a New ID?

IDs in SharePoint are typically just GUIDs—a big long number that uniquely identifies items in SharePoint. You can easily create new GUIDs from within Visual Studio 2010 by selecting Create GUID from the Tools menu. SharePoint uses registry format GUIDs so make sure you select that option in the Create GUID dialog. Then paste the resulting GUID into your Elements.xml file.

4. The Elements.xml file contents with a new Field element added is shown in Listing 7-5.

Listing 7-5: Empty Element's Elements.xml Defining a New Site Column

```
<?xml version="1.0" encoding="utf-8"?>
<Elements xmlns="http://schemas.microsoft.com/sharepoint/">
  <Field ID="{AF26A84D-ADE1-4B69-A393-266B09ABF0E4}" Name="CameraModel"
Type="Text" Group="My Columns" DisplayName="Camera Used"/>
</Elements>
```

5. We must reference this site column from the content type's Elements.xml file. We can do this exactly the same way we did it for existing site columns. Open the content type Elements.xml and add the following line within the FieldRefs element. The ID you use here is the same ID you used in the Empty Element project item's Elements.xml file.

```
<FieldRef ID="{AF26A84D-ADE1-4B69-A393-266B09ABF0E4}"/>
```

6. Press F5 to deploy the project.

7. Click on the MyFirstContentType – ContentType1 link.

8. Notice the CameraModel field with the display name Camera Used is in the content type as shown in Figure 7-20.

Columns			
Name	Type	Status	Source
Name	File	Required	Document
Preview	Computed	Optional	Picture
Title	Single line of text	Optional	Item
File Type	Computed	Optional	Picture
Comments	Multiple lines of text	Optional	Picture
Keywords	Multiple lines of text	Optional	Picture
Preview Image URL	Hyperlink or Picture	Optional	Picture
Where was this picture taken?	Single line of text	Optional	
Camera Used	Single line of text	Optional	

Figure 7-20: A new site column "Camera Used" in the MyFirstContentType content type

There are some problems with our current implementation however. If you retract this solution, you will notice that the CameraModel site column doesn't get removed. This is because we are creating the CameraModel field with an Empty Element and Visual Studio doesn't know anything about the contents of Empty Element and how to uninstall it. A second problem that can occur is that we really need to ensure that our site column definition always gets activated before the content type. Otherwise, the activation of the content type could fail because it refers to CameraModel, a site column that might get installed after the content type.

To remedy these two issues, we are going to create a second feature and install the site column definition with the second feature and the content type with the first feature. Then we'll create a feature dependency between the two features that tells Visual Studio that the second feature (where our site column definition is) must be installed before the first feature (where our content type is). Finally, we'll write an event handler for the second feature that removes the CameraModel site column when the second feature is uninstalled.

1. Right click the Features folder.

2. Select Add Feature.

A new feature is added to the project and the feature designer is opened.

3. Double-click the SiteColumns feature from the Items in the Solution list to add to the feature.

    Once the site columns are added to the feature, the feature designer should look like Figure 7-21.

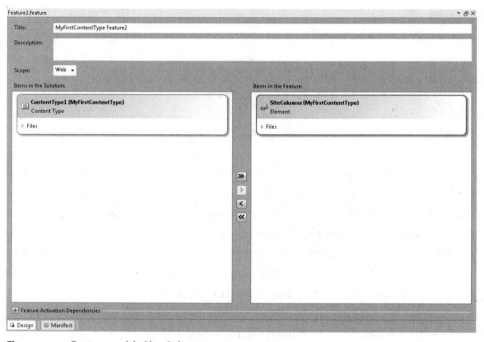

Figure 7-21: Feature2 with Site Columns

4. Because we are deploying the site columns in the second feature now, we should go and remove it from the first feature. Double click Feature1 to open the feature designer.

5. Double click the SiteColumns feature in the Items in the Feature list to remove it from the feature.

    After we've done that, the Feature1 designer looks like Figure 7-22.

6. Now that we have two features, Feature1 for the content type and Feature2 for the site column type, let's set a feature activation depen-

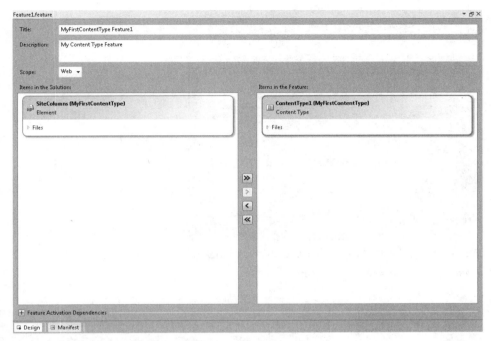

Figure 7-22: Feature1 with Content Type

dency to make sure that Feature2 is activated before Feature1. If we don't do this then our content type could be activated before the Camera site column definition is activated and this would cause the activation of our content type to fail. In the designer for Feature1, expand the Feature Activation Dependencies pane at the bottom of the designer.

7. Click Add… to add a feature activation dependency.

The Add Feature Activation Dependencies dialog opens as shown in Figure 7-23.

8. Select Feature2 from the list and click Add to add the dependency.

The Feature designer for Feature1 is displayed again and the activation dependency on Feature2 has been added as shown in Figure 7-24.

9. Now, right click Feature2 in Solution Explorer and select Add Event Receiver.

A file called Feature2.EventReceiver.cs is added to the project.

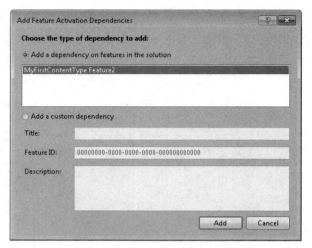

Figure 7-23: Using the Activation Dependencies dialog to make Feature1 dependent on Feature2

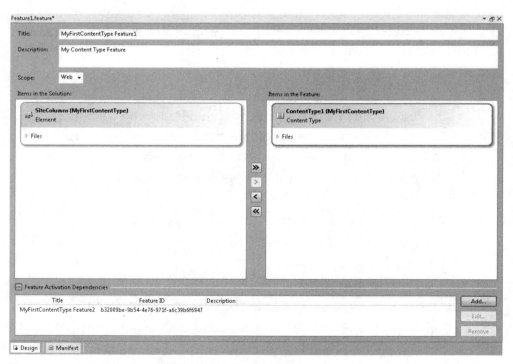

Figure 7-24: Feature1 with activation dependency on Feature2

10. Uncomment the FeatureUninstalling method in this file and add the code to remove the site column definition when Feature2 is uninstalled. The completed method is displayed in Listing 7-6.

Listing 7-6: FeatureUninstalling Method for Feature2

```
public override void FeatureUninstalling(SPFeatureReceiverProperties properties)
{
  SPWeb web = properties.Feature.Parent as SPWeb;
  string fieldId = "{44934FDB-3560-4507-BF74-F3CBE1FC59CD}";
  if (web.Fields.Contains (fieldId))
  {
    web.Fields[fieldId].Delete();
  }
}
```

Seeing the code in Listing 7-6 might inspire an idea of a different way to implement the site column. Instead of using an empty element to add the new site column, we could accomplish the same thing by writing a Feature-Installed method and programmatically creating the site column when the feature is installed. Note that if we uninstall the feature that contains fields, those fields will also be removed from any SharePoint artifacts that are using them. For example the uninstalled field "Camera Used" won't show up in the content type "MyFirstContentType – ContentType1" any more.

If we press F5 to deploy the SharePoint project it seems that the behavior hasn't changed. From the user experience view, the behavior is exactly the same: A content type with a custom site column has been deployed to the SharePoint. What actually happens on F5 (or deploy) is that the package file was created, deployed, and at activation time Feature2 containing SiteColumns was activated first followed by the Feature1 containing the content type.

Creating a List Definition from a Content Type

Visual Studio 2010 has one more template that is related to content types. In previous sections we created new site columns and added and removed columns from content types—all from within Visual Studio. The only thing we had to do from the SharePoint UI was to create a new library and associate the content type with it. Well, we can use Visual Studio 2010 for this as well. Open the project we created in previous sections and follow the steps below to create a list definition that uses our custom content type.

1. Right click the project name and select Add > New Item.
2. In the New Item dialog select the List Definition from Content Type template.
3. Name the new item MyPhotosListDefinition and click Add.

   Figure 7-25 shows the SharePoint Customization Wizard that is displayed. From this page we can change the display name for our list definition, select the content type we want to use for the list definition and decide if we want to add a list instance as well.

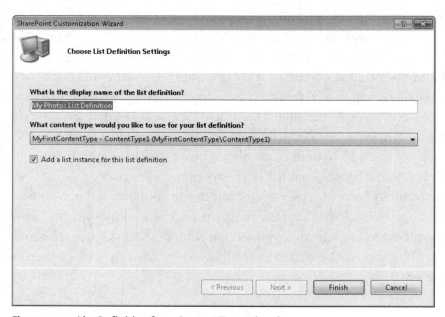

Figure 7-25: List Definition from Content Type Wizard

4. Change the display name to "My Photos List Definition."
5. The desired content type is already selected by default (the custom content type MyFirstContentType – ContentType1 in our project) so we don't have to change that setting.

6. Leave the check box checked so that a list instance will be created when the feature is activated, then click the Finish button to create the project item.

A list definition and a list instance project item are added to the SharePoint solution. Because we created a list definition from the custom content type in our project we must update the Type attribute in the ListTemplate as well as in the ListInstance Elements.xml file. By default the unique identifier is set to "10000." The identifier for the picture library is 109. You can refer to Table 7-6 for the default list template types.

TABLE 7-6: List Template Identifiers

Unique Identifier	List Template Name
100	Generic list
101	Document library
102	Survey
103	Links list
104	Announcements list
105	Contacts list
106	Events list
107	Tasks list
108	Discussion board
109	Picture library
110	Data sources
111	Site template gallery
112	User Information list
113	Web Part gallery

Continues

TABLE 7-6: List Template Identifiers *(Continued)*

Unique Identifier	List Template Name
114	List template gallery
115	XML Form library
116	Master pages gallery
117	No-Code Workflows
118	Custom Workflow Process
119	Wiki Page library
120	Custom grid for a list
130	Data Connection library
140	Workflow History
150	Gantt Tasks list
200	Meeting Series list
201	Meeting Agenda list
202	Meeting Attendees list
204	Meeting Decisions list
207	Meeting Objectives list
210	Meeting text box
211	Meeting Things To Bring list
212	Meeting Workspace Pages list
301	Blog Posts list
302	Blog Comments list
303	Blog Categories list
1100	Issue tracking
1200	Administrator tasks list

7. Open the Elements.xml file under the MyPhotosListDefinition item and change the Type attribute value to 109.

8. Open Elements.xml file under the ListInstance1 item and change the Type attribute value to 109.

9. Press F5 to deploy the project.

    When the Internet browser opens you will notice the MyFirstContent-Type – ListInstance1 under the Pictures group.

10. Click MyFirstContentType – ListInstance1 to open the picture library list instance.

When you click the Upload button and upload a picture you will get the same user experience as previously when we manually created a new picture library and added the content type to it.

Advanced Content Types

Earlier in this chapter we mentioned how content type site columns can be used with Office documents. This means we can access the data in a column from a client application such as Word. In this section we will show how to associate a Word document with a content type and how to use Word's Document Panel to show columns associated with the content type. We will also show how to use Word's content controls to display the data from the content type's columns directly in the document. We will also show how to associate a Visual Studio document customization with a document associated with a content type.

Another nice feature SharePoint offers in connection with content types is the ability to associate SharePoint workflows with content types. We will learn how to associate a workflow with a content type in this section as well. Workflow is considered in more detail in Chapter 8, "SharePoint Workflow."

Word Documents and Content Types

Word has a feature called the Document Panel that is used for displaying the content type associated with a document and columns defined by content type. It doesn't stop there, Word also allows you to edit the values of each column associated with the document by the content type. If you change the value of a column from the document panel and save the document back to the SharePoint library that information travels together with the document to the SharePoint library. It works in reverse as well—if you edit the document's columns in the SharePoint library and save the changes, the next time you open that document in Word you will see the changes in the Document Panel.

At the beginning of the chapter, we mentioned trip reports as a content type example. Imagine that an employee from a company goes to a conference or participates in training that happens outside of the company. In this case, the employee usually sends out a trip report that contains the information about the sessions they attended and what they learned. The company is currently using a standard document library called Trip Reports to store all the trip reports, but they want to update the library to use content types. Our job is to create a TripReport content type with custom site columns and associate it with a Word template. For the sake of simplicity we are going to store some additional information about the trip in three site columns:

- Conference name
- City where conference was held
- Was this a personal or business trip

We want these three columns to be displayed in the document library as well as in the document template. Let's start by opening Visual Studio 2010 and creating a content type project as we did in the previous example in this chapter.

1. Click File > New Project.
2. Under Visual C# > SharePoint > 2010 select the Content Type project and name it "TripReport." Click OK to start the SharePoint Customization wizard.
3. Accept the defaults in the first wizard page and click the Next button.

4. Select Document as the base content type and click Finish to create the project.

5. Right click the project name and select Add > New Item.

6. Select Empty Element from the list of templates and name it. "TripReportSiteColumns." Click Add to create the project item.

7. We now need to define our custom site columns in the Elements.xml file under the TripReportSiteColumns item. Refer to Listing 7-7 for the contents of the TripReportSiteColumn item's Elements.xml file.

Listing 7-7: TripReportSiteColumn's Elements.xml File Defining Three Site Columns

```
<?xml version="1.0" encoding="utf-8"?>
<Elements xmlns="http://schemas.microsoft.com/sharepoint/">
  <Field ID="{FAD46E37-4764-40BA-95A0-FA25CAF774E5}"
  Name="ConferenceName" Type="Text" DisplayName="Conference Name"/>
  <Field ID="{12F07E93-685E-4DE8-BA59-0E975F70AA58}"
  Name="ConferenceLocation" Type="Text"
  DisplayName="Conference Location"/>
  <Field ID="{146127DD-16E5-480F-A404-047DC92F8D7C}"
  Name="TripType" Type="Choice" DisplayName="Trip Type">
    <CHOICES>
      <CHOICE>Personal</CHOICE>
      <CHOICE>Business</CHOICE>
    </CHOICES>
  </Field>
</Elements>
```

8. Once the fields are defined we need to reference them from the content type's Elements.xml file. Listing 7-8 shows the contents of the content type TripReport's Elements.xml file.

Listing 7-8: Content Type TripReport's Elements.xml File

```
<?xml version="1.0" encoding="utf-8"?>
<Elements xmlns="http://schemas.microsoft.com/sharepoint/">
  <!-- Parent ContentType: Document (0x0101) -->
  <ContentType ID="0x010100b49ef71370e1432eaf39f54e69b75b4d"
    Name="TripReport - ContentType1"
    Group="Custom Content Types"
    Description="My Content Type"
    Inherits="TRUE"
    Version="0">
    <FieldRefs>
```

```
    <FieldRef ID="{FAD46E37-4764-40BA-95A0-FA25CAF774E5}"
     Name="ConferenceName" DisplayName="Conference Name"/>
    <FieldRef ID="{12F07E93-685E-4DE8-BA59-0E975F70AA58}"
     Name="ConferenceLocation" DisplayName="Conference Location"/>
    <FieldRef ID="{146127DD-16E5-480F-A404-047DC92F8D7C}"
     Name="TripType" DisplayName="Trip Type"/>
  </FieldRefs>
 </ContentType>
</Elements>
```

9. As before, we should separate the TripReportSiteColumns item and the TripReport content type into two different features. Right click the Features folder and select Add Feature to add a new feature.

10. Double click on the TripReportSiteColumns item in the Feature2 designer to add it to the feature.

11. Open Feature1 designer and remove the TripReportSiteColumns from this feature.

12. Right click Feature2 and select Add Event Receiver.

    We are going to use feature event receiver to remove our custom site columns from the SharePoint once feature is uninstalled.

13. Uncomment the FeatureUninstalling method and add the code to remove the custum column site columns. Listing 7-9 shows the implemented method.

Listing 7-9: FeatureUninstalling Method

```
public override void FeatureUninstalling(
  SPFeatureReceiverProperties properties)
{
  SPWeb web = properties.Feature.Parent as SPWeb;
  web.Fields["{FAD46E37-4764-40BA-95A0-FA25CAF774E5}"].Delete();
  web.Fields["{12F07E93-685E-4DE8-BA59-0E975F70AA58}"].Delete();
  web.Fields["{146127DD-16E5-480F-A404-047DC92F8D7C}"].Delete();
}
```

14. Right-click the project name and select Deploy to deploy the project.

Now that we have a basic content type project prepared, we can continue and create a Word document to use as a template for every trip report that is added to the Trip Reports library. Launch Word and create a simple trip report layout. You can look at our template in Figure 7-26.

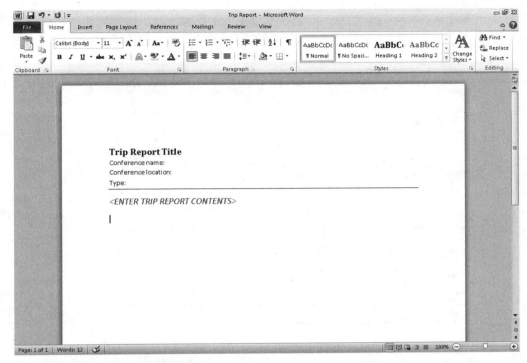

Figure 7-26: Word document template

Now that we have created a document template in Word, the next step is to upload the document template to SharePoint and assign it to the Trip-Report content type we created. Open the Internet browser, navigate to the SharePoint site home page, and follow the steps below.

1. From the home page, click the Site Actions menu and select Site Settings.

2. Click the Site content types link under Galleries.

3. Find the TripReport – ContentType1 content type and click it.

   Figure 7-27 shows the content type settings page that gets displayed. Notice the new site columns we created are listed under the Columns section.

4. Click the Advanced settings link.

   The Advanced settings page shown in Figure 7-28 opens.

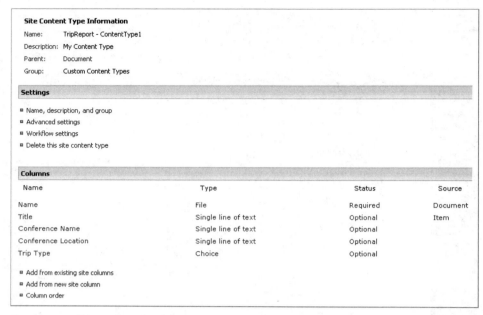

Site Content Type Information

Name: TripReport - ContentType1
Description: My Content Type
Parent: Document
Group: Custom Content Types

Settings

▫ Name, description, and group
▫ Advanced settings
▫ Workflow settings
▫ Delete this site content type

Columns

Name	Type	Status	Source
Name	File	Required	Document
Title	Single line of text	Optional	Item
Conference Name	Single line of text	Optional	
Conference Location	Single line of text	Optional	
Trip Type	Choice	Optional	

▫ Add from existing site columns
▫ Add from new site column
▫ Column order

Figure 7-27: Content Type settings page

Document Template

Specify the document template for this content type.

◉ Enter the URL of an existing document template:

◯ Upload a new document template:

[Browse..]

Read Only

Choose whether the content type is modifiable. This setting can be changed later from this page by anyone with permissions to edit this type.

Should this content type be read only?

◯ Yes
◉ No

Update Sites and Lists

Specify whether all child site and list content types using this type should be updated with the settings on this page. This operation can take a long time, and any customizations made to the child site and list content types will be lost.

Update all content types inheriting from this type?

◉ Yes
◯ No

[OK]   [Cancel]

Figure 7-28: Advanced settings page

5. In the Document Template section, click the radio button. "Upload a new document template" and click the Browse button to browse to the document template you just created in Word.

6. Click OK to save the changes.

We have assigned a document template to the content type. Next we have to apply the content type to a library named Trip Reports. You can create a new document library in SharePoint by clicking the Libraries link and selecting the Create link. From the list of templates displayed in Figure 7-29, select Document Library, name it Trip Reports, and click the Create button to create the library.

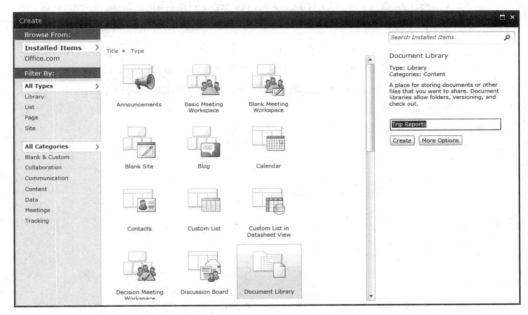

Figure 7-29: Creating a new document library

In the newly created document library, click the Library tab and then the Library Settings button to open the library settings page where we can add a content type. If you remember from the previous example, we first need to allow content types before we can add them. Follow the steps below to allow content types and to add the TripReport content type we created to the library.

1. From the Document Library Settings page click the Advanced settings link.

2. Choose Yes for the Allow management of content types question.

3. Click OK to apply the changes.

   We are redirected to the document library settings page. Next, we are going to add the TripReport content type.

4. Click the Add from existing site content types link.

5. Select the TripReport – ContentType1 from the list of content types and click the Add button to include it.

6. Click OK to close this page and return to the document library settings page.

   Notice in Figure 7-30 that the TripReport – ContentType1 is added to the library's content types. Since Document is still the default content type we should change that and make the TripReport content type the default.

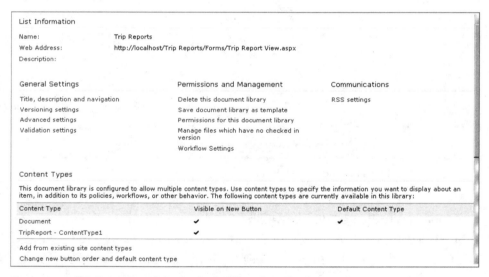

Figure 7-30: TripReport content type in the library

7. Click the Change new button order and default content type link. Figure 7-31 shows the settings page that opens.

Figure 7-31: Page that allows changing the button order

8. Uncheck the Document content type in the Visible column and change the TripReport – ContentType1 Position from Top to 1.

   After you're done the page should look like the one in Figure 7-32.

9. Click OK to return to the document library settings.

Figure 7-32: Changing the content type display settings

We set the TripReport content type as the default content type for the document library and almost everything is completed. We can navigate back to the Trip Reports library and click the Documents tab. As you click the New Document drop-down button you will notice the TripReport – ContentType1 template is the only option. Click it and the template we created in Word is opened. You may ask where the fields associated with the content type are, but don't worry they are there. Let's see them in the document panel first—follow the steps below to open the document panel.

1. Click the File tab in Word to bring up the Backstage view.
2. Click the Info item in the left bar if not selected by default.

3. Click the Properties drop-down just below the document thumbnail on the right side of the menu. Refer to Figure 7-33.

4. Click the Show Document Panel item.

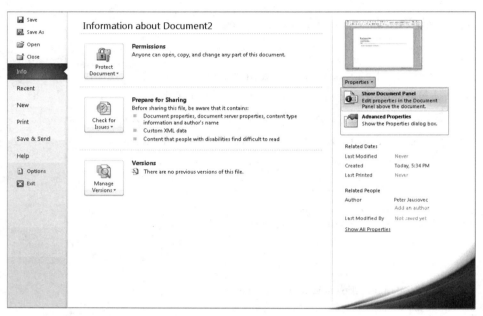

Figure 7-33: Displaying the document panel

The document panel opens and its title is set to the content type name associated with the document as shown in Figure 7-34. The panel also shows the columns for the content type we deployed with our SharePoint project.

Even though the document panel looks nice, we would rather have the columns for conference name, location, and trip type displayed directly within the document. We mentioned content controls before and now it's time to show how to use them. Our plan is to insert the content controls right after the text we have in the document. We will need three content controls: one for the conference name, one for the location, and one for the trip type. The steps below show how to insert the content controls into the

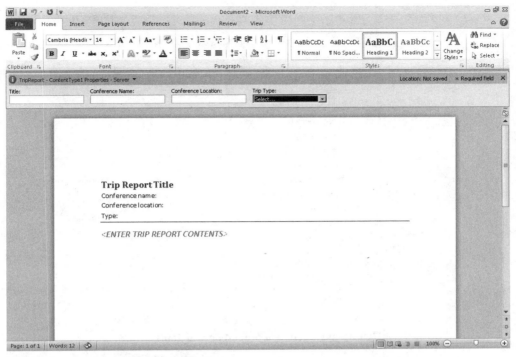

Figure 7-34: Document Panel in Word 2010

document. We assume you still have the document opened, if not go to the Trip Reports library and create a new report—this will open the document in Word.

1. Click the Insert tab in the ribbon.
2. Click the Quick Parts drop-down menu and select the Document Property submenu.

   Figure 7-35 shows the contents of the document property menu. You can see all the document specific properties as well as the site columns associated with the content type.

3. Click the column name to insert its content control into the document next to its corresponding label.

Figure 7-35: Document property menu items

Repeat step 3 above for the three fields we have associated with our content type (Conference Name, Conference Location, and Trip Type). When you are done, your document should look similar to the one in Figure 7-36.

Now, try typing something inside the content controls. Notice how the drop-down button works for the Trip Type content controls—it contains the values we specified in the SharePoint project. Save the document and then navigate to the Trip Reports SharePoint library to upload it. As you click Add document and upload the document you will notice the site columns and the values you entered while editing the document are displayed in the SharePoint edit form. This is shown in Figure 7-37.

If you wanted you could change the values again; but since we are OK with the values we set before we can click the Save button to save the document to the list. The experience of creating trip reports has changed—instead of each trip report having its own style and layout we used a content

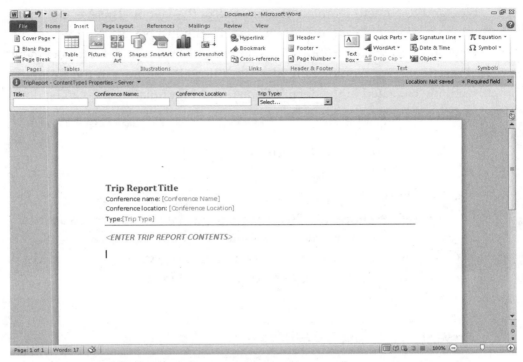

Figure 7-36: Document with content controls

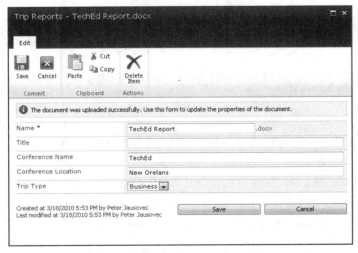

Figure 7-37: SharePoint edit form with custom columns

type and document template to standardize the layout. There is one more thing we need to do and the solutions will be almost perfect. Notice how the view of the document library hasn't changed from the default document library view. We would really like to see the site columns in the Columns section we created in the default library view. Fortunately this can be done easily by following the steps below.

1. Navigate to the Trip Reports document library.
2. Click the Library tab.
3. Click the Create View button.

    Figure 7-38 shows the Create View page that allows us to create new views. There are many view formats we could use to generate the new view, but since we want to have only one view and add the columns the easiest way is to modify an existing view.

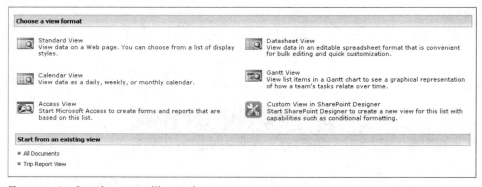

Figure 7-38: Creating a new library view

4. Click the All Documents link under the "Start from an existing view" heading.

    The page shown in Figure 7-39 opens and it allows us to add or remove columns from the view as well as to re-arrange them.

5. Click the check mark next to the Conference Name, Conference Location, and Trip Type columns.

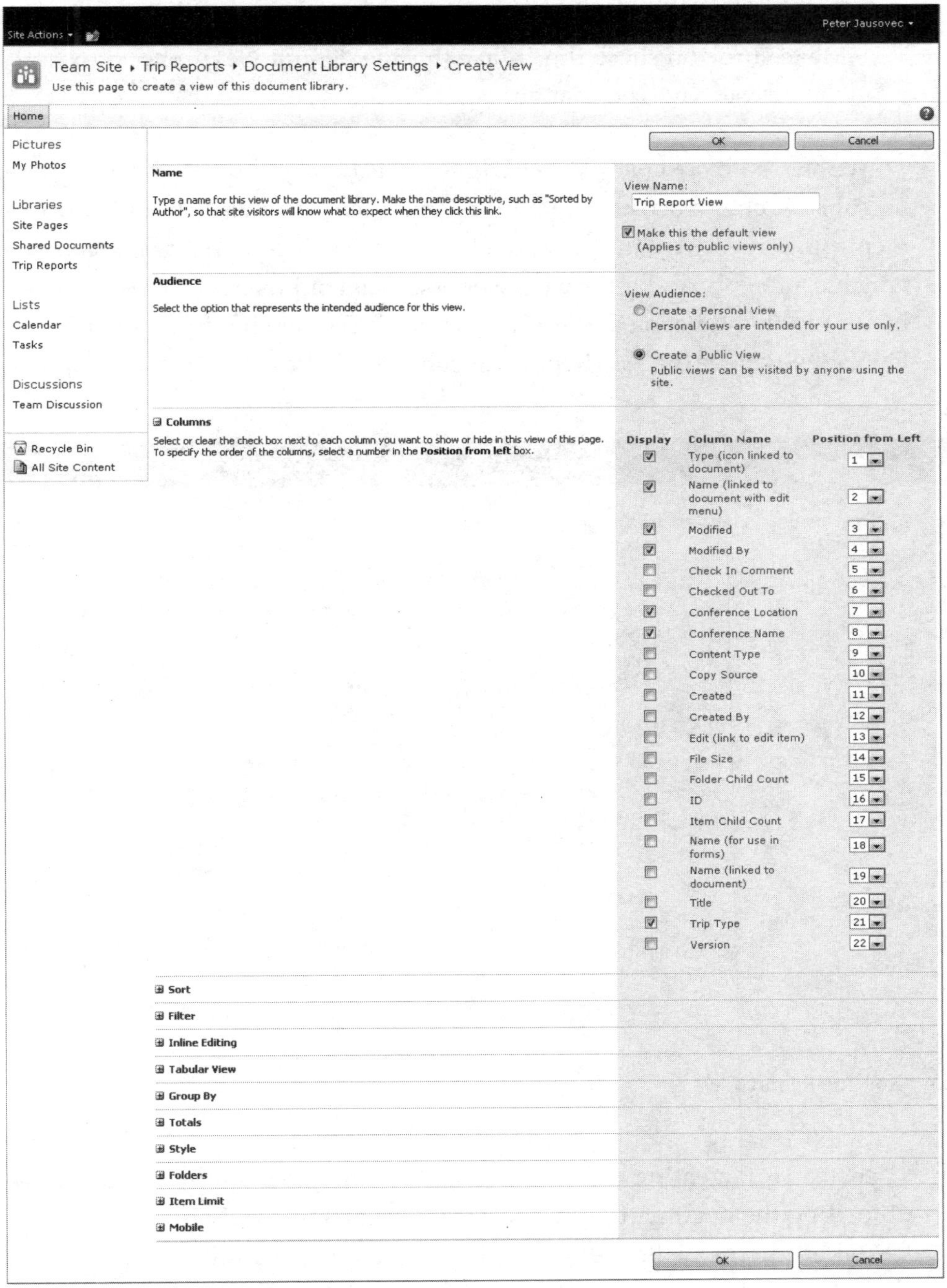

Figure 7-39: Re-arranging columns in SharePoint's Create View page

6. Type "Trip Report View" in the View Name textbox.

7. Make sure you check the "Make this the default view" checkbox and click OK to save the changes.

We are redirected back to the Trip Reports library and now it looks more useful than before because without opening the document or editing document properties we can immediately tell which trip report was made for which conference and if the trips were personal or business. We could even use the sorting function and sort the reports by conference location or name. Figure 7-40 shows the Trip Reports document library with new view applied.

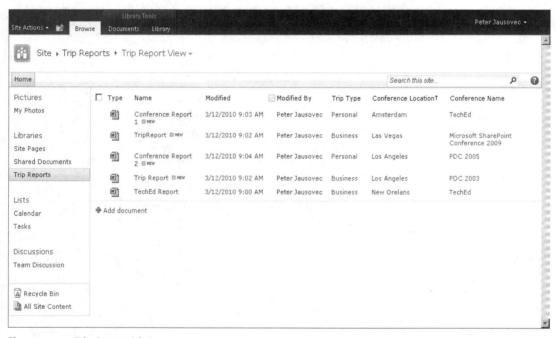

Figure 7-40: Trip Report View

Instead of creating the library, modifying the view, and manually uploading the document from the SharePoint UI we could do all that from Visual Studio as well. We do need to modify the SharePoint TripReport project a little bit. To automatically deploy the document we can add a DocumentTemplate element to the content type project. But even before we do this we need to deploy the document to the SharePoint server—we are going to use a mapped folder to do that. Open the TripReport project and follow the steps below to associate a document with the content type.

1. Right click the Trip Report project node and select SharePoint "Layouts" Mapped Folder to add a mapped folder.

   A layouts mapped folder with TripReport subfolder is added to the project.

2. Right click the TripReport folder under Layouts mapped folder and select Add > Existing Item…

3. Find the TripReport document template we created before and click Add to add it to the mapped folder.

4. Double click the Elements.xml file under the ContentType1 folder.

   In order to associate the content type with the document we are going to use the DocumentTemplate element.

5. Add the following XML after the FieldRefs element to the Elements.xml file:

```
<DocumentTemplate TargetName="/_layouts/TripReport/Trip Report.docx"/>
```

Don't be surprised to see an error when you press F5. The error saying that project item "Layouts" is not compatible with a package in a sandboxed solution is expected, because when we started creating the project we selected the sandboxed solution. Because our project has a mapped folder we need to change the solution from sandboxed to farm. Click the project node in Solution Explorer, open the Properties window, and change the Sandboxed Solution property from True to False. Press F5 again to deploy the project, this time without any errors. When the site with the list of content types opens, click the TripReport – ContentType1. It should be at the top of the page. On the site content type settings page, click the Advanced settings link. Notice the URL to existing document template is already set.

That was pretty easy. How about changing the view from our Visual Studio project? Since views are associated with a list definition we will have to add a List Definition from Content Type project item to our project. The list definition project item contains the Schema.xml file where all views for the list are defined. Follow the steps below to add a list definition from content type project item and to modify the default view.

1. Right click the TripReport project node and select Add > New Item....
2. Select the List Definition from Content Type project item template, name it "Trip Report List Definition," and click Add.

   The SharePoint Customization Wizard is displayed and TripReport – ContentType1 content type from out project is selected by default as shown in Figure 7-41.

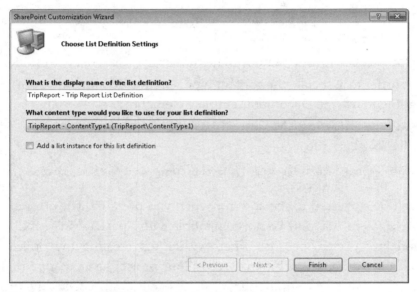

Figure 7-41: List Definition from Content Type wizard

3. Uncheck the Add a list instance for this list definition check box.
4. Click Finish to create the project item.

   Multiple SharePoint elements such as views, forms, fields, and content types are defined inside the Schema.xml file. Double click the file to open it. The Views element defines all views that are available for the SharePoint list that is created from this list definition. The one we are especially interested in is the View element that has the BasedViewID set to 1. This is the default view for the SharePoint library.

Changing the columns that show up in a view is fairly easy. Each View element has the ViewFields element that represents the fields that show up in the view. Listing 7-10 shows the ViewFields element with our custom fields added.

Listing 7-10: ViewFields

```
<ViewFields>
  <FieldRef Name="DocIcon">
  </FieldRef>
  <FieldRef Name="LinkFilename">
  </FieldRef>
  <FieldRef Name="Modified">
  </FieldRef>
  <FieldRef Name="Editor">
  </FieldRef>
  <FieldRef Name="ConferenceName"/>
  <FieldRef Name="ConferenceLocation"/>
  <FieldRef Name="TripType"/>
</ViewFields>
```

There is one small thing we need to change in the Schema.xml. Remember when we had to allow the content type management for the list in SharePoint? If you deploy the solution you would notice that the default document content type shows up for the list. To enable our content type in the list, add the following attribute to the List element in the Schema.xml file for the list definition:

```
EnableContentTypes="TRUE"
```

Now we can finally verify that the list definition works as expected. Press F5 to deploy the solution. When the Internet browser opens click the Lists link. Next, click the Create link to create a new list based on the list definition we just deployed. Select the "TripReport – Trip Report List" from the Create dialog and name it "Trip Reports" as shown in Figure 7-42.

When you click the Create button, a new list based on our custom list definition is created. You will notice the three fields we added: Conference Name, Conference Location, and Trip Type are in the default view as shown in Figure 7-43.

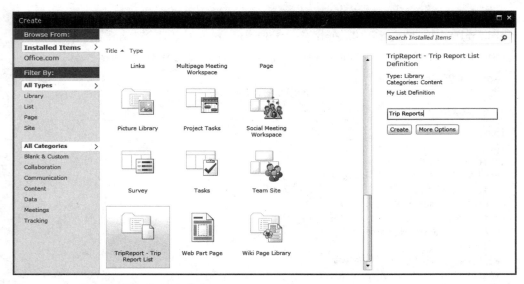

Figure 7-42: Creating Trip Reports list

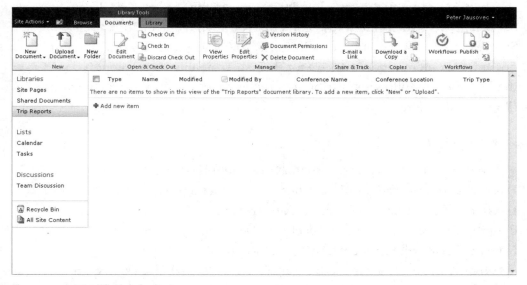

Figure 7-43: Modified default view

Also, if you click the Documents tab on the ribbon and then click the New Document drop-down you will see the Word document template we deployed.

Let's expand our scenario a little bit more. We have the document template but we want to include more functionality in the Word document template. Specifically, we want to automatically generate the trip report title once the user enters the conference name, location, and type. If you remember earlier, we added the content controls to a Word document in order to bind them to the columns in the content type. In order to automatically generate the trip report title we have to add similar content controls to our Word template.

Since we already deployed the Word template, content type, and list definition and we created the list instance we can navigate to that list instance and create a new trip report.

1. Open the Trip Reports list.
2. Click the Documents tab and select the TripReport – ContentType1 under the New Document menu.

    The document opens in Word. If the document is opened in a protected view, click the Enable Editing button to enable document editing.

3. Click the Insert tab and open the Quick Parts menu.
4. In the Document Property menu, click the Conference Name property.

    A content type control for Conference Name property is added to the document. Position the control right after the conference name text.

5. Repeat step 4 for Conference Location and Trip Type. After you are finished, the document should look like the one shown in Figure 7-44.

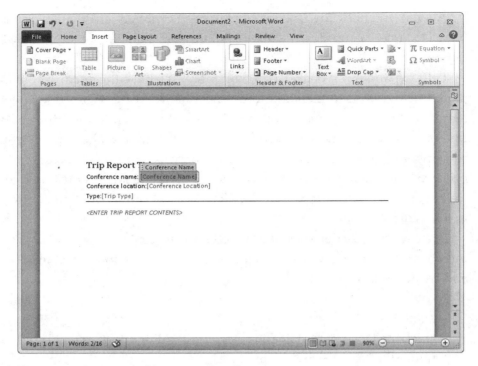

Figure 7-44: Document with content controls

Now that we added the content controls they are associated with the content type in our existing list. We can save this document to the desktop because we are going to use it as the basis for the VSTO document project we are about to create. Follow the steps below to add a new Word 2010 document project to the SharePoint solution.

1. Right click the solution name and select Add > New Project.
2. Expand the Office and 2010 nodes and select the Word 2010 document project.
3. Name the project "Trip Report Document" and click OK to create the project.
   Visual Studio Tools for Office Project Wizard opens.
4. Select the Copy an existing document radio button and browse to the trip report document with content controls that we just save with the

content type. The wizard with the document selected should look like the one in Figure 7-45.

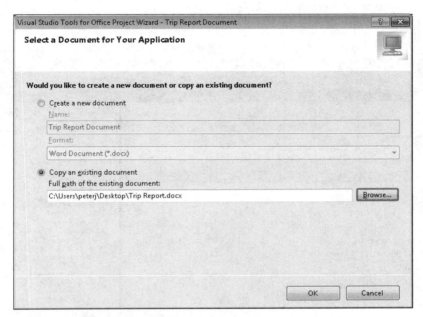

Figure 7-45: Word 2010 document wizard

5. Click OK to close the wizard.

If this is the first time you are creating a VSTO project a warning dialog as shown in Figure 7-46 is displayed. To use VSTO projects you need to enable access to the Microsoft Office Visual Basic for Applications (VBA) project system.

Figure 7-46: Enabling access to the VBA project system

6. Click OK to allow access and the project will be created.

When the project is created the trip report document opens in Visual Studio as shown in Figure 7-47.

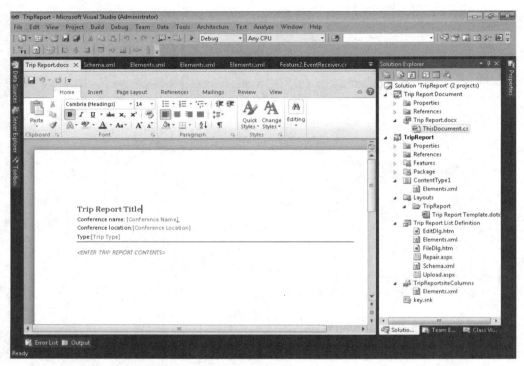

Figure 7-47: Word document in Visual Studio

The first thing we should do is to rename the content controls to something more meaningful than plain TextContentControl1. Click the Conference Name content control in the Word designer and open the Properties window. Change the (Name) property value to txtConferenceName. Repeat the same for conference location and trip type, naming them txtConference-Location and cmbTripType.

Because we want to automatically generate the trip report title we should add a bookmark control to the text that says Trip Report Title. This way we can access that text from the code and change it. Follow the steps on the next page to add a bookmark control.

1. Open the Toolbox.

2. Drag and drop the bookmark control from the Word Controls tab to the Word designer.

   The Add Bookmark Control dialog is displayed.

3. Select the "Trip Report Title" in the document as shown in Figure 7-48 and click OK on the dialog to insert the bookmark control.

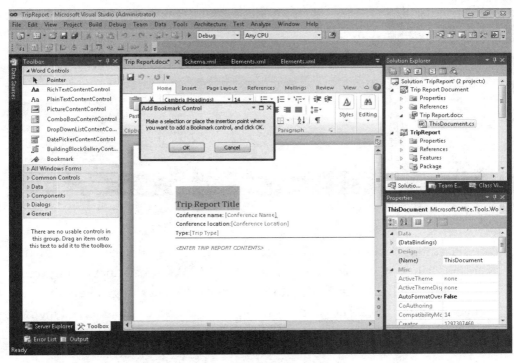

Figure 7-48: Inserting a bookmark control in the Word designer

4. Select the bookmark control on the document surface and open the Properties window.

5. Change the (Name) property to "txtTitle."

6. Drag and drop a button from the toolbox right next to the trip report title text on the document then use the Properties window to change the caption to "Create Title."

   Your document should look like the one shown in Figure 7-49.

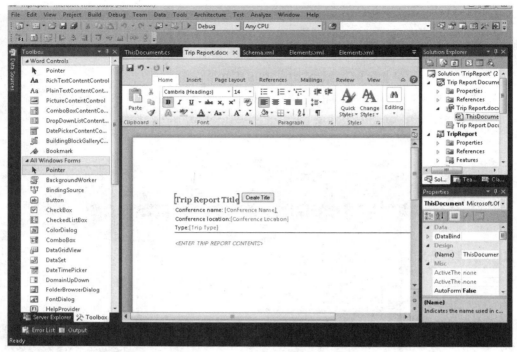

Figure 7-49: Document with controls

To make this really simple we are going to use a button control and when users click on it, we are going to create the title. We already have a button, so we only need to double click it in the Word designer to generate the click event handler code. The code in Listing 7-11 shows the implemented method in the ThisDocument.cs file.

Listing 7-11: Code for Creating the Title

```csharp
private void btnCreateTitle_Click(object sender, EventArgs e)
{
  txtTitle.Text = string.Format("{0} - {1} ({2})",
    txtConferenceName.Text,
    txtConferenceLocation.Text,
    cmbTripType.Text);
}
```

The code in Listing 7-11 reads the text from each of the content controls and displays it in the title. The document is ready now and we can deploy it. In order for the content type to use it we must deploy it to the same location as we deployed the document in the SharePoint project, that's in the _layouts/TripReport folder. Follow the steps below to deploy the VSTO document project.

1. Right click the Trip Report Document project and select Publish…
2. Type "http://localhost/_layouts/TripReport" into the location text box as shown in Figure 7-50.

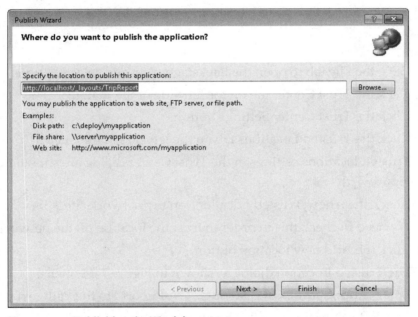

Figure 7-50: Publishing the Word document

3. Click Finish to publish the document.
4. Right click the Trip Report Document project and select Clean to clean the project and remove temporary settings that are created for development purposes.

Now we have deployed the VSTO document to the _layouts/TripReport folder on the SharePoint server. The content type can access the document from this location and it will open it when we create a new trip report.

Before we try this out, let's remove the mapped folder from the SharePoint project. To do this, select the Layouts folder in the SharePoint project and press the Delete key to remove it. Also, make sure the DocumentTemplate in the Elements.xml file is pointing to the right location: /_layouts/Trip-Report/Trip Report.docx. If you changed the document name in the VSTO project, make sure you change the name in the Elements.xml file and in the Schema.xml file as well.

In order for the customized document to install and load in Word, we need to make sure the location from which the document is being loaded is trusted. We can set the trusted locations in Word like this:

1. Open Word.
2. Click the File tab to open the Backstage view and select Options.
3. Click the Trust Center tab on the left side of the dialog.
4. Click the Trust Center Settings button.
5. Click the Trusted Locations tab on the left side of the dialog.

   Trusted locations settings in the Trust Center dialog are shown in Figure 7-51.

6. Check the Allow Trusted Locations on my network check box.

   We need to check this in order to trust the location on the network.

7. Click the Add new location button.

   The Trusted Location dialog as shown in Figure 7-52 opens.

8. Enter "http://localhost/_layouts/TripReport" to the Path text box.
9. Check the Subfolders of this location are also trusted check box and click the OK button.
10. Click the Add new location button again and add enter "http://localhost/Trip Reports" into the Path textbox.

    Because we are saving documents to the Trip Reports list we need to make sure documents in that location are trusted as well.

11. Close the dialogs and then close Word.

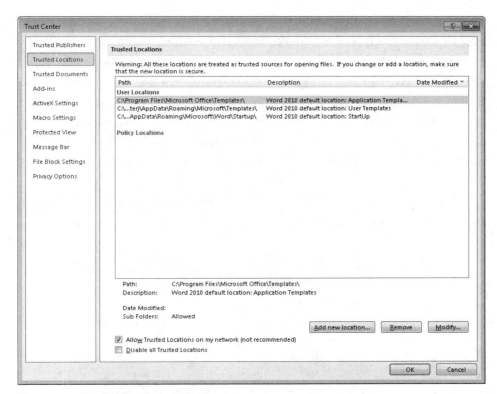

Figure 7-51: Trusted location settings

Figure 7-52: Adding trusted location

Everything is set. We deployed the customized document, the SharePoint project is deployed as well (make sure you re-deploy it if you made any changes), and security settings are set. We can test our solution now. Open the Internet browser and navigate to your SharePoint site. If you re-deployed the SharePoint project you need to create a new list based on the trip report list definition. Make sure the name you use for the list is the same one you added to the trusted locations in Word. Navigate to the Trip Reports list, click the New Document drop-down and select the TripReport – ContentType1 item.

When Word opens the document the Microsoft Office Customization Installer shown in Figure 7-53 is displayed.

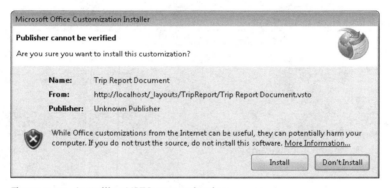

Figure 7-53: Installing VSTO customization

Click Install to install the customization. At this point the custom code we wrote is loaded and you can see the button as well as the content controls we added in Visual Studio. Use the Document Panel or type the conference name and location directly into the provided content controls. When you click the Create Title button you will notice the title changes according to the format we specified in the code. Figure 7-54 shows the document with the generated title.

There is much more to VSTO than we described in this section, but because this book is focused on SharePoint development we recommend that you read the book *Visual Studio Tools for Office* by Eric Carter and Eric Lippert for more information on this topic.

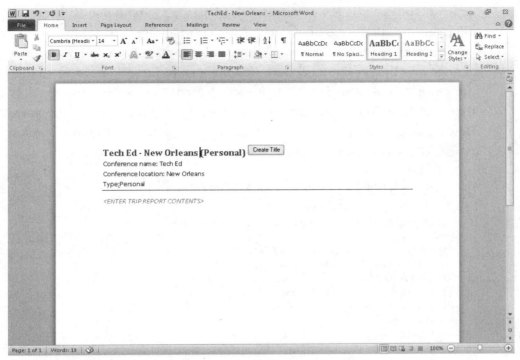

Figure 7-54: Customized document

Content Types and Workflows

It's natural to think that there has to be a way to associate SharePoint work-flows with content types. Since we already can associate workflows with SharePoint lists and sites why would content types be any different?

If you associate a workflow with a list based on the workflow settings the workflow starts as soon as users either upload a document to the list or change an existing document in the list. That works as long as you have one list and that list is the only place you want to run the workflow from. If we continue with the TripReport content type sample, imagine that you have multiple Trip Report libraries (maybe a separate library for each company department or division) and you want to start the same workflow on every item that gets uploaded to those lists. We could create multiple workflow associations and associate the same workflow to different lists but it would be more convenient if we could associate the workflow with the TripReport content type itself. This way we don't have to worry about manually associating the workflow each time a new Trip Report library is created.

To associate a SharePoint workflow with a content type we only need to change one line in the workflow's Elements.xml file. We need to change the value of the AssociationCategories element to ContentType to allow that workflow to be associated to a content type. An example of a workflow's Elements.xml that would allow it to be associated with a content type is shown in Listing 7-12.

Listing 7-12: Allowing Associating Workflows to Content Types

```xml
<?xml version="1.0" encoding="utf-8" ?>
<Elements xmlns="http://schemas.microsoft.com/sharepoint/">
  <Workflow
    Name="TripReportWorkflow - Workflow1"
    Description="My Trip Report Workflow"
    Id="a3bc35fe-318b-4054-9f81-5c977d15d01b"
    CodeBesideClass="TripReportWorkflow.Workflow1.Workflow1"
    CodeBesideAssembly="$assemblyname$">
    <Categories/>
    <MetaData>
      <AssociationCategories>ContentType</AssociationCategories>
      <StatusPageUrl>_layouts/WrkStat.aspx</StatusPageUrl>
    </MetaData>
  </Workflow>
</Elements>
```

Since this is the chapter about content types we will not go into any more details about this. In Chapter 8, "SharePoint Workflow," we will see how to associate a workflow to a content type. Changing the AssociationCategories merely allows us to make the workflow associable to content types.

Conclusion

In this chapter we explained what content types and site column definitions are and how they are used on a SharePoint site. We learned what content types are and explored the different content types that ship with SharePoint. We also learned how to use Visual Studio 2010 to deploy both site column definitions and content types. We also used the feature designer to create separate features in a project to allow us to deploy one feature before another one.

Since content types are not useful if they are not associated with a list instance or list definition, we showed an example of creating a list definition based on a content type and deployed it all together in one solution. At the end of the chapter we showed how to associate a content type with a document template, we saw the document panel, and how to insert content controls in Word documents that are linked to fields associated with the content type. We also saw how to associate a Visual Studio customization with a document template used by a content type.

■8■

SharePoint Workflow

SharePoint workflows offer a way of running multistep or multistate processes. Workflows are often long running, waiting for humans or external systems to complete tasks or other processes before continuing.

In this chapter we will describe workflow basics, the activities that make up workflows, and how to create custom forms to use with workflow in Visual Studio 2010 as well as in SharePoint Designer 2010.

Workflow Basics

Workflows are made up of one or more activities that are executed in a logical order to complete some function. All of us have encountered workflows before, even though we didn't think about them as workflows. The way your whole day goes could be represented with a workflow—you wake up in the morning, get coffee or tea, drive to the office, go to lunch, etc. Each part of your day could be separated into separate activities. Depending on the conditions of your day the order of activities you perform could be different. For example, on Sundays you probably won't go to the office or you might work from home on Mondays. Getting back to the software world: Every activity in a workflow has an Execute method and can be in one of a number of states (e.g., Executing, Closed, etc.), and some activities can have conditions that change the execution path of the workflow. Visual Studio supports the creation of two types of workflows, sequential and state machine.

Sequential workflows are represented in the form of a flowchart. They have a defined beginning and end. All execution paths through the sequential workflow can be easily identified just by looking at the workflow model. The path that is taken depends on the evaluated conditions, which are often influenced by data provided by users and/or external systems. Figure 8-1 shows a sequential workflow for a simple document approval process.

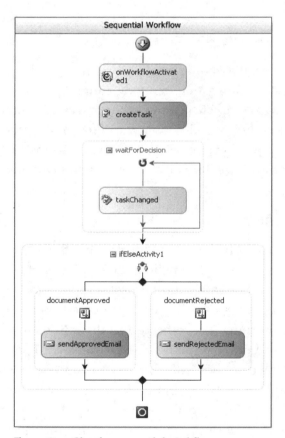

Figure 8-1: Simple sequential workflow

Just by looking at the workflow we know where it starts, what activities it includes, and where it ends. When the document is ready to be approved it is uploaded to a SharePoint list then the workflow starts and creates a task for the approver. Once the task is created and assigned, the workflow waits until the approver makes a decision and either approves or rejects the document. It then moves to the next activity and based on the approver's decision informs the author of the document about the decision by sending an e-mail.

State machine workflows introduce the concept of *states*, *events*, and *transitions*. State machine workflows are the route to take if you need to model a more complex business process. Every state machine workflow has a defined initial state and end state. The execution path taken between the start and end state depends on the transitions between states and events that trigger those transitions. In contrast to sequential workflows there is no prescribed path in state machine workflows. Because we can't be certain which event is triggered and which state is next, it is very hard to identify all execution paths just by looking at the state machine workflow. The sample state machine workflow in Figure 8-2 represents a document approval workflow similar to the sequential workflow discussed previously.

Just by comparing the sequential and state machine workflow figures you will see they look completely different. The state machine workflow in Figure 8-2 starts at the DocumentApprovalInitialState. When a document is uploaded the workflow moves to the DocumentUploaded state and so on.

Both types of workflows are flexible and can be used to model different business processes. The decision to choose one type over the other should be made based on the problem you are trying to solve. There is no right or wrong choice, but when you find a workflow becoming messy or complex, it should make you consider if you have used the best type. A good rule of thumb would be to choose a sequential workflow if you are modeling a well-defined process that does not have many state transitions and proceeds mostly down a single path. It can have branches along the way, but these branches should find their way back to the main flow. Workflows with many state transitions and branches that send the workflow permanently off in a different direction are usually better represented with a state machine workflow.

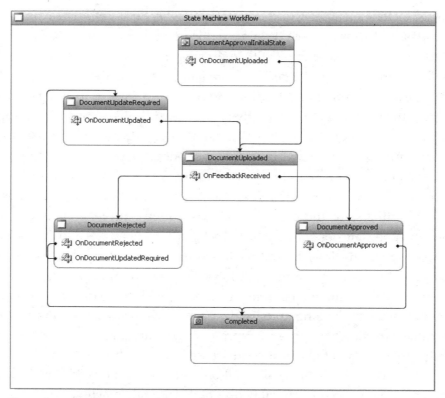

Figure 8-2: Simple state machine workflow

Workflow Activities

As mentioned earlier, activities are the building blocks of every workflow and should be atomic and reusable. The purpose of every activity is to complete a specific step in the workflow. Visual Studio 2010 ships with about 30 general workflow activities and an additional 26 SharePoint-related activities. These can be found in the Toolbox when a workflow is open in the Workflow designer in Visual Studio. If all those activities are not enough for you or you need specific functionality you can implement your own activity or even a library of workflow activities. In general we can separate activities into three groups.

1. Control flow activities
2. Container activities
3. Standard activities

Control Flow Activities

Control flow activities are used as decision points in workflows and control the execution path within a workflow. They have a condition attached to them; based on the evaluation of that condition an appropriate branch or path through the workflow is chosen. Examples of control flow activities are the While and IfElse activities. There are two types of conditions you can use in control flow activities, a declarative rule condition, and a code condition. Declarative rule conditions are created using the rule condition editor and are stored in an XML file with a .rules suffix, while code condition rules are created by writing .NET code.

Container Activities

Container Activities serve as a grouping mechanism and can contain multiple activities. An example of a container activity would be the Sequence activity. We could also consider activities like While and IfElse as container activities, because they contain other activities.

Standard Activities

Standard activities are used to execute some task. Tasks could be anything from method written in .NET (Code activity) to invoking a web service (InvokeWebService activity) to terminating the workflow (Terminate activity) or even throwing an exception (Throw activity).

Table 8-1 contains the list of general workflow activities in Visual Studio 2010 and their purposes.

TABLE 8-1: Workflow Activities and Their Purposes

Activity	Description
CallExternalMethod	Activity is used to send data from the workflow to an external host application.
Code	For executing .NET code.
ConditionedActivityGroup	Used for creating data-driven workflows.
Delay	Delays the workflow for a specified duration
EventDriven	Used for grouping an activity whose execution is started by an event.
EventHandlingScope	Similar to Listen activity, but it allows events to be received multiple times. This activity is heavily used in built-in SharePoint workflows.
FaultHandler	Activity is used for handling exceptions in workflow.
HandleExternalEvent	Opposite to CallExternalMethod, this activity is used to send data from an external host application back to the workflow.
IfElse	Behaves the same way as an if/else construct in C# or VB programming language; this activity is comprised of one or more branches that are executed based on the associated condition. Branch conditions are evaluated and the first branch to evaluate to True is executed. The other branches are not executed.
Listen	Activity is used for listening to an external event. It contains multiple branches and the branch that receives the first event is executed. Aside from other branches, there is a special timer branch. If timer goes off before anything else, the timer branch is executed. We could compare this activity to switch/case statement in VB or C# language, where multiple branches are case statements and timer branch is the default statement. This activity supports a workflow pattern to wait for one or more responses and then timeout if a response is not received within a preset duration.

TABLE 8-1: Workflow Activities and Their Purposes *(Continued)*

Activity	Description
Parallel	Activity is used for executing two or more branches at the same time; before the activity is completed, it waits until execution is completed in each of the branches.
Replicator	Activity is used to process or iterate through a number of elements in a serial or parallel fashion; if using serial execution, this activity is similar to the *for each statement* in VB or C#. The activity is critical for a number of scenarios in which, for example, a document needs to be approved by multiple approvers, or e-mails need to be sent to multiple recipients. This activity is heavily used in built-in SharePoint workflows.
Sequence	A container used for grouping one or more activities that need to be sequentially executed.
Terminate	Used to terminate a workflow.
While	This activity behaves the same as the *while* keyword in the C# or VB programming language. The activity loops while the associated condition remains True.

Activities in Table 8-2 are displayed in the Toolbox in Visual Studio, but they are not supported by SharePoint workflow.

TABLE 8-2: Workflow Activities not Supported by SharePoint

Activity	Description
Compensate	All compensation-related activities are used for undoing or compensating work that was previously done in case there's a failure.
CompensatableTransaction	Similar to TransactionScope activity; this activity uses compensation logic.
CompensatableSequence	Same purpose as Compensate activity.

Continues

TABLE 8-2: Workflow Activities not Supported by SharePoint *(Continued)*

Activity	Description
InvokeWebService	Activity is used for calling a web service from a workflow.
InvokeWorkflow	Activity is used to invoke another workflow.
Policy	Activity is used for storing the definition and execution logic of a RuleSet (collection of If-Then-Else expressions).
ReceiveActivity	Used for exposing a workflow as a WCF service.
SendActivity	Used for connecting to a WCF end-point.
Suspend	Activity suspends the workflow execution.
SynchronizationScope	Used for synchronizing the execution. For example, activity specifies data that is required before the contained activities are allowed to execute.
Throw	Activity is used for raising exceptions in a workflow.
TransactionScope	Used for grouping activities into a transaction scope.
WebServiceInput	Used for exposing a workflow as a web service.
WebServiceOutput	Used for exposing a workflow as a web service.
WebServiceFault	Used for sending a fault from the workflow to the web service.

SharePoint Workflow Activities

In addition to an extensive set of general workflow activities, there are number of SharePoint-specific activities that ship in Visual Studio 2010 (Table 8-3). We can separate these SharePoint workflow activities into four groups; task-related activities, item-related activities, workflow-related activities, and event activities. Event activities enable developers to have an event handler attached to a specific event (e.g., OnTaskCreated).

TABLE 8-3: SharePoint Workflow Activities and Their Descriptions

Activity	Description
ApplyActivation	Updates initial workflow status with new information (from the class SPWorkflowActivationProperties).
CompleteTask	Activity marks a task as completed. Activity-specific parameters: • MethodInvoking • TaskOutcome • TaskId
CreateTask	Activity creates a new task in associated task list. Activity-specific properties: • MethodInvoking • ListItemId • SpecialPermissions • TaskId • TaskProperties
CreateTaskWithContentType	Used for creating tasks with content types in SharePoint.
DeleteTask	Activity deletes a task. Activity specific properties: • TaskId
EnableWorkflowModification	This activity enables a workflow modification form in SharePoint.
InitializeWorkflow	Activity is used for initializing workflow
LogToHistoryListActivity	Activity is used for writing messages (logging) to workflow history list.
OnTaskChanged	Event that fires when a task is changed.
OnTaskCreated	Event that fires when a task is created.
OnTaskDeleted	Event that fires when a task is deleted.

Continues

TABLE 8-3:   SharePoint Workflow Activities and Their Descriptions *(Continued)*

Activity	Description
OnWorkflowActivated	Event that fires when workflow is activated; this is the first activity in every SharePoint 2010 workflow. It is added automatically when a SharePoint workflow item is added to a project.
OnWorkflowItemChanged	Event that fires when a workflow item is changed.
OnWorkflowItemDeleted	Event that fires when a workflow item is deleted.
OnWorkflowModified	Event that fires when a workflow is modified by use of the EnableWorkflowModification activity and a workflow modification form.
RollbackTask	Activity rolls a workflow task back to its previous state.
SendEmail	Activity sends an e-mail message using the data provided in the properties .
SetState	Activity to set the next state in state machine workflows.
UpdateAllTasks	Same as UpdateTask, except it updates all tasks that a workflow instance has created.
UpdateTask	Activity updates an existing task with new information. Activity-specific properties: • TaskId • TaskProperties
CheckInItemActivity	Activity checks in an item to the list. Activity-specific properties: • Context • Comment • ListId • ListItem
CheckOutItemActivity	Activity checks out an item from the list. Activity-specific properties: • Context • ListId • ListItem

TABLE 8-3:   SharePoint Workflow Activities and Their Descriptions *(Continued)*

Activity	Description
CopyItemActivity	Activity allows copying an item or a file to a specified list. Activity-specific properties: • Context • ListId (source list id or name) • ListItem • Overwrite • ToListId (target list id or name)
CreateItemActivity	This activity creates a new list item or a file using the defined properties. In order to use this activity the following properties need to be set: • ListId (GUID or name of the list) • ItemProperties (contains properties for the new item) • Overwrite (should the activity overwrite the item if the item already exists) • Context Once the activity is completed (and the item is created), the ItemID property contains the GUID of a newly created item.
DeleteItemActivity	This activity deletes an item from a list. Activity-specific properties: • Context • ListId • ListItem
UpdateItemActivity	Activity updates an existing item. Activity-specific properties: • Context • ItemProperties (this should contain the new properties for the updated item) • ListId • ListItem

If the activities in Table 8-1 and 8-3 don't cover the functionality you're looking for, you can develop your own custom activities. A custom activity is just a regular class that inherits from System.Workflow.Component-Model.Activity and overrides methods like Initialize, Execute, and Cancel. These activities can be made to show up in the Toolbox and then used in workflows just like the built-in activities. Custom-made activities will show up in the Toolbox when you build the project that contains a custom activity class that inherits from System.Workflow.ComponentModel.Activity class.

SharePoint Workflows

By now you probably can guess that SharePoint workflows are not that different from workflows hosted inside a console application or Windows Forms application. Regardless of their host, the principle of workflow is the same. Because SharePoint is more document and list centric, workflows hosted in SharePoint often work with documents and tasks. Tasks, lists, documents, and items are central to SharePoint workflow because every Share-Point workflow needs to have a task list assigned to it.

Before a SharePoint workflow can be used it must be associated with a list in a SharePoint site (a list workflow) or with the SharePoint site itself (a site workflow). In addition, there are other settings that affect how the workflow is started that must be set before the SharePoint workflow can be used, such as the workflow's association list, history list, and task list. To better understand workflow associations and other settings, let's create a simple SharePoint workflow project with a CreateTask activity that creates a task and assigns it to a user when the workflow completes successfully.

1. Start Visual Studio 2010 in elevated mode.
2. In the Project dialog, select SharePoint > 2010 from the left side and then Sequential Workflow from the center of the form (see Figure 8-3 for reference).
3. Click OK to create the project.

   The first wizard page shows up and the only thing we can change here is the local site to use for debugging. By default it is set to your

Figure 8-3: New Project dialog

local machine name. Change this to the site collection you created in Chapter 2. The "Deploy as a sandboxed solution" option is disabled because workflows cannot be deployed to SharePoint as sandboxed solutions. Figure 8-4 shows the wizard page.

4. Click Next to advance to the second wizard page.

On the second wizard page shown in Figure 8-5 you can specify the name of the workflow association and decide if this will be a list or site workflow. Remember, a list workflow is associated with a specific list which will need to be identified in an upcoming wizard page, whereas a site workflow is associated with a specific SharePoint site, specifically the one identified previously.

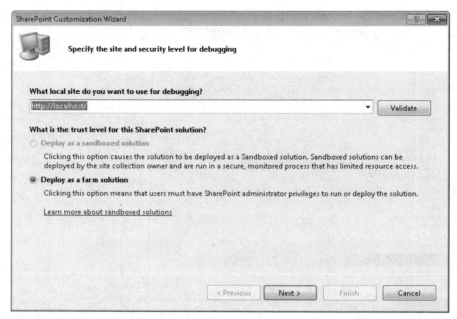

Figure 8-4: First SharePoint Customization Wizard page for workflow

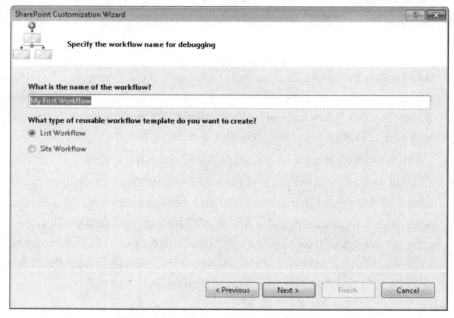

Figure 8-5: Second SharePoint Customization Wizard page for workflow

5. Change the workflow name to "My First Workflow." The name you are supplying is not the name of the workflow item that will be created in the project, but the name of the association when the workflow is associated to a list. There are actually three names that are used when creating workflows in Visual Studio 2010. The first is the name of the project item, the second the name of the workflow itself—as defined in the Elements.xml file under the workflow project item folder—and the third is the name of the association, the one we are supplying here, which is used when the project is run (assuming the auto-association check box is checked on the next page). Ensure the *List Workflow* option is set and click Next.

On the next wizard page shown in Figure 8-6, you can determine if you want the workflow automatically associated with a list when you run the project. Assuming you do, and we do for this first example, you must also select the list with which you want the workflow associated. In fact, we need to select three lists; an association list, a history list, and a task list. The *association list* is the list our workflow is

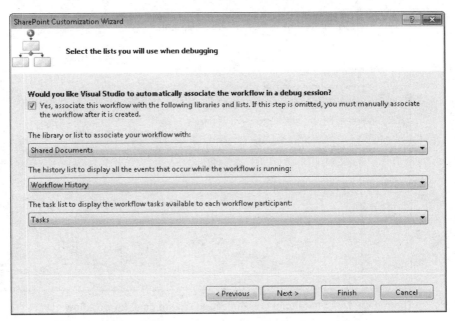

Figure 8-6: Third SharePoint Customization Wizard page for workflow

going to be associated with. This means if you accept the default list, Shared Documents, you will be only able to start the workflow on this list. You cannot start the same workflow on another list unless it is associated with that list. The *Workflow history list* is used to store all events that occur while workflow is running. Lastly, the *Task list* is used to add, update, and delete any tasks used by the workflow.

6. Click Next to proceed to the last wizard page.

   The last wizard page shown in Figure 8-7 contains additional workflow settings pertaining to the association. On this page you define when the workflow is started. The first option determines if the user can manually start it. The next two options determine if the workflow should be started automatically when an item is created (e.g., when you create or upload a document to the SharePoint list) or when an item is changed (e.g., when you change an item in a list).

7. Click Finish to close the wizard and create the project.

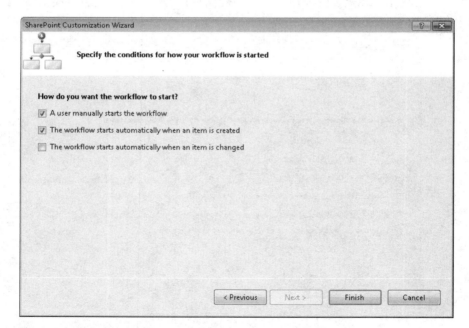

Figure 8-7: Last SharePoint Customization Wizard page for workflow

When you close the wizard a SharePoint workflow project is created that contains a single project item, Workflow1, and the Workflow designer is displayed. You screen should look similar to Figure 8-8.

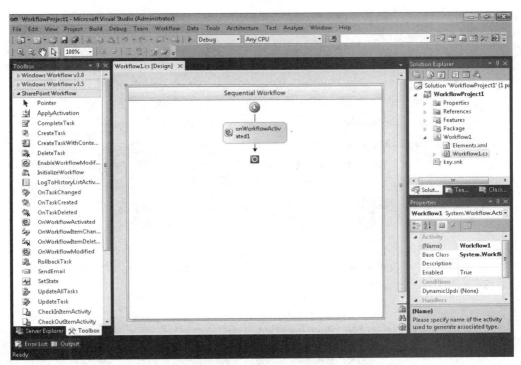

Figure 8-8: SharePoint Workflow designer inside Visual Studio 2010

If you created SharePoint workflows in Visual Studio 2008 you will notice the project structure is different. In Visual Studio 2010 all SharePoint project items have the same basic structure. Two common items in every SharePoint project are the Features and Package folders. The Features folder typically contains one or more feature items that in turn is associated with one or more project items. Each of these project items, such as the Workflow1 item in the current example, is made up of a folder with a special icon and one or more files. The folder is just a container for the one or more files that make up the item. Both the project item folder and the files within it have specific SharePoint knowledge so these items are called

SharePoint project items. The Package folder represents the SharePoint solution that will be packaged into a .WSP file when you package and/or deploy the project. You can learn more about packaging and deployment in Chapter 11, "Packaging and Deployment."

What about My Visual Studio 2008 Workflows?

Unfortunately you can't directly convert a Visual Studio 2008 SharePoint workflow project to a Visual Studio 2010 SharePoint. You will have to manually convert your Visual Studio 2008 SharePoint workflow projects and the easiest way to do this is to create a new Visual Studio 2010 SharePoint workflow project and copy and paste the workflow code-behind and move all custom classes and items in your 2008 project to the new Visual Studio 2010 SharePoint workflow project.

Files that are found in the Workflow1 project item folder are listed in Table 8-4.

TABLE 8-4:   Files under SharePoint Workflow Project Item Folder

File name	Description
Elements.xml	This is a file that describes the workflow to SharePoint. It can be named whatever you want, but for consistency sake the name Elements.xml is used for all of the SharePoint project items you add to your project.
	This file is used to store the name and description of the workflow, any forms that it uses, and other information.
Workflow1.cs Workflow1.designer.cs file	These are the files that make up the activities and code for the workflow. The activities are displayed in the Workflow designer and the code exists in the code-behind file, just like many other Visual Studio designers, such as an ASP.NET page.

TABLE 8-4: Files under SharePoint Workflow Project Item Folder *(Continued)*

File name	Description
SharePointProjectItem.spdata	By default this file is hidden and it should not be modified manually.
	The .spdata file contains information about the SharePoint project item. Each SharePoint project item has an .spdata file that contains some common information and optionally some information that is specific to that type of item. For example, the workflow would have information about the workflow type (list vs. site).

To have our workflow do something more interesting, let's add a CreateTask activity to it. With the CreateTask activity you can create a new task in the SharePoint task list associated with the workflow. We are going to set the task title and assign it to a user. This activity is heavily used in SharePoint workflows—take for example a document approval process or expense report approval—as soon as an approval is part of your business process you can be sure that you will have to use SharePoint tasks. In the approval part of the process you create tasks and assign them to users for approval. Once tasks are approved (completed), you can use an OnTaskChange activity to detect that event; your business process and workflow can then continue to execute.

1. Drag and drop a CreateTask activity from the Toolbox to the Workflow designer, right below the onWorkflowActivated1 activity.

   As you drag the activity onto the designer you will be given feedback as to where an activity can and cannot be dropped. When you do drop the CreateTask activity onto the designer you will notice the red exclamation mark on the top right side of the activity. This exclamation mark is telling us that there is a required property we have not set.

2. Click the createTask1 activity in the designer and open the Properties window. (We will be using the Properties window quite a bit; it would be a good idea to dock it within the IDE.)

3. Locate the CorrelationToken property and set the value to "taskToken." You have to use a unique correlation token for each task you are referencing in a workflow. You must use the same correlation token if you want multiple activities to reference the same task (such as in a CreateTask activity at the beginning of a workflow and then later in a CompleteTask or other task-related activity that is referring to the task that was created in the workflow).

Correlation Token? What's That?

Correlation token is a unique string identifier within your workflow that enables mapping between the items in your workflow, hosting environment, and workflow runtime. The most common errors SharePoint workflow developers experience are due to incorrectly set correlation tokens. The guidance is to have a separate correlation token for the workflow itself and each task you need to reference in the workflow. If you are creating a new task and are then changing an existing one you would need two separate correlation tokens to represent those two tasks. However, if you want to reference the same task you created in the OnTaskChanged or CompleteTask activity for example you would use the same correlation token throughout the workflow.

4. Expand the CorrelationToken property and set OwnerActivityName to "Workflow1."

5. Find and click on the TaskId property in the Properties window. This will display the ellipsis (...) button; click it to display the Bind dialog as shown in Figure 8-9. The Bind dialog is used to link a workflow property to a field or property in the code-behind file. This can be either an existing member or you can choose to create a new one.

6. Click Bind to a new member tab.

7. Type "taskId" in the New member name textbox.

8. Select Create Property radio button.

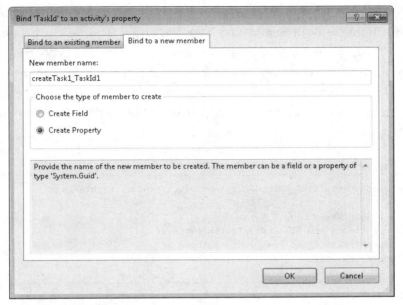

Figure 8-9: Binding dialog

9. Click OK.

10. Repeat steps 5–9 for the TaskProperties property and use "task-Properties" for the New member name.

Binding activity properties is usually the first thing you need to do after you add an activity to the designer. Above, you created new member variables for the TaskId and TaskProperties properties in order to be able to access them from code. We still need to set the taskId and taskProperties in order for the activity to create a new task once workflow is started. The best place to do this is before the activity is executed. Follow these steps to add the event handler.

1. Double click on the createTask1 activity to open the code view.

   A method is created in the Workflow1.cs code file called createTask1_MethodInvoking.

2. In this method, initialize taskId and taskProperties.

In order to be able to reference the new task and to set its properties we need to initialize both taskId and taskProperties. The taskId property is merely a GUID that represents the new task, and taskProperties is an instance of the SPWorkflowTaskProperties object that contains properties that pertain to SharePoint tasks, such as title, description, due date, etc.

An implementation for the createTask1_MethodInvoking method is shown in Listing 8-1.

Listing 8-1: MethodInvoking for createTask1

```
private void createTask1_MethodInvoking(object sender, EventArgs e)
{
  taskId = Guid.NewGuid();
  taskProperties = new SPWorkflowTaskProperties();
  taskProperties.AssignedTo = "contoso\\user";
  taskProperties.Title = "Task created from workflow";
}
```

The above code creates a new GUID and assigns it to the taskId property we created using the Bind dialog. For taskProperties we create a new instance of the SPWorkflowTaskProperties class and set a few properties. In the above example we used two of the most common properties: AssignedTo and Title. The SPWorkflowTaskProperties class contains more properties that you can use, such as StartDate, PercentComplete, and Due-Date. Make sure to assign your own user account to the AssignedTo property, otherwise the workflow will not complete successfully.

Now let's add a breakpoint to the CreateTask activity and deploy the project. To add a breakpoint, switch to the Workflow designer, select the desired activity, and press F9. Press F5 to package and deploy the workflow and start debugging it. When deployment completes, an web browser opens up to the Shared Documents library with which you associated the workflow. In the wizard we chose to automatically associate workflow, so you can just upload a new document to the Shared Documents list to start the workflow. To upload a new document to the Shared Document list, click the Add document link at the bottom of the list, browse to the file you want to upload, and click OK to upload it. As soon as the document is uploaded to the list, the workflow is started, and the breakpoint on the CreateTask activity is hit. Press F5 to continue running the workflow.

When the workflow completes, a new column with the name "My First Workflow" is added to the Shared Documents list as shown in Figure 8-10. This column shows the current status of the workflow. If everything finishes as expected, the value in the column should be "Completed." If workflow is still running, the value in the column should read "In Progress," and if something went wrong, "Error Occurred" will be displayed.

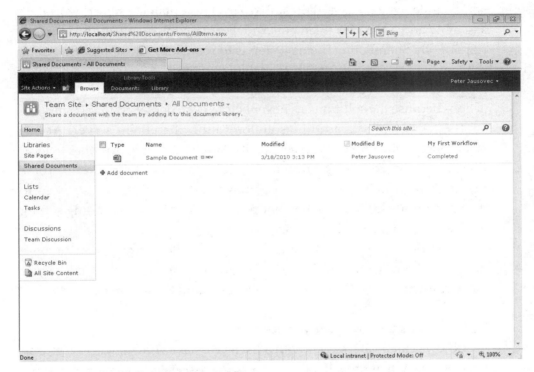

Figure 8-10: Successfully completed workflow

To verify if workflow created the task correctly, click the Tasks link in the left navigation area and you should see a task with the title "Task created from workflow" as set by Listing 8-1.

How Does Workflow Deployment Work?

As you started debugging this project you probably noticed there was a lot going on before the web browser was displayed, especially if the Output window happened to be open. Workflow deployment and debugging consists of several steps.

From the project standpoint, a SharePoint 2010 workflow project is not that different from a regular class library that gets compiled to a .NET assembly file. But, there are other steps that need to happen after the compilation in order to successfully deploy and start the workflow.

After the project is built, packaging kicks in and creates a SharePoint solution file, which has a .WSP suffix. This file contains a signed workflow assembly and XML files (Elements.xml, Feature.xml, manifest.xml) that are required by SharePoint. The next step is to recycle the IIS application pool, then retract any previous versions of this solution. The first time you deploy a solution, the recycle and retract steps don't actually perform the normal actions because the solution has never before been deployed to this site.

The next step is to add the solution to the SharePoint server. At this stage, SharePoint copies the package file and extracts the XML files to locations on the server and/or into the content database. In the last step the feature is activated on the SharePoint site and workflow is associated to the appropriate list. Association happens only if the corresponding setting was selected in the workflow wizard.

Steps for deploying other SharePoint project items are similar to those described here. To get even more detailed information about packaging and deployment, see Chapter 11, "Packaging and Deployment."

List, Site, and Content Type Associations

Workflows can be associated with a list as we have shown, with a site, and also with a content type. If a workflow is not associated as a part of deployment, you need to associate it manually once the workflow is deployed to the SharePoint server. Remember that an unassociated workflow is basically a useless workflow, because you cannot run it. It is similar with site-level association—a workflow must be associated with a site before it can be run on that site, either manually or by using the SharePoint object model.

Associating workflows with content types means that for each list or site to which the content type is added the list or site will inherit the workflows associated with that content type. For example, suppose you have multiple document libraries which are storing expense reports. Further, suppose that each of the document libraries are using the same expense report content type. Instead of manually associating an expense approval workflow with each of those libraries you could associate the expense approval workflow with the expense report content type.

Workflow association information is stored in the Elements.xml file for the workflow project item. More precisely, the value in the Association-Categories element determines if a workflow can be associated to a list, site, or content type. The line below shows a portion of the Elements.xml file that indicates that a workflow can be associated with a list:

```
<AssociationCategories>List</AssociationCategories>
```

When a workflow can be associated with a site, the AssociationCategories element looks like this:

```
<AssociationCategories>Site</AssociationCategories>
```

If you remember from the earlier example, there are only two options in the workflow wizard: list or site workflow. So how do you associate workflow with a content type? In order to associate workflow with a content type you have to change the AssociationCategories element value in the workflow's Elements.xml file to ContentType. In Chapter 7, "SharePoint Content Types," you learned about what content types are and how to create them. In that chapter we created a TripReport content type. As we mentioned we could have multiple SharePoint lists in which to store trip reports and if we wanted to use the same workflow on all those lists we could associate the workflow to a content type used by all the lists (instead of associating the workflow with a specific list). Here's how you can associate workflows to content types.

1. Double click the Elements.xml file for the workflow to open it.

2. Locate the AssociationCategories element and change its value to ContentType as shown below:

```
<AssociationCategories>ContentType</AssociationCategories>
```

3. Click on the Workflow1 project item folder and open the Properties window.

4. Change the value of the Auto Associate property from True to False. We do this because we want to associate the workflow with a content type ourselves, we don't want to do it automatically on F5.

5. Press F5 to build, package, and deploy the project.

6. In the browser, click Site Actions in the upper left corner and choose the Site Settings item from the menu.

7. Click the Site Content Types link under the Galleries section.

8. Under Document Content Types, click the Document content type. The Document content type page will be displayed as shown in Figure 8-11.

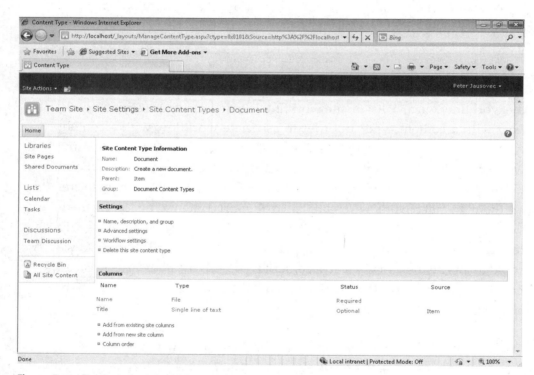

Figure 8-11: Document content type page

9. Click the Workflow settings link. The Workflow settings page is displayed; here you can add a workflow to a content type.

10. Click the Add a Workflow link.

The Add a Workflow page is displayed as shown in Figure 8-12. This page contains all the settings required to associate the workflow.

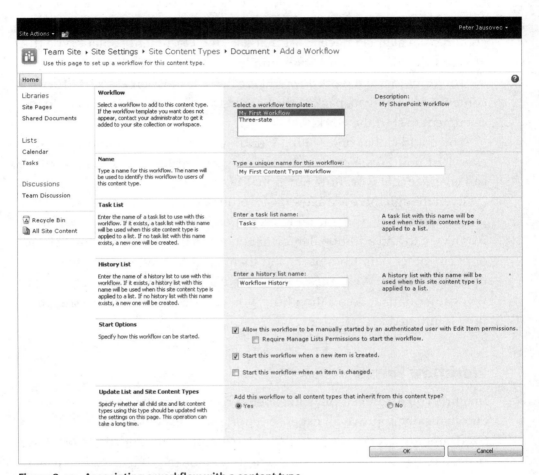

Figure 8-12: Associating a workflow with a content type

11. Select My First Workflow from the list of workflow templates.

12. Type "My First Content Type Workflow" in the unique workflow name textbox.

13. Under Start Options, check the Start this workflow when a new item is created checkbox.

14. Click OK to associate the workflow with the content type.

The settings displayed in Figure 8-12 are essentially the same settings you supply through the workflow wizard. But since we didn't automatically associate the workflow during deployment we need to set these using the SharePoint web UI when we associate the workflow to the content type. Now that the workflow is associated to the Document content type it should be available in every list that uses the Document content type (the Shared Documents library, for example).

To verify that the workflow still creates a task when associated with a content type, navigate back to the Shared Documents library and upload a document to start the workflow.

You could call a content type workflow a multi-list workflow; because every list that uses a content type that has a workflow associated with it can leverage that workflow functionality.

Even though there are a few basic settings you can set when a workflow is associated, such as name and description, it would be really nice if there was a way to add additional information when the workflow is associated, or even gather data from users and then use it to configure the workflow upon association. Well, guess what—there's a way to do that! Not only can you gather data at association time, you can also do it right before workflow is initiated.

Workflow Forms

Imagine you are developing an expense report workflow and you want to automatically approve all expense reports with expenses that are below a fixed amount—let's say $100. Why hard code $100 into the workflow? Instead of hard-coding this value, wouldn't it be nice if there was a way to establish it as part of the association of the workflow and then use it throughout? This would also allow you to associate the workflow with a different list—maybe a list of expense reports for senior executives—and set the minimum approval value to a higher amount for expense reports submitted to that list.

An association form is a regular ASPX form that gets deployed together with your workflow and is displayed to the person who is responsible for associating the workflow. Note that end users usually won't be the ones who associate workflows; this is typically done by a site owner or administrator.

In addition to association forms that allow for input when the workflow is associated with a list, site, or content type, SharePoint workflows also support an initiation form that allows the workflow to gather input each time the workflow is started. Initiation forms are only displayed when a workflow is started manually by a user, not when a workflow is automatically started when an item is added or updated in a list.

A workflow can only have one association form and one initiation form. These workflow forms are linked to the workflow using the Elements.xml file's AssociationUrl and InstantiationUrl attributes. Those two attributes point to the ASPX form that is to be displayed on workflow association and instantiation. To demonstrate how to use association forms, let's modify the sample workflow we created at the beginning of this chapter.

Currently, the sample workflow is associated with a list and once a document is uploaded it immediately creates a task. What we want to do is to create a task for approval only if an expense is greater than a value specified at workflow initiation time (like $100) and write a message to the history list if an expense report doesn't require approval. We are going to start by adding an association form to the project. Open the workflow project you created at the beginning of this chapter and follow these steps.

1. Right click the Workflow1 project item folder, remember that it does not have a normal folder icon but an icon that represents the workflow, and select Add > New Item….

   The Add New Item dialog opens.

2. Select the Workflow Association Form from the list of templates and click Add.

   An ASPX association form is added to the project and opened in the designer. A nice thing the project system does for us is it automatically updates the Elements.xml file to set the AssociationUrl for us. Since visual designer support is not available in Visual Studio for workflow association forms, we will have to work using the source view.

3. Drag and drop a Label and TextBox control from the Toolbox inside the `<asp:Content ID="Main"...` tag. This generates the code shown in Listing 8-2.

Listing 8-2: ASPX Page Markup

```
<asp:Label ID="Label1" runat="server"
  Text="Auto Approval Amount:">
</asp:Label>
<asp:TextBox ID="TextBox1" runat="server"></asp:TextBox>
```

4. Change the ID attribute in the TextBox element to "txtAutoApproval-Amount."

5. Right click on WorkflowAssociationForm1.aspx in Solution Explorer and select View Code.

   The code file contains methods that are needed to associate the workflow. Most of the methods do not typically need to be modified. There is one method that is called just before the workflow is associated called GetAssociationData, which returns a string. Whatever data needs to be passed into the workflow should be returned from this method. Because the return type is a string, if more than one value needs to be returned, typically an XML document is built up and returned as a string. Once in the workflow we can use the AssociationData property of the WorkflowProperties object to access the value returned from the GetAssociationData method.

6. Locate the GetAssociationData method and add the following code:

   ```
   return txtAutoApprovalAmount.Text;
   ```

We now have the mechanism for setting the auto approval amount in place. But how are we going to find out what the actual expense was? Parsing the document is complicated and a lot of work, and we really don't have enough time to do it—we just want to get the workflow running. This is where we will use the initiation form that we mentioned earlier. As we said, this form is displayed to the user just before workflow is started, assuming the workflow was started manually. Let's continue where we left off and add an initiation form to the project.

1. Right click on the Workflow1 folder and select Add > New Item….

2. Select the Workflow Initiation Form from the list of templates and click Add.

   An ASPX initiation form is added to the project and the Elements.xml file is updated to set InstantiationUrl properly.

3. Drag and drop a Label and TextBox control from the Toolbox inside the <asp:Content ID="Main"... tag as shown in Listing 8-3.

Listing 8-3: ASPX Page Markup

```
<asp:Label ID="Label1" runat="server"
  Text="Total Amount:">
</asp:Label>
<asp:TextBox ID="TextBox1" runat="server"></asp:TextBox>
```

4. Change the ID attribute in the TextBox element to "txtTotalAmount."

5. Right click on WorkflowInitiationForm1.aspx in Solution Explorer and select View Code.

   The initiation form code contains methods that are required to start the workflow. Just as with association forms, there is a similar method called GetInitiationData, which returns a string and can be accessed from the WorkflowProperties object from within the workflow.

6. Locate the GetInitiationData method and add the following code to return the expense report amount the user types in the initiation form:

   ```
   return txtTotalAmount.Text;
   ```

Now that we have both association and initiation forms in the project we need to modify the workflow to use the data provided by these forms. We are going to use IfElse activity to determine if the total expense amount gathered by the initiation form is greater than the auto approval amount gathered by the association form, and create either a task or log a message to history list.

1. Double click the Workflow1 project item folder to open the workflow designer.

2. Drag and drop an IfElse activity onto the designer and place it before the createTask1 activity.

The IfElse activity is under the Windows Workflow v3.0 tab in the Toolbox.

3. Click on ifElseBranchActivity1 to select it and open the Properties window.

4. Change the Condition property to Declarative Rule Condition and expand it.

5. Click the (…) button next to ConditionName property.

   The Rule Condition Editor opens.

6. Click New….

7. In the Condition textbox, type the following condition:

```
Convert.ToInt32(workflowProperties.InitiationData) >
    Convert.ToInt32(workflowProperties.AssociationData)
```

We are getting the data from the initiation and association forms, converting it to integer values and then comparing them. The Rule Condition Editor with the code should look like the one in Figure 8-13.

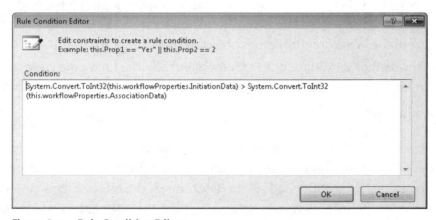

Figure 8-13: Rule Condition Editor

8. Click OK to close the Rule Condition Editor.

9. You can click the Rename… button in the Select Condition dialog to rename the condition to "IsApprovalRequired."

10. Click OK to close the dialog.

At this point you will notice that the red exclamation mark next to the IfElse activity is gone.

We have the condition in place and we have the CreateTask activity already on the designer. Drag and drop the createTask1 activity to ifElse-BranchActivity1. Then double click the activity to open the code view and change the Title property as follows:

```
taskProperties.Title = "Please approve this expense: " +
    workflowProperties.InitiationData;
```

This way the person the task is assigned to will know what he needs to do. One branch of the IfElse is handled, now it is time to handle the second.

1. Drag and drop a LogToHistoryListActivity to ifElseBranchActivity2.
2. Bind the HistoryDescription property to a new field or property named "historyDescription."
3. Bind the HistoryOutcome property to a new field or property named "historyOutcome."
4. Type "LogEvent" in MethodInvoking property and press ENTER to generate the method.
5. Code that should go in the LogEvent method is shown in Listing 8-4.

Listing 8-4: LogEvent Method Implementation

```
historyDescription = "Expense approval workflow";
historyOutcome = "Auto Approved: " + workflowProperties.InitiationData;
```

It's time to put the workflow to the test; press F5 to start debugging. Because we want to set the auto approval amount using the association form, we have to manually associate the workflow. Follow these steps to associate the workflow.

1. Navigate to a list with which you want to associate the workflow.

   If you followed the steps above you should have Shared Documents library open in the web browser.
2. Click the Library tab on the ribbon.

3. Click the Add a Workflow button.

4. Select the workflow template My First Workflow from the list of templates.

5. Name the workflow "My Expense Workflow."

6. Click OK.

   After you click OK, the association form we created should be displayed and it should look like the one in Figure 8-14.

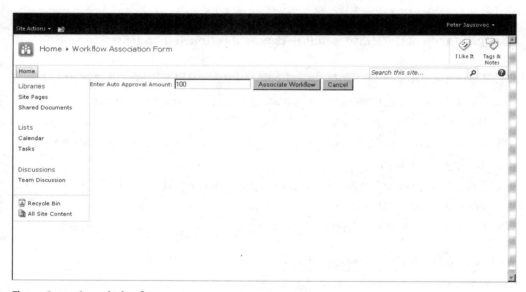

Figure 8-14: Association form

7. Enter an auto approval amount (100 for our example) then click the Associate Workflow button in the association form to finish the association.

8. Navigate back to the Shared Documents list.

9. Hover the mouse over an item in the Shared Documents list and click the drop-down button to reveal the context menu (see Figure 8-15).

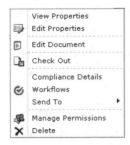

Figure 8-15: Context menu on documents in the SharePoint list

10. Click the Workflows menu item.

11. On the Start a New Workflow page, click the "My Expense Workflow" link to start the workflow.

    Before the workflow is started, the initiation form is displayed. It will look like the one in Figure 8-16.

12. Type "1000" into the textbox and click Start Workflow.

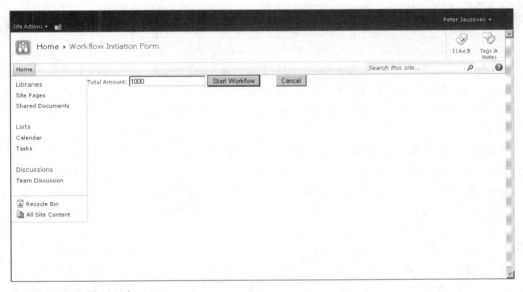

Figure 8-16: Initiation form

Since the total amount we entered (1,000) is greater than the auto approval amount (100) the first branch in the IfElse activity should be executed and a task should be created. Navigate to the Tasks list and verify that a task with the title "Please approve this expense: 1000" has been created.

To verify the second branch of the IfElse activity, navigate back to the Shared Documents list to start the workflow again—this time enter an amount that is less than 100. Once the workflow is completed click on the Completed link that is displayed under the "My Expense Workflow" column in the same row as the document on which you started the workflow. The workflow status page is opened. Under the Workflow History notice an entry that says that expense was auto approved. See Figure 8-17.

Workflow History

◘ View workflow reports
The following events have occurred in this workflow.

	Date Occurred	Event Type	User ID	Description	Outcome
	1/19/2010 2:40 PM	Comment	System Account	Expense approval workflow	Auto Approved: 50

Figure 8-17: Entry in Workflow History list

In addition to workflow association and initiation forms, SharePoint workflow also supports task and modification forms.

Task forms, as the name suggests, have something to do with tasks. You've probably seen a SharePoint task form before; it's a form that is displayed when you're editing a task in the SharePoint tasks list as shown in Figure 8-18.

You may want to customize the task form for example to track how much time a user spent working on a task that was assigned to him. To do this you can use a workflow task form and add a custom field that tracks that information. An example of a customized workflow task form is shown in Figure 8-19.

Unfortunately, Visual Studio 2010 only supports the creation of association and initiation forms. There are no project item templates in Visual Studio 2010 allowing you to create modification or task forms. You could use

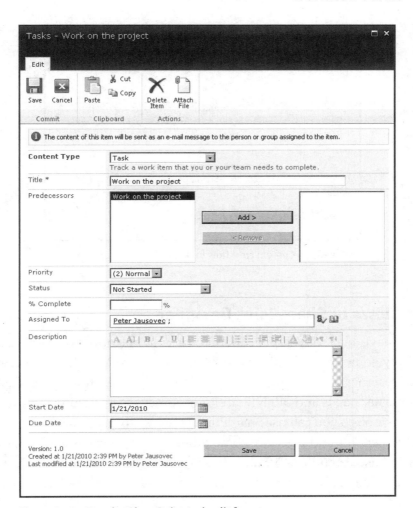

Figure 8-18: Regular SharePoint task edit form

an application page project item to create a workflow task form or modification form, but the process isn't straightforward and it involves a lot of steps. If you don't want to go down that path you can use SharePoint Designer 2010 to create task and modification forms and then import the SharePoint Designer .WSP file to Visual Studio. In the next section we will describe how to use SharePoint Designer 2010 to create workflows and how to import those workflows into Visual Studio.

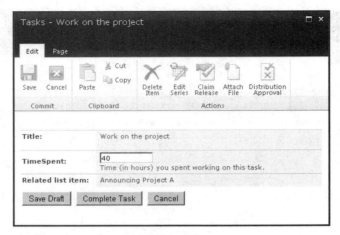

Figure 8-19: Custom workflow task form

Workflows in SharePoint Designer

If you have ever developed SharePoint customizations before you are probably somewhat familiar with Microsoft SharePoint Designer. Share-Point Designer offers a large number of features, everything from customizing master pages and other SharePoint content to designing workflows.

Even though you can use SharePoint Designer to develop workflows you should keep in mind there are some differences between workflows developed in Visual Studio 2010 and those developed in SharePoint Designer. You can find some of the most important differences in the following list.

- Only declarative workflows are supported in SharePoint Designer whereas Visual Studio workflows can have .NET code and are compiled.
- Workflow debugging is not available in SharePoint Designer whereas Visual Studio supports debugging on both the designer surface and in the code-behind.
- Only sequential workflows can be created in SharePoint Designer. If you need to develop state machine workflows you must use Visual Studio 2010.

We are going to develop the same workflow as in the previous section, but this time we will use SharePoint Designer. We will have to re-design the workflow because some features are not available in SharePoint Designer when only SharePoint Foundation is installed (e.g., association forms). Association form support is available in SharePoint Designer if you're creating workflows for SharePoint Server. With SharePoint Designer you can create list or site workflows and reusable workflows. As a part of our re-design we will create a reusable workflow. This will allow us to export the reusable workflow to a .WSP file and then import it into Visual Studio 2010.

1. Open SharePoint Designer 2010.
2. Click Sites and select Open Site.

   The first time you start the application you need to open the SharePoint site you want to customize. The sites you open will be remembered so you can easily open them the next time you use SharePoint Designer.

3. Type "http://localhost/" and click Open to open the default SharePoint site on your local machine.
4. Click Workflows in the Navigation area on the left.

   All globally reusable workflows are displayed in the main area of the window, as shown in Figure 8-20.

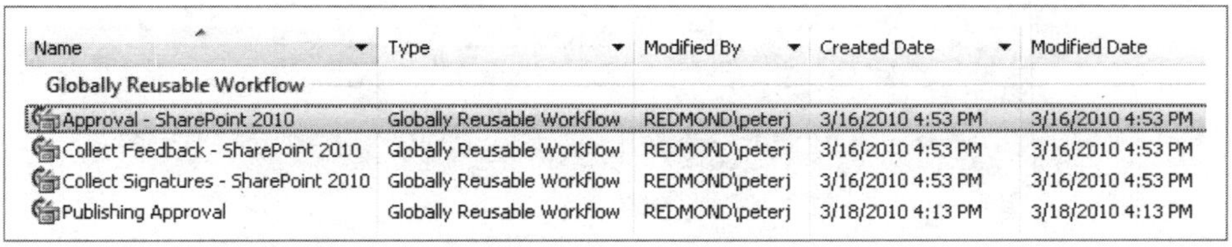

Name ▲	Type	Modified By	Created Date	Modified Date
Globally Reusable Workflow				
Approval - SharePoint 2010	Globally Reusable Workflow	REDMOND\peterj	3/16/2010 4:53 PM	3/16/2010 4:53 PM
Collect Feedback - SharePoint 2010	Globally Reusable Workflow	REDMOND\peterj	3/16/2010 4:53 PM	3/16/2010 4:53 PM
Collect Signatures - SharePoint 2010	Globally Reusable Workflow	REDMOND\peterj	3/16/2010 4:53 PM	3/16/2010 4:53 PM
Publishing Approval	Globally Reusable Workflow	REDMOND\peterj	3/18/2010 4:13 PM	3/18/2010 4:13 PM

Figure 8-20: Globally reusable workflows on SharePoint site

5. Click the Reusable Workflow button on the ribbon.

   The dialog for creating a new reusable workflow is displayed, as shown in Figure 8-21.

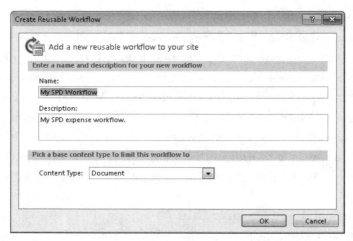

Figure 8-21: Creating Reusable Workflows

6. Enter "My SPD Workflow" in the Name textbox and select Document in the Content Type combo box and then click OK.

   Setting the content type to Document will limit this workflow to be associated only to lists that have Document as a base content type. When you click OK, SharePoint Designer will connect to SharePoint and retrieve some necessary data for workflow creation. Once completed, the newly created workflow is opened as shown in Figure 8-22.

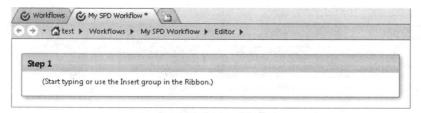

Figure 8-22: Workflow designer in SharePoint Designer

7. Click the Local Variables button in the ribbon.

   Since we cannot design an association form in SharePoint Designer on a machine with only SharePoint Foundation installed we are hard-coding the auto approval amount in a local variable.

8. Click Add… on the Local Variables dialog.

9. Type "AutoApprovalAmount" in the Name textbox, and choose Number in the Type combo box as shown in Figure 8-23.

Figure 8-23: Adding local
variable to workflow

10. Click OK to close the Edit Variable dialog.

11. Click OK to close the Local Variables dialog.

12. Click the Initiation Form Parameters button in the ribbon.

Now, we will create a new parameter for the initiation form. This parameter will represent the total expense amount. We did something similar in Visual Studio 2010 when we designed the initiation form.

13. Click Add… in the Association and Initiation Form Parameters dialog.

14. Type "Total Amount" in the Field name textbox and change the Information Type to Number as shown in Figure 8-24.

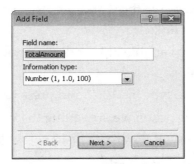

Figure 8-24: Adding a field

15. Click Next.

    This dialog allows you to set the default value.

16. Click Finish to close the Add Field dialog.

    The field is added to the list and it will show up on the initiation form as shown in Figure 8-25.

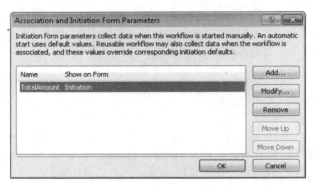

Figure 8-25: Parameter TotalAmount will be displayed on the initiation form

17. Click OK to close the Association and Initiation Form Parameters.

    Now, we are ready to start adding activities to our workflow. In Step 1 we need to set the AutoApprovalAmount value.

18. Select Step 1 on the workflow designer and click the Action drop-down in the ribbon and select "Set Workflow Variable" under Core Actions.

    A new action is added to the workflow. The parameters that are required appear as links.

19. Click the workflow variable link, and select the Variable: Auto-ApprovalAmount.

20. Click the value link, type in "100," and press Enter.

    With this workflow action we are setting the value of the variable AutoApprovalAmount that we defined earlier to 100.

21. Move the selection below Step 1.

22. Click the Step button in the ribbon to create a new step.

23. Select Step 2 on the designer and click the Condition drop-down in the ribbon, and select If any value equals value under Common Conditions.

    The condition is added to the workflow and you can set left and right values and the operation between them by clicking on respective links.

24. Click the left "value" link and then click the function button.

    Clicking the function button opens a new dialog that lets you select the data source and field from which the data will come.

25. Select Workflow Variables and Parameters from the Data source combo box.

26. Select Parameter: TotalAmount from the Field from source combo box.

27. Click OK to close the dialog.

28. Click the equals link and select "is greater than."

29. Click the right value link and then click the function button.

30. Select Workflow Variables and Parameters from the first combo box and then select Variable: AutoApprovalAmount from the second combo box.

31. Click OK to close the dialog.

By now, the workflow should look like Figure 8-26.

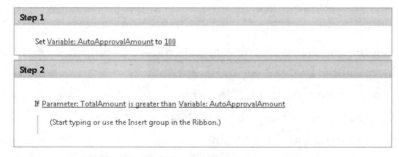

Figure 8-26: SharePoint Designer workflow with two steps

In step 1 we are setting the AutoApprovalAmount value to 100. In step 2 we have an If action that checks to see if the TotalAmount is greater than the AutoApprovalAmount. We need to create a task for when this condition evaluates to True. We also need to add an Else statement that runs when the TotalAmount is less than the AutoApprovalAmount. Finally we must log a message to the workflow history list. Let's continue and add an action that creates a task.

1. Move the selection below the If action in step 2 and click the Step button in the ribbon.

2. Click the Action button in the ribbon, and select Assign a To-do Item under Task Actions.

3. Click the "a to-do item" link to open the Custom Task Wizard.

4. Click Next on the first page of the Custom Task Wizard.

5. Type "Please approve this report" for the name of the task.

6. Click Finish to close the dialog.

7. Click the "these users" link to choose the users to whom the task should be assigned.

8. Type the name or e-mail address of the user and click Add to add it to the Selected Users list.

9. Click OK to close the dialog.

10. Click under the If statement and type "Else."

11. Press ENTER to insert the Else statement.

12. Click the Actions button on the ribbon and select "Log to History List" under Core Actions.

13. Click the "this message" link and then the (…) button to open the String Builder dialog.

14. Type the following text in the Name textbox: "Auto Approved:."

15. Click the Add or Change Lookup button.

    We want to include the amount in the message so we have to look up a field that represents that amount, which is TotalAmount.

16. Select Workflow Variables and Parameters from the data source combo box.

17. Select Parameter: TotalAmount from the Field from source combo box.

18. Click OK to close the dialog.

The text in the string builder dialog should look like this:

```
Auto Approved: (%Parameter: TotalAmount%)
```

19. Click OK to close the String Builder dialog.

At this point we have everything we need, and the workflow we have created works similar to the one we created with Visual Studio 2010. The finished workflow inside SharePoint Designer should look like the one in Figure 8-27.

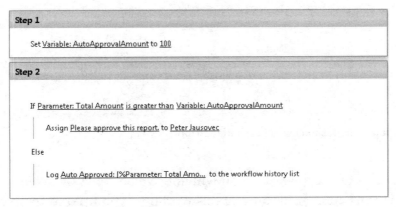

Figure 8-27: Finished workflow

The last thing we need to do is publish the workflow by clicking the Publish button in the ribbon. SharePoint Designer validates the workflow and deploys it to the SharePoint server. Since the workflow is associated with the Document content type, we can use it in any SharePoint list that supports Document content type, such as Shared Documents library.

To verify the behavior, launch your web browser and navigate to the Shared Documents library. You can upload a document or use an existing document from the library to start the workflow. The initiation form is displayed as soon as you start the workflow as shown in Figure 8-28, prompting you to enter the TotalAmount value. Enter a value greater than 100 and click Start.

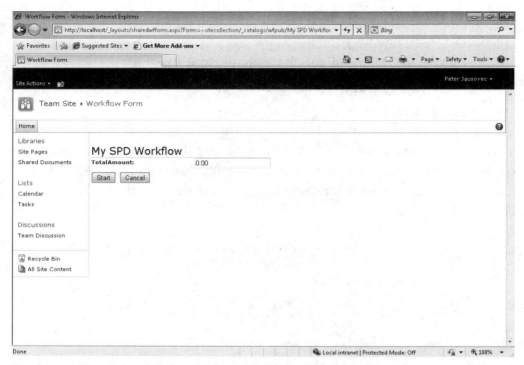

Figure 8-28: SharePoint Designer workflow initiation form

If you open the Tasks list you will notice a new task is created. Before you can start another instance of this workflow you need to complete the task first. To do so, click on the task title and select Edit Task. Now click the Complete Task button to complete the task.

Try running the workflow again and make the amount less than 100 this time. When the workflow completes, click the Completed link and notice a new entry in the workflow history list that says that the expense report was auto approved and lists the total amount as well.

Importing SharePoint Designer Workflow Into Visual Studio 2010

From the wide range of SharePoint templates Visual Studio 2010 offers, there are two import templates. These templates allow you to import a .WSP file that contains a reusable workflow or even a whole SharePoint site into to Visual Studio 2010. If you started developing your SharePoint solution in SharePoint Designer, for example, and you hit a roadblock or a feature you require is only available in Visual Studio 2010, you can import your solution to Visual Studio 2010 and continue your development.

The main reason for importing a .WSP to Visual Studio 2010 is that you want to leverage features available in Visual Studio 2010 to further customize your SharePoint site or your workflows. For example, you spent a substantial amount of time to develop a workflow and workflow task forms in SharePoint Designer and you don't want to throw that work away, yet you need to use Visual Studio 2010 to extend your workflow by adding custom activities and using .NET code. Importing a workflow sounds like a much better solution than spending time re-designing and re-developing workflows you already developed once.

Before we can import the workflow we created in the previous section we need to export it to a .WSP file. This can be done with either SharePoint Designer or through a SharePoint site. Note that from a SharePoint site you can only export the full site and not just workflows. To export workflow only, you need to use SharePoint Designer. If for any reason you can't use SharePoint Designer to export the workflow you can still export the whole site from SharePoint and when importing the .WSP you can choose which SharePoint items you want to bring over to Visual Studio 2010.

Let's try exporting a reusable workflow to a .WSP file from SharePoint Designer.

1. Open SharePoint Designer and select the Workflows item in the Site Objects pane.
2. Select My SPD Workflow from the list of Reusable Workflows as shown in Figure 8-29.
3. Click the Save as Template button.

   SharePoint Designer packages the workflow in a .WSP file and uploads it to the Site Assets library on the SharePoint site.
4. Open the Internet browser and navigate to the Site Assets library.

   You can click the Libraries link to get to the list of all libraries on the current SharePoint site and then navigate to the Site Assets Library shown in Figure 8-30.
5. Click on the exported workflow and save the file.

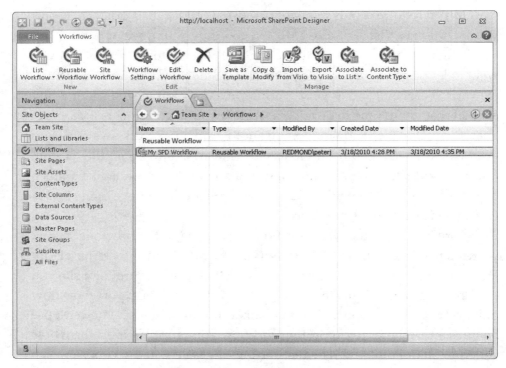

Figure 8-29: Reusable workflows in SharePoint Designer

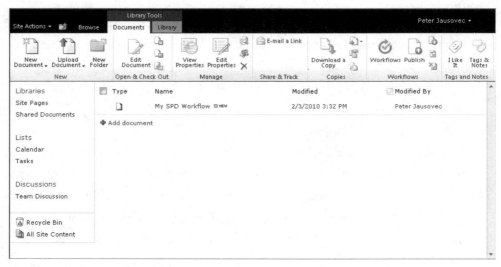

Figure 8-30: The Site Assets Library in SharePoint

If you want to export the complete SharePoint site instead of exporting just workflow, you can follow these steps.

1. Open the web browser and navigate to your SharePoint site.
2. Click Site Actions and select Site Settings.

   The Site Settings page is opened.
3. Click Save site as template under Site Actions heading.

   The Save as Template page appears, as shown in Figure 8-31.
4. Enter the name for the template file in the file name textbox.
5. Enter the template name and description.

   If you want to include contents of all lists and libraries check the Include Content check box.
6. Click OK.

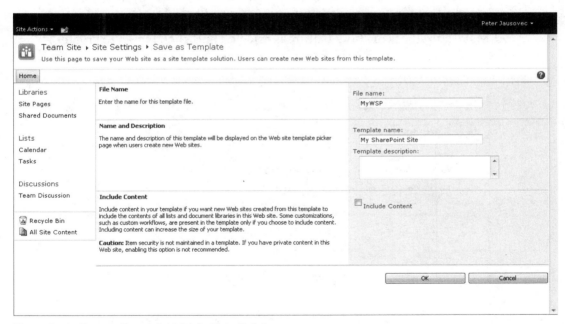

Figure 8-31: Save as Template page in SharePoint

The saved .WSP file will be placed in the Solution Gallery. You can navigate there to download the .WSP file. Now that we have a .WSP file we can move to Visual Studio 2010 and import it.

1. Open Visual Studio 2010.
2. Click File > New Project....

   The New Project dialog opens.
3. Select SharePoint and 2010 from the list of templates.
4. Select Import Reusable Workflow template and click OK.

   First the wizard page is displayed; it's exactly the same as the workflow wizard page.
5. Verify that the local site URL is set to http://localhost and click Next.
6. Browse to the .WSP file we exported before and click Next.

   Visual Studio 2010 parses the .WSP file and displays all the features from that file. There should be only one feature in the file, and the wizard page should look like the one in Figure 8-32.
7. Make sure the workflow feature is selected and click Finish to create the project.

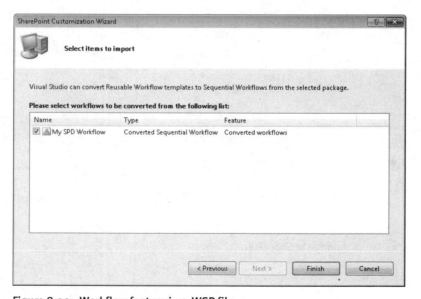

Figure 8-32: Workflow feature in a .WSP file

Visual Studio will convert the reusable workflow from .WSP and create a workflow project. The first time you convert a reusable workflow you may be surprised by what you see in the workflow designer. Open the workflow designer (double click the My_SPD_WorkflowFT folder) and take a look (see Figure 8-33).

We only took two steps and a few actions (set variable, if-else statement, logging to history list), but the converted workflow looks much more complicated than the original one we created in Visual Studio 2010. Even though it looks complicated, it's not that hard to understand what's going on. In common scenarios you probably won't change the activities that are already performing as expected, but you will probably customize them by adding .NET code or additional activities.

We are going to implement some simple archive functionality in our imported workflow. After the expense report is approved we are going to copy it to an archive location. We are going to create a new list called "Expense Report Archive" as the archive location.

We are going to use a CodeActivity to implement this functionality. Since workflows created in SharePoint Designer don't contain any code we will need a way to get access to the document, list, etc. For this purpose we are going to use properties on the ApplyActivation activity that is already part of the workflow and shown in the designer. Unfortunately, we can't access the activities directly (remember, no-code workflows) and we will have to use the collection of all activities to get the correct one by name.

1. Open the workflow designer in Visual Studio 2010.
2. Drag and drop CodeActivity to the Workflow designer and move it to the bottom of the workflow. See Figure 8-34 for reference.
3. Double click codeActivity1 to open the code view.
4. Add the following using statement to the code file:

   ```
   using Microsoft.SharePoint;
   ```

5. Put the code in Listing 8-5 in the codeActivity1_ExecuteCode method. Note that there are two underscores (_) in front of the Work-flowProperties variable.

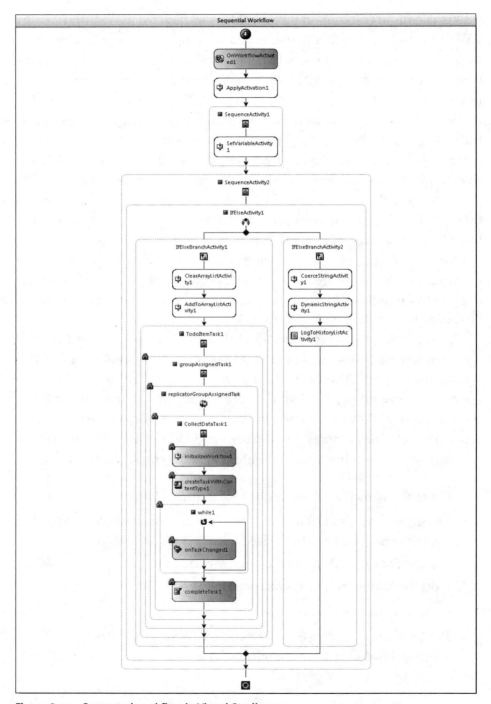

Figure 8-33: Converted workflow in Visual Studio 2010

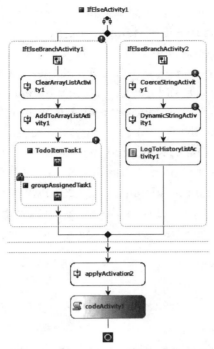

Figure 8-34: CodeActivity in imported workflow

Listing 8-5: ExecuteCode Method Implementation

```
string archiveListTitle = "Expense Report Archive";
ApplyActivation activationActivity =
  (ApplyActivation)base.Activities["ApplyActivation1"];
SPSite site = activationActivity.__WorkflowProperties.Site;
SPWeb web = site.RootWeb;
SPList archiveList = site.RootWeb.Lists.TryGetList(archiveListTitle);

if (archiveList == null)
{
  Guid archiveListGuid = web.Lists.Add(
    archiveListTitle, "Archives", SPListTemplateType.DocumentLibrary);
  archiveList = web.Lists[archiveListGuid];
}

SPList docLibrary = activationActivity.__WorkflowProperties.List;
SPListItem currentItem =
  docLibrary.Items[activationActivity.__WorkflowProperties.ItemId];
currentItem.CopyTo(
  site.Url + @"/" + archiveListTitle + @"/" + currentItem.Name);
```

In the first couple of lines of code we are getting the SharePoint site and web information. Because we don't know if the archive site is already created we are calling the TryGetList method. This method returns the actual list or returns null if the list doesn't exist. In the if statement block we check to see whether the list is there yet, and if it isn't there we create it. To create the list we pass the list title, description, and list template type to the Add method.

Now that the archive list is created we get the source list and the actual item we want to copy. Finally, we just copy the current item to the target list.

You can press F5 at this point to deploy the workflow and then verify that the activity we added in Visual Studio 2010 works together with the functionality created in SharePoint Designer. After the workflow completes, the workflow copies the item on which you started the workflow to the archive list.

Conclusion

In this chapter we sailed through the world of workflows trying to touch upon the most important and interesting things. You learned about the base building blocks of workflow—activities. The tables provided in this chapter with descriptions of available activities can serve as a starting point when trying to decide if you need to develop a custom activity or use an existing one. The examples provided in this chapter are simple yet they contain the elements that every workflow uses.

We also saw how workflow support in SharePoint Designer could be the right tool for you to get started with workflow development. You can import your reusable workflows to Visual Studio 2010, modify them, and try to learn as much as you can from them, and you will be developing SharePoint code workflows in no time.

9

SharePoint Web Parts

Introduction to Web Parts

Web parts are a great way to structure your SharePoint site to make different data or different applications accessible on the same page. Think about a SharePoint intranet site that is used by executives to get sales reports on their different products, headcount information for their different divisions, and the latest financial news. Because executives usually want to have all the important information in one place, web parts are a great solution to have all this data displayed on a single SharePoint web part page. The page could have a web part showing the reports from a reporting server or analysis server, another web part showing divisional headcount information, and a web part for reading a news feed from the *Financial Times*. Since web parts run in the security context of the user of the SharePoint site, the executive would be able to access the data from the reporting server or the other data stores without reentering credentials.

In the past, developing SharePoint web parts hasn't been as easy as developing ASP.NET web parts. The main reason is that there were no visual designers available to develop those types of web parts. The differences in deploying a web part to an ASP.NET site versus deploying a web part to a SharePoint site was also an issue. With the introduction of the visual web part designer in Visual Studio 2010 creating web parts has never been easier.

In this chapter we will learn how to create visual web parts, web parts created with code only, and Silverlight web parts.

Web Part Fundamentals

Before we start building our first web parts we should have a look at the web part infrastructure in SharePoint. If you have already worked with ASP.NET web parts you should consider this section to be a refresher.

Web parts are ASP.NET server side controls that run in the context of a web part page and allow users to edit and modify the controls in the browser. A web part page is an ASP.NET page that has web part zones defined that serve as placeholders for the web parts to be added. Each web part page has a web part manager object that tracks which web parts have been added to each particular zone, and stores and retrieves data about how each web part has been customized and personalized. A SharePoint web part page does not use the ASP.NET WebPartManager and WebPartZones classes directly—instead it uses its own classes called SPWebPartManager and SPWebPartZone, which inherit from the corresponding ASP.NET classes.

SharePoint 2010 supports two types of web parts: ASP.NET 2.0 web parts, which derive from System.Web.UI.WebControls.WebParts.Web-Part, and older style SharePoint web parts, which derive from Microsoft.SharePoint.WebPartPages.WebPart. In this chapter we will use the newer ASP.NET 2.0 web parts, which derive from System.Web.UI.WebControls.WebParts.WebPart.

When Should I Create the "Older Style" SharePoint Web Parts?

Generally you should always create ASP.NET web parts. That's the reason why all web parts in Visual Studio 2010 derive from ASP.NET web parts by default. However, you may need to build the older style SharePoint web parts when you want to create cross-page web part connections or connections between web parts that are outside of web part zones. Also, you would use the older style SharePoint web parts if you want to take advantage of the SharePoint data-caching infrastructure that allows caching to the content database.

Creating a Visual Web Part

We will start our exploration of web parts by creating a visual web part. It's called a visual web part because we use the visual web designer that edits ASP.NET pages in Visual Studio to design the web part. In Visual Studio 2010 you can also develop a different type of web parts, which are developed with code only and simply called web parts or "code-only web parts" to distinguish them from visual web parts. We will look at developing code-only web parts later in this chapter.

Launch Visual Studio 2010 to get started with our first visual web part. Once Visual Studio opens, select File > New > Project. In the New Project dialog that appears, navigate to the SharePoint templates folder and chose 2010. Select Visual Web Part and name the project "CreateTaskWebPart." Figure 9-1 shows the New Project dialog.

Click the OK button to get to the SharePoint Customization Wizard. In the SharePoint Customization Wizard leave the entry for the debugging site set to the default site. Figure 9-2 shows the SharePoint Customization Wizard. As you can see, the Deploy as sandboxed solution radio button is disabled. This is because visual web parts can only be deployed as farm solutions.

Figure 9-1: The New Project dialog for creating a visual web part

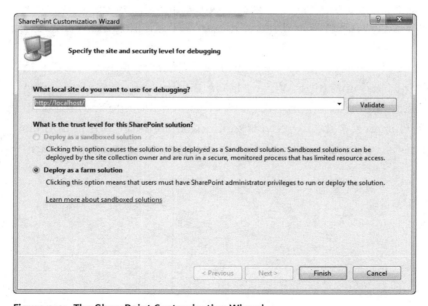

Figure 9-2: The SharePoint Customization Wizard

Why Can Visual Web Parts Only Be Deployed as Farm Solutions?

The reason is that the visual web part project uses an ASP.NET user control, which must be deployed to the "~/_CONTROLTEMPLATES" folder in the SharePoint hive. In order to access this folder, the web part needs to have farm permissions. Later we will see how to create a code-only web part that can be deployed as a sandboxed solution.

After you have clicked the Finish button in the SharePoint Customization Wizard, Visual Studio creates the project and opens the source view of the visual web designer. Figure 9-3 shows Visual Studio after the project has been created.

Before we start implementing the visual web part we should take a look at what files Visual Studio has created for us. Click on the VisualWebPart1 project item folder in the Solution Explorer to show the files under the folder. Figure 9-4 shows the expanded VisualWebPart1 project item folder.

The first file we see under the VisualWebPart1 folder is the Elements .xml file. This file contains the information for the module associated with the web part. The module contains deployment instructions and the files needed to deploy the visual web part. (See Chapter 11, "Packaging and Deployment" for more information on modules.)

The second file is called VisualWebPart1.cs, which contains the actual code for the web part.

The third file is called VisualWebPart1.webpart, and it's an XML file required by SharePoint that contains properties that describe the web part, such as the title, description, and error message if the web part import fails. The .webpart file also makes the web part discoverable in the web part gallery.

The fourth file is called VisualWebPart1UserControl.ascx. As its name indicates, this is the actual ASP.NET user control that is hosted by the code in VisualWebPart1.cs, and this is the file that you can actually edit in the visual web designer.

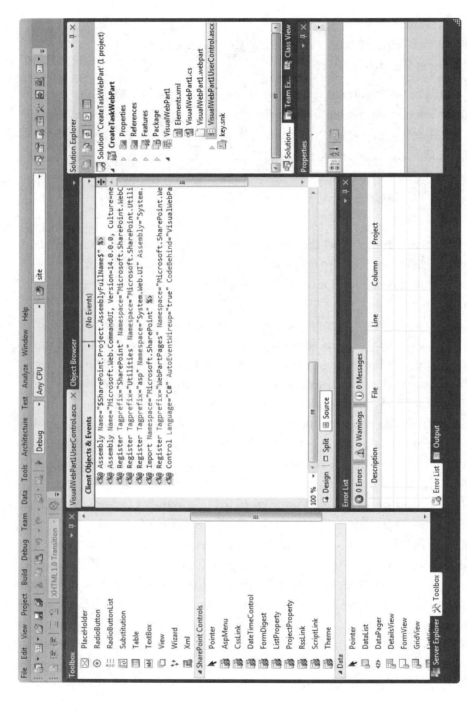

Figure 9-3: CreateTaskWebPart project created in Visual Studio

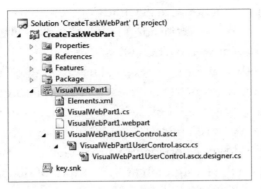

Figure 9-4: Web part files in Solution Explorer

Let's have a closer look at how these files all fit together. Double-click the VisualWebPart1.cs file in the Solution Explorer to bring up a code view. Listing 9-1 shows the code for VisualWebPart1.cs.

Listing 9-1: Code for VisualWebPart1.cs

```
[ToolboxItemAttribute(false)]
public class VisualWebPart1 : WebPart
{
  // Visual Studio might automatically update this path when
  // you change the Visual Web Part project item.
  private const string _ascxPath =
    @"~/_CONTROLTEMPLATES/CreateTaskWebPart/VisualWebPart1" +
    @"/VisualWebPart1UserControl.ascx";

  protected override void CreateChildControls()
  {
    Control control = Page.LoadControl(_ascxPath);
    Controls.Add(control);
  }
}
```

As you can see there is a private constant defined in Listing 9-1 called _ascxPath. It has a string value assigned that points to the path where the VisualWebPart1UserControl.ascx file will be installed when the solution is installed in the SharePoint hive. You should not change this value because Visual Studio will take care of it automatically if you rename the user control file.

Now look at the function CreateChildControls. This function adds the user control to the Controls collection in the web part class. Visual Studio is creating a SharePoint web part that hosts an ASP.NET user control.

That's enough theory for now. Let's start creating our first visual web part, which will allow users to add tasks to a SharePoint task list. We will start with implementing the UI of the web part. In Solution Explorer double click on the file VisualWebPart1UserControl.ascx to bring up the visual web designer. The designer opens in source view. We need to switch to design view. Locate the Design tab at the bottom of the source view window and click on it. Figure 9-5 shows the Design tab.

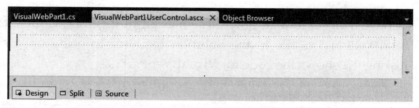

Figure 9-5: The Design tab of the visual web designer

We are now presented with a visual design surface where we can start creating the UI. First we should give our web part some heading text. With the cursor at the top of the visual designer, type "Create Tasks." We can now change the text properties of the heading text we typed, such as font size and color, by using the formatting toolbar shown in Figure 9-6.

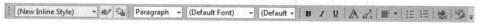

Figure 9-6: The formatting toolbar of the visual web designer

We want to make our heading text bigger and give it a different color. Highlight the text you typed and select "x-large (24pt)" as the font size by using the font size drop-down shown in Figure 9-7.

Now we want to change the color. Click on the icon in the formatting toolbar. This opens the More Colors dialog. Figure 9-8 shows the More Colors dialog.

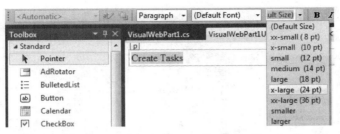

Figure 9-7: The font size drop-down in the formatting toolbar of the visual web designer

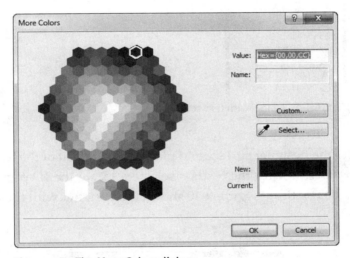

Figure 9-8: The More Colors dialog

In the dialog enter "Hex={00,00,CC}" as the value and click the OK button. This will set the color of our heading text to blue. Of course we can use any other color provided by the dialog or even define a custom color.

Next we need to add a couple of controls to the visual web part. Locate the label control in the Toolbox and drag it onto the designer underneath the heading text. In the Properties window change its Text property to "Title" followed by a colon. Figure 9-9 shows the label in the designer.

Now we need to add a textbox control to allow users to enter the actual title of the task. Go to the Toolbox and locate the textbox control. Drag the

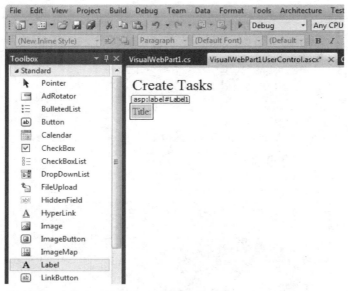

Figure 9-9: A label with text set to Title

control onto the designer surface and place it to the right of the label. In the Properties window with the textbox selected, locate the ID property and enter "uxTitleTextBox." Figure 9-10 shows the designer with the new controls added.

Figure 9-10: Designer with a textbox control for inputting a task title

The next user input we want to capture is the due date of the task. Drag another label on the designer and change its Text property to "Due date:". Add a calendar control for the user to select a due date for the task. In the Toolbox locate the calendar control and drag it next to the label with the title "Due date." Change the ID of the calendar control to uxDueDate using the Properties window.

Finally we need to add a button control that users can click to create the task. Drag a new button control from the Toolbox onto the designer and place it under the calendar control. Change the Text property of the button to Create Task and its ID property to uxCreateTask. The designer should now look like Figure 9-11.

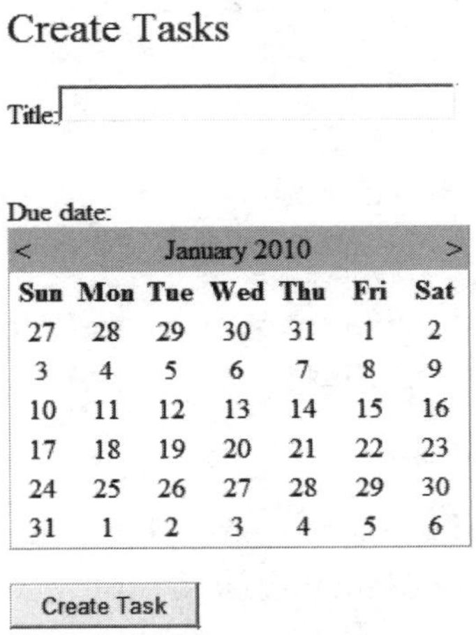

Create Tasks

Title:

Due date:

<		January 2010				>
Sun	Mon	Tue	Wed	Thu	Fri	Sat
27	28	29	30	31	1	2
3	4	5	6	7	8	9
10	11	12	13	14	15	16
17	18	19	20	21	22	23
24	25	26	27	28	29	30
31	1	2	3	4	5	6

Create Task

Figure 9-11: The final web part UI in the designer

So far the experience of creating a visual web part hasn't been much different from creating an ASP.NET user control. Now that we have created the UI for the web part we need to write some code. Double click the Create Task button to create an event handler for it. Visual Studio displays the code view for VisualWebPart1UserControl.ascx as shown in Figure 9-12.

Don't get confused by Source View and Code View. Source View is a view in the designer that shows the markup of the user control Visual-WebPart1UserControl.ascx. Code view is the code-behind view of the code file associated with the ASP.NET user control called VisualWebPart1User-Control.ascx.cs.

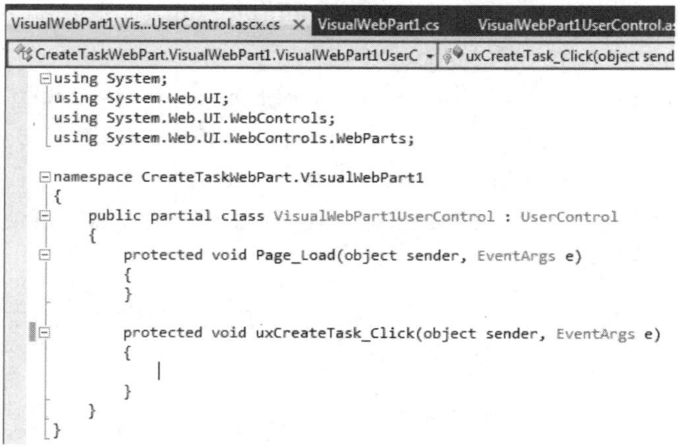

```
VisualWebPart1\Vis...UserControl.ascx.cs  ×   VisualWebPart1.cs        VisualWebPart1UserControl.as
CreateTaskWebPart.VisualWebPart1.VisualWebPart1UserC  ▼   uxCreateTask_Click(object send
    using System;
    using System.Web.UI;
    using System.Web.UI.WebControls;
    using System.Web.UI.WebControls.WebParts;

    namespace CreateTaskWebPart.VisualWebPart1
    {
        public partial class VisualWebPart1UserControl : UserControl
        {
            protected void Page_Load(object sender, EventArgs e)
            {
            }

            protected void uxCreateTask_Click(object sender, EventArgs e)
            {
                |
            }
        }
    }
```

Figure 9-12: Code view for the web part UI in the designer

Let's add some code to create a new SharePoint task. First we need to add the following using directive to the code file:

```
using Microsoft.SharePoint;
```

We don't need to add a reference to Microsoft.SharePoint because the visual web part project template in Visual Studio already has a reference to the Microsoft.SharePoint assembly. The Microsoft.SharePoint assembly contains the SharePoint server side object model, which we will use to add a SharePoint task. (See Chapter 3, "Introduction to the SharePoint Object Model," for more information on SharePoint object models.)

With the using statement added to our code file, we can go ahead and implement the code for the event handler uxCreateTask_Click. We want the event handler to create a new task in the task list. Listing 9-2 shows code that creates a new task.

Listing 9-2: Code for Creating a Task in the CreateTaskWebPart's uxCreateTask_Click event handler

```
protected void uxCreateTask_Click(object sender, EventArgs e)
{
  SPSite site = SPContext.Current.Site;
  using (SPWeb web = site.OpenWeb())
  {
    SPList tasks = web.Lists["Tasks"];
    SPListItem myTask = tasks.Items.Add();
```

```
    myTask["Title"] = uxTitleText.Text;
    myTask["DueDate"] = uxDueDate.SelectedDate;
    myTask.Update();
  }
}
```

Before we can create a task we need to get the Task list. In the first line of the code in Listing 9-2, we create an SPSite object from the current context. This gives us access to the site collection of the site where our web part is hosted. Once we obtain the site object we need to get the web object, which represents the SharePoint site where the task list resides. Because the SPSite is returned by the SPContext we don't need to dispose of it (an SPSite object returned by an SPContext object is managed by the Share-Point framework and should not be explicitly disposed in your code). The SPWeb object however must be instantiated in a using directive because it implements the IDisposable interface and must be cleaned up properly.

With the SPWeb object created we can access the task list and update its properties. (See Chapter 4, "SharePoint Lists," for more information on working with lists)

Before we test our web part we should change its title. Remember that the .webpart file contains the Title property for web parts. Double click the .webpart file in the solution explorer and edit the XML to change the Title property to "CreateTaskWebPart" and the Description property to "This web part creates new tasks in the task list." The XML should now look like Listing 9-3.

Listing 9-3: .webpart File for CreateTaskWebPart

```xml
<webParts>
  <webPart xmlns="http://schemas.microsoft.com/WebPart/v3">
    <metaData>
      <type name="CreateTaskWebPart.VisualWebPart1.VisualWebPart1,
        $SharePoint.Project.AssemblyFullName$" />
      <importErrorMessage>
      $Resources:core,ImportErrorMessage;
      </importErrorMessage>
    </metaData>
  <data>
    <properties>
      <property name="Title" type="string">CreateTaskWebPart</property>
      <property name="Description" type="string">
```

```
        This web part creates new tasks in the task list</property>
      </properties>
    </data>
  </webPart>
</webParts>
```

Shouldn't the Visual Web Part Title Get Updated When I Rename the VisualWebPart1 Project Item Folder?

Renaming and refactoring are two weaknesses in Visual Web Part projects. You can rename the VisualWebPart1 project item folder, but the .webpart file will not have its title updated. The same applies if you change the class name and namespace of the web part.

Now it is time to test our web part. Set a breakpoint on the first line of the code in Listing 9-2 and press F5. Visual Studio launches the browser with the site we specified when we created the project.

In order to debug our web part we should create a web part page first. We could also add the web part to an existing web part page but by creating a new one and only adding our web part we will have better performance as well as better diagnostic possibilities as the page only needs to render our web part. Also if the page throws an error we know that our web part and not some other web part on the page is causing the error.

In the Site Actions menu of the SharePoint site, select "More Options..." as shown in Figure 9-13.

In the Create dialog that appears as shown in Figure 9-14, click Page under Filter By: and then click Web Part Page and click the Create button.

The new web part page appears. This page allows users to create web part pages and select various layouts for the page. Layouts let you define how web parts are laid out on the page itself by specifying the layout and number of web part zones. The create web part page also lets you choose a Save Location to store the new web part page. Name the new page Create-TaskWebPartHost, leave the default template selected (Header, Footer, 3

Figure 9-13: More Options
item in the Site Actions menu

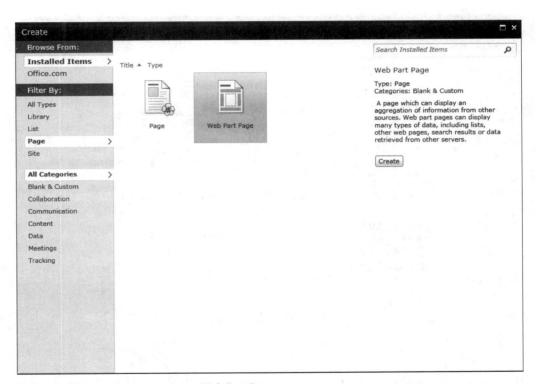

Figure 9-14: Create page to create a Web Part Page

Columns, which will define a total of five web part zones), select Site Pages as the Save Location, and click the Create button. Figure 9-15 shows the New Web Part page with these settings.

The new page CreateTaskWebPartHost is created and displayed in the browser. Now click the Add a web part link in the header section of the page. Once you click it the page enters an editing mode and the SharePoint ribbon appears. In the Categories list select the Custom folder. This is the folder that contains all the user-created web parts. Figure 9-16 shows the page CreateTaskWebPartHost in Edit mode with the Custom folder selected in the Categories list.

Our web part CreateTaskWebPart shows up under the Web Parts list, and when we select it the description entered in the .webpart file is displayed

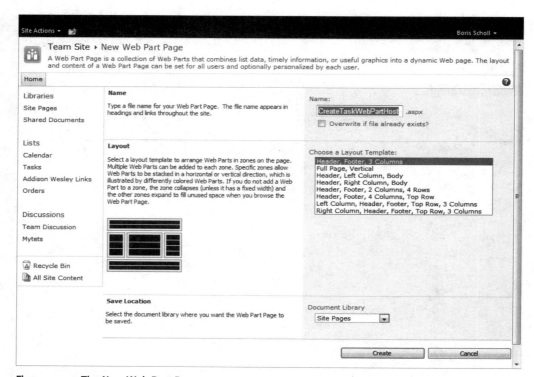

Figure 9-15: The New Web Part Page

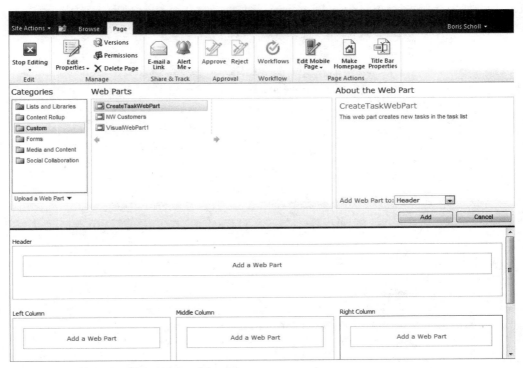

Figure 9-16: CreateTaskWebPartHost in Edit mode

in the About the Web Part section. Click the Add button to add the web part to the page. Click the Stop Editing button to get back to normal view. Figure 9-17 shows the web part CreateTaskWebPart added to the page.

What we have done so far is set up the infrastructure to test our web part. We deployed the visual web part for the first time, created a new web part page to host our web part, and added our web part to the newly created page.

Now it's time to debug. Enter "Need to write about web parts" as the title of the task to create and set the due date to any date. Then click the Create Task button. We hit the breakpoint in the code and can debug as shown in Figure 9-18. Press F5 to run the event handler for the Create Task button to completion.

Figure 9-17: CreateTaskWebPart added
to the page

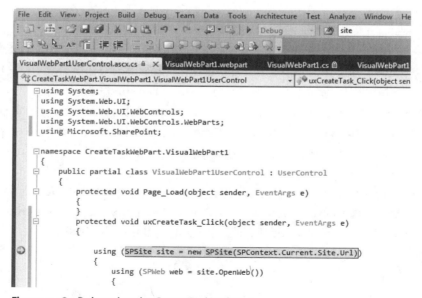

Figure 9-18: Debugging the CreateTaskWebPart

Let's check if the new task was added to the task list. Navigate to your SharePoint site's homepage and click the Tasks list in the left navigation menu. Once the task list is displayed you can see the newly created task "Need to write about web parts." Figure 9-19 shows the newly created task in the task list.

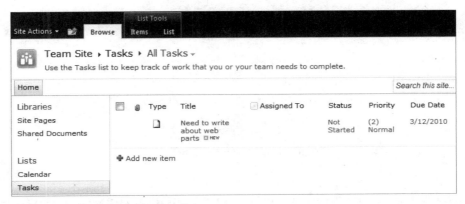

Figure 9-19: New task in the task list

Creating Web Parts with AJAX That Update without Having to Reload the Entire Web Page

We now consider how to modify our web part so it can update without requiring a full page refresh. We do that using a development pattern called Asynchronous JavaScript and XML or AJAX. SharePoint pages are already AJAX enabled. Every SharePoint page has a ScriptManager object, which is an ASP.NET object that enables AJAX style updating of a control. If you want to enable partial page updates with AJAX, you must use the UpdatePanel control in your user control.

To modify our visual web part to enable partial updating we will add a new label to the web part that tells us whether a task was created or not. In the Design view for VisualWebPart1UserControl.ascx open the Toolbox and drag a label next to the button Create Task as shown in Figure 9-20. Clear its Text property and enter "lblResult" as the ID.

We want to implement a partial page update so we need to add the UpdatePanel control to the web part and include the controls that should

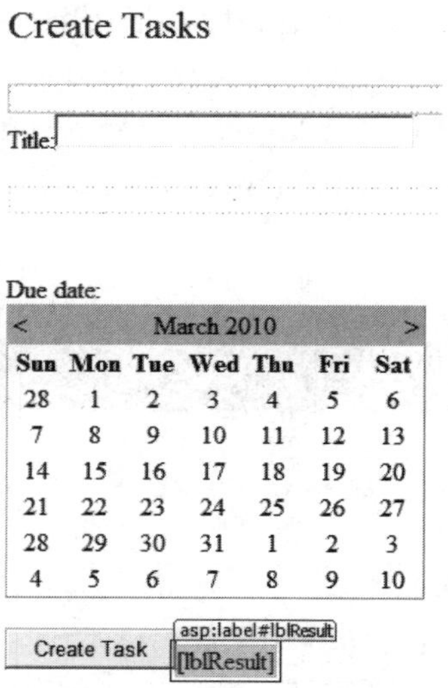

Create Tasks

Figure 9-20: Add a new label

be included in the partial update in its ContentTemplate elements. Open the Source view for VisualWebPart1UserControl.ascx. From the Toolbox category AJAX Extensions, drag the UpdatePanel control onto the source view right above the label Label1. Cut the closing tag of UpdatePanel, </asp:UpdatePanel>, and paste it under the label lblResult. Next we need to add the ContentTemplate opening tag, <ContentTemplate>, right under the opening tag of the UpdatePanel element and the ContentTemplate closing tag, </ContentTemplate>, right above the closing tag of the Update-Panel element. By doing this we tell ASP.NET's AJAX runtime that all the controls included in the UpdatePanel control are supposed to be updated without reloading the entire page. Listing 9-4 shows the new markup of our control after adding the UpdatePanel control and the label.

Listing 9-4: UpdatePanel Markup for VisualWebPart1UserControl.ascx

```
<p class="style2">
    Create Tasks</p>
<p class="style1">
 <asp:UpdatePanel ID="UpdatePanel1" runat="server">
    <ContentTemplate>
      <asp:Label ID="Label1" runat="server"
              style="color: #000000"
              Text="Title:"></asp:Label>
```

```
        <asp:TextBox ID="uxTitleText"
                runat="server"
                Width="223px"></asp:TextBox>
      </p>
      <br/>
      <asp:Label ID="Label4" runat="server" Text="Due date:">
      </asp:Label>
      <asp:Calendar ID="uxDueDate" runat="server"></asp:Calendar>
      <p>
      <asp:Button ID="uxCreateTask"
              runat="server"
              onclick="uxCreateTask_Click"
              Text="Create Task" />
      <asp:Label ID="lblResult" runat="server"></asp:Label>
    </ContentTemplate>
 </asp:UpdatePanel>
</p>
```

With the UpdatePanel control added we can now modify our code. Listing 9-5 shows the updated code for creating a task in CreateTaskWebPart's uxCreateTask_Click event handler.

Listing 9-5: Code for Creating a Task in the CreateTaskWebPart's uxCreateTask_Click Event Handler

```
protected void uxCreateTask_Click(object sender, EventArgs e)
{
  SPSite site = SPContext.Current.Site;
  using (SPWeb web = site.OpenWeb())
  {
    try
    {
      SPList tasks = web.Lists["Tasks"];
      SPListItem myTask = tasks.Items.Add();
      myTask["Title"] = uxTitleText.Text;
      myTask["DueDate"] = uxDueDate.SelectedDate;
      myTask.Update();
      lblResult.Text = uxTitleText.Text + " successfully created!";
      uxTitleText.Text = "";
      uxDueDate.SelectedDate = DateTime.Today.Date;
    }
    catch (Exception ex)
    {
      lblResult.Text = "Task failed to create. ErrMsg: " + ex.Message;
    }
  }
}
```

We modified the code that creates the tasks and included it in a try catch statement to determine if the task was created successfully. If the myTask's Update() method is successful we write the status to lblResult and clear the text in the title textbox. In addition we set the date in the calendar control to Today. If the creation fails we write an error message to the lblResult. To see the impact of using AJAX, try removing the UpdatePanel and ContentTemplate tags and run it then put the tags back and run it again. You will see that with AJAX enabled, the label and the selected date on the calendar update without an entire page reload.

To recap, we've learned what visual web parts are, how to design them, and how to deploy and debug them. There is one more thing we should be aware of. When debugging stops, Visual Studio automatically retracts the visual web part, which means that if you navigate to the web part page after debugging you will see an error that the web part cannot be found. To test the web part without debugging again you need to explicitly deploy it. This can be done by right clicking the project CreateTaskWebPart in the Solution Explorer and selecting Deploy in the context menu as shown in Figure 9-21.

Figure 9-21: Deploying the visual web part

Web Part Customization

Visual web parts and web parts can be customized and personalized by the end user. Customization and Personalization refer to different concepts. Customization means that a setting in the web part, for example which task list in which site collection is used by the web part, can be configured by the site owner and then that configuration can be used by all users of the web part instance.

Personalization means that certain developer-specified properties can be exposed by the web part so they are modifiable by the end user when they are in Edit mode for the SharePoint web part page. Modifications made to the individual user's web part instance are saved and displayed on a per user basis.

Let's look at the CreateTaskWebPart behavior at runtime to see what customization means. As we noted before, Visual Studio automatically retracts the web part after debugging, so we need to deploy it again. Right click the project CreateTaskWebPart and select "Deploy."

Once the visual web part has been successfully deployed we need to open the browser and navigate to the web part page CreateTaskWeb-PartHost.aspx. In the top right corner of the header section click the drop down arrow to open the web part menu. Figure 9-22 shows the web part menu for the visual web part CreateTaskWebPart.

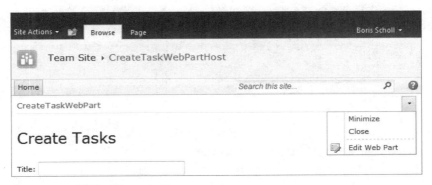

Figure 9-22: Web part menu

In the web part menu click Edit Web Part to bring up the editing view shown in Figure 9-23. The editing view provides an edit side bar at the right of the web page that allows users to change the look and feel and behavior of a selected web part.

As mentioned before there are situations in which you want users to be able to provide information that is used by the web part code. For example, you might have an RSS feed web part for which users can enter an URL for the feed they want to display in the web part. In our sample, we would like to provide a way for users to pick a different task list in which to create tasks. To allow the user to provide us with the task list to use, we will create a custom property on our web part that end users can edit.

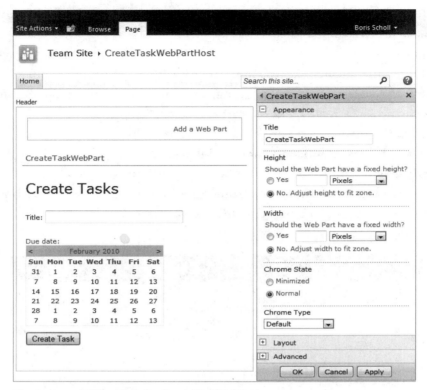

Figure 9-23: Editing View for CreateTaskWebPart

All custom properties that we want to show up in the web part editing view must be implemented by a public property in the web part class. This property must also have some attributes added to it so SharePoint recognizes that the property is one that can be modified by the end user in the web part editing view.

Remember the actual web part for a visual web part is defined by the class named VisualWebPart1.cs. Right now, our code in VisualWebPart1.cs doesn't do much—it just hosts the ASP.NET user control we designed and wrote code behind. But now, we need to add some custom properties to our web part class in VisualWebPart1.cs so they will be configurable in the web part editing view.

In Listing 9-6, we add a public string property called SiteCollectionUrl. This property will allow end users to choose the site collection containing the task list we want our CreateTaskWebPart to add tasks to.

Listing 9-6: Custom Property SiteCollectionUrl Defined for CreateTaskWebPart

```
[Personalizable(PersonalizationScope.Shared),
 WebBrowsable(true),
 WebDisplayName("Site collection url"),
 WebDescription("Set the url if you want to create tasks in a " +
   "different site collection"),
 Category("Configuration")]
 public string SiteCollectionUrl { get; set; }
```

There are five attributes added to our SiteCollectionUrl property. Table 9-1 describes these attributes.

TABLE 9-1: Attributes for Web Part Custom Properties

Attribute	Description
Personalizable	Tells SharePoint that this is a custom property with a given scope—in Listing 9-6 we use the scope Personalization-Scope.Shared, which means that when set this custom property impacts all web parts in the site collection. If set to PersonalizationScope.User then the custom property will be set on a per user basis.
WebBrowsable	When set to True, this attribute makes the custom property appear in the web part editing view.
WebDisplayName	The name that is displayed for the property in the web part editing view.
WebDescription	The description of the property; this description will be shown in a tooltip when the user hovers the mouse over the property in the web part editing view.
Category	Defines the category in which the custom property will appear; this can be an arbitrary string for creating a new category or the name of an existing category.

All these properties are defined in the System.Web.UI.WebControls
.WebParts namespace. The first attribute, Personalizable, tells the Share-
Point web part manager to store the value of our custom property Site-
CollectionUrl. It is instantiated with a PersonalizationScope parameter.
PersonalizationScope is an enumeration with two values: Shared and

User. The personalization scope for our property is set to Personalization-Scope.Shared, which means SiteCollectionUrl is not set on a per user basis. This makes this property a "Configuration" property as described earlier—changing this property affects all users of the web part in the site collection. PersonalizationScope.User means that the property is saved on a per user basis, which means the property is a "Personalization" property as described earlier.

With the property added to the web part class we can now deploy our web part again and see if the property is available in the web part editing view. Right click the project CreateTaskWebPart and select "Deploy."

Once the solution is deployed put the web part in editing view by using the steps previously described. Figure 9-24 shows the visual web part and

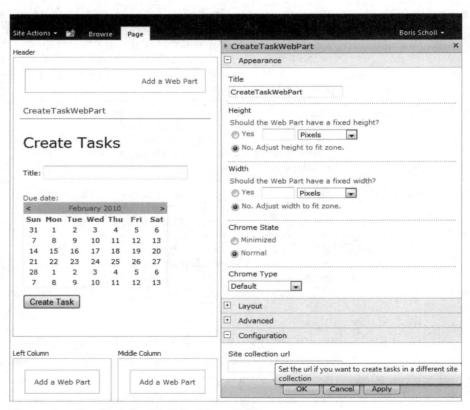

Figure 9-24: The SiteCollectionUrl editing experience

the editing experience for the newly added property SiteCollectionUrl. Note that in Figure 9-24, we hovered the mouse over the property to display the tooltip showing the WebDescription property.

Great, so now we can let users edit our custom property in the Share-Point UI, but of course nothing will happen yet as we haven't implemented the code to use the new custom property.

The first obstacle you will face as you think about how to use the new custom property is figuring out how to use the property defined in VisualWebPart1.cs in the ASP.NET user control defined in VisualWebPart-UserControl.cs as these are two separate classes. One way is by defining a public property in the user control class VisualWebPartUserControl and assigning the value of the custom property before the user control is loaded. Listing 9-7 shows this approach.

Listing 9-7: VisualWebPart1UserControl Class Implementation

```csharp
public partial class VisualWebPart1UserControl : UserControl
{
  public string ToolPartSiteUrl {get;set;}
  string siteUrl = string.Empty;

  protected void Page_Load(object sender, EventArgs e)
  {
    siteUrl = ToolPartSiteUrl;
  }

  protected void uxCreateTask_Click(object sender, EventArgs e)
  {
    if (siteUrl == string.Empty)
    {
      siteUrl = SPContext.Current.Site.Url;
    }
    using (SPSite site = new SPSite(siteUrl))
    {
      using (SPWeb web = site.OpenWeb())
      {
        try
        {
          web.AllowUnsafeUpdates = true;
          SPList tasks = web.Lists["Tasks"];
          SPListItem myTask = tasks.Items.Add();
          myTask["Title"] = uxTitleText.Text;
```

```
            myTask["DueDate"] = uxDueDate.SelectedDate;
            myTask.Update();
            lblResult.Text = uxTitleText.Text + " successfully created!";
            uxTitleText.Text = "";
            uxDueDate.SelectedDate = DateTime.Today.Date;
        }
        catch (Exception ex)
        {
            lblResult.Text =
                "Task failed to create. ErrMsg: " + ex.Message;
        }
    }
  }
 }
}
```

In the first line of the class we declare a public property named Tool-PartSiteUrl, which we will use from our class VisualWebPart1 to move the value of the custom property SiteCollectionUrl from VisualWebPart1 to the VisualWebPart1UserControl class.

Next we declare a variable named siteUrl and assign an empty string to it. In the Page_Load method of the user control we assign the value of the property ToolPartSiteUrl to the variable siteUrl. If a URL was not provided by the user an empty string will be assigned. Listing 9-8 shows how we assign the site URL entered by the user to the property ToolPartSiteUrl.

In Listing 9-7, in the uxCreateTask_Click method we check if the siteUrl has a value assigned and if there is no value we assign the URL of the current site collection by using SPContext.Current.Site.Url property. Otherwise, we will use the URL provided by the user. Finally we create the SPSite object for a site with the URLstored in siteUrl and create the appropriate web object.

Before we can actually create a task we need to set the AllowUnsafeUpdate property of the web object to true. This is because we may be crossing site collections, which means we may be calling from one web application into another. If your server is set up in a way that both site collections use the same web application you may not need this code. For more information on site collections and web applications, see Chapter 1, "Introduction to SharePoint."

Listing 9-8: Assigning a Value to a Property Defined in the User Control in the VisualWebPart1 Class

```
protected override void CreateChildControls()
{
  Control control = Page.LoadControl(_ascxPath);
  VisualWebPart1UserControl vwpCtrl = control
    as VisualWebPart1UserControl;
  vwpCtrl.ToolPartSiteUrl = SiteCollectionUrl;
  Controls.Add(control);
}
```

The first line of the CreateChildControls method gets generated by Visual Studio and it loads the user control and uses the control base class (Control). In the second line we create a variable of type VisualWebPart1UserControl and cast the control object we loaded in the first line to VisualWebPart1UserControl to access the ToolPartSiteUrl property we defined in the user control. Now that we have a strongly typed variable for our user control we can access the ToolPartSiteUrl property and assign it the value of the SiteCollectionUrl property. The last line is generated by default by Visual Studio and it just adds the control to the controls collection of the web part.

Now we can go ahead and test our custom property for our visual web part. First we will need to create a new site collection with a task list so we can create tasks. For more information on how to create a new site collection, see Chapter 1, "Introduction to SharePoint."

Deploy the web part again then navigate to the web part page called CreateTaskWebPartHost.aspx and select Edit Web Part in the web part menu. In the configuration section of the web part editing view enter the URL to the second site collection and click the OK button. Figure 9-25 shows the web part tool part with a value for another site collection URL.

Now, exit editing mode and enter a task title and a due date in the web part and click the Create Task button. Navigate to the task list in your new site collection and check if the task has been created. Figure 9-26 shows the newly created task in a task list of a different site collection.

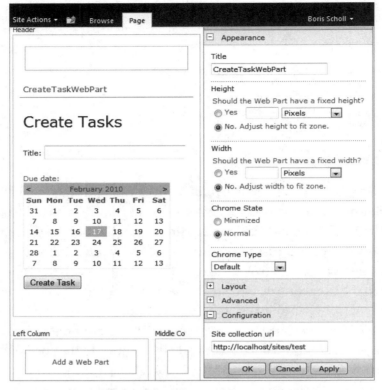

Figure 9-25: Setting a new site collection URL for the web part

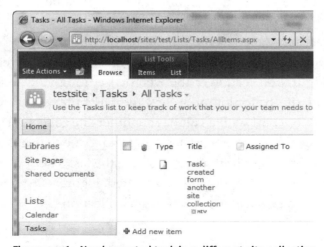

Figure 9-26: Newly created task in a different site collection

Custom properties are implemented in exactly the same way for code only web parts as for visual web parts. We will now look into how to create code only web parts.

Creating a Code-only Web Part (Sandboxed)

As mentioned earlier in this chapter, you can also create code-only web parts in Visual Studio. As we have seen visual web parts are actually SharePoint web parts hosting an ASP.NET user control, so that we can use the Visual Studio web designer. A code only web part is a SharePoint web part without an ASP.NET user control component.

When would you want to create a code-only web part? There are a few reasons to use code-only web part projects. The first reason is if your corporate policy prevents you from creating files under the ControlTemplates folder in the SharePoint hive. A second more important reason is that code-only web parts can be deployed as sandboxed solutions. If you want to develop for SharePoint Online for example, you can only create sandboxed solutions because these are the only supported solutions for SharePoint Online.

What Is SharePoint Online?

SharePoint Online is an offering by Microsoft to host SharePoint for customers. Basically you can take advantage of SharePoint functionality without the need to set up and maintain a your own servers. For more information see http://www.microsoft.com/online/sharepoint-online.mspx.

We will now consider how to create web parts for sandboxed solutions and discuss important concepts associated with them. A sandboxed solution means that your web parts are running in isolated processes so that your SharePoint farm is at less risk. Sandboxed solutions have some additional limitations. First, web service calls are not supported in a sandboxed solution. Second, not all of the object, properties, and methods provided by the server or client side object model are accessible so you must check the documentation to find out what parts of the object model you can use. Visual Studio IntelliSense can also help here—if you are developing a sandboxed solution, Visual Studio will hide the portion of the object model that is not accessible in a sandboxed solution. But this is only a design time help— Visual Studio doesn't check if you are using the right portion of the object model at compile time, so your solution might throw an error during runtime if the parts of the object model are not supported in a sandboxed environment. For this reason, you should be careful when pasting code from samples, such as online samples that may have been written for full trust Farm solutions and may compile but cause runtime errors for sandboxed solutions.

Visual Studio 2010 SharePoint Power Tools

Visual Studio 2010 SharePoint Power Tools contain a Visual Web Part template that can be deployed as a sandboxed solution as well as a sandbox compile feature. The sandbox compile feature will throw an error at compile time if you are using objects, properties, and methods that are not allowed in a sandbox solution.

Let's create a simple web part that shows a summary of the tasks in the task list based on their status. The web part will show the user how many completed, not started, and other status tasks are in the task list. Figure 9-27 shows how the web part will look once we have implemented it.

Figure 9-27: The SummaryTasksWebPart web part

Open Visual Studio and select New Project. In the New Project dialog navigate to the SharePoint 2010 node. The first noticeable difference from visual web parts is that there is no Visual Studio project template for code-only web parts. We need to create an empty SharePoint project and add a code-only web part as a new project item. Select Empty SharePoint project, name it "SummaryOfTasks," and click the OK button.

The SharePoint Customization Wizard comes up; leave the debugging URL to the default set by Visual Studio. Because we want to create a sandboxed web part, leave the Deploy as sandboxed solution radio button selected and click the Finish button.

Once Visual Studio has created the empty SharePoint project we can add the web part project item to it. Right click the SummaryOfTasks solution folder to bring up the context menu. In the menu select Add then New Item… In the Add New Item dialog select the Web Part template and name it "SummaryTasksWebPart" then click the Add button. Figure 9-28 shows the Add New Item dialog.

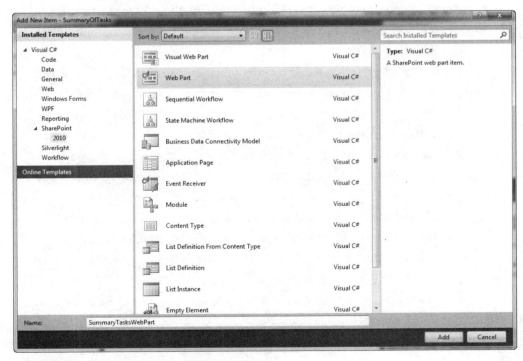

Figure 9-28: Add New Item dialog—Add Web Part

Visual Studio adds the web part as a SharePoint project item. It also adds the web part to the feature designer and the package designer so it can be deployed by the project. All the namespaces and the web part title are set by Visual Studio based on our initial SummaryTasksWebPart name, so there is no additional editing needed and we can go right into writing the code.

The SummaryTasksWebPart class already has a method signature for CreateChildControls, which overrides the method in the base web part class from which SummaryTasksWebPart derives. That is the method we need to use to add our UI controls.

Why Use the CreateChildControls Method?

Well we could say to use the CreateChildControls method because that's the method Visual Studio creates by default, but there is more to it. If you look at other literature about creating web parts you will notice that some of the articles suggest overriding the methods RenderContents and Render. While RenderContents is safe to use, you should never use the Render method. The reason lies in the way web parts are being rendered on the SharePoint page.

Web parts are rendered in a ‹Table› element that has two rows. One of the rows contains a ‹DIV› tag and that's where the RenderContents and CreateChildControls methods put their output. The Render method will overwrite the entire table, which can easily break the SharePoint web page. Another way to look at it is that the CreateChildControls method is the method intended to build the control tree. The controls receive and process their events and go through the page life cycle. On the other hand the Render method should only render final HTML, it should not create controls.

For simple controls (for example if we want to write a control that displays an image and a hyperlink) we can use the Render method but if we need more advanced features, such as events, or we need to use some built-in ASP.NET controls like TextBox, then we will use the CreateChildControls method.

Let's create a helper class that we will use to represent a group of tasks that share the same status. Right click the SummaryTasksWebPart folder then select Add then New Item... In the Add New Item dialog select Code under the Visual C# node and select Class in the main part of the dialog. Name the new class TaskGroup.cs. Once Visual Studio has added the class we can implement it. Listing 9-9 shows our implementation of the Task-Group class.

Listing 9-9: TaskGroup.cs

```csharp
class TaskGroup
{
  public string TaskState {get; private set;}
  public int TaskCount { get; private set; }

  public TaskGroup(string taskState, int taskCount)
  {
    this.TaskState = taskState;
    this.TaskCount = taskCount;
  }
}
```

The TaskGroup class has two public properties called TaskState and TaskCount. We will use the TaskState property to store the status of the tasks and TaskCount to store the number of tasks with a certain status. The constructor of the class assigns the value of its parameters to the properties when an object of the class TaskGroup is created.

The next step is to create the actual web part. We need to add a reference to the System.Drawing assembly as our web part will show the results in a table and we want a color code from System.Drawing to set the row's color to red if the task group's status is "Waiting." Right click the References folder and select Add Reference. In the Add Reference dialog select the .NET tab and scroll to the component named System.Drawing. Figure 9-29 shows the Add Reference dialog.

After the reference is added to the project we need to add two new using directives to the top of SummaryTasksWebPart.cs. The first using directive is for System.Drawing and the second for System.Collections .Generic as we will use a generic list to store our tasks groups.

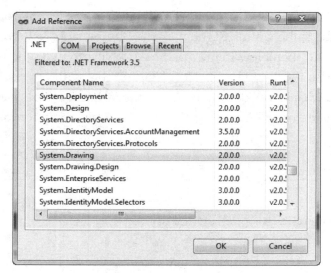

Figure 9-29: Add Reference dialog

With the two using statements added we can go ahead and implement our web part class. Listing 9-10 shows the code for the SummaryTasks-WebPart class.

Listing 9-10: SummaryTasksWebPart.cs

```
public class SummaryTasksWebPart : WebPart
{
  private SPListItemCollection collNotStartedTasks;
  private SPListItemCollection collInProgTasks;
  private SPListItemCollection collCompletedTasks;
  private SPListItemCollection collWaitingTasks;
  private SPListItemCollection collDeferredTasks;
  private List<TaskGroup> taskGroupsList;
  Table table;

  protected override void CreateChildControls()
  {
    GetTaskGroups();
    taskGroupsList = GetTaskGroupList();
    table = new Table();
    table.Width = Unit.Percentage(25);
    TableHeaderRow headerRow = new TableHeaderRow();
    headerRow.BackColor = Color.LightBlue;
    TableHeaderCell headerTableCell1 = new TableHeaderCell();
```

```
TableHeaderCell headerTableCell2 = new TableHeaderCell();
headerTableCell1.Text = "Task Status";
headerTableCell2.Text = "Task Count";
headerRow.Cells.Add(headerTableCell1);
headerRow.Cells.Add(headerTableCell2);
table.Rows.Add(headerRow);
for (int i = 0; i < taskGroupsList.Count; i++)
{
  TableRow row = new TableRow();
  TableCell cell1 = new TableCell();
  cell1.Text = taskGroupsList[i].TaskState;
  cell1.HorizontalAlign = HorizontalAlign.Center;
  if(taskGroupsList[i].TaskState == "Waiting")
    row.BackColor = Color.Red;
  TableCell cell2 = new TableCell();
  cell2.Text = taskGroupsList[i].TaskCount.ToString();
  cell2.HorizontalAlign = HorizontalAlign.Center;
  row.Cells.Add(cell1);
  row.Cells.Add(cell2);
  table.Rows.Add(row);
}
  this.Controls.Add(table);
}

private void GetTaskGroups()
{
  SPWeb mySite = SPContext.Current.Web
  SPList taskList = mySite.Lists["Tasks"];

  SPQuery camlQuery = new SPQuery();
  camlQuery.Query = "<Where><Eq><FieldRef Name='Status'/>" +
    "<Value Type='Choice'>Not Started</Value></Eq></Where>";
  collNotStartedTasks = taskList.GetItems(camlQuery);

  SPQuery camlQuery2 = new SPQuery();
  camlQuery2.Query = "<Where><Eq><FieldRef Name='Status'/>" +
    "<Value Type='Choice'>In Progress</Value></Eq></Where>";
  collInProgTasks = taskList.GetItems(camlQuery2);

  SPQuery camlQuery3 = new SPQuery();
  camlQuery3.Query = "<Where><Eq><FieldRef Name='Status'/>" +
    "<Value Type='Choice'>Completed</Value></Eq></Where>";
  collCompletedTasks = taskList.GetItems(camlQuery3);

  SPQuery camlQuery4 = new SPQuery();
  camlQuery4.Query = "<Where><Eq><FieldRef Name='Status'/>" +
    "<Value Type='Choice'>Waiting on someone else" +
    "</Value></Eq></Where>";
  collWaitingTasks = taskList.GetItems(camlQuery4);
```

```
    SPQuery camlQuery5 = new SPQuery();
    camlQuery5.Query = "<Where><Eq><FieldRef Name='Status'/>" +
      "<Value Type='Choice'>Deferred</Value></Eq></Where>";
    collDeferredTasks = taskList.GetItems(camlQuery5);

  }

  private List<TaskGroup> GetTaskGroupList()
  {
    List<TaskGroup> taskgroupsList = new List<TaskGroup>();
    taskgroupsList.Add(new TaskGroup
      ("Not Started", collNotStartedTasks.Count));
    taskgroupsList.Add(new TaskGroup
      ("In progress", collInProgTasks.Count));
    taskgroupsList.Add(new TaskGroup
      ("Completed", collCompletedTasks.Count));
    taskgroupsList.Add(new TaskGroup
      ("Waiting", collWaitingTasks.Count));
    taskgroupsList.Add(new TaskGroup
      ("Deferred", collDeferredTasks.Count));
    return taskgroupsList;
  }
}
```

Let's start exploring the code. First we create a couple of SPListItem-Collection objects to store task list items with a certain status. As a task can have five different statuses we create five SPListItemCollection objects, each representing a collection of tasks with a certain status. For example, the collNotStartedTasks collection stores task items that have the status Not Started. We will use these objects to determine how many tasks with a certain status exist. Refer to Chapter 4, "SharePoint Lists," for more information about list items and how to work with them.

Secondly, we create a list to store TaskGroup objects that we will create and a Table object that will be used to display the task groups. The first line of the method CreateChildControls calls the method GetTaskGroups. This method puts task items into five different collections based on CAML queries. Note that we could have also used SPLINQ as we are only making list queries and SPLINQ fully supports querying for items in a list

Taking a closer look at the first couple of lines we set the variable taskList to an SPList object representing the tasks list. Remember that sandboxed solutions only allow access to SharePoint objects within the same site collection that the solution is running, so we couldn't use the cross-site SiteCollectionUrl we used in the previous section. SPList has a method called GetItems, which takes an SPQuery representing a CAML query as a parameter and returns a filtered set of list items.

We create an SPQuery object for each of the task statuses and assign a query string to its Query property. Then we call the GetItems method of the taskList object and pass in the SPQuery object to return a collection of tasks with a certain status. We then assign the result to an SPListItem-Collection object. Representative code is shown below.

```
SPQuery camlQuery = new SPQuery();
camlQuery.Query = "<Where><Eq><FieldRef Name='Status'/>" +
  "<Value Type='Choice'>Not Started</Value></Eq></Where>";
collNotStartedTasks = taskList.GetItems(camlQuery);
```

The code creates an SPQuery object called camlQuery and sets its Query property to return all the tasks that have the status Not Started. The SPQuery object is passed to SPList's GetItems method to return an SPList-ItemsCollection object, which is assigned to colNotStartedTasks.

In the second line of the CreateChildControls method we get a list of TaskGroup objects returned by GetTaskGroupList. The GetTaskGroupList method creates a new list of type List<TaskGroup>. Then it adds five Task-Group objects to the list, one for each possible SharePoint task status. When creating each new TaskGroup object we pass the task status and task count into the constructor where the values get assigned to the properties TaskCount and TaskState of the TaskGroup object.

Now that we have all the information we need from the task list we can start implementing the table that will display the results in the web part. First we instantiate a new Table object and assign it to our table variable. We set the width property to 25% so the table only uses 25% of the control space.

Next we create a TableHeaderRow object and set its back color property to Color.LightBlue. To finish our header row we create two Table-HeaderCell objects: headerTableCell1 and headerTableCell2, and assign the values "Task Status" and "Task Count" to their respective Text properties. Finally we add the cells to headerRow and headerRow to the table.

With the table header implemented we can now create the other rows dynamically. We create a for loop to iterate through the TaskGroup objects stored in taskGroupLists. With each iteration we create a new TableRow object row that has two TableCell objects (cell1 and cell2). The values of the TaskState and TaskCount properties of each TaskGroup object are assigned to the respective Text property of the cells. The HorizontalAlign property of each cell is set to HorizontalAlign.Center to center the text in the cells. Because we want to highlight the row for tasks with the status "Waiting" in red, we check the value of TaskState, and if it is "Waiting" we set the row's back color to Color.Red. Finally we add the cell objects to the row and the row object to the table. The last thing we do after we exit the loop is add the table control to the controls collection of the web part.

Before testing the web part we should make sure that we have a couple of tasks in the task list, so that the web part has some data to display. Once some tasks have been added, we can test if the web part works. Set a breakpoint at GetTaskGroups in the method CreateChildControls and press F5. As you can see, debugging a code-only web part is no different from debugging a visual web part.

When your browser comes up you can either use the web part page you created for the visual web part before or create a new web part page. We went through the steps of setting up a web part page earlier in this chapter, so we will skip the detailed steps on how to do this here.

Once we have a web part page, we can put the page in the Edit mode and add the web part to the page. Figure 9-30 shows the web part Summary-TaskWebPart in the web part gallery.

Once the web part is added and the page is refreshed the breakpoint in CreateChildControls is hit. We can now step through the code and after the code has been executed we will see the web part shown in Figure 9-27.

Personalization and Customization for a code-only web part works exactly the same way as we saw in the visual web part section. In fact it is easier for a code-only web part because you don't have to worry about passing property data between the web part class and the associated ASP.NET user control class.

As we have seen in this chapter, Visual Studio provides us with an easy way to develop visual web parts for farm solutions. We can also create

Figure 9-30: SummaryTaskWebPart in the
web part gallery

code-only web parts for sandboxed solutions. So far our web parts have
been ASP.NET based with a little AJAX thrown in. To create an even more
interactive web part, Visual Studio allows you to create Silverlight web
parts as well.

Creating a Silverlight Web Part

Before we start diving into the world of Silverlight web parts we need a
basic understanding of what Silverlight is and how SharePoint handles Silverlight applications.

Silverlight is a powerful development platform for creating engaging,
interactive user experiences for web, desktop, and mobile applications
whether online or offline. Silverlight applications are browser indepen-
dent and are executed in a browser plug-in that works cross-platform and
cross-device. For more information on Silverlight visit the official Silverlight developer center at http://silverlight.net.

When would you use Silverlight in a web part? With Silverlight you can
build very powerful and rich Internet applications, also called RIA applications, combining animation, video, layout, vector graphics, perspective
3D, special effects, and features like Deep Zoom. In other words you can
really "light up" your user experience in SharePoint.

What If I Don't Have Silverlight Installed?

You need to have the Silverlight plug-in installed to get the Silverlight experience for SharePoint. Don't worry if you don't have Silverlight installed. SharePoint will fall back to an HTML view, so you still will be able to create new items. If you want to build and test the Silverlight web part sample that we will create later in this chapter you must install Silverlight. As soon as you try to show the Silverlight web part developed in this section you will be prompted to download and install the Silverlight runtime.

How does SharePoint support Silverlight? Silverlight is hosted by adding script or markup to a web page. In the SharePoint context that means that we can develop application pages, web part pages and web parts that host Silverlight. Even some features in SharePoint itself are implemented in Silverlight. When we created a new web part page—the dialog that shows available web parts pages is actually implemented using Silverlight. In addition SharePoint comes with a Silverlight web part that can be used to host custom Silverlight applications. This web part has the markup and script already implemented, so that we only need to point it to the Silverlight package containing our Silverlight control.

We start our exploration of Silverlight web parts by creating a Silverlight web part that displays the task groups in a pie chart control. The pie chart control is part of the Silverlight 3 Toolkit available on http://silverlight .codeplex.com/releases. In order to use this control you will have to download and install the Silverlight Toolkit on your development machine.

To build our Silverlight web part, we will first create a Visual Studio solution with a Silverlight application project that implements the pie chart, and an empty SharePoint project that we will use to deploy the Silverlight application to SharePoint. Once the application is deployed we will use the Silverlight web part included in SharePoint to host our Silverlight application.

To get started, open Visual Studio in elevated mode and select new project. In the New Project dialog select SharePoint then 2010 and pick the project template Empty SharePoint Project. Name the new project "SL-SummaryTaskWebPart." After clicking the OK button, the customization wizard comes up. Leave the default settings and click the Finish button. Note that our approach for creating Silverlight web parts works for both sandboxed and farm solutions.

Create a New Silverlight Application

As mentioned earlier we are using the empty SharePoint project to deploy the Silverlight application. Right now there is nothing left to do in this project and we can move on and create the Silverlight application project. Right click the solution node SLSummaryTaskWebpart in Solution Explorer, select Add, then select New Project… from the context menu. In the New Project dialog select Silverlight in the templates section and chose Silverlight Application as shown in Figure 9-31.

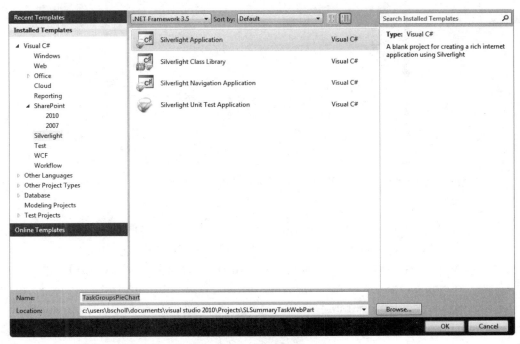

Figure 9-31: Adding a New Silverlight project to the solution

Name the project TaskGroupsPieChart and click the OK button. The New Silverlight application dialog comes up. This dialog is used to configure a test page that hosts the Silverlight application and it also configures the Silverlight version to be used.

By default the dialog assumes that you want to create a new web site and the check box Host the Silverlight application in a new web site is checked. We don't need a test web site because we will test and debug the Silverlight application in the SharePoint Silverlight web part. Uncheck Host the Silverlight application in a new web site and make sure that Silverlight 3 is set as the Silverlight version as shown in Figure 9-32.

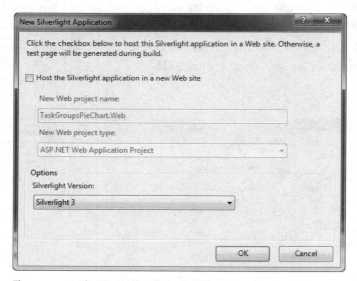

Figure 9-32: The New Silverlight Application dialog

A new Silverlight project is created and the Silverlight designer, also called the XAML editor, is displayed. XAML is the name of the markup language used to describe a Silverlight application. In the solution explorer you can see two XAML files were added: App.xaml and MainPage.xaml. App.xaml is comparable to the Main method in a console application. It starts the application and creates a new MainPage object. MainPage.xaml file is where we will write our implementation.

Before we can implement the code that retrieves the task groups we need to add the PieChart control to the Toolbox in Visual Studio and add a reference to the SharePoint Silverlight client object model assembly to our project. Actually there are two ways to work with SharePoint data in Silverlight applications. The first way is to use the SharePoint Silverlight Client Object model and the second way is to use SharePoint Soap and WCF data services. In our sample we will leverage the SharePoint Silverlight client object model.

To add the pie chart control to the toolbox, right click the Silverlight control bar in the toolbox and select Choose Items… from the context menu. Figure 9-33 shows the context menu.

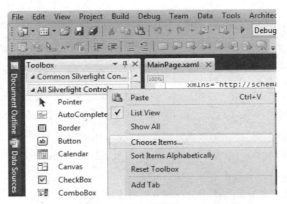

Figure 9-33: Context menu to add new Silverlight controls to the toolbox

In the Choose Items dialog select the Silverlight Components tab and scroll down until you find the PieSeries entry, which represents pie chart data rendered by the Chart control. You will use both the Chart control and the PieSeries control to create the final Silverlight control. Figure 9-34 shows the PieSeries control in the Silverlight controls list. Check the entry and click the OK button to add the PieSeries to the toolbox. Note: You must have the Silverlight toolkit installed to use this control.

The next step is to add a reference to the SharePoint Silverlight Client Object Model. Right click the References Folder in the TaskGroupsPieChart

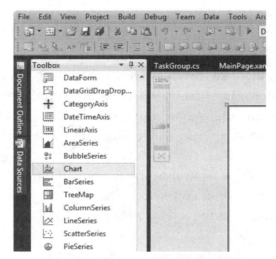

Figure 9-34: The Chart and PieSeries controls
in the Silverlight controls list

project to bring up the Add Reference dialog. In the dialog select the
Browse tab and browse to the {SharePointRoot}\Template\Layouts\ClientBin
directory. Select the assemblies Microsoft.SharePoint.Client.Silverlight.dll
and Microsoft.SharePoint.Client.Silverlight.Runtime.dll and click the OK
button.

The last thing we need to do is to add the following using directives to
MainPage.xaml.cs.

```
using Microsoft.SharePoint.Client;
using System.Collections.ObjectModel;
```

We need the first using directive to access the SharePoint client object
model and the second one to create an ObservableCollection object for
TaskGroup objects.

Add a new class to the TaskGroupsPieChart project and name it Task-
Group. Add the same code as shown in Listing 9-9 to the TaskGroup class.

Now we're ready to create the pie chart control and add code to it. Double click the MainPage.xaml to bring up the Silverlight designer. In the

Toolbox locate the Chart control and drag it onto the designer surface. In the designer increase the size of the Chart control by dragging it to the desired size. In the Properties window change the chart name to "ctTask-GroupsChart" and set its Title property to "TaskGroups."

In the XAML section at the bottom of the designer locate the <charting-Toolkit:Chart...> element and delete everything between the element opening tag and the element closing tag.

Now we'll need to add a PieSeries control inside the Chart control by dragging it from the Toolbox to the XAML editor. Put the control inside the <chartingToolkit:Chart> tags. Listing 9-11 shows the XAML for the chart after removing the default data in the <chartingToolkit:Chart> element and adding the PieSeries control.

Listing 9-11: Chart XAML

```
<chartingToolkit:Chart
  HorizontalAlignment="Left"
  Margin="21,12,0,0"
  Name="ctTaskGroupsChart"
  Title="Task Groups"
  VerticalAlignment="Top" Width="356" Height="285">
  <chartingToolkit:PieSeries />
</chartingToolkit:Chart>
```

Put your cursor on the line <chartingToolkit:PieSeries/> to bring up the Properties window for the PieSeries control. In the Properties window click the icon to sort the properties by category.

Table 9-2 shows the values we need to assign to corresponding properties in the Properties window. The most important ones are Dependent-ValuePath, IndependentValuePath, and ItemBinding because those values tell the PieSeries control that the data for the chart will come from our code. Figure 9-35 shows the designer once the settings in Table 9-2 are set.

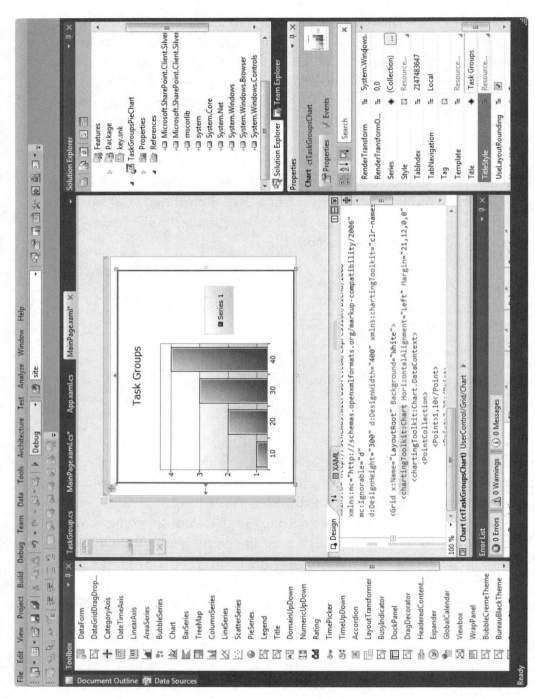

Figure 9-35: XAML designer showing the design view of the PieChart

TABLE 9-2: Properties and Values for the PieSeries Control

Property	Value
DependentValuePath	**TaskCount** We will use the TaskCount property of the TaskGroup class as the dependent value.
AnimationSequence	**FirstToLast** This will add the pie segments in order from first to last.
IndependentValuePath	**TaskState** We will use the TaskState property of the TaskGroup class as the independent value.
IsSelectionEnabled	**Checked** Provides a nice animation when hovering the mouse over the pie chart.
ItemBinding	**Binding...** Click on the little icon in the ItemBinding cell and select Apply DataBinding in the context menu. A menu dialog will pop up that you can close.

With the UI designed we can go ahead and implement the code to get a list of TaskGroup objects set up. Listing 9-12 shows the code for the Main-Page class. Remember this is the code-behind class for the MainPage.xaml file. You can think of it as being similar to the code-behind file for an ASPX file. It will run when the Silverlight application executes.

Listing 9-12: MainPage.xaml.cs

```
public partial class MainPage : UserControl
{
    private ListItemCollection collNotStartedTasks;
    private ListItemCollection collInProgTasks;
    private ListItemCollection collCompletedTasks;
    private ListItemCollection collWaitingTasks;
    private ListItemCollection collDeferredTasks;

    public ObservableCollection<TaskGroup> taskgroupsList;

    public MainPage()
    {
        InitializeComponent();
        GetTaskGroups();
    }

    private void GetTaskGroups()
    {
```

```
ClientContext context = ClientContext.Current;
List taskList = context.Web.Lists.GetByTitle("Tasks");
CamlQuery camlQuery = new CamlQuery();
camlQuery.ViewXml =
  "<View><Query><Where><Eq><FieldRef Name='Status'/>" +
  "<Value Type='Choice'>Not " +
  "Started</Value></Eq></Where></Query></View>";
collNotStartedTasks = taskList.GetItems(camlQuery);
CamlQuery camlQuery2 = new CamlQuery();
camlQuery2.ViewXml =
  "<View><Query><Where><Eq><FieldRef Name='Status'/>" +
  "<Value Type='Choice'>In " +
  "Progress</Value></Eq></Where></Query></View>";
collInProgTasks = taskList.GetItems(camlQuery2);
CamlQuery camlQuery3 = new CamlQuery();
camlQuery3.ViewXml =
  "<View><Query><Where><Eq><FieldRef Name='Status'/>" +
  "<Value Type='Choice'>Completed</Value>" +
  "</Eq></Where></Query></View>";
collCompletedTasks = taskList.GetItems(camlQuery3);
CamlQuery camlQuery4 = new CamlQuery();
camlQuery4.ViewXml =
  "<View><Query><Where><Eq><FieldRef Name='Status'/>" +
  "<Value Type='Choice'>Waiting on someone " +
  "else</Value></Eq></Where></Query></View>";
collWaitingTasks = taskList.GetItems(camlQuery4);
CamlQuery camlQuery5 = new CamlQuery();
camlQuery5.ViewXml =
  "<View><Query><Where><Eq><FieldRef Name='Status'/>" +
  "<Value Type='Choice'>Deferred</Value></Eq>" +
  "</Where></Query></View>";
collDeferredTasks = taskList.GetItems(camlQuery5);

context.Load(collNotStartedTasks);
context.Load(collInProgTasks);
context.Load(collCompletedTasks);
context.Load(collWaitingTasks);
context.Load(collDeferredTasks);

context.ExecuteQueryAsync(ClientRequestSucceeded,
  ClientRequestFailed);
}

public void BindDataToChart()
{
  if (taskgroupsList != null && taskgroupsList.Count > 0)
  {
    ctTaskGroupsChart.DataContext = taskgroupsList;
  }
}
```

```
private void ClientRequestSucceeded(object sender,
  ClientRequestSucceededEventArgs args)
{
  taskgroupsList = new ObservableCollection<TaskGroup>();
  taskgroupsList.Add(new TaskGroup
    ("Not Started", collNotStartedTasks.Count));
  taskgroupsList.Add
    (new TaskGroup("In progress", collInProgTasks.Count));
  taskgroupsList.Add(new TaskGroup
    ("Completed", collCompletedTasks.Count));
  taskgroupsList.Add(new TaskGroup
    ("Waiting", collWaitingTasks.Count));
  taskgroupsList.Add(new TaskGroup
    ("Deferred", collDeferredTasks.Count));
  this.Dispatcher.BeginInvoke(BindDataToChart);
}
private void ClientRequestFailed(object sender,
  ClientRequestFailedEventArgs args)
{
  lblResult.Content = "request failed";
}
}
```

Because the Silverlight PieChart is reusing the code from our previous web part we don't need to walk through it to understand how the code works and we can focus on the differences instead. We are now using the objects provided by the Silverlight client object model, meaning we are now using ListItemCollection instead of SPListItemCollection from the server object model. We also add code to create an ObservableCollection of Task-Group. ObservableCollection can provide notification if an item is added to the collection and trigger a refresh of the pie chart. To keep the code sample smaller our code hasn't implemented such a notification event.

The client object model objects are used to retrieve the task list items in the GetTaskGroups method. Please see Chapter 4, "SharePoint Lists," for more information on how to use the client object model to retrieve data from SharePoint lists.

The biggest difference from the previous web part implementation is that we now have to use the ExecuteQueryAsync method on the context object because all queries using the SharePoint Silverlight client object model need to be asynchronous. The ExecuteQueryAsync method takes two delegates as parameters: ClientRequestSucceeded and ClientRequestFailed.

So let's have a look at the ClientRequestSucceeded and ClientRequest-Failed delegates. In case the query request fails the handler ClientRequest-Failed is called and a message box with a detailed error message is shown to the user. If the request is successful the ClientRequestSucceeded event fires and we add new TaskGroup objects containing the status and the task count to the taskgroupList.

In the last line `this.Dispatcher.BeginInvoke(BindDataToChart)` we call back to the UI thread using the Dispatcher object of the thread that created the UI by calling BeginInvoke method.

Simply said, the Silverlight application creates a UI thread then calls the query asynchronously on another thread created to run the query. After we have received the results we need to update the UI, which means we need to delegate the control back to the UI thread. This always needs to be done if changes to the UI are made through the SharePoint Silverlight object model.

Once the UI thread has control again, the BindDataToChart method is executed. As the name implies, this method binds the collection of Task-Group objects to the chart control.

Deploying a Silverlight Web Part to SharePoint

Let's build the project TaskGroupsPieChart. This creates an .XAP file that will be used by the SharePoint Silverlight web part.

What Is a .XAP File?

A .XAP file is basically the executable for a Silverlight application and it includes an .XAML file named "AppManifest.xaml" and .DLL files referenced by the application. A .XAP file is a compressed zip file and you can investigate its content by renaming the file extension to .ZIP and opening it with a ZIP utility.

Before we deploy the .XAP file we need a place to store it. It is recommended that you store all .XAP files in a document library. The document library can either be an existing one or a new one dedicated to storing Silverlight applications. The document library can be hidden, so that normal SharePoint users can't see it. To create a new document library, open your SharePoint home page and select New Document Library from the Site Actions menu. In the Create dialog that appears, name the new document library "SLApps" and leave the Navigation and Document History settings as they are set by default. Because there is no template for .XAP files select None in the Document Template drop-down. Figure 9-36 shows the Create dialog with these options selected.

With the document library created we can now go ahead and work on the SharePoint project to deploy the .XAP file. A SharePoint module can be used to deploy files to SharePoint, for example to document libraries. We will take advantage of modules to deploy the .XAP file to the document library SLApps.

Right click the project SLSummaryTaskWebPart and select Add then New Item. In the New Item dialog select Module and name it "PieChartModule." Then click the Add button. Visual Studio adds the module including a sample file to the project. We don't need the sample file, so we can just

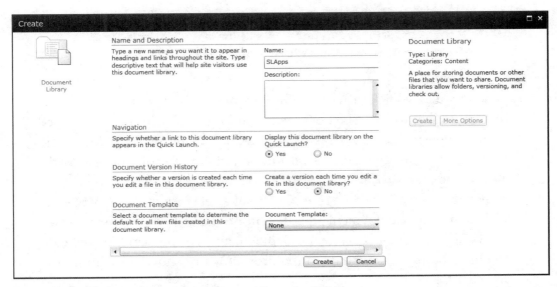

Figure 9-36: Create dialog for a New Document Library for .XAP files

delete it. Notice that Visual Studio updates the Elements.xml automatically when you delete the file so that Elements.xml no longer refers to the deleted sample file.

Select the SharePoint project item folder PieChartModule. In the Properties window locate the property "Project Output References" and click the ellipsis button next to the (Collection) property. Click the button to bring up the Project Output References dialog shown in Figure 9-37.

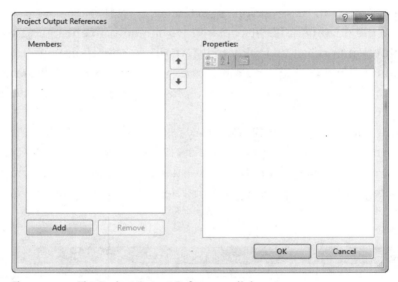

Figure 9-37: The Project Output References dialog

In this dialog click the Add button. By default Visual Studio adds the current project to the members list. In the right grid locate the Project Name property and select TaskGroupPieChart from the drop-down list. Visual Studio detects and lists all the projects in the solution and adds them to the drop-down.

Because we want to deploy the .XAP file as an element file (see Chapter 11, "Packaging and Deployment" for more information on deployment of element files) we need to change the Deployment Type property to Element-File by choosing ElementFile in the drop-down as shown in Figure 9-38 and click OK.

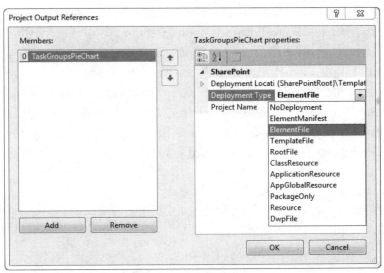

Figure 9-38: Select ElementFile as deployment type

Visual Studio updates the Elements.xml file. We need to make some additional manual updates to the Elements.xml file, which are described below. Listing 9-13 shows the updated Elements.xml file.

Listing 9-13: Elements.XML File for the Module Deploying the .XAP File

```
<?xml version="1.0" encoding="utf-8"?>
<Elements xmlns="http://schemas.microsoft.com/sharepoint/">
   <Module Name="PieChartModule" Url="SLApps">
     <File Path="PieChartModule\TaskGroupsPieChart.xap"
       Url="TaskGroupsPieChart.xap"
       Type="GhostableInLibrary" />
   </Module>
</Elements>
```

The additional updates we made to Elements.XML are as follows. First, we added the Url attribute to the Module element. This tells SharePoint to which document library the .XAP should be added and here we specify the document library we just created for storing .XAP files. Second, we removed "PieChartModule/" from the Url property in the File element because we don't need the full path and we can instead specify just the name of the .XAP file. Third, we added the Type attribute and set its value to GhostableIn-Library, which tells SharePoint to create a list item for the .XAP file.

Our project is now ready to be deployed. Let's test and debug it. Before we can debug a Silverlight project we need to enable Silverlight debugging. Right click the project SLSummaryTaskWebPart and select Properties. In the Properties page of Visual Studio select the SharePoint tab. In the Edit Configurations area check Enable Silverlight debugging (instead of Script debugging) as shown in Figure 9-39.

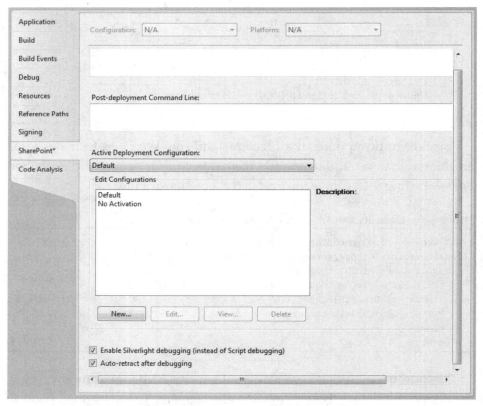

Figure 9-39: Enabling Silverlight debugging in a SharePoint project

Set a breakpoint in the ClientRequestSucceeded event handler of the MainPage class in the TaskGroupsPieChart and hit F5. Once the browser comes up we can navigate to the SLApps document library to verify that the .XAP file was deployed correctly.

Now we need to create the Silverlight web part and point it to the .XAP file. Remember we didn't have to create a custom web part because Share-Point includes a generic Silverlight web part that can be pointed at any .XAP file. Create or use the test web part page we created earlier in this chapter and switch to editing mode. In the Insert Web Part section select Media and Content as the category and SilverlightWebPart as the web part. If you click the Add button a new dialog appears asking for the URL to the .XAP file. Enter "/SLApps/TaskGroupsPieChart.xap" and click the OK button. Figure 9-40 shows the dialog for entering the URL to the .XAP file.

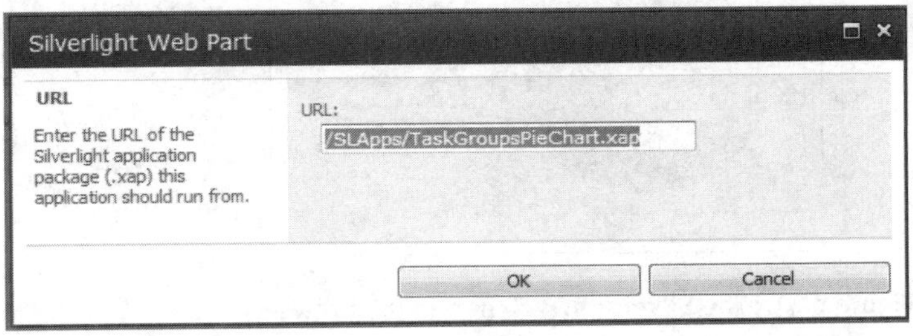

Silverlight Web Part

URL

Enter the URL of the Silverlight application package (.xap) this application should run from.

URL:

/SLApps/TaskGroupsPieChart.xap

OK Cancel

Figure 9-40: Specifying the URL to the TaskGroupsPieChart.xap file

Once the web part is added, the breakpoint is hit and we can keep debugging our code. Figure 9-41 shows the final web part in the browser.

You can clear the breakpoint or stop debugging and refresh the page to see the entire Silverlight animation of the pie chart. Unlike web part and visual web part projects, we don't need to deploy the solution again after debugging because the .XAP file is not retracted when we stop debugging.

Well, that was easy, wasn't it? But you may have wondered about having to tell your users to insert a generic SilverlightWebPart and then telling them to set the .XAP file to the URL of the .XAP file. There is another way to create Silverlight web parts, which is to create a custom web part to host the .XAP file and not use the generic out-of-the-box SharePoint Silverlight web part. This approach provides a slight advantage because we can write the code to automatically pick the desired .XAP file and to size the web part as desired.

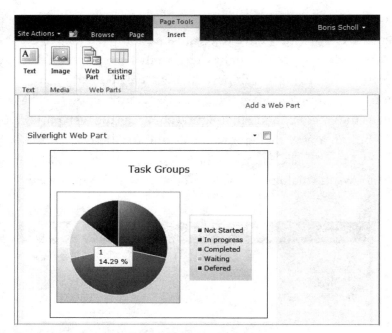

Figure 9-41: The Silverlight web part in the browser

Luckily we don't need to write a bunch of custom code to create such a Silverlight web part because Microsoft has released project extensions that ship with a web part template for this approach. The extension including documentation can be downloaded from the MSDN Code Gallery at http:// code.msdn.microsoft.com/vsixforsp.

Silverlight web parts provide a richer user interface for the end user and they can really light up the end user experience. They can be deployed as sandboxed solutions, either using a custom web part or using the out-of-the-box SharePoint Silverlight web part. This has served as an introduction to this approach, but for really interesting Silverlight web parts, you're going to have to learn more about Silverlight, which is beyond the scope of this book. For more information about Silverlight see www.silverlight.net.

Web Part Connections

In Chapter 6, "Working with Business Data," we saw a good example of what connected web parts are. The business data list web part and the business data related list web part in SharePoint Server are connected web parts. Let's say we want a web part showing a list of customers in the business data list web part and we want to see the orders for the customer selected in the business data list web part. We can use the business data related list web part to see all the orders for the customer selected in the business data list web part. As you might guess, these two web parts must talk to each other to make this happen and they do so via a web part connection.

In this section we will look at how to create your own connected web parts. There are two types of connections that web parts can use: static and dynamic. Static connections are only used for web parts pairs in which one web part does not reside in a web part zone. This would require writing a non-ASP.NET web part that derives from the Microsoft.SharePoint.Web-PartPages.WebPart class, which is beyond the scope of this book. Dynamic connections can be created using ASP.NET web parts, so we will consider how to create such a connection.

In a connected pair of web parts one web part is the provider and the other one is the consumer. You can also think of this as a master/detail relationship. To enable a dynamic connection between two web parts the web parts need to have a common interface to talk through and the connection itself needs to have the ConnectionProvider and Connection-Consumer attribute assigned to it.

It is easier to understand the concept by looking at the code. We will get right into building a simple example. In our example the provider web part has a drop-down list of names and the consumer web part will display the name selected in the drop-down box plus a string. So if you select Boris from the drop-down list in the provider web part, the consumer web part will show "Boris recommends the book *SharePoint 2010 Development with Visual Studio 2010* (.NET Development Series)." It's a simple example but it will teach us the concepts very well.

Open Visual Studio and create a new Empty SharePoint project, name the project ConnectedWebParts. In the SharePoint Customization Wizard select "Deploy as Farm Solution" and click the Finish button. We need to deploy the solution as a farm solution because SharePoint does not allow web part connections to be used in sandboxed solutions.

First we need to implement an interface. Right click the project Connected-WebParts and select Add then New Item. In the Add New Item dialog select Code under installed templates. In the main area select Interface and name it "IAuthorProvider." In our IAuthorProvider interface, we will provide a simple read-only property called AuthorName of type string. Listing 9-14 shows the IAuthorProvider interface.

Listing 9-14: IAuthorProvider Interface

```
interface IAuthorProvider
{
  string AuthorName { get; }
}
```

We will use this interface in both the provider and the consumer web parts. Let's create the provider web part first by right clicking the project ConnectedWebParts and selecting Add then New Item.... Choose Web Part template under SharePoint 2010 and name the web part Author-ProviderWebPart.

Once Visual Studio has added the web part project item we can implement the code for our provider web part. Listing 9-15 shows the code for the AuthorProviderWebPart class.

Listing 9-15: Implementation of the AuthorProviderWebPart

```
public class AuthorProviderWebPart : WebPart,  ConnectedWebParts.IAuthorProvider
{
  DropDownList cboAuthors = null;
  protected override void CreateChildControls()
  {
    cboAuthors = new DropDownList();
    cboAuthors.Items.Add(new ListItem("Boris"));
    cboAuthors.Items.Add(new ListItem("Eric"));
    cboAuthors.Items.Add(new ListItem("Peter"));
    cboAuthors.AutoPostBack = true;
    this.Controls.Add(cboAuthors);
  }

  public string AuthorName
  {
    get { return cboAuthors.SelectedValue; }
  }
```

```
[ConnectionProvider("Author Name", AllowsMultipleConnections = true)]
public IAuthorProvider GetAuthorProvider()
{
  return this;
}
}
```

In the AuthorProviderWebPart class we create a new drop-down list object that we instantiate and add values to in the CreateChildControls method. Finally we set the AutoPostBack property to true to force a page refresh when the user selects a new item from the drop-down list. Finally we add the drop-down list object to the Controls collection.

Next we implement the AuthorName read only property of the IAuthorInterface in our web part class—we just return the text of the currently selected item in the drop-down list.

The last step is to create the provider connection point. Remember we want to provide the consumer web part with an author name. To create a provider connection point we create a method that returns the IAuthorProvider interface implemented by our web part. To tell SharePoint this is a connection point, we add the ConnectionProvider Attribute to the public method. The first parameter sets the display name of the connection and is exposed in the connection UI in the web part menu. The second parameter, AllowMultipleConnections, indicates whether our provider web part can connect to multiple consumers at the same time. We set the value to true, so our provider web part can connect to more than one consumer web part.

This is all we need to do for the provider web part. When the web part is executed SharePoint detects that this web part is participating in a connection as a provider and enables the UI to connect it to the consumer web part.

To create a consumer web part right click the project ConnectedWebParts and select Add then New Item…. Choose Web Part template under SharePoint 2010 and name the web part "AuthorConsumerWebPart." Once Visual Studio has added the web part project item we can implement the code for our consumer web part. Listing 9-16 shows the code for the AuthorConsumerWebPart.

Listing 9-16: Implementation of the AuthorConsumerWebPart

```
public class AuthorConsumerWebPart : WebPart
{
  string authorName = string.Empty;
  ConnectedWebParts.IAuthorProvider AuthorProvider = null;
  Label lblResult = null;
  protected override void CreateChildControls()
  {
    lblResult = new Label();
    lblResult.Text = "No Author selected";
    this.Controls.Add(lblResult);
  }

  protected override void OnPreRender(EventArgs e)
  {
    if (this.AuthorProvider != null)
      this.authorName = this.AuthorProvider.AuthorName;
  }

  protected override void RenderContents(HtmlTextWriter writer)
  {
    if (this.authorName != String.Empty)
    {
      lblResult.Text = this.authorName +
        " recommends the book SharePoint 2010 Development" +
        " with Visual Studio 2010" +
        " (Microsoft .NET Development Series)";
    }
    base.RenderContents(writer);
  }

  [ConnectionConsumer("Author Name")]
  public void GetProviderInterface
    (ConnectedWebParts.IAuthorProvider authorprovider)
  {
    this.AuthorProvider = authorprovider;
  }
}
```

In the AuthorConsumerWebPart class we create a new string called authorName and initialize it to an empty string. Whatever author's name is selected in the drop-down box of the AuthorProviderWebPart will be stored in the authorName field.

We also need to create an object to store the instance of the IAuthor-Provider interface provided to the control by the AuthorProviderWebPart and a label to display the selected author's name and our appended string containing a shameless plug for this book.

In the CreateChildControls method we instantiate the label and set the text to "No Author selected." There are two reasons why we do this. First of all, the web part might not be connected at all and thus we won't have an author's name to display. Secondly and more importantly the Create-ChildControls method is executed very early in a web part page life cycle and is executed before a connection is established, so we cannot use this method to assign the correct value to the label even if there was a connection established.

To retrieve the value after a connection has been established we need to override the OnPreRender method, which is executed after the Create-ChildControls method. The OnPreRender method retrieves the name of the author selected via the AuthorName property of the IAuthorName interface and assigns it to the authorName field. Remember we set the value of that property in the provider web part.

In the web part life cycle the method RenderContents is executed after the method OnPreRender so it is safe for us to set the new value of the label lblResult in that method.

The last method of the code shown in Listing 9-16 is the method that gets the instance of the IAuthorName interface from the AuthorProvider-WebPart. It is this method that allows the AuthorConsumerWebPart to participate in the connection as the consumer.

The method GetProviderInterface accepts an object of type IAuthor-Provider and assigns it to the IAuthorProvider object AuthorProvider. Finally we need to assign the ConnectionConsumer attribute to the method, so that the SharePoint runtime can detect the role of this web part in the connection.

Debugging connected web parts is the same as debugging any other web part so we will skip that step and deploy the web parts right away. Right click the project ConnectedWebParts and select Deploy. Once Visual Studio says deployment has succeeded, open a web part page in the browser and add the web parts AuthorProviderWebPart and AuthorConsumerWebPart. Figure 9-42 shows both web parts on the page.

As expected the provider web part AuthorProviderWebPart shows Boris in the drop-down box and the consumer web part AuthorConsumerWebPart

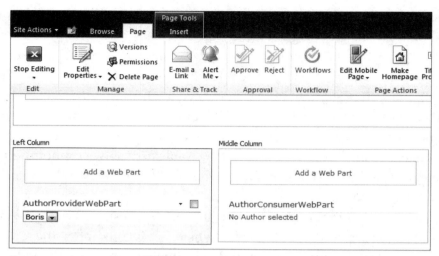

Figure 9-42: The connected web parts on the web part page

part shows No author is displayed on the label because the web parts are not yet connected. To connect both web parts click on the web part menu that drops down from the upper right corner of a web part when you hover over it. Select Connections in the drop-down menu as shown in Figure 9-43.

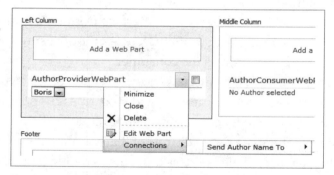

Figure 9-43: Connections item in the web part menu

The menu item expands and says Send Author Name to. The text "Author Name" comes from the first parameter we passed to the Connection-Provider attribute in the AuthorProviderWebPart's GetAuthorProvider method. If you click on this menu, it will show the web part Author-ConsumerWebPart as an available consumer. Click the AuthorConsumer-

WebPart menu web part. SharePoint establishes the connection between our producer and consumer web part. The consumer web part now displays the correct label as shown in Figure 9-44.

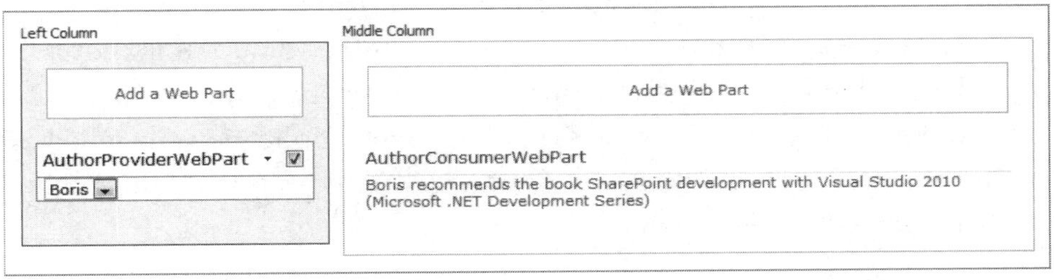

Left Column

Add a Web Part

AuthorProviderWebPart

Boris

Middle Column

Add a Web Part

AuthorConsumerWebPart

Boris recommends the book SharePoint development with Visual Studio 2010 (Microsoft .NET Development Series)

Figure 9-44: Connected web parts

The web parts are now connected and when you choose another author from the drop-down list it will update the consumer web part.

We have learned what connected web parts are and how to implement them. To summarize, connected web parts are a great way to display master/ detail information if this is required, all you need to do is to implement a common interface and use the ConnectionProvider and Connection-Consumer attribute. When you develop connected web parts keep in mind that connections are not enabled in sandboxed environments.

Configuration of Web Parts

Connection Strings

Over the last couple of pages we looked into how to create different kinds of web parts but all of our samples were either displaying values from SharePoint objects, such as lists or from the code itself.

You will probably run into situations in which you need to display data from databases or REST and SOAP services. Accessing data from such data sources requires either connection strings or at least the URL of the endpoints of the services to be stored somewhere, so you might wonder, where can I store this information?

The first decision to make is whether we are developing a sandboxed solution or not. Let's look at the farm solution first. As you might have surmised by now, farm solutions have access to the file system. How else can they get to the ASCX file installed to the SharePoint hive? Because every site collection is hosted in a web application and every web application has a web.config file, the web.config file associated with your farm solution is one place you can store connection strings or other data.

Let's take a look at the web.config file. Open the Windows Explorer on your development machine and browse to the folder C:\inetpub\wwwroot\. This folder contains the directories of all the web applications installed on the machine. If you open the folder wwwroot you can find a folder called WSS. Figure 9-45 shows the WSS folder.

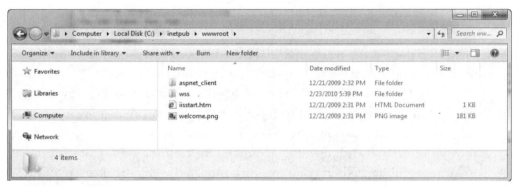

Figure 9-45: WSS folder in the wwwroot folder

If you open the WSS folder you get to a new folder called Virtual-Directories. This folder contains all the web applications in your farm. If you haven't created a new web application you should see two folders, one named 80 and one with a different number. The folder 80 is the one we are after because it represents the web application we are using in our test environment. The other folder represents the SharePoint Central Administration site. Note: If you have created additional web applications to host other site collections, you need to open the folder with the name matching the port number of your web application.

If you open the 80 folder you can find the web.config file. To add a connection string to the web.config file you can simply add a connectionStrings section between the closing element </SharePoint> and the opening element <system.web> in the web.config. Listing 9-17 shows a sample connection-Strings section. The name of the connection string is MyConnectionString and the connectionString attribute stores the actual connection string.

Listing 9-17: connectionStrings Section

```
</SharePoint>
  <connectionStrings>
  <add name="MyConnectionString" connectionString="Data
    Source=serverName;Initial
    Catalog=DemoDB;Persist
    Security Info=True;User ID=userName;Password=password;"/>
  </connectionStrings >
<system.web>
```

For the purpose of readability you can see the password for the connection string in Listing 9-17, but in production environments you should always encrypt passwords before storing them in the web.config file. For more information about how to encrypt a password in a file, see http://msdn.microsoft.com/en-us/library/ms178372.aspx.

You can read the connection string during runtime in your web part by using the WebConfigurationManager object available in the System.Web .Configuration namespace and use its ConnectionStrings collection to access the element containing the connection string. All you need to do is reference System.Configuration to your code and add a using directive for it. The following line shows you how to access the connection string in code.

```
string connectionString = WebConfigurationManager.
  ConnectionStrings["MyConnectionString"].ConnectionString;
```

The only problem with our approach so far is that you need to manually add the connection string element to the connectionStrings section in the web.config. This also needs to be done in the web.config files of the target web applications on the destination servers.

Another approach for adding connection strings to the connection-Strings section of the web.config file is to use the SPWebConfigModification class in a feature event receiver to make changes to the SharePoint web.config file automatically. Using a feature event receiver has the advantage that the connection strings will be automatically added to the web.config files at the destination servers when the feature is activated and also can be removed when the feature is deactivated (for more information on feature event receivers see Chapter 5, "SharePoint Event Receivers"). Listing 9-18 shows the code that adds a connection string to the connectionStrings section in the web.config in a FeatureActivated event handler.

Listing 9-18: Code for Adding a Connection String to the connectionStrings Section in the web.config

```
public override void FeatureActivated(
  SPFeatureReceiverProperties properties)
{
  SPWebService myService = SPWebService.ContentService;
  SPWebConfigModification myModification =
    new SPWebConfigModification();
  myModification.Path = "configuration/connectionStrings";
  myModification.Name = "add[@name='MyConnectionString']" +
    "[@connectionString='DataSource=serverName;" +
    "Initial Catalog=DemoDB;" +
    "Persist Security Info=True;" +
    "User ID=userName;Password=password;']";
  myModification.Sequence = 0;
  myModification.Owner = "UniqueOwner";
  myModification.Type = SPWebConfigModification.
    SPWebConfigModificationType.EnsureChildNode;
  myModification.Value = "<add name='MyConnectionString'" +
    "connectionString='DataSource=serverName;" +
    "Initial Catalog=DemoDB;" +
    "Persist Security Info=True;" +
    "User ID=userName;Password=password;'/>";
  myService.WebConfigModifications.Add(myModification);
  myService.Update();
  myService.ApplyWebConfigModifications();
}
```

In order to access the web.config and make updates we need to get the current web application first. We want the modifications to apply to all web applications in a farm so we create an object of SPWebService rather than accessing the farm instance through SPWebApplication. SPWebService serves as a container for all the web applications in a SharePoint farm. After that we create the SPWebConfigModification object. The Path property sets an XPath expression that is used to locate the node that is being modified or created, which is in our case the connectionStrings section node. The Name property sets the name of the attribute or section node to be modified or created, which is the attributes name in our case and connectionString. The Sequence property is set to 0 because we only have one notification. If we had more we would need to increment the sequence number. The Owner property needs a unique string, which we set in our sample to UniqueOwner.

The modification type is set to EnsureChildNode, which basically makes sure that there is a child node. Other values for the modification type are EnsureSection and EnsureAttribute. When creating a new section you should use the EnsureChildNode modification type value instead of EnsureSection. EnsureChildNode will allow us to remove the section programmatically if needed. The Value property contains the actual value of our connection string. Next we must add the modification object to the WebConfigModifications collection of the service object and call the Update method on the service object. The Update method causes this web service to save its state and to propagate changes to all the machines in the farm. Finally we call the ApplyWebConfigModifications method on the service object, which applies the list of web.config modifications to all web applications in this web service across the farm.

Can We Use the Same Techniques for Sandboxed Solutions?

No we can't, as we already know, sandboxed solutions do not have access to the web.config files. To be honest there is not even a need to store connection information in sandboxed solutions. You can't reference a web service or access a database in a sandboxed solution.

Code Access Security (CAS)

Code Access Security provides a security model that restricts operations that can be performed or resources that can be accessed by code. In the case of web parts it restricts or allows operations performed by the web part assembly.

If you are not familiar with Code Access Security principles you should read the code access security introduction on the MSDN Visual Studio library http://msdn.microsoft.com/en-us/library/930b76w0.aspx.

Now you might wonder why we need code access security at all. If we want to limit the web part assembly access to the resources or restrict its operations you could just create a sandboxed web part.

While this is generally true, you might want to grant more rights to your web part than a sandboxed solution allows. Remember sandboxed solutions are very limited, they don't allow database access, they don't allow web services or data services calls, and they don't allow access to all the objects in the SharePoint object model. All you can do is work with objects within the site collection to which the sandboxed solution is deployed.

Perhaps then you might say, "Why bother with Code Access Security— I'll just develop my web part as a farm solution." While this would work you should keep in mind that the web part assembly gets deployed to the GAC, which means it runs in full trust. Full trust is against the policy of many companies, especially large enterprises. Also, it is generally good design principle to only give your code the trust and access necessary to make it difficult to use a bug to gain full trust access to the machine on which it is running. So what can we do? We can use code access security to strike a middle ground between full trust farm solutions and very low trust sandboxed solutions.

Let's start with a simple sample by creating a new Empty SharePoint project in Visual Studio and naming it "CASWebPart." In the SharePoint Customization Wizard select Deploy as farm solution. Once the project is created add a new code-only web part item (not a visual web part) and name it "CASWebPart." Let's add some code to the CASWebPart.cs file. The code reads the current logged on user of the SharePoint site and writes the information to a label. Listing 9-19 shows the code.

Listing 9-19: Code for CASWebPart

```
public class CASWebPart : WebPart
{
  protected override void CreateChildControls()
  {
    Label lblName = new Label();
    SPUser user = SPContext.Current.Web.CurrentUser;
```

```
        lblName.Text = "Hello " + user.LoginName;
        this.Controls.Add(lblName);
    }
}
```

The way the project is created it will by default deploy the web part assembly to the GAC. But we want to change this to make it deploy to the web application bin directory and thereby require less trust. Let's test what happens if we change the Assembly Deployment Target property of the project to WebApplication as shown in Figure 9-46.

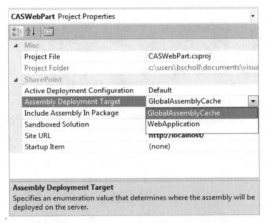

Figure 9-46: Change deployment location for the project

After changing the Assembly Deployment Target property to Web-Application, deploy the web part again and see what happens. We end up getting a security exception. In our case this is caused by us trying to access the SharePoint object model in our code from an assembly that no longer has full trust since it has been moved from the GAC to the web application bin directory. Figure 9-47 shows the exception.

The assembly no longer has full trust because it is deployed to the web application rather than to the GAC. What does it mean to be "deployed to the web application"? If we browse to the root folder of the web application and open the bin folder (C:\inetpub\wwwroot\wss\VirtualDirectories\80\bin) we will find the web part assembly there. So apparently assemblies in that location are not allowed to access the SharePoint object model.

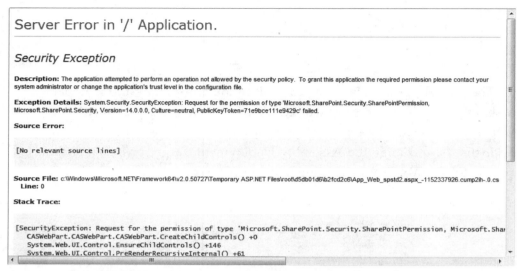

Figure 9-47: Security exception when deploying the web part to a web application

How can we fix this? There are two options. The first one is to increase the overall trust level of the server farm in the web.config file. Because this is a high security risk it is not a recommended approach. The second one is to create a custom trust level for your web part.

You Lost Me. What Is a Trust Level?

The default settings in the web.config of a SharePoint web application give minimal trust to any web part assemblies not running from the GAC. The custom trust levels that SharePoint defines and runs under are wss_minimaltrust and wss_mediumtrust. The definitions of those levels are stored in files that can be found under {SharePointRoot}\Config. SharePoint can also have additional custom trust levels that would be stored in a wss_custom file. To find more information on how to create custom trust policies see http://msdn.microsoft.com/en-us/library/ff649312.aspx.

SharePoint allows us to add a custom code access security policy directly to the solution manifest. In Visual Studio, open the Package designer by double clicking the Package.package item. In the designer click the Manifest tab and expand the Edit options. (See Chapter 11, "Packaging and Deployment," for more information on the Package designer.) Figure 9-48 shows the Package designer with the Manifest tab selected.

We can now paste additional custom elements in the textbox at the bottom of the Package designer's Manifest tab and Visual Studio will merge our items with the ones already created for the feature.xml file. Listing 9-20 shows the XML we need to paste between the <Solution> element tags in the Package designer.

Listing 9-20: Code for CASWebPart

```
<CodeAccessSecurity>
  <PolicyItem>
    <PermissionSet class="NamedPermissionSet"
      version="1" Description="Permission set for CASWebPart">
      <IPermission class="AspNetHostingPermission"
        version="1"
        Level="Minimal" />
      <IPermission class="SecurityPermission"
        version="1"
        Flags="Execution,ControlPrincipal,
          ControlAppDomain,ControlDomainPolicy,
          ControlEvidence,ControlThread" />
      <IPermission class="Microsoft.SharePoint
        .Security.SharePointPermission,
        Microsoft.SharePoint.Security,
        Version=14.0.0.0,
        Culture=neutral,
        PublicKeyToken=71e9bce111e9429c"
        version="1"
        ObjectModel="True" />
      <IPermission class="System.Security.Permissions
        .EnvironmentPermission,
        mscorlib, Version=2.0.0.0,
        Culture=neutral,
        PublicKeyToken=b77a5c561934e089"
        version="1" Read="UserName" />
    </PermissionSet>
    <Assemblies>
      <Assembly Name="CASWebPart"  />
    </Assemblies>
  </PolicyItem>
</CodeAccessSecurity>
```

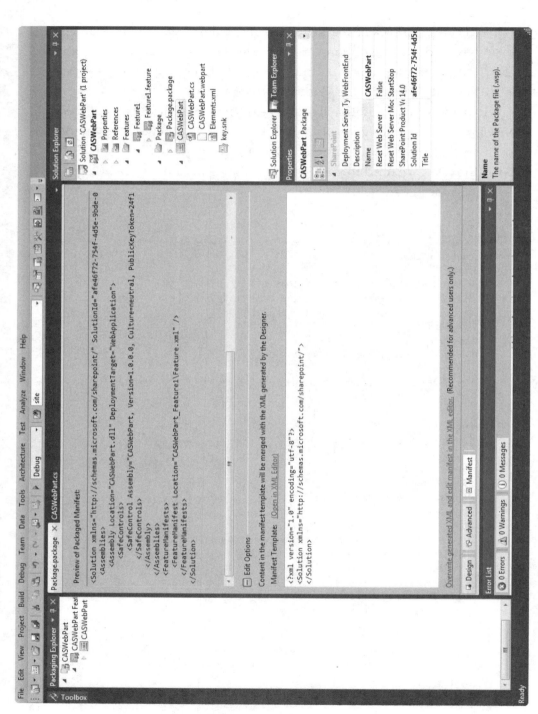

Figure 9-48: Package designer in the CASWebPart project

Listing 9-20 creates a named permission set for our CAS web part. The permissions we provide are common permissions for SharePoint applications:

- **AspNetHostingPermissions**—permission to access ASP.NET controls
- **SecurityPermissions**—defines permissions, such as ControlThread, Assertion, etc.
- **SharePointSecurityPermission**—defines permissions to access the object model and impersonation. In our sample we didn't set the impersonation property.
- **SystemSecurityPermission**—permissions to access the environment

In addition to these custom permissions, note that we have added an Assemblies element and a single Assembly element whose Name attribute is set to the name of our web part, CASWebPart. This will tell SharePoint to apply the permissions we have specified to our web part.

Code access security is a huge area and we certainly can't cover every security setting in this chapter. For more information on securing web parts using CAS policies check out the MSDN article at http://msdn .microsoft.com/en-us/library/cc768613.aspx.

We can see that Visual Studio has successfully merged our elements by looking at the Preview Package Manifest section and deploying the web part to see if it works. Right click the project CASWebPart and select the Deploy command. After the deployment test the web part. It will now run successfully from the web application's bin directory.

Bug Alert!

There is a bug in the first release of Visual Studio 2010 that prevents users from deploying SharePoint artifacts, such as web parts with CAS policies added to the solution manifest. To work around that issue you need to create a custom targets file to insert a custom target post-package that opens the package manifest, removes the class attribute from each PermissionSet element, and saves the modified manifest. The workaround is described in the knowledge base article 2022463 and can be found at http://support .microsoft.com/default. aspx?scid=kb;en-US;2022463.

Conclusion

In this chapter we looked at several different types of web parts: visual web parts, code-only web parts, and Silverlight web parts. We have seen how to use Visual Studio to build and customize these web parts. Finally, we looked at some more advanced web part topics, such as web part connections and creating custom CAS permissions to allow a farm web part to be deployed to the web application bin directory rather than the GAC.

As mentioned in the beginning of this chapter, creating web parts is one of the most useful developer scenarios in a SharePoint environment. Web parts are also the perfect starting point for ASP.NET developers to get started with SharePoint development because the web part concepts in ASP.NET and SharePoint are the same.

10

SharePoint Pages

Introduction to SharePoint Pages

SharePoint is built on top of ASP.NET and thus the SharePoint user interface consists entirely of ASP.NET pages. This makes it fairly simple for a developer with ASP.NET experience to customize and develop SharePoint pages. Although SharePoint provides great out-of-the-box capabilities to change the look and feel of the SharePoint user interface, there are certain requirements that cannot be met with the out-of-the-box customization capabilities that can only be met by customizing ASP.NET pages. For example, suppose your customer doesn't like the default navigation structure of a SharePoint site, your customer needs a customized web part page that is different from the in-box templates, or your customer wants to integrate an existing ASP.NET application into a SharePoint site. These are all scenarios that require custom ASP.NET development and this is exactly what this chapter is about—customizing and developing SharePoint pages in ASP.NET.

SharePoint Architecture

Before we learn how to customize and create SharePoint pages we will take another look at the SharePoint architecture. So far we have learned that SharePoint uses web applications to host site collections, but what is a web application? A web application in SharePoint is an IIS web application that has its own application pool. An application pool is a worker process (a process started up by IIS) that runs to receive requests from IIS and process responses—SharePoint runs in this process to return web pages when a request to IIS is made.

During installation SharePoint creates two IIS web applications. The first one hosts the default site collection and the second one hosts the SharePoint Central Administration web site. Because two web applications cannot share the same port, the SharePoint Central Administration web site is usually accessible through the URL http://yourserverurl:portnumber and the web application hosting the default site collection is available through the default port and so can be accessed using the URL http://yourserverurl. The port number for the SharePoint Central Administration web site depends on the available ports on the machine. If you want to create additional site collections you always need to tell SharePoint which existing web application will host the new site collection (since a web application can host multiple site collections), or you need to create a new web application to host the site collection.

Now you might wonder why you might want to create more than one web application rather than just have one web application host all the site collections you might create. One key reason to create a new web application is to isolate content. Every time a new web application is created, SharePoint creates a new content database. All the data in the sites associated with the web application is stored in this content database. If site collections grow really fast and the content database approaches the size limit, administrators can move one site collection to a new content database while continuing to use the same web application. This is called splitting the content database.

A second key reason to create a new web application has to do with security. All the execution of all the site collections associated with a web application occurs in the application pool. If you want to ensure that certain code from one site collection is never allowed to run in the same process as the code from another site collection, you can use a different web application to host the second site collection. This ensures that different application pools are used for the two site collections.

A site collection, as the name suggests, is a collection of SharePoint sites and pages. For each site collection you can allow an entirely different group of people to be administrators, you can have separate, unique users, groups, and permissions, you can back up that site collection, and you can associate with it unique workflows, site templates, list templates, content types, and site columns. Think about a company that needs SharePoint sites that has an Engineering department and a Marketing department. Not only will the content for each department be different but it's very likely that the users for the engineering sites will be different from the users for the marketing sites. For this case you would create one site collection for Engineering and second one for Marketing. By using different site collections you can prevent Marketing from looking at information used internally by Engineering by limiting or disallowing access to the Engineering sites.

A site collection is represented by the SPSite object in the server side object model or the Site object in the client side object model. As mentioned before a site collection contains sites and pages.

So what is the difference between a site collection and a site? A site collection and a site seem similar from an end user's perspective since a site collection always has a default site associated with it. Subsites that are created within the site collection inherit the permissions and navigation structure from the parent site. Sometimes you might wonder when to create a new subsite and when to create a new site collection. There is a lot of discussion about when to use what. If you want more information on that topic you can read the following article on MSDN: http://technet.microsoft.com/en-us/library/cc742548.aspx.

A SharePoint site is represented by the SPWeb object in the server side object model and the Web object in the client side object model. Figure 10-1 shows a site architecture with two site collections in one web application. Both site collections have a single default site created. Of course, a site collection can contain multiple sites beyond the default site—this happens when you create additional subsites.

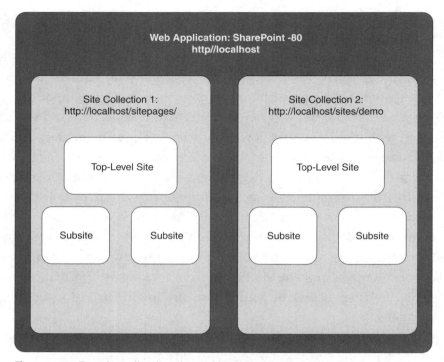

Figure 10-1: Two site collections hosted by a single web application

The last objects to discuss in the SharePoint architecture are pages associated with a site collection or site. There are three types of pages in a SharePoint environment that are interesting to developers: master pages, site pages, and application pages.

Master Pages are pages in SharePoint that define the look and feel of multiple pages in SharePoint. For example master pages define the ribbon, the AJAX script manager object, and the site navigation. Every page that uses the same master page has the same layout. Pages that use a master page are called content pages. Each content page benefits from the shared look and feel provided by the master page. A developer can extend the master page by using replaceable placeholders to add unique content. Figure 10-2 shows the relationship between master pages and content pages. On the left is a single master page called V4.master that provides common functionality to both the Home.aspx page and the Mywebpartpage.aspx.

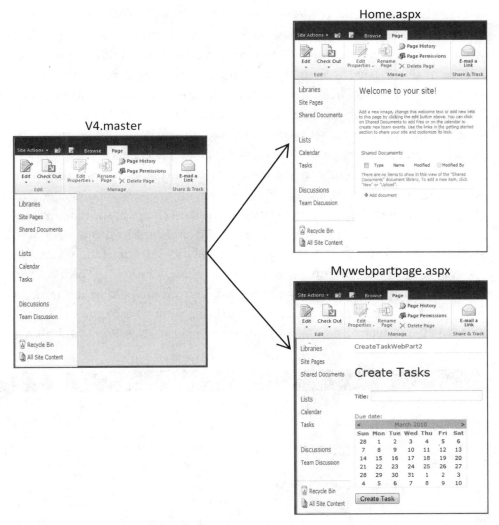

Figure 10-2: Two different content pages that share the same master page

SharePoint is built on ASP.NET, therefore master pages are implemented as ASP.NET master pages. Master pages in SharePoint have the file extension .master.

The second page type of interest is the site page. These are pages that support user customization through the SharePoint user interface and tools such as SharePoint Designer. It's important to understand that SharePoint stores customized site pages in the content database. This applies to all pages created and customized using SharePoint Designer. Now why might that be important? Think about a large SharePoint farm with thousands of pages. If every page was customized then all the pages requested would need to be retrieved from the content database and loaded into memory. This has an impact on performance and scalability. Nonetheless customization of site pages provides great options to the user and administrator. A good example of a site page is the top-level page home.aspx.

Finally there are application pages. As with site pages, you can use application pages to surface functionality and content to the SharePoint user. The biggest difference between application pages and site pages is that application pages don't support customization and are deployed once per web server to the file system (not to the content database). All application pages are stored in the SharePoint hive at the location {SharePointRoot}\TEMPLATE\ LAYOUTS. Application pages are accessible from any site in the farm. A very good example of an application page is the Settings.aspx page shown in Figure 10-3, which is accessible from every site in SharePoint and allows

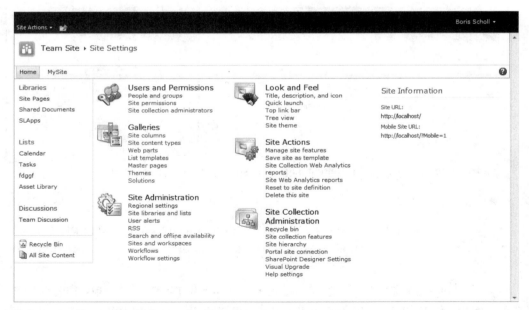

Figure 10-3: An application page: Settings.aspx

users with advanced permission, such as site collection administrators, to make changes to SharePoint objects.

With this introduction to SharePoint architecture and the types of SharePoint pages a developer can create, we are ready to consider the customization and creation of SharePoint pages in the next section.

Customizing and Developing SharePoint Pages

This book is about SharePoint development in Visual Studio 2010 and we will mainly focus on how to create application pages in this chapter. This is the only page type for which Visual Studio provides an out-of-the-box template. However, we will first take a brief look at master pages and site pages to get you started with creating those page types.

Customizing and Creating Master Pages

Master pages are used to define a common look and feel for a SharePoint page. SharePoint uses the file v4.master as the primary master page for its content and application pages. To have a look at the v4.master master page we can use SharePoint Designer.

Open SharePoint Designer and connect to your SharePoint site. Under Site Objects click on Master Pages as shown in Figure 10-4.

There are three master pages listed. You can also see all the master pages available in SharePoint by going directly to the SharePoint Master Page Gallery, which is accessible by entering http://localhost/_catalogs/masterpage/Forms/AllItems.aspx in the browser. The default.master file is used mainly for backward compatibility with previous versions of SharePoint. SharePoint 2010 has a compatibility mode that was added to give SharePoint users time to adapt to the new SharePoint user interface during a migration process. The minimal.master is a master page with the minimal requirements for a SharePoint master page.

v4.master is the primary master page for SharePoint and is the one we will take a look at. Double click on v4.master to open the view and manage settings page for the master page file as shown in Figure 10-5.

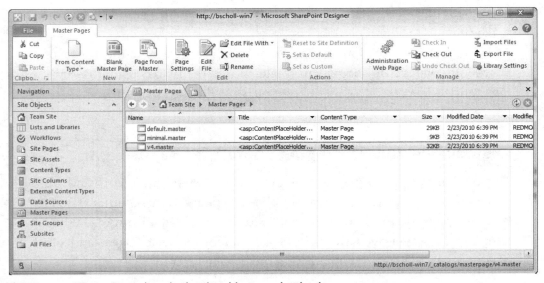

Figure 10-4: Master Pages item in the site objects navigation bar

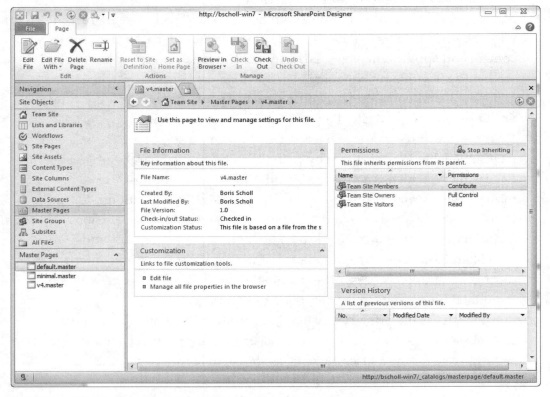

Figure 10-5: View and manage settings page for v4.master master page

Click on the Edit file link in the Customization area of the view and manage settings page. SharePoint Designer opens the master page in the page editor. The page editor is based on the visual web designer in Visual Studio and thus you can switch between design view, split view, and code view. Figure 10-6 shows the design view.

Let's make a simple customization to the v4.master master page. It is a good practice to not edit the v4.master master page file directly until you have tested changes in a separate master page file. We will do that by creating a new master page using SharePoint Designer.

Click on the Master Pages item in the left navigation bar to get to the view that lists all the master pages. This shows the Master Pages ribbon tab that contains a Blank Master Page button in the ribbon. Figure 10-7 shows the Blank Master Page button.

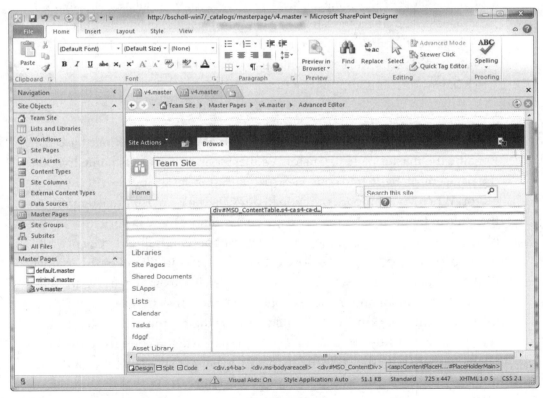

Figure 10-6: The v4.master master page in the SharePoint Designer page editor

Figure 10-7: The Blank Master Page button

It Is Usually a Good Idea to Create a Copy of V4.Master Rather Than Modifying V4.Master Directly

You should usually create a copy of the v4.master file rather than edit it directly to ensure you don't break the SharePoint site since so many pages use the v4.master file. Then when you are sure your changes work, you can apply them to the v4.master file. In case you make changes directly to v4.master and break the site, you can always reset v4.master to the original site definition. You can find more information on that topic here: http://office.microsoft.com/search/redir.aspx?AssetID=HA101741451033&CTT=5&Origin=HA101009061033.

Click the Blank Master Page button to create a new blank master page. Rename the master page to CustomV4.master and click on its name to open the page editor. Switch to code view using the tabs at the bottom of the page editor. When you compare the code in our CustomV4.master master page to the code in the v4.master master page you will note there is very little in the blank master page—even the SharePoint ribbon is missing. Let's copy the markup code from v4.master to CustomV4.master. In SharePoint Designer switch back to the v4.master file and select code view as shown in Figure 10-8.

Place the cursor somewhere in the code and press Ctrl+A then Ctrl+C to copy all the markup code. Switch back to the customV4.master editor, select all the markup code and use Ctrl+V to paste the code from the clipboard to overwrite the code in customV4.master. There is a lot of markup in there now, switch the editor to split view using the tabs at the bottom of

Figure 10-8: Code view of v4.master

the page editor. With the split view we can select the area we want to customize in the designer and easily locate the corresponding markup for it.

Click on the site image in the top left corner of the page editor. SharePoint Designer highlights the markup that defines the site image as shown in Figure 10-9.

Now we can change the site image for all of our sites by changing the value of the LogoImageUrl attribute in the selected markup with a URL to a new image. In this case we have manually copied an image called awsiteicon .png to the SharePoint hive in the folder {SharePointRoot}\templates\ images. In Chapter 11, "Packaging and Deployment," we will see how you could deploy such an image to the SharePoint hive as part of your packaging and deployment of your SharePoint solution using Visual Studio. After changing the value of the LogoImageUrl attribute, SharePoint Designer updates the design view of the master page with the new icon as shown in Figure 10-10.

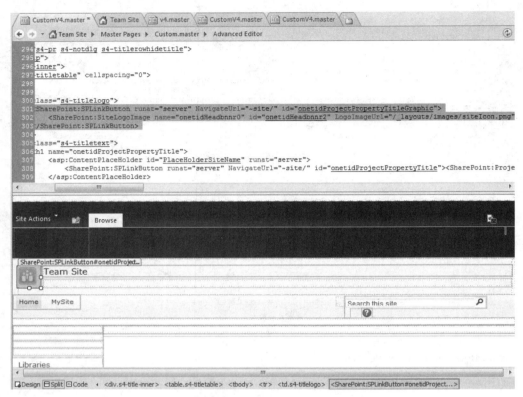

```
294 s4-pr s4-notdlg s4-titlerowhidetitle">
295 p">
296 inner">
297 titletable" cellspacing="0">
298
299
300 lass="s4-titlelogo">
301 SharePoint:SPLinkButton runat="server" NavigateUrl="~site/" id="onetidProjectPropertyTitleGraphic">
302     <SharePoint:SiteLogoImage name="onetidHeadbnnr0" id="onetidHeadbnnr2" LogoImageUrl="/_layouts/images/siteIcon.png"
303 /SharePoint:SPLinkButton>
304
305 lass="s4-titletext">
306 h1 name="onetidProjectPropertyTitle">
307     <asp:ContentPlaceHolder id="PlaceHolderSiteName" runat="server">
308         <SharePoint:SPLinkButton runat="server" NavigateUrl="~site/" id="onetidProjectPropertyTitle"><SharePoint:Proje
309     </asp:ContentPlaceHolder>
```

Figure 10-9: The site image selected in the split view of CustomV4.master

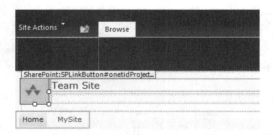

Figure 10-10: The new site icon for CustomV4.master

To make all the current and future SharePoint pages use our customized master page we need to make it the default master page. Click on Master Pages in the left navigation of SharePoint Designer to get to the master pages overview page. Right click on the CustomV4.master file and select Set as Default Master Page from the context menu as shown in Figure 10-11.

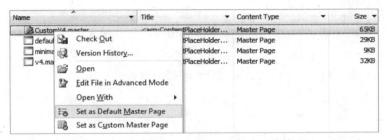

Figure 10-11: Setting customV4.master as the default master page in
SharePoint Designer

If we now go to the homepage for the SharePoint site we will see that the new master page is being used. If we create a new page it will also use our master page. Figure 10-12 shows the CustomV4.master master page in use on the home page of our site.

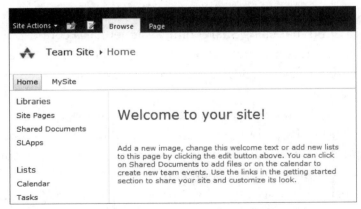

Figure 10-12: Home page using the CustomV4.master as master page

As we have seen it is really easy to use SharePoint Designer to customize master pages. Granted our last sample was simple but it showed how to get started with SharePoint Designer.

Additional Tips for Building a Master Page from Scratch

As we saw in this section, the easiest way is to copy the markup code from an existing master page, such as the v4.master master page and customize it to meet specific requirements. Also you can use start with one of the master page templates provided by the community, such as the SharePoint 2010 Starter Master pages on CodePlex http://startermasterpages .codeplex.com/ and customize it. These two approaches require just enough understanding of ASP.NET to be able to identify what markup code is responsible for which functionality.

SharePoint ships with a master page called minimal.master that provides minimal functionality that can be another good starting point if you want to create your own master page. MSDN has a great list of placeholders and controls used in the v4.master master page that you can use as reference material when creating a master page from scratch http://msdn .microsoft.com/en-us/library/ee539981(office.14).aspx.

Keep in mind that using SharePoint Designer has a couple of tradeoffs. First of all, the customizations done in SharePoint Designer are stored in the content database. Second, there is no way to use source code control to track your changes.

Visual Studio can help us with the second issue even though it doesn't provide a Master Page designer. You can use Visual Studio's support for source control with any type of SharePoint project. So the question is, how do you add a master page to a SharePoint project?

Let's create an Empty SharePoint project by opening Visual Studio in elevated mode and naming the project CustomMaster. If we wanted to add our master page project to source control we could check the Add to Source Control check box. In the SharePoint customization wizard select

Deploy as a farm Solution. We could have also selected Deploy as sand-boxed solution.

The next step is to add a Module. As you may remember, a Module is a special SharePoint project item that can be used to deploy even SharePoint artifacts, such as master pages, which Visual Studio doesn't have any built-in support for. We will use a Module to deploy our master page. For more information on modules, see Chapter 11, "Packaging and Deployment." Right click on the solution CustomMaster in the Solution Explorer and choose Add > New Item. In the Add New Item dialog select Module and name it MasterPage.

We are at the point where we can add the master page to the module. Again there is no designer available in Visual Studio for master pages and Visual Studio does not provide us with a way to even add an ASP.NET master page through the Add New Item dialog, so we need to create a new master page file outside the SharePoint project and add it to the module once we are done creating the master page.

Why Doesn't the SharePoint Project Let You Add an ASP.NET Master Page to It Directly?

In the beginning of the development of the Visual Studio SharePoint Developer tools the Visual Studio team made the decision not to support any SharePoint artifacts that need to be directly deployed to the content database. That's why even ASP.NET pages and ASP.NET master pages cannot be added directly to a SharePoint project. Visual Studio uses modules to deploy SharePoint artifacts to the content database as we shall see later in this chapter.

In the Visual Studio File menu select File > New > File... In the New File dialog navigate to Web > C#, select Master Page, and click the Open button. Visual Studio creates the new master page and we can add our markup. For this example we are just using the markup found in the file minimal.master. You can easily copy this markup by opening the file minimal.master in SharePoint Designer.

Next we need to save the master page to disk. Press Ctrl+S to bring up the Save As dialog and name the master page CustomMinimal.master. Then click the Save button to save the file.

If you already have a master page you can skip the steps of creating a new master page in Visual Studio and proceed with the next step, which is to add the existing master page to the module. Right click on the module MasterPage and select Add > Existing Item. In the Add Existing Item dialog browse to the folder containing CustomMinimal.master and click the Add button. The next step is to delete the file Sample.txt, which is created by default. Right click on the file Sample.txt under the MasterPage Module project item and select Delete.

Double click on the file Elements.xml under the MasterPage Module project item to open it in the editor. We need to update the Elements.xml file to deploy our new master page to the master page gallery. Listing 10-1 shows the markup.

Listing 10-1: Elements.xml File for a Module That Deploys a Master Page File

```xml
<?xml version="1.0" encoding="utf-8"?>
<Elements xmlns="http://schemas.microsoft.com/sharepoint/">
  <Module Name="MasterPage" Url="_catalogs/masterpage">
  <File Path="MasterPage\CustomMinimal.master"
    Url="CustomMinimal.master"
    Type="GhostableInLibrary" />
</Module>
</Elements>
```

We need to add two attributes to the Elements.xml file created by Visual Studio. The first attribute is the Url attribute in the Module element. By setting the Url attribute value to "_catalogs/masterpage" we tell SharePoint to deploy the file CustomMinimal.master to the master page gallery. Now you might wonder what the difference between a gallery and a list is. The answer is there is no difference. So the master page gallery is a special SharePoint list that stores master pages. Secondly we remove "MasterPage/" from the Url attribute of the File element. If we left it there it would create a new folder called MasterPage in the master page gallery. Lastly we add the

Type attribute and set its value to "GhostableInLibrary," which makes the file show up in the gallery. (See Chapter 11, "Packaging and Deployment," for more information on deploying files using Modules.)

Now we are all set and can deploy our master page to SharePoint. We can ignore the warnings and messages as Visual Studio tries to validate the master page but can't because it doesn't have the SharePoint context. Right click on the project CustomMaster and select Deploy.

Once the deployment completes we can check to see if the master page is in the master page gallery. Open the top-level SharePoint site, and select Site Settings from the Site Actions menu. In the settings page select Master pages in the Galleries section. Once the master page gallery shows up we can see our CustomMinimal.master page along with the CustomV4.master we created in SharePoint Designer and the out-of-the-box SharePoint master pages. Figure 10-13 shows the Master page gallery.

We have learned what master pages are and how we can create and customize them. We intentionally didn't look at all the placeholders and components in the v4.master master page because this would go beyond the scope of this chapter. If you are interested in building your very own master page from scratch you may find the list of all the placeholders available on MSDN at the link http://msdn.microsoft.com/en-us/library/ee539981(office.14).aspx.

	Type	Name	Modified	Modified By	Checked Out To	Compatible UI Version(s)
		CustomMinimal.master	3/21/2010 7:58 PM	Boris Scholl		4
		CustomV4.master	3/21/2010 1:46 PM	Boris Scholl		4
		default.master	2/23/2010 5:39 PM	Boris Scholl		3
		minimal.master	2/23/2010 5:39 PM	Boris Scholl		4
		v4.master	2/23/2010 5:39 PM	Boris Scholl		4

Team Site ▸ Master Page Gallery ▸ All Master Pages ▾
Use the master page gallery to store master pages. The master pages in this gallery are available to this site and any sites underneath it.

Site Actions ▾   Browse   Documents   Library   Library Tools   Boris Scholl ▾

Home   MySite   Search this site...

Libraries
Site Pages
Shared Documents
SLApps
Lists
Calendar

Figure 10-13: Master page gallery

Creating Site Pages

As with master pages, Visual Studio doesn't provide a designer for site pages, but SharePoint Designer can help us here again. In this section we will look at using SharePoint Designer to create SharePoint site pages. Open SharePoint Designer and connect to your SharePoint site by using the Open Site button or clicking on the SharePoint site in the Recent Sites section. On the left side bar select Site Pages to open the Site Pages home page, which lists all the site pages. Figure 10-14 shows the Site Pages home page.

Where Did the All the Site Pages in Figure 10-14 Come From?

Figure 10-14 shows several site pages. How did these get created? Home .aspx and How to use this library.aspx were created when we installed and provisioned SharePoint. The other pages were created throughout the book and were used as samples, for example to demo web parts.

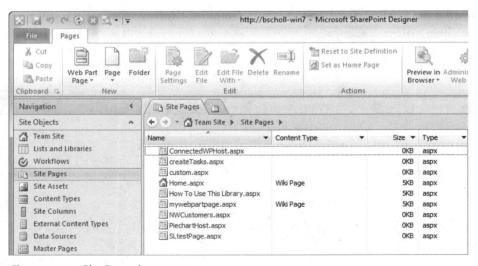

Figure 10-14: Site Pages home page

The Site Pages home page allows us to customize existing site pages and create new ones. Depending on what type of site page we want to create we can either choose the Web Part Page button or the Page button in the ribbon. As the name suggests we can create web part pages by using the Web Part Page button and plain aspx and html pages by using the Page button. For this example, we will create a new web part page. Click on the Web Part Page button and select the Full Page Vertical template as shown in Figure 10-15. When you click the Create Web Part Page button, SharePoint Designer provides you with eight web part page templates to start from, which are also offered by the SharePoint UI when you create a new web part page from within SharePoint.

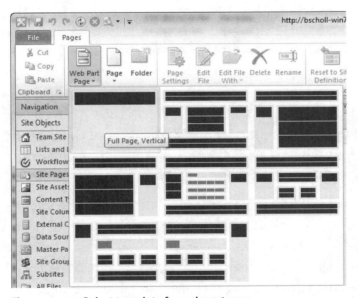

Figure 10-15: Select template for web part page

Now that you've created a new web part page, rename the file to Custom-WebPart.aspx and double click on the file. This will show the view and manage settings page for the CustomWebPart.aspx. Figure 10-16 shows the view and manage settings page.

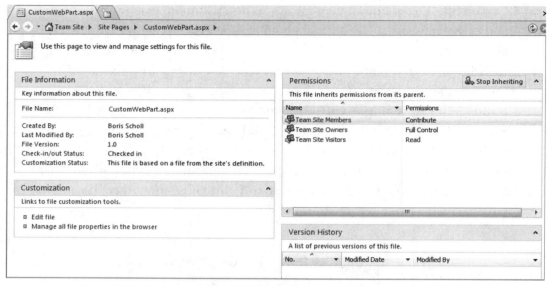

Figure 10-16: View and manage settings page for CustomWebPart.aspx

Site Pages Are Customizable by the User—I Understand That for Web Part Pages, but How Are Plain ASPX or HTML Pages User Customizable?

Earlier in this chapter, we mentioned that what sets a site page apart from application pages is that it is end-user customizable and stored in the content database. For a web part page, it is clear that the end user can customize it by configuring the web parts it displays and other settings pertaining to web part containers. But if you create a plain ASPX or HTML page, how is that user customizable and why would it have to be stored in the content database? As soon as the page references a master page including the SharePoint ribbon users can customize even a simple ASPX page by adding objects such as tables and pictures to the page's placeholders.

In the Customization section click on the Edit file link. This opens the web page designer of SharePoint Designer. SharePoint Designer is using the same web page designer as Visual Studio for ASP.NET pages. It has a design view that allows you to design the page, a split view that allows you to design the pages and edit the HTML markup in the same view, and a source view that allows you to edit the HTML markup directly. We just want to make some minor changes to the site page, which can best be done in the split view. Switch to split view and locate the TitleWebPart in the design view. Click on the Untitled_1 placeholder in the design view. This will highlight the corresponding HTML markup as shown in Figure 10-17.

Figure 10-17: The split view in the web page designer for CustomWebPart

In the highlighted TitleWebPart element locate the attribute Header-Title and change its value to "New Site Page." We could also add new HTML, ASP.NET, and SharePoint controls by using the controls buttons in the ribbon. Figure 10-18 shows the ASP.NET controls that can be added to the page by using the ribbon.

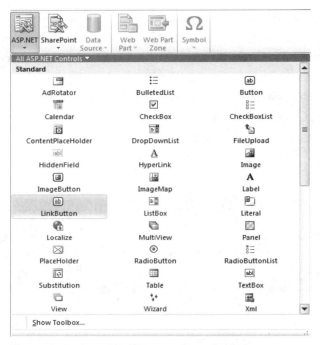

Figure 10-18: New ASP.NET controls available from
SharePoint Designer's ribbon in the web page designer

We will resist the temptation to add additional controls and just save our file with the changed title. Click the Save button in the ribbon. This will save the new site page to the content database.

Since SharePoint Designer Works with Site Pages in the Content Database, How Do I Get File-Based Visual Studio to Work with Site Pages in the Content Database?

When you create a SharePoint site page in SharePoint designer, it is saving and opening from the content database associated with the site collection.

You probably see some problems here—first, how can you get a site page you created in SharePoint designer out of the content database and into a file that you can add to a Visual Studio project? Second, how can you make Visual Studio deploy the site page to the content database? Unfortunately there is no way that Visual Studio can extract a site page from the content database. Later in this chapter we will see how you can create site pages without SharePoint Designer and use Visual Studio to deploy site pages to the content database.

Next, open the browser and navigate to your SharePoint site. In the left navigation pane, click on Site Pages under the Libraries category. This opens the Site Pages gallery. As shown in Figure 10-19 our new site page shows up in the gallery.

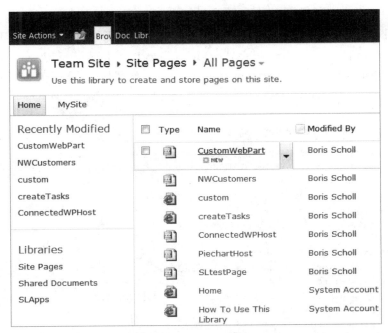

Figure 10-19: CustomWebPart in the Site Pages gallery

Click on CustomWebPart to open the site page in the browser. Figure 10-20 shows our new site page with the custom title "New Site Page."

Figure 10-20: CustomWebPart in browser

Now that we've created a site page in SharePoint Designer, let's consider how to create a site page in Visual Studio. We will create a new web part page with two web part zones so that users can add two web parts to it. First, we need to work around the fact that we cannot add an ASP.NET page directly to a SharePoint project. Open Visual Studio in elevated mode and select File > New > File. In the New File dialog select Web > C# and Web Form. Click the Open button. Visual Studio creates a web form with some standard HTML. We can delete the entire HTML markup and replace it with the markup needed for our custom web part page. Listing 10-2 shows the HTML markup needed to create a custom web part page with two web part zones.

Listing 10-2: The Markup in the Custom Web Part Page

```
<%@ Page Language="C#" MasterPageFile="~masterurl/default.master"
  Inherits="Microsoft.SharePoint.WebPartPages.WebPartPage,
  Microsoft.SharePoint,Version=14.0.0.0,
  Culture=neutral,PublicKeyToken=71e9bce111e9429c"
  meta:webpartpageexpansion="full"
  meta:progid="SharePoint.WebPartPage.Document" %>

<%@ Register Tagprefix="SharePoint"
  Namespace="Microsoft.SharePoint.WebControls"
  Assembly="Microsoft.SharePoint, Version=14.0.0.0,
  Culture=neutral, PublicKeyToken=71e9bce111e9429c" %>
<%@ Register Tagprefix="Utilities"
  Namespace="Microsoft.SharePoint.Utilities"
  Assembly="Microsoft.SharePoint,
  Version=14.0.0.0, Culture=neutral,
  PublicKeyToken=71e9bce111e9429c" %>
```

```
<%@ Import Namespace="Microsoft.SharePoint" %>
<%@ Assembly Name="Microsoft.Web.CommandUI, Version=14.0.0.0,
   Culture=neutral,
   PublicKeyToken=71e9bce111e9429c" %>
<%@ Register Tagprefix="WebPartPages"
   Namespace="Microsoft.SharePoint.WebPartPages"
   Assembly="Microsoft.SharePoint, Version=14.0.0.0,
   Culture=neutral, PublicKeyToken=71e9bce111e9429c" %>
<asp:Content ID="main" runat="server"
   ContentPlaceHolderID="PlaceHolderMain">
   <h1> Custom web part site page</h1>
     <table style="width: 100%;">
       <tr>
         <td>
           <WebPartPages:WebPartZone ID="LeftWebPart"
             runat="server">
           </WebPartPages:WebPartZone>
         </td>
         <td>
           <WebPartPages:WebPartZone ID="RightWebPart"
             runat="server">
           </WebPartPages:WebPartZone>
         </td>
       </tr>
     </table>
</asp:Content>
```

The first directive that needs to be added is the @Page directive. We need to add the MasterPageFile attribute and set its value to the master page we want to use. In our case we want to use the default master page thus we set the value to the token ~masterurl/default.master. We also need to derive our new page from the SharePoint web part pages. This is done by setting the Inherits attribute to "Microsoft.SharePoint.WebPartPages.WebPartPage, Microsoft.SharePoint, Version=14.0.0.0, Culture=neutral, PublicKeyToken=71e9bce111e9429c."

If we look closer at this very long value, we can see that we use the WebPartPages namespace in the Microsoft.SharePoint assembly. Version 14.0.0.0 indicates that we are using the 2010 version of Microsoft.SharePoint. You will also see green squiggles under the master page token in Visual Studio. Unfortunately, this prevents us from switching to the Design view of the web page designer because Visual Studio won't be able to load the SharePoint master page because we are not in a SharePoint context, so we have to create our custom site page in Source view.

Next we need to add an @Register directive to register the SharePoint web controls available in Microsoft.SharePoint.WebControls and set their tag prefix to SharePoint. We do the same for Microsoft.SharePoint.Utilities. Objects in the Utilities namespace can be used for utility tasks such as string encoding and the processing of user information. We also include the assembly Microsoft.Web.CommandUI, which is located in the GAC and contains the logic for the SharePoint ribbon. Finally we need to register Microsoft.SharePoint.WebPartPages and prefix it with WebPartPages.

Can I Also Register Other Controls Defined in Other Assemblies or Add Custom Controls?

Yes, it's possible but in order to use those controls you need to register them as safe controls in the web.config of your SharePoint web application. This is required because SharePoint parses site pages in a mode called "safe mode," which requires all controls in the page to be registered as safe. If you open the web.config (if you have installed SharePoint on port 80 the web.config is located in C:\inetpub\wwwroot\wss\Virtual-Directories\80) you can search for SafeControls, which shows all the controls registered as safe.

Now we can go ahead and build the rest of the page. As we want our web part zones to show up in the main part of the page we add the content place holder PlaceHolderMain to the site page. In the element <H1> we set the headline of our site page. Next we create a table by dragging and dropping a Table element from the HTML section of the toolbox. Visual Studio adds a table with three rows and three columns. Because we only need one row and two columns we can delete two rows and one column. Next we can drag the web part zones from the toolbox to the columns. Figure 10-21 shows the WebParts section of the toolbox in Visual Studio.

As you can see the prefix for the web part zone is "asp:" when it is added to the page. We need to change the prefix to "WebPartPages:" otherwise

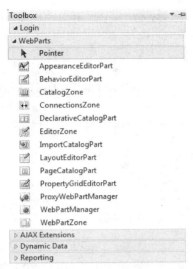

Figure 10-21: Web parts controls in
the Visual Studio Toolbox

SharePoint won't recognize those web part zones and the user won't be able
to add web parts. Now we need to drag the second web part zone to the second column. After setting the web part zone properties to the values shown
in Listing 10-2 we can save the page as MyWebPartPage.aspx.

The next step is to deploy MyWebPartPage.aspx to the content database. We will use the same technique as we did for master pages. Create a
new empty SharePoint project and name it WebPartPage. In the Share-
Point customization wizard select Deploy as a farm solution (we could also
create a sandboxed solution) and click the Finish button. Now we add a
module by right clicking on the project WebPartPage and selecting Add >
New Item in the context menu. Select Module in the New Item dialog and
name it WebPartPage and click the Add button. We can delete the file sam-
ple.txt by right clicking on it and selecting Delete in the context menu. We
can now add our custom site page to the module. Right click on the module folder WebPartPage and select Add > Existing Item.

In the Add Existing Item dialog browse to the location where you have
stored the page MyWebPartPage.aspx, select it and click the Add button.

The last thing we need to do is to change the Elements.xml file so that our page gets deployed to the Site Pages library. Listing 10-3 shows the modified Elements.xml file.

Listing 10-3: Elements.xml File for a Module That Deploys a Site Page File

```
<?xml version="1.0" encoding="utf-8"?>
<Elements xmlns="http://schemas.microsoft.com/sharepoint/">
  <Module Name=" WebPartPage" Url="SitePages">
  <File Path="WebPartPage\MyWebPartPage.aspx"
    Url="MyWebPartPage.aspx"
    Type="GhostableInLibrary" />
</Module>
</Elements>
```

Just as we've done for master pages we have to change the default Elements.xml file a little bit. We need to add two attributes to the xml created by Visual Studio. The first attribute is the Url attribute in the Module element. By setting the Url attribute value to "SitePages" we tell SharePoint to deploy our custom page to the Site Pages library. Secondly we remove "WebPartPage/" from the Url attribute of the File element. If we left it there SharePoint would create a new folder called WebPartPage in the Site Pages library. Lastly we add the Type attribute and set its value to "GhostableInLibrary," which makes the file show up in the gallery.

Now we can deploy our custom page. Right click on the project WebPartPage and select Deploy in the context menu. Once Visual Studio shows the Deploy succeeded message in the lower left corner we can open the browser and navigate to the home page. We can find our new site page in the left navigation side bar—click on Site Pages under Libraries.

Click on the site page to open it in the browser. Once the page is rendered in the browser click the Page tab in the ribbon. To test if our page can be edited click the Edit Page button. The page is now in edit mode and the two web part zones appear. Users can now add web parts to our custom web part page. Figure 10-22 shows our custom web part page in edit mode.

Creating Application Pages

Application pages are used to surface content and functionality to SharePoint users just as site pages do, but application pages are accessible from all

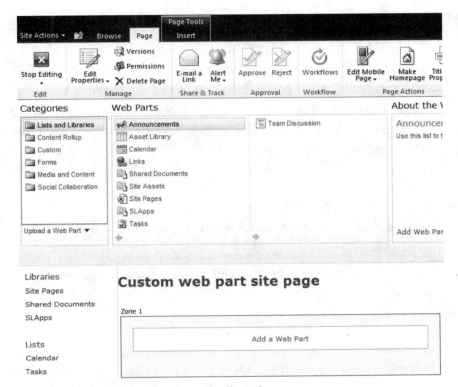

Figure 10-22: MyWebPartPage.aspx in edit mode

sites and site collections within a farm. Furthermore application pages provide a performance advantage over site pages as they cannot be customized, which eliminates the need to store many copies of the page in the content database. Also, an application page is always compiled into a single DLL, which makes it perform better than site pages. From a developer's perspective the biggest difference between site pages and application pages is that application pages allow the use of inline code in the page markup.

We will now build a custom application page. Open Visual Studio in elevated mode and select New Project. Because application pages are only available as SharePoint project items (e.g., you can't create an Application Page Project that has precreated in it an Application Page project item) we must create an Empty project first. In the New Project dialog select Empty SharePoint Project and name it "CustomApplicationPage." Then click the OK button.

I Can't Use Code in Site Pages?

You can't use inline code in the page markup of a site page because users can customize site pages, they could modify the page in a way that misused the inline code in the markup—for example, add references to scripts containing malicious code. Also it is not possible to associate code-behind with site pages.

Can I Deploy an Application Page in a Sandboxed Solution?

The short answer is no because application pages are meant to be available in any site in a farm. Sandboxed solutions are only available from a site within a site collection.

In the SharePoint Customization Wizard select Deploy as a farm solution and click the Finish button. Once the project has been created right click on the project CustomApplicationPage in the Solution Explorer and select Add > New Item from the context menu.

In the New Item dialog select Application Page and name it Custom .aspx. Visual Studio adds the application page and opens the source view for the ASPX page. There is no design view available for application pages, so we need to add the markup manually. The application page item template already contains definitions that make it easy to identify the places where you can add controls to build a custom application page. Listing 10-4 shows the initial markup for an application page item template.

Why Is There No Design View for Application Pages?

The short answer is that there was just not enough time and resources to get a designer working for version 1. Sound like any projects you've worked on?

Listing 10-4: The Markup in the Application Page Item Template

```
<%@ Assembly Name="$SharePoint.Project.AssemblyFullName$" %>
<%@ Import Namespace="Microsoft.SharePoint.ApplicationPages" %>
<%@ Register Tagprefix="SharePoint"
  Namespace="Microsoft.SharePoint.WebControls"
  Assembly="Microsoft.SharePoint, Version=14.0.0.0,
  Culture=neutral, PublicKeyToken=71e9bce111e9429c" %>
<%@ Register Tagprefix="Utilities"
  Namespace="Microsoft.SharePoint.Utilities"
  Assembly="Microsoft.SharePoint, Version=14.0.0.0,
  Culture=neutral, PublicKeyToken=71e9bce111e9429c" %>
<%@ Register Tagprefix="asp"
  Namespace="System.Web.UI"
  Assembly="System.Web.Extensions, Version=3.5.0.0,
  Culture=neutral, PublicKeyToken=31bf3856ad364e35" %>
<%@ Import Namespace="Microsoft.SharePoint" %>
<%@ Assembly Name="Microsoft.Web.CommandUI, Version=14.0.0.0,
  Culture=neutral, PublicKeyToken=71e9bce111e9429c" %>
<%@ Page Language="C#" AutoEventWireup="true"
  CodeBehind="Custom.aspx.cs"
  Inherits="CustomApplicationPage.Layouts.CustomApplicationPage.Custom"
  DynamicMasterPageFile="~masterurl/default.master" %>
<asp:Content ID="PageHead"
  ContentPlaceHolderID="PlaceHolderAdditionalPageHead" runat="server">
</asp:Content>

<asp:Content ID="Main" ContentPlaceHolderID="PlaceHolderMain"
  runat="server">
</asp:Content>

<asp:Content ID="PageTitle" ContentPlaceHolderID="PlaceHolderPageTitle"
  runat="server">
Application Page
</asp:Content>

<asp:Content ID="PageTitleInTitleArea"
  ContentPlaceHolderID="PlaceHolderPageTitleInTitleArea"
  runat="server">
My Application Page
</asp:Content>
```

The very first line of the HTML markup is an assembly directive that references the project output assembly that contains the compiled code-behind. Since the application page is in the Layouts folder in the SharePoint hive it needs to reference an assembly that will be placed in the GAC. In the second line, the page imports the namespace Microsoft.SharePoint.ApplicationPages, which SharePoint needs for internal processing. Members and types of this namespace are not supposed to be used directly by user code.

Next, the HTML markup contains a couple of register directives to register prefixes for controls and objects referenced in the namespace attribute of the register directive. Those prefixes associate aliases with namespaces and class names.

One interesting directive to consider is the Page directive, especially given our prior discussion about master pages. In addition to pointing to the code-behind file through the CodeBehind attribute it also contains an attribute that tells the page which master page to use. By default it has the DynamicMasterPageFile attribute set to "~masterurl/default.master," which points to the default master page for SharePoint. If we want our application page to use a different master page we need to replace the attribute DynamicMasterPageFile with the attribute MasterPageFile and set its value to the URL for the specific master page we want to use.

Why Is DynamicMasterPageFile Set to ~masterurl/default.master, I Thought v4.master Is the Default Master Page?

DynamicMasterPageFile can only take two tokens as its value. It can either take ~masterurl/default.master or ~masterurl/custom.master. These tokens will be resolved by SharePoint to the current site's default master (v4.master) or a custom master page. You can check programmatically which master page is used by using the SPWeb object's MasterUrl property.

The last part of the application item template markup contains the content placeholders. Visual Studio adds four content placeholders to the item template. Table 10-1 shows the placeholders and their functions.

Before we continue creating the application page, let's take a deeper look at the project structure in the Solution Explorer of Visual Studio. Note that Visual Studio has created a folder in the solution called Layouts—this

TABLE 10-1:   Content Placeholders in the Application Page Item Template

Placeholder	Description
PlaceHolderAdditional-PageHead	Contains content that needs to be within the <head> tag of the page, such as script references and style sheet references. Note that the title of the page does not go here because it has its own placeholder called PlaceHolderPageTitle.
PlaceHolderMain	The main content of the page.
PlaceHolderPageTitle	The page <Title> that is shown in the browser's title bar.
PlaceHolderPageTitleIn-TitleArea	The title of the page, which appears in the title area on the page.

folder is mapped to the folder in the SharePoint hive where the application page will be deployed at deployment time. Further, Visual Studio has created a subfolder based on the project's name called CustomApplication-Page under the Layouts folder. Finally our application page is added to the CustomApplicationPage folder. Every application page added to this project will be stored in this subfolder. From a deployment perspective it is great that Visual Studio creates subfolders as opposed to storing all of the master pages directly in the layouts folder; this makes it easier to locate and logically group the custom application pages. Figure 10-23 shows the Solution Explorer view for the project.

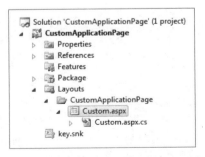

Figure 10-23: New application page Custom.aspx
created in the solution's folder hierarchy

With this knowledge we can go ahead and complete our first application page. We will build an application page that shows usage information for the current site collection. First we need to add the HTML markup to the placeholders of the page that we saw in Table 10-1. Listing 10-5 shows the HTML markup.

Listing 10-5: The HTML Markup for the Application Page

```
<asp:Content ID="PageHead" ContentPlaceHolderID="PlaceHolderAdditionalPageHead"
  runat="server">

</asp:Content>

<asp:Content ID="Main" ContentPlaceHolderID="PlaceHolderMain"
  runat="server">
  <table border ="1" width="100%">
    <tr>
      <td>Site Collection:</td>
      <td>
        <asp:Label ID="lblSiteUrl" runat="server"></asp:Label>
      </td>
    </tr>
    <tr>
      <td>Hits:</td>
      <td>
        <asp:Label ID="lblHits" runat="server"></asp:Label>
      </td>
    </tr>
    <tr>
      <td>Visits</td>
      <td>
        <asp:Label ID="lblVisits" runat="server"></asp:Label>
      </td>
    </tr>
    <tr>
      <td>Bandwidth:</td>
      <td>
        <asp:Label ID="lblBandWidth" runat="server"></asp:Label>
      </td>
    </tr>
    <tr>
      <td>Storage:</td>
      <td>
        <asp:Label ID="lblStorage" runat="server"></asp:Label>
      </td>
    </tr>
    <tr>
```

```
        <td>Discussion storage:</td>
        <td>
            <asp:Label ID="lblDiscStorage" runat="server"></asp:Label>
        </td>
    </tr>
  </table>
</asp:Content>

<asp:Content ID="PageTitle" ContentPlaceHolderID="PlaceHolderPageTitle"
  runat="server">
Site Collection Usage Statistics
</asp:Content>

<asp:Content ID="PageTitleInTitleArea"
  ContentPlaceHolderID="PlaceHolderPageTitleInTitleArea"
  runat="server">
Site Collection Usage Statistics
</asp:Content>
```

We didn't use the placeholder PlaceHolderAdditionalPageHead because we do not need to reference any style sheets or scripts. In the placeholder PlaceHolderMain we create an HTML table showing the usage statistics for the site collection. The table contains 6 rows, created using the <tr> elements with two cells per row created using the <td> element. The first cell contains the description of the usage statistic and the second cell contains a label to store the actual statistic. The title for the application page is added to the placeholder PlaceHolderPageTitle and the placeholder PlaceHolderPage-TitleInTitleArea.

With the HTML designed we can go ahead and implement the code to assign values to the labels in the table. Right click on the source view surface and select View Code in the context menu. This will open the code-behind file, Custom.aspx.cs, for the application page. As we want to have the values shown in the table as soon as the page is loaded we will add the code shown in Listing 10-6 to the Page_Load event.

Listing 10-6: A Page_Load Event Handler That Assigns Values to the Labels in the HTML Table

```
protected void Page_Load(object sender, EventArgs e)
{
    SPSite site = SPContext.Current.Site;
    SPSite.UsageInfo usage = site.Usage;
    lblSiteUrl.Text = site.Url;
```

```
lblDiscStorage.Text = usage.DiscussionStorage.ToString();
lblStorage.Text = usage.Storage.ToString();
lblBandWidth.Text = usage.Bandwidth.ToString();
lblHits.Text = usage.Hits.ToString();
lblVisits.Text = usage.Visits.ToString();
}
```

In the first line of the Page_Load event we obtain an SPSite object from the current SharePoint context SPContext.Current. (See Chapter 3, "Introduction to the SharePoint Object Model," for more information on working with the SharePoint object model.) In the second line we create a UsageInfo object that will provide us with the usage statistics for the site collection. After this we set the values of the respective labels using usage information from the SharePoint site collection.

Why Don't We Need to Dispose the SPSite Object in This Sample?

According to SharePoint best practices, SPSite and SPWeb objects returned by SPContext.Site, SPContext.Current.Site, SPContext.Web, and SPContext.Current.Web should not be explicitly disposed by user code.

With the code implemented we can now go ahead and debug the application page. We can set the application page as the Startup item of the project. This has the advantage that Visual Studio will browse to the page directly after hitting F5. Locate the Startup Item property in the Properties window for the project CustomApplicationPage and select Custom.aspx in the drop-down as shown in Figure 10-24. After that we can set a breakpoint in the first line of the Page_Load event and hit F5.

Remember that application pages are deployed to the Layouts folder in the SharePoint hive and that Visual Studio creates a subfolder under the Layouts folder set to the name of the project. Debug through the code and finally the application page Custom.aspx is rendered. Figure 10-25 shows the rendered application page. Don't forget that Visual Studio retracts the

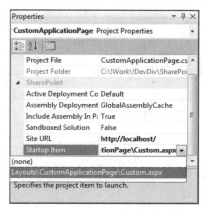

Figure 10-24: Setting Custom.aspx as
the Startup Item of the project

solution after you have stopped debugging, so if you want to check the page after you have finished debugging you have to deploy it again by right clicking the project in the Solution Explorer and selecting Deploy in the context menu.

Figure 10-25: Application page Custom.aspx in the browser

Now that we have successfully built our first application page let's recap what we have done to create an application page. We created an empty Visual Studio project and added an application page as a new item to the project. Visual Studio creates mapped folders to mirror the structure in the SharePoint Layouts folder in the SharePoint hive. As developers we need to design the layout of the application page through adding HTML markup to the Main placeholder of the ASP.NET page (Visual Studio doesn't provide a visual designer for application pages) and implement the code in the code-behind aspx.cs file. We can then deploy and debug an application page by hitting F5.

Security and Application Pages

Next we are going to take this one step further and think about security. You might think that SharePoint is taking care of security so why does the developer have to consider this? Developers can often write code in an application page that circumvents SharePoint's integrated security logic. Doing this can make application pages vulnerable and expose SharePoint sites to great risk. In our sample, every user of the SharePoint site can access the application page and check the site statistics of the site collection. In SharePoint however, most users aren't allowed to see this information. So it might be a good idea to restrict the access of this information to site collection administrators.

There are several approaches to implementing permissions for application pages. In this chapter we will look at the three most common ones. The first approach is to secure access to application pages by validating permission levels. Permission levels are defined by a set of base permissions, such as ManageWeb, OpenItems, etc., that can be granted to users or SharePoint groups on SharePoint items such as lists, library, sites, etc. The SharePoint object model represents permission levels as role definitions with the SPRoleDefinition object. Out of the box, SharePoint has five permission levels as shown in Table 10-2. Administrators can also create new custom permission levels or edit and delete existing ones.

To make our application page more secure, we will check for the Full Control permission level before showing site usage information to the user. Listing 10-7 shows how to check for the Full Control permission level before we execute the code to fill the table with the site usage information.

TABLE 10-2: SharePoint Permission Levels

Permission Level	Description
Limited Access	The Limited Access permission level is designed to be combined with base permissions to give users access to a specific list, document library, item, or document, without giving them access to the entire site. The Limited Access permission level cannot be customized or deleted.
Read	Users and groups with this permission level have read-only access to the web site, which means they can view items and pages and open items and documents.
Contribute	Users can add, edit, and delete items in existing lists and document libraries.
Design	Users or groups with this permission level can create lists and document libraries; edit pages; and apply themes, borders, and style sheets in the web site.
Full Control	This permission level contains all base permissions. This permission level cannot be customized or deleted.

Listing 10-7: Checking the Permission Level before Executing the Code

```
protected void Page_Load(object sender, EventArgs e)
{
   SPSite site = SPContext.Current.Site;
   using (SPWeb web = site.OpenWeb())
   {
      SPRoleDefinitionBindingCollection usersRoles =
      web.AllRolesForCurrentUser;
      SPRoleDefinitionCollection siteRoleCollection =
        web.RoleDefinitions;
      SPRoleDefinition roleDefinition =
        siteRoleCollection["Full Control"];
      if (usersRoles.Contains(roleDefinition))
      {
         SPSite.UsageInfo usage = site.Usage;
         lblSiteUrl.Text = site.Url;
         lblDiscStorage.Text = usage.DiscussionStorage.ToString();
         lblStorage.Text = usage.Storage.ToString();
         lblBandWidth.Text = usage.Bandwidth.ToString();
         lblHits.Text = usage.Hits.ToString();
         lblVisits.Text = usage.Visits.ToString();
```

```
    }
    else
    {
        Response.Redirect("/_layouts/accessdenied.aspx");
    }
  }
}
```

To check for the permission level, we need to obtain the SPWeb object first. We obtain the SPWeb object by using the OpenWeb method of the SPSite object. This method returns the top-level site in the site collection since we don't pass a parameter in the constructor. Next we need to create an SPRoleDefinitionBindingCollection object assigned to userRoles to store all the roles the logged on user is assigned to by using SPWeb's AllRolesForCurrentUser property. In the next line we create an SPRoleDefinitionCollection object assigned to siteRoleCollection to store all the role definitions available for the site. After that we need to create an SPRoleDefinition object assigned to roleDefinition to which we assign the Full Control permissions set.

In the "if" condition we check if the user is a member of the permission set Full Control and if so, we execute the code to show the usage data for the site collection. If not we use Response.Redirect to redirect the response to the standard SharePoint access denied page (accessdenied.aspx), which is also an application page by the way.

The second approach to implementing permissions for an application page is to check for group membership permissions. Checking group membership permissions means that we check to see if the user is part of a certain SharePoint group. SharePoint by default creates three groups for each site. Table 10-3 shows the three groups and their descriptions. You can manage the groups for your site collection by opening the SharePoint site and selecting the Site Permissions item in the Site Actions menu. As with permission levels, administrators can create custom groups and customize and delete existing groups. SharePoint groups have a default permission level assigned to them.

Listing 10-8 shows how to check if the user requesting access to our application page is a member of the site owners group.

TABLE 10-3: SharePoint Groups

Group	Description	Default Permission Level
Site name owners	Owners of the SharePoint site with full control	Full Control
Site name members	Users who contribute to the site	Contribute
Site name visitors	Users who have read-only rights	Read

Listing 10-8: Checking If the User Is a Member of a SharePoint Group before Executing the Code

```
protected void Page_Load(object sender, EventArgs e)
{
    SPSite site = SPContext.Current.Site;
    using (SPWeb web = site.OpenWeb())
    {
        SPGroup group = web.Groups["Team Site Owners"];
        if (group.ContainsCurrentUser)
        {
            SPSite.UsageInfo usage = site.Usage;
            lblSiteUrl.Text = site.Url;
            lblDiscStorage.Text = usage.DiscussionStorage.ToString();
            lblStorage.Text = usage.Storage.ToString();
            lblBandWidth.Text = usage.Bandwidth.ToString();
            lblHits.Text = usage.Hits.ToString();
            lblVisits.Text = usage.Visits.ToString();
        }
        else
        {
            Response.Redirect("/_layouts/accessdenied.aspx");
        }
    }
}
```

After we have obtained the SPWeb object we create a variable called "group" that we set to the group Team Site Owners. The group is called Team Site Owners because our site has the name "Team Site." Then we check to see if the current user is a member of this group by using the method ContainsCurrentUser on the group object. If the user is a member of the Team Site Owners group we return the site collection statistics and if not we redirect the user to the access denied page.

The third approach to implementing permissions for an application page is to only allow site collection administrators to access the application page. We can accomplish this by simply overriding the property Require-SiteAdministrator (a property in the base class LayoutsPageBase, which is used for a SharePoint application page) and returning true. Listing 10-9 shows the code for our application page using the RequireSiteAdministrator property.

Listing 10-9: Overriding the RequireSiteAdministrator Property

```
public partial class Custom : LayoutsPageBase
{
  protected override bool RequireSiteAdministrator
  {
    get { return true; }
  }

  protected void Page_Load(object sender, EventArgs e)
  {
    SPSite site = SPContext.Current.Site;
    SPSite.UsageInfo usage = site.Usage;
    lblSiteUrl.Text = site.Url;
    lblDiscStorage.Text = usage.DiscussionStorage.ToString();
    lblStorage.Text = usage.Storage.ToString();
    lblBandWidth.Text = usage.Bandwidth.ToString();
    lblHits.Text = usage.Hits.ToString();
    lblVisits.Text = usage.Visits.ToString();
  }
}
```

In our application page Custom we override the base class Layouts-PageBase's property RequireSiteAdministrator and return true, which tells SharePoint that only the site collection administrators can access this application page. The nice thing about this approach is that we don't need to redirect users to the access denied page, SharePoint takes care of this if the current user is not a site collection administrator.

Layouts or _layouts?

In this chapter we frequently referred to the Layouts folder. This folder is where application pages must reside and is found in the SharePoint hive, typically in the directory C:\Program Files\Common Files\Microsoft Shared\ Web Server Extensions\14\TEMPLATE\LAYOUTS for a standard SharePoint Foundation installation. You also might have noticed some reference to _layouts, for example in Listing 10-8 when we redirect to the application page for access denied, we used the URL "/_layouts/accessdenied.aspx." The Layouts folder is mapped to the URL http://localhost/_layouts for the default site collection's root site. For another site the Layouts folder is mapped to a URL starting with the root URL for that site, e.g. for the site http://localhost/subsite the URL to the Layouts folder is http://localhost/ subsite/_layouts. So for our application page Custom.aspx which was created in a directory within the LAYOUTS directory called CustomApplication-Page, the path to its location on disk in the SharePoint hive is C:\Program Files\Common Files\Microsoft Shared\Web Server Extensions\14\TEMPLATE\ LAYOUTS\CustomApplicationPage\Custom.aspx but the URL where Share-Point serves the page from for the default collection's root site is http:// localhost/_layouts/CustomApplicationPage/Custom.aspx.

Conclusion

We started this chapter with a high level look at the SharePoint architecture and briefly touched on creating master pages and site pages using SharePoint Designer. We also learned the differences between site pages and application pages. Visual Studio has no templates for master and site pages but offers a project item template for application pages. Finally we looked into how to create application pages and how to restrict access to them by using various techniques.

■ 11 ■
Packaging and Deployment

The Basics and Beyond

Throughout this book you have seen a number of examples in which we created various types of SharePoint artifacts and then deployed these artifacts to SharePoint. In most cases we were able to add these artifacts (lists, web parts, event receivers, etc.) to the project and then press F5 to package and deploy everything to SharePoint.

In this chapter we will discuss what is happening behind the scenes in regards to the packaging and deployment of your SharePoint artifacts when F5 is pressed. In addition, we will discuss how, when, and why to change the default packaging and deployment settings. We are also going to show you how to use Visual Studio extensibility to create your own custom deployment steps and deployment configurations.

SharePoint Features

In order to fully understand all the packaging and deployment features that Visual Studio 2010 offers we need to step back and start with the basic building blocks of SharePoint deployment: SharePoint features. After you understand the manual process of creating, deploying, and activating SharePoint features you will quickly realize how much has been done in Visual Studio 2010 to help developers easily deploy SharePoint features.

Whenever someone is talking about SharePoint features you probably immediately think about how a SharePoint feature adds additional functionality to SharePoint. A SharePoint feature contains some functionality that can be used on the SharePoint site once the feature is deployed and activated. From a technical standpoint, a SharePoint feature is just an XML file that is conveniently named Feature.xml. The Feature.xml file is called the feature manifest file. This file contains general information about the feature, such as its ID, name, and scope.

A feature's ID and name are pretty much self-explanatory—these two attributes are there to uniquely define the feature. The name is just an arbitrary string. The ID is a GUID—a globally unique identifier in the format "xxxxxxxx-xxxx-xxxx-xxxx-xxxxxxxxxxxx." The "x" in the format can be any hexadecimal digit—digits 0 through 9 and a, b, c, d, e, and f. Most of the time, Visual Studio will automatically create a GUID for you when you need it—for example, when you create a new SharePoint feature in Visual Studio, the GUID will automatically be created. Occasionally, you need to create your own GUID, however do not create the GUID manually. When you need to create your own GUID, use the Create GUID command in the Tools menu of Visual Studio to automatically create a GUID and copy it to the clipboard and then you can paste it into the file that needs the GUID.

All SharePoint functionality is available at a particular scope: Farm, Web Application, Site, or Web. A feature with scope Farm is available to any site or site collection on the server. A feature with scope Web is only available to the SharePoint site in which the feature was installed and activated. The four scopes at which a feature can be deployed and activated are shown in Table 11-1. Note that you cannot just arbitrarily use any scope you want for any type of SharePoint customization—some SharePoint customizations can only be installed at a particular scope, for example content types and workflows can only be installed at Site scope while custom actions can be installed at every scope. We will talk more about SharePoint customizations and the scopes at which each type can be installed later in the SharePoint Elements section.

TABLE 11-1: SharePoint Feature Scopes

Scope	Description
Farm	A feature with this scope can be used by all sites within the Farm where the feature was installed and activated.
Web Application	A feature with this scope can be used by all sites within the web application where the feature was installed and activated.
Site	A feature with this scope can be used by all sites within the site collection where the feature was installed and activated.
Web	A feature with this scope can be used by the site where the feature was installed and activated.

At least name, ID, and scope are necessary to define an empty feature as shown in Listing 11-1, but in most cases you would want a Feature.xml file to include additional attributes to specify the functionality or customization associated with the feature.

Listing 11-1: The Simplest Possible Feature.xml Feature Manifest

```
<Feature Title="SharePoint Feature"
  Id="b52f4b52-5d79-4e8a-a663-fc11d4a10ff9" Scope="Site">
</Feature>
```

If we wanted to, we could deploy the feature in Listing 11-1 to the SharePoint server but there's no point in doing that, because the feature is empty—it only contains the minimum feature definition without any functionality.

The feature manifest file typically includes an XML element called ElementManifests, which can contain a collection of ElementManifest elements that point to an Elements.xml file that includes the actual information needed to install the functionality associated with the feature. If you remember from previous chapters, every SharePoint project item we created had an Elements.xml file. The Elements.xml file is the file that an ElementManifest element from a Feature.xml file points at. For example if we wanted to deploy a SharePoint project item called MyElement1 using the empty feature file we created in Listing 11-1, we would add the ElementManifests element with an ElementManifest child element with its Location attribute set to the Elements.xml file associated with MyElement1 as shown in Listing 11-2.

Listing 11-2: Feature.xml

```
<Feature Title="SharePoint feature"
  Id="b52f4b52-5d79-4e8a-a663-fc11d4a10ff9" Scope="Site">
  <ElementManifests>
    <ElementManifest Location="MyElement1\Elements.xml" />
  </ElementManifests>
</Feature>
```

If we wanted to deploy more SharePoint project items with the same feature, we just have to add more ElementManifest child elements to the ElementManifests element and point to the Elements.xml file associated with each additional SharePoint project item.

Apart from ElementManifests and ElementManifest, there are some other XML elements that can be used in the feature manifest file. The structure of the feature manifest file with all available elements is shown in Listing 11-3.

Listing 11-3: All Possible XML Elements That Can Be Included in the Feature.xml file

```
<Feature>
  <ActivationDependencies>
    <ActivationDependency/>
    <ActivationDependency/>
  </ActivationDependencies>
  <ElementManifests>
    <ElementFile/>
    <ElementManifest/>
  </ElementManifests>
  <Properties>
    <Property/>
    <Property/>
  </Properties>
  <UpgradeActions>
    <AddContentTypeField/>
    <ApplyElementManifests>
      <ElementFile/>
      <ElementManifest/>
    </ApplyElementManifests>
```

```
    <CustomUpgradeAction>
      <Parameters>
        <Parameter/>
      </Parameters>
    </CustomUpgradeAction>
    <MapFile/>
    <VersionRange/>
  </UpgradeActions>
</Feature>
```

Table 11-2 shows all the possible Feature.xml elements we showed in Listing 11-3 with descriptions and a sample of how each element is used. Note that this table doesn't contain elements under the UpgradeActions element. The UpgradeActions element is new to SharePoint 2010 and will be described later in this chapter.

TABLE 11-2: Features.xml Element Descriptions

Element	Description	Sample
Activation-Dependency	The ActivationDependency element specifies a feature by ID on which activation of the current feature depends. **Example:** One way this could be used is when deploying a list and an associated workflow that has a dependency on the list. The activation dependency can be used to ensure the list is activated first and then the workflow.	`<ActivationDependency FeatureId="{51AE94E5-9735-4C15-9688-A47168AC371D}"/>`
ElementFile	The ElementFile element is used to specify supporting files that are required by the feature. **Example:** You can use ElementFile to deploy resource files, text files, images, ASPX files, XML files, and other files needed by the feature.	`<ElementFile Location="Resources\ Resources.resx" />`

Continues

Table 11-2:   Features.xml Element Descriptions *(Continued)*

Element	Description	Sample
ElementManifest	The ElementManifest element is used to point to the Elements.xml file associated with a SharePoint project item you want the feature to deploy.	`<ElementManifest Location="Workflow1\ Elements.xml" />`
Property	The Property element is used to define feature properties. Feature properties can be defined by specifying a name for the property along with a default value. You can access the feature properties from code within a feature event receiver using the 'properties' parameter (SPFeature-ReceiverProperties type) passed to the event handler method like this: properties.Feature.Properties["Color"].Value.	`<Property Key="Color" Value="Blue"/>`

SharePoint 2010 adds a new element called the UpgradeActions element. This element is used for specifying upgrade actions to take for a specified feature. The purpose of this element is to specify how to upgrade an existing feature instance. For example you have deployed a content type and site columns feature and now you want to delete a site column and update the content type accordingly. You could use the Upgrade-Actions element to specify the CustomUpgradeAction and a parameter that contains the name of the site column you want to delete. Next you would implement the FeatureUpgrading event receiver method and use the parameters passed to that method to determine the upgrade action name and the parameters. Table 11-3 below lists the upgrade action elements that can be placed in the feature manifest file.

TABLE 11-3: Feature Upgrade Actions Elements

Element	Description	Sample
AddContent-TypeField	Adds a new column to an existing content type. **Example:** You deployed a feature with a content type and you want to add a new column to that content type.	`<AddContentTypeField ContentTypeId="[CONTENT TYPE ID]" FieldId="{[FIELD ID]}" PushDown="TRUE"/>`
Custom-UpgradeAction	Inside the custom upgrade action you can specify a list of parameters. These parameters are the passed to the FeatureUpgrading method in the feature event receiver. See Chapter 5, "SharePoint Event Receivers," on more information about SharePoint event receivers.	`<CustomUpgradeAction Name="MyUpgradeAction"/>`
ApplyElement-Manifests	Used for provisioning all the elements that are referenced in the element. This element can contain ElementManifest and ElementFile elements. **Example:** You want to include an element manifest file that deploys additional elements to SharePoint.	`<ApplyElementManifests>` `<ElementManifest Location="MyFeature\ UpgradeManifest.xml"/>` `</ApplyElementManifests>`
Parameter	Used for specifying a parameter that gets passed to the FeatureUpgrading method of the feature event receiver.	`<Parameter Name="Parameter-Name">ParameterValue </Parameter>`
MapFile	This element can be used to either rename or move a file. It has two attributes: FromPath and ToPath, which can be used to specify the source and target file. **Example:** You want to move the images deployed with the feature to a new location.	`<MapFile FromPath="OldLogo.png" ToPath="NewLogo.png"/>`
VersionRange	Used for versioning. You can specify a specific version range and which upgrade actions to apply. **Example:** You can use the VersionRange element to update specific versions of the deployed feature.	`<VersionRange BeginVersion="3.0.0.0" EndVersion="5.0.0.0"/>`

What we've learned so far is that SharePoint features provide a mechanism for deploying one or more SharePoint project items by pointing at the Elements.xml file associated with each project item through Feature.xml's ElementManifest element. We've also learned that we can specify additional elements and properties in the feature manifest such as upgrade actions or custom properties. But it's not enough to just point to the desired Elements.xml file. Depending on the type of SharePoint project items we are including in the Feature.xml file, we also need to correctly scope the feature. Also, you need to be aware that not all types of SharePoint project items can be deployed at the same scope. Before we show what the correct scopes for different SharePoint project items are, let's talk more about SharePoint elements.

SharePoint Elements

So far in the chapter, the word "elements" has been highly overloaded. Unfortunately, we're about to overload it even more. When we talk about elements in this chapter we sometimes mean an XML element like the XML element <Feature> in the Feature.xml file. We also have talked about the XML elements ElementManifests and ElementManifest that are used in a Feature.xml file to associate a feature with the Elements.xml file associated with a SharePoint project item. That Elements.xml file is yet another overload of the word "elements"—the Elements.xml file associated with each SharePoint project item and has the information in it that SharePoint needs to deploy the functionality contained in the SharePoint project item.

The further overloading of the word "elements" that we must introduce here is the notion of SharePoint elements. Most of the chapters in this book have been focused on one or more SharePoint elements, such as content types, workflows, list definitions, andlist instances. In most cases, Visual Studio provides a SharePoint project item for these SharePoint elements, so thus far in this book we have gotten away with not calling these "SharePoint elements" but instead "SharePoint project items." However, there are more SharePoint elements you can create and deploy that don't have a corresponding SharePoint project item. Table 11-4 lists all SharePoint elements and their descriptions.

TABLE 11-4: SharePoint Elements Descriptions and Their Associated SharePoint Project Item if Available

Element	Associated SharePoint Project Item	Description
Content Type	Content Type	Content type element as described in Chapter 7, "SharePoint Content Types."
Content Type Binding	N/A	Used for defining a content type for lists that can't be modified directly (lists defined in the onet.xml schema).
Custom Action	N/A	Allows adding custom actions for a link or toolbar item.
Custom Action Group	N/A	Used for grouping custom actions.
Delegate Controls	N/A	Used for specifying controls for a particular functionality and to choose a functionality provider for those controls. For example, you could specify a control and then add tooltips to that control.
Document Converter	N/A	Used for defining document converters.
Event Receiver	Event Receiver	Event receivers as described in Chapter 5, "SharePoint Event Receivers."
Feature/Site Template Association	N/A	Used for including specific features as part of the site definition configuration.
Field Element	N/A	Used for creating site columns.
Hide Custom Action	N/A	Allows hiding of custom actions.
List Instance	List Instance	Used for defining list instances.
List Template	List Definition	Used for defining list templates.
Module	Module	Modules are used to deploy files that support a feature.
Workflow	Workflow	SharePoint Workflows as described in Chapter 8, "SharePoint Workflow."

Where Are Visual Studio 2010 Project Items for These Elements?

You probably noticed some elements in the above table don't have Visual Studio 2010 project items. Not all elements mentioned above are available as project items—although they may be added in future releases of Visual Studio. However, this doesn't mean you can't use Visual Studio 2010 to create and deploy SharePoint elements that don't have a corresponding Visual Studio project item. If you want to deploy a custom action, for example, you can use the Empty Element project item template. This is why the Empty Element project item exists—to fill in the gap where Visual Studio doesn't have a project item for a particular SharePoint element. The Empty Element project item is a blank project item with an Elements.xml file below it in which you can put the XML markup that describes the SharePoint element you want to add to the project.

It Seems Like Some Things Are Missing from Table 11-4—For Example, Where Are Web Part and Application Page?

Web Parts, Visual Web Parts, and Application Pages are missing from Table 11-4 because they don't have their own SharePoint element. If you open the Elements.xml file of a Web Part project you would notice that it is being deployed as a Module. The web part definition is in the .webpart file and this file is deployed to the SharePoint with the help of the Module element. Since Application Page is just an .aspx file there's no need to use a dedicated SharePoint element to deploy it—Application Pages are deployed to SharePoint as template files that are part of the SharePoint package.

Each of the elements described in Table 11-4 can be deployed to a specific set of scopes. Table 11-5 shows all the SharePoint elements and the scopes at which each element can be deployed and activated.

TABLE 11-5: Elements and Supported Scopes

	Scope			
Element	**Farm**	**Web Application**	**Site**	**Web**
Content Type			X	
Content Type Binding			X	
Custom Action	X	X	X	X
Custom Action Group	X	X	X	X
Delegate Controls	X	X	X	X
Document Converter				X
Event Receiver			X	X
Feature/Site Template Association	X	X	X	
Field Element			X	
Hide Custom Action	X	X	X	X
List Instance			X	X
List Template			X	X
Module			X	X
Workflow			X	

Deploying SharePoint Features

Now that we know what SharePoint elements are and how they should be scoped we now consider how to deploy a feature to the SharePoint server.

When a feature is deployed, the Feature.xml and associated Elements.xml files are copied to the file system of the SharePoint server. All feature and element files that have been installed on a server are stored under the features folder in the SharePoint hive, which is located at the following location.

```
Program Files\Common Files\Microsoft Shared\web server
    extensions\14\TEMPLATE\FEATURES\
```

Typically, the way to install features is to package them in a .WSP file and then run stsadm.exe on the .WSP file—stsadm.exe will copy the files in the package to the appropriate place in the SharePoint hive and then install the files. But in this section, we are going to do the copying of our files to the SharePoint hive ourselves without using a .WSP file and then run stsadm.exe on the files directly. Follow the steps below to create a new folder and copy Feature.xml file to that folder.

1. Navigate to the FEATURES folder in the SharePoint hive where all features are stored (shown above)
2. Create a subfolder called "MyFeature."
3. Copy the Feature.xml file to the MyFeature subfolder.

Our Feature.xml file has three SharePoint elements called: "MyElement1," "MyElement2," and "MyElement3." Listing 11-4 shows our Feature.xml file.

Listing 11-4: Feature.xml

```
<Feature Title="Myfeature" Id="b52f4b52-5d79-4e8a-a663-fc11d4a10ff9"
  Scope="Site">
  <ElementManifests>
    <ElementManifest Location="MyElement1\Elements.xml" />
    <ElementManifest Location="MyElement2\Elements.xml" />
    <ElementManifest Location="MyElement3\Elements.xml" />
  </ElementManifests>
</Feature>
```

Because we have three SharePoint elements, we need to create three subfolders under the MyFeature folder. Each of these element folders should contain the Elements.xml file we are referencing from Feature.xml. The structure of the MyFeature folder should look like this:

MyFeature
>   Feature.xml
>   MyElement1
>>   Elements.xml
>   MyElement2
>>   Elements.xml
>   MyElement3
>>   Elements.xml

Now that we have everything in place we can use stsadm.exe to install the feature. From the command line we can navigate to the stsadm.exe location, which is in the following folder on the SharePoint server: C:\Program Files\Common Files\Microsoft Shared\Web Server Extensions\14\BIN. To make accessing the stsadm.exe easier you can put the directory name in the PATH environment variable. Once the stsadm.exe directory is in the path variable you can run the stsadm.exe regardless of the folder where the command line was opened. Next, go to the C:\Program Files\Common Files\Microsoft Shared\Web Server Extensions\14\TEMPLATE\FEATURES folder and then run this command to install the feature:

```
Stsadm -o installfeature -filename MyFeature\feature.xml
```

Using the same tool we could issue a different command to uninstall the feature:

```
Stsadm -o uninstallfeature -filename MyFeature\feature.xml -url http://localhost
```

Once the install feature command runs successfully we can navigate to the SharePoint site and manually activate the feature. We could also use stsadm.exe to activate the feature with the following command:

```
Stsadm -o activatefeature -filename MyFeature\feature.xml -url http://localhost
```

The command for deactivating SharePoint features is similar:

```
Stsadm –o deactivatefeature –filename MyFeature\feature.xml –url http://localhost
```

We've now seen how features and their associated Element.xml files get stored in the SharePoint hive and how to manually install, uninstall, activate, and deactivate SharePoint features. As long as you have only one SharePoint feature to install, the process is not hard. But what happens if you would want to install multiple SharePoint features at once? Yes, you could create a script that would run all manual steps for each feature. What would be really nice is if there was some mechanism that could group or package all the features together and then we could just install that group and all of our features would be installed. Luckily for us, there is a way to do this and it's called SharePoint solution packaging.

SharePoint Solution Packaging

A SharePoint solution is a set of one or more SharePoint features. Figure 11-1 below shows the relationships between a SharePoint solution, features, and elements.

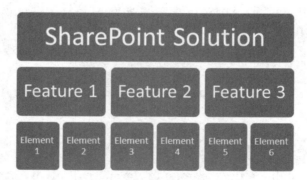

Figure 11-1: A SharePoint Solution with features and elements

The concept of a solution is similar to the concept of the feature. Just as we can use features to group different SharePoint elements together, we can use a solution to group different SharePoint features together. A SharePoint solution is a cabinet file (.CAB) that has a .WSP extension. This file is sometimes called a solution package or package file. The heart of a SharePoint solution is the solution manifest file, which is an XML file called Manifest .xml. This file indicates what's contained in the solution and information about where to deploy the solution contents. It also has a SolutionId, which is a GUID that uniquely identifies the solution. As we will see later, a solution manifest can also hold other settings such as Safe Control settings, resources, and Code Access Security settings. A sample solution manifest file that could be used to deploy three features is shown in Listing 11-5.

Listing 11-5: A Manifest.xml Solution Manifest to Install Three SharePoint Features

```
<Solution SolutionId="e16f0bec-15c1-4adb-872a-d2824bfd9669"
  SharePointProductVersion="14.0">
  <FeatureManifests>
    <FeatureManifest Location="Feature1\Feature.xml" />
    <FeatureManifest Location="Feature2\Feature.xml" />
    <FeatureManifest Location="Feature3\Feature.xml" />
  </FeatureManifests>
</Solution>
```

As is evident from the above listing, the FeatureManifests element and FeatureManifest elements are used to identify the Feature.xml feature manifest files that describe the features. Just as with a feature manifest, a solution manifest can contain more information than just pointers to feature manifests. The solution manifest structure with all possible XML elements is shown in Listing 11-6.

Listing 11-6: All Possible XML Elements That Can Be Included in the Manifest.xml File

```
<Solution>
  <ActivationDependencies>
    <ActivationDependency>
  </ActivationDependencies>
  <Assemblies>
    <Assembly>
      <BindingRedirects/>
      <ClassResources/>
      <SafeControls/>
    </Assembly>
  </Assemblies>
```

```
<ApplicationResourceFiles>
  <App_GlobalResourceFile/>
  <ApplicationResourceFile/>
</ApplicationResourceFiles>
<CodeAccessSecurity>
  <PolicyItem>
    <Assemblies>
      <Assembly/>
    </Assemblies>
    <PermissionSet>
      <IPermission/>
    </PermissionSet>
  </PolicyItem>
</CodeAccessSecurity>
<DwpFiles>
  <DwpFile/>
</DwpFiles>
<FeatureManifests>
  <FeatureManifest/>
</FeatureManifests>
<Resources>
  <Resource/>
</Resources>
<RootFiles>
  <RootFile/>
</RootFiles>
<SiteDefinitionManifests>
  <SiteDefinitionManifest>
    <WebTempFile/>
  </SiteDefinitionManifest>
</SiteDefinitionManifests>
<TemplateFiles>
  <TemplateFile/>
</TemplateFiles>
</Solution>
```

All the XML elements that can be used in the solution manifest file with their descriptions are shown in Table 11-6.

Based on Table 11-6 it is clear that solution manifests are not used just for deploying a particular feature. They can be used for more, such as defining safe controls for web parts, deploying resource files and deploying site definitions.

TABLE 11-6: Solution Manifest XML Elements

Element	Description	Sample

Activation-Dependencies	This element can be used like the ActivationDependencies element in the feature manifest file. With it we can specify the ID of a package on which activation of the current package depends. **Example:** Your SharePoint solution is separated into two packages: a base package with basic functionality and SharePoint elements and a second package that deploys the additional features that require the base package to be deployed.	`<ActivationDependencies>`
		`<ActivationDependency`
		`SolutionId="{GUID}"`
		`SolutionName="BaseSolution"/>`
		`</ActivationDependencies>`

Application-ResourceFiles	This element specifies any application resource files that need to be included in the solution. **Example:** You need to deploy resources required by your solution like some image files.	`<ApplicationResourceFiles>`
		`<ApplicationResourceFile`
		`Location="MyResource.jpg"/>`
		`<App_GlobalResourceFile`
		`Location="GlobalResource.jpg"/>`
		`</ApplicationResourceFiles>`

Assemblies	This element specifies assemblies that should be included in the solution.	`<Assemblies>`
		`<Assembly Location="MyWorkflow`
		`.dll" DeploymentTarget=`
		`"GlobalAssemblyCache" />`
		`</Assemblies>`

SafeControls	This element specifies safe controls from an assembly that should be added to the safe control list, typically used for web parts. **Example:** When deploying web parts, Visual Studio automatically adds a SafeControl entry for the web part project.	`<SafeControls>`
		`<SafeControl Assembly="MyWebPart,`
		`Version=1.0.0.0, Culture=neutral,`
		`PublicKeyToken=669efd360d838364"`
		`Namespace="MyWebPart.VWP"`
		`TypeName="*" />`
		`</SafeControls>`

Continues

TABLE 11-6: Solution Manifest XML Elements *(Continued)*

Element	Description	Sample

ClassResources	This element specifies any class resources for an assembly. **Example:** ClassResources type is used to deploy any resources that are required by the controls in your assembly. These resources can be accessed programmatically from code file as well.	`<ClassResources>`
		`<ClassResource`
		`Location="Picture.jpg " />`
		`</ClassResources>`

CodeAccess-Security	This element defines the trust level and custom policy files for specific assemblies. If your assembly requires a higher trust level you can create custom policy instead of increasing the trust level of the entire server.	See Chapter 9, "SharePoint Web Parts," for an example of how to use the CodeAccessSecurity element.

DwpFiles	The DwpFiles element allows you to deploy web parts to SharePoint.	`<DwpFiles>`
		`<DwpFile Location="MyDwp.dwp" />`
		`</DwpFiles>`

FeatureManifests	This element points to feature manifests to deploy with this solution.	`<FeatureManifests>`
		`<FeatureManifest`
		`Location="Feature1\Feature.xml" />`
		`<FeatureManifest`
		`Location="Feature2\Feature.xml" />`
		`</FeatureManifests>`

Resources	This element defines resources to be included in the solution.	`<Resources>`
		`<Resource`
		`Location="MyResources.resx" />`
		`</Resources>`

RootFiles	Used for copying certain files to the folders in the Share-Point hive folder structure. All root files are deployed under the SharePoint hive on the SharePoint server: Program Files\Common Files\Microsoft Shared\web server extensions\14	`<RootFiles>`
		`<RootFile Location="MyFile.xml" />`
		`</RootFiles>`

TABLE 11-6: Solution Manifest XML Elements *(Continued)*

Element	Description	Sample
SiteDefinition-Manifests	This element allows us to include site definitions in the solution.	```<SiteDefinitionManifests> <SiteDefinitionManifest Location="STS"/> </SiteDefinitionManifests>```
WebTempFile	Web template specification file is associated with the site definition that is included in the solution.	```<WebTempFile Location="1033\STS\webtempSTS.xml"/>```
TemplateFiles	This element is similar to the RootFiles element. It can be used to copy certain files to the TEMPLATE folder. Most commonly this element is used to copy files to the _layouts virtual directory, which is mapped to the \TEMPLATE_LAYOUTS folder. **Example:** Application Pages and workflow forms are deployed as TemplateFiles.	```<TemplateFiles> <TemplateFile Location="LAYOUTS\ Page1.aspx" /> </TemplateFiles>```

Installing solutions to the SharePoint server requires more work than installing features. Before a solution can be installed to the server it needs to be packaged as a .WSP file. In the following section we will describe how to manually create a solution stsadm.exe. Once we've manually created a solution package, we will use stsadm.exe to install it to the SharePoint server. Later, we'll find that Visual Studio automates all of this for us, but for now we are going to do things the hard way to better understand what Visual Studio is doing for us behind the scenes.

Deploying SharePoint Solutions

In order to create a SharePoint solution package, we need to prepare the solution folder structure and copy the required files to their respective folders. When creating solution package files we start with an empty root folder and place the package manifest file (Manifest.xml) in that folder. For each feature associated with the solution, we create a separate folder and put the Feature.xml file for the feature in that folder. Since every feature usually includes a SharePoint element with its associated Elements.xml file, we need to create the element folders under the feature folder and place the corresponding Elements.xml file there.

For this example, we have a solution with two features. First, Feature1 that has two elements: Element1 and Element2. Second, Feature2 with one element: Element3. If we created the solution folder structure based on the rules above, it should look like this:

```
Root Folder
      Manifest.xml
      Feature1
            Feature.xml
            Element1
                  Elements.xml
            Element2
                  Elements.xml
      Feature2
            Feature.xml
            Element3
                  Elements.xml
```

With the folder structure defined we already know what the package manifest file should look like. Listing 11-7 shows the manifest.xml file for the above example.

Listing 11-7: Manifest.xml for a SharePoint Solution with Two Features

```xml
<Solution SolutionId="e16f0bec-15c1-4adb-872a-d2824bfd9669"
 SharePointProductVersion="14.0">
 <FeatureManifests>
   <FeatureManifest Location="Feature1\Feature.xml" />
   <FeatureManifest Location="Feature2\Feature.xml" />
 </FeatureManifests>
</Solution>
```

Both Feature.xml files would look similar to the one we discussed in the SharePoint features section; Feature1's Feature.xml would reference two elements and Feature2's Feature.xml would reference one element. You also would copy the Elements.xml files to their respective folders to complete the folder and file structure on disc.

Now that we have the folder and files structure in place, the next step is to create a solution package. In order to do that we need to create a Diamond Directive File (or .DDF file) that defines the folder structure of the package. A .DDF file is just a text file following a specific syntax. The .DDF file for the solution we defined above is shown in Listing 11-8.

Listing 11-8: MySolution.DDF

```
HEADER
.OPTION EXPLICIT
.Set CabinetNameTemplate=MySolution.wsp
.Set DiskDirectoryTemplate=CDROM
.Set CompressionType=MSZIP
.Set UniqueFiles=Off
.Set Cabinet=On
.Set DiskDirectory1=Package

; ROOT FOLDER
manifest.xml

; Feature1 folder
.Set DestinationDir=Feature1
Feature1\Feature.xml

; Feature2 folder
.Set DestinationDir=Feature2
Feature2\Feature.xml
```

Once you save the file with a .DDF extension you have to run the MAKECAB tool that is part of the operating system that creates the .CAB file. Before you run the command to create the .CAB file from the .DDF file make sure you are in the same folder where the .DDF file is. The command to create the .CAB file looks like this:

```
Makecab /f Solution.DDF
```

This command creates a subfolder called "Package" in the folder where the Makecab was executed and places the MySolution.wsp file in it. Now that we have the .WSP file we can use stsadm.exe to install the solution on the SharePoint server. The command to add the solution to the SharePoint solution store would look like this:

```
Stsadm -o addsolution -filename MySolution.wsp
```

This command just adds the solution to the SharePoint solution store. The solution store is a centralized collection of all SharePoint solutions for the server farm. A second command is required to make the features in the solution usable—this command actually puts the necessary files from the solution into the respective folders. We can say that the deploysolution command below is similar to the installfeature command we used to install a single feature and copy all the files to the hive. The command that does all this looks like this:

```
Stsadm -o deploysolution -name MySolution.wsp -immediate
```

The above command will deploy the solution to all the servers in the farm. There are additional options you could pass to stsadm.exe when deploying the solution, such as allowing GAC deployment, deploying only to the local server, etc. If we wanted to remove the solution from the solution store, there is an opposite action to the deploy solution called retract solution. The command for retracting a solution would look like this:

```
Stsadm -o retractsolution -name MySolution.wsp -immediate
```

Retract removes all the features included in the solution from the SharePoint server. Retract doesn't remove or delete the solution though. In order to delete the solution from the store, you can use the delete solution command:

```
Stsadm -o deletesolution -name MySolution.wsp
```

We did things the hard way thus far to get familiar with how features and solutions work. As you saw from these simple examples, it can be a lot of work to prepare the features and create a solution, then package it and finally deploy it. In the remainder of this chapter we are going to explain how to achieve everything from packaging to deployment the easy way—using the new features of Visual Studio 2010.

The SharePoint Project Structure in Visual Studio

Some of the SharePoint elements we talked about in this chapter are represented as project templates or project item templates in Visual Studio 2010. When you create a new SharePoint 2010 project, Visual Studio automatically creates a project structure for you. The project structure of every SharePoint project follows the same pattern. Each SharePoint project has the following elements:

- A Features folder
- A Package folder
- 0 or more SharePoint project item folders

Let's take the workflow project as an example; the structure of the workflow project is shown in Figure 11-2.

Figure 11-2: Workflow Project Structure

You can easily locate the Features and Package folders, and there is also a SharePoint project item for the workflow. The workflow project item, Workflow1 in our example, is actually a folder that contains the Elements .xml file we discussed earlier, which describes the workflow so it can be installed and deployed. In addition to the Elements.xml file, the Workflow1 project item folder also contains a Workflow1.cs code file. These files inside the project item folder are called project item files.

Every project item file in the Visual Studio SharePoint project item has properties set that define where the file will be deployed on the SharePoint server. When you click on a project item file and show the Properties window, you can see these properties under the SharePoint category. Figure 11-3 shows the properties that are displayed when you click on the Elements.xml file for the Workflow project item. The properties in the SharePoint category determine where the specific project item file will be deployed.

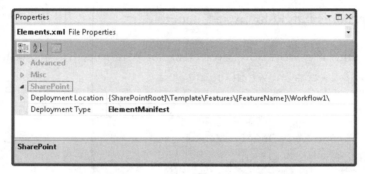

Figure 11-3: Deployment Properties in the SharePoint Category for Elements.xml

The Deployment Type property determines where the file will be deployed. If you change this property, the value of the Deployment Location will change as appropriate. Because the Elements.xml file is a SharePoint element manifest, the deployment type is set to ElementManifest. The Deployment Location property is built from two parts: Root and Path. The Deployment Location property can be expanded in the Properties window so you can see both parts of it. You can refer to Table 11-7 for default Root values based on the selected deployment types. Also note that Visual Studio uses some variables specified in { } brackets to specify names in an indirect way. {SharePointRoot} maps to the root of the SharePoint hive, {FeatureName} maps to the name of the feature the file is associated with, and so on.

TABLE 11-7: Deployment Types and Default Root and Path Values

Deployment Type	Root	Path
NoDeployment	/	N/A
ElementManifest	{SharePointRoot}\Template\Features\{FeatureName}\	{ProjectItemName}
ElementFile	{SharePointRoot}\Template\Features\{FeatureName}\	{ProjectItemName}
TemplateFile	{SharePointRoot}\Template\	{ProjectName}\{ProjectItemName}
RootFile	{SharePointRoot}\	{ProjectName}\{ProjectItemName}
ClassResource	{ClassResourcePath}\	{ProjectName}\{ProjectItemName}
Application-Resource	{WebApplicationRoot}\Resources\	{ProjectName}\{ProjectItemName}
AppGlobal-Resource	{WebApplicationRoot}\App_GlobalResources\	{ProjectName}\{ProjectItemName}
PackageOnly	/	{ProjectName}\{ProjectItemName}
Resource	{SharePointRoot}\Template\Features\	N/A
DwpFile	{WebApplicationRoot}\wpcatalog\	{ProjectName}\{ProjectItemName}

You probably remember some of the deployment types in the above table. We mentioned them in the section about the SharePoint solution manifest and you can see that these deployment types map to XML elements used in the solution manifest described in Table 11-6. When a project is packaged all the files in the project are enumerated and their deployment types are checked. If a file has the deployment type set to TemplateFile for example, the XML element TemplateFile is added to the Manifest.xml solution manifest file for the project.

Files that have the deployment type set to NoDeployment are ignored and they are not packaged. If you select the Workflow1.cs file you will notice that the deployment type for this file is set to NoDeployment, because we don't want to deploy the code file. But if we changed the deployment type, for example, to RootFile, the code file would get packaged and deployed. The XML element RootFile would be used in the Manifest.xml solution manifest file for the project.

You will note that the NoDeployment deployment type doesn't have a root path set. There is a second deployment type that doesn't have the root path set. If a file is marked with the PackageOnly deployment type it is included in the package, but it won't contain any information on how to deploy it. Sometimes developers want to include additional files (such as PDB files or even code files) in the package but they don't want to deploy them to the SharePoint server.

Next we have deployment types that can be used for deploying resources. Depending on what we are trying to localize and where we want the resource file to be deployed we can set the deployment type either to ClassResource, ApplicationResource, AppGlobalResource, or Resource.

The ClassResource deployment type should be used for any resource that is required by the controls in your assembly—this applies to Web Part projects. If you are using resources such as images, scripts, style sheets, and similar resources that are not included in the assembly you would mark them with the ClassResource deployment type and they will end up at the correct location on the SharePoint server. The location of the resources deployed as a ClassResource type depends on the assembly deployment location—GAC or web application. From the web part code file you can access the resources using the GetServerRelativeClassResourcePath method in the SPWebPartManager class.

Files deployed as ApplicationResource type will end up in the resource folder of the SharePoint web application. For example if we deployed a MyResource.xml file as an ApplicationResource from a web part project, the file would end up in the following location: C:\inetpub\wwwroot\wss\VirtualDirectories\[PORTNUMBER]\resources\MyProjectName\MyProjectItemName\MyResource.xml.

The AppGlobalResource deployment type is meant for resource files that are used by ASPX pages and assemblies. Resources marked with this deployment type get deployed to C:\inetpub\wwwroot\wss\Virtual-Directories\[PORT NUMBER]\App_GlobalResources where they can be used from assemblies and ASPX pages.

In order to deploy resources that are specific to the feature you are deploying you should use the Resource deployment type. Files marked with Resource deployment type are deployed to the SharePoint hive's TEMPLATE\FEATURES\{Feature Name}\Resources folder. If you want to share the same resources across the features on the SharePoint server you should deploy it to the Resources folder in the SharePoint hive.

The second part of the Deployment Location property is the Path property. Based on the selected deployment type, the Path property is usually set either to the project name, project item folder or both using the bracketed ({ }) variable notation. The value of this property is appended to the Root property value. During packaging, the bracketed variables are resolved and the Root and Path properties are combined to create the final full deployment path of a file. The root property is fully managed by the deployment type meaning it is read-only and cannot be changed directly. The Path property is not read-only and it can be changed to different values if needed.

Feature Designer

The Features folder is a folder where all the features created in the SharePoint project are located. The nicest thing about the features inside the Features folder is that by double-clicking the feature we can get to the Feature designer shown in Figure 11-4.

The Feature designer offers you a designer view of the feature manifest file (Feature.xml). From the designer and the Properties window shown when the Feature designer is active as in Figure 11-5 we can set everything we were able to edit directly in the Feature.xml file.

Table 11-8 lists all the properties shown in the Properties window for the Feature designer and their descriptions.

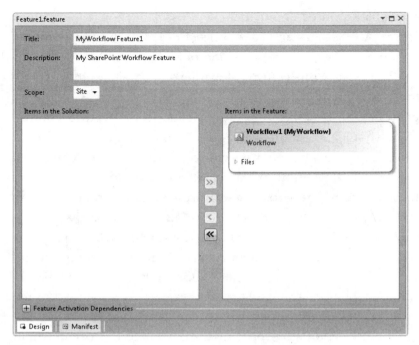

Figure 11-4: Feature designer

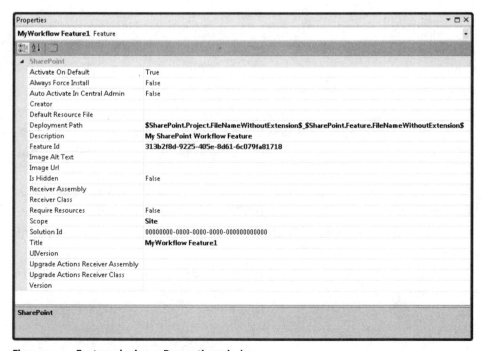

Figure 11-5: Feature designer Properties window

TABLE 11-8: Feature Designer Properties

Property	Description
Activate On Default	Indicates whether the feature is activated during deployment; set to True by default.
Always Force Install	If set to True, the feature will be installed by force, which means it will overwrite the same feature if it is already installed. This property is set to False by default.
Auto Activate In Central Admin	Indicates if the feature is activated for administrators; set to False by default.
Creator	Name of the developer who created the feature.
Default Resource File	Resource file from which feature resources are retrieved.
Deployment Path	The path to which the feature is deployed.
Description	Description of the feature.
Feature Id	Unique ID of the feature, a GUID.
Image Alt Text	The text for the image that is associated with the feature.
Image Url	The URL for the feature image: this image is shown in the Site Features or Site Collection Features pages within SharePoint.
Is Hidden	Indicates if a feature is hidden from the list of available features to activate on the SharePoint; set to False by default.
Receiver Assembly	Fully qualified name of the feature event receiver assembly if the feature has an event receiver associated with it.
Receiver Class	Class name of the feature event receiver if the feature has an event receiver associated with it.
Requires Resources	Indicates whether SharePoint checks for resources for a particular language and culture; set to False by default.
Scope	Scope of the feature as discussed earlier in this chapter.
Solution Id	For internal use only, this is the ID of the SharePoint server in which the feature will be installed.

Continues

TABLE 11-8: Feature Designer Properties *(Continued)*

Property	Description
Title	Title of the feature.
UIVersion	Compatible UI versions of the SharePoint site; this property can accept two values: 3 or 4. If UIVersion of a feature is set to 3 the feature can only be activated on SharePoint sites whose UI is set to version 3 (e.g., SharePoint 2007).
Upgrade Actions Receiver Assembly	Fully qualified name of the feature event receiver that handles custom upgrade actions.
Upgrade Actions Receiver Class	Class name of the feature event receiver that handles custom upgrade actions.
Version	Represents the feature version.

We will now present an example to learn more about the Feature designer and how to use it. We are going to show how to hide a feature, set an image for the feature, and how to use the Empty Element project item to create SharePoint elements that don't have their own project item templates in Visual Studio 2010. Let's start with an Empty SharePoint project.

1. Open Visual Studio 2010 with administrator privileges.
2. Click File > New Project.
3. Expand the Visual C# > SharePoint > 2010 node and select the Empty SharePoint Project template.
4. Name the project "HiddenFeatureAndImage" and click OK to start the SharePoint Customization Wizard.

   The wizard page shown in Figure 11-6 appears.
5. Select Deploy as a farm solution and click Finish to create the project.

   We selected the farm solution deployment because we will add the CustomAction element that cannot be deployed as a sandboxed solution.

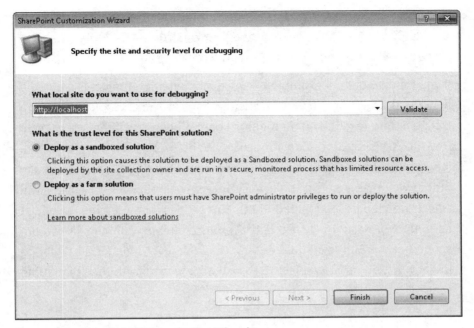

Figure 11-6: SharePoint Customization Wizard

We created an Empty SharePoint project. By default Empty SharePoint projects don't have any features. There are two ways features can be created: by adding SharePoint project items or by directly adding a new empty feature.

Every time you add a SharePoint project item to the project it will automatically reuse an existing feature of compatible scope in the project or if there is no feature with a compatible scope in the project (or no features at all) it will create a new feature. For example, if you create a list definition project, a new feature with the scope set to Web (SharePoint Site) is created. If you add a workflow project item to this project a new feature will get created, because workflows can only be deployed at Site (SharePoint Site Collection) scope and since we can't add the workflow to the existing, Web-scoped feature, Visual Studio creates a new feature. If we added another list definition project item or list instance, the project item would be added to the existing Web-scoped feature.

Some SharePoint Elements Are Compatible with Multiple Scopes—How Does Visual Studio Pick One?

If you think about our example—when a list definition project is created a new feature with scope Web is created—but in Table 11-5 it says that a List Template (e.g., List Definition) is compatible with either Site or Web. How does Visual Studio decide to use Web (site) scope instead of Site (site collection) scope? When creating new SharePoint projects Visual Studio will always select the lowest of the available scopes—e.g., it will select the Web scope instead of the Site scope when creating a new list definition project. However, if the project already contains a feature scoped at the Site level (higher than the Web level), Visual Studio adds the new list definition project to the existing feature with the compatible scope.

The second way to add new features to the project is by right clicking the Features folder and selecting Add Feature from the context menu. This adds a new feature to the project. The initial title of the new feature is set to the project and feature name concatenated with a unique number (e.g., MyProject Feature1, MyProject Feature2, etc.).

Because our current empty project includes a single feature and no SharePoint project items it is not very interesting, so let's add a SharePoint project item.

1. Right click the project name and select Add > New Item....

   Instead of right clicking you can also click the project node and press CTRL+SHIFT+A to open the Add New Item dialog.

2. Select the Empty Element project item template and name it "My Custom Action."

3. Click Add to add the item to the project.

What's an Empty Element?

Remember earlier in this chapter when we discussed all the different SharePoint elements, such as Custom Action, Document Converters, etc. that can be added to the SharePoint in Table 11-4? You will also remember that the project and project item templates for some of these elements are not available. The Empty Element project item is your friend in this case. An Empty Element is just a simple SharePoint project item with an empty Elements.xml file. With a little knowledge you can transform this empty Element project item into a Custom Action, a Document Converter, a Field element, or any other SharePoint element that doesn't have a project template in Visual Studio 2010 by putting the appropriate markup in the Elements.xml file.

The hardest part when creating SharePoint elements from an Empty Element project item is determining what markup to put in the Elements .xml file. When you add an Empty Element project item you are presented with an empty Elements.xml file. In order to make the element do something useful you need to write some XML. IntelliSense that shows when you are trying to write the XML can be very helpful because it shows you what XML elements and attributes are available in the Elements.xml file. Another helpful piece of information when developing SharePoint actions is the schema for the elements that can be found on MSDN. You can find the custom action schema here for example: http://msdn.microsoft.com/en-us/library/ms460194.aspx.

For this example we are going to create a custom action element that adds a link to the Bing search engine to the Site Actions menu on SharePoint. In order to do this we will need to specify the link URL (e.g., www.bing .com) and we need to tell SharePoint where to put the link (e.g., the Site Actions menu). The schema for the custom action's Elements.xml file shows attributes such as ID, GroupId, Location, and Title. In order to show the link in the Site Actions menu we need to set all those attributes. You can find all possible values for GroupId and Location property on MSDN (http://msdn.microsoft.com/en-us/library/bb802730.aspx). At this URL we find that the Microsoft.SharePoint.StandardMenu is the location we need, and from the corresponding GroupIds for the StandardMenu the location is Site-Actions. Writing this up in the Elements.xml file we get Listing 11-9.

Listing 11-9: An Elements.xml File Specifying a CustomAction to Display a Link to the Bing Search Engine in the Site Actions Menu

```
<Elements xmlns="http://schemas.microsoft.com/sharepoint/">
  <CustomAction Id="BingLink" GroupId="SiteActions"
    Location="Microsoft.SharePoint.StandardMenu" Title="Bing">
    <UrlAction Url="http://www.bing.com"/>
  </CustomAction>
</Elements>
```

Now that we have the XML shown in Listing 11-9 in the Elements.xml file we can try and deploy the project by pressing F5. In the web browser, navigate to the SharePoint home page and open the Site Actions menu. A "Bing" menu item is added as shown in Figure 11-7. The reason this worked is that when we added the Empty Element project item to the project, Visual Studio was smart enough to add the Elements.xml for our empty element to the Features.xml associated with the feature created in the project.

We should make our custom action prettier— right now it's just a regular item with a title. We should add a description and an image. Adding a description is easy—simply add the Description attribute to the Custom-Action element. What about the image? If you noticed there is an ImageUrl attribute we could use. We only need to point to an image we want to show for the menu item. We could just point to any URL that contains an image, but what we want to do is deploy our own image to the SharePoint server as part of our deployment and then point to the deployed image. To deploy the image we are going to use a mapped folder. In the next section we are going to describe what a mapped folder is and then use it to deploy the image.

Figure 11-7: A custom menu Item
in the Site Actions menu

Mapped Folders

A mapped folder in a Visual Studio SharePoint project is a construct that allows deploying files from the Visual Studio project to folders that are under the SharePoint hive (e.g., Program Files\Common Files\Microsoft Shared\web server extensions\14). There are two ways you can add a mapped folder to the SharePoint project: adding a predefined mapped folder, such as Images and Layouts or using the SharePoint Mapped Folder dialog.

To add a predefined mapped folder you can right click the project name and select the Add menu. The context menu shown Figure 11-8 opens and you can click either SharePoint "Images" Mapped Folder or SharePoint "Layouts" Mapped Folder to add a mapped folder to the Images or Layouts folder in the SharePoint hive. Images and Layouts are available in this predefined way because they are used so commonly in SharePoint development.

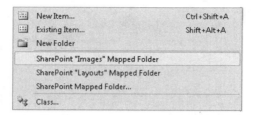

Figure 11-8: The Project Context Menu with the SharePoint "Images" Mapped Folder menu item

If you click the SharePoint Mapped Folder... menu item in Figure 11-8 the SharePoint Mapped Folder dialog shown in Figure 11-9 appears. From that dialog you can add a mapped folder for any of the folders in the Share-Point hive to your project.

Figure 11-9: Mapped Folder dialog

Since we are trying to deploy an image we will need the Images mapped folder. Right click the project name and select Add > SharePoint "Images" Mapped Folder. This adds the Images mapped folder to the project and the project structure will now look like Figure 11-10.

Figure 11-10: Project with an Images
Mapped Folder

Each mapped folder that gets added to the project is represented with the mapped folder icon. Under a particular mapped folder (e.g., Images) a new folder is always created with a name matching the project name.

Now that we have an Images mapped folder we can right click on the project name folder under the Images mapped folder and select Add > Existing item. In the Add Existing Item dialog, select the image, and click the Add button to add it to the mapped folder.

By default the Deployment Type of any file you add to a mapped folder is set to TemplateFile. This means that files added to mapped folders are not part of any feature, but deployed with the solution itself. The entry in Manifest.xml for a file deployed through the mapped folder is specified with the XML element TemplateFile.

For the image we just added to the mapped folder, the Deployment Type for the image is set to TemplateFile, which means the image is going to to be deployed to the SharePoint hive's \TEMPLATE\IMAGES\Hidden-FeatureAndImage folder. In order to display the image next to the custom link in the Site Actions dialog we need to set the ImageUrl property. To do this, we must update the Elements.xml file associated with our custom action with a Description and ImageUrl attribute as shown in Listing 11-10.

Listing 11-10: Updated CustomAction Element

```
<Elements xmlns="http://schemas.microsoft.com/sharepoint/">
  <CustomAction Id="BingLink"
    GroupId="SiteActions"
    Location="Microsoft.SharePoint.StandardMenu"
    Description="Open Bing.com"
    Title="Bing"
    ImageUrl="/_layouts/Images/HiddenFeatureAndImage/BingLogo.jpg">
    <UrlAction Url="http://www.bing.com"/>
  </CustomAction>
</Elements>
```

If we deploy the project and open the Site Actions menu on the Share-Point home page, we should see the Bing menu item with image and description as shown in Figure 11-11.

Figure 11-11: Custom Action with an image
that was deployed with the solution

Why Does the IMAGES Folder Map to _layouts/Images and Not _images?

There is a little surprise here in Listing 11-10. The image we deployed to the SharePoint hive at \TEMPLATE\IMAGES\HiddenFeatureAndImage\ BingLogo.jpg has the URL "http://localhost/_layouts/Images/Hidden-FeaturesAndImage/BingLogo.jpg." This is because SharePoint maps the SharePoint hive directory \TEMPLATE\LAYOUTS to http://localhost/_layouts and the SharePoint hive directory \TEMPLATE\IMAGES to http://localhost/_layouts/images.

What we should do next is to use the same image for the feature image. So, instead of using the generic feature image on the list of site features as shown in Figure 11-12 we could display our custom image there. To get to the site features page, go to the home page of the SharePoint site and drop down the Site Actions menu and select Site Settings from the menu. Then, in the Site Settings page, click on the Manage Site Features link in the Site Actions setting as shown in Figure 11-13.

HiddenFeatureAndImage Feature1

Deactivate   Active

Figure 11-12: Our feature without a custom image

Since we are already deploying the image we just need to tell the feature where to get the image from.

1. Double click the Feature1.feature file to open the Feature designer.
2. With Feature designer selected, open the Properties window.
3. Locate the Image Url property and set it to: HiddenFeatureAndImage/BingLogo.jpg.

Notice that in step 3 we didn't have to reference the image with the full folder path (_layouts/Images) as we did in the Elements.xml file. SharePoint already assumes the image is coming from the /_layouts/Images folder. Let's deploy the project again and check if the image shows up in the list of site features.

1. Press CTRL+F5 to deploy the project and start the web browser.
2. Click the Site Actions menu and select Site Settings.
   The Site Settings page shown in Figure 11-13 opens.
3. Click the Manage site features link to open the list of site features.

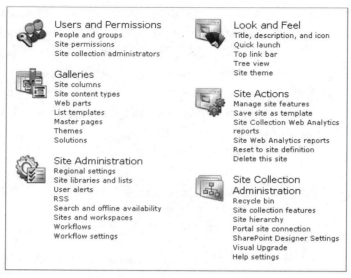

Figure 11-13: Site Settings page

On the Manage site features page you should find the feature we deployed and you should notice it uses the custom image we deployed. Depending on which image you used you should see the image shown together with the feature just like in Figure 11-14.

Figure 11-14: Feature with custom image

Let's say that the users of the SharePoint site we are managing really like the Bing feature. Due to the high popularity of this feature we want to make this a default part of our SharePoint sites from now on and prevent SharePoint users from ever deactivating this feature. To do so, we only need to change the value of the Is Hidden property on the feature designer to True and deploy the project again. If we navigate to the list of site features again, our cool Bing feature with the nice image is hidden and it doesn't show up on the page—but it can't be deactivated.

You can probably think of another way to deploy the image for our feature that wouldn't require the use of a mapped folder. We could just move the image file as a file under our Empty Element project item and change its SharePoint deployment properties to deploy it to the images folder. This is true, but consider how the picture is now being deployed. If you deploy the file through the mapped folder mechanism, this means that the file will be directly referenced from the Manifest.xml solution manifest via the Template-Files XML element. If you deploy the image file as a file associated with a SharePoint project item, the file would still get deployed to the right location, but instead of being part of the package it would be deployed as a part of a feature. Imagine this scenario: We have multiple SharePoint project items each installed by their own feature. In one of the project items we have some images that are used by all the project items but we are deploying those images as a part of one feature. What happens to other features if we uninstall the feature that was used to deploy those images? Well, the images won't show up in other features anymore because they were a part of the feature that got uninstalled. In this case using the mapped folder would be the right choice. Even if any of the features are uninstalled, the images are still there because they were deployed as a part of the solution.

Of course there could also be cases when deploying files through SharePoint project items would make more sense than deploying them through mapped folders. You could have several features, each associated with a particular language that holds resources specific to that language. That way you could send your users several features that hold language specific files and they could install or uninstall just the feature they need for their language as a sort of language pack.

Feature Activation Dependencies

We used the feature activation dependency functionality in Chapter 7, "SharePoint Content Types," when we were deploying a content type that was dependent on particular site columns. Our requirement there was to deploy and activate site columns before the content type was activated. We had two separate features—one that held site columns and one that held the content type. To make sure the site column feature was activated before the content type feature we used feature activation dependencies.

Feature activation dependencies can be configured through the Feature designer UI. First you need to open the Feature designer and at the bottom of the designer expand the Feature Activation Dependencies panel as shown in Figure 11-15.

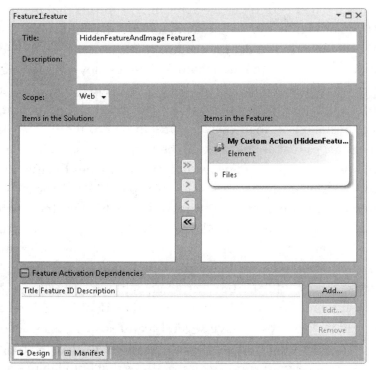

Figure 11-15: Expanded Feature Activation Dependencies panel

In order to show how activation dependencies work we should create two new empty SharePoint projects with one feature in each project and one Empty Element SharePoint project item in each project. Create an Empty SharePoint project and then right click the project name and select Add New Item. From the list of SharePoint project item templates, select the Empty Element template and click Add to add it to the project. Do the same action again for the second project.

By default activation dependencies are not set, but what we want to do is allow activation of the EmptyElement1 in the first project only if the EmptyElement1 in the second project is already activated. To do this, open the Feature designer in the first SharePoint project, expand the Feature Activation Dependencies panel and then click the Add... button to open the Add Feature Activation Dependencies dialog shown in Figure 11-16.

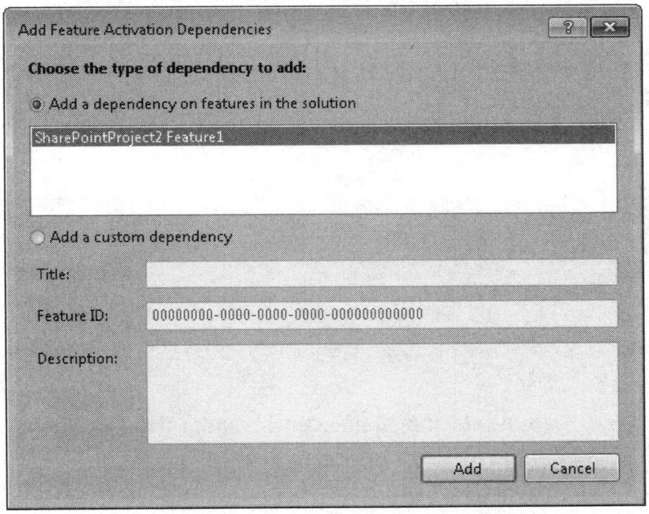

Figure 11-16: Add Feature Activation Dependencies dialog

From the Add Feature Activation Dependencies dialog we could either choose an existing feature in the solution or we could add a custom dependency. In order to add the custom dependency you need to specify the feature ID and title of the dependent feature. Let's create a dependency on the feature in the second SharePoint project (SharePointProject2.Feature1) and when we click the Add button, the dependency is added to the Feature Activation Dependencies panel as shown in Figure 11-17.

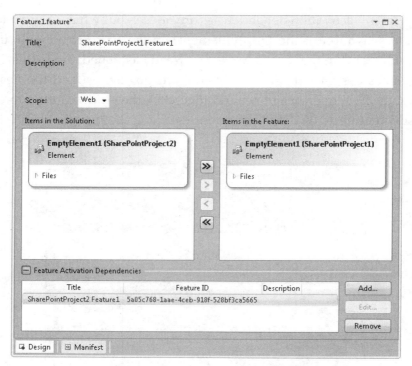

Figure 11-17: Feature Activation Dependencies with a dependency in
SharePointProject1.Feature1 on SharePointProject2.Feature1

Let's try and deploy the first SharePoint project. Right click the Share-
PointProject1 node and select Deploy. An error message like the one below
is displayed:

```
Error occurred in deployment step 'Activate Features':
Dependency feature with id 5a05c768-1aae-4ceb-918f-528bf3ca5665 for feature
'SharePointProject1_Feature1' (id: 925104e4-3ff8-44f4-98af-5f8d0a937491)
is not installed.
```

This error is actually expected because we set the feature activation
dependency. In order to successfully deploy and activate the feature in the
first project we need to deploy and activate the feature in the second
project first. Go ahead and right click the SharePointProject2 and select
Deploy to deploy it. Now try deploying the first project again—no errors
occur this time because the dependent feature is installed.

All changes made in the Feature designer are really editing the underlying Features.xml feature manifest file. But what if you want to take control over the Features.xml feature manifest file and edit it directly? For example, you may want to add a custom property to the feature manifest file. Unfortunately there is no way to do this from the Feature designer, but there is an option that lets you modify the underlying feature manifest file. In the next section we will explain the feature manifest editing options for advanced users and scenarios the Feature designer does not support.

Feature Designer for Advanced Users

Let's say you want to include some custom properties with your feature. The Feature designer offers you two different views: the Design view we already discussed, the view of interest to us now is the Manifest view. To switch between the two views you have to click the Design or Manifest buttons at the bottom of the Feature designer. The manifest view of the Feature designer is shown in Figure 11-18.

Figure 11-18: Manifest view in the Feature designer

The manifest view gives you a preview of the Feature.xml feature manifest file. You can now see the XML markup specifying the activation dependency we added earlier. The preview window is read-only and doesn't allow you to make any changes. However, if you expand the Edit Options panel at the bottom of the manifest view as shown in Figure 11-19 you will notice an editable textbox with XML.

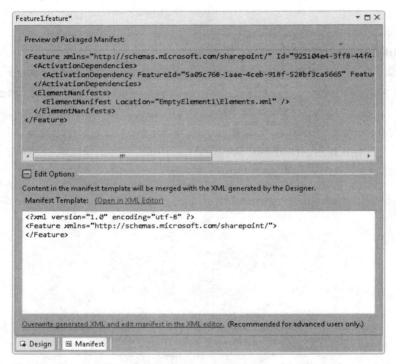

Figure 11-19: Manifest view in the Feature designer with Edit Options panel expanded

Whatever you type into the Edit Options panel's textbox is merged with the existing XML generated by the Feature designer. Type the following XML between the feature elements into the textbox in the Edit Options panel to add a custom property to the feature:

```
<Properties>
  <Property Key="MyProperty" Value="MyValue"/>
</Properties>
```

As you start typing XML you will notice that the manifest in the preview window changes. Once you type the complete XML it will get merged with the XML already in the feature manifest file.

There is one more option for editing feature manifests but it's recommended for advanced users only. Clicking the "Overwrite generated XML and edit manifest in the XML Editor" link allows you to take total control over editing the Feature.xml feature manifest. When you click that link a dialog prompting you if you want to disable the designer is displayed as shown in Figure 11-20.

Figure 11-20: Disabling the Feature designer

If you click Yes in the dialog you are disabling the Feature designer and overwriting the generated manifest file. Once the dialog is closed you will see a message on the Feature designer saying that designer is disabled and you have an option of editing the manifest file in the XML editor or discarding the changes and re-enabling the designer again.

Package Designer

You can use the Package designer in Visual Studio to manage creation of a .WSP file containing the SharePoint features in your solution. The Package designer can be opened by double clicking the Package folder in Solution Explorer. The Package designer is shown in Figure 11-21 and it has a similar layout to the Feature designer.

The purpose of the Package designer is to help you quickly group together SharePoint features into a .WSP file. From the designer itself you

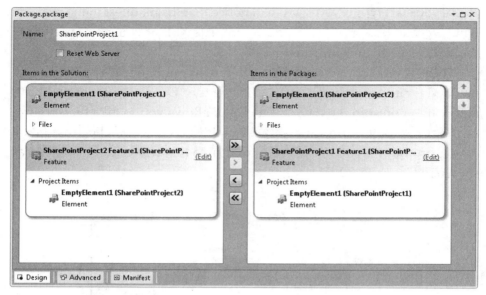

Figure 11-21: Package designer

can specify the package name and decide if you want to reset the web server during the deployment. If you open the Properties window with the designer active, you can access more package properties. The properties with their names and descriptions are shown in Table 11-9.

TABLE 11-9: Package Designer Properties

Property	Description
Deployment Server Type	Specifies the type of server that hosts the package; you can choose between WebFrontEnd (default selection) and ApplicationServer
Description	Package description
Name	Package file name (e.g., SharePointProject1.wsp)
Reset Web Server	Indicates whether IIS should be restarted after the package is installed

TABLE 11-9: Package Designer Properties *(Continued)*

Property	Description
Reset Web Server Mode On Upgrade	Specifies the type of web server reset; the default setting is StartStop, but you can also use the Recycle setting, which recycles the IIS worker process
SharePoint Product Version	This property specifies the SharePoint product version and is used by SharePoint for compatibility purposes
Solution Id	The ID of the package, a GUID
Title	The title of the package

Packaging Explorer

The Packaging Explorer shown in Figure 11-22 offers you a different view of the features and packages in your Visual Studio solution. It shows you all packages and features available in the solution as well as the SharePoint project item associated with each feature with its associated project item files (e.g., Elements.xml).

Figure 11-22: Packaging Explorer

The Packaging Explorer is an alternate view of your project from the Solution Explorer view. If you prefer working with the Packaging Explorer by all means do that. From the Packaging Explorer you can access the properties of every SharePoint project item that is in the solution along with every feature and package in the solution.

You can also re-arrange features and SharePoint project items—you can drag and drop a SharePoint project item from one feature to another feature in the same or a different package. Using the Packaging Explorer can prove very helpful if you have a large SharePoint solution with a large number of SharePoint project items and features. In that case, opening every single feature just to check which SharePoint project items are in there can be very time consuming. With the Packaging Explorer you can see all your packages with features and rearrange them to your liking much easier and faster than clicking through designers.

Package Designer for Advanced Users

From the Package Designer you can also perform some advanced tasks. If you click the Advanced tab at the bottom of the Package Designer the designer will change to a view that allows you to add additional assemblies to the deployment shown in Figure 11-23.

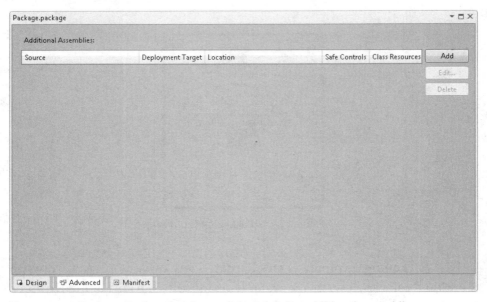

Figure 11-23: Package Designer's Advanced view showing additional assemblies

You can add additional assemblies to the package from the advanced view of the Package Designer. If you click the Add button you are presented with two options: Add Existing Assembly and Add Assembly from Project Output. The Add Existing Assembly dialog shown in Figure 11-24 allows you to add an existing assembly to the package.

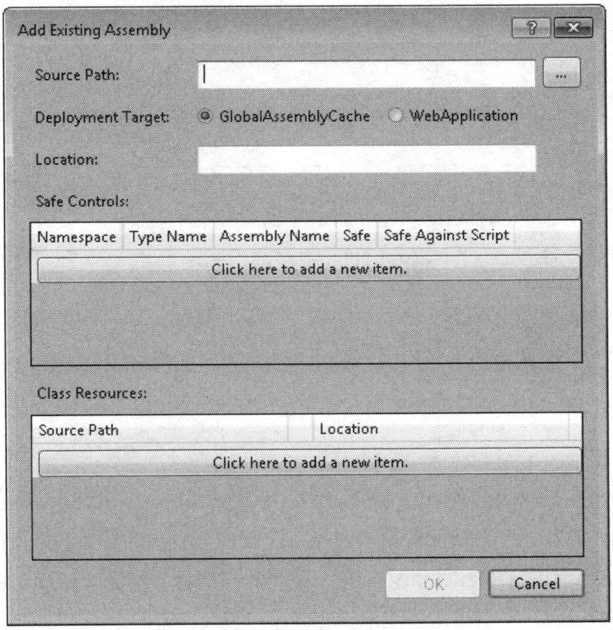

Figure 11-24: Add Existing Assembly dialog

From this dialog you can specify the desired assembly and where you want to deploy it. You can also register safe controls and add class resources that are in the selected assembly. The dialog for adding an assembly from the project output shown in Figure 11-25 is very similar to the previous dialog.

The only difference is that instead of having an option to browse to an existing assembly, you have the option to select a project from your current solution. The output assembly of the selected project is then added to the package. Just as with existing assemblies you can also specify the safe controls as well as class resources.

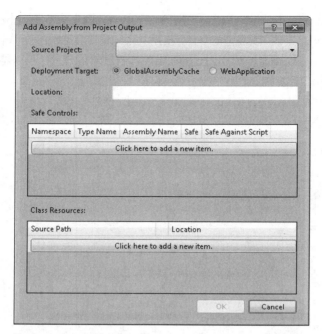

Figure 11-25: Add Assembly from Project Output dialog

Any changes made from this part of the designer are reflected in the package manifest file (Manifest.xml). As in Feature Designer, the Package Designer gives you an option to fully control the package manifest without the designer. If you click the Manifest tab the designer changes to the view shown in Figure 11-26.

You have two options for updating the package manifest. You can either enter the package manifest XML elements into the provided textbox and the XML you type is merged with the XML generated by the Package designer. The other advanced option is to overwrite the generated package manifest by clicking the link: Overwrite generated XML and edit manifest in the XML editor. If you decide to do this, you will be able to control the Manifest.xml package manifest file directly and change it to your liking and requirements. However, if you decide to go back and re-activate the Package designer, all the changes you made in the Manifest.xml package manifest will get overwritten.

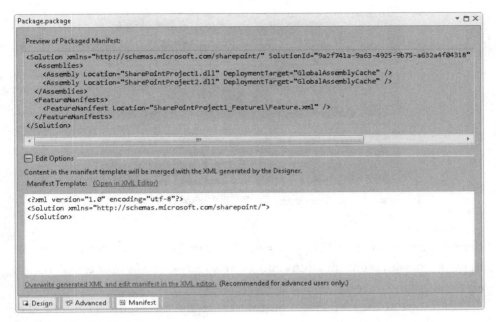

Figure 11-26: Manifest view

Configurable Deployment

Deployment of SharePoint projects from Visual Studio is done with the help of configurable deployment. Configurable deployment lets you configure the way SharePoint projects are deployed and retracted from the server. Visual Studio 2010 ships with two deployment configurations: default deployment and no activation deployment. Before we explain what the difference is between these two we should look at the deployment configuration structure. Figure 11-27 shows how deployment configuration is structured.

Each deployment configuration consists of two parts: deployment and retraction. When a SharePoint project is deployed Visual Studio executes a series of deployment steps in a specific order. Something similar happens when you retract the project. Retraction steps are executed in a specific order. Both parts (deployment and retraction) are built from steps. Since

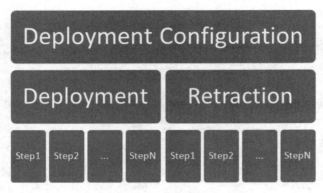

Figure 11-27: Deployment configuration structure

deployment is configurable you can use zero, one, or multiple steps for both the deployment and retraction parts of the configuration. You can also control the order in which steps are executed.

Let's start at the steps level and move up the hierarchy. Visual Studio ships with a number of reusable deployment steps shown in Table 11-10. You can use these steps to build your own deployment configuration.

TABLE 11-10: Deployment Steps

Step	Description
Run Pre-Deployment Command	Specifies a command that gets called before the deployment of the SharePoint project starts; you can use MS-DOS or MSBuild commands.
Run Post-Deployment Command	Specifies a command that gets called after the Share-Point project is deployed; you can use MS-DOS or MSBuild commands.
Recycle IIS Application Pool	When executed it will recycle the IIS application pool.
Retract Solution	Retracts the SharePoint solution from the server.
Add Solution	Adds the SharePoint solution to the server.
Activate Features	Activates the features on the SharePoint server.

When you create any SharePoint project the active deployment configuration is set to the built-in deployment configuration "Default Deployment." The numbered list shows the steps and the order in which they are performed when the SharePoint project is deployed using the default deployment configuration:

1. Run Pre-Deployment Command.
2. Recycle IIS Application Pool.
3. Retract Solution.
4. Add Solution.
5. Activate Features.
6. Run Post-Deployment Command.

The list of retraction steps in the default deployment configuration is much shorter and it looks like this:

1. Recycle IIS Application Pool.
2. Retract Solution.

The built-in deployment configuration, "No activation deployment," is very similar to the default deployment. The only difference is that when using No activation deployment, the Activate Features step is not performed. All the other steps and their order are identical. If you have read the previous chapters you probably remember that we used No activation deployment when we were debugging feature event receivers. As explained in Chapter 5, "SharePoint Event Receivers," in order to debug the Feature-Activated event we had to deploy it without activating it. We used the No activation deployment to deploy the feature event receiver and when we activated the feature from the SharePoint UI, the breakpoint in the Feature-Activated event was hit.

Switching between the default and no activation deployment configurations can be done in two places in the Visual Studio UI. The most common place to change the active deployment configuration is in the Properties window. If you click the project name in the Solution Explorer and open the Properties window you will notice the Active Deployment Configuration property as shown in Figure 11-28.

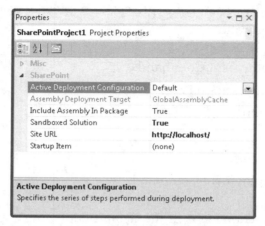

Figure 11-28: Active Deployment Configuration property

The second place where you can change the active deployment configuration is from the property pages shown when you right click the project and choose Properties... The SharePoint property page can also be used to view the existing deployment configurations (default and no activation) as well as to create new deployment configurations. Let's use the SharePoint property page to create a simple deployment configuration. As a base we are going to use the same steps and order used in the default deployment configuration. In our new deployment configuration we will define custom pre- and post-deployment commands to write something to the Output window. We also won't use the retract solution or the recycle IIS application pool steps. Follow the steps below to open the SharePoint property page and start creating new deployment configurations.

1. Open Visual Studio in elevated mode.
2. Click File > New Project.
3. Create a new Empty SharePoint project.
   Accept the default in the SharePoint Customization Wizard and click Finish to create the project.

4. Right click the project name in the Solution Explorer and select Properties from the context menu.

   The Project property pages open as shown in Figure 11-29.

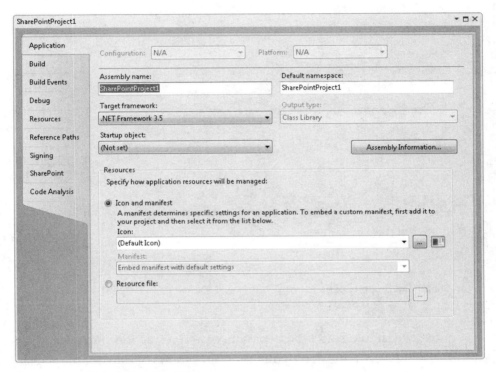

Figure 11-29: Project property pages

5. Click the SharePoint tab to open the SharePoint property page.

   The SharePoint property page shown in Figure 11-30 is displayed. From this page we can create, edit, view, and delete deployment configurations and set additional settings that affect debugging.

6. Click the New… button.

   The Add New Deployment Configuration dialog shows the available deployment and retractions steps we can use in our deployment configuration. The dialog is shown in Figure 11-31.

7. Change the deployment configuration name to "My Deployment Configuration."

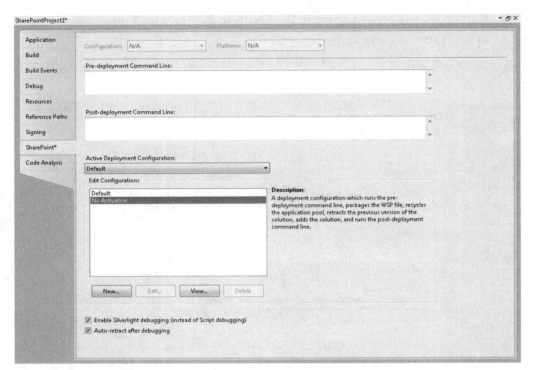

Figure 11-30: SharePoint property page

Next, we should select the deployment and retraction steps. To include a step in the deployment configuration you can double click it in the list of Available Deployment Steps on the left or click the > button with the step selected on the left. This will move the step from the left to the right side of the dialog to the list of Selected Deployment Steps. There are also buttons on the right side of the dialog to reorder steps once you have them in the Selected Deployment Steps list and to remove a step from the Selected Deployment Steps list.

8. Add the following steps to the selected deployment steps list:

Run Pre-Deployment Command.

Add Solution.

Activate Features.

Run Post-Deployment Command.

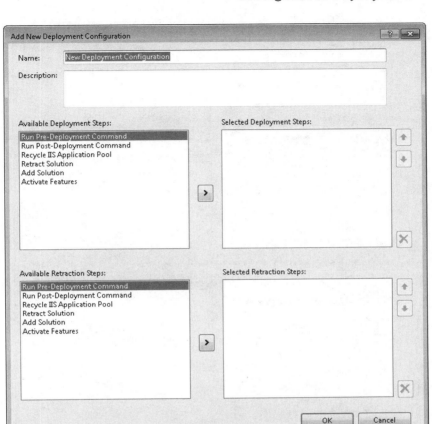

Figure 11-31: New Deployment Configuration dialog

9. Add the following steps to the selected retraction steps list:

Recycle IIS Application Pool.
Retract Solution.

10. Use the arrow buttons to the right of the Selected Deployment Steps and Selected Retraction Steps lists to arrange the steps in the right order. After you've done this, the Add New Deployment Configuration dialog should look like the one in Figure 11-32.

11. Click OK to close the dialog.

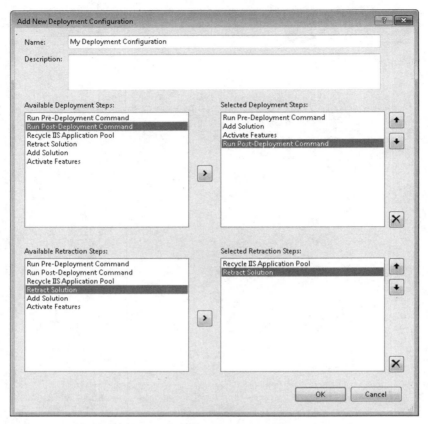

Figure 11-32: Add New Deployment Configuration dialog

You will notice a new entry in the list of deployment configurations. Since we said we are going to add custom pre- and post-deployment steps we need to add some custom commands to the provided textboxes at the top of the SharePoint properties page shown in Figure 11-30. Note that pre- and post-deployment commands are not specific to each deployment configuration. If you set the pre- and post-deployment commands for Default deployment configuration and then switch to the No Activation deployment configuration, the same pre- and post-deployment steps will be executed.

Type the following command into the Pre-deployment Command Line textbox:

```
echo Project deployment started...
```

When we deploy the project, this message is going to be included in the Output window. Let's do something similar with the post-deployment command. Type the following command into the Post-deployment Command Line textbox:

```
echo Project deployed!
```

In order to use the new deployment configuration we need to set it as the active deployment configuration. To do this use the Active Deployment Configuration combo box on the SharePoint property page to select it, or set the Active Deployment Configuration property in the Properties window for the project. Once you've set the new active deployment configuration, right click the project name in the Solution Explorer and select Deploy. Once deployment is finished, the following text appears in the Output window:

```
Active Deployment Configuration: My Deployment Configuration
Run Pre-Deployment Command:
Project deployment started...
Add Solution:
  Adding solution 'SharePointProject1.wsp'...
  Deploying solution 'SharePointProject1.wsp'...
Activate Features:
  Configuring SharePoint Sandboxed Code service...
  Restarting SharePoint Sandboxed Code service...
  No features in this solution were activated.
Run Post-Deployment Command:
Project deployed!
```

This output tells us which deployment configuration we used and which steps were executed. Each step also outputs what it is doing, e.g., "No features in this solution were activated" or "Deploying solution 'SharePointProject1.wsp'." If we retract the project we will see a similar output in the Output window. It should look similar to this:

```
Active Deployment Configuration: My Deployment Configuration
Recycle IIS Application Pool:
  Skipping application pool recycle because a sandboxed solution is being
  deployed.
Retract Solution:
  Retracting solution 'SharePointProject1.wsp'...
  Deleting solution 'SharePointProject1.wsp'...
```

Notice that since we didn't include the pre- and post-deployment steps for the Retraction steps in our custom deployment configuration, no custom output is displayed during retraction. Also notice how the recycle IIS application pool step is smart enough to detect that the SharePoint project is a sandboxed solution and so it skips the application pool recycle.

Sometimes there are situations where you would want to develop your own custom steps and use them during deployment or retraction. In the following section we will show an example of how to build your custom deployment steps using Visual Studio extensibility.

Custom Deployment Steps

To develop a custom deployment step you have to install the Visual Studio 2010 SDK. We are going to use the VSIX Project template that is part of the Visual Studio 2010 SDK. This template will be used to deploy the custom deployment step. You can download the Visual Studio 2010 SDK at this location: http://www.microsoft.com/downloads/details.aspx?FamilyID=47305cf4-2bea-43c0-91cd-1b853602dcc5&displaylang=en. Let's start by creating the extension project that will contain our custom deployment step.

1. Open Visual Studio.
2. Click File > New Project.
3. In the New Project dialog expand the Visual C# node and click the Windows node.
4. Select the Class Library template and name the project "DeploymentStepExtension."
5. Click OK to create the project.

Because we want to create a custom deployment step we have to add some references to the assemblies where the SharePoint configurable deployment API is stored. Add references to the following two assemblies: Microsoft.VisualStudio.SharePoint and System.ComponentModel.Composition. You can find both assemblies in the .NET tab of the Add References dialog. Before we start adding code, let's rename the class file to "MyStep.cs" and the class to "MyStep."

A custom deployment step is a class that inherits from the IDeployment-Step interface and exports the type of IDeploymentStep so it can be found by Visual Studio. To start your class, add the following using statements at the top of the class file:

```
using Microsoft.VisualStudio.SharePoint;
using Microsoft.VisualStudio.SharePoint.Deployment;
using System.ComponentModel.Composition;
```

Now we can inherit from the IDeploymentStep interface that is declared in the Microsoft.VisualStudio.SharePoint.Deployment namespace. With the help of Visual Studio IntelliSense we can automatically implement the interface. You will notice there are three methods we can use: CanExecute, Execute, and Initialize as shown in Listing 11-11.

Listing 11-11: Initial Implementation of the MyStep Class

```
public class MyStep : IDeploymentStep
{
  public bool CanExecute(IDeploymentContext context)
  {
    throw new NotImplementedException();
  }

  public void Execute(IDeploymentContext context)
  {
    throw new NotImplementedException();
  }
  public void Initialize(IDeploymentStepInfo stepInfo)
  {
    throw new NotImplementedException();
  }
}
```

The CanExecute method gets called before the step is actually executed to determine if the step should be executed or not. For example if our step is relying on some other action we can use the CanExecute method to check if that required action is done and return true if we want the step to execute or false if the step shouldn't get executed.

The Execute method is self-explanatory—this method is called when a step is executed. If the main idea of your step is to copy some files to the

SharePoint server or make backups, this is the method in which you will implement that functionality.

The Initialize method is used to initialize the step. For example we can use this method to set the step name, description, and status bar message that is displayed before the step is executed.

Before we actually start implementing the step, let's decide what we want our step to do. Our step is going to backup the .WSP file to a folder on the server. We are only going to copy the .WSP file if the SharePoint project is a farm solution. If it's a sandboxed solution we won't execute the step.

Let's start by implementing the Initialize method. The Initialize method implementation is shown in Listing 11-12.

Listing 11-12: Initialize Method

```
public void Initialize(IDeploymentStepInfo stepInfo)
{
  stepInfo.Name = "Copy WSP File";
  stepInfo.StatusBarMessage = "Creating Backup ...";
  stepInfo.Description = "Copy the WSP file to the defined location.";
}
```

Because we only want the step to work for a farm solution we should implement the CanExecute method. In this method we check if the solution is a sandboxed solution and throw an exception if it is. Otherwise we return true, telling the Visual Studio to continue executing the step. The CanExecute method implementation is shown in Listing 11-13.

Listing 11-13: CanExecute Method

```
public bool CanExecute(IDeploymentContext context)
{
  if (context.Project.IsSandboxedSolution)
  {
    string message = "This step doesn't support sandboxed solutions.";
    context.Logger.WriteLine(message, LogCategory.Error);
    throw new InvalidOperationException(message);
  }
  return true;
}
```

Finally, we implement the Execute method. We write a message to the Output window informing the developer that we are copying the .WSP file to the backup location. To get to the .WSP file we are using the deployment context parameter that is passed to this method. The implementation of the Execute method is in Listing 11-14.

Listing 11-14: Execute Method

```
public void Execute(IDeploymentContext context)
{
  context.Logger.WriteLine("Copying WSP file to backup location.",
    LogCategory.Status);

  string backupPath = @"C:\Backups";
  if (!Directory.Exists(backupPath))
  {
    Directory.CreateDirectory(backupPath);
  }

  string backupName = string.Format ("{0}{1}-{2}.{3},
    context.Project.Name, DateTime.Now.Hour,
    DateTime.Now.Minute, "wsp");
  string package = context.Project.Package.OutputPath;
  try
  {
    File.Copy(package, Path.Combine (backupPath, backupName));
  }
  catch (Exception ex)
  {
    context.Logger.WriteLine("Error copying file: " +
      ex.Message, LogCategory.Error);
  }
}
```

In the Execute method we first check to see if the backup location exists and if it doesn't we create a new folder. Next we create the name of the backup .WSP that will contain the name of the project and the current hour and minute. Finally we try to copy the file to the backup location. If there are any exceptions during the copying process we write an error message to the Errors window.

In order for our custom step to be recognized as a SharePoint deployment step we need to add a couple of attributes to the MyStep class. The finished class with all methods implemented and with required attributes is shown in Listing 11-15.

Listing 11-15: Implemented MyStep Class

```
[Export (typeof (IDeploymentStep))]
[DeploymentStep("MyStep.CopyWspFile")]
public class MyStep : IDeploymentStep
{
  public bool CanExecute(IDeploymentContext context)
  {
    if (context.Project.IsSandboxedSolution)
    {
      string message =
        "This step doesn't support sandboxed solutions.";
      context.Logger.WriteLine(message, LogCategory.Error);
      throw new InvalidOperationException(message);
    }
    return true;
  }

  public void Execute(IDeploymentContext context)
  {
    context.Logger.WriteLine("Copying WSP file to backup location.",
      LogCategory.Status);

    string backupPath = @"C:\Backups";
    if (!Directory.Exists(backupPath))
    {
      Directory.CreateDirectory(backupPath);
    }

    string backupName = context.Project.Name + DateTime.Now.Hour +
      "-" + DateTime.Now.Minute + ".wsp";
    string package = context.Project.Package.OutputPath;
    try
    {
      File.Copy(package, Path.Combine (backupPath, backupName));
    }
    catch (Exception ex)
    {
      context.Logger.WriteLine("Error copying file: " +
        ex.Message, LogCategory.Error);
    }
  }
}
```

```
public void Initialize(IDeploymentStepInfo stepInfo)
{
  stepInfo.Name = "Copy WSP file";
  stepInfo.StatusBarMessage = "Creating Backup ...";
  stepInfo.Description =
    "Step copies the WSP file to the backup location.";
}
}
```

With the Export attribute we are enabling Visual Studio to discover and load our custom deployment step and with the DeploymentStep attribute we are specifying the deployment step ID. In order to deploy and test the custom step we have to create the VSIX project so our step can be installed to a Visual Studio installation.

1. Right click the solution node in the Solution Explorer and select Add > New Project.
2. In the New Project dialog expand the Visual C# node and click the Extensibility node.
3. Select the VSIX Project template and name the project "Custom-DeploymentStep" as shown in Figure 11-33.
4. Click OK to create the project.

Now that we have the VSIX project we need to configure it to include our deployment step. To do so, double click the source.extension.vsixmanifest file. A designer shown in Figure 11-34 opens.

From this designer we can specify the general information about the package, such as Product Name, Author, Version, Descriptions, and so on. The part in the designer that is most interesting for us is the Add Content dialog. This is where the contents of the package can be added or removed. Click the Add Content button so we can include our custom deployment step in the VSIX package. Our content type is a MEF Component and since the custom deployment step project is in the same solution we can select the DeploymentStepExtension as the source. The Add Content dialog with the content type and source selected is shown in Figure 11-35.

Figure 11-33: VSIX project template

This is all we need to do to prepare the VSIX package. Now we can build the project—this can take a minute or so. When the project is successfully built you can right click the VSIX project node in Solution Explorer and select Open Folder in Windows Explorer. Because we are installing a Visual Studio extension we should close all Visual Studio instances.

Open the bin\debug folder of the VSIX project in which the built VSIX package is located. The VSIX package file should have the same name as the VSIX project: CustomDeploymentStep. Double click this file to install it to Visual Studio. The Visual Studio Extension Installer dialog is displayed as shown in Figure 11-36.

Click Install to install the extension. The dialog shown in Figure 11-37 is displayed when installation is completed. Click the Close button to close the dialog.

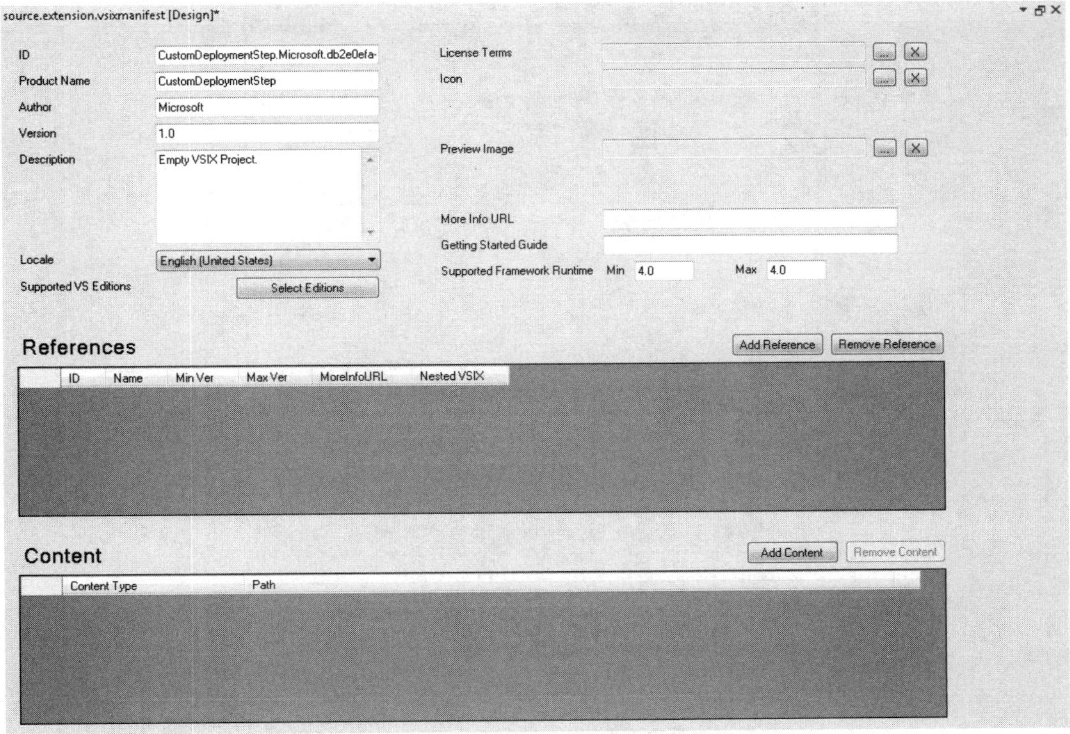

Figure 11-34: VSIX manifest designer

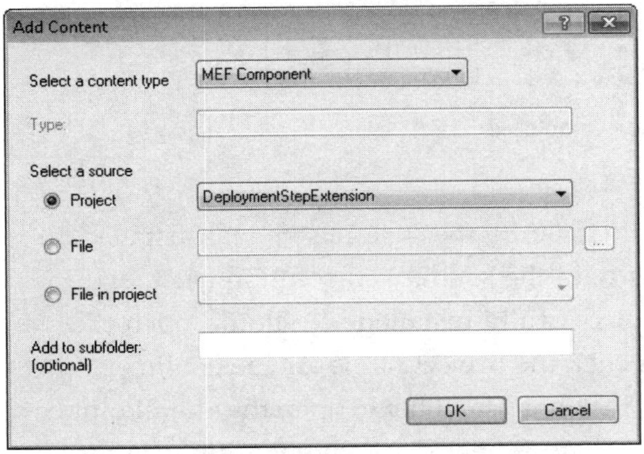

Figure 11-35: Add Content dialog

Figure 11-36: Installing custom deployment step

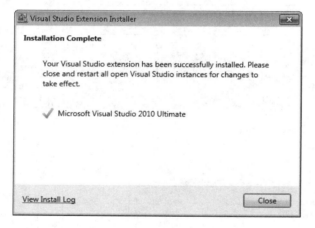

Figure 11-37: Installation Completed

We can now open Visual Studio to verify the custom step was installed. Let's just create an empty project with the sandboxed solution trust level. To verify our custom step was successfully installed we should open the SharePoint property page. Right click the project name and select Properties from the context menu. Click the SharePoint tab to open the SharePoint property page. We are going to create a new deployment configuration that will use our custom step. Click the New button and the Add New Deployment Configuration dialog as shown in Figure 11-38 opens.

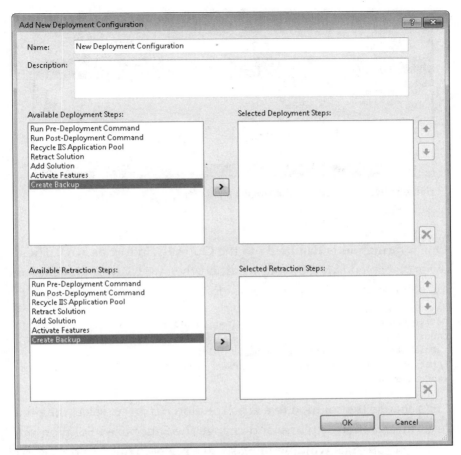

Figure 11-38: The Add New Deployment configuration with custom step "Create Backup" installed

Notice that our custom Create Backup step we created is installed and it shows in the list of available deployment and retraction steps. Double click the step name and add it to the selected deployment steps. Click OK to close the dialog and set the deployment configuration you just created as the active one. Next, right click the project name and click Deploy to deploy the project. What happens is exactly what we wanted to happen— the project we created is a sandboxed project therefore we are getting the error we implemented in the Error List as shown in Figure 11-39.

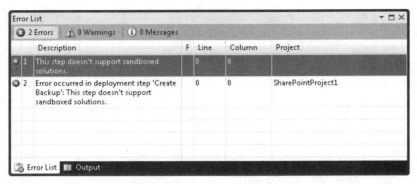

Figure 11-39: Error using custom deployment step

Our information is displayed to the Output window as well. The text below is displayed in the Output window when we try to deploy the sandboxed solution that uses our custom step.

```
Active Deployment Configuration: My Configuration
Create Backup:
  This step doesn't support sandboxed solutions.
Error occurred in deployment step 'Create Backup': This step doesn't support
sandboxed solutions.
```

Let's change the solution to a farm solution. To do so, select the project node in the Solution Explorer and change the Sandboxed Solution property in the Properties window to False. Try re-deploying the project. This time the custom step executes successfully and copies the .WSP file to the location we specified in our code (C:\Backups). The text in the Output window is shown below:

```
Active Deployment Configuration: My Configuration
Create Backup:
  Copying WSP file to backup location.
```

Even though the custom step was installed and we are able to use it, we still had to manually create a new deployment configuration. If we ship the custom deployment step as it is right now the developers would still need to create the deployment configuration that uses this step. What would be really nice is if we could install the extension and a custom deployment configuration that used it as well. We can do that as well. We can create our own custom deployment configuration from code. Once we have that we can deploy both the extension and the deployment configuration and ensure that all users are using the same configuration.

Just like with the custom deployment step, to create a custom deployment configuration we have to create a new class, add an attribute, and inherit from an interface called ISharePointProjectExtension. Open the DeploymentStepExtension project and add a new class to the project. Name the class "MyDeploymentConfiguration." Open the class file once it's created and add the following using statements at the top of the file:

```
using Microsoft.VisualStudio.SharePoint;
using Microsoft.VisualStudio.SharePoint.Deployment;
using System.ComponentModel.Composition;
```

The newly created deployment configuration class has to inherit from the ISharePointProjectExtension interface. Type :ISharePointProject-Extension right after the class name and then click the IntelliSense menu that is displayed under the interface name and click the Implement interface ISharePointProjectExtension to implement the interface as shown in Figure 11-40.

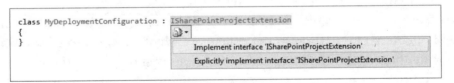

Figure 11-40: Implementing interfaces

We should also make this class discoverable by adding the Export attribute just as we did with the custom deployment step. The MyDeployment-Configuration class with implemented interface and Export attribute is shown in Listing 11-16.

Listing 11-16: MyDeploymentConfiguration.cs

```
[Export (typeof (ISharePointProjectExtension))]
class MyDeploymentConfiguration : ISharePointProjectExtension
{
  public void Initialize(ISharePointProjectService projectService)
  {
    throw new NotImplementedException();
  }
}
```

The projectService parameter that is passed to the Initialize method has properties, methods, and events we can use to extend the SharePoint project and create the new deployment step. What we want to achieve is to have the custom deployment configuration available as soon as a Share-Point project is created. We can use the ProjectInitialized event to do that. First, let's remove the exception code from the Initialize method and hook up the ProjectInitialized handler by adding the following line to the Initialize method:

```
projectService.ProjectInitialized +=
  new EventHandler<SharePointProjectEventArgs>(
  projectService_ProjectInitialized);
```

In the ProjectInitialized method handler we will create a custom deployment configuration. The SharePointProjectEventArgs parameter passed to the event handler method exposes the Project instance in which we can access the DeploymentConfigurations collection and add a new deployment configuration to the collection. What we need to pass to the Add method of the DeploymentConfigurations collection is the name of the deployment configuration as well as the list of deployment step IDs and retraction step IDs. Let's decide that for our custom configuration we are going to use the same order of deployment and retraction steps as the default configuration does. The only difference in our custom deployment configuration will be our custom CreateBackup step, which is going to be executed as the last in the list of deployment steps.

Add the code in Listing 11-17 to the projectService_ProjectInitialized method to create the list of deployment and retraction steps and a custom deployment configuration.

Listing 11-17: ProjectInitialized Method

```
void projectService_ProjectInitialized(object sender,
  SharePointProjectEventArgs e)
{
  string [] deploymentSteps = new string []
  {
    DeploymentStepIds.PreDeploymentCommand,
    DeploymentStepIds.RecycleApplicationPool,
    DeploymentStepIds.RetractSolution,
    DeploymentStepIds.AddSolution,
    DeploymentStepIds.ActivateFeatures,
    DeploymentStepIds.PostDeploymentCommand,
    "MyStep.CopyWspFile"
  };
  string [] retractionSteps = new string []
  {
    DeploymentStepIds.RecycleApplicationPool,
    DeploymentStepIds.RetractSolution
  };
  IDeploymentConfiguration myConfig =
    e.Project.DeploymentConfigurations.Add(
    "Default Configuration With Backup", deploymentSteps,
    retractionSteps);
  myConfig.Description =
    "Default deployment configuration which makes the WSP file copy.";
}
```

In the code in Listing 11-17 we are defining the deployment and retraction steps and then adding the new deployment configuration to the collection of deployment configurations. Since this class is in the same assembly as the custom step we can just rebuild the project as well as the VSIX project. Before we install the new extension, we should remove the one that we installed previously. In Visual Studio, click the Tools menu and select Extension Manager. The Extension Manager dialog as shown in Figure 11-41 appears.

Click the Uninstall button to uninstall the extension and then close Visual Studio. We can now install the new extension by double clicking the CustomDeploymentStep.vsix file in the bin\debug directory of the project. After you install the extension, open Visual Studio and create a new SharePoint project. Open the project properties and the SharePoint property page. You will notice the configuration Default Configuration With Backup is in the list of available deployment configurations as shown in Figure 11-42.

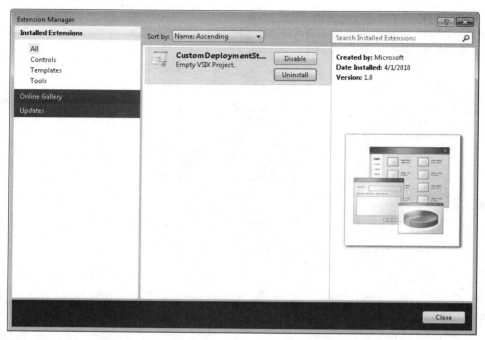

Figure 11-41: Extension Manager dialog

To verify the new deployment configuration you can set it as the active configuration and deploy the project. The behavior is the same as with the default configuration but in our configuration we are also copying the .WSP file to the location we specified in the code.

Deployment Conflicts

During the development process you are usually deploying the same project over and over again to the same location on the SharePoint server as you test it. We already know that before each deployment the Share-Point solution is retracted from the server but in some cases we would like to be prompted if we want to overwrite the solution or items that are already on the SharePoint server. Visual Studio will detect collisions in cases when an item on the server has the same name, URL, or ID as an item in your SharePoint solution. If this happens the deployment conflict dialog shown in Figure 11-43 is displayed.

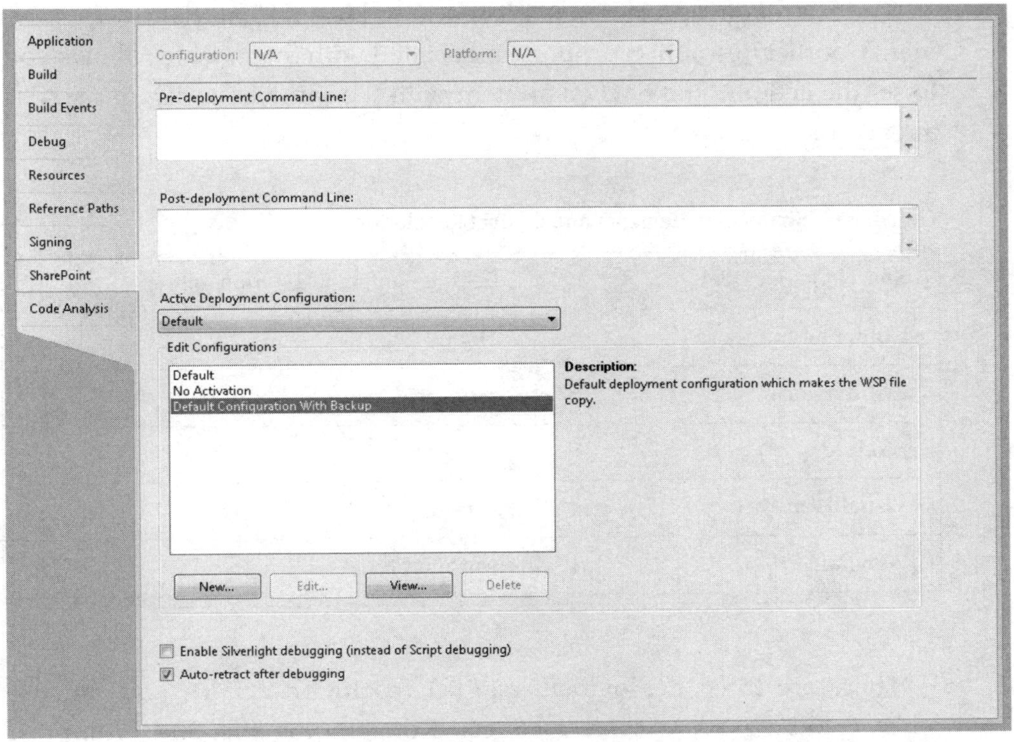

Figure 11-42: Custom Deployment Configuration added by our Project_Initialized Handler

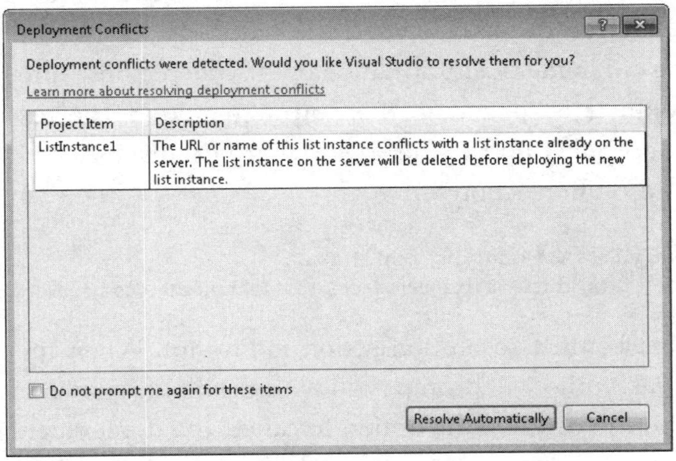

Figure 11-43: Deployment Conflicts dialog

The SharePoint project items listed in Table 11-10 all have a Deployment Conflict Resolution property associated with them, which allows you to set the action to take when an item with the same URL, ID, or name is already on the server.

TABLE 11-11:　SharePoint Elements and Conflict Resolution

SharePoint Element	Default Conflict Resolution Action
Content Type	None
List Instance	Prompt
Module	Automatic
Visual Web Part	Automatic
Web Part	Automatic

There are three deployment conflict resolution actions you can use when resolving deployment conflicts: None, Automatic, and Prompt. If None is selected, Visual Studio won't bother detecting the collisions—this means that the SharePoint element will be overwritten if there's an item with the same name, ID, or URL already on the server. If Automatic is selected, Visual Studio detects the collision and automatically resolves the conflict by deleting the old item. The information on discovered and automatically resolved conflicts is logged in the output window. The text below is written to the output window when deploying a list instance with an Automatic conflict resolution action set:

```
Found 1 deployment conflict(s).  Resolving conflicts ...
Deleted list instance 'Lists/ListDefinitionProject1-ListInstance1' from server.
```

The last deployment conflict resolution action is Prompt. When this option is selected, Visual Studio will prompt you with the dialog shown in Figure 11-43. At this point you have the option to cancel the deployment by clicking the Cancel button or automatically resolve the conflict by clicking the Resolve Automatically button. You can also choose to ignore this dialog in the future by checking the Do not prompt me again for these items check box. If you do so, the deployment conflict resolution action for the project item will be set to Automatic and you won't be bothered with this dialog anymore.

Apart from collision detection at the SharePoint project item level, there is another detection that happens at the SharePoint package level. At deployment time Visual Studio will check if a package with the same name is already on the server. If that is the case, the dialog shown in Figure 11-44 is displayed.

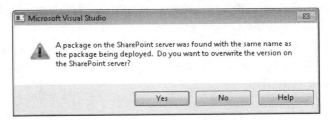

Figure 11-44: Package Name Conflict dialog

If you click Yes, the package that's on the server will be retracted and the new package will be deployed. If you click No, the existing package is not retracted and deployment of the new package will fail.

Sandboxed and Farm Solutions

Throughout the book you have been creating and deploying both sandboxed and farm SharePoint solutions. Sandboxed solutions are a new feature in SharePoint 2010 that allows users to upload their own solutions to the SharePoint server. The most common use of the sandboxed solution is for deploying code-only web parts. Sandboxed SharePoint solutions run in a secure and monitored process that has a limited access to the rest of the SharePoint farm. An example where sandboxed solutions are extremely attractive is for SharePoint hosting providers—they would like to allow their users to deploy their own custom solutions, yet they don't want to give them full access to the entire server farm. Also, deploying a solution that could affect the whole farm is not a wise thing. With sandboxed solutions you are isolating that particular solution to a specific site collection.

To achieve better protection of the server, the sandboxed solution assemblies are loaded into a different process than the one used for farm solutions. The SPUCWorkerProecess.exe where all sandboxed solution assemblies are loaded is monitored and it allows setting quotas in order to further protect the farm.

The flip side of sandboxed solutions is that they are somewhat limited compared to the farm solutions. This means that not all SharePoint items available in Visual Studio can be deployed as part of the sandboxed solution. Besides that, you can't use the object model types in the SharePoint 2010 server assembly Microsoft.Office.Server. However, you can still use many of the objects, properties, and methods in the Microsoft.SharePoint assembly. Table 11-12 shows all SharePoint elements that are supported in sandboxed solutions.

TABLE 11-12:   SharePoint Elements Supported in Sandboxed Solutions

SharePoint Element
Content Types
Custom Actions
Event Receivers
Fields
List Definitions
List Instances
Modules
Web Parts

The SharePoint items available in Visual Studio 2010 that can't be used in a sandboxed solution are workflows, visual web parts, mapped folders, application pages, and all farm and web application-scoped features.

Auto-Retract

The purpose of the auto-retract feature is to decrease the time required to either deploy or debug a SharePoint project. The way auto-retract works is that when you finish your debugging session it automatically retracts the solution and recycles the IIS application pool and prepares the SharePoint server for the next deployment or debugging session. This happens in the background when Visual Studio switches from the debugging mode to the design mode. The next time you deploy the project or start debugging the deployment steps in the active deployment configuration are executed. Each time the recycle IIS and retract steps are executed they perform a check to verify if they actually need to be executed. Since both steps were executed when the debugging session was stopped by auto-retract, there is no need to execute them again and in this scenario recycle and retract steps can be skipped. This makes it so your debugging sessions can start more quickly.

One thing to note is that auto-retract only executes when the debugging session is stopped. This means that even if this feature is enabled, SharePoint solutions are not auto retracted if you use the Deploy command from the context menu or the Visual Studio menu. A solution also won't be retracted if you start the project without attaching the debugger (e.g., Ctrl + F5).

The auto-retract feature is enabled by default for every SharePoint project. You can modify this setting by unchecking the Auto-retract after debugging check box from the SharePoint property page, which can be accessed by right clicking the SharePoint project name, selecting Properties and then clicking the SharePoint tab.

Silverlight Debugging

The Enable Silverlight debugging option in the SharePoint property page shown in Figure 11-45 allows you to debug a Silverlight XAP file you deployed together with the SharePoint project—typically this is used for a web part or application page development scenario.

We showed how to build and deploy Silverlight web parts in Chapter 9, "SharePoint Web Parts." Here we will show how to build and deploy an application page that uses Silverlight. We want to place the Silverlight control in the ASPX application page and when we click the button that's on

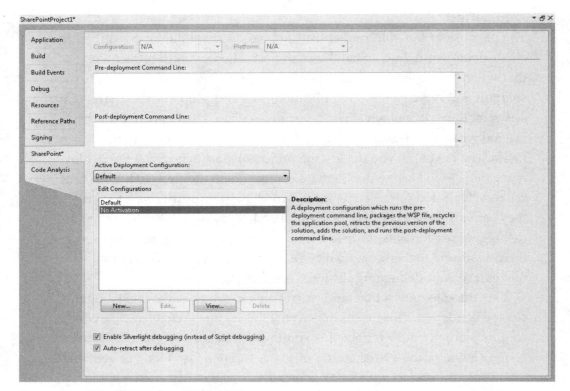

Figure 11-45: Silverlight Debugging check box

the Silverlight page we would like the breakpoint in the event handler method to be hit. Follow the steps below to create the Silverlight project.

1. Open Visual Studio.
2. Click File > New Project.
3. Expand the Visual C# node and select Silverlight.
4. Select the Silverlight Application template and name it "MySilverlightApp."
5. Click OK.

   The New Silverlight application dialog shown in Figure 11-46 is displayed.

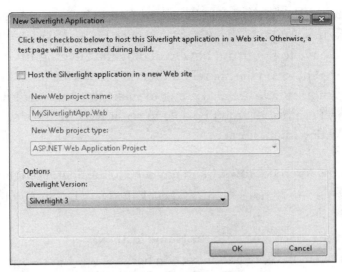

Figure 11-46: New Silverlight Application dialog

6. Uncheck the Host the Silverlight application in a new Web site check box and click OK to create the project.

7. Add the XAML in Listing 11-18 inside the UserControl tag in the MainPage.xaml.

Listing 11-18: MainPage.xaml

```
<Grid x:Name="LayoutRoot" Background="White">
  <Button x:Name="btnMyButton" Content="Click Me!"/>
</Grid>
```

8. Double click the button on the designer to create the click event handler.

9. Insert a breakpoint in the btnMyButton_Click method.

This is a very simple Silverlight page yet it's enough to show how debugging Silverlight applications from SharePoint projects works. Next, we have to create an Empty SharePoint project. Right click the solution name and select Add > New Project. Choose the Empty SharePoint Project template, name the project "SPSilverlight," and click OK. Make sure you select the farm solution in the wizard and click Finish to create the project.

Now we have to figure out how to deploy the Silverlight XAP file. The recommended place on the SharePoint server for storing all .XAP files is in a document library. We are also going to make the document library hidden so SharePoint users won't be able to see it. Follow the steps below to create a new document library:

1. Open the Internet browser and navigate to the SharePoint home page.
2. Open the Site Actions menu and click the New Document Library item.
3. Type the name "XAPs" in the Name textbox.
4. Select No in the Navigation section because we don't want to display the library on the Quick Launch.
5. Select None in the Document Template drop-down.
   The Create dialog should look like the one shown in Figure 11-47.
6. Click the Create button to create the document library.

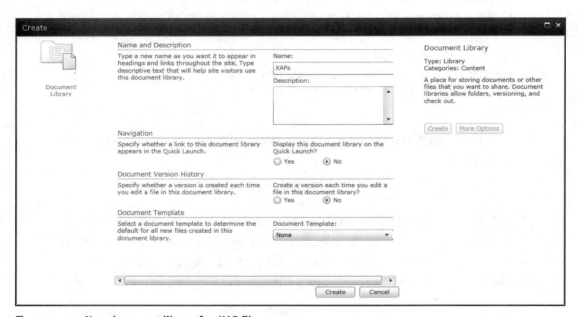

Figure 11-47: New document library for .XAP files

Now that we have the place to store the .XAP file we need a way to deploy it to the document library. We are going to use the Module project item to deploy the .XAP file to the document library. Switch back to the Visual Studio and follow the steps below to add a new Module project item.

1. Right click the SPSilverlight SharePoint project node and select Add > New Item.
2. Select the Module project item template and name it "XapModule."
3. Click Add to create the project item.

By default Visual Studio creates a Sample.txt file that gets deployed with the module element. Because we are deploying the .XAP file we don't need that text file so go ahead and delete it. We are going to use the Project Output References dialog to deploy the .XAP file. Select the XapModule folder in Solution Explorer and open the Properties window. Find the Project Output References property and click the (…) button. The Project Output References dialog as shown in Figure 11-48 appears.

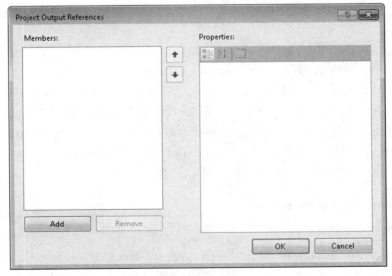

Figure 11-48: Project Output References dialog

Click the Add button to add a new reference. In the Properties window of the Project Output References dialog change the Project name property to MySilverlightApp. Change the Deployment Type to ElementFile and click OK to close the dialog. In order to deploy the .XAP file to the document library we will add the Url attribute to the Module element in the Elements.xml file and modify the Url attribute of the File element. With the Url attribute value changed to "XAPs" we are telling SharePoint that we want to deploy this module to the XAPs document library we created earlier. We also removed the project item name (XapModule) from the Url attribute in the File element, because just having the file name is enough. The last change to the Elements.xml file is adding the Type attribute with value GhostableInLibrary to the File element. This attribute is telling SharePoint to create a new list item in the library for the XAP file. The final Elements.xml file for the XapModule is shown in Listing 11-19.

Listing 11-19: Elements.xml for XapModule

```xml
<?xml version="1.0" encoding="utf-8"?>
<Elements xmlns="http://schemas.microsoft.com/sharepoint/">
  <Module Name="XapModule" Url="XAPs">
  <File Path="XapModule\MySilverlightApp.xap"
    Url="MySilverlightApp.xap"
    Type="GhostableInLibrary"/>
  </Module>
</Elements>
```

Finally we can add an application page and reference the XAP file from the document library. Right click the SPSilverlight project and select Add > New Item. Select the Application Page template and click Add to add the ASPX page to the project. We are going to use the object tag to embed the deployed .XAP file to the ASPX page. Let's modify the Main asp:Content tag so it looks like Listing 11-20.

Listing 11-20: ApplicationPage1.aspx

```
<asp:Content ID="Main" ContentPlaceHolderID="PlaceHolderMain"
  runat="server">
  <object type="application/x-silverlight" width="100%" height="100%"
    id="slc">
```

```
    <param name="source"
      value="http://localhost/XAPs/SilverlightApplication1.xap"/>
  </object>
</asp:Content>
```

Finally we should enable the Silverlight debugging from the SharePoint property page and set the application page as the startup item. Right click the SharePoint project and select Properties. Click the SharePoint tab to open the SharePoint property page and check the Enable Silverlight debugging (instead of Script debugging) check box. To set the application page as the startup item, right click the ApplicationPage1.aspx file and select Set As Startup Item from the context menu. Press F5 to deploy the SharePoint project.

When the Internet browser opens it should navigate to the application page and the button we created in the Silverlight application should show up as shown in Figure 11-49.

If you click the button the breakpoint on the click handler is hit. The breakpoint would not be hit if we hadn't enabled the Silverlight debugging.

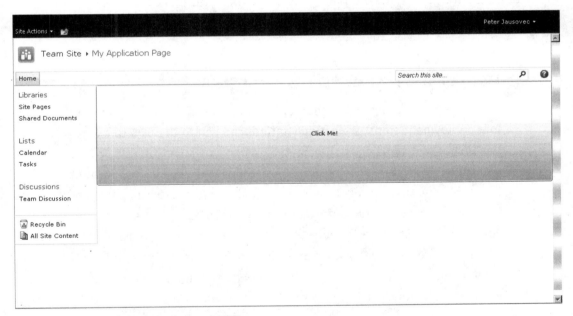

Figure 11-49: Silverlight control on an ASPX page

Conclusion

In this chapter we explored the packaging and deployment features that are available in Visual Studio. At the beginning of this chapter we explained the basics of SharePoint solutions, features, and packages. We also showed how to author Elements.xml files, Feature.xml feature manifest files, and manifest.xml package manifest files by hand and how to deploy the feature using stsadm.exe. Hopefully this helped you to understand and appreciate all that Visual Studio does behind the scenes to make packaging and deployment easier.

Next, we moved to Visual Studio and explained the cool features that are available for packaging and deployment. We showed the feature and package designers how easy it is to add and remove features or move a SharePoint project item to be associated with a different feature. All this can be done through designers or the Packaging Explorer.

In the last part of the chapter we talked about configurable deployment. Using configurable deployment you can create your own configurations; not only that but with the help of extensibility you can even create your own, custom deployment steps, as well as deployment configurations.

Much More than Custom Deployment Steps

We did a sneaky thing in this chapter when we talked about creating custom deployment steps. We actually introduced you to the SDK to extend the SharePoint tools in Visual Studio. When you used objects in the namespace Microsoft.VisualStudio.SharePoint you were using parts of that SDK. You can do much more than just create custom deployment steps with this SDK. You can extend the SharePoint project system and add your own SharePoint project item types. You can also extend the Server Explorer that we have used in this book. For more information on extending the Visual Studio SharePoint tools, see http://msdn.microsoft.com/en-us/library/ee256693.aspx.

A.
Preparing for SharePoint Development

The first challenge you will face when starting to develop solutions for SharePoint is preparing your development machine. In order to use Visual Studio and SharePoint on your development machine you will need to install a 64-bit operating system, which is supported by SharePoint 2010. Once you've installed a 64-bit operating system, you can then install Visual Studio 2010 Professional (or higher) and SharePoint 2010.

In this chapter we will describe how to install and configure the required software components in order to successfully develop SharePoint solutions with Visual Studio 2010.

Supported Operating Systems

SharePoint 2010 only supports 64-bit operating systems. The operating systems in which SharePoint 2010 is fully supported are the server operating systems: Microsoft Windows Server 2008 and Microsoft Windows Server 2008 R2. But what about the client operating systems like Windows Vista and Windows 7?

SharePoint 2010 can also be installed on 64-bit client operating systems running Microsoft Windows Vista SP1 (or later) or Microsoft Windows 7. Although SharePoint 2010 can be installed on these client operating systems, this configuration is intended only for development, not production use. This is not a fully supported configuration, and if product support is required, you may be requested to duplicate the issue you are seeking assistance for on one of the fully supported, server operating systems. Even though SharePoint 2010 isn't fully supported for production environments on a client operating system, we have found this to be an ideal environment for development. So for this book, we recommend the use of SharePoint 2010 on 64-bit Windows 7.

The following installation steps assume you have a clean install of one of the above operating systems. As far as system resources required for developing SharePoint solutions using Visual Studio 2010, it is suggested you have at least 4GB of memory and 4GB of free disc space.

Installing SharePoint 2010

You can choose between installing Microsoft SharePoint Foundation 2010 (the previous version was known as Microsoft Windows SharePoint Services 3.0 or WSS 3.0) or the higher end Microsoft SharePoint Server 2010 (the previous version was known as Microsoft Office SharePoint Server 2007 or MOSS 2007).

The only feature in Visual Studio that requires the higher end SharePoint Server 2010 to be installed is the deployment of Business Data Connectivity (BDC) models. If you have SharePoint Foundation 2010 installed, BDC models can still be created using the new BDC model designer in Visual Studio, but they cannot be deployed to the Business Connectivity Services Metadata Catalog without adding a custom feature event receiver. See Chapter 6, "Working with Business Data," for more information on BDC models and sample code for a custom feature event receiver to be used to deploy BDC models on SharePoint Foundation 2010.

As mentioned above, SharePoint 2010 can be installed on a server operating system or a client operating system. We will provide details for either installation, although remember that installation on a client operating system is for development purposes only; it cannot be used for a production installation.

The installation of SharePoint 2010 occurs in three steps. First, some prerequisites and other configuration must be done; this is the pre-install step. Second, the installation of SharePoint 2010 itself is completed. Finally, the SharePoint 2010 Configuration wizard must be run. The first step is the only one that varies between server and client installations, the other two are the same.

The distribution of SharePoint 2010 may be in the form of a single compressed file named SharePoint.exe or OfficeServer.exe, depending on which product you are installing, or it may be many uncompressed folders and files. Regardless, copy these file(s) to a location on your development machine; we will assume these are copied to "C:\SharePointFiles" in the following steps.

Pre-Installation on a Client Operating System

Using a client operating system like Windows 7 on your development machine has some benefits. A number of developers today use laptops, albeit fairly powerful ones, to do SharePoint and other types of development. As Windows 7 is more suited to laptop use, this allows them to take their development environment on the road wherever it may be needed. Running your development environment on Microsoft Windows Vista SP1 (or later) or Microsoft Windows 7 allows you to use the client operating system features to which you are accustomed, such as sleep and hibernate. It also means the many drivers you may need are more readily available.

As stated above, installing SharePoint on a client operating system is only allowed for development machines. In addition, when installing on a client operating system you can only install SharePoint in a standalone configuration, a server farm configuration is not allowed.

There are a few specific steps required if you are installing on Microsoft Windows Vista SP1. These steps are necessary because some components required by SharePoint are not installed on Microsoft Windows Vista SP1.

These steps are not necessary for Microsoft Windows Windows 7. Perform the following steps in order to install these components.

1. Install Microsoft .NET Framework 3.5 SP1 from here: http://www.microsoft.com/downloads/details.aspx?familyid=AB99342F-5D1A-413D-8319-81DA479AB0D7.

2. Install the Windows Management Framework Core package, which includes WindowsPowerShell 2.0 and WinRm 2.0 (KB968930) from here: http://www.microsoft.com/downloads/details.aspx?FamilyId=0f73efa2-f8d6-45f3-a8f8-5cdc205b119a&displaylang=en.

3. Install the Microsoft Windows Installer 4.5 redistributable from here: http://www.microsoft.com/downloads/details.aspx?FamilyID=5a58b56f-60b6-4412-95b9-54d056d6f9f4.

The remaining steps are required for installation on both Microsoft Vista SP1 and Microsoft Windows 7. Perform the following steps in order to complete the installation and configuration.

1. If your distribution is a single compressed file (e.g., SharePoint-Foundation.exe) that you've copied to C:\SharePointFiles, extract the SharePoint files by opening a command prompt, navigating to C:\SharePointFiles, and running one of the following commands: For SharePoint Foundation 2010 run:

   ```
   SharePointFoundation.exe /extract:C:\SharePointFiles
   ```

   OR

   For SharePoint Server 2010 run:

   ```
   OfficeServer.exe /extract:C:\SharePointFiles
   ```

2. Find the file C:\SharePointFiles\Files\Setup\config.xml and check the properties of this file. Make sure it is not marked as "Read-only."

3. Open this file in Notepad and add the following line just above the closing "</Configuration>" node—the file is case-sensitive so capitalization is important:

   ```
   <Setting Id="AllowWindowsClientInstall" Value="True" />
   ```

The file should now look like the file shown in Listing A-1 if you are installing SharePoint Foundation 2010. The file will be longer for SharePoint Server 2010, but should have the same Setting node with the Allow-WindowsClientInstall attribute set to True.

Listing A-1: The config.xml XML File Allowing Client Install

```xml
<Configuration>
  <Package Id="sts">
    <Setting Id="SETUPTYPE" Value="CLEAN_INSTALL"/>
  </Package>
  <DATADIR Value="%CommonProgramFiles%\Microsoft Shared\Web Server
    Extensions\14\Data"/>
  <Logging Type="verbose" Path="%temp%" Template="Microsoft SharePoint
    Foundation 2010 Setup *.log"/>
  <Setting Id="UsingUIInstallMode" Value="1"/>
  <Setting Id="SETUP_REBOOT" Value="Never" />
  <Setting Id="AllowWindowsClientInstall" Value="True" />
</Configuration>
```

You can close and save the config.xml file now and continue with the installation of the prerequisites.

1. Install the Microsoft Filter Pack 2.0 by launching the installer from your extracted SharePoint files:
   C:\SharePointFiles\PrerequisiteInstallerFiles\FilterPack\ FilterPack.msi

2. Install the Microsoft Sync Framework Runtime from the following location:
   http://go.microsoft.com/fwlink/?LinkID=141237.

3. Install Microsoft SQL Server 2008 Native Client support from the following location:
   http://go.microsoft.com/fwlink/?LinkId=123718.

4. Install Windows Identity Foundation from the following location:
   http://support.microsoft.com/kb/974405.

5. Install Microsoft ADO.NET Data Services Update (KB976127), which is required for the REST support that is part of SharePoint.

If you are installing SharePoint on the Windows Vista operating system, install the update from here:

http://www.microsoft.com/downloads/details.aspx?FamilyID= a71060eb-454e-4475-81a6-e9552b1034fc.

If you are installing SharePoint on the Windows 7 operating system, install the update from here:

http://www.microsoft.com/downloads/details.aspx?familyid= 79D7F6F8-D6E9-4B8C-8640-17F89452148E&displaylang=en.

6. Install the Chart Controls (this is not required for SharePoint Foundation) from here:

http://go.microsoft.com/fwlink/?LinkID=122517.

7. Install SQL Server Analysis Services - ADOMD.Net (this is not required for SharePoint Foundation) from here:

http://download.microsoft.com/download/A/D/0/AD021EF1-9CBC-4D11-AB51-6A65019D4706/SQLSERVER2008_ASADOMD10.msi.

8. Turn on the required Windows features in one of the following two ways:

Open a command prompt and run the following command:

```
start /w pkgmgr /iu:IIS-WebServerRole;IIS-WebServer;
IIS-CommonHttpFeatures;IIS-StaticContent;IIS-DefaultDocument;
IIS-DirectoryBrowsing;IIS-HttpErrors;IIS-ApplicationDevelopment;
IIS-ASPNET;IIS-NetFxExtensibility;IIS-ISAPIExtensions;IIS-ISAPIFilter;
IIS-HealthAndDiagnostics;IIS-HttpLogging;IIS-LoggingLibraries;
IIS-RequestMonitor;IIS-HttpTracing;IIS-CustomLogging;IIS-Security;
IIS-BasicAuthentication;IIS-WindowsAuthentication;
IIS-DigestAuthentication;IIS-RequestFiltering;IIS-Performance;
IIS-HttpCompressionStatic;IIS-HttpCompressionDynamic;
IIS-WebServerManagementTools;IIS-ManagementConsole;
IIS-IIS6ManagementCompatibility;IIS-Metabase;IIS-WMICompatibility;
WAS-WindowsActivationService;WAS-ProcessModel;WAS-NetFxEnvironment;
WAS-ConfigurationAPI;WCF-HTTP-Activation
```

OR

Go to Control Panel > Programs then choose Turn Windows features on or off from under the Programs and Feature section. Make sure all of the features under Internet Information Services are checked. Figures A-1 and A-2 show the features that need to be checked. Press OK once to close the dialog.

Figure A-1: Web Management Tools features required to be on

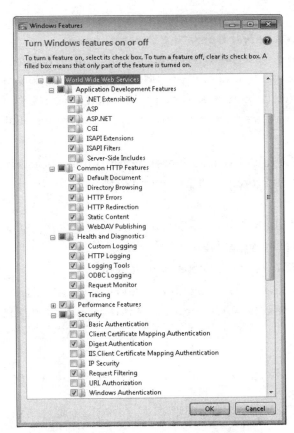

Figure A-2: World Wide Web Services features required to be on

9. If you are installing SharePoint on the Windows Vista operating system, install KB976394 from:

   http://code.msdn.microsoft.com/KB976394/Release/ ProjectReleases .aspx?ReleaseId=357.

   If you are installing SharePoint on the Windows 7 operating system, install KB976462 from:

   http://code.msdn.microsoft.com/KB976462/Release/ ProjectReleases.aspx?ReleaseId=3571.

This completes the pre-installation required on a client operating system. At this point you should reboot your computer and proceed to the section titled "Installation and Configuration of SharePoint 2010" if you are using a client operating system.

Pre-Installation on a Server Operating System

The pre-installation on a server operating system is much easier than configuring a client machine. SharePoint provides a pre-installation process that performs the required configuration and preparation of your server machine. Complete the following steps in order to complete the pre-installation:

1. Navigate to the folder where SharePoint installation files are located and double click PrerequisiteInstaller.exe to start the SharePoint 2010 pre-installation.

   The Microsoft SharePoint 2010 Products Preparation Tool window will display as shown in Figure A-3.

2. Click Next and accept the license agreement.

3. Click Next to start the preparation tool. When installation is completed a dialog as shown in Figure A-4 is displayed. Click Finish to close it.

This completes the prerequisites installation on a server operating system.

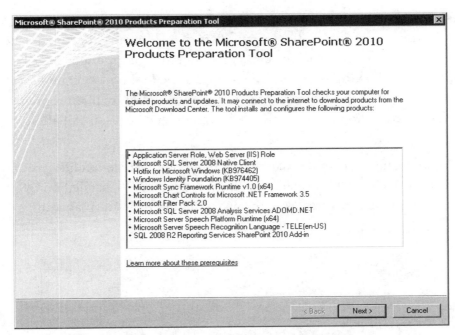

Figure A-3: Microsoft SharePoint 2010 Products Preparation Tool

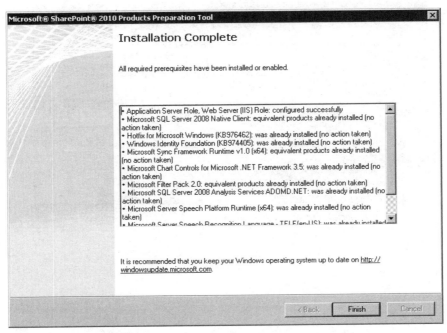

Figure A-4: Completed installation of prerequisites

Installation and Configuration of SharePoint 2010

At this point, pre-installation is complete, which means all prerequisites are installed on your machine and any required configurations have been made. The following steps, which are applicable for both client and server machines, will install SharePoint 2010 and then configure it appropriately. Complete the following steps in order to complete the pre-installation:

1. Navigate to the folder where the SharePoint installation files are and double click setup.exe to start the SharePoint 2010 installation. A page with license terms as the one in Figure A-5 is displayed.

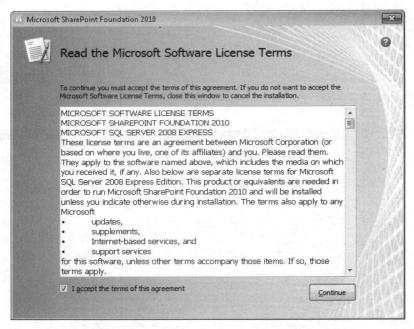

Figure A-5: Accepting terms of the agreement

2. After you accept the end user license agreement and click Continue you will see a dialog similar to Figure A-6; choose the "Standalone" option to begin the installation of SharePoint 2010.

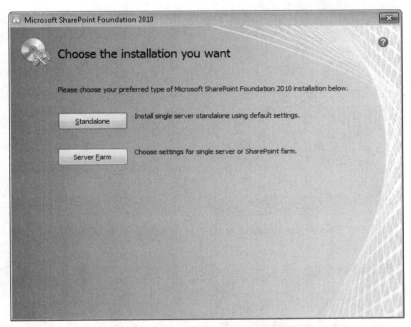

Figure A-6: SharePoint 2010 setup wizard—Choose installation type

3. When the installation is complete a dialog similar to the one shown in Figure A-7 will be displayed; make sure the check box is checked, and then click Close to run the SharePoint Configuration Wizard.

4. When the first dialog of the SharePoint Configuration Wizard is displayed, similar to Figure A-8, click Next.

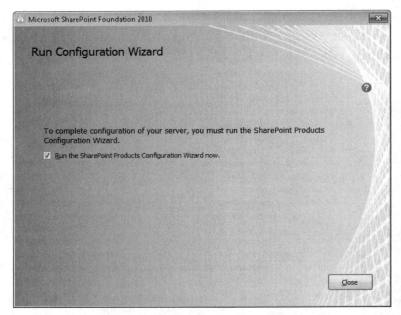

Figure A-7: SharePoint 2010 setup wizard—Installation complete

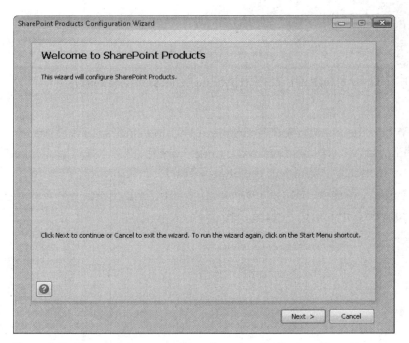

Figure A-8: SharePoint 2010 configuration wizard—Start configuration

5. At this point, if you are installing on a client operating system, you will be reminded that you are installing SharePoint 2010 on a client operating system by a dialog similar to the one shown in Figure A-9. Click OK to continue.

Figure A-9: Confirm installation on client operating system

6. You will be prompted to start or reset some services with a dialog similar to the one shown in Figure A-10. Click Yes to continue.

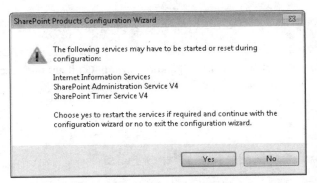

Figure A-10: Confirm start or reset of services

7. After a few minutes you will see a dialog similar to the one shown in Figure A-11, stating that the configuration was successful; click Finish.

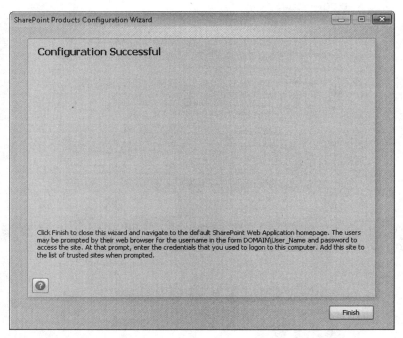

Figure A-11: SharePoint 2010 configuration wizard—Configuration successful

SharePoint Configuration Wizard Fails!

The SharePoint configuration wizard may fail if you are using a computer that is joined to a domain but that is not connected to a domain controller. To fix this problem you can either connect to a domain controller or use the New-SPConfigurationDatabase command in Windows Power Shell. This command allows you to specify none domain credentials for the farm. To execute this command, launch the SharePoint 2010 management shell located in the same location as the central admin link and simply type the above command in the command window; press Enter.

After the command completes you will find a new configuration database in SQL and an admin content database. The simplest way to complete the installation is to return to the configuration wizard because you are now starting with the server that is already joined to the farm.

If you choose to install SharePoint Server 2010, you have an additional step to choose the template or site that will be created as the root web of the default site collection. A browser window will be displayed with a page similar to Figure A-12; select a site template and click the OK button.

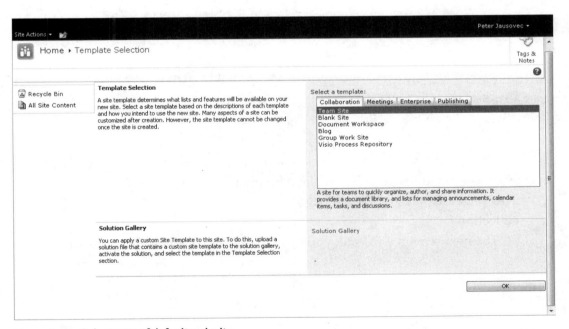

Figure A-12: Select type of default web site

The last step to configure site collection is to set the groups for the site. A dialog similar to Figure A-13 is displayed. You can accept the default settings and click OK.

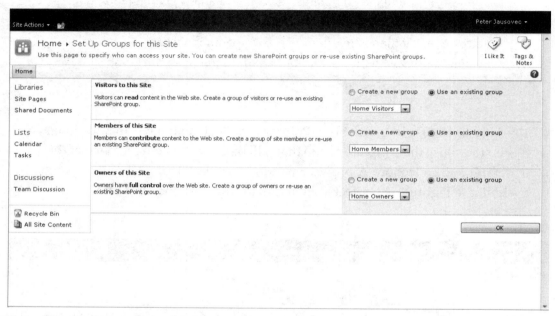

Figure A-13: Setting groups for the site

This completes the installation and configuration of SharePoint 2010! A browser window will be displayed with a page similar to Figure A-14. This page displays the home page of the root web site in the default site collection.

The next section will walk you through installing Visual Studio 2010.

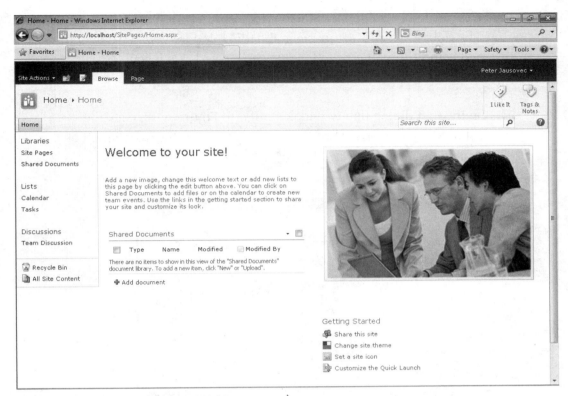

Figure A-14: Home page of default web site

Installing Visual Studio 2010

The SharePoint development templates and tools are included in Microsoft Visual Studio 2010 Professional, Microsoft Visual Studio 2010 Premium, and Microsoft Visual Studio 2010 Ultimate. You will need to install one of these versions of Visual Studio on your development machine; that machine must have a 64-bit operating system installed on it. Note that Visual Studio 2010 is a 32-bit application, but will run fine on a 64-bit operating system, using Windows on Windows 64-bit (WOW64) emulation.

After acquiring one of the above listed versions of Visual Studio 2010, save any open documents or other data and shut down any applications you may be using; the installation will likely require a reboot. Launch the setup wizard by double clicking setup.exe in the root folder of your Visual Studio 2010 media and complete the following steps in order to install Visual Studio 2010.

1. On the first dialog that will look similar to Figure A-15, click the Install Microsoft Visual Studio 2010 link to begin the installation of Visual Studio 2010.

Figure A-15: Visual Studio 2010 setup wizard—Start installation

2. On the next two pages click Next to continue.
3. On the next dialog, which will look similar to Figure A-16, select either Full or Custom install, and then click the Install or Next button.
4. If you choose to do a custom install you can select the features you want to install by checking the box for each one desired. You can select any you want, but you must select Visual Basic and/or Visual C#, Visual Web Developer, and Microsoft SharePoint Development Tools in order to have the necessary features installed for doing SharePoint development in Visual Studio 2010. Choose the features you want installed and click Install to begin the installation.

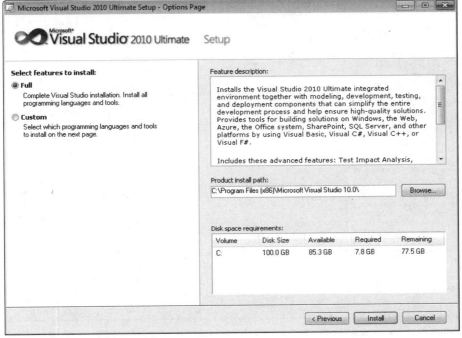

Figure A-16: SharePoint 2010 setup wizard—Choose type of install

5. A dialog similar to the one shown in Figure A-17 will be displayed, showing you the progress of the installation.

   The Microsoft .NET Framework 4 will be installed as part of Visual Studio 2010. Part way through the installation you will likely be prompted to restart your computer, most likely just after the framework is installed. After the restart, setup will continue automatically when you log back in.

6. When the installation is complete a dialog similar to the one shown in Figure A-18 will be displayed, indicating a successful installation. Click Finish.

7. The original setup dialog will be displayed; click Exit to complete the installation of Visual Studio 2010.

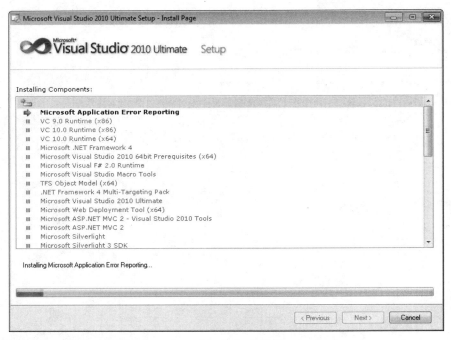

Figure A-17: SharePoint 2010 setup wizard—Installation progress

Figure A-18: SharePoint 2010 setup wizard—Installation succeeded

This completes the installation of Microsoft Visual Studio 2010. The next section will walk you through installing SharePoint Designer 2010.

Installing SharePoint Designer 2010

Now that you have SharePoint 2010 and Visual Studio 2010 installed, there is one more application that is often handy to have on your development machine—Microsoft SharePoint Designer 2010.

Some of the chapters in this book will use SharePoint Designer 2010 to accomplish certain tasks and introduce you to how SharePoint Designer 2010 can be used in conjunction with Visual Studio 2010 to build SharePoint solutions. Therefore, follow these steps to obtain and install SharePoint Designer 2010 on your development machine.

1. Download SharePoint Designer 2010 from http://r.office.microsoft .com/r/rlidBrowserToSPD and double click the downloaded file to extract the SharePoint Designer 2010 files and start the setup.

2. After you accept the end user license agreement you will see a dialog similar to Figure A-19; choose the Install Now option to begin the installation of SharePoint Designer 2010.

3. When the installation is complete a dialog similar to Figure A-20 will be displayed; click Close to complete the installation of SharePoint Designer 2010.

With SharePoint Designer 2010 now installed, we have installed all of the required software to begin developing SharePoint solutions. The last section in this chapter will walk you through creating a site collection to use for this development.

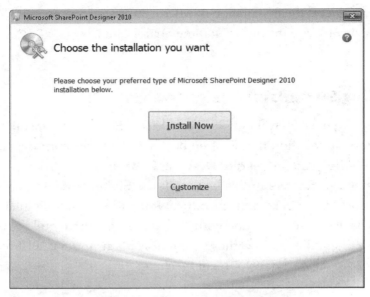

Figure A-19: SharePoint Designer 2010 installation wizard

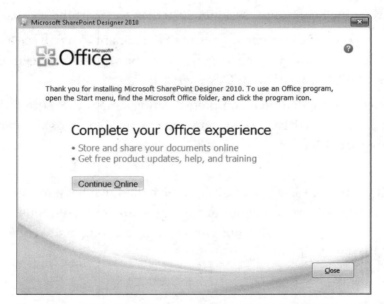

Figure A-20: SharePoint Designer 2010 setup wizard—Installation complete

Creating a Site Collection

While developing SharePoint solutions you will inevitably deploy an artifact, feature, or solution that causes the SharePoint site to have problems. This can be caused by incorrectly written artifacts and code, or sometimes just because the same solution has been deployed multiple times during the iterative process of development.

For this reason we suggest you create a new site collection prior to beginning the development of a new SharePoint solution, and do your development in that new site collection. This will make it more likely that you will always be able to access the default site collection and root web site created during SharePoint installation and configuration.

This is not required; many developers use the default site collection for all of their development. If you would like to follow our guidance, perform the following steps to create a new site collection to use for the development of SharePoint solutions.

In order to create a new site collection you need to use the SharePoint 2010 Central Administration site. To bring up this site click the Windows Start button, then click All Programs, and under Microsoft SharePoint 2010 Products click the SharePoint 2010 Central Administration menu.

From the main page of the Central Administration site under the Application Management section, click the Create site collections link. This will display a page similar to Figure A-21.

Fill in the Title textbox with the name of the site collection you want to create. Use a name that is representative of the solution or site you will be creating; in Figure A-21 you will see we used the name Dev1. You also need to fill in the URL textbox. It is common to use the name of the site collection in the URL, but you may want to avoid using spaces or other special characters that will be URL-encoded, which can make the URL confusing. Set the drop-down portion of the URL to sites.

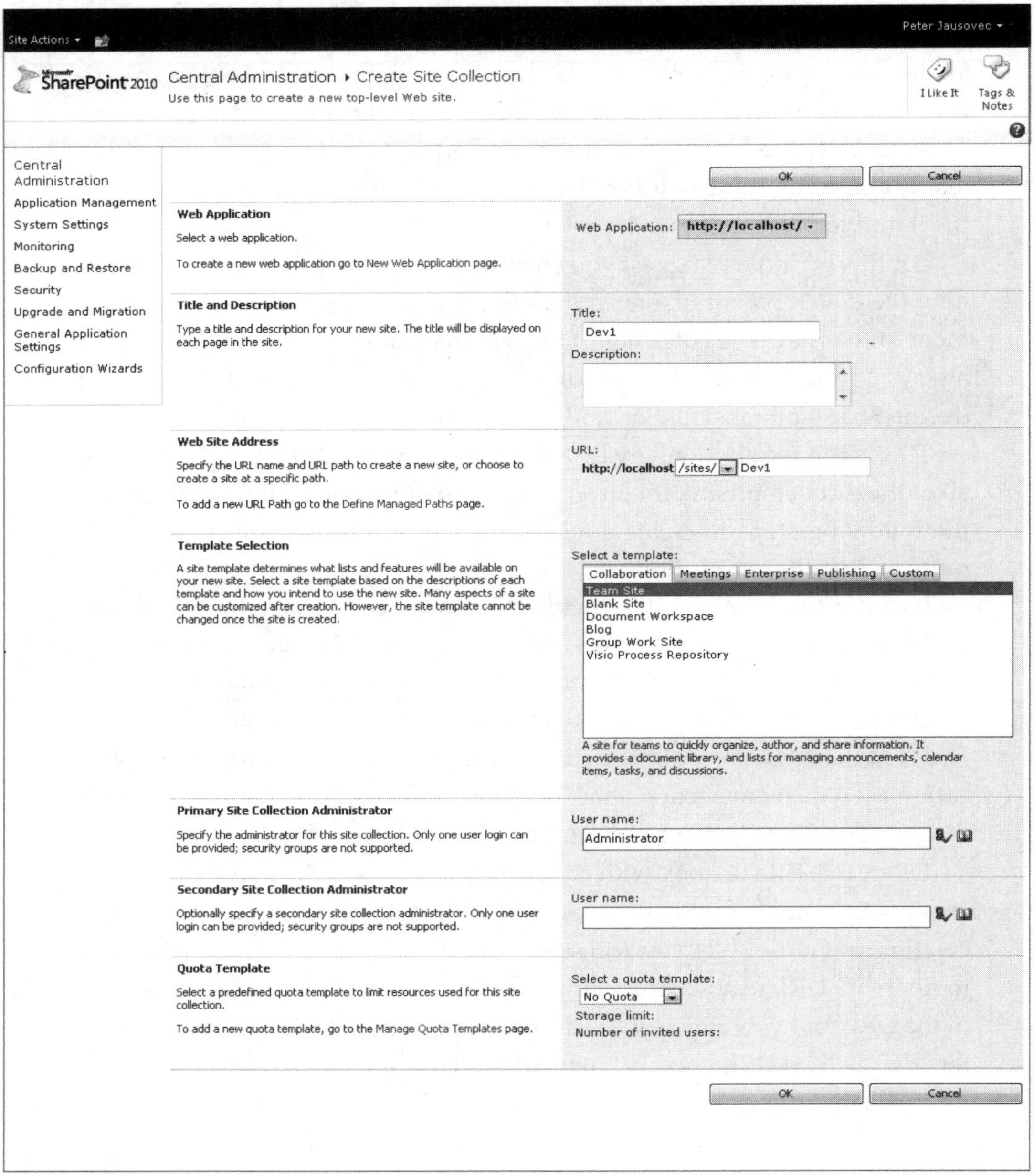

Figure A-21: SharePoint Central Administration—Create site collection

Next you need to select a site template. You can click on each one and see a description of the site that will be created; select the one that makes the most sense for your solution. If you are not sure at this point, just select Team Site; it is a good one to start with. The last field you need to supply on this page is the User name for the primary site collection administrator. Since this is a site collection you will be using for development, enter the domain\ username that you will be using on this machine for development.

Finally, click OK and the new site collection will be created. You will see a page similar to Figure A-22.

You can click on the link in the middle of the page to bring up a new browser window displaying the root web site of the new site collection just created.

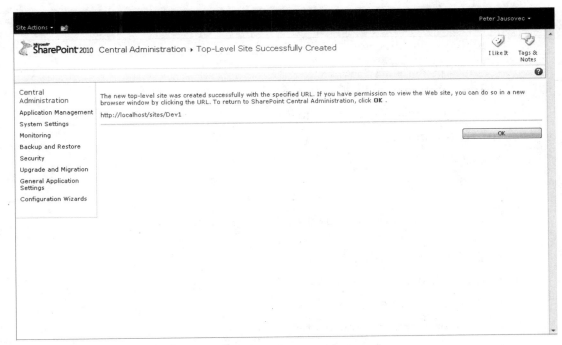

Figure A-22: SharePoint Central Administration—Site collection created

Developer Dashboard

The Developer Dashboard in SharePoint is a diagnostics tool that can help to diagnose a class of bugs that can be introduced through custom code. A good example of how developer dashboard can help you to diagnose various issues is a web part that retrieves tons of data in its load event and thus makes the page less responsive. With the help of an extensible mechanism for measuring various performance counters at various scopes that's part of the developer dashboard you can monitor usage and resource consumption at each stage of the request. Within developer dashboard you can find the following counter types: per-thread counters, per-process counters, client counters, and system counters.

Per-thread counters measure the actual values for the current request or timer jobs and can give you information for the following:

- Execution time
- SPRequests Allocated
- Number of SQL queries performed
- The duration of each SQL query
- The query text of each SQL query
- URL (or timer job name)
- Current user
- Start time

Per-process counters include the following information:

- Global heap size
- Total size of all native heaps
- Number of native heaps
- Number of active native heaps
- Number of SharePoint operations in progress

In the client counters group there is only one measurement: page size. The last group of counters is called the System counters, which can include any system performance counter. Here are some examples of system counters:

- Managed memory heap size
- Hard page faults
- Processor utilization
- Available memory on the machine

Note that any values that exceed acceptable ranges will be shown in red. As a developer you can monitor any piece of custom code by wrapping it with the SPMonitoredScope or create your own custom monitors by implementing the ISPScopedPerformanceMonitor interface and adding the monitor to the SPMonitoredScope. In order to use the developer dashboard, you will need to enable it. The developer dashboard can work in three modes, default, on mode, and on demand mode. Default mode is the setting where the dashboard is turned off. In the On mode, developer dashboard is shown on every page render. Finally, in the OnDemand mode the dashboard is enabled but it won't be visible until the user manually activates it by selecting the DevDashboard icon.

There are three ways to change the Developer Dashboard mode. You can either use stsadm.exe tool, SharePoint 2010 Management Shell, or change the mode through object model. Stsadm.exe is a command line administrator tool for SharePoint servers and sites and it's located at the following path on the drive where SharePoint is installed: %COMMONPROGRAMFILES%\ Microsoft Shared\Web Server Extensions\14\bin.

To change the developer dashboard to On mode using stsadm.exe you can run the following command:

```
STSADM -o setproperty -pn developer-dashboard -pv On
```

Commands for Off and OnDemand mode are very similar to the one above. To turn off the developer dashboard, run the following command:

```
STSADM -o setproperty -pn developer-dashboard -pv Off
```

Finally, to activate the OnDemand mode you can execute this command:

```
STSADM -o setproperty -pn developer-dashboard -pv OnDemand
```

With the help of SharePoint 2010 Management Shell you can write the PowerShell script that does the same as the previous stsadm.exe commands. As an example let's start Notepad and type the script in Listing A-2.

Listing A-2: Enabling Developer Dashboard with PowerShell Script

```
$DevDashboardSettings = [Microsoft.SharePoint.Administration.SPWebService]
  ::ContentService.DeveloperDashboardSettings;
$DevDashboardSettings.DisplayLevel = 'OnDemand';
$DevDashboardSettings.RequiredPermissions = 'EmptyMask';
$DevDashboardSettings.TraceEnabled = $true;
$DevDashboardsettings.Update()
```

Note that the script in Listing A-2 will change the mode to On-Demand—if you want to use On or Off mode you can just change that value. If you change the developer dashboard mode to OnDemand the icon as shown in Figure A-23 is displayed on the SharePoint site.

Figure A-23: Developer
Dashboard icon

Next, save the script and name it DeveloperDashboard.ps1 and then run it inside the SharePoint 2010 Management Shell, which is located under All Programs > Microsoft SharePoint 2010 Products.

If you prefer to work with code you can use the SharePoint object model to change the developer dashboard modes. The code in Listing A-3 shows how to enable the dashboard and set its mode to OnDemand.

Listing A-3: Enabling Developer Dashboard from Code

```
SPWebService cs = SPWebService.ContentService;
cs.DeveloperDashboardSettings.DisplayLevel = SPDeveloperDashboardLevel.OnDemand;
cs.DeveloperDashboardSettings.Update();
```

If you execute the code in Listing A-3 an icon as shown in Figure A-23 is displayed on the SharePoint site and if you click that icon you can bring up the developer dashboard shown in Figure A-24.

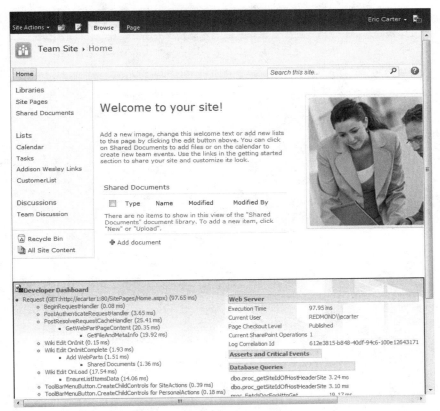

Figure A-24: Developer Dashboard on the SharePoint Site

Conclusion

This chapter described what is required in order to prepare your machine for SharePoint development. By now, you should have SharePoint 2010, Visual Studio 2010, and SharePoint Designer 2010 installed and configured on your client or server machine. In addition, if you chose to do so, we showed you how to create a new site collection to use during the development activities described in this book and how to enable Developer Dashboard.

Index

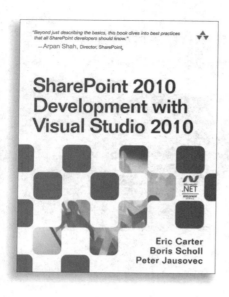

"Beyond just describing the basics, this book dives into best practices that all SharePoint developers should know."
—Arpan Shah, Director, SharePoint

SharePoint 2010
Development with
Visual Studio 2010

Eric Carter
Boris Scholl
Peter Jausovec

FREE Online Edition

Your purchase of *SharePoint 2010 Development with Visual Studio 2010* includes access to a free online edition for 45 days through the Safari Books Online subscription service. Nearly every Addison-Wesley Professional book is available online through Safari Books Online, along with more than 5,000 other technical books and videos from publishers such as Cisco Press, Exam Cram, IBM Press, O'Reilly, Prentice Hall, Que, and Sams.

SAFARI BOOKS ONLINE allows you to search for a specific answer, cut and paste code, download chapters, and stay current with emerging technologies.

Activate your FREE Online Edition at
www.informit.com/safarifree

> **STEP 1:** Enter the coupon code: TNLWNCB.

> **STEP 2:** New Safari users, complete the brief registration form.
> Safari subscribers, just log in.

If you have difficulty registering on Safari or accessing the online edition,
please e-mail customer-service@safaribooksonline.com